Annual Review of Anthropology

Production Editors: Jennifer E. Mann, Claire Insel
Bibliographic Quality Control: Mary A. Glass
Color Graphics Coordinator: Emé O. Akpabio
Electronic Content Coordinator: Suzanne K. Moses
Subject Indexer: Suzanne Copenhagen

ANNUAL REVIEW OF ANTHROPOLOGY

VOLUME 31, 2002

WILLIAM H. DURHAM, *Editor*
Stanford University

JEAN COMAROFF, *Associate Editor*
University of Chicago

JANE HILL, *Associate Editor*
University of Arizona

www.annualreviews.org science@annualreviews.org 650-493-4400

ANNUAL REVIEWS
4139 El Camino Way • P.O. BOX 10139 • Palo Alto, California 94303-0139

ANNUAL REVIEWS
Palo Alto, California, USA

International Standard Serial Number: 0084-6570
International Standard Book Number: 0-8243-1931-1
Library of Congress Catalog Card Number: 72-821360

∞ The paper used in this publication meets the minimum requirements of American National Standards for Information Sciences—Permanence of Paper for Printed Library Materials, ANSI Z39.48-1992.

TYPESET BY TECHBOOKS, FAIRFAX, VA
PRINTED AND BOUND IN THE UNITED STATES OF AMERICA

PREFACE: A Forty-Year Review of the Annual Review

With this volume of the *Annual Review of Anthropology* (*ARA*) we begin our fourth decade of publication. That fact, together with a timely invitation to present a report on the *ARA* at the November 2001 meetings of the American Anthropological Association, prompted me to undertake a retrospective review and self-study of our work. By also including the *ARA*'s predecessor, the *Biennial Review of Anthropology* (*BRA*), which was published every other year from 1959 to 1971, I was able to look back over four sequential decades of published reviews in anthropology, roughly corresponding to the 1960s, 1970s, 1980s, and 1990s.

Including the *BRA* in this analysis was doubly appropriate, I felt, because the *Biennial Review* imparted a significant historical legacy to the *ARA*. Although the publishing house changed when the series became annual, from Stanford University Press to Annual Reviews, Inc., the founding editor of the *ARA*—my esteemed colleague and good friend Prof. Bernard J. Siegel—had also served as originator and editor of the *Biennial Review*. In founding the *ARA*, there were deliberate and explicit efforts not only to build the new publication on the base of the *BRA*, but also to intensify and broaden its coverage by publishing every year with more chapters. As befit this transition, *ARA* Editor Siegel was joined in 1971 by Associate Editors Stephen Tyler (a linguist) and Alan Beals (a biological anthropologist), and this "founding triumvirate," as they are affectionately known, was to supervise the *ARA* from first publication in 1972 to 1992 when Prof. Siegel retired and I was brought on board as *ARA* Editor.

As I began this review, I chose to focus on some quantitative measures of this history, the better to show temporal trends and continuities across the 40 years of coverage. More qualitative themes and topics had already been explored in Professor Siegel's earlier retrospective, featured in *ARA* volume 22 (1993). I therefore created a quantitative database representing all 612 *BRA* and *ARA* chapters spread over 36 total volumes—an average of 17.0 chapters per volume. In this task, I was greatly aided by the diligent, cheerful assistance of Stanford Postdoc, Beverly Humphrey, even though I did not divulge to her the questions and hypotheses I was eager to explore. Dr. Humphrey carefully compiled a spreadsheet of basic facts and figures for each article in all volumes (e.g., number of pages, number of figures and tables, number of references cited, etc.). In addition to these relatively objective measures, Dr. Humphrey also coded the "relative topical specificity" of all *ARA* and *BRA* chapters on a scale of 1 to 4 according to the level of specificity implied by their titles:

1. A broad *subfield* (e.g., archeology, biological anthropology, etc.)

2. A *named specialization* within a subfield (e.g., historical archeology, classical archeology, etc.)
3. A generally *recognized topic* within a specialization (e.g., historical archeology of slavery)
4. A *focused topic* within a specialization (e.g., historical archeology of slavery in the 17th century)

In subsequent analysis, I focused on temporal trends and correlations within this large matrix of data.

As I undertook this review, I had a number of specific questions in mind that I have often wondered about during my years as Editor. The first concerned possible long-term trends in the format of our publication: How have the numbers of chapters and lengths of chapters changed over these four decades of publication? Obviously, there were big changes in these features when the *Biennial Review* became annual, and the number of chapters per volume was deliberately increased. But what about changes since that time? In 1992, for example, we began efforts to expand each volume slightly with the goal of improving coverage of diverse subfields: Had we been successful? Figure 1 summarizes the four-decade trend in these measures. The figure shows, first, that a quick adjustment in average length of chapters was achieved when the *BRA* became the *ARA*, and that the average length of *ARA* chapters has been impressively constant ever since, fluctuating around 25 pages per chapter. Second, Figure 1 shows a corresponding quick change in the number of chapters per volume, from 6 to 8 in the *BRA* to 16 to 18 in the *ARA*, and confirms a modest upward trend since 1992. Currently, we aim to publish 20–22 chapters per volume, although the final number is often determined by deadlines and constraints on authors' time beyond our control.

Another question that concerned me was subfield balance: Have we improved over the decades the attention the *ARA* gives to smaller subfields in anthropology, such as biological anthropology and anthropological linguistics? As a legacy of its origin in the *BRA*, the *ARA* began with an over-representation in the coverage of sociocultural anthropology. This was certainly understandable in the early days, given that sociocultural anthropology was (and is) the subfield with the largest number of active scholars and was (is) especially prominent in shaping the field as a whole. Yet the explicit goal in the founding of the *ARA* was to improve coverage of *all* of anthropology. I wondered whether the change from *BRA* to *ARA* had been fairly easy to achieve in the structural dimensions summarized in Figure 1, but more difficult and thus slower to emerge with respect to subfield balance.

Figure 2 confirms this general expectation. It shows, as an example, the percentage of published reviews in sociocultural anthropology and biological anthropology over the four decades of this study. The diminishing gap between the two curves represents improving subfield balance: Over the decades, reviews in sociocultural anthropology settled downward from 50% or more, in days of the *Biennial Review*, to 30 to 40 percent of all reviews today, in a trajectory that shows declining year-to-year variation as well. Meanwhile biological anthropology has increased

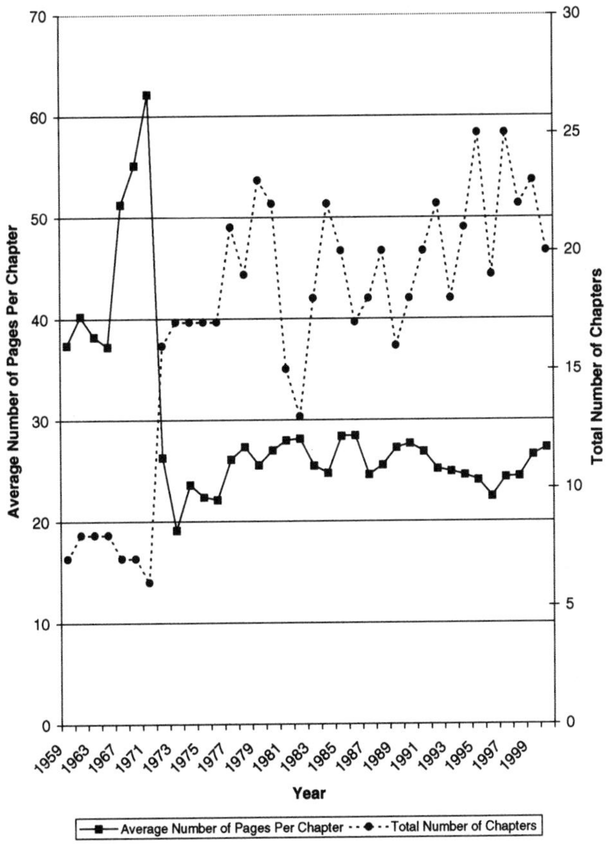

Figure 1 Structural features of the *Annual Review of Anthropology* (*ARA*) and its predecessor, the *Biennial Review of Anthropology* (*BRA*), across four decades of publication. Two curves are plotted: average number of pages per chapter (solid line), scaled at *left*, and total number of chapters per volume (dotted line), scaled at *right*.

from 12%–14% of all reviews published to normally 20%–22% today, though with considerable remaining annual variation. I found similar trajectories (not shown, but available online) for the percentage of archeology and linguistics chapters as well, each tending upward toward an average today of 20% or so. In my view, a 40:20:20:20 breakdown for the main subfields represents a reasonable balance for anthropology today. A remaining goal is to reduce the year-to-year variation in subfield coverage (the wobble or "flutter" in the curve). But it is also important to note that we achieved this improved subfield balance without disadvantaging the *ARA*'s coverage of sociocultural anthropology. In the 1990s, the *ARA* featured a total of 73 reviews in sociocultural anthropology, an actual *increase* from the 58 and 61 reviews in the 1970s and 1980s respectively. As the overall size of the *ARA*

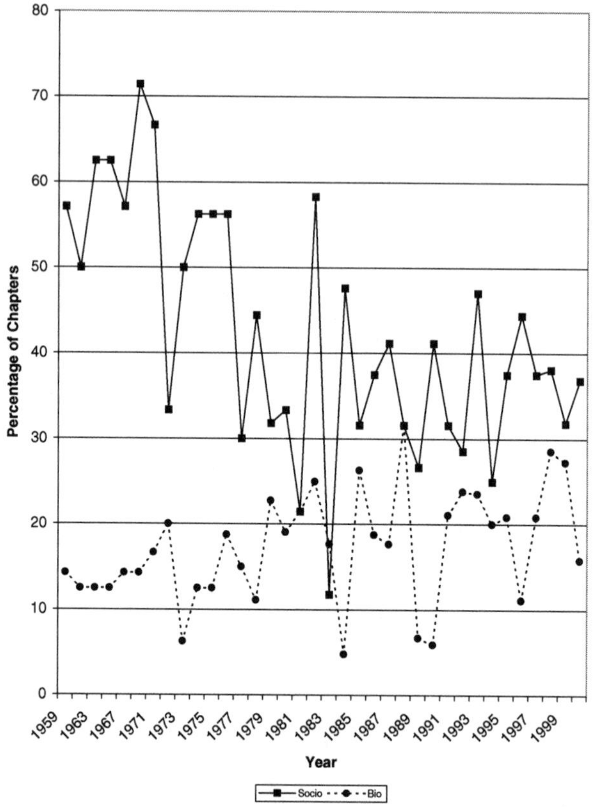

Figure 2 Subfield composition across four decades of publication. Two curves are plotted, both scaled at *left*: reviews in sociocultural anthropology (solid line) and reviews in biological anthropology (dotted line) as a percent of all reviews published in the *ARA*.

increased, we were able to improve subfield balance while even slightly expanding our coverage in the largest subfield.

From the start, the ambition of the *ARA* has been to provide annual review of world anthropology, not just North American anthropology. But such ambition has been far easier said than done, especially in the decades before reliable international email. By itself, the time and effort required to communicate back then with scholars at a distance almost inevitably produced some degree of bias against overseas authors: In some cases, invitations may simply never have arrived. It took little imagination to predict some improvement over the four decades in the number of non-U.S. authors. The question was really, how much? I hypothesized similar improvements, but for different reasons, with regard to gender. We have made deliberate efforts over the years to bring about gender balance in *ARA* authorship: How much have these efforts helped? A 1994 study of gender ratios in academic

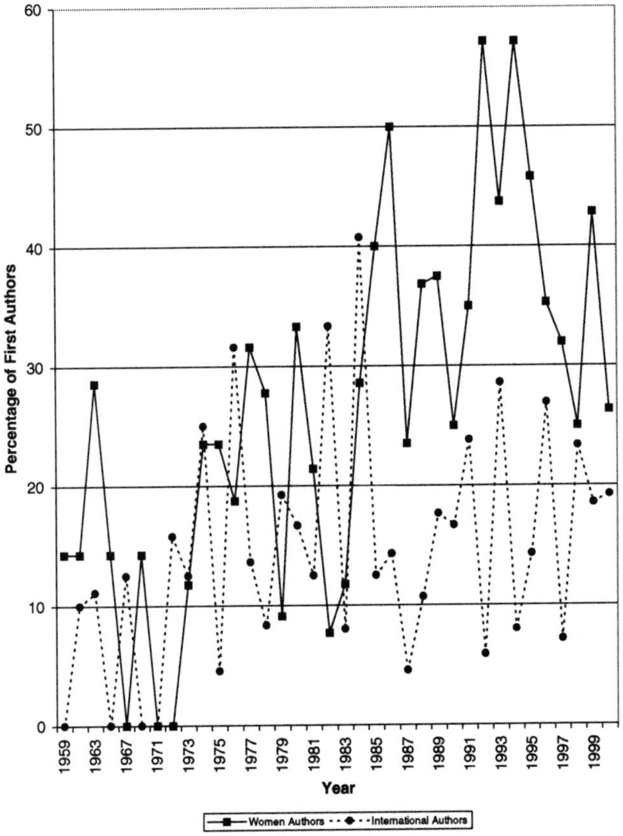

Figure 3 Authorship across four decades of publication. Two curves are plotted: the percentage of all first authors in the *ARA* who are women (solid line) and the percentage of all first authors who have a non-U.S. address (dotted line).

employment in the United States[1] by Burton, Watson, Quinn, and Webster found that women in academic positions, across all ranks, had increased to 31% of the total employed in 1992. Granted, not all female anthropologists work in academia. Still it was useful to know, had authorship by women in the *ARA* increased to levels like those for women in academic employment in anthropology?

Figure 3 shows the historical record of the *ARA* in these important areas. First, with respect to international authorship, the overall trend is, yes, a gradually increasing proportion of reviews whose first (or sole) author has an overseas address.

[1]Burton M, Watson PJ, Quinn N, Webster C. 1994. Academic employment of women in anthropology. *Anthropol. News*, October. http://www.aaanet.org/committees/coswa/burton.htm

One also can see a modest reduction in year-to-year variation in that proportion, although considerable variation or "flutter" remains. On the other hand, the magnitude of the overall increase is disappointingly modest: From an average of only 5% international authors in the first decade of the *BRA*, the average increased quickly to 15.9% in the 1970s but only moved up to 16.6% in the 1990s. An important goal for the *ARA* today remains to increase international authorship. Toward this end, we implemented an active program of "International Correspondents" in the 1990s, but certainly more can be done.

With regard to the gender ratio of authorship the record is somewhat more encouraging. As Figure 3 shows, there has been a steeper increase in the percentage of women as first (or sole) authors than there has been for international authors, as can be seen from the enduring gap that opens up in the late 1980s between the two curves. In some years in the 1990s female first authors surpassed 50% of the total, although there remains considerable year-to-year variation (including a couple of years in the 1990s under 30%). When one looks at decade totals, the trend is even clearer: From 12.5% first authors in the 1960s, women increased to 18% in the 1970s, 30% in the 1980s, and on to just over 40% in the 1990s. These most recent figures compare favorably with the 1992 academic workplace figure, 31%, described above. But there is still much room for improvement, particularly to reduce the year-to-year variation.

Finally, I was also interested in testing a very general impression that *ARA* reviews have been getting increasingly specific in their focus over the years. Both because anthropological knowledge is arguably cumulative over time, and because of "repeated sampling" in certain areas (i.e., the appeal of re-reviewing key topics at regular intervals, like once a decade or so), I expected to find a discernable trend toward increasing specificity in the topics reviewed in our pages. I expected the trend to show in all subfields, especially the smaller ones (with fewer active scholars, and thus a smaller base of research for review), but also in sociocultural anthropology where there has been something of a deliberate avoidance of generalizing scholarship in recent decades.

Figures 4 and 5 summarize two noteworthy dimensions in the trend toward increasing topical specificity in the *ARA*. Figure 4 shows the average level of topical specificity implied by the titles of *ARA* reviews across the 40 years of our publication, according to the subjective 4-point scale mentioned earlier (from "1" meaning review of an entire subfield, to "4" meaning review of a focused topic within a specialization). Consider, first, the plot for biological anthropology: From level-2 specificity during most of the *BRA* years, topical focus jumped quickly with the onset of the *ARA* to annual averages of 3.0 or more most years, where it has remained ever since, with some annual fluctuation. Compare biological anthropology now with topical specificity across *all* published chapters in the *ARA*, and three trends become apparent. First, the increasing specificity of topics is apparent across all the reviews that we publish, from roughly level-2 specificity in the days of the *BRA* to an average of level 3 today. Second, the annual variation or "flutter" is small in this instance, which suggests that the trend is not spurious

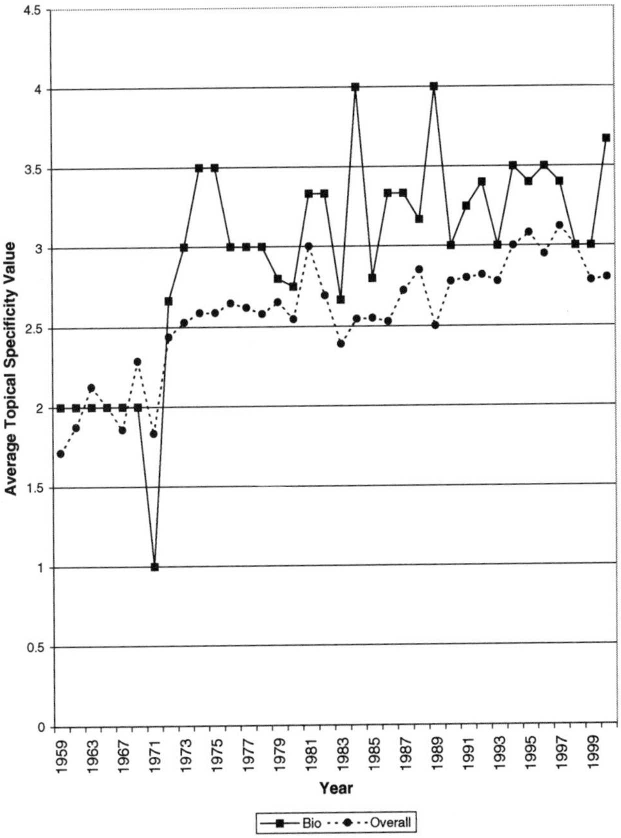

Figure 4 Topical specificity across four decades of publication. Two curves are plotted: the overall average "specificity value" of titles for *all* reviews published in a given year of the *ARA* (dotted line), and the average specificity value for reviews in biological anthropology alone (solid line). "Specificity value," defined in the text, runs from 1.0 (most general or broadly focused) to 4.0 (most specific or narrowly focused).

or a by-product of our yearly subfield sampling procedures. Third, the average specificity value for biological anthropology remains consistently higher, across the 1970s, 1980s, and 1990s, than the average value for all reviews. To some extent, this is inevitable, given that biological anthropology is a relatively small and relatively specialized subfield. But it also suggests that we could well renew our efforts in this and other subfields to invite every year a number of broader subfield reviews, as may well be more interesting to the general reader anyway.

Finally, Figure 5 confirms my long-held suspicion that chapter titles in the *ARA* are growing longer and longer as the years go by. The average review title of the 1990s (running about 7 words on average) was more than double the length of its

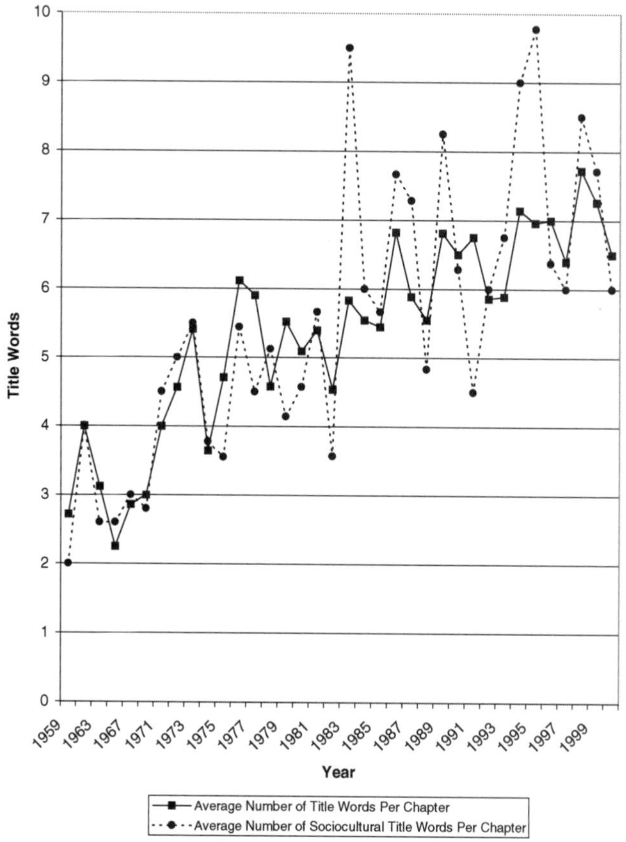

Figure 5 Length of chapter titles across four decades of publication. Two curves are plotted: the overall average number of title words per chapter in the *ARA* (solid line), and the average number of title words in chapters pertaining to sociocultural anthropology alone (dotted line).

counterpart in the 1960s (about 3 words, on average). And reviews from the sociocultural subfield, shown by the broken line in the figure, have sometimes featured an average *triple* that of the 1960s (9 or more words, on average, versus 3). Several factors no doubt contribute to this trend, including the growing specificity of topics, a desire for comprehensive computer searching and bibliographic retrieval, and the fashionability of colons (a high proportion of chapter titles today feature colons). But title length may also be indicative of some more general increase in verbosity and circumlocution in anthropological publication; whereas copyediting routinely tightens the body of text in the *ARA*, we rarely edit an author's preferred title. I am hopeful that we will soon see a leveling-off, if not a reversal, in this trend. We at the *ARA* remain committed in our quest to publish the best concise reviews that we can. With more and more colleagues complaining that they have less and less time to read, the pressure is on each and every author to entice a broad readership by being as concise as possible.

We thus enter our fourth decade of publishing hopeful of continued improvement in the *Annual Review of Anthropology* as highlighted by this review of our past. Perhaps the single most helpful person as we confront this challenge is the *ARA*'s Production Editor. This year we bid a fond farewell to Clare Insel, who served so diligently in that regard for the last couple of volumes, and welcome Jennifer Mann to take her place. With Jennifer's ever-positive attitude, I am hopeful that we will begin to see tighter reviews and shorter titles in the years ahead. Other changes this year include rotation off the Editorial Committee of two esteemed members, Margaret Lock (of McGill University) and Alessandro Duranti (of UCLA), both ever helpful in our search for timely topics and the very best authors. We welcome in their places Susan Greenhalgh (Irvine) and Greg Urban (Pennsylvania). We are also happy to announce that the *ARA* has begun to offer "Reviews in Advance": Chapters will henceforth be available online at the *ARA* website before the printed book appears, once they have been accepted and edited. No longer will authors—or their admiring readers—have to wait for a book in print before sharing URLs for their published work. And finally, we hope within the year to be able to offer our authors and readers the possibility of "Continuous Review Updates." For up to one year after publication, authors will be able to update their online reviews (sorry, this applies to the online version only) with as many as 3 pages of additional text and references. My colleagues and I on the Editorial Committee hope these improvements will serve the *ARA* well as it begins its next four decades of publication.

William H. Durham
Editor

Annual Review of Anthropology
Volume 31, 2002

CONTENTS

INDEXES

ERRATA

An online log of corrections to *Annual Review of Anthropology* chapters (if any, 1997 to the present) may be found at http://anthro.annualreviews.org/errata.shtml

Related Articles

From the ***Annual Review of Ecology and Systematics***, Volume 32 (2001)

Urban Ecological Systems: Linking Terrestrial Ecological, Physical, and Socioeconomic Components of Metropolitan Areas, S. T. A. Pickett, M. L. Cadenasso, J. M. Grove, C. H. Nilon, R.V. Pouyat, W. C. Zipperer, and R. Costanza

Ecology, Conservation, and Public Policy, Donald Ludwig, Marc Mangel, and Brent M. Haddad

From the ***Annual Review of Genomics and Human Genetics***, Volume 3 (2002)

Human Migrations and Population Structure: What We Know and Why It Matters, David B. Goldstein and Lounès Chikhi

Balanced Polymorphism Selected By Genetic Versus Infectious Human Disease, Michael Dean, Mary Carrington, and Stephen J. O'Brien

Patenting Genes and Genetic Research Tools: Good or Bad for Innovation? Beth E. Arnold and Eva Ogielska-Zei

From the ***Annual Review of Nutrition***, Volume 22 (2002)

Malnutrition and Poverty, Manuel Peña and Jorge Bacallao

From the ***Annual Review of Political Science***, Volume 5 (2002)

The Origins, Development, and Possible Decline of the Modern State, Hendrik Spruyt

From the ***Annual Review of Psychology***, Volume 53 (2002)

Human Aggression, Craig A. Anderson and Brad J. Bushman

Self and Social Identity, Naomi Ellemers, Russell Spears, and Bertjan Doosje

Cultural Influences on Personality, Harry C. Triandis and Eunkook M. Suh

From the ***Annual Review of Sociology***, Volume 28 (2002)

Global Ethnography, Zsuzsa Gille and Seán Ó Riain

Integrating Models of Diffusion of Innovations: A Conceptual Framework, Barbara Wejnert

Violence in Social Life, Mary R. Jackman

ANNUAL REVIEWS is a nonprofit scientific publisher established to promote the advancement of the sciences. Beginning in 1932 with the *Annual Review of Biochemistry*, the Company has pursued as its principal function the publication of high-quality, reasonably priced *Annual Review* volumes. The volumes are organized by Editors and Editorial Committees who invite qualified authors to contribute critical articles reviewing significant developments within each major discipline. The Editor-in-Chief invites those interested in serving as future Editorial Committee members to communicate directly with him. Annual Reviews is administered by a Board of Directors, whose members serve without compensation.

Annual Reviews of

Anthropology
Astronomy and Astrophysics
Biochemistry
Biomedical Engineering
Biophysics and Biomolecular Structure
Cell and Developmental Biology
Earth and Planetary Sciences
Ecology and Systematics
Energy and the Environment
Entomology
Fluid Mechanics
Genetics
Genomics and Human Genetics
Immunology
Materials Research
Medicine
Microbiology
Neuroscience
Nuclear and Particle Science
Nutrition
Pharmacology and Toxicology
Physical Chemistry
Physiology
Phytopathology
Plant Biology
Political Science
Psychology
Public Health
Sociology

SPECIAL PUBLICATIONS

Excitement and Fascination of Science, Vols. 1, 2, 3, and 4

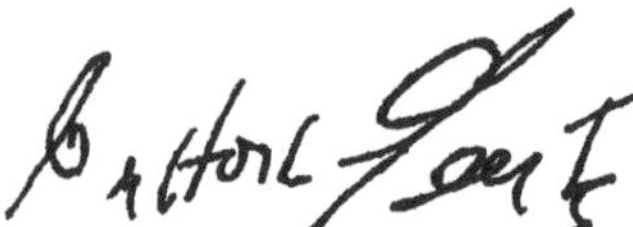

Annu. Rev. Anthropol. 2002. 31:1–19
doi: 10.1146/annurev.anthro.31.040402.085449

AN INCONSTANT PROFESSION: The Anthropological Life in Interesting Times

Clifford Geertz
Institute for Advanced Study, Einstein Drive, Princeton, New Jersey 08540; email: geertz@ias.edu

Key Words social sciences, history, third world, modernization, Cold War

■ **Abstract** I give an overall view of anthropology and of my career within it over the past fifty years, relating them to changes in the world in general during that time. All lessons are implicit, all morals unstated, all conclusions undrawn.

INTRODUCTION

I have arrived, it seems, at that point in my life and my career when what people most want to hear from me is not some new fact or idea, but how I got to this point in my life and my career. This is a bit discouraging, not just because of its *momento mori* overtones (when you are seventy-five, everything has *memento mori* overtones), but because, having spent the whole of my adult life trying to push things forward in the human sciences, I am now being asked to consider what that has entailed—why I think my direction can be called forward, and what, if that direction is to be sustained, the next necessary thing might be. As a result, I have engaged in the past few years in at least two more or less organized attempts to describe the general curve of my life as a working anthropologist, and this essay will be the third, and, I trust, the last. Talking about one's self and one's experiences in a homiletical manner—"go thou and do likewise"—is a bit much the first time around. Recycled, it loses charm altogether.

The first of these essays in apologetical retrospection, originally given as a Harvard-Jerusalem lecture in 1990, became the chapter entitled "Disciplines" in my book *After the Fact* (Geertz 1995a). There I concentrated mostly on matters of research and scholarship, most especially on my long-term fieldwork in Indonesia and Morocco—a story of projects leading to outcomes leading to other projects leading to other outcomes. The second, originally given as an American Council of Learned Societies "Life of Learning" lecture in 1999, became the first chapter, entitled "Passage and Accident," of my most recent book, *Available Light* (Geertz 2000). There I presented a more personal, semi-introspective account of both my life and my career; a sort of sociointellectual autobiography and self-accounting. This time—this last time—I want to do something else: namely, to trace the development of anthropology as a field of study over the more than half-century, 1950–2002, I have been involved in it, and to trace, too, the relationships between that development and the broader movements of contemporary history. Though this also, of necessity, produces something of a "the things I have been through and the things I have done" sort of narrative, I am, for the most part, not concerned with either my work or my persona. I am concerned with what has happened around me, both in the profession in which I have been, however loosely and at times uncomfortably, enclosed, and in what we are pleased to call "the wider world," in which that profession has been, however marginally and insecurely, enclosed. That world is with us late and soon: There is very little in anthropology that is genuinely autonomous; pretensions to the contrary, however dressed in the borrowed clothes of "science," are self-serving. We are, like everybody else, creatures of our time, relics of our engagements.

Admittedly, this is a little vast for a short essay, and I am obliged to pass over some very large matters very quickly, ignoring detail and suppressing nuance and qualification. But my intent is not to present a proper history, an inclusive summary, or a systematic analysis. It is, instead,

1) To outline the succession of phases, periods, eras, generations, or whatever, both generally and in anthropology as such, as I have lived through it, and them, in the last half of the last century, and,
2) To trace the interplay between (for the most part, American and European) cultural, political, social, and intellectual life overall and anthropology as a special and specialized profession, a trade, a craft, a *métier*.

Whether such broad-stroke, impressionistic, the-view-from-here sketching will yield much in the way of insight into how things are, and have been, heading in our field remains to be seen. But, absent a crystal ball, I know of no other way.

So far as phases, periods, eras, and the like are concerned, I shall, for my own convenience, mark out four of them. None of them is internally homogeneous, none of them is sharply bounded; but they can serve as useful place-markers in a lurching, tangled, digressive history. The first, roughly between 1946 and 1960—all dates are movable—was a period of after-the-war exuberance, when a wave of optimism, ambition, and a sense of improving purpose swept through the human sciences. The second, about 1960 to about the mid-1970s, was dominated, on the one hand, by the divisions of the universalized cold war, and, on the other, by the romances and disappointments of Third-Worldism. From 1975 or so to, shall we say, in honor of the fall of The Wall, 1989, there was, first, a proliferation of new, or anyway newfangled, approaches to social and cultural analysis, various sorts of theoretical and methodological "turns," *Kehre*, *tournures d'esprit*; and then, on the heels of these, the rise of radically critical and dispersive "post-" movements, brought on by increasing uncertainty, self-doubt, and self-examination, both within anthropology and in Western culture generally. Finally, from the 1990s until now, interest has begun to shift toward ethnic conflict, violence, world-disorder, globalization, transnationalism, human rights, and the like, although where that is going, especially after September 11, is far from clear. These, again, are not the only cuts that could be made, nor even the best. They are but the reflections, diffuse and refracted, in my own mind of the way of the world and the ways of anthropology within the way of the world.

POSTWAR EXUBERANCE

During the second world war, American anthropologists were, like American sociologists, historians, psychologists, and political scientists, drawn, almost to the man or woman, into government service. After it ended, in what was, in the United States anyway, not that long a time, three or four years, they returned, immediately, again almost to the man or woman, to academia with their conception of themselves and their profession radically altered. What had been an obscure, isolate, even reclusive, lone-wolf sort of discipline, concerned mainly with tribal ethnography, racial and linguistic classification, cultural evolution, and prehistory, changed in the course of a decade into the very model of a modern, policy-conscious, corporate social science. Having experienced working (mostly in connection with propaganda, psychological warfare, or intelligence efforts) in large, intellectually diverse groups, problem-focused collections of thrown-together specialists, most of whom they had previously known little about and had less to do with, anthropologists came back to their universities in a distinctly experimental frame of mind. Multi- (or inter-, or cross-) disciplinary work, team projects, and concern with the immediate problems of the contemporary world were combined with boldness, inventiveness, and a sense, based mainly on the sudden availability of large-scale material support both from the government and from the new mega-foundations, that things were, finally and certainly, on the move. It was a heady time.

I encountered all this at what may have been its point of highest concentration, greatest reach, and wildest confusion: Harvard in the 1950s. An extraordinary collection of persons and personalities had gathered there, and at the nearby Massachusetts Institute of Technology, launching programs in all directions. There was the Department of Social Relations, which—chaired by the systematic sociologist Talcott Parsons, and animated, rather diffusely, by his rather diffuse "General Theory of Social Action "—combined sociology, anthropology, clinical psychology, and social psychology into an at least terminologically integrated whole (Parsons & Shils 1951). There was the Russian Research Center, headed by the cultural anthropologist Clyde Kluckhohn (1951); the Psychological Clinic, headed by the psychoanalyst Henry Murray (1938); the Laboratory of Social Relations, headed by the social statistician Samuel Stouffer (Stouffer 1949). John and Beatrice Whiting, in from Yale, assembled a team and began exploiting the newly created Human Relations Area Files for comparative correlation studies of socialization (BB Whiting & J Whiting 1975). And at MIT, there was the Center for International Studies dedicated to stimulating modernization, democratization, and takeoff in the new states of Asia and Africa and the stranded ones of Eastern Europe and Latin America (Millikan & Blackmer 1961). Just about everything that was in any way in the air in the social or, as they soon came to be called as the pressures toward unification intensified, the behavioral sciences—from group dynamics (Homans 1950), learning theory (Tolman 1958), and experimental psychology (Bruner & Krech 1950) to structural linguistics (Jakobson 1952), attitude measurement (Allport 1954), content analysis (Inkeles 1950), and cybernetics (Wiener 1962)—was represented by one or another Institute, one or another Center, one or another Project, one or another entrepreneur. Only Marxism was missing, and a number of the students happily provided that (for a general critique from the left of all this, see Diamond 1992).

For me, as a would-be anthropologist—one who had never had an anthropology course and had no particular aim in mind except to render himself somehow employable—the figure I had most to come to terms with in this swarm of talkative authorities was Clyde Kluckhohn. A driven, imperious, rather haunted man, with an enormous range of interests, a continuously restless mind, and an impassioned, somewhat sectarian sense of vocation, he had read Classics at Oxford as a Rhodes Scholar. He had studied the Navajo and other peoples in the American Southwest since having been sent there as a teenager for his health, and he knew his way around the corridors of power, both in Washington (where he had worked as consultant to the Secretary of War and directed morale surveys for the Office of War Information) and, an even greater achievement (considering he had been born obscure in Iowa) at Harvard. The author of what was then the most widely read, and best written, statement of what anthropology was all about, *Mirror for Man* (1949), a past president of the American Anthropological Association, a fierce controversialist, a player of favorites, and a master money-raiser, Kluckhohn was rather a presence.

Of the various collective enterprises (thinking back, I count at least eight, and there were probably more) that Kluckhohn was at that moment either directing, planning, or otherwise animating, I myself became involved, in turn, in three, which, taken together, not only launched my career but also fixed its direction.

The first, and smallest, was the compendium of definitions of culture Kluckhohn was preparing in collaboration with Alfred Kroeber, then in his late seventies and concluding a sovereign career in detached retirement (Kroeber & Kluckhohn 1952). I was given what, with the aid of other, more senior, graduate students, they had assembled and what they had written in the way of commentary, and I was asked to review it and offer suggestions. I had some suggestions, most of them expository, a few of which were attended to; but the most fateful result of the experience for me was that I was inducted into the thought-ways of the particular form of anthropology then called, rather awkwardly, pattern theory or configurationalism. In this dispensation, stemming from work before and during the war by the comparative linguist Edward Sapir at Yale and the cultural holist Ruth Benedict at Columbia, it was the interrelation of elements, the gestalt they formed, not their particular, atomistic character, as in previous diffusion and culture area studies, that was taken to be the heart of the matter. A phoneme, a practice, a role, an attitude, a habit, a trait, an idea, a custom was, as the slogan had it, "a point in a pattern"; it was systems we were after, forms, structures, shapes, contexts—the social geometry of sense (Kluckhohn 1962, Sapir 1949, Benedict 1934).

A large number of expressions of this approach to things current in anthropology appeared at that time. Perhaps the most visible and influential, though as it turned out not so long-lived, was the so-called culture and personality movement, in the service of which Kluckhohn, Murray, and a junior member of the Social Relations Department, David Schneider, put together a more or less definitive reader (Kluckhohn et al. 1949). Strongly influenced by psychoanalytical ideas and by projective testing methods, it sought to relate the processes of individual psychological development to the cultural institutions of various societies. Abram Kardiner and Ralph Linton at Columbia, Cora DuBois, first at Berkeley then at Harvard, Erik Erikson, also first at Berkeley and then at Harvard, and Kluckhohn himself in his Navajo work (Kardiner & Linton 1939, Du Bois et al. 1944, Erikson 1950, Leighton & Kluckhohn 1947) were perhaps the most prominent figures in the movement, and Margaret Mead was its battle-fit, out-front tribune; but it was very widespread (Hallowell 1955, Piers & Singer 1953, Wallace 1970). Closely allied to culture and personality there were the so-called national character or culture-at-a-distance studies, such as Benedict's on Japan, and Mead's, Rhoda Métraux's and Geoffrey Gorer's on Europe and America (Benedict 1949; Mead 1942; Mead & Métraux 1953; Métraux & Mead 1954; Mead & Rickman 1951; Gorer 1948, 1955; Gorer & Rickman 1963), and, of course, those of the Russian Research Center, where sociologists, psychologists, political scientists, and anthropologists attempted to assemble a collective portrait of "the new Soviet man" out of the analysis of communist writings and refugee life-histories (Bauer 1959, Bauer et al. 1956).

My interest in all this was limited by what seemed to me its somewhat mechanical, destiny-in-the-nursery quality and the vastness of its explanatory ambitions. So I drifted instead toward another of Kluckhohn's large-scale, long-term, multi-discipline, multi-inquirer, systematical enterprises in the interpretation of cultures, the so-called Comparative Study of Values or Ramah (later Rimrock) Project. This project, methodical and well financed, was dedicated to describing the value systems (world-views, mental attitudes, moral styles) of five geographically adjacent but culturally discrete, small communities in northwestern New Mexico—Navajo, Zuni, Spanish American, Mormon, and Anglo (or Texan). Over a period that finally stretched to twenty years or so, dozens of researchers from a wide variety of crossbred specialties—moral philosophers, regional historians, rural sociologists, American Indianists, child psychologists—were dispatched to one or another of these sites to describe one or another aspect of the life being lived there. Their fieldnotes, hundreds upon hundreds of pages of them, were then typed up on cards and filed in the Human Relation Area Files manner at the Peabody Museum of Anthropology, where they could be commonly consulted and a long string of special studies, and finally a collective volume, written (Vogt & Albert 1966, Vogt 1955, Kluckhohn & Strodtbeck 1961, Smith & Roberts 1954, Ladd 1957). As for me, I did not go to the Southwest but worked for some months in the files, then already vast and varied, on a subject set by Kluckhohn—the differential responses of the five groups to problems set to them all by the common conditions of their existence as small, rural, more or less encapsulated communities: drought, death, and alcohol. Mormon technological rationalism, Zuni rain dancing, Spanish-American dramatic fatalism in the face of drought, Navajo fear of ghosts, Mormon eschatological schemes, Anglo grief-avoidance in the face of death, Zuni sobriety, Mormon puritanism, and Navajo spree drinking in the face of alcohol—all were outlined, rather schematically, and attributed, rather speculatively, to their differing value systems (Geertz, unpublished observations). But whatever the limitations of the report I produced (and it wasn't all that bad as a first pass at things), the experience turned out to be both a sort of dry-run for the kind of field research—comparative, collaborative, and addressed to questions of meaning and significance—that I would spend the rest of my life pursuing; and a transition to the next phase or period of the immersion of anthropology in the movement of the times: the age of modernization, nation-building, and the all-enveloping Cold War.

MODERNIZATION AND THE COLD WAR

The Center for International Studies at the Massachusetts Institute of Technology, which I mentioned earlier as part of the cluster of social science holding-companies emerging in post-war Cambridge, was set up in 1952 as a combination intelligence gathering and policy planning organization dedicated to providing political and economic advice both to the rapidly expanding U.S. foreign aid program and to those it was ostensibly aiding—the "developing," "under-developed," or, for the less sanguine, "backward" countries of Asia, Africa, and Latin America. At first, the Center, something of an anomaly in an engineering school not much given at that time to social studies of any sort, was hardly more than a secretary, a suite of offices, a name, a large amount of money, and a national agenda. In an effort simply to get it up and running, Kluckhohn, who, still moving in mysterious ways, had again been somehow involved in its formation, proposed that a team of doctoral candidates from Harvard social science departments be formed and sent to Indonesia under its auspices to carry out field research in cooperation with students from that country's new, European-style universities. Five anthropologists, including myself and my then wife, Hildred, also a Social Relations student; a sociologist who was a historian of China; a social psychologist; and a clinical psychologist were given a year of intensive work in the Indonesian language and sent off for two years to the rice fields of eastern Java (not all of them got there, but that's another story) to carry out, ensemble, parallel, interconnected, and, so it was hoped, cumulative researches: the Ramah Project model updated, concentrated, and projected abroad.

The ups and downs of this enterprise, which itself came to be called "The Modjokuto Project" and the degree to which it achieved the ends proposed to it, have been retailed elsewhere (Geertz 1995a). For the present "March of Time" sort of story, its significance lies in the fact that it was, if not the first, surely one of the earliest of what soon turned into a flood of efforts by anthropologists, or teams of them, to adapt themselves and their tribes-and-islands discipline to the study of large-scale societies with written histories, established governments, and composite cultures–nations, states, civilizations. (For another early effort in this direction, see Steward et al. 1956.) In the years immediately following, the number of such country-focused projects multiplied (as did, of course, as a result of decolonization, the number of countries), and a sort of super-discipline called area studies, eclectic, synoptical, reformative, and policy-conscious, came into being to support them (Steward 1950; Singer 1956; Redfield 1953, 1956).

When the Modjokuto team left for Southeast Asia, the Center, as I mentioned, did not yet really exist as a going concern, so its connection with the work we did there—essentially historical and ethnographic, a refitted community study—was nominal at best. By the time we returned to Cambridge, three years further on, however, it had become a large, bureaucratized organization with dozens of specialized researchers, most of them economists, demographers, agronomists, or political scientists, engaged in development planning of one sort or another or serving as in-country policy consultants to particular governments, including that of Indonesia. The work of our team seemed, both to the Center staff and to ourselves, to be rather to the side of the Center's mission, inconsonant with its "applied" emphasis and too concerned with what the program-minded types took to be parochial matters. We drifted away into writing our separate theses on religion, kinship, village life, market selling, and other irrelevancies, and beginning, finally, our academic careers. I, however, was rather more interested in developmental questions, and in state formation, than my colleagues, and I wished to return as soon as possible to Indonesia to take them up. So, after gaining my doctorate, I rejoined the Center and became more directly involved in its work and with the master idea that governed it: modernization.

This idea, or theory, ubiquitous in Third World studies during the 1960s and early 1970s, and, of course, not all that dead yet, stemmed from a variety of sources. Most particularly, it grew out of the writings of the German sociologist Max Weber and his American followers (of whom, Talcott Parsons was perhaps the most prominent, and certainly the most insistent) on the rise of capitalism in the West (Weber 1950a,b, 1947, 1965; Tawney 1947; Parsons 1937; Bendix 1962; Levy 1960; Eisenstadt 1966; Black 1976). Weber's conception of the history of the West since the Renaissance and the Reformation was that it consisted of a relentless process of economic, political, and cultural rationalization, the instrumental adjustment of ends and means, and he saw everything from bureaucracy, science, individualism, and double-entry bookkeeping to the industrial organization of labor and the disciplined management of inner life as expressions of such a process. The systematic ordering of the entirety of human existence in rational terms, its imprisonment in an "iron cage" of rule and method, was what, in its essence, modernity was. In particular, his famous, in some quarters infamous, Protestant Ethic thesis—that the harsh, predestinarian beliefs of Calvinism and related inner-worldly ascetic doctrines of the sixteenth and seventeenth centuries provided the moral legitimation and driving force for the tireless pursuit of profit under bourgeois capitalism—spurred a whole host of studies designed to support and extend it, to find signs and portents of such progress-producing value systems in that most residual of residual categories, the nonmodern, nonrational, noncapitalist non-West (Bellah 1957, 1965; Eisenstadt 1968; Geertz 1956, 1963b).

As for me, my original thesis proposal, put temporarily aside to address myself to describing Javanese religion more generally for the purposes of the common project, was to pursue the possibility that reformist (or modernist) Islam might play a role in Indonesia similar to that which Weber's Calvinism supposedly played in the West. So, after writing a short book at the Center on the history of Javanese agriculture, which ascribed its failure to rationalize along the capital-intensive, labor-saving lines experienced earlier in the West and, in a somewhat different way, in Japan, to the colonial policies of the Dutch (Geertz 1963a), I headed back to Indonesia hoping to address the Weberian thesis in a more direct and systematic, hypothesis-testing way. I would, I thought, spend four or five months each in a strongly Islamic region in Sumatra, a strongly Calvinist region in Sulawesi, and a Hindu region in Bali and try to ferret out the effects, if any, of different varieties of religious belief on the modernization of economic behavior.

But a funny thing happened on the way to the field. The cold war, previously fought out (the rather special case of Korea perhaps excepted) in the client and satellite states of Europe, shifted its center of gravity to the Third World, and most especially to Southeast Asia. All this—the Malaya emergency, the Vietnam war, the Khmer Rouge, the Huk rebellion, the Indonesian massacres—is much visited, much disputed, history, and I will not rehearse it again here. Suffice it to say this development altered the whole scene of action for those of us trying to carry out field studies in such suddenly world-critical places. The induction of the obsessions and machinations of the East-West confrontation into entrenched, long-standing divisions in religious, ethnic, and cultural life—another, less foreseen, form of modernization—brought local, hand-to-hand politics to a furious boil just about everywhere it occurred, and it occurred just about everywhere.

From the end of the 1950s to the beginning of the 1970s, the charismatical, hero-leaders of the new states—Nehru, Nkrumah, Nasser, Ben Bellah, U Nu, Ayub Khan, Azikwe, Bandanaraike, Sihanouk, Ho, Magsaysay, Sukarno—bedeviled within and without by these pressures toward ideological polarization, struggled to position their countries in the ever-narrowing, unfilled space between the powers: neutral, nonaligned, newly emerging, "*tiers monde*." Indonesia, which soon found itself with both the largest Communist Party outside the Sino-Soviet bloc and an American-trained and -financed army, was in the very forefront of this effort, especially after Sukarno organized the Bandung Conference of 29 Asian and African nations, or would-be nations, in that west Javanese city in 1955 (Kahin 1956, Wright 1995). Nehru, Chou, Nasser, and Sukarno himself all addressed the Conference, which led on to the formal creation of the nonaligned movement. All this, and the general unfolding of things, made of Indonesia perhaps the most critical battleground after Vietnam in the Asian cold war. And in the mid-1960s it collapsed under the weight: failed coup, near civil-war, political breakdown, economic ruin, and mass killings. Sukarno, his regime, and the dreams of Bandung, never more than dreams, or self-intoxications, were consumed, and the grimmer, less romantic age of the kleptocrats, Suharto, Marcos, Mobutu, Amin, and Assad emerged. Whatever was happening in the Third World, it did not seem to be the progressive advance of rationality, however defined. Some sort of course correction in our procedures, our assumptions, and our styles of work, in our very conception of what it was we were trying to do, seemed, as they say, indicated.

AN EXPLOSION OF PARADIGMS

By the time I got back to the United States toward the beginning of the 1960s (my neat little three-way project spoiled by the outbreak of anti-Sukarno rebellions in Sumatra and Sulawesi, I had spent most of the year in Bali), the destabilizing effects of the deepening of the great power confrontation in Southeast Asia were beginning to be felt with some force there as well. The profession itself was torn apart by charges and countercharges concerning the activities, or supposed activities, of anthropologists working in Vietnam. There was civil rights and "The Letter from Birmingham Jail," civil liberties and the Chicago Seven. The universities—Berkeley, Harvard, Columbia, Cornell, Kent State, Chicago—erupted, dividing faculty, inflaming students, and alienating the general public. Academic research on "underdeveloped" countries in general, and on "modernization" in particular, was put under something of a cloud as a species of neoimperialism, when it wasn't being condemned as liberal do-goodism. Questions multiplied rapidly about anthropology's colonial past, its orientalist biases, and the very possibility of disinterestedness or objective knowledge in the human sciences, or indeed whether they should be called sciences in the first place. If the discipline was not to retreat into its traditional isolation, detached from the immediacies of contemporary life—and there were those who recommended that, as well as some who wished to turn it into a social movement—new paradigms, to borrow Thomas Kuhn's famous term, first introduced around this time (Kuhn 1962), were called for. And soon, and in spades, they came.

For the next fifteen years or so, proposals for new directions in anthropological theory and method appeared almost by the month, one more clamorous than the next. Some, like French structuralism, had been around for awhile but took on greater appeal as Claude Lévi-Strauss, its proprietor-founder, moved on from kinship studies to distributional analyses of symbolic forms—myths, rituals, categorical systems—and promised us a general account of the foundations of thought (Lévi-Strauss 1963a,b, 1966, 1964–1967; Boon 1972). Others, like "sociobiology" (Chagnon & Irons 1979), "cognitive anthropology" (Tyler 1969, D'Andrade 1995), "the ethnography of speaking" (Gumperz & Hymes 1964, Tedlock 1983), or "cultural materialism," (Harris 1979, Rappaport 1968) were stimulated, sometimes overstimulated, by advances in biology, information theory, semiotics, or ecology. There was neo-Marxism (Wolf 1982), neo-evolutionism (Service 1971, Steward 1957), neo-functionalism (Gluckman 1963, Turner 1957), and neo-Durkheimianism (Douglas 1989). Pierre Bourdieu gave us "practice theory" (1977), Victor Turner "the anthropology of experience" (Turner & Bruner 1986), Louis Dumont "the social anthropology of civilizations" (1970), Renajit Guha, "subaltern studies" (1982). Edmund Leach talked of "culture and communication" (1974), Jack Goody of "the written and the oral" (1977), Rodney Needham of "language and experience" (1972), David Schneider of "kinship as a cultural system" (1968), Marshall Sahlins of "structure and conjuncture" (1981). As for me, I contributed to the merriment with "interpretive anthropology," an extension, broadened and redirected by developments in literature, philosophy, and the analysis of language, of my concern with the systems of meaning—beliefs, values, world views, forms of feeling, styles of thought—in terms of which particular peoples construct their existence and live out their particular lives (1973, 1983). New or reconditioned social movements, feminism (Rosaldo & Lamphere 1974, Ortner & Whitehead 1981, McCormack & Strathern 1980, Weiner 1976), antiimperialism (Said 1978), indigenous rights (Deloria 1969), and gay liberation (Newton 1979), added to the mix, as did new departures in neighboring fields—the *Annales* movement in history (Le Roi Ladurie 1980), the "new historicism" in literature (Greenblatt 1980), science studies in sociology (Latour & Woolgar 1986, Traweek 1988), hermeneutics and phenomenology in philosophy (Gadamer 1975, Ricoeur 1981, Habermas 1972), and that elusive and equivocal movement, known, elusively and equivocally, as "post-structuralism" (Foucault 1970, Lacan 1977, Derrida 1976, Deleuze & Guattari 1977). There were more than enough perspectives to go around.

What was lacking was any means of ordering them within a broadly accepted disciplinary frame or rationale, an encompassing paradigm. The sense that the field was breaking up into smaller and smaller, incommensurable fragments, that a primordial oneness was being lost in a swarm of fads and fashions, grew, producing cries, angry, desperate, or merely puzzled, for some sort of reunification (Lewis 1998). Types or varieties of anthropology, separately conceived and organized, appeared, one on top of the next: medical anthropology, psychological anthropology, feminist anthropology, economic anthropology, symbolic anthropology, visual anthropology; the anthropology of work, of education, of law, of consciousness; ethnohistory, ethnophilosophy, ethnolinguistics, ethnomusicology. What had been, when I stumbled into it in the early 1950s, a group of a few hundred, argumentative but similarly minded ethnologists, as they tended then to call themselves, most of whom knew one another personally, became by the late 1970s a vast crowd of scholars whose sole commonality often seemed to be that they had passed through one or another doctoral program labeled anthropology (there are more than a hundred in the United States alone, and perhaps that many more around the world).

Much of this was expectable and unavoidable, a reflex of the growth of the field and the advance of technical specialization, as well as, once again, the workings of the World Spirit as it made its way toward the conclusion of things. But change nonetheless produced both an intensification of polemical combat and, in some quarters anyway, angst and malaise. Not only did there appear a series of trumped-up "wars" between imaginary combatants over artificial issues (materialists vs.

idealists, universalists vs. relativists, scientists vs. humanists, realists vs. subjectivists), but a generalized and oddly self-lacerating skepticism about the anthropological enterprise as such—about representing The Other or, worse yet, purporting to speak for him—settled in, hardened, and began to spread (Clifford 1988, Fabian 1983).

In time, as the impulses that drove the optimism of the 1950s and the turbulence of the 1960s died away into the routines and immobilities of Reagan's America, this doubt, disillusion, and autocritique gathered itself together under the broad and indefinite, rather suddenly popular banner of postmodernism (Lyotard 1984, Harvey 1989). Defined against modernism in reproof and repudiation—"goodbye to all that"—postmodernism was, and is, more a mood and an attitude than a connected theory: a rhetorical tag applied to a deepening sense of moral and epistemological crisis, the supposed exhaustion, or, worse, corruption of the received modes of judgment and knowledge. Issues of ethnographic representation, authority, political positioning, and ethical justification all came in for a thorough going-over; the anthropologist's very "right to write" got put into question. "Why have ethnographic accounts recently lost so much of their authority?"—the jacket copy of James Clifford's and George Marcus' *Writing Culture* collection (1986), something of a bellwether in all of this, cried:

> Why were they ever believable? Who has the right to challenge an 'objective' cultural description?. . . Are not all ethnographies rhetorical performances determined by the need to tell an effective story? Can the claims of ideology and desire ever be fully reconciled with the needs of theory and observation?

Most of the work in this manner (not all of it so flat-out or so excited as this, nor so densely populated with rhetorical questions) tended to center around one or the other of two concerns: either the construction of anthropological texts, that is, ethnographical writing, or the moral status of anthropological work, that is, ethnographical practice. The first led off into essentially literary matters: authorship, genre, style, narrative, metaphor, representation, discourse, fiction, figuration, persuasion (Geertz 1988, Boon 1982, Fernandez 1986, Sapir & Crocker 1977, Pratt 1992); the second, into essentially political matters: the social foundations of anthropological authority, the modes of power inscribed in its practices, its ideological assumptions, its complicity with colonialism, racism, exploitation, and exoticism, its dependency on the master narratives of Western self-understanding (Hymes 1972, Asad 1973, Marcus & Fischer 1986, Rosaldo 1989). These interlinked critiques of anthropology, the one inward-looking and brooding, the other outward-looking and recriminatory, may not have produced the "fully dialectical ethnography acting powerfully in the postmodern world system," to quote that *Writing Culture* blast again, nor did they exactly go unresisted (Gellner 1992, cf. Geertz 1995b). But they did induce a certain self-awareness, and a certain candor also, into a discipline not without need of them.

However that may be, I spent these years of assertion and denial, promise and counterpromise, first at the University of Chicago, from 1960 to 1970, then at the Institute for Advanced Study in Princeton, from 1970 on, mostly trying to keep my balance, to remember who I was, and to go on doing whatever it was I had, before everything came loose, set out to do.

At Chicago, I was once again involved in, and this time ultimately as its director, an interdisciplinary program focused on the prospects of the by now quite stalled and shredded—Biafra, Bangladesh, Southern Yemen—third world: the Committee for the Comparative Study of New Nations. This committee, which remained in being for more than a decade, was not concerned as such with policy questions nor with constructing a general theory of development, nor indeed with goal-directed team research of any sort. It consisted of a dozen or so faculty members at the university—sociologists, political scientists, economists, and anthropologists—working on or in one or another of the decolonized new states, plus a half-dozen or so postdoctoral research fellows, mostly from elsewhere, similarly engaged. Its main collective activity was a long weekly seminar at which one of the members led a discussion of his or her work, which in turn formed the basis for a smaller core group of, if not precisely collaborators, for we all worked independently, similarly minded, experienced field workers directed toward a related set of issues in what was then called, rather hopefully, considering the general state of things, nation building (Geertz 1963b). Unable, for the moment, to return to Indonesia, by then fully in the grip of pervasive rage, I organized a team of doctoral students from the anthropology department, of which I was also a member, to study a town comparable in size, complexity, and general representativeness to Modjokuto, but at the far other, Maghrebian, end of the Islamic world: Morocco (Geertz et al. 1979).

The Chicago department of anthropology, presided over at that time by an unusually open and supportive group of elders (Fred Eggan, Sol Tax, Norman MacQuown, and Robert Braidwood; Robert Redfield having only just died), provided an unusually congenial setting for this sort of free-style, thousand-flowers approach to things anthropological. Lloyd Fallers, Victor Turner, David Schneider, McKim Marriott, Robert Adams, Manning Nash, Melford Spiro, Robert LeVine, Nur Yalman, Julian Pitt-Rivers, Paul Friedrich, and Milton Singer were all there crying up, as I was also, one or another line of cultural analysis, and the interaction among us was intense, productive, and surprisingly, given the range of temperaments involved, generally amicable (Stocking n.d.). But when, in the late 1960s, the Director of the Institute for Advanced Study in Princeton, the economist Carl Kaysen, invited me to come there and start up a new school in the Social Sciences to complement the schools in Mathematics, Natural Science, and Historical Studies in existence since Einstein, Weyl, von Neumann, Panofsky, and other worthies had put the place in motion in the late 1930s and early 1940s, I, after a couple of years backing and filling, accepted. However exposed and full of hazard it might be, especially in a time of such division within the academy and the dubiousness of the very idea of "the social sciences" in the eyes of many humanists and "real scientists," the prospect of being given a blank and unmarked page upon which to write was, for someone by now addicted to good fortune, simply too attractive to resist.

CONCLUSION

It is always very difficult to determine just when it was that "now" began. Virginia Woolf thought it was "on or about December 1, 1910," for W.H. Auden it was "September 1, 1939," for many of us who worried our way through the balance of terror, it was 1989 and the Fall of the Wall. And now, having survived all that, there is September 11, 2001.

My years, thirty-one and counting, at the Institute for Advanced Study have proved, after some initial difficulties with the resident mandarins, soon disposed of (the difficulties, not the mandarins), to be an excellent vantage from which to watch the present come into being in the social sciences (Geertz 2001). Setting up a new enterprise in the field from a standing start—the whole field from economics, politics, philosophy, and law, to sociology, psychology, history, and anthropology, with a few scholars from literature, art, and religion thrown in for leavening—demanded much closer attention to what was going on in these areas, not only in the United States but abroad as well. And with more than five hundred scholars from more than thirty countries spending a year as visiting fellows at one time or another (nearly a fifth of them anthropologists of various kinds, origins, ages, and degrees of celebrity), one had the extraordinary experience of seeing "now" arrive, live and in color.

All that is well and good, but as the present immediate is, in the nature of the case, entirely in motion, confused and unsettled, it does not yield so readily to sorting out as does, at least apparently, the perfected, distanced past. It is easier to recognize the new as new than to say exactly what it is that is new about it, and to try to discern which way it is in general moving is but to be reminded again of Hegel's Dictum: the future can be an object of hope or of anxiety, of expectation or of misgiving, but it cannot be an object of knowledge. I confine myself, then, in finishing up this picaresque tale of questing adventure, to just a few brief and evasive remarks about how things anthropological seem to have been going in the last decade or so.

At the world-history level I have been invoking throughout as active background, the major developments are, of course, the end of the cold war, the dissolution of the bipolar international system, and the emergence of a system, if it can be called a system, which comes more and more each day to look like a strangely paradoxical combination of global interdependence (capital flow, multinationals, trade zones, the Net) and ethnic, religious and other intensely parochial provincialisms (The Balkans, Sri Lanka, Ruanda-Burundi, Chechnya, Northern Ireland, the Basque country). Whether this "Jihad vs. McWorld" (Barber 1995), is genuinely a paradox, or, as I tend to think, a single, deeply interconnected phenomenon, it has clearly begun to affect the anthropological agenda in ways that September 11 can only accelerate.

Studies of ethnic discord (Daniel 1996), of transnational identities (Appadurai 1996), of collective violence (Das 2000), of migration (Foner 2000), refugees (Malkki 1995), and intrusive minorities (Kelly 1991), of nationalism (Gellner 1983), of separatism (Tambiah 1986), of citizenship, civic and cultural (Rosaldo

1997), and of the operation of supra-national quasi-governmental institutions [e.g., the World Bank, the International Monetary Fund, UN bodies, etc. (Klitgaard 1990)]—studies which were not thought to be part of anthropology's purview even a few short years ago—are now appearing on all sides. There are works, and very good ones, on the advertising business in Sri Lanka (Kemper 2001), on television in India (Rajagopal 2001), on legal conceptions in Islam (Rosen 1989, 2000), on the world trade in sushi (Bestor 2000), on the political implications of witchcraft beliefs in the new South Africa (Ashforth 2000). Insofar as I myself have been directly involved in all this, it has been in connection with the paradox, real or otherwise, of the simultaneous increase in cosmopolitanism and parochialism I just mentioned; with what I called in some lectures I gave in Vienna a few years ago (and hope soon to expand) "The World in Pieces" calling for an anthropological rethinking of our master political conceptions, nation, state, country, society, people (Geertz 2000).

Things are thus not, or at least in my view they are not, coming progressively together as the discipline moves raggedly on. And this, too, reflects the direction, if it can be called a direction, in which the wider world is moving: toward fragmentation, dispersion, pluralism, disassembly, -multi, multi-, multi-. Anthropologists are going to have to work under conditions even less orderly, shapely, and predictable, and even less susceptible of moral and ideological reduction and political quick fixes, than those I have worked under, which I hope I have shown were irregular enough. A born fox (there is a gene for it, along with restlessness, elusiveness, and a passionate dislike of hedgehogs), this seems to me the natural habitat of the cultural . . . social . . . symbolic . . . interpretive anthropologist. Interesting times, an inconstant profession: I envy those about to inherit them.

The *Annual Review of Anthropology* is online at http://anthro.annualreviews.org

LITERATURE CITED

Allport GW. 1954. *The Nature of Prejudice*. Cambridge, MA: Addison-Wesley

Appadurai A. 1996. *Modernity at Large: Cultural Dimensions of Globalization*. Minneapolis: Univ. Minn. Press

Asad T, ed. 1973. *Anthropology and the Colonial Encounter*. New York: Humanities

Ashforth A. 2000. *Madumo: a Man Bewitched*. Chicago: Univ. Chicago Press

Barber BR. 1995. *Jihad vs. McWorld*. New York: Times Books

Bauer R. 1959. *The New Man in Soviet Psychology*. Cambridge, MA: Harvard Univ. Press

Bauer R, Inkeles A, Kluckhohn C. 1956. *How the Soviet System Works: Cultural, Psychological, and Social Themes*. Cambridge, MA: Harvard Univ. Press

Bellah RN. 1957. *Tokugawa Religion: the Values of Pre-Industrial Japan*. New York: Free Press

Bellah RN, ed. 1965. *Religion and Progress in Modern Asia*. New York: Free Press

Bendix R. 1962. *Max Weber: an Intellectual Portrait*. Garden City, NY: Doubleday

Benedict RF. 1934. *Patterns of Culture*. Boston: Houghton Mifflin

Benedict R. 1949. *The Chrysanthemum and the Sword: Patterns of Japanese Culture*. Boston: Houghton Mifflin

Bestor TC. 2000. When sushi went global. *Foreign Aff.*: Nov.–Dec.

Black C, ed. 1976. *Comparative Modernization: a Reader*. New York: Free Press

Boon JA. 1972. *From Symbolism to Structuralism: Lévi-Strauss in a Literary Tradition*. Oxford: Blackwells

Boon JA. 1982. *Other Tribes, Other Scribes: Symbolic Anthropology in the Comparative Study of Cultures, Histories, Religions, and Text*. New York: Cambridge Univ. Press

Bourdieu P. 1977. *Outline of a Theory of Practice*. New York: Cambridge Univ. Press

Bruner JS, Krech D, eds. 1950. *Perception and Personality*. Durham, NC: Duke Univ. Press

Chagnon N, Irons W, eds. 1979. *Evolutionary Biology and Human Social Behavior*. North Scituate, MA: Duxbury

Clifford J. 1988. *The Predicament of Culture: Twentieth Century Ethnography, Literature, and Art*. Cambridge, MA: Harvard Univ. Press

Clifford J, Marcus G, eds. 1986. *Writing Culture: the Poetics and Politics of Culture*. Berkeley: Univ. Calif. Press

D'Andrade RG. 1995. *The Development of Cognitive Anthropology*. New York: Cambridge Univ. Press

Daniel EV. 1996. *Charred Lullabies: Chapters in an Anthropology of Violence*. Princeton, NJ: Princeton Univ. Press

Das V, ed. 2000. *Violence and Subjectivity*. Berkeley: Univ. Calif. Press

Deleuze G, Guattari F. 1977. *Anti-Oedipus: Capitalism and Schizophrenia*. New York: Viking

Deloria V. 1969. *Custer Died for Your Sins: an Indian Manifesto*. New York: Macmillan

Derrida J. 1976. *Of Grammatology*. Baltimore, MD: Johns Hopkins Univ. Press

Diamond S. 1992. *Compromised Campus: the Collaboration of the Universities with the Intelligence Community, 1945–1955*. New York: Oxford Univ. Press

Douglas M. 1989. *How Institutions Think*. Syracuse, NY: Syracuse Univ. Press

Du Bois C, Kardiner A, Oberholzer E, et al. 1944. *The People of Alor: a Social-Psychological Study of an East Indian Island*. Minneapolis: Univ. Minn. Press

Dumont L. 1970. *Homo Hierarchicus: an Essay on the Caste System*. Chicago: Univ. Chicago Press

Eisenstadt S, ed. 1968. *The Protestant Ethic and Modernization: a Comparative View*. New York: Basic Books

Eisenstadt SN. 1966. *Modernization: Protest and Change*. Englewood Cliffs, NJ: Prentice-Hall

Erikson EH. 1950. *Childhood and Society*. New York: Norton

Fabian J. 1983. *Time and the Other: How Anthropology Makes Its Object*. New York: Columbia Univ. Press

Fernandez JA. 1986. *Persuasions and Performances: the Play of Tropes in Culture*. Bloomington: Ind. Univ. Press

Foner N. 2000. *From Ellis Island to JFK: New York's Two Great Waves of Immigration*. New Haven, CT: Yale Univ. Press

Foucault M. 1970. *The Order of Things, an Archaeology of the Human Sciences*. New York: Pantheon

Gadamer H-G. 1975. *Truth and Method*. London: Sheed & Ward

Geertz C. 1956. Religious belief and economic behavior in a central Javanese town: some preliminary considerations. *Econ. Dev. Cult. Change* 2:134–58

Geertz C. 1963a. *Agricultural Involution: the Process of Ecological Change in Indonesia*. Berkeley: Univ. Calif. Press

Geertz C, ed. 1963b. *Old Societies and New States*. New York: Free Press

Geertz C. 1973. *The Interpretation of Cultures, Selected Essays*. New York: Basic Books

Geertz C. 1983. *Local Knowledge: Further Essays in Interpretive Anthropology*. New York: Basic

Geertz C. 1988. *Works and Lives: the Anthropologist as Author*. Stanford, CA: Stanford Univ. Press

Geertz C. 1995a. *After the Fact: Two Countries, Four Decades, One Anthropologist*. Cambridge, MA: Harvard Univ. Press

Geertz C. 1995b. Reason, religion and Professor Gellner. In *The Limits of Pluralism: Neo-absolutism and Relativism*, ed. HR Hoetink, n.p. Amsterdam: Praemium Erasmanium Found.

Geertz C. 2000. *Available Light: Anthropological Reflections on Philosophical Topics.* Princeton, NJ: Princeton Univ. Press

Geertz C. 2001. School building: a retrospective preface. In *Schools of Thought: Twenty-five Years of Interpretive Social Science*, ed. JW Scott, D Keates, pp. 1–11. Princeton, NJ: Princeton Univ. Press

Geertz C, Geertz H, Rosen L. 1979. *Meaning and Order in Moroccan Society.* New York: Cambridge Univ. Press

Gellner E. 1983. *Nations and Nationalism.* Oxford: Basil Blackwell

Gellner E. 1992. *Postmodernism, Reason, and Religion.* New York: Routledge

Gluckman M. 1963. *Order and Rebellion in Tribal Africa, Collected Essays.* Glencoe, IL: Free Press

Goody J. 1977. *The Domestication of the Savage Mind.* New York: Cambridge Univ. Press

Gorer G. 1948. *The American People: a Study in National Character.* New York: Norton

Gorer G. 1955. *Exploring English Character.* London: Cresset

Gorer G, Rickman J. 1963. *The People of Great Russia, a Psychological Study.* London: Cresset

Greenblatt SJ. 1980. *Renaissance Self-Fashioning: From More to Shakespeare.* Chicago: Univ. Chicago Press

Guha R, ed. 1982. *Subaltern Studies: Writings on South Asian History and Society.* New York: Oxford Univ. Press

Gumperz JJ, Hymes D, eds. 1964. *The Ethnography of Communication.* Washington, DC: Am. Anthropol. Assoc.

Habermas J. 1972. *Knowledge and Human Interests.* Boston: Beacon

Hallowell AI. 1955. *Culture and Experience.* Phila.: Univ. Penn. Press

Harris M. 1979. *Cultural Materialism: the Struggle for a Science of Culture.* New York: Random House

Harvey D. 1989. *The Condition of Post Modernity.* Cambridge, UK: Blackwell

Homans G. 1950. *The Human Group.* New York: Harcourt-Brace

Hymes DH, ed. 1972. *Reinventing Anthropology.* New York: Pantheon

Inkeles A. 1950. *Public Opinion in Soviet Russia: a Study of Mass Persuasion.* Cambridge, MA: Harvard Univ. Press

Jakobson R. 1952. *Preliminaries to Speech Analysis: the Distinctive Features and Their Correlates.* Cambridge: MIT Acoust. Libr. Tech. Rep. No. 13

Kahin GMcT. 1956. *The Asian African Conference, Bandung, Indonesia, April 1958.* Ithaca, NY: Cornell Univ. Press.

Kardiner A, Linton R. 1939. *The Individual and His Society: the Psychodynamics of Primitive Social Organization.* New York: Columbia Univ. Press

Kelly JD. 1991. *The Politics of Virtue: Hinduism, Sexuality, and Counter Colonial Discourse in Fiji.* Chicago: Univ. Chicago Press

Kemper S. 2001. *Buying and Believing: Sri Lankan Advertising and Consumers in a Transnational World.* Chicago: Univ. Chicago Press

Klitgaard R. 1990. *Tropical Gangsters.* New York: Basic Books

Kluckhohn C. 1949. *Mirror for Man: the Relation of Anthropology to Modern Life.* New York: McGraw-Hill

Kluckhohn C. 1951. *Project on the Soviet Social System.* Cambridge, MA: Harvard Russ. Res. Cent.

Kluckhohn C. 1962. *Culture and Behavior: Collected Essays*, ed. R Kluckhohn. New York: Free Press

Kluckhohn C, Murray HA, Schneider DM. 1949. *Personality in Nature, Society, and Culture.* New York: Knopf

Kluckhohn FR, Strodtbeck F. 1961. *Variations in Value Orientations.* Evanston, IL: Northwestern Univ. Press

Kroeber AL, Kluckhohn C. 1952. *Culture: a Critical Review of Concepts and Definitions.* Cambridge, MA: Pap. Peabody Mus. Archaeol. Ethnol., Harvard Univ., 57(1)

Kuhn TS. 1962. *The Structure of Scientific Revolutions.* Chicago: Univ. Chicago Press

Lacan J. 1977. *Ecrits, a Selection*. New York: Norton

Ladd J. 1957. *The Structure of a Moral Code: a Philosophical Analysis of Ethical Discourse as Applied to the Ethics of the Navaho Indians*. Cambridge, MA: Harvard Univ. Press

Latour B, Woolgar S. 1986. *Laboratory Life: the Construction of Scientific Facts*. Princeton, NJ: Princeton Univ. Press

Leach ER. 1974. *Culture and Communication*. New York: Cambridge Univ. Press

Leighton DC, Kluckhohn C. 1947. *Children of the People: the Navaho Individual and His Development*. Cambridge, MA: Harvard Univ. Press

Le Roy Ladurie E. 1980. *Montaillou: Cathars and Catholics in a French Village, 1294–1324*. New York: Penguin

Lévi-Strauss C. 1963a. *Structural Anthropology*. New York: Basic Books

Lévi-Strauss C. 1963b. *Totemism*. Boston: Beacon

Lévi-Strauss C. 1964–1967. *Mythologiques*. 4 Vols. Paris: Plon

Lévi-Strauss C. 1966. *The Savage Mind*. Chicago: Univ. Chicago Press

Levy M. 1960. *Modernization and the Structure of Societies: a Setting for International Relations*. Princeton, NJ: Princeton Univ. Press

Lewis HS. 1998. The misrepresentation of anthropology and its consequences. *Am. Anthropol.* 100(3):716–31

Lyotard J-F. 1984. *The Post-Modern Condition: a Report on Knowledge*. Minneapolis: Univ. Minn. Press

Malkki L. 1995. *Purity and Exile: Violence, Memory, and National Cosmology Among the Hutu Refugees of Tanzania*. Chicago: Univ. Chicago Press

Marcus G, Fischer M. 1986. *Anthropology as Cultural Critique: an Experimental Moment in the Human Sciences*. Chicago: Univ. Chicago Press

McCormack CP, Strathern M, eds. 1980. *Nature, Culture, and Gender*. Cambridge, UK: Cambridge Univ. Press

Mead M. 1942. *And Keep Your Powder Dry: an Anthropologist Looks at America*. New York: Norton

Mead M, Métraux R. 1953. *The Study of Culture at a Distance*. Chicago: Univ. Chicago Press

Mead M, Rickman J. 1951. *Soviet Attitudes Toward Authority: an Interdisciplinary Approach to the Study of Soviet Character*. NewYork: McGraw-Hill

Métraux R, Mead M. 1954. *Themes in French Culture*. Stanford, CA: Stanford Univ. Press

Millikan M, Blackmer D, eds. 1961. *The Emerging Nations: Their Growth and United States Policy*. Boston: Little Brown

Murray HA, ed. 1938. *Explorations in Personality: a Clinical Exploratory Study of Fifty Men of College Age*. New York: Oxford Univ. Press

Needham R. 1972. *Belief, Language, and Experience*. Oxford: Blackwell

Newton E. 1979. *Mother Camp: Female Impersonators in America*. Chicago: Univ. Chicago Press

Ortner SB, Whitehead H, eds. 1981. *Sexual Meanings: the Cultural Construction of Sexuality*. New York: Cambridge Univ. Press

Parsons T. 1937. *The Structure of Social Action: a Study in Social Theory with Special Reference to a Group of Recent European Writers*. New York: McGraw-Hill

Parsons T, Shils E, eds. 1951. *Toward a General Theory of Action*. Cambridge, MA: Harvard Univ. Press

Piers G, Singer MB. 1953. *Shame and Guilt, a Psychoanalytical and a Cultural Study*. Springfield, IL: Thomas

Pratt ML. 1992. *Imperial Eyes: Travel Writing and Transculturation*. New York: Routledge

Rajagopal A. 2001. *Politics After Television: Hindu Nationalism and the Reshaping of the Public in India*. Cambridge, UK: Cambridge Univ. Press

Rappaport RA. 1968. *Pigs for the Ancestors: Ritual in the Ecology of a New Guinea People*. New Haven, CT: Yale Univ. Press

Redfield R. 1953. *The Primitive World and its Transformations*. Ithaca, NY: Cornell Univ. Press

Redfield R. 1956. *Peasant Society and Culture: an Anthropological Approach to Civilization*. Chicago: Univ. Chicago Press

Ricoeur P. 1981. *Hermeneutics and the Human Sciences*. Cambridge, UK: Cambridge Univ. Press

Rosaldo M, Lamphere L, eds. 1974. *Woman, Culture, and Society*. Stanford, CA: Stanford Univ. Press

Rosaldo R. 1989. *Culture and Truth: the Reworking of Social Analysis*. Boston: Beacon

Rosaldo R. 1997. Cultural citizenship, inequality, and multiculturalism. In *Latino Cultural Citizenship: Claiming Identity, Space, and Right*, ed. W Flores, R Benmajor, pp. 27–33. Boston: Beacon

Rosen L. 1989. *The Anthropology of Justice: Law as Culture in Islamic Society*. New York: Cambridge Univ. Press

Rosen L. 2000. *The Justice of Islam: Comparative Perspectives of Islamic Law and Society*. Oxford, UK: Oxford Univ. Press

Sahlins M. 1981. *Historical Metaphors and Mythical Realities: Structure in the Early History of the Sandwich Islands*. Ann Arbor: Univ. Mich. Press

Said EW. 1978. *Orientalism*. New York: Pantheon

Sapir E. 1949. *Culture, Language, and Personality*. Berkeley: Univ. Calif. Press

Sapir JD, Crocker JC, eds. 1977. *The Social Use of Metaphor: Essays on the Anthropology of Rhetoric*. Phila.: Univ. Penn. Press

Schneider DM. 1968. *American Kinship: a Cultural Account*. Englewood Cliffs, NJ: Prentice-Hall

Service ER. 1971. *Cultural Evolutionism: Theory and Practice*. New York: Holt, Rinehart & Winston

Singer M. 1956. *Traditional India, Structure and Change*. Phila.: Am. Folklore Soc.

Smith W, Roberts JM. 1954. *Zuni Law: a Field of Values*. Cambridge, MA: Pap. Peabody Mus. Archaeol. Ethnol., Harvard Univ., 43(1)

Steward JH. 1950. *Area Research: Theory and Practice*. New York: Soc. Sci. Res. Counc.

Steward JH. 1957. *Theory of Culture Change: the Methodology of Multilinear Evolution*. Urbana: Univ. Ill. Press

Steward JH, Manners R, Wolf ER, Padilla Seda E, Mintz SW, et al. 1956. *The People of Puerto Rico*. Urbana: Univ. Ill Press

Stocking GW. n.d. "From the Paleolithic to Palo Alto," "The Boom Years," "Untying the Sacred Bundle," cases 19, 20, 21. http://anthropology.uchicago.edu/about.html

Stouffer SA, ed. 1949. *The American Soldier*. 4 Vols. Princeton, NJ: Princeton Univ. Press

Tambiah SJ. 1986. *Sri Lanka: Ethnic Fratricide and the Dismantling of Democracy*. Chicago: Univ. Chicago Press

Tawney RH. 1947. *Religion and the Rise of Capitalism: a Historical Study*. New York: Harcourt-Brace

Tedlock D. 1983. *The Spoken Word and the Work of Interpretation*. Phila.: Univ. Penn. Press

Tolman EC. 1958. *Essays in Motivation and Learning*. Berkeley: Univ. Calif. Press

Traweek S. 1988. *Beamtimes and Lifetimes*. Cambridge: Harvard Univ. Press

Turner VW. 1957. *Schism and Continuity in an African Society*. Manchester, UK: Manchester Univ. Press

Turner VW, Bruner E, eds. 1986. *The Anthropology of Experience*. Urbana: Univ. Ill Press

Tyler SA, ed. 1969. *Cognitive Anthropology: Readings*. New York: Rinehart & Winston

Vogt EZ. 1955. *Modern Homesteaders*. Cambridge: Harvard Univ. Press

Vogt EZ, Albert EM, eds. 1966. *People of Rimrock: a Study of Values in Five Cultures*. Cambridge, MA: Harvard Univ. Press

Wallace AFC. 1970. *Culture and Personality*. New York: Random House

Weber M. 1947. *The Theory of Social and Economic Organization*. Glencoe, IL: Free Press

Weber M. 1950a. *The Protestant Ethic and the Spirit of Capitalism*. New York: Scribner

Weber M. 1950b. *General Economic History*. Glencoe, IL: Free Press

Weber M. 1965. *The Sociology of Religion*. Boston: Beacon

Weiner AB. 1976. *Women of Value, Men of Renown: New Perspectives in Trobriand Exchange*. Austin: Univ. Tex. Press
Whiting BB, Whiting J. 1975. *Children of Six Cultures: a Psycho-Cultural Analysis*. Cambridge, MA: Harvard Univ. Press
Wiener N. 1962. *Cybernetics; or Control and Communication in the Animal and the Machine*. Cambridge, MA: MIT Press
Wolf ER. 1982. *Europe and the People Without History*. Berkeley: Univ. Calif. Press
Wright R. 1995. *The Color Curtain: a Report on the Bandung Conference*. Jackson: Univ. Press Miss.

Annu. Rev. Anthropol. 2002. 31:21–44
doi: 10.1146/annurev.anthro.31.032902.101743

First published online as a Review in Advance on April 23, 2002

THE FORM AND FUNCTION OF RECONCILIATION IN PRIMATES

Joan B. Silk
Department of Anthropology, University of California, Los Angeles, Los Angeles, California 90095; email: jsilk@anthro.ucla.edu

Key Words peacemaking, conflict resolution, aggression, remediation, sociality

■ **Abstract** Sociality is favored by natural selection because it enhances group members' access to valued resources or reduces their vulnerability to predators, but group living also generates conflict among group members. To enjoy the benefits of sociality, group living animals must somehow overcome the costs of conflict. Nonhuman primates have developed an effective mechanism for resolving conflicts: They participate in peaceful postconflict (PC) reunions with former opponents. These peaceful PC interactions are collectively labeled reconciliation. There is a broad consensus that peaceful contacts among former opponents relieve stressful effects of conflict and permit former opponents to interact peacefully. Primates may reconcile to obtain short-term objectives, such as access to desirable resources. Alternatively, reconciliation may preserve valuable relationships damaged by conflict. Some researchers view these explanations as complementary, but they generate different predictions about the patterning of reconciliation that can be partially tested with available data. There are good reasons to question the validity of the relationship-repair model, but it remains firmly entrenched in the reconciliation literature, perhaps because it fits our own folk model of how and why we resolve conflicts ourselves. It is possible that the function of reconciliation varies within the primate order, much as other aspects of cognitive abilities do.

MAKING AMENDS

Conflict is a common consequence of group living. Sociality is favored among primates by natural selection because it enhances group members' access to valued resources (Wrangham 1980, 1987) or reduces their vulnerability to predators (van Schaik 1983, van Schaik & van Hooff 1983), but group living also generates competition and conflict among group members (Isbell 1991, van Schaik 1983, van Schaik & van Hooff 1983). To enjoy the benefits of sociality, group living animals must somehow overcome the disruptive effects of competition and conflict.

Many species of nonhuman primates have developed an effective mechanism for resolving conflicts. Although disputes seem likely to drive antagonists apart, conflict often has the opposite effect. For example, a female baboon who has just attacked a lower ranking female may subsequently approach her former victim

0084-6570/02/1021-0021$14.00

and grunt softly to her (Castles 1998, Gore 1994, Silk et al. 1996). Experimental and observational evidence indicates that these grunts reassure the victim that the conflict has ended (Cheney et al. 1995) and facilitate peaceful interactions among former opponents (Cheney & Seyfarth 1997, Silk et al. 1996). In a wide range of primate species, former opponents are much more likely to interact peacefully or sit together in the minutes that follow conflicts than they are at other times. The behaviors that constitute these peaceful postconflict reunions are collectively labeled reconciliation.

Reconciliation has now been documented in more than two dozen species of nonhuman primates (Aureli & de Waal 2000b), as well as in feral sheep (Rowell & Rowell 1993), domestic goats (Schino 1998), spotted hyenas (Hofer & East 2000), and bottle-nosed dolphins (Samuels & Flaherty 2000). Reconciliation occurs in all major taxa within the primate order, including prosimians, monkeys, apes, and humans, and has become a major focus of empirical and theoretical work in primatology over the last two decades.

THE FUNCTION OF RECONCILIATION

Reconciliation may be favored by natural selection because it settles conflicts swiftly and unambiguously. This might be useful because agonistic interactions have abrupt beginnings but quite indefinite endings. A conflict may end after one episode of aggression, or it may continue and even escalate to a more dangerous level. The recipient of aggression may submit, retaliate, or recruit support from powerful allies. This uncertainty makes the period following conflict stressful for both aggressors and their victims (Aureli et al. 1989, Aureli & van Schaik 1991, Das et al. 1997). Uncertainty also precludes further contact among former opponents because it is risky to reestablish contact when the intentions of former opponents are uncertain.

Reconciliatory behaviors, such as female baboons' grunts, may be signals that inform the recipient that the current conflict is over and the actor's intentions are now benign (Silk 1996, 1997). Signals of nonaggressive intent may be favored by selection because they enable former opponents to coordinate their interactions (Silk 1997). Imagine that a conflict takes place between two female monkeys. The aggressor does not intend to continue fighting; she would like to be groomed. The victim aims to avoid further aggression and would rather groom her former aggressor than retaliate against her. In this situation, it is important for females to be able to signal their intentions because there is real uncertainty about what will happen next. If no signals that convey this information are given, both parties may be wary of each other and reluctant to approach. If dishonest signals are given neither will benefit. For instance, if the aggressor signals that her intentions are nonaggressive and then resumes her attack, the victim will flee, and there will be no grooming. Similarly, if the victim signals peaceful intentions and then retaliates, the aggressor will either fight or flee, but will not groom. If grooming is more beneficial than fighting at this juncture, then both parties benefit from sending truthful signals about their peaceful inclinations. Since there is no incentive for deception, these signals are expected to be inexpensive and inconspicuous (Silk et al. 2000).

Alternatively, reconciliation may be adaptive because it preserves the quality of valuable social bonds. De Waal & van Roosmalen (1979) originally chose the term reconciliation to describe peaceful postconflict reunions among captive chimpanzees because it was their subjective "impression that such body contacts have a calming effect and serve an important socially homeostatic function" (1979:65). This "homeostatic function" was hypothesized to be important because it preserves the cohesion of social groups by reducing the disruptive effects of conflict. In more recent formulations of this model, the emphasis has shifted from the maintenance of group cohesion to the preservation of valuable[1] social relationships among individuals (e.g., Cords 1988; de Waal 1989, 1993; de Waal & Aureli 1996; Kappeler & van Schaik 1992). Peaceful contact among former opponents is favored by natural selection because it contributes to the stability of social bonds, which ultimately enhances reproductive fitness.

Some workers have argued that the benign-intent and relationship-repair models are complementary, not alternative, explanations of why reconciliation occurs (de Waal 2000, Cords & Aureli 1996). According to this view, the long-term effects on social relationships may be incidental, albeit advantageous, side effects of reconciliatory behavior: "The habit of reconciling conflicts might make social partners get along better over the long run by increasing a dominant's tolerance of the subordinate, and by decreasing chronic stress in the subordinate. Repeated occasions in which partners communicate their common interest in each other by reconciling after conflict may increase the predictability of their interaction patterns, and hence their ability to interact in adaptive ways" (Cords & Aureli 1996:45).

All interactions between two individuals contribute incrementally to the history of events that define their relationship (Hinde 1983), so peaceful reunions after conflicts will inevitably, but indirectly, influence the nature and quality of social bonds. But this does not necessarily mean that natural selection has favored the evolution of reconciliatory behaviors *because* they enhance long-term social bonds. This is an important distinction because the selective forces that favor the evolution of signals of benign intent may be quite different from the selective forces that shape the evolution of social bonds among females. The distinction also becomes meaningful when we consider how reconciliation is patterned in nature. The two

[1]In this context, value is defined in terms of reproductive fitness. According to evolutionary theory, natural selection is expected to favor the evolution of behaviors that enhance the fitness of individuals. Altruistic behaviors, which enhance the fitness of others and reduce the fitness of the actors, can evolve via kin selection (Hamilton 1964) or reciprocal altruism (Trivers 1971). Kummer (1978) suggested that the same logic applies to evolutionary forces shaping the formation and maintenance of social relationships. Animals are expected to selectively invest in relationships from which they gain benefits that exceed their costs, and work hardest to cultivate relationships from which they derive the greatest profits. Again, benefits and costs are defined in terms of their effects on reproductive fitness.

models generate different predictions about the frequency of reconciliation across species, groups, and dyads (Silk 1996, 1997, 2000). Thus, the empirical record holds important clues about the function of these interactions.

Alternative Strategies for Resolving Conflicts

It is important to emphasize that reconciliation is not the only tactic that primates use to resolve conflict. Redirected aggression provides another means for reducing the stressful consequences of conflict in some species. After conflicts, monkeys sometimes initiate aggression against third parties who were not involved in the original dispute (Watts et al. 2000). Male baboons who characteristically redirect aggression tend to have lower levels of basal glucocorticoids, hormones secreted in response to stress, than males who do not do so (Ray & Sapolsky 1992, Sapolsky & Ray 1989, Sapolsky 2000, Virgin & Sapolsky 1997). It is not entirely clear why redirected aggression has this effect, but it may be linked to the fact that monkeys are able to reduce uncertainty about subsequent events by redirecting aggression (Aureli & van Schaik 1991). Long-tailed macaques who redirected aggression to third parties during postconflict periods were less likely to become the targets of further aggression themselves than monkeys who did not redirect aggression or reconcile with their former opponents. Redirected aggression and reconciliation were equally effective in protecting the victim against further harassment from former aggressors. This was directly reflected in change in rates of some self-directed behaviors. Monkeys that redirected aggression or reconciled conflicts peacefully scratched themselves less often than monkeys who did not reconcile or redirect aggression (Aureli & van Schaik 1991).

In some species, reconciliation apparently does not occur at all. Red-bellied tamarins, ring-tailed lemurs, and white-faced capuchins all live in cohesive social groups, but apparently do not reconcile after conflicts (Schaffner & Caine 2000, Perry 1995, Kappeler 1993).

Measuring Reconciliation

Reconciliation is a functional label, like affiliation or aggression, not a descriptive one, like grooming or biting (Cords 1993, de Waal & van Roosmalen 1979). In ordinary English, reconciliation refers to the settlement of conflicts or inconsistencies and the restoration of peaceful or amicable relations,[2] a meaning that is embodied

[2]De Waal (2000) writes "According to my English dictionaries, 'reconciliation' refers to the reestablishment of close relationships and the settlement of conflict" (p. 21). However, the closeness of relationships does not figure prominently in definitions of 'reconciliation' in at least two major dictionaries. The *Random House Dictionary* defines reconcile as: "(1) To render no longer opposed, bring to acquiescence or acceptance; (2) to win over to friendliness, cause to become amicable; (3) to compose or settle (a quarrel, dispute, etc.); (4) bring into settlement or harmony; make compatible or consistent." (There are a number of additional definitions that are used in religious contexts.) The *Oxford English Dictionary* lists a number of definitions that are related to conflict resolution: "(1) To bring a person

in both of the working models described above. The use of this term is justified if we can demonstrate that nonaggressive interactions after conflicts enable former opponents to settle disputes and restore peace (Silk 1998). Despite this, most studies of reconciliation have relied on an operational definition of the behavior, and it is "assumed that behavior that fits the prescribed criteria of operationally defined reconciliation does actually function to restore, or at least improve, the relationship between former opponents after aggressive conflicts" (Cords 1993:256).

Studies that make use of operational definitions of reconciliation rely on comparisons between the sequence and timing of events that occur after conflicts and the sequence and timing of events that occur at other times (Veenema 2000). This is done by comparing events during a specified period of time after conflicts (the postconflict period) with events observed during a control period [the matched-control (MC) period]. Control samples are generally matched for time, activity, and sometimes for proximity among former opponents. In the PC-MC method, for example, former opponents are said to be "attracted" if they make contact during the postconflict period but not the MC period, or if they make contact earlier in the postconflict period than in the MC period (de Waal & Ren 1988). The timed-rule method (Aureli et al. 1989) is based on the fact that former opponents often make initial affiliative contact very early in the postconflict period, whereas first contacts are more evenly distributed through MC observations. Reconciliation is thus defined as any affiliative contact among former opponents that occurs during the interval in which the two distributions are disjunct (Figure 1).

Some studies have developed explicitly functional assays of reconciliation. For example, Cords (1993) investigated how nonaggressive postconflict interactions among captive long-tailed macaques influence their tolerance of one another at drinking bottles. After conflicts, monkeys were normally less willing to drink in close proximity to higher-ranking opponents. But monkeys who made physical contact, sat together, or exchanged friendly signals with their former opponents were more tolerant of their former opponents while drinking than monkeys who did not participate in these kinds of behaviors. Thus, these peaceful postconflict interactions were apparently effective in reconciling former opponents. Similarly, free-ranging female baboons who grunted to their former opponents after conflicts were more likely to subsequently interact peacefully and less likely to harass or supplant their former opponents than females who remained silent after conflicts (Figure 2). Thus, postconflict grunts were interpreted as reconciliatory signals that facilitated peaceful interactions among former opponents (Silk et al. 1996).

These two studies have also examined the effectiveness of particular kinds of signals in resolving conflicts. In long-tailed macaques, proximity is as effective in

---

again into friendly relations to or with (oneself or another) after an estrangement; (2) to win over (a person) again to friendship with oneself or another; (3) to set (estranged persons or parties) at one again; to bring back into concord, to reunite (persons or things) in harmony; (4) to bring (a person) back to, into peace, favour, etc . . . (7) to conciliate, recover (a person's favour, etc.); to gain credit, (9) to adjust, settle, bring to agreement."

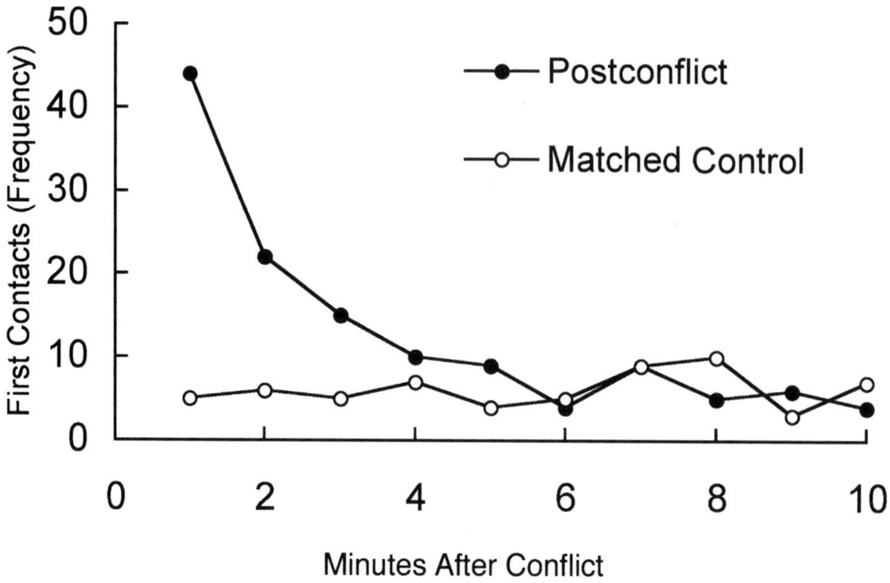

Figure 1 Among captive long-tailed macaques, the frequency of nonaggressive contacts between former opponents (*solid circles*) peaks in the first few minutes after conflicts and then declines to baseline levels. When no conflicts occur (*open circles*), the rate of nonaggressive contacts is uniformly low. (Adapted from Aureli et al. 1989, Figure 1.)

restoring tolerance among former opponents as are more intimate forms of contact (Cords 1993). Proximity maintenance also plays an important role in reconciliation among rhesus and stump-tailed macaques (Call et al. 1996, 1999). Among baboons, however, proximity alone is not sufficient to resolve conflicts: Females must grunt to their former opponents. Field experiments in which reconciliation is simulated by playing the aggressor's tape-recorded grunt to her former victim indicate that grunts by former aggressors are sufficient to reconcile conflicts, even in the absence of any other behavioral cues (Cheney & Seyfarth 1997).[3]

[3]A number of studies report the sequences of behaviors observed during postconflict and MC observations, attempting to determine whether specific behavioral elements were characteristic of the initial postconflict contact between former opponents. In some species, certain behaviors are more likely to occur earlier in postconflict periods than later in postconflict periods or during MC periods (e.g., de Waal & van Roosmalen 1979, de Waal & Yoshihara 1983, de Waal & Ren 1988, Ren et al. 1991). These studies have two shortcomings. First, they do not examine the efficacy of different types of behaviors in facilitating subsequent affiliation and tolerance or inhibiting further aggression. Second, vocalizations are not included in most of these analyses, although they may play a role in facilitating peaceful postconflict reunions.

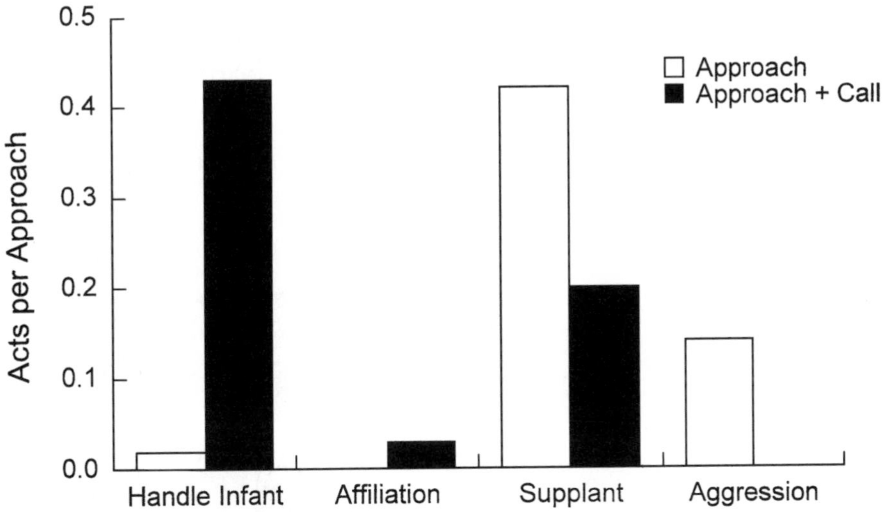

Figure 2 When female baboons approach and grunt to their former opponents during the postconflict period, they are more likely to handle their former opponents' infant and less likely to supplant their former opponents than if they approach and remain silent. (Adapted from Silk et al. 1996, Figure 2.)

FIRST-ORDER EFFECTS OF RECONCILIATION

For primates, conflict is stressful. The heart rates of female rhesus macaques increase sharply after conflicts and remain elevated over baseline levels for several minutes (Smith et al. 1986 cited in Aureli & Smucny 2000, Smucny et al. 1997). Rates of self-directed behaviors, including scratching, yawning, and body shaking, which are associated with physiological measures of stress, also increase after conflict and remain elevated for several minutes (Aureli 1992, 1997; Aureli & van Schaik 1991; Aureli et al. 1989; Castles & Whiten 1998b; Das et al. 1998). Stress is an adaptive short-term response to crises because it produces a set of physiological responses that facilitate rapid responses to danger (Sapolsky 1998, 2000). However, prolonged activation of the stress response is quite debilitating.

Peaceful contact among former opponents reduces stress levels. When female rhesus macaques make peaceful contact with their former opponents in the moments that follow conflicts, their heart rates rapidly decline to baseline levels. This effect is much more marked when females interact with their former opponents than when they interact with other group members or do not interact at all (Smucny et al. 1997). In long-tailed macaques and baboons, rates of self-directed behavior also decline rapidly to baseline levels after peaceful reunions with former opponents, whereas rates of self-directed behavior remain elevated for several minutes if former opponents do not reconcile (Figure 3; Aureli & van Schaik 1991, Castles & Whiten 1998b, Das et al. 1998).

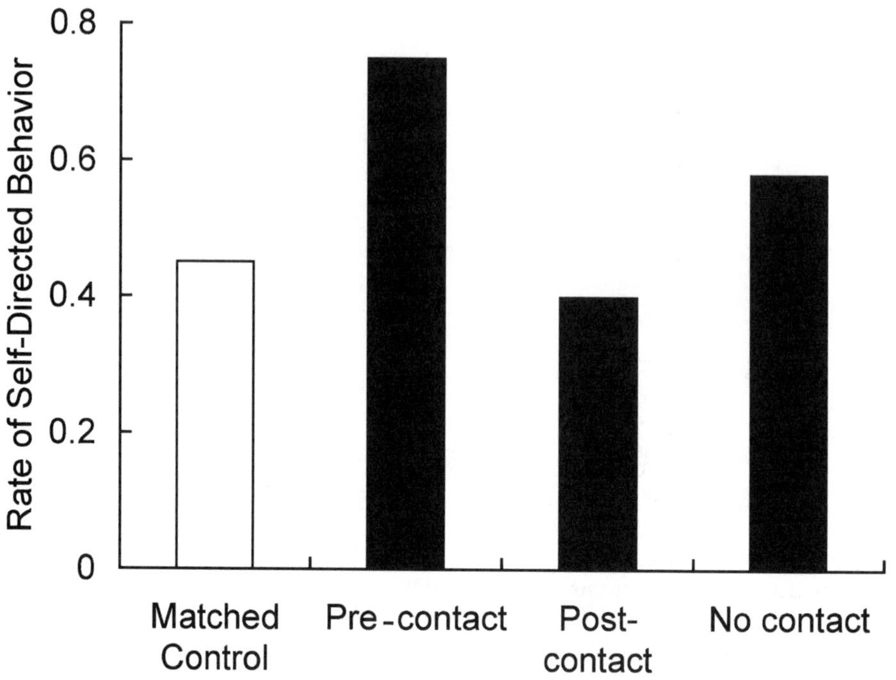

Figure 3 The rate of self-directed behavior by female baboons exceeds baseline rates during post-conflict periods in the minutes preceding peaceful contact and when no peaceful contact occurs. The rate of self-directed behavior falls to baseline levels during the postconflict period after peaceful contact occurs. (Adapted from Castles & Whiten 1998b, Figure 6.)

Further evidence in support of the hypothesis that reconciliation reduces stress because it alleviates uncertainty about subsequent events comes from a playback experiment conducted on free-ranging baboons (Cheney et al. 1995). This experiment took advantage of the fact that female baboons sometimes screamed when other group members attacked them, and victims of aggression sometimes redirected aggression toward lower ranking individuals. Thus, a female who heard the scream of a higher-ranking female might soon become the target of redirected aggression. To determine whether grunting during the postconflict period reduces females' anxiety about whether former aggressors would harass them, the investigators played tape-recorded screams of aggressors to their former victims (*a*) shortly after they had fought and the aggressor had grunted to her former victim, (*b*) shortly after they had fought but the aggressor had not grunted to her former victim, and (*c*) as a control, after a period of 45 minutes in which they had not interacted at all. Females reacted most strongly when they had fought, but the aggressor had not grunted to the victim. Females' responses after grunts had been given matched their responses when they had not interacted at all. Thus, the stressful effects of prior conflicts were remedied by grunts.

Uncertainty Makes Reconciliation More Likely

If the proximate function of reconciliation is to reduce stress that arises from uncertainty about the intentions of others, then we should expect conciliatory tendencies to vary in relation to the degree of uncertainty that exists. Several lines of evidence suggest that this is the case:

1. Conflicts that do not have clearly decided outcomes are more likely to be reconciled than conflicts with clear and unambiguous outcomes (Aureli et al. 1989, 1993; Kappeler 1993).
2. Dyads in which both partners give aggressive signals are more likely to reconcile than dyads in which one partner consistently submits to the other (Aureli et al. 1989).
3. Dyads that are close in dominance rank, and presumably have roughly equivalent competitive ability, tend to reconcile at higher rates than dyads that are more distantly ranked (Aureli et al. 1993, Judge 1991, Silk et al. 1996), and this effect is not entirely due to the fact that kin tend to occupy adjacent ranks (Judge 1991).
4. Reconciliation is more common when aggression is directed up the hierarchy (and contravenes the established dominance order) than when aggression is directed down the hierarchy (Judge 1991).
5. Interspecific comparisons among macaque species indicate that the likelihood of reconciliation is consistently linked to the likelihood that aggression will be directed up the hierarchy. For example, despotic rhesus and Japanese macaques reconcile at lower rates than more egalitarian stumptailed macaques (de Waal & Luttrell 1989, de Waal & Ren 1988). Similarly, the degree of symmetry in aggression is related to the tendency to reconcile among rhesus, long-tailed, Japanese, and Tonkean macaques (Figure 4) (Thierry 1986, 1990). Finally, comparisons of two groups of long-tailed macaques housed under very similar conditions suggest that despotic dominance styles are associated with lower levels of reconciliation than more egalitarian dominance styles (Butovskya et al. 1996).
6. Nonhuman primates reconcile after aggressive disputes, but they typically do not reconcile after naturally occurring disputes over food [4] (e.g., Castles & Whiten 1998a, Verbeek & de Waal 1997, Watts 1995, Aureli 1992). This may reflect the fact that disputes over food are unlikely to continue once the victim has relinquished the contested food item, and thus they produce little uncertainty and stress.
7. The severity of aggression has little consistent effect on the likelihood of reconciling (Castles & Whiten 1998a, Cords & Aureli 1993, de Waal &

[4]In a number of experimental studies of reconciliation, disputes are provoked by offering a desirable food item to the subordinate member of a dyad (Cords 1988, Cords & Thurnheer 1993). In these cases, disputes are sometimes reconciled.

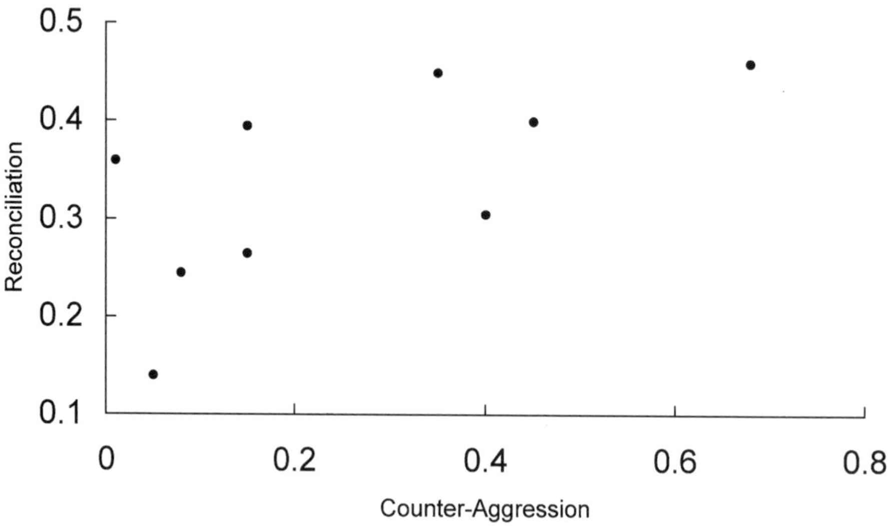

Figure 4 In macaques, the proportion of agonistic contests that involve aggressive signals by both parties is positively associated with the proportion of conflicts that are reconciled ($r = 0.70$, $n = 9$, 1-tailed $p = 0.02$). Data on rates of counter-aggression drawn from Thierry et al. 1997; data on rates of reconciliation drawn from Aureli & de Waal 2000b, Appendix A.

Ren 1988; but see Schino et al. 1998). Since mild conflicts can escalate into severe aggression and severe conflicts may continue for long periods, mild and severe aggression may be equally stressful even though they are not equally dangerous.

DISENTANGLING PROXIMATE AND ULTIMATE BENEFITS OF RECONCILIATION

The data reviewed to this point provide a compelling account of the short-term effects of reconciliation—reconciliation reduces uncertainty about the intentions of former opponents and thereby relieves stress that is associated with not knowing whether hostilities will continue. However, these data do not fully resolve functional questions about why reconciliation occurs. Does natural selection favor the evolution of reconciliation because it preserves valuable social bonds, as the relationship-repair model hypothesizes, or does natural selection favor reconciliation because it permits former opponents to resume peaceful contact as the benign-intent model suggests?

The relationship-repair model predicts that the value, security, and compatibility of a pair's social relationship will influence the likelihood that they reconcile. By contrast, the benign-intent model predicts that primates will reconcile to gain short-term objectives, which may include access to favored partners or desirable resources. Below, I review evidence that is relevant to evaluating these predictions in an effort to weigh the plausibility of these two functional hypotheses. Readers will soon realize that this is not a straightforward exercise because the two models do not generate orthogonal predictions; multiple interpretations of the same observation are often possible. This means that evidence that supports one hypothesis does not necessarily disconfirm the other and vice versa.

Reconciliation Preserves Valuable Bonds

The relationship-repair model rests on the idea that reconciliation preserves valuable social bonds. This means that the likelihood that two individuals will reconcile is expected to vary in relation to the value of the pair's social relationship. It is difficult to test this prediction directly because we cannot assess the adaptive value of social relationships in quantitative terms. This problem is common to almost all studies of the adaptive function of social behavior in animals. Instead, researchers rely on what Grafen (1991) calls the phenotypic gambit, the assumption that the short-term benefits that individuals derive from social interactions are ultimately translated into long-term differences in fitness. Animals who are regularly supported in agonistic confrontations, protected from harassment, or allowed to share access to desirable resources are expected to gain short-term benefits that are ultimately translated into fitness gains (Cords & Aureli 2000, van Schaik & Aureli 2000). Thus, relationships with allies, protectors, and tolerant group members would be particularly valuable.

Some studies have reported associations between conciliatory tendencies and the frequency of affiliative interactions (see below), and cite these data as evidence that primates reconcile selectively with valuable partners. However, Cords & Aureli (2000) caution against conflating the value of social bonds with the compatibility of partners. They point out that "partners with whom one is especially friendly are often, but not necessarily, very valuable" (p. 187).

Comparisons of the rates of reconciliation among dyads within groups provide some support for the hypothesis that primates reconcile selectively with valuable partners. Thus, monkeys tend to reconcile at higher rates with kin (Schino et al. 1998; Koyama 1997; Call et al. 1996; Castles et al. 1996; Silk et al. 1996; Demaria & Thierry 1992; Judge 1991; Aureli et al. 1989, 1993, 1997; Cheney & Seyfarth 1989; de Waal & Ren 1988; York & Rowell 1988; de Waal & Yoshihara 1983) who are most likely to provide coalitionary support. These data suggest that the value of social bonds influences the tendency to reconcile, but this conclusion must be viewed with some caution. First, there is little evidence that the frequency of coalitionary support is directly linked to reconciliatory tendencies. Even if such correlations were established, conclusions about the causal processes underlying the correlations would not be justified. Monkeys may reconcile and support kin because they gain important inclusive fitness benefits from interacting with kin, generating a spurious correlation between coalitionary support and conciliatory tendencies (Hemelrijk & Ek 1991).

To my knowledge, only two studies have assessed the relationship between coalitionary support and reconciliation directly. In a study of juvenile macaques, Cords & Aureli (1993) monitored patterns of support in agonistic contests. Juveniles were equally likely to reconcile with monkeys that had previously supported them as with monkeys who had not done so.[5] Similarly, captive chimpanzees did not reconcile selectively with those that supported them most often (Preuschoft et al. 2002).

Evidence from great apes provides support for the idea that primates reconcile selectively with valuable partners. Thus, male chimpanzees, who rely on one another for coalitionary support (Boesch & Boesch-Achermann 2000, de Waal 1986, Goodall 1986), reconcile at higher rates than do females (de Waal 1986, Goodall 1986). Female gorillas selectively reconcile disputes with resident males, on whom they rely for protection from strange males (Watts 1995). However, there is no direct evidence linking support or protection and conciliatory tendencies in chimpanzees (Preuschoft et al. 2002) or gorillas, and alternative explanations cannot be ruled out.

In response to the difficulties of measuring the value of social relationships, Cords & Thurnheer (1993) designed an experiment in which they artificially manipulated the value of other individuals in the group and examined the subsequent effect on reconciliation. The study focused on seven pairs of female long-tailed macaques drawn from a large and stable captive group. In the first phase of the experiment, reconciliatory tendencies in each dyad were evaluated by the pair's behavior after conflicts were artificially provoked. In the second phase of the experiment, each pair was trained to perform a cooperative task in which access to a desirable food was contingent on their mutual tolerance. In the third phase of the experiment, the reconciliatory tendencies were evaluated again, using the same methods as in the first phase of the experiment. If reconciliation is influenced by the value of social bonds, then an increase in the rate of reconciliation was expected to be observed. Six of the seven dyads performed as expected; rates of reconciliation increased after monkeys had been trained to cooperate on the feeding task. It is not known whether the tenor of females' social relationships was altered when they returned to their social groups. Cords & Thurnheer (1993) concluded that their results were "consistent with the hypothesis that monkeys reconcile more often with a former opponent when that opponent is more valuable to them."

Reconciliation is Influenced by the Security of Social Bonds

The security of social bonds may also influence the benefits of reconciling (Cords 1988). Dyads that have valuable, but insecure, relationships are expected to be particularly motivated to reconcile because conflict is likely to be especially disruptive. By the same token, dyads whose relationships are valuable, but secure,

[5]In this case, the categorical distinction between supporters and others may be problematic. A more fine-grained measure of alliance support, taking into account the amount and type of support provided, might generate different results.

should have little need to reconcile because their relationships are unlikely to be disrupted by conflict. This prediction has not been tested directly, partly because methods for measuring the security of social bonds have not been developed and validated (Cords & Aureli 2000). However, the theory of kin selection (Hamilton 1964) suggests that social relationships among close relatives will be particularly resilient because individuals can enhance their inclusive fitness when they help their relatives. Among kin, altruism is favored whenever the $br > c$, where $b =$ the fitness benefits gained by the recipient, $r =$ the degree of relatedness between the actor and the recipient, and $c =$ the fitness costs incurred by the actor.

If relationships among kin are less likely to be disrupted by conflict than relationships among nonkin, then it should require less effort to maintain bonds among them (Cords 1988). This prediction does not figure in recent writings about the pattern of reconciliation (e.g., Cords & Aureli 2000, de Waal & Aureli 1996), but the logic seems compelling. In all but one study, kin reconciled at least as often as nonkin did (Cords 1988). High rates of reconcilation among kin seem to contradict the predicted relationship between reconciliatory tendencies and the security of social bonds.

Reconciliation is Influenced by Compatibility

All other things being equal, compatible dyads are expected to reconcile at higher rates than others because they are more accessible to one another: "When the members of a dyad are in the habit of interacting in nonantagonistic ways in many contexts, it may be easier for them to engage in a friendly postconflict reunion because this is the sort of interaction they usually have with each other, and so it is a familiar course of action" (Cords & Aureli 2000). Compatibility is typically measured by the frequency of affiliative and agonistic interactions within dyads, but methods of assessing social bonds have not been fully standardized.

Compatibility is linked to reconciliation in a number of groups, as those with close and friendly relationships reconcile a greater proportion of their conflicts than those with hostile or weak relationships (Call et al. 1999, Schino et al. 1998, Castles et al. 1996, Cords & Aureli 1993, Aureli et al. 1989, de Waal & Ren 1988, de Waal & Yoshihara 1983). This result is not entirely due to the confounding effects of kinship[6] (Call et al. 1999, Schino et al. 1998, Cords & Aureli 1993, Aureli et al. 1989, de Waal & Yoshihara 1983).

Reconciliation Facilitates Short-Term Objectives

The benign-intent model suggests that primates reconcile primarily in order to obtain short-term objectives, such as access to a desirable resource or tolerance by a preferred partner. Preferences may be based on ephemeral features, such as

[6]In some cases, the confounding effects of kinship are eliminated by examining the effects of relationship quality only among nonkin. In other cases, the effects of both kinship and relationship quality on conciliatory tendencies are examined in multivariate analyses.

reproductive status or possession of a valuable resource, or on more stable features, such as kinship.

Although many researchers argue that Cords & Thurnheer's (1993) experimental results provide compelling support for the relationship-repair model, the results are also compatible with the hypothesis that monkeys can learn to use reconciliation in an instrumental way to gain access to a valued resource. In Cords & Thurnheer's experiment, monkeys were allowed to feed on the desirable food item only if their partner fed simultaneously. If females anticipated being chased or attacked when they approached the feeding site or their partner, they might avoid coming close, thus preventing their partner from feeding. To avoid this undesirable outcome, both partners may benefit from communicating their intention to behave peacefully. Thus, monkeys may become more conciliatory to enhance prospects for tolerance, not because they came to value their relationships with their partners more highly.

Studies of captive chimpanzees suggest that they sometimes use conciliatory behaviors for instrumental purposes. Koyama & Dunbar (1996) found that rates of grooming and proximity were substantially elevated during the hour that preceded the regularly scheduled presentation of tightly clumped foods. After the food was presented, the chimpanzees spent the most time near the individuals that they had previously groomed and sat near. This suggests that they were "attempting to increase tolerance and facilitate co-feeding" (Koyama 2000).

Further evidence that primates may use reconciliation to gain strategic short-term objectives comes from studies of free-ranging baboons. Female monkeys are strongly attracted to infants, particularly newborns, and eager to handle them (e.g., Altmann 1980, Bauers 1993, Silk 1999). Although handling seems relatively benign in most cases, mothers respond warily when others try to handle their infants. Female macaques and baboons typically grunt as they approach new mothers, and these grunts facilitate infant handling (Silk et al. 2000). Female baboons reconcile selectively with the mothers of young infants (Silk et al. 1996). Moreover, the rate of reconciliation tracks changes in the rate of infant handling as infants mature. Females are most likely to reconcile conflicts with females whose infants they are most eager to handle (Silk 2000; Figure 5). These data suggest that females' decisions to reconcile were based on their motivation to obtain access to infants, not on the value of their long-term relationship with the mother.

RECONCILIATION IN *HOMO SAPIENS*

Reconciliation is an anthropomorphic concept (de Waal & van Roosmalen 1979), so it is not surprising that researchers have begun to delineate conflict resolution strategies in humans. Much of this work is explicitly based on de Waal's hypothesis that reconciliation repairs relationships that have been damaged by conflicts.

Detailed studies of conflict resolution have been conducted on children in the United States and Europe (Butovskaya et al. 2000, Cords & Killen 1998, Schmitt & Grammer 1997, Verbeek et al. 2000). This body of work reveals a number

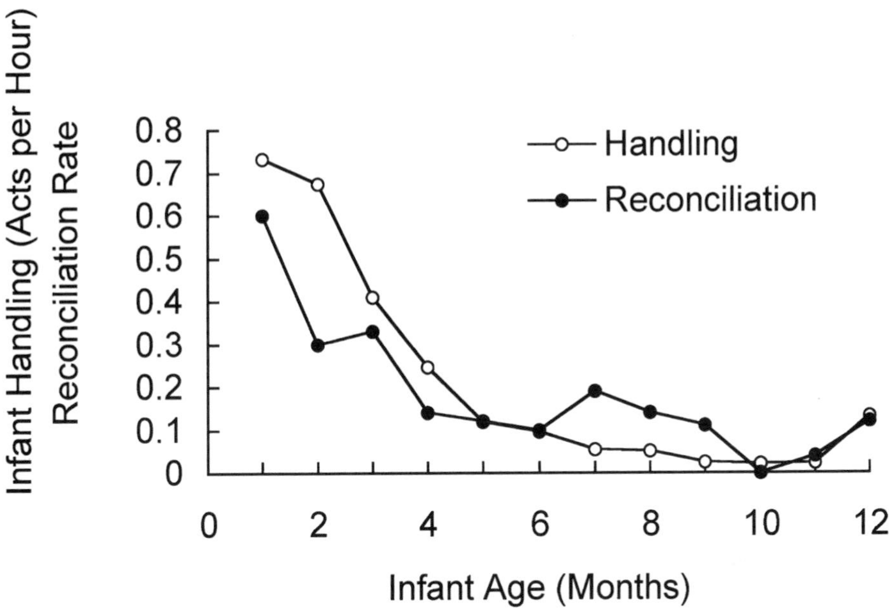

Figure 5 Among female baboons, rates of reconciliation with mothers closely track rates of infant handling. Females are most likely to reconcile with females when they have young, attractive infants. (From Silk 2000.)

of parallels between the reconciliatory behavior of children and other primates. Children often approach one another and make peaceful contact of some sort in the minutes that follow conflicts. The form and timing of these events is remarkably similar to the timing of peaceful postconflict contacts among monkeys (Verbeek 1996; Figure 6). Reconciliatory behaviors sometimes involve physical gestures, such as hugs or embraces, behaviors that are also seen among other primates. Reconciliatory behaviors by children also include verbal apologies, offers to share, and invitations to resume play. In other cases, "implicit" peacemaking strategies are inferred when children resume friendly play without any overt reference to the previous dispute.[7] Young children do not often attempt to mediate conflicts among their peers (Butovskaya et al. 2000), although they often intervene in conflicts on behalf of one of the disputants (Butovskaya et al. 2000, Verbeek et al. 2000).

Several studies have examined how the nature of children's relationships influences the likelihood of reconciling conflicts. In these studies, the quality of children's relationships is assessed by tabulating how often they are together or

[7]Although "implicit" conflict resolution may seem to be an oxymoron, it is analogous to the elevated level of nonaggressive behavior seen soon after conflicts in many monkey species. Thus, engagement in peaceful interactions by former opponents is interpreted as a tactic for resolving conflicts.

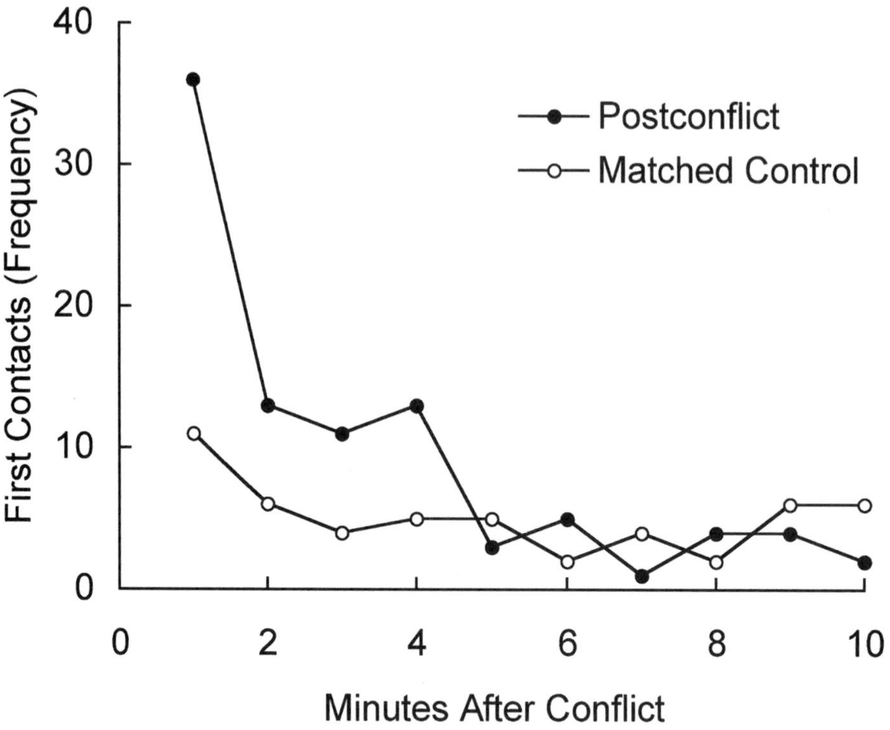

Figure 6 For human children, rates of friendly contact among former opponents peak in the minutes following conflicts and then fall to baseline levels. Note similarities in the course of postconflict interactions among macaques (Figure 1) and children. (Adapted from Verbeek 1996, Figure 3.1.)

how often they play. Friends spend more time together and play more than acquaintances, and acquaintances spend more time together and play more than "nonfriends." For children, Cords & Killen (1998) suggest that friendships, defined in this way, constitute valuable relationships: "Because friends are desirable social partners, and because there is much evidence that relationships with friends are important to children's development, it seems reasonable to take friends as an indicator of value measured in the currency of lifetime reproductive success."

In some studies, children reconcile less often with friends than with acquaintances or nonfriends, while in other studies friends reconcile more often. Drawing on a body of studies conducted by child psychologists, Cords & Killen (1998) conclude that children resolve conflicts with friends at higher rates than with nonfriends. Two studies using methods originally developed for studying conflict resolution in nonhuman primates present a different picture. Russian schoolchildren are nearly twice as likely to reconcile with acquaintances as with their friends (Butovskaya & Kozintsev 1999). When American children part after conflicts, friends and acquaintances are equally likely to reconcile. However, friends are more likely to stay together after conflicts have ended than are acquaintances (Verbeek 1996, Verbeek et al. 2000).[8] Butovskaya et al. (2000) note that the results of these two studies "do not provide clear evidence that postconflict peacemaking specifically aims at restoring close relationships among children" (p. 253). It is not clear whether the discrepancy between the results cited by Cords & Killen and by Butovskya and her colleagues reflect differences in the methodologies used to assess conflict resolution or differences between the subject pools.

Fry (2000) draws on the ethnographic record to examine conflict resolution strategies in traditional human societies. Reconciliation tends to involve certain common elements in most cultures. These include gift giving or gift exchange; payment of restitution; food sharing; physical contact (i.e., kissing, shaking hands); appeasement postures and gestures; apologies and expressions of remorse and contrition; and mediation by third parties. Fry's review indicates that "... conflict resolution often focuses on restoring relationships and involves interested parties beyond the disputants themselves" (p. 347). Relationships that have important economic, social, or political utility are most likely to be reconciled.

Among young children, reconciliation is only weakly linked to friendship and rarely involves the intervention of third parties. In contrast, among adults reconciliation is consistently associated with the maintenance of relationships and frequently involves the intervention of third parties as mediators. This difference in the reconciliation behavior of children and adults may reflect the fact that young children have a limited ability to attribute knowledge, feelings, and intentions to others and to see things from another's perspective. These cognitive properties, collectively termed a theory of mind, are poorly developed in young children (Wellman 1990). De Waal & Yoshihara (1983) have argued that reconciliation does not rely on complex cognitive abilities. All that is needed is the ability to recognize individuals, remember past interactions, and a conciliatory disposition. However, "... if reconciliation is selectively employed to manipulate relationship quality, a 'Machiavellian' dimension is added to the cognitive challenge" (Castles 2000:189). To use reconciliation to preserve social bonds, individuals must exercise their conciliatory tendencies selectively. This selectivity is based on the likelihood that conflicts with certain partners in certain situations will have lasting, negative effects on the relationship. It is possible that children and adults may learn the contingencies between conflict and the impact on their relationships with others, or they may rely on innate proclivities to reconcile in certain situations and with certain partners. However, it seems more likely that the selectivity is based on

[8]Schmitt & Grammer (1997) provide a brief description of the results of a study of conflict resolution among kindergartners. They report that "the probability of reconciliation does not co-vary with friendship, power, dominance, and rank in attention structure, whereas there is a strong and significant correlation with conflict intensity" (p. 99). The authors do not describe the methods that they used to conduct the study or provide details about the subjects of their study.

the ability to understand the impact of conflict on other individuals and requires at least some knowledge of others' minds (Silk 1998). Triadic interactions, including third party mediation, are cognitively demanding (Castles 2000, Tomasello & Call 1997). To mediate disputes among others, individuals must know something about their own relationship to the disputants and the disputants' relationship to one another.

WHAT IS THE MISSING LINK?

The relationship-repair model has been widely accepted in the literature (c.f. Aureli & de Waal 2000b), even though there are substantive reasons to question its validity when applied to nonhuman primates (and human children). The relationship-repair model may be compelling because it fits our own folk model of how and why we resolve conflicts. In daily life, we make frequent use of conflict resolution tactics such as apologies, and we are well aware of the deleterious effects of frequent, unresolved conflicts on our social relationships.

De Waal acknowledges that the relationship-repair model "rests on an anthropomorphic interpretation of animal behavior and as such comes with inevitable human connotations" (de Waal 2000). He defends the application of an anthropomorphic approach to the study of the behavior of monkeys and apes: "The decision making underlying much of what these animals do strikes the human observer as very familiar. Provided that it is based on intimate knowledge and translated into testable hypotheses, anthropomorphism is a very useful first step toward understanding a psychology similar to and almost as complex as ours" (De Waal 1989:25). Contemporary social scientists generally think of anthropomorphism in pejorative terms, but it can be a useful device when employed with caution: "Heuristic anthropomorphism, when pursued as an explicit strategy, is a straightforward example of the use of analogy in scientific hypothesizing, and demands the usual care in distinguishing positive, negative, and neutral correspondences between the two domains under comparison... care must be taken to distinguish the empirical and conceptual attractions of an analogy from the covertly anthropocentric attractions of mere familiarity" (Daston 1997:140).

De Waal's defense of anthropomorphism as a means of generating hypotheses about the behavior of other primates relies on the fact that monkeys and apes have "similar" psychologies. However, a considerable body of evidence indicates that there are important differences in the cognitive abilities of monkeys, apes, and humans (Povinelli & Eddy 1996, Tomasello & Call 1997). If mind-reading plays an important role in the development of reconciliatory strategies (Castles 2000, Silk 1998), then it is important to take into account how differences in theories of mind among monkeys, apes, and humans may influence the function of reconciliation. This does not mean that we cannot gain important insights about the evolutionary forces shaping conflict resolution in humans by studying other primates, but it may limit the usefulness of our own intuition in understanding why other primates reconcile.

THE EVOLUTIONARY HISTORY OF RECONCILIATION

Reconstructing the functional origins of reconciliation is a perilous exercise because we can study only the end points of this process, the behavior of ourselves and other living primates. Writing about the difficulties of studying the evolutionary history of a trait's function, Povinelli & Eddy (1996) note: "When it comes to understanding the continuous chain of processes that have led to the evolution of a given biological system or structure, it is one thing to speak of precursors, foundations, or building blocks, but quite another to tackle the more difficult problem of function. Because we inhabit only a very narrow slide of evolutionary time, we are privy to only a thin cross section of the diversity it has produced.... Extinction, coupled with the imperfections of the fossil record, virtually guarantees that during a period of rapid evolutionary change we can never accurately identify the exact origin and subsequent elaboration of a given trait" (p. 184).

Although we cannot reconstruct the evolutionary history of reconciliation with great confidence, the empirical record provides some clues about how and when the function of reconciliation has been transformed over the last five million years (Silk 1998). Reconciliation may have initially evolved from signals that are used in a broad range of social situations to communicate information about intentions and subsequent events. Having little understanding of others' minds, monkeys use reconciliatory behavior to propitiate former opponents. These conciliatory efforts reduce uncertainty about whether hostilities will continue and facilitate peaceful interactions among former adversaries. Even though monkeys have little knowledge of their partners' minds, they can learn to use reconciliation instrumentally for strategic purposes. Apes, who may have a more powerful theory of mind than monkeys do, may use reconciliation for their own strategic purposes and may mediate disputes among others. Human children, who have not yet developed a powerful theory of mind, may use reconciliation primarily as a means to settle conflicts and reestablish contact with former opponents. As they grow older and develop a fuller knowledge of others' feelings, intentions, and knowledge, reconciliation acquires broader functions. It is used to mend and preserve relationships that have particular social, economic, or political value. Reconciliation often extends beyond the original parties in the dispute, involving consolation, mediation by thirty parties, and institutionalized remedies for conflict that are built into legal and judicial systems (Yarn 2000).

ACKNOWLEDGMENTS

The empirical work that shaped some of my ideas about reconciliation was conducted in collaboration with Robert Seyfarth and Dorothy Cheney and was partially supported by National Science Foundation Grant 9213586. I am grateful to a number of my colleagues for stimulating discussions, in person and in print, about the function of reconciliation, particularly Felipo Aureli, Robert Boyd, Marina Cords, Joseph Manson, Susan Perry, and Darlene Smucny.

The *Annual Review of Anthropology* is online at http://anthro.annualreviews.org

LITERATURE CITED

Altmann J. 1980. *Baboon Mothers and Infants*. Cambridge, MA: Harvard Univ.

Aureli F. 1992. Postconflict behaviour among wild long-tailed macaques (*Macaca fasicularis*). *Behav. Ecol. Sociobiol.* 31:329–37

Aureli F. 1997. Post-conflict anxiety in nonhuman primates: the mediating role of emotion in conflict resolution. *Aggr. Behav.* 23: 315–28

Aureli F, Das M, Veenema HC. 1997. Differential kinship effect on reconciliation in three species of macaques (*Macaca fasicularis, M. fuscata*, and *M. sylvanus*). *J. Comp. Psychol.* 111:91–99

Aureli F, de Waal FBM, eds. 2000a. *Natural Conflict Resolution*. Berkeley, CA: Univ. Calif. Press

Aureli F, de Waal FBM. 2000b. Why natural conflict resolution? See Aureli & de Waal 2000a, pp. 3–10

Aureli F, Smucny DA. 2000. The role of emotion in conflict and conflict resolution. See Aureli & de Waal 2000a, pp. 199–224

Aureli F, van Schaik CP. 1991. Post conflict behaviour in long-tailed macaques (*Macaca fasicularis*). II. Coping with the uncertainty. *Ethology* 89:101–14

Aureli F, van Schaik CP, van Hooff JARAM. 1989. Functional aspects of reconciliation among captive long-tailed macaques (*Macaca fasicularis*). *Am. J. Primatol.* 19: 39–51

Aureli F, Veenema HC, van Panthaleon van Eck CJ, van Hooff JARAM. 1993. Reconciliation, consolation, and redirection in Japanese macaques (*Macaca fuscata*). *Behaviour* 124:1–21

Bauers KA. 1993. A functional analysis of staccato grunt vocalizations in the stump-tailed macaque (*Macaca arctoides*). *Ethology* 94:147–61

Boesch C, Boesch-Achermann H. 2000. *The Chimpanzees of the Taï Forest*. Oxford: Oxford Univ. Press

Butovskya M, Kozintsev A, Welker C. 1996. Conflict and reconciliation in two groups of crab-eating monkeys differing in social status by birth. *Primates* 37:261–70

Butovskya M, Verbeek P, Ljungberg T, Lunardini A. 2000. A multicultural view of peacemaking among young children. See Aureli & de Waal 2000a, pp. 243–58

Butovskya ML, Kozintsev AG. 1998. Aggression, friendship, and reconciliation in Russian primary school children. *Aggr. Behav.* 25:125–39

Call J, Aureli F, de Waal FBM. 1999. Reconciliation patterns among stumptail macaques: a multivariate approach. *Anim. Behav.* 58:165–72

Call J, Judge PG, de Waal FBM. 1996. Influence of kinship and spatial density on reconciliation and grooming in rhesus monkeys. *Am. J. Primatol.* 39:35–45

Castles DL. 2000. Triadic versus dyadic resolutions: cognitive implications. See Aureli & de Waal 2000a, pp. 289–91

Castles DL, Aureli F, de Waal FBM. 1996. Variation in conciliatory tendency and relationship quality across groups of pigtail macaques. *Anim. Behav.* 52:389–403

Castles DL, Whiten A. 1998a. Post-conflict behaviour of wild olive baboons. I. Reconciliation, redirection and consolation. *Ethology* 104:126–47

Castles DL, Whiten A. 1998b. Post-conflict behaviour of wild olive baboons. II. Stress and self-directed behaviour. *Ethology* 104:148–60

Cheney DL, Seyfarth RM. 1989. Redirected aggression and reconciliation among vervet monkeys, *Cercopithecus aethiops*. *Behaviour* 110:258–75

Cheney DL, Seyfarth RM. 1997. Reconciliatory grunts by dominant female baboons influence victims' behaviour. *Anim. Behav.* 54:409–18

Cheney DL, Seyfarth RM, Silk JB. 1995. The role of grunts in reconciling opponents and facilitating interactions among adult female baboons. *Anim. Behav.* 50:249–57

Cords M. 1988. Resolution of aggressive conflicts by immature long-tailed macaques *Macaca fasicularis*. *Anim. Behav.* 36:1124–35

Cords M. 1993. On operationally defining reconciliation. *Am. J. Primatol.* 29:255–67

Cords M, Aureli F. 1993. Patterns of reconciliation among juvenile long-tailed macaques. In *Juvenile Primates: Life History, Development, and Behavior*, ed. ME Pereira, LA Fairbanks, pp. 271–84. Oxford: Oxford Univ. Press

Cords M, Aureli F. 1996. Reasons for reconciling. *Evol. Anthropol.* 5:42–45

Cords M, Aureli F. 2000. Reconciliation and relationship qualities. See Aureli & de Waal 2000a, pp. 177–98

Cords M, Killen M. 1998. Conflict resolution in human and non-human primates. In *Piaget, Evolution, and Development*, ed. J Langer, M Killen, pp. 193–218. Mahwah, NJ: Lawrence Erlbaum Assoc.

Cords M, Thurnheer S. 1993. Reconciliation with valuable partners by long-tailed macaques. *Ethology* 93:315–25

Das M, Penke Zs, van Hooff JARAM. 1997. Affiliation between aggressors and third parties following conflicts in long-tailed macaques (*Macaca fasicularis*). *Intl. J. Primatol.* 18:159–81

Das M, Penke Zs, van Hooff JARAM. 1998. Postconflict affiliation and stress-related behavior of long-tailed macaque aggressors. *Intl. J. Primatol.* 19:53–71

Daston L. 1997. Anthropomorphism. In *Human by Nature*, ed. P Weingart, PJ Richerson, SD Mitchell, S Maasen, pp. 134–42. Mahwah, NJ: Erlbaum Assoc.

de Waal FBM. 1986. The integration of dominance and social bonding in primates. *Q. Rev. Biol.* 61:459–69

de Waal FBM. 1989. *Peacemaking Among Primates*. Cambridge, MA: Harvard Univ. Press

de Waal FBM. 1993. Reconciliation among primates: a review of empirical evidence and unresolved issues. In *Primate Social Conflict*, ed. WA Mason, SP Mendoza, pp. 111–44. Albany, NY: SUNY Press

de Waal FBM. 2000. The first kiss: foundations of conflict resolution research in animals. See Aureli & de Waal 2000a, pp. 15–33

de Waal FBM, Aureli F. 1996. Consolation, reconciliation, and a possible cognitive difference between macaques and chimpanzees. In *Reaching into Thought*, ed. AE Russon, KA Bard, ST Parker, pp. 80–110. Cambridge, UK: Cambridge Univ. Press

de Waal FBM, Luttrell L. 1989. Toward a comparative socioecology of the genus *Macaca*: different dominance styles in rhesus and stumptailed macaques. *Am. J. Primatol.* 19: 83–109

de Waal FBM, Ren R. 1988. Comparison of the reconciliation behavior of stumptail and rhesus macaques. *Ethology* 78:129–42

de Waal FBM, van Roosmalen A. 1979. Reconciliation and consolation among chimpanzees. *Behav. Ecol. Sociobiol.* 5:55–66

de Waal FBM, Yoshihara D. 1983. Reconciliation and redirected affection in rhesus monkeys. *Behaviour* 85:224–41

Demaria C, Thierry B. 1992. The ability to reconcile in Tonkean and rhesus macaques. *Abstr. XIV Cong. Int. Primatol. Soc.*, p. 101. Strasbourg: SICOP

Fry DP. 2000. Conflict management in cross-cultural perspective. See Aureli & de Waal 2000a, pp. 334–51

Goodall J. 1986. *The Chimpanzees of Gombe:*

Patterns of Behavior. Cambridge, MA.: Belknap

Gore MA. 1994. Dyadic and triadic aggression in adult female rhesus monkeys, *Macaca mulatta*, and hamadryas baboons, *Papio hamadryas*. *Anim. Behav.* 48:385–92

Grafen A. 1991. Modelling in behavioural ecology. In *Behavioural Ecology*, ed. JR Krebs, NB Davies, pp. 5–31. Oxford: Blackwell

Hamilton WD. 1964. The genetical evolution of social behavior. I and II. *J. Theor. Biol.* 7: 1–52

Hemelrijk CK, Ek A. 1991. Reciprocity and interchange of grooming and 'support' in captive chimpanzees. *Anim. Behav.* 41:923–35

Hinde RA. 1983. A conceptual approach. In *Primate Social Relationships*, ed. RA Hinde, pp. 1–7. Sunderland, MA: Sinauer Assoc.

Hofer H, East ML. 2000. Conflict management in female-dominated spotted hyenas. See Aureli & de Waal 2000a, pp. 232–34

Isbell L. 1991. Contest and scramble competition: patterns of female aggression and ranging behaviour among primates. *Behavioral Ecology* 2:43–55

Judge PG. 1991. Dyadic and triadic reconciliation in pigtail macaques (*Macaca nemestrina*). *Am. J. Primatol.* 23:225–37

Kappeler P, van Schaik CP. 1992. Methodological and evolutionary aspects of reconciliation among primates. *Ethology* 92:51–69

Kappeler PM. 1993. Reconciliation and post-conflict behavior in ringtailed lemurs, *Lemur catta*, and red-fronted lemurs, *Eulemur fulvus fulvus*. *Anim. Behav.* 45:901–15

Koyama NF. 1997. *Reconciliation in Japanese macaques* (*Macaca fuscata*). PhD thesis, Univ. Liverpool, 289 pp.

Koyama NF. 2000. Conflict prevention before feeding. See Aureli & de Waal 2000a, pp. 130–32

Koyama NF, Dunbar RIM. 1996. Anticipation of conflict by chimpanzees. *Primates* 37:79–86

Kummer H. 1978. On the value of social relationships to nonhuman primates: a heuristic scheme. *Social Science Information* 17:687–705

Perry S. 1995. *Social relationships in wild white-faced capuchin monkeys, Cebus capucinus*. PhD thesis, Univ. Michigan

Povinelli DJ, Eddy TJ. 1996. *What Young Chimpanzees Know About Seeing*. *Monogr. Soc. Res. Child Dev.* Vol. 61, No. 3

Preuschoft S, Wang X, Aureli F, de Waal FBM. 2002. Reconciliation in captive chimpanzees: a reevaluation with controlled methods. *Int. J. Primatol.* 34:29–50

Ray J, Sapolsky R. 1992. Styles of male social behavior and their endocrine correlates among high ranking baboons. *Am. J. Primatol.* 28:231–40

Ren R, Yan K, Su Y, Qi H, Liang B, Bao W, de Waal FBM. 1991. The reconciliation behavior of golden monkeys (*Rhinopithecus roxellanae roxellanae*) in small breeding groups. *Primates* 32:321–27

Rowell TE, Rowell CA. 1993. The social organisation of feral *Ovis aries* ram groups in the pre-rut period. *Ethology* 95:213–32

Samuels A, Flaherty C. 2000. Peaceful conflict resolution in the sea? See Aureli & de Waal 2000a, pp. 229–31

Sapolsky R. 1998. *Why Zebras Don't Get Ulcers: a Guide to Stress, Stress-Related Diseases and Coping*. 2nd ed. New York: WH Freeman

Sapolsky R. 2000. Physiological correlates of individual dominance style. See Aureli & de Waal 2000a, pp. 114–16

Sapolsky R, Ray J. 1989. Styles of dominance and their physiological correlates among wild baboons. *Am. J. Primatol.* 18:1–12

Schaffner CN, Caine NG. 2000. The peacefulness of cooperatively breeding primates. See Aureli & de Waal 2000a, pp. 155–69

Schino G. 1998. Reconciliation in domestic goats. *Behaviour* 135:343–56

Schino G, Rosati L, Aureli F. 1998. Intragroup variation in reconciliation tendencies in captive Japanese macaques. *Behaviour* 135:897–912

Schmitt A, Grammer K. 1997. Social intelligence and success: Don't be too clever in order to be smart. In *Machiavellian Intelligence II. Extensions and Evaluations*, ed. A

Whiten, RW Byrne, pp. 86–111. Cambridge, UK: Cambridge Univ. Press

Silk JB. 1996. Why do primates reconcile? *Evol. Anthropol.* 5:39–42

Silk JB. 1997. The function of peaceful post-conflict contacts among primates. *Primates* 38:265–79

Silk JB. 1998. Making amends: adaptive perspectives on conflict remediation in monkeys, apes, and humans. *Human Nature* 9: 341–68

Silk JB. 1999. Why are infants so attractive to others? The form and function of infant handling in bonnet macaques. *Anim. Behav.* 57:1021–32

Silk JB. 2000. The function of peaceful post-conflict interactions: an alternate view. See Aureli & de Waal 2000a, pp. 179–81

Silk JB, Cheney DL, Seyfarth RM. 1996. The form and function of post-conflict interactions between female baboons. *Anim. Behav.* 52:259–68

Silk JB, Kaldor E, Boyd R. 2000. Cheap talk when interests conflict. *Anim. Behav.* 59:423–32

Smith OA, Astley CA, Chesney MA, Taylor DJ, Spelman FA. 1986. Personality, stress and cardiovascular disease. In *Neural Mechanisms and Cardiovascular Disease*, ed. B Lown, A Malliani, M Prosdomici, pp. 471–84. Padua, Italy: Liviana

Smucny DA, Price CS, Byrne EA. 1997. Post-conflict affiliation and stress reduction in captive rhesus macaques. *Adv. Ethol.* 32: 157

Thierry B. 1986. A comparative study of aggression and response to aggresion in three species of macaque. In *Primate Ontogeny, Cognition, and Social Behaviour*, ed. JG Else, PC Lee, pp. 307–13. Cambridge, UK: Cambridge Univ. Press

Thierry B. 1990. The state of equilibrium among agonistic behavior patterns in a group of Japanese macaques (*Macaca fuscata*). *C. Royal Acad. Sci., Paris* 310:35–40

Thierry B, Aureli F, de Waal FBM, Petit O. 1997. Variations in reconciliation patterns and social organization across nine species of macaques. *Adv. Ethol.* 32:S39

Tomasello MJ, Call J. 1997. *Primate Cognition.* Oxford: Oxford Univ. Press.

Trivers RL. 1971. The evolution of reciprocal altruism. *Q. Rev. Biol.* 46:35–57

Van Schaik CP. 1983. Why are diurnal primates living in groups? *Behaviour* 87:120–144

Van Schaik CP, Aureli F. 2000. The natural history of valuable relationships in primates. See Aureli & de Waal 2000a, pp. 307–33

Van Schaik CP, van Hooff JARAM. 1983. On the ultimate causes of primate social systems. *Behaviour* 85:91–117

Veenema HC. 2000. Methodological progress in post-conflict research. See Aureli & de Waal 2000a, pp. 21–23

Verbeek P. 1996. *Peacemaking of young children.* PhD thesis, Emory Univ.

Verbeek P, de Waal FBM. 1997. Postconflict behavior of captive brown capuchins in the presence and absence of attractive food. *Intl. J. Primatol.* 18:703–26

Verbeek P, Hartup WW, Collins WA. 2000. Conflict management in children and adolescents. See Aureli & de Waal 2000a, pp. 34–53

Virgin C, Sapolsky R. 1997. Styles of male social behavior and their endocrine correlates among low-ranking baboons. *Am. J. Primatol.* 42:25–34

Watts DP. 1995. Post-conflict social events in wild mountain gorillas (*Mammalia, Hominoidea*) I. Social interactions between opponents. *Ethology*, 100:139–57

Watts DP, Colemnares F, Arnold K. 2000. Redirection, consolation, and male policing: how targets of aggression interact with bystanders. See Aureli & de Waal 2000a, pp. 281–301

Wellman HM. 1990. *The Child's Theory of Mind.* Cambridge, MA: MIT Press

Wrangham RW. 1980. An ecological model of female-bonded primate groups. *Behaviour* 75:262–300

Wrangham, RW. 1987. Evolution of social structure. In *Primate Societies*, ed. BB

Smuts, DL Cheney, RM Seyfarth, RW Wrangham, TT Struhsaker, pp 282–97. Chicago: Univ. Chicago Press

Yarn DH. 2000. Law, love, and reconciliation: searching for natural conflict resolution in *Homo sapiens*. See Aureli & de Waal 2000a, pp. 54–70

York AD, Rowell TE. 1988. Reconciliation following aggression in patas monkeys, *Erythrocebus patas*. *Anim. Behav.* 36:502–9

Annu. Rev. Anthropol. 2002. 31:45–67
doi: 10.1146/annurev.anthro.31.040202.105553

First published online as a Review in Advance on May 1, 2002

CURRENT TOPICS IN PRIMATE SOCIOENDOCRINOLOGY

Fred B. Bercovitch[1] and Toni E. Ziegler[2]
[1]*Division of Behavioral Biology, Center for Reproduction of Endangered Species, Zoological Society of San Diego, San Diego, California 92112-0551; email: fbercovitch@sandiegozoo.org*
[2]*Wisconsin Regional Primate Research Center and Department of Psychology, University of Wisconsin, Madison, Wisconsin 53715-1299; email: ziegler@primate.wisc.edu*

Key Words reproductive maturation, stress, scent communication, adolescent subfecundity, paternal care

■ **Abstract** Socioendocrinology is the study of the effect of the social environment on the interactions between hormones and behavior. Individuals have evolved a physiological flexibility that enables them to respond to their social surroundings in a manner that maximizes reproductive success. We present evidence that (*a*) males who have evolved to participate in infant care have different endocrine profiles around offspring from males who have not evolved to regularly participate in infant care, (*b*) the energetic costs of reproduction in both males and females creates conditions conducive to elevated levels of both stress and sex hormones, (*c*) adolescent subfecundity among females evolved as a mechanism fostering mate choice, (*d*) some primate species are probably facultative ovulators, and (*e*) endocrine suppression of subordinate males probably does not contribute to delayed onset of reproduction but does contribute to reduced access to females, which hampers progeny production. Hormones and behavior are inextricably intertwined in a feedback relationship that regulates each other.

INTRODUCTION

Socioendocrinology is the study of the effect of the social environment on the interactions between hormones and behavior (Figure 1). Understanding the dynamic interactions that link the social environment with neuroendocrine mechanisms and behavior provides a foundation for determining factors regulating differential reproductive success among individuals. Socioendocrine factors construct ontogenetic trajectories beginning in utero and operating until death. For example, neuroendocrine feedback mechanisms achieve a prominent role in mediating reproductive processes in postpubescent animals, but differences in fetal and neonatal development influence adult neuroendocrine profiles. Prenatally stressed rhesus macaques (*Macaca mulatta*) develop different neuroendocrine feedback

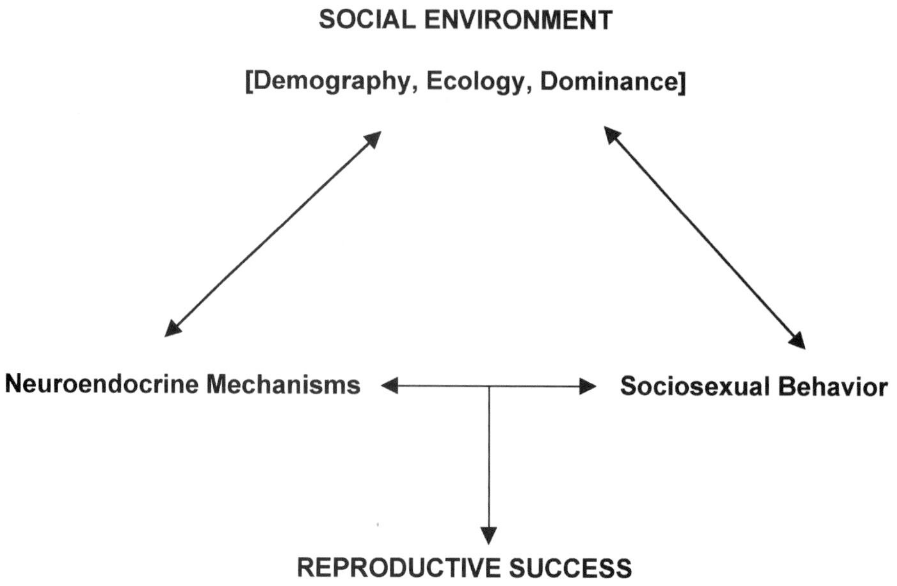

Figure 1 The basic paths of socioendocrinology. Modified from Bercovitch & Ziegler 1990 and Dixson 1998.

sensitivities compared with control subjects (Clarke et al. 1994), and blockage of elevated neonatal testosterone levels in male common marmosets (*Callithrix jacchus*) results in attenuation of the pubertal rise in testosterone (Lunn et al. 1994).

One fundamental tenet of socioendocrinology is that individuals have evolved an adaptive flexibility enabling them to adjust both mating effort and parental effort according to social surroundings, which yields alternative mating strategies promoting individual reproductive success. All animals need not continually strive to achieve the alpha slot in a hierarchy in order to maximize their chances of contributing to subsequent generations. Animals respond to their social surroundings in a manner that balances the benefits of current reproduction against the costs of future reproduction, even if such a calculation involves retarded reproductive maturation or reproductive restraint. A socioendocrinological perspective provides a framework for connecting reproductive endocrinology with evolutionary biology.

Rather than give an extensive review of the literature, this contribution provides a critical assessment of four key topics: (*a*) associations between male parental care, paternity, and endocrine state, (*b*) relationships among stress, social strategies, and reproduction, (*c*) the socioendocrinology of reproductive maturation in females, and (*d*) the socioendocrinology of reproductive maturation in males. These four subjects were chosen because they are some of the most active and controversial areas posing challenges for future research projects in the field of primate socioendocrinology.

ASSOCIATIONS AMONG MALE PARENTAL CARE, PATERNITY, AND ENDOCRINE STATE

Direct male parental care is rare in mammals. Only 10% of mammalian species exhibit some type of paternal care, but male care of infant primates occurs in approximately 40% of primate genera (Kleiman & Malcom 1981). Among nonhuman primates, extensive paternal care is most often associated with monogamous, or polyandrous, species such as siamangs (*Symphalangus* spp.), owl monkeys (*Aotus* spp.), titi monkeys (*Callicebus* spp.), goeldii's monkeys (*Callimico goeldii*), marmosets (*Callithrix* spp.), and tamarins (*Saguinus* spp.), with several cercopithecine species also displaying strong male-infant bonds (Whitten 1987, Smuts & Gubernick 1992). The evolutionary explanation(s) for paternal care are controversial; the leading contenders are protection from nonparental infanticidal males (van Schaik & Paul 1997, van Schaik & Janson 2000), care of probable offspring that enhances survivorship prospects (Bernstein 1976, Bercovitch 1995), sharing the energetic burden of raising descendants because of metabolic constraints of lactation (Heymann 2000), and using infants as devices to increase prospects for future matings (Price 1990, Smuts & Gubernick 1992).

The most extensive studies on the socioendocrinology of paternal care in primates have been conducted on cotton-top tamarins (*Saguinus oedipus*) (Figure 2, see color figure). Cotton-top tamarins are cooperative breeders, with the entire family participating in caring for the twin infants. Tamarin fathers begin carrying their young on the day of birth and spend as much time as do mothers with their infants during the first five days after birth (Ziegler & Snowdon 2000; Ziegler et al. 2000a,b). Sons and daughters delay their emigration from the family to help rear younger brothers and sisters. In captivity, both experienced fathers and their sons show elevated levels of prolactin following the birth of infants compared with nonfather tamarins (Ziegler et al. 1996).

Although prolactin is often thought of as a "female" hormone associated with lactation, blood concentrations in men and women are comparable, and newborn infants have higher prolactin levels than do nursing mothers (Norman & Litwack 1997). Evidence that prolactin was involved in male parenting behavior in primates initially emerged from studies of the common marmoset and the cotton-top tamarin. Marmoset males have elevated prolactin concentrations following the birth of infants (Dixson & George 1982, Torii et al. 1998, Mota & Sousa 2000), which was thought to be related to infant contact because prolactin levels were higher in males carrying infants than in males not carrying infants. Lowering endogenous prolactin in young, inexperienced marmosets, using bromocriptine, caused an increase in the time to retrieval of marmoset infants, compared with control subjects,which suggests that prolactin promotes responsiveness to infants (Roberts et al. 2001).

Prolactin levels are elevated in cotton-top tamarin fathers throughout the first six weeks following the birth of their infants, whereas elevated prolactin in mothers is dependent on viable nursing infants (Ziegler et al. 2000a). Prolactin levels are positively correlated with the number of previous births with which a male has been involved. Although hyperprolactinemia suppresses testosterone concentrations in men (Norman & Litwack 1997), and many biparental birds display inverse relationships between prolactin and testosterone (Ziegler 2000), prolactin and testosterone levels do not change significantly from pre- to postpartum in cotton-top tamarin fathers. Figure 3 shows levels of prolactin, testosterone, and dihydrotestosterone (DHT), a potent androgenic metabolite of testosterone) among cotton-top tamarin males under a variety of conditions. Mean prolactin levels by month of gestation (6-month gestation period for the cotton-top tamarin) reveal a difference in prolactin for experienced and inexperienced father tamarins (Ziegler & Snowdon 2000). For experienced fathers, a significant rise in prolactin occurs during the second and third gestational month, whereas inexperienced fathers show elevated prolactin levels during the last month prior to birth. Cortisol levels show little change in males thoughout the pregnancy of their mate, regardless of level of experience of the father, but cortisol levels are elevated in new, inexperienced fathers (Ziegler et al. 1996). Tamarins have a postpartum ovulation that occurs within a couple of weeks following parturition and, therefore, have a simultaneous period of parenting and breeding. In fact, testosterone levels are significantly elevated in male tamarins around the time of the postpartum ovulation (Ziegler et al. 2000a).

Prepartum changes in male cotton-top tamarin endocrine profiles during their mate's pregnancy indicate how the social environment modifies the endocrine state. Cues emitted from the female mate could signal impending birth and provide an adaptive milieu for paternal care. Male cotton-top tamarins are known to receive arousal cues from female tamarins' periovulatory scent marks (Ziegler et al. 1993). Olfactory cues during pregnancy, stimulated by hormonal changes or produced by direct male-female contact, could regulate male parent endocrine state. Male tamarins have well-developed vomeronasal organs (Wysocki 1979) and female tamarins have well-developed scent glands (Epple 1986). Female tamarins scent mark substrates in their environment (Epple 1986, Savage et al. 1988) and are known to scent mark throughout pregnancy (Epple 1976). Social stimulus through increased contact time with the pregnant female can also initiate a cascade of hormonal events (Uvnas 1997), and these events might be important in initiating male parental behaviors. Although the physiological mechanism triggering pre- and postpartum endocrine changes in males is unknown, the socioendocrinology of cotton-top tamarin mating and rearing systems indicates a coordinated network that prepares the pair for parenthood and implicates multiple caregivers in the survival of offspring.

→

Figure 3 Mean + SEM percentage changes in urinary (*A*) prolactin, (*B*) testosterone and DHT, and (*C*) cortisol from the first month of gestation in experienced and inexperienced male cotton-top tamarins. Months with the same letters are not significantly different from each other, whereas months with different letters indicate statistically significant differences. Modified from Ziegler & Snowdon (2000).

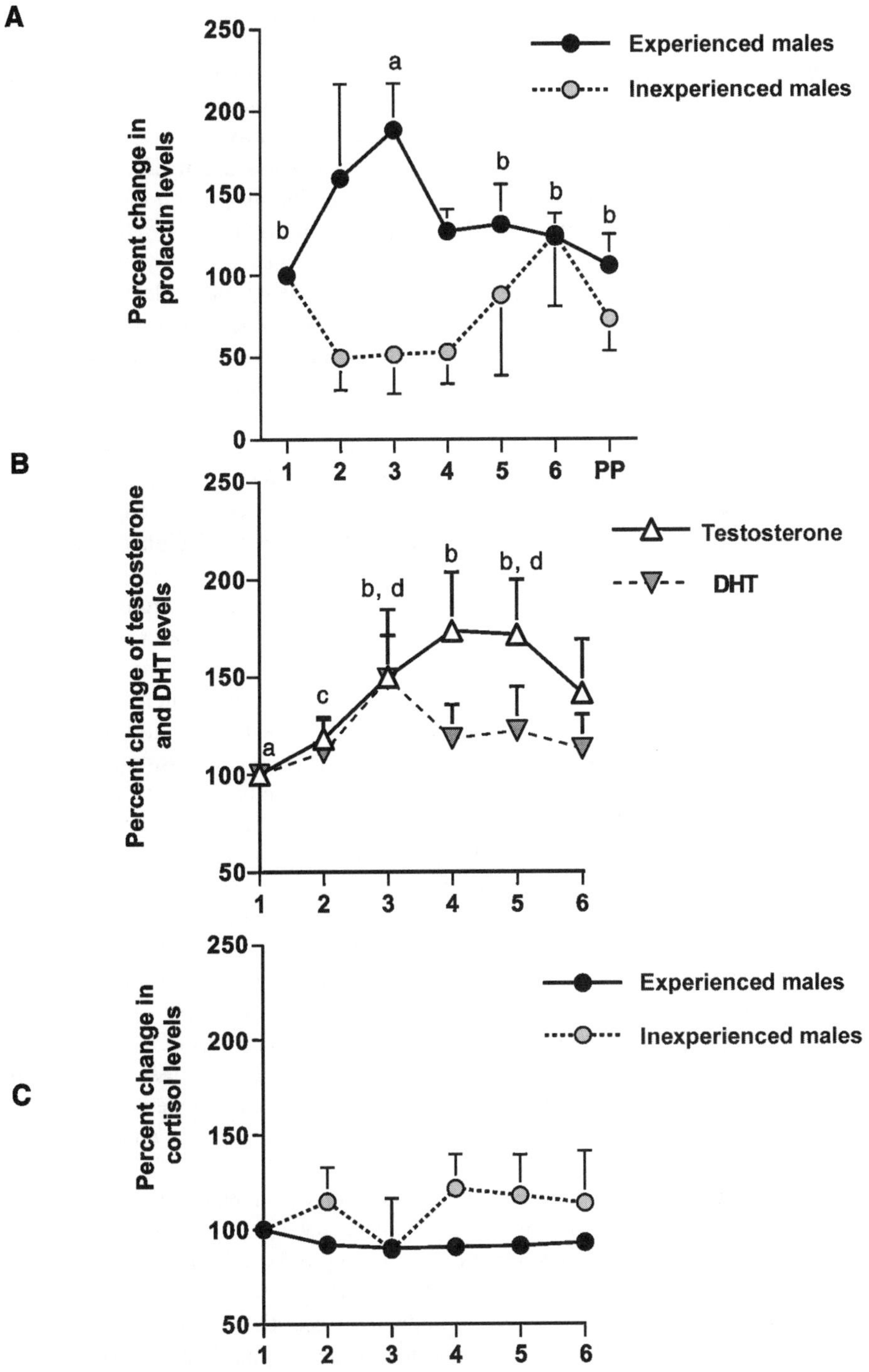
A
250
200
150
100
50
0
Percent change in prolactin levels
Experienced males
Inexperienced males
a
b
b
b
b
1
2
3
4
5
6
PP
B
250
200
150
100
50
Percent change of testosterone and DHT levels
Testosterone
DHT
a
c
b, d
b
b, d
1
2
3
4
5
6
C
250
200
150
100
50
Percent change in cortisol levels
Experienced males
Inexperienced males
1
2
3
4
5
6

The socioendocrinology of parental care in cotton-top tamarins has many similarities to that of humans. For example, the endocrine changes associated with pregnancy and parturition not only prepare a mother for delivering an infant but also stimulate neurochemical changes within the brain to influence maternal behavior (Numan 1994, Bridges 1996). Similar life history stage–specific differences appear in some hormone levels for both females and males, e.g., higher concentrations of prolactin and cortisol in the period just before the birth of an infant are accompanied by lower levels of sex steroids postnatally (Storey et al. 2000). Additionally, men who experience more pregnancy-like symptoms (couvade) during their wife's pregnancy have higher mean prolactin levels than men with fewer symptoms. Testosterone levels in men appear to be lower following infant birth, whereas cortisol levels are higher prior to parturition (Berg & Wynne-Edwards 2001). Hormonal changes occur prior, and in response, to parturition in both mother and father in both cotton-top tamarins and people. Father participation in the direct care of his children has increased over the past 30 years in many areas of Europe and America (Lamb 1981, 1987), with research into the motivational factors and benefits of father participation receiving increasing attention. In both sexes, hormonal patterns may have evolved to facilitate infant care behaviors.

Children who have positive involvement with both parents throughout childhood are more likely to be confident, social individuals (Lieberman et al. 1999), and fathers are more likely to invest care in their biological children than in their step children (Daly & Wilson 1988). Cultural factors play a prominent role in shaping whether or not fathers are likely to be directly involved with their children (Hewlett 1992a). Since cultural factors are one component of the social environment, studying the relationship between cultural practices and the endocrinology of fatherhood falls within the domain of primate socioendocrinology. Even in societies where father participation is encouraged, considerable variation exists among fathers in patterns of paternal care. But, as with the cotton-top tamarins, some of the variability in human fathers' responses to infants is associated with periparturitional hormonal changes within the father (Storey et al. 2000, Berg & Wynne-Edwards 2001).

We suggest that evolution has molded a malleable endocrine state among males that responds to the social environment by regulating internal milieu among fathers in a fashion that promotes the survival of their offspring. In species where male care of infants is crucial, we expect endocrine changes in males that will augment their parental roles, whereas in primate species in which male care is unimportant for infant survivorship, pre- and/or postpartum modifications in endocrine state are less likely to occur.

Continuing to examine socioendocrine influences on male parental behaviors in primates is important for understanding mechanisms involved in fostering male reproductive success. We propose that hormonal profiles will have coevolved with social behavior during the evolution of breeding systems to ensure that patterns of parental investment maximize reproductive success. Therefore, studying the socioendocrinology of paternal care can provide insights into the evolutionary foundations of different mating systems.

STRESS, SOCIAL STRATEGIES, AND REPRODUCTION

Primates are often challenged by conspecifics or predators. The fight-or-flight response demands increased energy mobilization, which is achieved by activation of the endocrine stress response. The stress response is a biological mechanism that operates by dampening digestive, immune, and reproductive systems while stimulating cardiovascular and musculoskeletal activity (Sapolsky 1994, Norman & Litwack 1997). Glucocorticoids flood the circulatory system and mediate metabolic processes by converting amino acids to carbohydrates, which conserve glucose as an energy source. Elevated glucocorticoids, or corticosteroids, inhibit both antibody production and the inflammatory response, which is one reason why topical application of cortisone ointment alleviates itching. Cortisol is the major primate glucocorticoid and belongs to the same "superfamily" of hormones as the sex steroids because all are derived from cholesterol and all share similar receptor binding properties.

A standard paradigm has developed that assumes that low-ranking primates are subject to high levels of social or nutritional stress and, therefore, are characterized by higher cortisol levels and reduced reproductive success (e.g., Dunbar 1988). However, this scenario has proved increasingly inadequate among a number of species. We describe an alternative model that links reproductive activity to increased metabolic demands and elevated "stress." We propose that animals have evolved a physiological flexibility enabling them to meet the energetic demands of mating activity by increasing both adrenal and sex steroid concentrations without detriment to reproductive success. The effects of stress are modulated by positive social interactions among primates that decrease the potentially adverse impact of circulating glucocorticoids on reproductive processes.

Consider the situation among a number of nonprimate species. Breeding female green turtles (*Chelonia mydas*) have elevated levels of both corticosterone (the major glucocorticoid in most species) and progesterone; the catabolic properties of corticosterone probably facilitate the energetic demands associated with nest construction and egg laying (Jessop et al. 2000). In many passerine birds, such as the dark-eyed junco (*Junco hyemalis*), mating season elevations of both testosterone and corticosterone jeopardize immune function but are beneficial for shunting nutritional reserves into behavioral patterns and for exhibiting secondary sexual traits that promote reproductive success (Casto et al. 2001). Male copperhead snake (*Agkistrodon cantortrix*) fighting involves lots of physical contact without biting. Defeated males display significantly elevated corticosterone concentrations, but winners and losers have similar testosterone levels, which demonstrates a disconnect between the two hormones as well as shows how endocrine levels respond to social stimuli in snakes (Schuett et al. 1996). Finally, male marsupial mice (*Antechinus stuartii*), who all die after a one- to two-week mating season, are characterized by eightfold increases in testosterone and a doubling of cortisol levels, from the pre- to peak breeding period (McAllen 1998).

Among nonhuman primates, exposure to estrous females results in elevated concentrations of both testosterone and cortisol in long-tailed macaques (*Macaca fascicularis*) (Glick 1984), talapoins (*Miopithecus talapoin*) (Martensz et al. 1987), capuchins (*Cebus apella*) (Lynch et al. 2002), and squirrel monkeys (*Saimiri sciurius*) (Mendoza & Mason 1991). Among male rhesus macaques (*M. mulatta*), cortisol concentrations are neither related to social status nor negatively associated with testosterone concentrations (Bercovitch & Clarke 1995). Dominant male lesser mouse lemurs (*Microcebus murinus*) have significantly higher testosterone concentrations than do subordinate males, but the two classes of males do not differ in cortisol levels (Perret 1992), whereas dominant male squirrel monkeys have higher concentrations of both testosterone and cortisol than do subordinate males (Coe et al. 1979). Dominant male savanna baboons (*Papio cynocephalus*) have lower cortisol levels than subordinate males when the social hierarchy is stable, but low-ranking males who have extensive social affiliations and are adept at displacing aggression also have low cortisol concentrations (Sapolsky 1994). Male mountain gorillas (*Gorilla gorilla*) living in Rwanda show no evidence of rank-related differences in cortisol concentrations (Robbins & Czekala 1997), and rank effects on both cortisol and testosterone are absent among male muriquis (*Brachyteles arachnoides*) living in Brazil (Strier et al. 1999).

Social skills have a tremendous impact on male reproduction among primates (Strum 1987, Bercovitch 1991) and contribute to mitigating the expression of the endocrine stress response (Sapolsky 1994). Furthermore, among male primates, differences in reproductive success are more likely to arise from adoption of alternative reproductive strategies than from testosterone concentrations (Bercovitch & Goy 1990). Even under conditions of stress-mediated cortisol suppression of testosterone, spermatogenesis continues and males are capable of impregnating females. However, intense stress does interfere with the ability to achieve and sustain an erection (Sapolsky 1994, Bercovitch 1999).

Both nutritional and social stress operate along similar neuroendocrine pathways that can interfere with regular ovarian cyclicity and dampen female reproductive success (Bercovitch & Goy 1990, Bercovitch & Strum 1993). One might expect, therefore, a more pronounced connection between increased cortisol concentrations and reduced reproductive success in female compared with male primates. Semi-free-ranging female Barbary macaques (*Macaca sylvanus*) who are subjected to aggression from conspecifics excrete increased amounts of glucocorticoids (Wallner et al. 1999). In the same population, breeding lifespan accounts for 61% of the variance in female reproductive success, and low-ranking females initiate reproductive senescence at a younger age than high-ranking females (Paul & Kuester 1996). The detrimental consequences of stress in this population do not seem to modify reproductive rate but do appear to have negative consequences for life expectancy.

In captive long-tailed macaques, serum cortisol concentrations were not related to dominance rank under conditions of social stability (Stavisky et al. 2001), and limited evidence suggests that urinary cortisol is independent of female rank among wild long-tailed macaques (van Schaik et al. 1991). In female cotton-top tamarins, cortisol levels are higher during the periovulatory than the nonperiovulatory phase, with fertility suppression of postpubescent females not associated with increased cortisol concentrations (Ziegler et al. 1995). The highest cortisol levels were documented for pregnant females, who also occupied the dominant position. Among female common marmosets, cortisol levels were higher in dominant, cycling females than in subordinate anovulatory females (Saltzman et al. 1994). Reproductive condition accounted for the elevated cortisol concentrations in dominant females in both species (Saltzman et al. 1994, Ziegler et al. 1995). The connection between high rank and high cortisol in these callitrichids was not a consequence of cooperative rearing and associated reproductive suppression because a similar pattern has been found among ring-tailed lemurs (*Lemur catta*), who reside in a different type of mating system.

Ring-tailed lemurs live in extremely seasonal habitats in Madagascar. They live in female-bonded social groups where the females are dominant to the males (Richard 1987, Gould 1999). Breeding seasonality is tightly constrained, with matings occurring during a one-month period. Toward the end of the dry season, when food resources are limited and predator pressure intensifies, cortisol concentrations of females increases slightly, but the best predictor of cortisol concentrations is female dominance status (Cavigelli 1999). Low-ranking females have low cortisol concentrations.

Chronic stress could decrease lifespan and thereby hinder reproductive output, but we suggest that the energetic costs of mating, especially among males, result in physiological adjustments that boost both sex and adrenal steroids. During the premating season, male rhesus macaques accumulate substantial fat deposits that are drawn upon during the mating season as males decrease feeding time and increase time spent in sociosexual activities (Bercovitch 1997). Male rhesus macaques not only have elevated levels of testosterone and estrogen during the mating season (Bercovitch 1992), but cortisol concentrations among high-ranking males, who also have the greatest fat deposits (Bercovitch & Nürnberg 1996), are much higher during the peak mating season than during the postmating season (Bercovitch & Clarke 1995). Casto et al. (2001) have proposed that the breeding season elevations of testosterone and corticosterone in birds are costly in two ways: a high-energy reproductive behavior and a shorter life history, because the hormonal increases reduce survivorship prospects and suppress immune function. A similar life history profile might characterize males of many primate species, but whether longevity is reduced among the most reproductively active males has not yet been evaluated.

The situation among females is more complex, but it could be similar. A concurrent increase in glucocorticoids and ovarian steroids might reflect the energetic costs of mating among females. Although female savanna baboons in consort relationships with males do not travel more than nonconsort females, they significantly reduce feeding time (Bercovitch 1983), and estrogen has suppressive effects on appetite (Bielert & Busse 1983). Callitrichids have severe energy hurdles for raising twin offspring, and while the energetic costs of mating in captivity are not profound, the possibility remains that links between high rank and high cortisol are reflecting metabolic adjustments prior to gestation. We suggest that the energetic costs of reproduction in both males and females might create conditions conducive to elevations in both adrenal and sex steroids and that the role of cortisol and stress on reproductive suppression has been overestimated.

In conclusion, male reproductive strategies are stressful, and the metabolic challenges of mate guarding and mate acquisition require extensive energy use, which, in turn, demands the mobilization of glucocorticoids. Female reproductive strategies are more mysterious with respect to the role of adrenal steroids on reproductive processes. Evidence from field and laboratory studies demonstrate that fertility enhancement, not suppression, can be accompanied by high levels of glucocorticoids.

THE SOCIOENDOCRINOLOGY OF REPRODUCTIVE MATURATION IN FEMALES

Puberty begins with alterations in the hypothalamic GnRH pulse generator, a complex of neurons responsible for regulating the timing of release of gonadotropins (Terasawa et al. 1983, Norman & Litwack 1997, Plant 1999). Nocturnal outbursts of GnRH stimulate increased pulsatile secretion of LH (luteinizing hormone), which triggers output of ovarian and testicular sex steroids, which drive development of reproductive potential and processes. Covert neuroendocrine adjustments prompting the transition from puberty to adulthood occur before outward manifestations of reproductive maturation. Ontogenetic physiological patterns bridging the period from pubescence to adulthood have been documented in detail, but primates are characterized by a fairly unique, and lengthy, phase of adolescent subfecundity (see Dixson 1998). Why a neuroendocrine system triggers gonadotropin pulsatility in the absence of concurrent and regular ovarian changes resulting in ovulation is unclear. We explain how social factors are partially responsible for regulating this life history stage, and suggest that prosimians, and possibly other primates, are facultatively reflex ovulators.

One resolution to the riddle of adolescent subfecundity might reside in female choice operating via two different pathways. One mechanism is reflex ovulation as a form of cryptic female choice (Eberhard 1996). Cryptic female choice occurs when females control sirehood in such a way that the rate at which they mate with a given partner is not correlated with the rate at which they co-reproduce with them. The other mechanism is neophyte mate choice designed to patiently adjudicate potential partners, given the costs of mating and producing offspring.

Primates are spontaneous ovulators, but reflex ovulation and spontaneous ovulation are not two discrete species-specific traits in mammals (Zarrow & Clark 1968, Conaway 1971, Jöchle 1975, Milligan 1982, Martin 1990). Rats ovulate spontaneously, but cervicovaginal stimulation increases output of eggs (Zarrow & Clark 1968), whereas camels are reflex ovulators, with about 5% of females ovulating spontaneously (van Tienhoven 1983). Coitus-induced ovulation has been reasoned to represent the primitive (Zarrow & Clark 1968) and the derived (Weir & Rowlands 1973) state, with the variety of ovarian dynamics across mammals failing to follow phylogenetic, ecological, or social classification (Conaway 1971, van Tienhoven 1983). Some animals are considered "facultative reflex ovulators" (Jöchle 1975), where exposure to a male or coital activity can trigger the LH surge responsible for ovulation.

Prosimians and New World monkeys are the most likely candidates for facultative reflex ovulation. Reflex ovulation predominates in nongregarious mammalian species with penile spines (Zarrow & Clark 1968). Most prosimians live in nongregarious mating systems (Bearder 1987, Dunbar 1988, Nash 1993) and possess prominent penile spines (Dixson 1987, 1998; Harcourt & Gardiner 1994). Among primates, penile spines and dispersed mating systems tend to coincide (Dixson 1987, Harcourt & Gardiner 1994). Although New World monkeys generally reside in large social configurations, some species have extensive penile spines. Regardless of the form of the mating system, the presence of penile spines in primates suggests that facultative reflex ovulation might contribute to delayed first pregancy following onset of ovarian processes. Sexually attracting, and mating with, an adult male establishes a necessary, but not sufficient, condition for reflex ovulation among adolescents.

Both prosimians and New World monkeys transmit chemosignals that alter the reproductive endocrinology of conspecifics, providing a second clue to how social factors regulate the timing of adolescent subfecundity. Among cotton-top tamarins, exposure to a novel male facilitates onset of ovarian cyclicity but does not influence the maintenance of ovarian function (Ziegler et al. 1987, Savage et al. 1988, Widowski et al. 1992). Pairing lesser galagos with an adult male accelerates onset of first estrus (Izard 1990), whereas introduction of an adult male to group-living squirrel monkeys results in elevated estradiol output within 24 h (Mendoza & Mason 1991). Copulation in squirrel monkeys intensifies the midcycle estradiol surge, which could ensure ovulation, facilitate gamete transport, promote luteal function, or enhance implantation prospects (Yeoman et al. 1991). In common marmosets, young postpubescent females are significantly more likely to ovulate when living with an unrelated male than when living with their father (Saltzman et al. 1997). In peer groups of common marmosets, subordinate females, who tended to copulate with subordinate males, did not ovulate, whereas the dominant female, who copulated mostly with the dominant male, became pregnant (Abbott & Hearn 1978), indicating that facultative reflex ovulation might be stymied by low social status. Among nonprimates, a wealth of data reveals that chemical, tactile, and auditory cues from male mice modify the reproductive status of females by inhibiting or potentiating ovulation, as well as by interfering with implantation (Bronson 1989, Vandenbergh 1994), despite classification as spontaneous ovulators (see Weir & Rowlands 1973, van Tienhoven 1983). Male induction of ovulation and female suppression of ovarian function represent a continuum of socioendocrine processes that regulate reproductive success. Reproductive development can be either accelerated or decelerated as a function of social stimuli.

Two other life history traits of prosimians and New World monkeys intimate facultative reflex ovulation as a reproductive strategy. New World monkeys tend to display relatively short estrous cycles, which are common among species where formation of a functional corpus luteum requires a mating stimulus (Martin 1990). Reflex ovulation and coitus-induced luteinization often co-occur. Second, postpartum estrus is frequently exhibited by reflex ovulators and is common among small-sized prosimians (e.g., mouse lemurs, lesser galagos) and Callitrichids (e.g., common marmosets, cotton-top tamarins), who reproduce aseasonally (Martin 1990, Ziegler et al. 1990).

In both prosimians and New World monkeys, morphological characteristics and male modification of female reproductive endocrinology establish a foundation for possible facultative reflex ovulation. In these species, adolescent subfecundity could be adaptive by postponing initial ovulation until females are presented with appropriate socioecological conditions favoring offspring survival. Prosimians are ideal candidates for further investigation of facultative reflex ovulation because they share many traits with reflex ovulators: They often live in dispersed social systems, display brief periods of sexual receptivity, scent mark in accordance with stage of ovarian cycle, attract multiple males while in estrus, alter reproductive endocrinology as a function of social cues, and have spiny penises, elongated os baculum, and engage in prolonged intromission (Dixson 1998).

Another means by which female choice could account for adolescent subfecundity is to enable neophyte females the opportunity to hone mate selection judgment capabilities prior to first conception. Appraising suitable sires is facilitated by proceptive behavior, but maintaining a constant follicular state for this purpose is not physiologically feasible. Continuous high estradiol levels interfere with development of the feedback relationship required to stimulate a sharp spike triggering the gonadotropin surge responsible for ovulation (Bercovitch et al. 1987). Retaining high gonadotropin levels would facilitate downregulation of receptor quantity and reduce subsequent gonadotropin output. Therefore, prolonged proceptivity is not an option due to physiological constraints imposed on reproductive cycles, but anovulatory cycles provide an opportunity for proceptive behavior without risking impregnation. Among cercopithecines, female body mass at puberty is significantly less than at adulthood (Bercovitch 2000), and, among captive pigtailed macaques, *M. nemestrina*, infant mortality due to dystocia is more pronounced among primiparous than multiparous mothers (Dazey & Erwin 1976). Primates tend to have longer follicular stages than other mammals (Zeleznick & Fairchild-Benyo 1994), and multiple nonovulatory cycles increase female chances for scrutinizing males. Across Primates, the span of adolescent subfecundity is extraordinarily variable but tends to be longest among females residing in multimale mating systems and shortest among those living in paired mating systems (Figure 4).

Adolescent subfecundity could be a nonadaptive consequence of the evolution of an exceedingly fine-tuned neuroendocrine system that requires a lengthy interval to coordinate the various components. It could be a "physiologial atavism" that has not been removed from primates during evolution (Zarrow & Clark 1968). It could be adaptive by postponing first conception until socioecological conditions are favorable for induced ovulation and subsequent pregnancy. Or it could be adaptive by permitting females time to imbibe male traits as a precursor to mate selection.

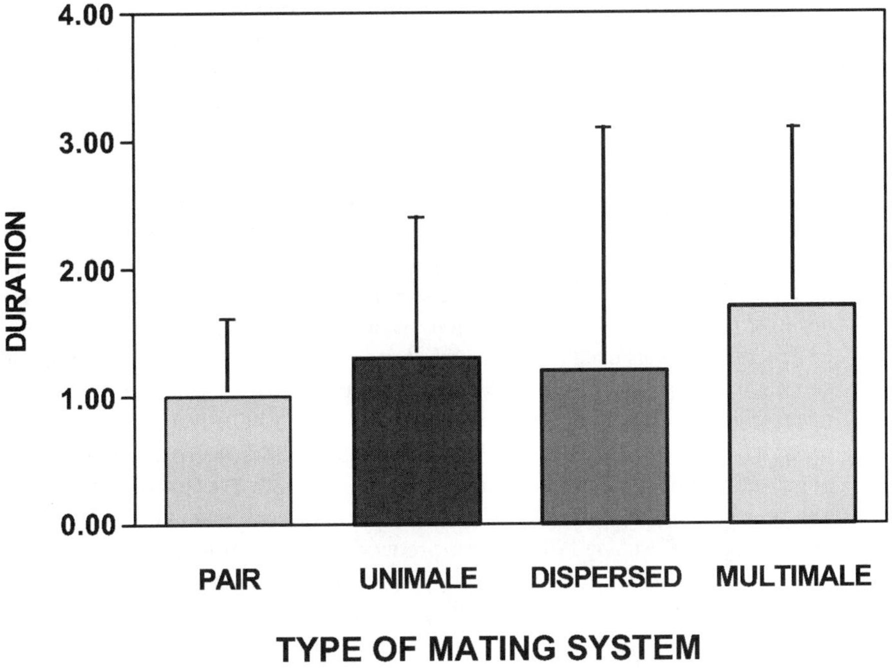

Figure 4 The relationship between duration of adolescent subfecundity and structure of the mating system. Histogram bars plot the mean plus standard deviation. Classification of mating systems follows Dixson (1991, 1995) and Harcourt et al. (1995). Differences in duration of adolescent subfecundity are absent when the four mating systems are compared (Kruskal-Wallis = 5.794, $P > 0.10$) but nearly significant when weight is held constant (ANCOVA: $F(3,35) = 2.780$, $P = 0.055$, multiple $r = 0.737$). The length of the adolescent subfecundity stage in multimale mating systems is significantly longer than that of the other systems combined (Mann-Whitney $U = 105$, $P = 0.03$).

Adolescent female sexuality in primates has received little systematic attention, and understanding the evolution of this life history period requires more detailed investigations.

THE SOCIOENDOCRINOLOGY OF MALE REPRODUCTIVE MATURATION

Neuroendocrine pathways guiding male reproductive maturation are identical to those of females, except that instead of fine-tuning pulsatile GnRH discharges into a cyclical pattern regulating ovulation, males develop a more stable rhythmicity that fosters continuous sperm production. Social stimuli retarding or accelerating reproductive maturation in males have not been scrutinized as solidly as those in females. Most information comes from papionins (i.e., macaques, mandrills, baboons, and mangabeys), but social factors have also been identified as promoting alternative paths of reproductive development in orangutans (*Pongo pygmaeus*). One difficulty encountered in studying the socioendocrinology of male reproductive maturation is that the most likely candidates are species that live in multimale-multifemale social systems, yet, in these same systems, females regularly mate with multiple partners, so evaluating the reproductive consequences of suppressed or accelerated maturation requires genetic analysis of sirehood. In addition, as noted earlier, thwarted reproductive endocrinology among males need not have negative repercussions on spermatogenesis and reproductive success.

Spermatogenesis occurs in the seminiferous tubules of the testes, with follicle stimulating hormone (FSH), the key hormone regulating spermatogenesis in primates (Sharpe 1994, Norman & Litwack 1997, Jones 1997). Testosterone exerts a secondary influence on sperm production. Circulating androgen concentrations are not correlated with rates of spermatogenesis (Johnson & Everitt 1984, Rommerts 1988), and testicular androgen concentrations do not correlate with sperm count (Weinbauer & Nieschlag 1991). Sperm production is related to testis size, but sperm output depends on ejaculatory frequency, epididymal efficiency, sperm storage capacity, and degree of precopulatory stimulation (Bercovitch 1989, Johnson 1989). Male cotton-top tamarins residing in their cooperative breeding family group are not developmentally suppressed but require exposure to an unrelated female in order to initiate their reproductive careers (Ginther et al. 2002). Hence, reproductive suppression among males involving endocrine profiles is unlikely to hamper sperm production, and, even in the presence of diminished sperm production, the fundamental factor promoting paternity is access to females and not sperm count (see Bercovitch 1989).

The most detailed information about the socioendocrinology of male reproductive maturation comes from studies of rhesus macaques. Among adolescent males within a cohort, higher ranking animals and those whose mothers are dominant tend to have elevated testosterone concentrations and larger testicles than lower ranking peers or those whose mothers are subordinant (Bercovitch & Goy 1990, Bercovitch 1993, Dixson & Nevison 1997). Among adult male rhesus macaques, a cluster of traits, including high dominance status, large body mass, relatively large testes, and good body condition are associated with actual progeny production (Bercovitch & Nürnberg 1996). Sons of high-ranking mothers are heavier than peers from one year of age (Figure 5) through adulthood, and infant weight accounts for a small fraction of the variance in adult male reproductive success (Bercovitch et al. 2000). High-ranking young males are more likely to sire offspring in their natal troop than are low-ranking peers (Bercovitch et al. 2000).

Dominant male rhesus macaques tend to remain in their natal troop longer than subordinate males (Colvin 1986), and some evidence implicates neuroendocrine factors as a variable influencing the timing of natal dispersal. Males who disperse at relatively young ages tend to have lower levels of cerebrospinal fluid concentrations of 5-hydroxyindoleacetic acid (CSF 5-HIAA), a serotonin metabolite, with low

Figure 2 A cotton-top tamarin father transporting one of his twin offspring on his back. Photo by Carla Boe.

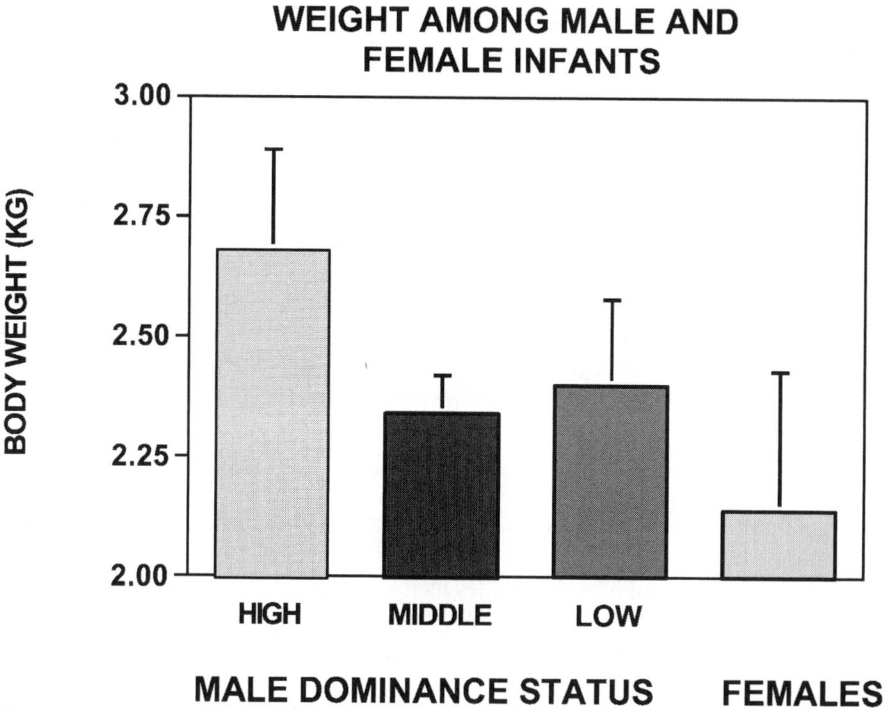

Figure 5 The influence of dominance rank on male mass at one year of age. Histogram bars plot the mean plus standard deviation. High-ranking males weigh significantly more than lower ranking peers (ANOVA: $F(2,8) = 4.823$, $P = 0.04$), and females weigh significantly less than males ($t = -3.329$, $df = 26$, $P < 0.01$). Modified from Bercovitch et al. 2000.

levels of CSF 5-HIAA associated with reduced social competence, excessive aggression, and increased mortality risks (Mehlman et al. 1995, Higley et al. 1996).

Delayed dispersal among male rhesus macaques is therefore linked with reduced mortality risks, high dominance rank, accelerated reproductive development, and earlier onset of reproductive career. However, the primary determinant of short-term reproduction in males is not body condition or status, but the number of females with which they have mated (Bercovitch & Nürnberg 1996). Dominant males not only mate with more females than subordinate males, but also they have longer mount series (Carpenter 1942, Kaufmann 1965). The longer mount series is accompanied by a greater number of thrusts per intromission, or mounts before ejaculation, which should maximize the number of sperm delivered into a female (Bercovitch & Nürnberg 1996). In summary, dominant males appear to have a reproductive edge in rhesus macaques because they are characterized by a number of social, sexual, and physiological traits that foster mating with multiple females, but subordinate males do adopt surreptitious tactics that have been linked with actual reproductive success (Berard et al. 1994).

Patterns documented in rhesus macaques have been found in other papionins. Sons of high-ranking female savanna baboons undergo accelerated reproductive maturation (Alberts & Altmann 1995), and evidence that high-ranking young natal males have sired offspring in their troop of birth has been reported from a number of study sites (Packer 1979, Smuts 1985, Bulger & Hamilton 1988, Altmann et al. 1996). Alpha male mandrills (*Mandrillus sphinx*) have more pronounced secondary sexual developments, higher testosterone concentrations, and greater reproductive success than subordinate males (Wickings & Dixson 1992, Dixson et al. 1993), with abrupt changes in social status associated with changes in physical appearance and reproductive activity (Setchell & Dixson 2001). Subordinate male mandrills develop more slowly than do dominant conspecifics (Setchell & Dixson 2002). Young sons of high-ranking Barbary macaques (*M. sylvanus*) have a higher mating success than sons of low-ranking females (Paul & Kuester 1990), and mating success is strongly tied to actual reproductive success in this population (Paul et al. 1993).

Orangutans (*P. pygmaeus*) are unusual among primates because the socioendocrinology of male development results in the co-existence of two "morphs": those with or without secondary sexual traits (Kingsley 1982, Graham & Nadler 1990). Suppression of endocrine levels is associated with failure to develop secondary sexual traits but not with reduced fertility (Maggioncalda et al. 1999, 2000; Dixson et al. 1982). Development of secondary features, such as cheek flanges, enlarged laryngeal sacs, and lengthy beards, seems suppressed under conditions of high male density and is possibly in the wild a response to the negative effects of vocal signals, i.e., male loud calls (Maggioncalda et al. 1999). Whether the alternative developmental strategies have comparable reproductive success among orangutans in the wild is unknown.

Male access to females is not only a consequence of agonistic competition among some primate species but is also related to the adoption of complex social strategies (Strum 1987, Bercovitch 1991). Among cercopithecines, male reproductive maturation begins significantly later in life, lasts for a longer period of time, and is more variable in duration than it is among females (Bercovitch 2000). A lengthy period of development permits males the opportunity to boost body mass prior to engaging in costly male competition, as well as reducing susceptibility to predators and buffering against feeding uncertainties during dispersal. Large size enhances endurance rivalry, or the ability to withstand long periods of feeding deprivation while mate guarding (Andersson 1994, Bercovitch 1997). A long life history stage devoted to male reproductive maturation also allows males the opportunity to learn complex social skills, which could be quite important in troop integration following dispersal and in forming nonkin alliances (see Bercovitch 1988, Silk 1993, Widdig et al. 2000). In some cercopithecines, new male migrants enter a troop at the lower echelons of the dominance hierarchy, while in other species, males enter at the upper echelons of the status structure, but in both types of cercopithecine primates, sexually receptive females actively solicit newcomers (Berard 1999). Female mate choice for novel males provides a genetic hedge against inbreeding, as well as diversifying genetic composition of offspring (Bercovitch 1997). The advantage of selecting novel males is unclear, but the behavior conforms with Darwin's (1882) observation that "... females often prefer strangers to their old companions." Translating sexual invitations into reproductive opportunities in the face of resident male competition probably requires brains as well as brawn.

In summary, we suggest that socioendocrine factors play a substantial role in regulating male reproductive development. Although a direct connection between suppressed endocrine status and sperm production is lacking, males with retarded physiological development appear to be at a disadvantage compared with peers in terms of social behaviors related to obtaining and maintaining access to sexually receptive females. Therefore, males with accelerated sexual maturation probably sire offspring at earlier ages than their peers with retarded sexual maturation, but the differences are more likely to be due to social skills than a direct consequence of endocrine suppression of fertility, as is the case with females.

CONCLUSION

Primate socioendocrinology is a challenging field. The growing use of noninvasive methods for determining endocrine profiles, as well as genetic relationships, provides multiple opportunities to advance our understanding of primate socioendocrinology. One of the hallmarks of primates is their extensive ability to establish and maintain complex social relationships. This capacity has undoubtedly been constructed during evolution by developing a flexible physiological system responsive to the social environment. Hormones and behavior are inextricably intertwined in a feedback relationship in which each regulates the other.

ACKNOWLEDGMENTS

Financial support has been provided by NIH Grant RR00167 to the WRPRC and by the Zoological Society of San Diego. This is publication No. 41-011 of the WRPRC.

LITERATURE CITED

Abbott DH, Hearn JP. 1978. Physical, hormonal and behavioral aspects of sexual development in the marmoset monkey, *Callithrix jacchus*. *J. Reprod. Fert.* 53:155–66

Alberts SC, Altmann J. 1995. Preparation and activation: determinants of age at reproductive maturity in male baboons. *Behav. Ecol. Sociobiol.* 36:397–406

Altmann J, Alberts SC, Haines SA, Dubach J, Muruthi P, et al. 1996. Behavior predicts genetic structure in a wild primate group. *Proc. Natl. Acad. Sci. USA* 93:5797–801

Andersson M. 1994. *Sexual Selection*. Princeton, NJ: Princeton Univ. Press

Bagatell CJ, Bremner WJ. 1990. Sperm counts

and reproductive hormones in male marathoners and lean controls. *Fert. Steril.* 53: 688–92

Bearder SK. 1987. Lorises, bushbabies, and tarsiers: diverse societies in solitary foragers. See Smuts et al. 1987, pp. 11–24

Berard JD. 1999. A four-year study of the association between male dominance rank, residency status, and reproductive activity in rhesus macaques (*Macaca mulatta*). *Primates* 40:159–75

Berard JD, Nürnberg P, Epplen JT, Schmidtke J. 1994. Alternative reproductive tactics and reproductive success in male rhesus macaques. *Behaviour* 129:177–201

Bercovitch FB. 1983. Time budgets and consortships in olive baboons (*Papio anubis*). *Folia Primatol.* 41:180–90

Bercovitch FB. 1988. Coalitions, cooperation, and reproductive tactics in savanna baboons. *Anim. Behav.* 36:1198–209

Bercovitch FB. 1989. Body size, sperm competition, and determinants of male reproductive success in savanna baboons. *Evolution* 43:1507–21

Bercovitch FB. 1991. Social stratification, social strategies, and reproductive success in primates. *Ethol. Sociobiol.* 12:315–33

Bercovitch FB. 1992. Estradiol concentrations, fat deposits, and reproductive strategies in male rhesus macaques. *Horm. Behav.* 26: 272–82

Bercovitch FB. 1993. Dominance rank and reproductive maturation in male rhesus macaques (*Macaca mulatta*). *J. Reprod. Fert.* 99: 113–20

Bercovitch FB. 1995. Female cooperation, consortship maintenance, and male mating success in savanna baboons. *Anim. Behav.* 50: 137–49

Bercovitch FB. 1997. Reproductive strategies of rhesus macaques. *Primates* 38:247–63

Bercovitch FB. 1999. The physiology of male reproductive strategies. See Dolhinow & Fuentes 1999, pp. 237–44

Bercovitch FB. 2000. Behavioral ecology and socioendocrinology of reproductive maturation in cercopithecine monkeys. In *Old World Monkeys*, ed. PF Whitehead, CJ Jolly, pp. 298–320. Cambridge, MA: Cambridge Univ. Press

Bercovitch FB, Clarke AS. 1995. Dominance rank, cortisol concentrations, and reproductive maturation in male rhesus macaques. *Physiol. Behav.* 58:215–21

Bercovitch FB, Goy RW. 1990. The socioendocrinology of reproductive development and reproductive success in macaques. See Ziegler & Bercovitch 1990, pp. 59–93

Bercovitch FB, Goy RW, Scheffler G, Wittwer DJ, Hempel M. 1987. A benign method for maintaining ovulatory estrogen levels in cycling rhesus macaques. *Am. J. Primatol.* 13: 67–72

Bercovitch FB, Nürnberg P. 1996. Socioendocrine and morphological correlates of paternity in rhesus macaques. *J. Reprod. Fert.* 107: 59–68

Bercovitch FB, Strum SC. 1993. Dominance rank, resource availability, and reproductive maturation among female savanna baboons. *Behav. Ecol. Sociobiol.* 33:313–18

Bercovitch FB, Widdig A, Nürnberg P. 2000. Maternal investment in rhesus macaques (*Macaca mulatta*): reproductive costs and consequences of raising sons. *Behav. Ecol. Sociobiol.* 48:1–11

Bercovitch FB, Ziegler TE. 1990. Introduction to socioendocrinology. See Ziegler & Bercovitch 1990, pp. 1–9

Berg SJ, Wynne-Edwards KE. 2001. Changes in testosterone, cortisol, and estradiol levels in men becoming fathers. *Mayo Clin. Proc.* 76:582–92

Bernstein IS. 1976. Dominance, aggression, and reproduction in primate societies. *J. Theor. Biol.* 60:459–72

Bielert C, Busse C. 1983. Influences of ovarian hormones on the food intake and feeding of captive and wild female chacma baboons (*Papio ursinus*). *Phys. Behav.* 30:103–11

Bridges RS. 1996. Biochemical basis of parental behavior in the rat. In *Parental Care: Evolution, Mechanisms, and Adaptive Significance*, ed. JS Rosenblatt, CT Snowdon, pp. 215–42. San Diego: Academic

Bronson FH. 1989. *Mammalian Reproductive Biology*. Chicago: Univ. Chicago Press

Bulger J, Hamilton WJ III. 1988. Inbreeding and reproductive success in a natural chacma baboon, *Papio cynocephalus ursinus*, population. *Anim. Behav.* 36:574–78

Carpenter CR. 1942. Sexual behavior of free-ranging rhesus monkeys (*Macaca mulatta*). I. Specimens, procedures and behavioral characteristics of estrus. *J. Comp. Psychol.* 33:113–42

Casto JM, Nolan V Jr, Ketterson ED. 2001. Steroid hormones and immune function: experimental studies in wild and captive dark-eyed juncos (*Junco hyemalis*). *Am. Nat.* 157:408–20

Cavigelli SA. 1999. Behavioural patterns associated with faecal cortisol levels in free-ranging female ring-tailed lemurs, *Lemur catta*. *Anim. Behav.* 57:935–44

Clarke AS, Wittwer DJ, Abbott DH, Schnider ML. 1994. Long-term effects of prenatal stress on HPA axis activity in juvenile rhesus monkeys. *Dev. Psychobiol.* 27:257–69

Coe CL, Mendoza SP, Levine S. 1979. Social status constrains the stress response in the squirrel monkey. *Phys. Behav.* 23:633–38

Colvin JD. 1986. Proximate causes of male emigration at puberty in rhesus monkeys. In *The Cayo Santiago Macaques*, ed. RG Rawlins, MJ Kessler, pp. 131–57. Albany, NY: SUNY Press

Conaway CH. 1971. Ecological adaptation and mammalian reproduction. *Biol. Rev.* 4:239–47

Daly M, Wilson M. 1988. Evolutionary social psychology and family homicide. *Science* 242:519–23

Darwin CR. 1882. A preliminary notice: "on the modification of a race of Syrian street-dogs by means of sexual selection." *Proc. Zool. Soc. London* 25:367–70

Dazey J, Erwin J. 1976. Infant mortality in *Macaca nemestrina*: neonatal and post-natal mortality at the Regional Primate Research Field Station, Univ. Washington, 1967–1974. *Theriogenology* 5:267–76

Dixson AF. 1987. Baculum length and copulatory behavior in primates. *Am. J. Primatol.* 13:51–60

Dixson AF. 1991. Sexual selection, natural selection and copulatory patterns in male primates. *Folia Primatol.* 57:96–101

Dixson AF. 1995. Sexual selection and ejaculatory frequency in primates. *Folia Primatol.* 64:146–52

Dixson AF. 1998. *Primate Sexuality*. Oxford: Oxford Univ. Press

Dixson AF, Bossi T, Wickings EJ. 1993. Male dominance and genetically determined reproductive success in the mandrill (*Mandrillus sphinx*). *Primates* 34:525–32

Dixson AF, George L. 1982. Prolactin and parental behaviour in a male New World primate. *Nature* 299:551–53

Dixson AF, Knight J, Moore HDM, Carman M. 1982. Observations on sexual development in male orangutans, *Pongo pygmaeus*. *Int. Zoo Yearb.* 22:222–27

Dixson AF, Nevison CM. 1997. The socioendocrinology of adolescent male development in male rhesus monkeys (*Macaca mulatta*). *Horm. Behav.* 31:126–35

Dolhinow P, Fuentes A, eds. 1999. *The Nonhuman Primates*. Mountain View, CA: Mayfield

Dunbar RIM. 1988. *Primate Social Systems*. Ithaca, NY: Cornell Univ. Press

Eberhard W. 1996. *Female Control: Sexual Selection by Cryptic Female Choice*. Princeton: Princeton Univ. Press

Epple G. 1976. Chemical communication and reproductive processes in non-human primates. In *Mammalian Olfaction, Reproductive Processes and Behavior*, ed. RL Doty, pp. 257–82. New York: Academic

Epple G. 1986. Communication by chemical signals. In *Comparative Primate Biology*, Vol. 2, Part A. *Behavior, Conservation and Ecology*, ed. G Mitchell, J Erwin, pp. 531–80. New York: Liss

Ginther AJ, Carlson AA, Ziegler TE, Snowdon CT. 2002. Neonatal and pubertal development in males of a cooperatively breeding primate, the cotton-top tamarin (*Saguinus oedipus oedipus*). *Biol. Reprod.* 66:282–90

Glick BB. 1984. Male endocrine responses to females: effects of social cues in cynomologus macaques. *Am. J. Primatol.* 6:229–39

Gould L. 1999. How female dominance and reproductive seasonality affect the social lives of adult male ringtailed lemurs. See Dolhinow & Fuentes 1999, pp. 133–39

Graham CE, Nadler RD. 1990. Socioendocrine interactions in Great Ape reproduction. See Ziegler & Bercovitch 1990, pp. 33–58

Harcourt AH, Gardiner J. 1994. Sexual selection and genital anatomy of male primates. *Proc. R. Soc. London Ser. B* 255:47–53

Harcourt AH, Purvis A, Liles L. 1995. Sperm competition: mating system, not breeding season, affects testes size of primates. *Funct. Ecol.* 9:468–76

Hewlett BS. 1992a. Introduction. See Hewlett 1992b, pp. xi–xix

Hewlett BS, ed. 1992b. *Father-Child Relations: Cultural and Biosocial Contexts.* New York: Aldine de Gruyter

Heymann EW. 2000. The number of adult males in callitrichine groups and its implications for callitrichine social evolution. In *Primate Males*, ed. P Kappeler pp. 64–71. Cambridge, MA: Cambridge Univ. Press

Higley JD, Mehlman PT, Higley SB, Fernald B, Vickers J, et al. 1996. Excessive mortality in young free-ranging male nonhuman primates with low cerebrospinal fluid 5-hydroxyindoleactic acid concentrations. *Arch. Gen. Psychol.* 53:537–43

Izard MK. 1990. Social influences on the reproductive success and reproductive endocrinology of prosimian primates. See Ziegler & Bercovitch 1990, pp. 159–86

Jessop TS, Hamann M, Read MA, Limpus CJ. 2000. Evidence for a hormonal tactic maximizing green turtle reproduction in response to a pervasive ecological stressor. *Gen. Comp. Endocrinol.* 118:407–17

Jöchle W. 1975. Current research in coitus-induced ovulation: a review. *J. Reprod. Fert. Suppl.* 22:165–207

Johnson A, Josephson R, Hawke M. 1985. Clinical and histological evidence for the presence of the vomernasal (Jacobson's) organ in adult humans. *J. Otalaryngol.* 14:71–79

Johnson L. 1989. Evaluation of the human testis and its age-related dysfunction. In *Sperm Measures and Reproductive Success*, ed. EJ Burger, RG Tardiff, AR Scialli, H Zenick, pp. 35–67. New York: Liss

Johnson M, Everitt B. 1984. *Essential Reproduction.* Oxford: Blackwell Sci.

Jones RE. 1997. *Human Reproductive Biology.* San Diego: Academic

Kaufmann JH. 1965. A three-year study of mating behavior in a free-ranging band of rhesus monkeys. *Ecology* 46:500–12

Kingsley S. 1982. Causes of non-breeding and the development of the secondary sexual characteristics in the male orangutan: a hormonal study. In *The Orangutan: Its Biology and Conservation*, ed. LEM de Boer, pp. 215–29. The Hague: W Junk

Kleiman DG, Malcolm JR. 1981. The evolution of male parental investment. In *Parental Care in Mammals*, ed. DF Gubernick, PH Klopfer, pp. 347–87. New York: Plenum

Knobil E, Neill JD, eds. 1994. *The Physiology of Reproduction.* Vols. 1, 2. New York: Raven

Lamb ME. 1981. *The Role of Father in Child Development.* New York: Wiley. 2nd ed.

Lamb ME. 1987. *Father's Role: Cross-Cultural Perspective.* New York: Erlbaum

Lieberman M, Doyle AB, Markiewicz D. 1999. Developmental patterns in security of attachment to mother and father in late childhood and early adolescence: associations with peer relations. *Child Dev.* 70:202–13

Lunn SF, Recio R, Morris K, Fraser HM. 1994. Blockade of the neonatal rise in testosterone by a gonadotrophin-releasing hormone antagonist: effects on timing of puberty and sexual behaviour in the male marmoset monkey. *J. Endocrinol.* 141:439–47

Lynch JW, Ziegler TE, Strier KB. 2001. Individual and seasonal variatin in fecal testosterone and cortisol levels of wild male turfted capuchin monkeys, *Cebus apella nigritus. Horm. Behav.* In press

Maggioncalda AN, Czekala NM, Sapolsky RM.

2000. Growth hormone and thyroid stimulating hormone concentrations in captive male orangutans: implications for understanding developmental arrest. *Am. J. Primatol.* 50:67–76

Maggioncalda AN, Sapolsky RM, Czekala NM. 1999. Reproductive hormone profiles in captive male orangutans: implications for understanding developmental arrest. *Am. J. Phys. Anthropol.* 109:19–32

Martensz ND, Yellucci SV, Fuller LM, Everitt BJ, Keverne EB, Herbert J. 1987. Relation between aggressive behaviour and circadian rhythms in cortisol and testosterone in social groups of talapoin monkeys. *J. Endocrinol.* 115:107–20

Martin RD. 1990. *Primate Origins and Evolution.* Princeton: Princeton Univ. Press

McAllen BM. 1998. Effect of testosterone and cortisol administration on the reproductive tract of male *Antechinus stuartii* (Marsupialia). *J. Reprod. Fert.* 112:199–209

Mehlman PT, Higley JD, Faucher I, Lilly AA, Taub DM, et al. 1995. Correlation of CSF 5-HIAA concentrations with sociality and the timing of emigration in free-ranging primates. *Am. J. Psychol.* 152:907–13

Mendoza SP, Mason WA. 1991. Breeding readiness in squirrel monkeys: Female-primed females are triggered by males. *Phys. Behav.* 49:471–79

Milligan SR. 1982. Induced ovulation in mammals. *Oxford Rev. Reprod. Biol.* 4:1–46

Mota MT, Sousa MBC. 2000. Prolactin levels of fathers and helpers related to alloparental care in common marmosets, *Callithrix jacchus. Folia Primatol.* 71:22–26

Nash LT. 1993. Juveniles in nongregarious primates. In *Juvenile Primates*, ed. ME Periera, LA Fairbanks, pp. 119–37. Oxford: Oxford Univ. Press

Norman A, Litwack J. 1997. *Hormones.* New York: Academic

Numan M. 1994. Maternal behavior. See Knobil & Neill 1994, 2:221–302

Packer C. 1979. Inter-troop transfer and inbreeding avoidance in *Papio anubis. Anim. Behav.* 27:1–36

Paul A, Kuester J. 1990. Adaptive significance of sex ratio adjustment in semifree-ranging Barbary macaques (*Macaca sylvanus*) at Salem. *Behav. Ecol. Sociobiol.* 27:287–93

Paul A, Kuester J. 1996. Differential reproduction in male and female Barbary macaques. In *Evolution and Ecology of Macaque Societies*, ed. JE Fa, DG Lindburg, pp. 293–317. Cambridge, MA: Cambridge Univ. Press

Paul A, Kuester J, Timme A, Arnemann J. 1993. The association between rank, mating effort, and reproductive success in male Barbary macaques (*Macaca sylvanus*). *Primates* 34:491–502

Perret M. 1992. Environmental and social determinants of sexual function in the male lesser mouse lemur (*Microcebus murinus*). *Folia Primatol.* 59:1–25

Plant TM. 1999. Puberty in nonhuman primates. In *Encyclopedia of Reproduction*, ed. E Knobil, JD Neill, 4:135–42. San Diego: Academic

Price EC. 1990. Infant carrying as a courtship strategy of breeding male cotton-top tamarins. *Anim. Behav.* 40:784–86

Richard AF. 1987. Malagasy prosimians: female dominance. See Smuts et al. 1987, pp. 25–33

Robbins MM, Czekala NM. 1997. A preliminary investigation of urinary testosterone and cortisol levels in wild male mountain gorillas. *Am. J. Primatol.* 43:51–64

Roberts RL, Jenkins KT, Lawler T Jr, Wegner FH, Newman JD. 2001. Bromocriptine administration lowers serum prolactin and disrupts parental responsiveness in common marmosets (*Callithris jacchus*). *Horm. Behav.* 39:106–12

Rommerts FFG. 1988. How much androgen is required for maintenance of spermatogenesis? *J. Endocrinol.* 116:7–9

Saltzman W, Schultz-Darken NJ, Scheffler G, Wegner FH, Abbott DH. 1994. Social and reproductive influences on plasma cortisol in female marmoset monkeys. *Phys. Behav.* 56:801–10

Saltzman W, Severin JM, Schultz-Darken NJ, Abbott DH. 1997. Behavioral and social correlates of escape from suppression of ovulation in female common marmosets housed with the natal family. *Am. J. Primatol.* 41:1–21

Sapolsky RM. 1994. *Why Zebras Don't Get Ulcers*. New York: Freeman

Savage A, Ziegler TE, Snowdon CT. 1988. Sociosexual development, pair bond formation, and mechanisms of fertility suppression in female cotton-top tamarins (*Saguinus oedipus oedipus*). *Am. J. Primatol.* 14:345–59

Schuett GW, Harlow HJ, Rose JD, van Kirk EA, Murdoch WJ. 1996. Levels of plasma corticosterone and testosterone in male copperheads (*Agkistrodon contortrix*) following staged fights. *Horm. Behav.* 30:60–68

Setchell JM, Dixson AF. 2001. Changes in the secondary sexual adornments of male mandrills (*Mandrillus sphinx*) are associated with gain and loss of alpha status. *Horm. Behav.* 39:177–84

Setchell JM, Dixson AF. 2002. Developmental variables and dominance rank in adolescent male mandrills (*Mandrillus sphinx*). *Am. J. Primatol.* 56:9–25

Sharpe RM. 1994. Regulation of spermatogenesis. See Knobil & Neill 1994, 1:1363–434

Silk JB. 1993. Does participation in coalitions influence dominance relationships among male bonnet macaques? *Behaviour* 126:171–89

Smuts BB. 1985. *Sex and Friendship in Baboons*. New York: Aldine de Gruyter

Smuts BB, Cheney DL, Seyfarth RM, Wrangham RW, Struhsaker TT, eds. 1987. *Primate Societies*. Chicago: Univ. Chicago Press

Smuts BB, Gubernick DJ. 1992. Male-infant relationships in nonhuman primates: paternal investment or mating effort? See Hewlett 1992b, pp. 1–30

Stavisky RC, Adams MR, Watson SL, Kaplan JR. 2001. Dominance, cortisol, and behavior in small groups of female cynomolgus monkeys (*Macaca fascicularis*). *Horm. Behav.* 39:232–38

Storey AE, Walsh CJ, Quinton RL, Wynne-Edwards KE. 2000. Hormonal correlates of paternal responsiveness in new and expectant fathers. *Evol. Hum. Behav.* 21:79–95

Strier KB, Ziegler TE, Wittwer DJ. 1999. Seasonal and social correlates of fecal testosterone and cortisol levels in wild male muriquis (*Brachyteles arachnoides*). *Horm. Behav.* 35:125–34

Strum SC. 1987. *Almost Human*. New York: Random House

Terasawa E, Nass TE, Yeoman RR, Louse MD, Schultz NJ. 1983. Hypothalamic control of puberty in the female rhesus macaque. In *Neuroendocrine Aspects of Reproduction*, ed. RL Norman, pp. 149–82. New York: Academic

Torii R, Moro M, Abbott DH, Nigi H. 1998. Urine collection in the common marmoset, *Callithrix jacchus*, and its applicability to endocrinological studies. *Primates* 39:407–17

Uvnas MK. 1997. Physiological and endocrine effects of social contact. *Ann. NY Acad. Sci.* 807:146–63

Vandenbergh JG. 1994. Pheromones and mammalian reproduction. See Knobil & Neill 1994, 2:343–59

van Schaik CP, Janson CH, eds. 2000. *Infanticide by Males*. Cambridge, MA: Cambridge Univ. Press

van Schaik CP, Paul A. 1997. Male care in primates: Does it ever reflect paternity? *Evol. Anthropol.* 5:152–56

van Schaik CP, van Noordwijk MA, van Bragt T, Blankenstein MA. 1991. A pilot study of the social correlates of urinary cortisol, prolactin, and testosterone in wild long-tailed macaques (*Macaca fascicularis*). *Primates* 32:345–56

van Tienhoven A. 1983. *Reproductive Physiology of Vertebrates*. Ithaca, NY: Cornell Univ. Press. 2nd ed.

Wallner B, Möstl E, Dittami J, Prossinger H. 1999. Fecal glucocorticoids document stress in female Barbary macaques (*Macaca sylvanus*). *Gen. Comp. Endocrinol.* 113:80–86

Weinbauer GF, Nieschlag E. 1991. Peptide and steroid regulation of spermatogenesis in primates. *Ann. NY Acad. Sci.* 637:107–21

Weir BJ, Rowlands IW. 1973. Reproductive strategies of mammals. *Annu. Rev. Ecol. Syst.* 4:139–63

Whitten PL. 1987. Infants and adult males. See Smuts et al. 1987, pp. 343–57

Wickings EJ, Dixson AF. 1992. Testicular function, secondary sexual development, and social status in male mandrills (*Mandrillus sphinx*). *Phys. Behav.* 52:909–16

Widdig A, Streich WJ, Tembrock G. 2000. Coalition formation among male Barbary macaques (*Macaca sylvanus*). *Am. J. Primatol.* 50:37–51

Widowski TM, Porter TA, Ziegler TE, Snowdon CT. 1992. The stimulatory effect of males on the initiation but not the maintenance of ovarian cycling in cotton-top tamarins (*Saguinus oedipus*). *Am. J. Primatol.* 26:97–108

Wright PC. 1990. Patterns of paternal care in primates. *Int. J. Primatol.* 11:89–102

Wysocki CJ. 1979. Neurobehavioral evidence for the involvement of the vomernasal system in mammalian reproduction. *Neurosci. Biobehav. Rev.* 3:301–42

Yeoman RR, Williams LE, Aksal S, Abee CR. 1991. Mating-related estradiol fluctuations during the estrous cycle of the Bolivian squirrel monkey (*Saimiri bolivensis bolivensis*). *Biol. Reprod.* 44:640–47

Zarrow MX, Clark JH. 1968. Ovulation following vaginal stimulation in a spontaneous ovulator and its implications. *J. Endocrinol.* 40:343–52

Zeleznick AJ, Fairchild-Benyo D. 1994. Control of follicular development, corpus luteum function, and the recognition of pregnancy in higher primates. See Knobil & Neill 1994, 2:751–82

Ziegler TE. 2000. Hormones associated with non-maternal infant care: a review of mammalian and avian studies. *Folia Primatol.* 71:6–21

Ziegler TE, Bercovitch FB, eds. 1990. *Socioendocrinology of Primate Reproduction.* New York: Wiley-Liss

Ziegler TE, Carlson AA, Ginther AJ, Snowdon CT. 2000a. Gonadal source of testosterone metabolites in urine of male cotton-top tamarin monkeys (*Saguinus oedipus*). *Gen. Comp. Endocrinol.* 118:332–43

Ziegler TE, Epple G, Snowdon CT, Porter TA, Belcher AM, Kuderling I. 1993. Detection of the chemical signals of ovulation in the cotton-top tamarin, *Saguinus oedipus. Anim. Behav.* 45:313–22

Ziegler TE, Savage A, Scheffler G, Snowdon CT. 1987. The endocrinology of puberty and reproductive functioning in female cotton-top tamarins (*Saguinus oedipus*) under varying social conditions. *Biol. Reprod.* 37:618–27

Ziegler TE, Scheffler G, Snowdon CT. 1995. The relationship of cortisol levels to social envirnoment and reproductive functioning in female cotton-top tamarins, *Saguinus oedipus. Horm. Behav.* 29:407–24

Ziegler TE, Snowdon CT. 2000. Preparental hormone levels and parenting experience in male cotton-top tamarins, *Saguinus oedipus. Horm. Behav.* 38:159–67

Ziegler TE, Snowdon CT, Uno H. 1990. Social interactions and determinants of ovulation in tamarins (*Saguinus*). See Ziegler & Bercovitch 1990, pp. 113–33

Ziegler TE, Wegner FH, Carlson AA, Lazaro-Perea C, Snowdon CT. 2000b. Prolactin levels during the periparturitional period in the biparental cotton-top tamarin (*Saguinus oedipus*): interactions with gender, androgen levels and parenting. *Horm. Behav.* 38:111–12

Ziegler TE, Wegner FH, Snowdon CT. 1996. Hormonal responses to parental and nonparental conditions in male cotton-top tamarins, *Saguinus oedipus*, a New World primate. *Horm. Behav.* 30:287–97

Annu. Rev. Anthropol. 2002. 31:69–97
doi: 10.1146/annurev.anthro.31.020402.101302

First published online as a Review in Advance on June 26, 2002

SIGNS OF THEIR TIMES: Deaf Communities and the Culture of Language

Richard J. Senghas[1] and Leila Monaghan[2]
[1]*Sonoma State University, Department of Anthropology/Linguistics, 1801 East Cotati Avenue, Rohnert Park, California 94928-3609; email: Richard.Senghas@sonoma.edu*
[2]*Temple University, Department of Anthropology, 1115 West Berks Street, Philadelphia, Pennsylvania 19122; email: monaghan@temple.edu*

Key Words sign language, deafness, linguistic communities, Deaf culture

■ **Abstract** Because of their deafness, deaf people have been marked as different and treated problematically by their hearing societies. Until 25 years ago, academic literature addressing deafness typically described deafness as pathology, focusing on cures or mitigation of the perceived handicap. In ethnographic accounts, interactions involving deaf people are sometimes presented as examples of how communities treat atypical members. Recently, studies of deafness have adopted more complex sociocultural perspectives, raising issues of community identity, formation and maintenance, and language ideology.

Anthropological researchers have approached the study of d/Deaf communities from at least three useful angles. The first, focusing on the history of these communities, demonstrates that the current issues have roots in the past, including the central role of education in the creation and maintenance of communities. A second approach centers on emic perspectives, drawing on the voices of community members themselves and accounts of ethnographers. A third perspective studies linguistic issues and how particular linguistic issues involving deaf people articulate with those of their hearing societies.

> *To use a cultural definition is not only to assert a new frame of reference, but to consciously reject an older one. . . . But the cultural definition continues to perplex many. If Deaf people are indeed a cultural group, why then don't they seem more like the Pennan of the island of Borneo, or the Huichol of Mexico?*
>
> Carol Padden (1996a)

INTRODUCTION

Deafness is not merely the absence of hearing. An estimated 6.2 million people currently living are prelingually deaf, and many of these have formed Deaf communities, often with distinct languages and cultural practices.[1] Anthropological studies show us that deafness impinges on many aspects of human activity. Furthermore, studies involving deaf people reveal issues of general anthropological significance, even to those who may not (yet) have particular interest in issues of deafness. For example, social organization, identity, culture, ideology, and sociolinguistic variation are all issues that permeate the studies mentioned in this review. The social implications of deafness are often counterintuitive and merit more than commonsense assessments. Deafness is, at least in part, a social construction. Understanding the complex nature of communities with deaf members requires attending to how people use and think about language. In other words, we need to understand more about the culture of language.

Therefore, this article has two primary goals: first, to review studies about communities of people who are deaf, with an emphasis on sign languages and anthropological contributions; and second, to suggest theoretical and methodological avenues worth further pursuit. Especially over the last 25 years, linguistic and psycholinguistic research has often addressed sign languages and signing systems (cf., Klima & Bellugi 1979, Siple & Fischer 1991; cf., also Morford 1996). Stokoe (1980) and Washabaugh (1981) are among the few anthropological reviews considering deafness and sign language research. Our article here focuses on issues of community identity and related cultural phenomena, especially language, and appropriate theory and methods for analysis of such issues.

Since the time of Stokoe's (1980) and Washabaugh's (1981) review articles, sign languages have become accepted as genuine languages, and the notion of linguistic communities of (deaf) signers is no longer novel. Yet anthropological studies of Deaf communities are still in a relatively early stage, akin to the early phases of Boasian descriptive ethnography of the early twentieth century (cf., Barnard 2000). Anthropologists, sociologists, and scholars from other disciplines such as education have used ethnographic methods to study deaf populations, especially to address pedagogical theory and practice. But studies of Deaf communities as such, especially those outside the United States and Europe, are rare, with few book-length ethnographic monographs available (cf., Higgins 1980, Evans & Falk 1986; cf., also Lane 1984, Baynton 1996, and Plann 1997 for sociohistorical accounts of deafness in France, the United States, and Spain). Nevertheless, a growing body of literature is emerging, much of it addressing sociolinguistic variation, providing fodder for comparison and theorization.

---

[1]Prelingual deafness refers to deafness that occurs prior to the individual's acquisition of a first language and includes deafness at birth through 3 years. The estimate is based on the 1:1000 ratio used by Schein (1992), applied to the current estimate of the world population (6.2 billion) in 2002, as indicated by the U.S. Census Bureau. (See http://www.census.gov/cgi-bin/ipc/popclockw for details.) Prevocational deafness, as used by Schein (1992), refers to deafness prior to the age of 19 years and occurs at roughly twice the rate of prelingual deafness.

A core of sources has become an introductory canon, providing historical background and introductions to various perspectives. Most famous are Lane's (1984) *When the Mind Hears*, Padden & Humphries' *Deaf in America, Voices from a Culture* (1988), and more recently, *A Journey into the DEAF-WORLD* (Lane et al. 1996). Other accounts and anthologies such as Gannon (1981), Sacks (1989), Wilcox (1989), TRAIN GO SORRY (Cohen 1994), Lane (1992), and Fischer & Lane (1993) are also accessible sources aimed at general audiences. ["Children of a Lesser God" (Paramount Pictures 1992) and "Sound and Fury" (Filmakers Library 2000), the latter a documentary about cochlear implants, are among the few deaf-related movies that introduce sociocultural issues of deafness to popular audiences.] *The Deaf Way* (Erting et al. 1994) provides accounts from around the world with an unparalleled range of topics and contributors (see below), though several of the essays are not academic in orientation or form, which make those essays less useful as authoritative references for researchers; the book's size (and cost) sometimes proves intimidating for popular audiences. Groce (1985), Baynton (1996), and Plann (1997) are excellent accounts with extensive references for those pursuing the issues from sociohistorical perspectives.

DEFINITIONS

The growing field of Deaf studies has its own terminology. Definitions for these terms reveal ideological and disciplinary issues that affect Deaf studies and also suggest how such studies fit within larger sociopolitical processes. Occasionally, educators, activists, and researchers draw on each other's works without careful attention to the subtle but significant differences in the denotations made by the original authors—distinctions often indicative of disciplinary perspectives. Efforts at more explicitly defining terms can be seen in a recent lexicon of terms used by linguistic anthropologists (Duranti 2001), including definitions for "deaf" (Padden 2001), "gesture" (Haviland 2001), "orality" (Rumsey 2001), and "signing" (Monaghan 2001). We now discuss these terms in more specific detail.

The D/d and H/h Words

The most well-known terminological quirk associated with Deaf studies is a distinction no one can hear uttered: Deaf/deaf. By 1972, Woodward used this Deaf/deaf distinction to highlight cultural identity as distinct from physiological deafness. Though widely adopted since, some scholars have avoided Deaf because they hold that the notion of Deaf identity is a bounded sociohistorical phenomenon (cf., Plann 1997 and Polich 1998); others merely avoid the orthographic awkwardness of the two terms.

Conceptually, the Deaf/deaf distinction is significant. Separating audiological issues (that is, measurable hearing levels—deaf and hearing) from those of socialization, acculturation, and identity (that is, Deaf as sociological or cultural reference) makes otherwise confusing issues far more understandable. Those who lose their hearing late in life, for example, might be considered deaf but not Deaf. Even where this distinction is directly cited, however, usage can be inconsistent. Some authors directly address the problematic nature of the audiological and sociological distinctions by using the combined term d/Deaf. Wrigley, in his 1996 work on politics and d/Deafness in Thailand, argues that frequently the two phenomena need simultaneous attention. Therefore, adopting the term d/Deaf highlights the multidimensional nature of a complex situation.

For reasons presented, we use deaf and hearing to denote specifically audiological traits, Deaf and Hearing to denote (or emphasize) identity or sociocultural issues, and d/Deaf and h/Hearing to denote and highlight the often inherently mixed nature of the audiological and sociocultural conditions.

Within the United States, heavy emphasis on the use of "Deaf" can correlate with a strong stance on the sociopolitical nature of not being able to hear. For example, despite identifying the Deaf/deaf distinction, Baker's (1999) discussion of Deaf "ethnicity," uses the term "Deaf" to refer to both audiological and cultural situations. Though some of the groundwork for ethnic terms of Deafness was laid out as early as 1965 (Stokoe et al. 1965), by 1980, many sign language researchers had accepted the notion of cultural, if not ethnic, Deaf identity (Baker & Battison 1980, Washabaugh 1981). Johnson & Erting (1989) address ethnicity and socialization of young deaf children. By 1994, the concept of Deaf culture, identity, and ethnicity clearly can be seen to have had global influence: at grassroots community, governmental, and even international organizational levels (Erting et al. 1994). Lane et al. describe their own book as "about the 'new ethnicity'" and go so far as to consider that "a child who has not acquired spoken language and culture because of limited hearing is a culturally Deaf child, even if that child has not yet had the opportunity to learn DEAF-WORLD[2] language and culture" (1996:x, cf. also 160–61). Perhaps their approach is appropriate for introducing the DEAF-WORLD to hearing people, but such usage does collapse attained and ascribed identities and other distinctions sometimes useful to keep separate.

Complementing Deaf/deaf distinctions are analogous Hearing/hearing distinctions; "Hearing" refers to hearing-identified society and culture (and by extension, mainstream society and culture), and "hearing" is used to denote only audiological ability. Many researchers have adopted a Deaf/deaf distinction without any corresponding Hearing/hearing distinction, arguing that the latter is not a self-ascription generally used by hearing people. With these two sets of distinctions, we can now understand an American Sign Language (ASL) expression glossed as either HEARING-THINKING or HEARING-IN-THE-HEAD, a term used (sometimes pejoratively) by signers as a label for deaf individuals attributed as holding primary identification with Hearing society—what might be called passing in other contexts. This sign is sometimes used as a synonym for "oralist," meaning someone

[2]The term DEAF-WORLD (in this all-capitalized form) is a gloss representing a sign in American Sign Language. Linguists use glosses as one-word equivalents (though not as true definitions or translations) for indexing lexical items in a language. The issues of transcription are raised in the section on methodologies, below.

who has been trained to lip-read, or speechread, to use more precise terminology (cf., Berger 1972).

Of course, issues of deafness, whether sociocultural or audiological, are not limited to binary distinctions. Eckert (1989, 2000) has shown with the enduring U.S. cultural concepts of Jocks and Burnouts that even those individuals who resist categorization and identify themselves as "In-betweens" are doing so using terms consistent with a pervasive hegemonic ideology. Similar phenomena are likely occurring with social categorizations involving deafness, often as part of larger sociohistorical processes (cf., Baynton 1996, Plann 1997). Thus, two more problematic categories have already been identified: Hard-of-hearing (Grushkin 1996, 2003) and offspring of deaf parents (Preston 1994). Both these authors raise issues of these respective categories as not merely steps in-between along a bipolar spectrum, but rather, that each category can be its own center—to echo the call by Padden for recognition of Deaf views on their own terms (1980).

The additional question of multiple, at times conflicting, Deaf, ethnic, or cultural identities is not new and has been addressed in Deaf studies for some time now. For example, Woodward, Erting, and Markowicz examined Black signing in Atlanta, comparing patterns across Northern and Southern Black and White signers in the mid 1970s (Woodward 1976). LeMaster & Monaghan (2002) have identified the first 20 years of sign language studies as focused on whether sign languages were "real" and autonomous languages (cf., also Washabaugh 1981), with studies on variation dominated by issues of language contact and mixing along an ASL/English continuum, though with some scholars attending to other signed and spoken language in other countries (e.g., DeSantis 1977; Woodward & DeSantis 1977a,b; Deucher 1984; Boyes Braem 1985; Kyle & Woll 1985; Schermer 1985; LeMaster 1990). Pre-1980s sign language work was predominantly conducted by linguists (with a noted exception of Carol Erting); however, as anthropologists, including linguistic anthropologists, began to work on sign language issues in the 1980s, there began a shift toward studies of variation along the lines of Deaf identities—the 1990s were a watershed period for such scholarship. Variation within the United States is addressed in the works of LeMaster (1977, 1983, 1990), Carmel (1987), Erting (1981, 1985), Hall (1989), and Johnson & Erting (1989). Lucas's (1989) edited volume became a common reference, and other books began to disseminate the cultural aspects of Deaf identity to lay audiences, among the most famous sources being *Deaf in America: Voices from a Culture* (Padden & Humphries 1988).

Signing and Sign Language

As we have just seen, sign languages play a significant role in the sociocultural studies of d/Deaf people. Just as Boas (1911) and Malinowski (1984 [1922]) recognized that ethnographers need at least some command of the languages used by the peoples they study, researchers of d/Deaf communities have understood the role of language, and especially signing and sign languages, as a central concern. Whether language is studied to reveal taxonomies used by groups to categorize and communicate about phenomena in their environments or examined for its role as symbolically marking identity, alignment, or distance and difference (cf., Barth 1969, Markowicz & Woodward 1982 [1978]), the "languaculture" (Agar 1994) of many d/Deaf groups uses signing as a key element, and so signing and sign language have merited much focused attention.

For those unfamiliar with sign languages, a few preliminary points must be mentioned before going further. Linguists have developed clear distinctions between natural sign languages (i.e., sign languages not consciously invented), artificial sign languages, gesture, and homesign. Because issues addressing linguistic communities and ideologies involving sign languages are raised below, it is important to clarify these distinctions.

Natural sign languages are now generally accepted by linguists as complex, grammatical systems with all the core ingredients common to other human languages (e.g., Klima & Bellugi 1979, Foley 1997, p. 61). The fundamental distinction between sign and spoken language is that the sets of articulators are different; for spoken languages the articulators are those required to produce sound (the vocal tract), while for sign languages the hands and body (including face) are used to encode both lexical forms and grammatical relationships.[3] The use of these visible (rather than audible) articulators allows signers to use three-dimensional space in complex linguistic ways and gives sign languages a unique quality not shared with spoken languages. (Also, a tactile form of natural signing is sometimes used by deaf individuals without sight.) With spoken languages, distinct regions and groups often have their own distinct languages. Similarly, numerous distinct sign languages exist around the world. (This fact directly contradicts a persistent lay notion that there is a universal sign language used by most deaf people.) And like spoken languages, these languages do not neatly correspond to national or geographic boundaries, although their distribution and patterns of change are certainly affected by these factors.

Artificial signed languages have been developed in many countries, often as pedagogical tools for teaching spoken languages to deaf individuals, though sometimes intended as a primary means of signed communication in and of themselves. These are manually coded versions of their corresponding spoken languages, though they sometimes borrow from the lexicon of natural sign languages while employing morphosyntactic features to model the spoken language (for example, articles and the verb 'is' will be encoded in Signing Exact English (Gustason et al. 1980), while ASL has no corresponding elements).

Fingerspelling is a language contact phenomenon and reflects the social reality that dominant (written) languages need to be dealt with by signers. Fingerspelling systems are basically written alphabets represented in a signed modality and may

[3]The facial and other gestures are considered linguistic, not just communicative. For example, in ASL, facial gestures mark questions, indicate topic phrases, and even convey aspects of verbs, and specific movements of the body, hands, and arms can indicate subject, verb, and object agreement. However, Farnell (1995, 1999) does challenge where we draw the boundary between linguistic and nonlinguistic action.

employ one-handed (such as the one used with ASL) or two-handed forms [such as that used with British Sign Language (BSL)]. Because alphabets vary cross-linguistically, fingerspelling systems accommodating them vary also. The manner of representing particular letters may vary (e.g., one-handed vs. two-handed systems), but so might the set of letters represented. For instance, the written Spanish alphabet includes *ñ*, while English does not; Cyrillic alphabets differ from Roman alphabets. Thus, ASL uses a fingerspelling system that maps to English, and Nicaraguan Sign Language (ISN) uses a slightly different fingerspelling system to accommodate *ll*, *ñ*, *rr*. Other cultural factors creep in, as well, including local (nonlinguistic) gestures used by the local (hearing) society. The letter *t* as represented in ASL (a closed fist with the thumb protruding from between the index and middle finger) is a very rude gesture in countries such as Nicaragua, where the corresponding letter is made similarly, but with the index finger extended.

Sign language researchers generally regard nonlinguistic gesture (such as that used by the hearing population) as analytically distinct from sign language. *Gesture* is often communicative and may even be considered systematic, but regular linguistic traits such as grammatical agreement are not generally recognized as characteristics of gesture. McNeill (1992) and Kendon (1997) are major figures in the studies of gesture; Kendon is especially recognized for his anthropologically informed, crosscultural comparisons of gesture. Volterra & Erting (1994) have edited a significant collection of essays analyzing and comparing the gesture of hearing and deaf children, and Messing & Campbell (1999) provide a useful collection of recent work in the field. Farnell, however, reminds us that the boundary between what is generally recognized as language and gesture needs clearer theorizing, as her work with Plains Indian Sign Talk demonstrates nicely (1995).

Two other forms of signing warrant mention at this point, the first being *homesign* systems. These are ad hoc systems developed to meet an individual's or a small group's needs for communicating. Because 90% of deaf children are born into hearing families (Lane et al. 1996, p. 30), it is likely that these families will use signs that they themselves invent for their immediate needs. Morford has produced a useful review of homesign research (1996). Because homesign systems are reinvented with each case, they tend to be eclectic, idiosyncratic, and linguistically limited, and they are typically eclipsed by other more elaborate systems once children are identified as deaf and receive intervention, whether medical or through special education. Some homesign research focuses on the effects of delayed exposure to a complete language on child language acquisition, whereas other research addresses questions of innate vs. learned linguistic traits.

Contact signing is the final form of signing we mention here. As discussed above, early linguistic work on sign language focused considerable attention to determine whether or not signing (ASL in particular) was its own "real" language, and researchers discovered that signers vary their signing depending on whether or not hearing people are present. Though paradigms of pidginization or creolization were originally invoked for describing or explaining variation in signing owing to the presence or absence of hearing individuals (cf., Hymes 1971; but see also Holm 2000 for a current general introduction to pidgin and creole studies), some scholars find such characterization as not quite appropriate (cf., Washabaugh 1981, and so what had once been referred to as Pidgin Signed English (PSE) is now generally considered contact language (Lucas & Valli 1989, Lucas et al. 2001).

DEAF AND SIGNING COMMUNITIES

Though there has been a range of studies on signing, sign languages, and communicative issues affecting deaf pedagogy, until recently there have been relatively few extended studies of particular communities of d/Deaf people. The definition of community itself is problematic, as indicated by Padden (1980). The term has been used in varied ways in such accounts as Gannon (1981), Van Cleve & Crouch (1989), Wilcox (1989), Padden & Humphries (1988), Higgins (1980), Lane (1984), Evans & Falk (1986), Hall (1989, 1991), and in the range of pieces in *Deaf Way* (Erting et al. 1994). Constant attention must be given as to whether the term denotes any one or a combination of group, linguistic (speech) community (cf., Hymes 1971), social network (cf., Bott 1971), imagined community (cf., Anderson 1991), ethnic group (Barth 1969, Markowicz & Woodward 1982 [1978], Edwards 1985), or even simply a population of deaf individuals (with little indication of any actual social relationships among them) in a given geographic area.

Much of the ethnographic work addressing deafness and d/Deaf communities has been done within the United States. Foster (1987, 1988, 1989, 1996) provides a series of contributions that are representative of both the manner and content of U.S. research. Higgins (1980) and Evans & Falk (1986) are both extended accounts addressing the socialization of deaf individuals with respect to each other, on the one hand, and hearing society, on the other. Schein's (1992) sociological account theorizes about when, where, and why deaf communities may form (or not). An oft-cited sociocultural-historical reconstruction is Groce's (1985) study of Martha's Vineyard. As her title, *Everyone Here Spoke Sign*, suggests, Groce examines the pervasive use of signing by both hearing and deaf Vineyarders alike. (This may best be seen as a study of a community with deaf members, rather than a Deaf community or community of deaf individuals.)

Despite early anthropological references to deaf people using language patterns distinct from their hearing counterparts (Tylor 1878), focused and extended attention on d/Deaf individuals or communities outside the United States still remains limited (Preston 1994, p. 14). Earlier forerunners include Washabaugh's (1986) work on Providence Island, Johnson (1991) in the Yucatan, and LeMaster (1990) in Ireland. Since that time, the amount of research done on d/Deaf communities has increased considerably, much of it for doctoral dissertations[4] and so has not yet reached general circulation (e.g., Monaghan 1996, Reilly 1995, R. J. Senghas

---

[4]Both authors of this article recall their own difficulties convincing some of their respective faculty advisors of the anthropological significance of studying d/Deaf people as members of d/Deaf (linguistic) communities. We are happy to notice that this seems to be a passing problem.

1997, Polich 1998, Nakamura 2001, Fjord 2001). Over the last decade there have regularly been sessions with d/Deafness, d/Deaf communities, or sign languages as prominent themes at the annual meetings of the American Anthropological Association. Woodward has examined situations in Thailand and Viet Nam (2003); Devlieger has worked in Kenya (1994).

Two remarkable sources bear particular attention. First, the *Gallaudet Encyclopedia of Deaf People and Deafness* (Van Cleve 1987) provides short articles by recognized authorities on topics ranging from medical discussions of deafness to short historical accounts of many Deaf communities. Second, a number of short pieces on communities around the world are available in the 900-page volume *The Deaf Way* (Erting et al. 1994). This volume is a collection of papers originally presented at the first Deaf Way conference in 1989 and contains over 150 short works by authors from around the globe including many Deaf individuals, some organizers and activists, and quite a few scholars. The discussions and rhetoric in these and other works clearly show that research in Deaf studies has had considerable influence in the DEAF-WORLD (cf., Lane et al. 1996 for a discussion of this term), intended and otherwise, which demonstrates both the general relevance of academic studies of d/Deafness and the difficulties of bringing academic subtleties to widespread audiences.

THEORETICAL ISSUES

We mentioned above that the current state of research on d/Deaf communities might arguably be considered an early, descriptive phase akin to that of Boasian American ethnography of the early twentieth century. Nevertheless, the research on d/Deaf and signing communities provides data suitable for anthropological analyses according to several varied theoretical approaches and provides useful cases for anthropological comparison with cases that do not involve deafness or signing. The most promising theoretical issues can be categorized into general areas: agency and models of deafness, child socialization, imagined communities and social networks, linguistic (speech) communities, language and linguistic ideologies, World Systems, and global cultural flow. Let us take these in turn.

Agency and Models of Deafness

One theoretical paradigm that has received considerable attention juxtaposes the cultural model of Deafness with the entrenched medical, infirmity, clinical, or pathological model (Johnson et al. 1989; Woodward 1982; Lane 1989, 1990, 1992). Much of our discussion of the d/Deaf identities above reflects aspects of this central theme. Cokely & Baker (1980a, p. 16) provide an early discussion and review of the distinctions between these two different types of models. Perhaps it is unfortunate that these two contrasting models have been denoted as medical vs. cultural because clearly the medical model is one particular cultural model.

(Polich 1998 offers a third model, the eternal dependent, which she argues more accurately reflects other situations such as that of Nicaragua, and we expect that yet more models of deafness remain to be identified.)

The *medical model of deafness* is one based on deficit theory and holds that deafness is the pathological absence of hearing and that such a hearing-impaired individual is therefore disabled because of faulty hearing. This perspective is sometimes called the medical model because medical procedures (such as cochlear implants) are characteristic of responses made by (hearing) parents of deaf children and often involve extensive intervention by medical professionals. Higgins (1980), drawing on Goffman's notions of spoiled identity and stigma (Goffman 1963, also cf., 1959), discusses the predicament of deaf individuals in Chicago and how they negotiate their lives in light of the larger society's conception of them as disabled. Differing notions of deafness, treatment, and deaf pedagogy reveal enduring issues that directly affect daily lives of deaf children and their families, especially issues of child language socialization.

In contrast to the medical model, a *cultural* or *sociocultural model of d/Deafness* has emerged and has been widely adopted in one form or another (Markowicz & Woodward 1975; LeMaster 1983, 1984; Padden 1980, 1996; Padden & Humphries 1988; Lane 1990, 1992; Parasnis 1996). In this view, deafness is identified as one range within the larger spectrum of human variations, and this view assumes that deafness allows for an alternate constellation of very human adaptations, among the most central being sign languages. When individuals or groups accept sign languages, other language-associated practices are also recognized, including traditional story-telling, patterns of greetings, introductions, and word-play; deaf people are thus seen as part of larger social entities such as communities.

At least implicit in these models, though at times rising to explicit levels, are issues of agency ["the socioculturally mediated capacity to act," (Ahearn 2001, p. 112), particularly acting to change lived-in social structure] and social structure. If we see societies as processes that exist and endure while changing over time, then we must identify the components of such processes. "The components or units of social structure are persons, and a person is a human being considered not as an organism but as occupying position in a social structure" (Radcliffe-Brown 1952, pp. 9–10). But the person is not entirely dissociated from the organic, and notions of body, practice, and movement need attention (Farnell 1995, 1999), especially if we recognize those bodies as operating within cultural environments. A number of different theoretical models are useful in exploring these relationships. R. J. Senghas draws on Bourdieu (1977), Giddens (1979), Harris (1989), and Lave (1988) in his analysis of changing notions of Nicaraguan Deaf personhood (1997). Polich (1998) draws on Giddens (e.g., 1979, 1984) even more directly and extensively as she uses his Structuration Theory to understand the structural causes of d/Deaf community formation in Nicaragua during the late twentieth century. Nakamura (2001) addresses social agency and structure in the politics of Deaf identity in Japan, including issues of disability and culture (cf., Ingstad & Whyte 1995).

Imagined Communities and Social Networks

Since Anderson's (1991) discussion of nationalism, the notion of an imagined community has been a useful theoretical framing device, providing some linkage between the abstractions of idealized (potential) relationships and day-to-day actions of localized groups and individuals, especially with respect to national identities. Both Appadurai (1991) and Hannerz (1992), among many others, have discussed the need for contemporary anthropologists to account for the problematic nature of communities in light of the modern (or postmodern) life, including the global migration and transmission of people and cultural forms despite the boundaries marking nation-states.

The imagination can physically locate communities, and it is useful to consider how notions of socially marked places have proved compelling to d/Deaf people in the past. Van Cleve & Crouch, in their tellingly titled *A Place of Their Own* (1989), have shown that finding or establishing places have been explicit goals for many deaf individuals, though at times such efforts have been met with rebuttals from both d/Deaf and hearing opponents alike. For example, in the 1850s, John Flournoy called for a deaf commonwealth to be established in the American territories (Lane 1984, pp. 310–11, Van Cleve & Crouch 1989, pp. 60–70). Deaf clubs are common, both in the United States and elsewhere, and accounts highlight the importance of clubs both as Deaf places and points of transmission of Deaf culture. Carmel presents a Deaf club in a city in the U.S. Midwest (1987), Hall examines folklore in a Philadelphia club (1991, 1994), Andersson discusses a club in Stockholm, Sweden (1994), and Monaghan (1996) writes on the history of clubs in New Zealand. Sometimes individuals who identify with such places emphasize that they are Deaf places, not hearing ones. R.J. Senghas (1997, pp. 6–10) recounts a situation in a Deaf center in Managua, Nicaragua, where a d/Deaf individual was concerned that such a symbolic boundary was being violated through inappropriate language use.

For purposes of analysis, we might identify groups who maintain separate places (or patterns of social interaction separate from larger society) as *isolating communities*, marking themselves as distinct from others based on some unifying trait or ideal (cf., Barth 1969). Where these communities actively work to establish or maintain social or physical isolation, we could consider them separatist. These communities might be seen as either havens or virtual penal colonies, depending on the observer's position and perspective. *Assimilating communities* (a concept Bahan & Poole-Nash 1995 attribute to T. Supalla) might be seen as a complementary category, wherein deaf individuals are assimilated into a larger (hearing) community (cf., Lane et al. 1996, p. 206).[5] Assimilating communities might be seen as either *suppressing* or *accommodating* (audiological) difference. Of course,

---

[5]We have often heard Martha's Vineyard referred to in romanticized utopian terms, a once-upon-a-time-and-place where deaf people were considered fully human by their enlightened hearing counterparts. Sacks (1989) also discusses visiting Martha's Vineyard.

what might be considered suppressive would be open for debate, again, depending on one's position and perspective. The cultural model of Deafness (above) has been used to justify both separatist efforts and demands that hearing society be more accommodating (cf., Ingstad & Whyte 1995 for discussion of culture and disability).

These theoretical issues of assimilation and accommodation inevitably lead us to studies of race and ethnicity, including the "burgeoning field of whiteness studies" (Trechtor & Bucholtz 2001, p. 3). Hill's (2001) discussion of the "culture of racism," Harrison's (1995, 1998) discussions of the social construction of race, and Brodkin's (1998) and Hartigan's (1999) research have all demonstrated the centrality of these issues to anthropology, and much of this theoretical work applies to Deaf studies just as well. It is no coincidence that Alexander Graham Bell worried about the possibility of a "deaf race" (1969 [1884]). Furthermore, the notion of "disabling" societies (Ingstad & Whyte 1995) can be seen as one particular incarnation of the same underlying paradigms, and the call for a culturally pluralistic model of Deafness makes sense only in the racial and ethnic context analyzed in these whiteness studies. Baynton's (1996) historical account of a century-long campaign against sign language in the United States highlights the central role of nationalism, with a racial component pervading that nationalism.

Some Deaf people have proposed the terms DEAF-WORLD (Lane et al. 1996) and DEAF-WAY (Erting et al. 1994) as abstractions for imagining a social identity and cultural milieu that d/Deaf people can share, so long as a pluralistic cultural environment is established. The geographic metaphor of DEAF-WORLD is particularly salient. The DEAF-WORLD is seen as transcending national borders and invokes the experiences of d/Deaf individuals and groups as unifying events, while simultaneously celebrating the diversity of d/Deaf people in an antiessentialist manner. The DEAF-WORLD includes sympathetic hearing people such as family members who accept d/Deaf people on their own terms.

Efforts toward uniting or networking deaf people have had a long history. The first formal gathering, a Parisian banquet, was held in 1834 (Mottez 1993); the first international gathering (also in Paris) was held in 1889 (Lane 1984, p. 404). These activities were just a few of those that led to the formation of clubs and associations, including the National Association of the Deaf in the United States and the World Federation of the Deaf. These membership organizations, though, have recently been experiencing a decline, possibly owing to class-related issues (Padden 1996a). The networked nature of Deaf clubs and other social organizations in the United States (and elsewhere) has provided opportunities for deaf individuals to build and use social relationships. Some components of these social networks are comparable to the urban brotherhoods in African cities discussed by Fortes (1963), especially as d/Deaf individuals balance issues of work opportunities, housing, and social obligations. These networks are often reminiscent of those revealed by the sociolinguistic work of Labov (1972) and others (e.g., Eckert 1989, 2000).

W. Tarzia (personal communication) suggests that the notion of imagined communities resonates with Dundes' concept of folk groups as they are used in folklore studies (cf., Bauman 1972; Dundes 1972, 1980). In this view, when some number of people share a belief or way of life and communicate about it, a folk group is formed, and folklore is the group's shared property and consists of beliefs, sayings, jokes, anecdotes, stories, songs, rituals, and material artifacts (in effect, a very Tylorian definition of culture as used in anthropology). Indeed, Hall identifies her research as a study of the folklore among Deaf people (1989, 1991, 1994). T. Supalla has also begun a Deaf Folklife Film Collection Project (1991).

The social networks working within and between these imagined (but also very real) communities are key to understanding these communities, and the significance of communicative patterns along such networks brings us to the studies of speech communities.

Linguistic (Speech) Communities and Sociolinguistic Variation

Simply put, *linguistic communities* are people who can and do communicate with each other using language. Because communication, and especially sign language, has been a central issue in Deaf studies, it is not surprising that the notion of linguistic communities has been applied to much of the research on d/Deaf communities.

As part of his ethnography-of-speaking approach to the study of discourse, Hymes (1974) developed the notion of communicative competence to address the real-life, pragmatic contexts of human communication, in direct contrast to Chomsky's notions of the "ideal-speaker-listener, in a completely homogenous speech-community" (1965, p. 3). The approaches of Hymes and other sociolinguistic researchers recognize the heterogeneity of actual speech communities and treat linguistic variation as not (always) merely "error" or troublesome noise, but as possible indices of social context relevant to the communicative action. Thus, notions of register, dialects, and sociolects become interesting and useful, and integral even in the study of syntax and morphology.

Anthropologists and sociolinguists analyze patterns of linguistic behavior, frequently identifying correlations between patterns of linguistic variation and other social phenomena such as social networks, some of these being class-based (Labov 1972, Eckert 2000), some based on other social categories such as race and ethnicity (Trechter & Bucholtz 2001), gender, or age. Likewise, sign language and Deaf studies scholars also have addressed these issues. Patterns of linguistic variation along racial/ethnic lines have been documented by Woodward, Erting, and Markowicz (Woodward 1976), gender has been central to LeMaster's Irish studies (1990, 1997, 2002), and age has been a factor in the work of A. Senghas on Nicaragua (1995, A. Senghas & Coppola 2001) and R.J. Senghas (1997, 2002). Lucas et al. (2001) have shown the importance of regional and other kinds of variation in the United States. Zimmer (1989) and Monaghan (1991) have both studied U.S. register variation. There is also a significant literature on contact languages including that by Lucas & Valli (1989, 1989). See LeMaster & Monaghan (2002) for a short review of works on the sociolinguistic variation in sign languages.

Language Acquisition and Socialization

In order for any communities, including linguistic communities, to survive, they must have ways of perpetuating themselves and adapting to changing circumstances. Thus, children are systematically socialized to acquire the language/s of their communities. There is a long-standing anthropological interest in the socialization of children, from Mead (1928), to Heath (1996), to the more recent work of Ochs (1988) and Schieffelin (1990). Socialization to the pragmatic aspects of language is highlighted in anthropological studies, though other aspects are often studied as well, including acquisition of grammar and semantic categories.

The cognitive and linguistic development of deaf children also raises issues of bilingual language acquisition. Grosjean (1996), Hamers (1996), and Padden (1996b) discuss the bilingual-bicultural paradigm, in which deaf children are considered members of a linguistic minority as they acquire language. Multilingualism and bilingualism are also addressed by Woll et al. (2001). For multilingual children (deaf or hearing), not only must they learn each language, but they must also learn when to use these particular languages and how to switch among them effectively. And frequently, native speakers of minority languages (including sign languages) must deal with the stigma sometimes associated with those languages.

Issues of child language acquisition are central in recent studies of a new sign language emerging in Nicaragua (R. J. Senghas & Kegl 1994; R. J. Senghas et al. 1994; A. Senghas 1995; Kegl & McWhorter 1997; R. J. Senghas 1997, 2003; A. Senghas & Coppola 2001; Pyers 2001). This case is of particular interest to psycholinguists because it is seen as a natural experiment that provides circumstances where, it is hoped, innate linguistic capacities might be more easily identifiable. Psycholinguists are specifically testing Bickerton's (1984) Language Bioprogram Hypothesis (LBH), which posits that innate language acquisition capacities held by children would predict that creolization of a new language would happen quickly and would be driven by the children's contributions more than those of the adults (cf., A. Senghas 1995; Kegl & McWhorter 1997; A. Senghas & Coppola 2001). Most of the psycholinguistic research on Nicaraguan signers is based upon experimentally controlled elicitations, and these have been good at identifying language variation based on age and time of entry into the signing community (see especially A. Senghas 1995; A. Senghas & Coppola 2001). However, extended ethnographic observations of child language socialization have yet to be started and would need to be conducted before we could exclude sociocultural processes as sources for grammatical structures emerging in this new sign language. R. J. Senghas (1997, 2003) has begun ethnographic observations, but these have not yet provided enough data to suggest how much of these structures might be innate or cultural in origin.

Language Ideologies and Linguistic Ideologies

Ideas about language affect many social processes (especially education and child socialization), and systems of related ideas are often reinforced by the syntax and semantics a community uses. Thus, there are ideologies of language and ideologies through language. These issues have already received extensive attention within linguistic anthropology (e.g., Schieffelin et al. 1998, Kroskrity 2000; see Woolard & Schieffelin 1994 and Ahearn 2001 for reviews); therefore, only issues directly raised by studies of sign languages or d/Deaf communities are mentioned here.

The most central ideological issue addressed by sign language and Deaf studies scholars is that of *oralism*. In most discussions of language, *oral* is used to denote spoken (usually face-to-face) interaction, in contrast to *written*. However, in deaf pedagogy, Deaf studies, and sign language research, the term oral is used in contradistinction with *signed* or *manual* (this last term incorrectly implies that sign language is only on the hands). Oralism, then, is an ideology that privileges spoken (and written) languages over signed ones, often denying the validity or linguistic nature of signing altogether. Researchers have been explicitly aware of this ideology as early as Stokoe's (1960) work, but the ideological issues themselves go back centuries. Plann (1997) documents an emphasis on speech that goes back to sixteenth-century Spain, including accounts of deaf individuals being allowed to inherit estates or be ordained as priests only after demonstrating that they could speak, read, and write. There has been considerable tension between oralists and manualists, especially over the last 150 years, and much of this conflict has been waged within the circles of deaf pedagogy. The accounts of Lane (1984), Baynton (1996), Plann (1997), and Monaghan (2003) all discuss this conflict; Baynton's account connects the oralist ideologies to other sociohistorical phenomena in U.S. history, including gender, nationalism, and evolutionism. Monaghan provides an international historical overview.

One current and heated version of oralist ideology involves cochlear implants as a medical/technological solution for deaf children. This conflict pits well-intended—and frequently well-informed–Deaf community members against equally well-intended medical practitioners and parents who wish to implant an electronic device in deaf children to allow them the possibility to hear (cf., Fjord 1999–2000, 2001).[6] Yet hearing parents, wishing their deaf children to be socialized as members of their own families' sociocultural groups (with all their familiar traditions and language), often do not recognize grounds for any conflict, sometimes even considering Deaf activists against cochlear implants as inappropriately intruding upon family rights and obligations.

The contest between the ideologies of oralism and signing has received explicit attention in sign language studies for 40 years now. Discussions on the interactions between the sign language and literacy-oriented versions of the term, however, are much more recent. Monaghan (1996) and Branson et al. (1996) both look at how oral (in Ong's usage) can be used to discuss signed performances, whereas Farnell (1995, 1999) points out how literacy-influenced models of language often blind

---

[6]Unfortunately, the training of medical professionals, including those who specialize in deafness, often provides relatively cursory training in sociocultural theory and even less in epistemology.

researchers to the permeable boundaries between language and gesture. Rumsey (2001) addresses these issues in his explication of the term "orality," but [as Polich (2000), points out] most of the recent work on language ideologies (e.g., Woolard & Schieffelin 1994, Schieffelin et al. 1998, and Kroskrity 2000) does not address this dimension.

Other more specific ideologies have also been identified, including particular languages being used as symbols for their communities, such as ASL for the U.S. Deaf community (Padden 1980, Padden & Humphries 1988, Lane et al. 1996), or *Idioma de Señas de Nicaragua* (Nicaraguan Sign Language or ISN) in Nicaragua (R.J. Senghas 1997). Nakamura addresses the contest over signing as a mark of Deaf identity in Japan (2001, 2002), while Monaghan (1996) looks at how the close-knit Deaf clubs of New Zealand changed from supporting oralism to actively promoting New Zealand Sign Language. There is also much sociolinguistic and historical work needed to document variation in many locations to determine whether one or more sign languages are used in specific places. Van Cleve (1987) and Erting et al. (1994) provide numerous accounts of the existence of local sign languages, and they are often named after the countries (nation-states) in which they have arisen. The papers in *Many Ways to be Deaf* (Monaghan et al. 2003) review these issues in countries ranging from Switzerland to South Africa, including Woodward's carefully documented discussion of seven sign languages in Thailand and Viet Nam.

In another *Many Ways* article, Schmaling (2003) shows how linguistic colonialism has affected Deaf pedagogy in Northern Nigeria. Her title, "A is for Apple," makes reference to an imported ASL sign that is relatively meaningless to locals (because apples are not generally available to this community). Both R.J. Senghas (1997) and Polich (1998) observed similar issues in Nicaragua concerning the selection of signs for the ISN dictionary (ANSNIC 1997).

Bilingualism and biculturalism are ideological issues that affect d/Deaf communities. These topics have been addressed by Johnston et al. (1989), Davis (1989), Grosjean (1992), and Lucas & Valli (1992), among others. Parasnis (1996) has edited a useful collection that addresses several aspects of sign language bilingualism (especially in the United States). Chapters include Hakuta & Mostafapour's (1996), Meath-Lang's (1996), and Stone's (1996) work on education; Hamers' (1996) and Padden's (1996b) on the relationship of cognitive and language development to identity; Padden's (1996a) and Emerton's (1996) work on community and biculturalism; and Bateman's (1996) work on politics.

So far, we have focused on ideologies of or about languages. Linguistic ideology may be considered as ideology through language because grammatical structures and terms (i.e., lexicon and categories of concepts) may possibly influence actors' predispositions toward certain patterns of social thought and action (e.g., Whorf 1995 [1941], Lucy 1995 [1985], and Silverstein 2000; see also Hill & Mannheim 1992 for a review). Linguistic communities of signers may prove to be interesting groups to study because the visual/spatial modality of their language presents structural possibilities unseen in spoken languages. If different linguistic patterns are likely to induce or perpetuate different (perceptions of) realities, then sign/spoken language contrasts should be demonstrably linked to differing structures in conceptions of reality (cf., for studies of gesture, Volterra & Erting 1994; Messing & Campbell 1999).

World Systems and Global Cultural Flow

Anthropologists have recognized the global nature of culture and social relations, especially with regard to nationalism or socioeconomics [Wolf 1982, Appadurai 1991; cf., Foster's review (1991)]. Deaf communities have been particularly affected by these relationships, especially given the international transmission of deaf pedagogies (Lane 1984, Plann 1997, Monaghan 2003, Monaghan et al. 2003), which are so often linked to government policies on education. The 1880 Congress of Milan is the most well-known historical example. This meeting marked the inception of a worldwide campaign promoting oralist pedagogies and the active suppression of sign languages. At this conference of educators and pedagogues of deaf special education, deaf participants were procedurally excluded from participating in a vote which ultimately supported a policy proposal that promoted oralism and discouraged the use of sign language in deaf education. The same year, however, was also when the first national conference of deaf people in the United States was held in Cincinnati, Ohio. Delegates to this meeting roundly denounced the Milan proceedings, showing that both the suppression of and support for signing were international (Lane 1984, pp. 386ff, 394–95).

A number of recent ethnographic works highlight the complex relationships between larger sociocultural, political, and economic trends and local sociocultural phenomena. Bagga-Gupta & Domfors (2003) discuss how Sweden's reforms in the deaf education system were directly influenced by American sign language researchers, including Stokoe. R. J. Senghas (1997, 2003), in turn, shows how the Swedish National Association of the Deaf affected the Nicaraguan d/Deaf community during the early stages of its formation. Pursglove & Komarova's (2003) work on Russia and Aarons & Reynolds' (2003) on South Africa show how larger national reforms such as *Perestroika* and the end of apartheid affect local d/Deaf communities.

Hannerz's (1992) notion of global cultural flow is useful for analyzing such situations, as it separates the observable cultural forms involved from the meanings ascribed to them by recipients and observers of these forms. Hannerz's approach is also compatible with the identity and language ideology issues mentioned above, especially given the center-periphery nature of Deaf institutions such as Gallaudet University in Washington, DC, the World Federation of the Deaf, and the many national Deaf associations in numerous countries that are often based in capital or central cities. However, changes in communications technologies, especially the introduction of real-time, point-to-point video communications, may bring radical changes in the patterns and forms of the global cultural flow. Keating (2000) and Keating & Mirus (2000) have been looking at how signers modify their signing to accommodate video interaction through computers, a technology as significant for deaf signers as the telephone has been for hearing people. The implications of these developments bear further inquiry.

METHODOLOGICAL ISSUES

Methodological issues are certainly intertwined with theoretical ones, but a few particular central issues have arisen in the studies of d/Deaf communities and sign languages; these issues bear attention here. Transcription systems are proving problematic, with no single transcription system taking a dominant position yet. Other methodological issues are not limited to deaf studies or sign language research but reflect unresolved problems general to anthropology and ethnography, such as informed consent and the need for more ethnographic researchers working in teams.

Transcription Systems

For ethnographers, especially those wishing to document language use and variation, transcription of language is important for both data collection and subsequent analysis. Fine phonological analysis, for example, allowed Labov (1972) to find patterns in the distribution of vowel sounds among (hearing) fishermen on Martha's Vineyard or sales clerks in New York department stores (Labov 1972).

Similar fine-grained phonological[7] patternings can be found in sign languages, and documenting them can help us understand the significance of language variation among signers. For example, Nicaraguan signers use some signs nearly identical to ASL forms (e.g., ASSOCIATION and TREE), some that suggest a relation to ASL forms (e.g., CLEAN), while other signs are clearly unrelated (ANSNIC 1997). Analyzing distribution of use allows us to see which signers are most clearly allied with Nicaragua's national organization (cf., R.J. Senghas 1997, pp. 453–55). Because educational systems (including special education programs for deaf students) are often government-controlled, and frequently implicated in ideological processes, Baynton's (1996) and Plann's (1997) accounts would suggest that phonological analysis of sign language would also be useful in studying possible colonizing patterns of language use.

No community of signers has adopted any conventional transcription system for general use, at least, not one in any way analogous to the widespread literacy that has been adopted for spoken languages. Instead, signers often learn to read and write a spoken language. For example, ASL signers often learn to read and write English, and Nicaraguan signers will likely try to learn written Spanish. So, in

[7]Despite the original sound-oriented connotations of phonology, this is the term currently used in sign language linguistics to describe patterning in minimal units like handshape and place of signing.

the absence of a rapid sign writing system, videotaping sign language interactions makes the possibility of later transcription possible, but videotaping can also be inappropriate or too intrusive for certain circumstances. Thus, transcription systems of sign language remain a methodological challenge. We present here some of the current options for representing sign language, though due to space limitations, they are not addressed in detail here. Many texts use a number of these options at the same time. For example, *A Dictionary of New Zealand Sign Language* uses illustrations, English glosses, and the Hamburg Notation System, one sign-oriented transcription option (Kennedy et al. 1997).

Illustrations have frequently been used, especially for sign language dictionaries (e.g., O'Rourke 1978). The advantages are that we can see the shape of the signs, and even some movement, through the judicious use of arrows and additional cues. Illustrations, however, are both space- and time-consuming to use and are not sufficient for documenting discourse.

Glossing is more compact and conveys the central meanings in signs. Glosses are frequently used when presenting information via printed matter (e.g., papers, articles, books) and are useful indexes, especially with those already familiar with the signs discussed. (DEAF-WORLD has been a gloss we have used in this article.) Their disadvantages are that little linguistic form, especially phonology and grammatical agreement, is encoded in basic glossing. The advantage of glosses is that they are relatively easy to use, requiring minimal training. They are also easy to type or write by hand, making them flexible for spontaneous use.

Elaborated Glossing adds additional, especially grammatical, information to glosses. Much of the linguistic literature involving sign languages has adopted such systems. One standard glossing system can found in Baker & Cokely's introductory sign language text (1981). Elaborated glossing can show such suprasegmental features as eye-brow positions, eye-gaze, and body shifting, which allows both phonological and grammatical analysis. Though more complex than simple glossing and therefore requiring more training and skill, elaborated glossing is relatively easy to understand and use and is flexible enough to accommodate novel characteristics researchers might wish to incorporate. It is also relatively easy to write by hand, though it begins to become difficult when used with word processors.

Stokoe Notation was one of the first systematic efforts at sign language transcription and has had considerable influence. Stokoe (1960) and his colleagues (1965) introduced this componential transcription system originally to represent ASL. The starting point was the U.S. fingerspelling alphabet (e.g., B is used by Stokoe to represent a flat open hand with fingers together, similar to the ASL fingerspelling for the letter *b*, but without the thumb folded into the palm). However, this system does not capture fine enough phonological or morphological detail to allow for close analysis of utterances, especially for cross-linguistic comparison. Though relatively easy to write manually once mastered, it is complex and somewhat difficult to learn and is difficult to transcribe on computers.

Liddell & Johnson's (1989) *Movement-Hold* model of transcription has proved useful in fine analysis of sign languages, especially when studying aspects of verbs or grammatical agreement among subject, objects, indirect objects, and verbs. It sprung off of Stokoe Notation but is more refined phonologically, especially with regard to incorporating movement (and pauses in movement, hence "hold"). The Movement-Hold model would be useful for closer analysis of language, such as phonological or morphosyntactic variation that might be used in sociolinguistic studies, but this close level of analysis requires considerable time and the use of video.

Another system useful for fine-grained phonological analysis is the *Hamburg Notation System* (HamNoSys) originally developed by the Centre for German Sign Language. It uses symbols intended to indicate actual handshapes rather than basing the notation on any fingerspelling alphabet (the same open hand described as a B shape in Stokoe Notation would be the shape of a horseshoe with a bottom and a short line indicating where the thumb was) and also has categories for finger and palm orientation, location, and movement (Kennedy et al. 1997, pp. xxxv–xxxix). Like Stokoe Notation, it can be difficult to learn and is hard to use on computers without specialized software.

There are also a number of transcription systems that developed out of dance notation including *Sutton SignWriting* and *Labanotation*. Sutton SignWriting evolved out of the Sutton Movement writing and shorthand system and was adapted and optimized to represent sign language. It is intended to enable a sign language literacy analogous to what is prevalent for spoken languages. Examples of its use can be found at the SignWriting web site (http://www.signwriting.org) including a paper by Roald (2000) discussing the development for physics terminology in Norwegian Sign Language. SignWriting's simplified phonological/morphological basis (that is, the way signs are made from linguistic components such as handshapes, movement, and use of body locations) makes it a relatively accessible form of writing for signers, though phonological and morphological differences in sign languages require language-specific symbols.[8] SignWriting might be a useful method for ethnographers keeping ethnographic fieldnotes, where we often resort to less precise glosses.

Farnell draws on Labanotation to transcribe gesture and signing in her analysis of Plains Sign Talk (PST) used by tribes in the Plains region of North America (1995). Though more complex than Sutton SignWriting, Labanotation can also encode time, space, and a range of linguistic and nonlinguistic gesture not able to be encoded in Sutton SignWriting. Farnell's work shows that such a system is useful for analyzing sign and gesture used by hearing people, but Labanotation is again fairly technical.

Slobin and Hoiting and their colleagues have been developing the *Berkeley Transcription System* (*BTS*) (Slobin et al. 1999, 2000), which is designed to analyze the morphological level of sign languages rather than primarily the phonetic

---

[8]Computer fonts for numerous specific sign languages are available.

or phonological levels. By analyzing the morphological level, these researchers begin to link the semantic levels of language (i.e., meanings) to the phonological levels of the actual forms used to encode and decode language. BTS is an extension to the CHILDES (Child Language Data Exchange) system (Sokolov et al. 1994) being used for linguistic and psycholinguistic research of spoken languages, including studies of language acquisition and linguistic cognition. One current project is the analysis of sign language "classifiers" (Slobin et al. 2000). A collection commented upon by Lucy (2000) suggests that classifier systems in general (i.e., those of spoken languages, but certainly those of sign language should be included) are pertinent to studies of linguistic relativity (cf., Lucy 1992a,b). It is still too early to evaluate the success of the BTS project, though if successful, the implications would be significant for both signed and spoken languages.

Discourse Analysis

Despite impediments involving transcription, effective work has been done on identifying discourse structures in deaf interactions. For example, the extended nature of Deaf good-byes is also well known (cf., Johnson 1994, Lane et al. 1996, pp. 452–55), and ritualized patterns of introductions such as asking whether other family members are deaf are consciously taught as part of ASL classes (Cokely & Baker 1980b, pp. 60–77). The analysis of such discourse is assisted by specialized software packages such as SignStream 2.0 and MediaTagger, which make tiered transcriptions linked to video data far more easy to manipulate. Consumer-grade digital video cameras and software applications such as iMovie 2 make sophisticated video processes extremely affordable and portable, even in remote locations such as Nicaragua (cf., A. Senghas 2001, Pyers 2001). These technological breakthroughs should enable considerable advances in sign language discourse analysis (cf., Shiffrin 1994) by allowing capture and analysis of transitory discourse. Metzger & Bahan's (2001) discussion of discourse analysis suggests a promising future for these approaches in sign language research (cf., for example, Mather 1987, 1994 for adult-child interaction; Celo 1996 for work on interrogatives in Italian Sign Language; and Roush 1999 for indirection in ASL).

However, with the increasing use of video technology for transcription and discourse analysis methodologies, a serious ethical concern arises. Especially as video becomes linked to tiered transcription systems for sign language (such as with SignStream), presenting actual utterances as linguistic data without revealing informants becomes increasingly difficult. Though we certainly promote the goals of Human Subjects Review (HSR) processes (cf., American Anthropological Association's Statement on Ethics [1998], especially the first obligation of ethnographers being to the people they study), we must raise the issue that current HSR procedures do not adequately address the problems of videotaping sign language subjects, nor the complex issue of informed consent. Most university HSR procedures overlook completely how culturally bound the concepts of informed and consent are, not recognizing that Western legal concepts of the individual as a person do not accurately reflect concepts in many cultural systems. These issues are of central concern during ethnographic research, particularly during the collection of naturally occurring discourse involving children, especially outside the United States.

Extended Ethnographies and Research Teams

We would be nowhere near the first to suggest that anthropological ethnographers should work in teams more frequently. Yet the nature of anthropological research involving sign languages usually requires very time-consuming analysis owing to the visual modality of the languages involved, making the importance of teamwork of even greater concern for studies of Deaf communities. Interdisciplinary collaboration improves the development of theory and methods as well. One of the authors (R. J. Senghas) notes that he has often benefited considerably from the informal cooperative relationships he holds both in the field and back at home with several colleagues from other disciplines, especially his sister, A. Senghas. In fact, he began his first fieldwork session in Nicaragua as a field assistant and cameraman for her (R. J. Senghas 1997, p. 6), and a recent joint presentation (R. J. Senghas et al. 2001) presents fruits of ongoing collaborative relationships.

Teamwork also facilitates diachronic analysis. Considering that only recently have researchers focused on documenting d/Deaf communities, there is a great need for data collected over time so that trends may be analyzed. Many of the accounts of d/Deaf individuals or d/Deaf communities over the past several centuries are anecdotal; a number of these have no known origin, and few have been informed by the social science disciplines. We need to build up not just the sign language corpus available to researchers, but the detailed ethnographic data that provide crucial sociocultural context for interpreting this corpus. For example, ethnographic data would help support work on child language socialization (including ideological issues), as well, and would be central in studies of critical discourse analysis (CDA) (Blommaert & Bulcaen 2000). If we keep in mind the goal of developing ethnographically rich bodies of data, the advantages of longitudinal teamwork, including the establishment and maintenance of the research infrastructure (labs, equipment, field site quarters, not to mention the supporting social relationships), seem clearly worth the necessary investment.

CONCLUDING COMMENTS

The past twenty years have shown a remarkable increase in the research on sign languages and d/Deaf communities. Major advances are being made, but the ethnographic component is only just starting. As we build these ethnographic accounts, the research must be seen as conducted among particular deaf people(s) in their particular places, at particular times, while interacting within particular circumstances. Nevertheless, the groundwork has been established, and the findings from research on d/Deaf communities and their sign languages are already contributing to general theoretical discussions in anthropology and other disciplines.

The implications of this research have begun to receive widespread attention, both within and without the academy, and to affect even lay notions concerning deafness and sign languages. Given recent breakthroughs in transcription systems, video technologies, and transcription software applications, the next twenty years should be equally rewarding, bringing considerable advances in anthropological and linguistic theory, deaf pedagogy, and the appreciation of d/Deaf experience.

ACKNOWLEDGMENTS

Deep thanks to our friend and colleague, Wade Tarzia, whose timely help with the manuscript considerably improved its readability, and to the editorial staff at Annual Reviews for further help with improving it.

The *Annual Review of Anthropology* is online at http://anthro.annualreviews.org

LITERATURE CITED

Aarons D, Reynolds R. 2003. South African Sign Language: changing policies and practice. See Monaghan et al. 2003

Agar M. 1994. *Language Shock: Understanding the Culture of Conversation*. New York: Morrow

Ahearn L. 2001. Language and agency. *Annu. Rev. Anthropol.* 30:109–37

Anderson B. 1991. *Imagined Communities: Reflections on the Origin and Spread of Nationalism*. New York: Verso. 2nd ed.

American Anthropological Association. 1998. Statement on Ethics. http://www.aaanet.org/committees/ethics/ethcode.htm

ANSNIC (Asociación Nacional de Sordos de Nicaragua). 1997. *Diccionario del Idioma de Señas de Nicaragua*. Managua: ANSNIC

Appadurai A. 1991. Global ethnoscapes: notes and queries for a transnational anthropology. In *Recapturing Anthropology: Working in the Present*, ed. RG Fox, pp. 191–210. Santa Fe, NM: Sch. Am. Res.

Bagga-Gupta S, Domfors LA. 2003. Pedagogical isssues in Swedish deaf education. See Monaghan et al. 2003

Baker C. 1999. Sign language and the Deaf community. In *Handbook of Language & Ethnic Identity*, ed. J Fishman, pp. 122–39. New York: Oxford Univ. Press

Baker C, Battison R, eds. 1980. *Sign Language and the Deaf Community: Essays in Honor of William C. Stokoe*. Silver Spring, MD: Natl. Assoc. Deaf

Baker C, Cokely D. 1981. *American Sign Language: a Student Text, Units 10–18*. Silver Spring, MD: TJ

Barnard A. 2000. *History and Theory in Anthropology*. Cambridge, UK: Cambridge Univ. Press

Barth F, ed. 1969. *Ethnic Groups and Boundaries*. Oslo: Universitetsforlaget

Bateman GC. 1996. Attitudes of the Deaf community towards political activism. See Parasnis 1996, pp. 146–59

Bauman R. 1972. Differential identity and the social base of folklore. See Paredes & Bauman 1972, pp. 31–41

Baynton D. 1996. *Forbidden Signs: American Culture and the Campaign Against Sign Language*. Chicago: Univ. Chicago Press

Berger KW. 1972. *Speechreading: Principles and Methods*. Baltimore, MD: Natl. Education

Bickerton D. 1984. The Language Bioprogram Hypothesis. *Behav. Brain Sci.* 7:173–221

Blount BG, ed. 1995. *Language, Culture, and Society: a Book of Readings*. Prospect Heights, IL: Waveland. 2nd ed.

Boas F. 1911. Introduction. In *Handbook of*

American Indian Languages, Part I. Washington, DC: Gov. Print. Office. 83 pp.

Bott E. 1971. *Family and Social Network: Roles, Norms, and External Relationships in Ordinary Urban Families*. London: Tavistock

Boyes Braem P. 1985. Studying sign language dialects. In *SLR 1983: Proceed. III Int. Symp. Sign Lang. Res., Rome, 22–26 June 1983*, ed. W Stokoe, V Volterra, pp. 247–53. Silver Spring, MD: Linstok

Branson J, Miller D, Marsaja IG, Negara IW. 1996. Everyone here speaks sign language, too: a Deaf village in Bali, Indonesia. In *Multicultural Aspects of Sociolinguistics in Deaf Communities*, ed. C Lucas.Washington, DC: Gallaudet Univ. Press

Brodkin K. 1998. *How Jews Became White Folks and What That Says about Race in America*. New Brunswick, NJ: Rugers Univ. Press

Carmel S. 1987. *A study of Deaf culture in an American urban Deaf community*. PhD thesis, Am. Univ., Washington, DC

Chomsky N. 1965. *Aspects of the Theory of Syntax*. Cambridge, MA: MIT Press

Cohen LH. 1994. *TRAIN GO SORRY: Inside a Deaf World*. Boston: Houghton Mifflin

Cokely D, Baker C. 1980a. *American Sign Languages: a Teacher's Resource on Curriculum, Methods, and Evaluation*. Silver Spring, MD: TJ

Cokely D, Baker C. 1980b. *American Sign Language: a Student Text, Units 1–9*. Silver Spring, MD: TJ

DeSantis S. 1977. *Elbow to hand in French and American Sign Languages*. Presented at New Ways of Analyzing Variation (NWAV) Conf., Georgetown Univ., Washington, DC

Deucher M. 1984. *British Sign Language*. London: Routledge Kegan Paul

Dundes A. 1972. Folk ideas as units of world view. See Paredes & Bauman 1972, pp. 93–103

Dundes A. 1980. *Interpreting Folklore*. Bloomington: Ind. Univ. Press

Duranti A, ed. 2001. *Key Terms in Language and Culture*. Malden, MA: Blackwell

Eckert P. 1989. *Jocks and Burnouts: Social Categories and Identity in the High School*. New York: Teachers College

Eckert P. 2000. *Linguistic Variation as Social Practice: the Linguistic Construction of Identity in Belton High*. Malden, MA: Blackwell

Edwards J. 1985. *Language, Society, and Identity*. Oxford: Blackwell

Emerton RG. 1996. Marginality, biculturalism, and social identity of Deaf people. See Parasnis 1996, pp. 136–45

Erting CJ. 1981. An anthropological approach to the study of the communicative competence of Deaf children. *Sign Lang. Stud.* 32: 221–38

Erting CJ. 1985. Sociocultural dimensions of Deaf education: belief systems and communicative interaction. *Sign Lang. Stud.* 47: 111–26

Erting CJ, Johnson RC, Smith DL, Snider BD. 1994. *The Deaf Way: Perspectives from the International Conference on Deaf Culture*. Washington, DC: Gallaudet Univ. Press. 907 pp.

Evans AD, Falk WW. 1986. *Learning to be Deaf*. Berlin: Mouton de Gruyer

Farnell B. 1995. *Do You See What I Mean?: Plains Indian Sign Talk and the Embodiment of Action*. Austin: Univ. Texas Press

Farnell B. 1999. Moving bodies, acting selves. *Annu. Rev. Anthropol.* 28:341–73

Filmakers Library. 2000. *Sound and Fury*. Film/Videotape

Fischer R, Lane HH, eds. 1993. *Looking Back: a Reader on the History of Deaf Communities and Their Sign Languages*. Hamburg: Signum

Fjord L. 1999–2000. Voices offstage: how vision has become a symbol to resist in an audiology lab in the US. *Vis. Anthropol. Rev.* 15(2):121–38

Fjord L. 2001. *Contested signs: discursive disputes in the geography of pediatric cochlear implants, language, kinship, and embodiment*. PhD thesis, Univ. Virginia

Foley WA. 1997. *Anthropological Linguistics: an Introduction*. Malden, MA: Blackwell

Fortes M. 1963. *Social Structure: Studies Presented to AR Radcliffe Brown*. New York: Russell & Russell

Foster RJ. 1991. Making national cultures in the global ecumene. *Annu. Rev. Anthropol.* 20:235–60

Foster SB. 1987. Employment experiences of deaf RIT graduates: an interview study. *J. Rehab. Deaf* 21(1):1–15

Foster SB. 1988. Life in the mainstream: reflections of deaf college freshman on their experiences in the mainstreamed high school. *J. Rehab. Deaf* 22(2):27–35

Foster SB. 1989. Social alienation and peer identification: a study of the social construction of deafness. *Hum. Org.* 48(3):226–35

Foster SB. 1996. Communication experiences of Deaf people: an ethnographic account. See Parasnis 1996, pp. 117–36

Gannon J. 1981. *A Narrative History of Deaf America*. Silver Spring, MD: Natl. Assoc. Deaf

Giddens A. 1979. *Central Problems in Social Theory: Action, Structure and Contradiction in Social Analysis*. Berkeley: Univ. Calif. Press

Giddens A. 1984. *The Constitution of Society*. Berkeley: Univ. Calif. Press

Goffman E. 1959. *The Presentation of Self in Everyday Life*. New York: Anchor/Doubleday

Goffman E. 1963. *Stigma: Notes on the Management of Spoiled Identity*. Englewood Cliffs, NJ: Prentice Hall

Groce NE. 1985. *Everyone Here Spoke Sign Language: Hereditary Deafness on Martha's Vineyard*. Cambridge, MA: Harvard Univ. Press

Grosjean F. 1996. Living with two languages and two cultures. See Parasnis 1996, pp. 20–37

Grushkin DA. 1996. *Academic, linguistic, social and identity development in hard-of-hearing adolescents educated within an ASL/English bilingual/bicultural educational setting for Deaf and hard-of-hearing students*. PhD thesis, Univ. Arizona, Tucson

Grushkin DA. 2003. The dilemma of the hard-of-hearing within the United States Deaf community. See Monaghan et al. 2003

Gustason G, Pfetzing D, Zawolkow E. 1980. *Signing Exact English*. Los Alamitos, CA: Modern Signs

Hakuta K, Mostafapour EF. 1996. Perspectives from the history and the politics of bilingualism and bilingual education in the United States. See Parasnis 1996, pp. 38–50

Hall SA. 1989. *The Deaf club is like a second home: an ethnography of folklore communication in American Sign Language*. PhD thesis, Univ. Penn.

Hall SA. 1991. Door into American: folklore in an American Deaf social club. *Sign Lang. Stud.* 73:421–29

Hall SA. 1994. Silent club: an ethnographic study of folklore among the Deaf. See Erting et al. 1994, pp. 522–27

Hamers. 1996. Cognitive and language development of bilingual children. See Parasnis 1996, pp. 51–75

Hannerz U. 1992. *Cultural Complexity: Studies in the Social Organization of Meaning*. New York: Columbia Univ. Press

Harris G. 1989. Concepts of *individual, self,* and *person* in description and analysis. *Am. Anthropol.* 91(3):599–612

Harrison FV. 1995. The resistance of "race" in the cultural and political economy of racism. *Annu. Rev. Anthropol.* 24:47–74

Harrison FV, ed. 1998. Issues forum: race and racism. *Am. Anthropol.* 100(3):607–731

Hartigan J. 1999. *Racial Situations: Class Predicaments of Whiteness in Detroit*. Princeton, NJ: Princeton Univ. Press

Haviland JB. 2001. Gesture. See Duranti 2001, pp. 83–86

Heath SB. 1996. What no bedtime story means: narrative skills at home and school. In *The Matrix of Language: Contemporary Linguistic Anthropology*, ed. D Brenneis, RKS Macaulay, pp. 12–38. Boulder, CO: Westview

Higgins P. 1980. *Outsiders in a Hearing World: a Sociology of Deafness*. Beverly Hills, CA: Sage

Hill JH. 2001. Comments, questions, and

enthusiastic praise. *J. Ling. Anthropol.* 11(1): 79–83

Hill JH, Mannheim B. 1992. Language and worldview. *Annu. Rev. Anthropol.* 21:381–406

Holm JA. 2000. *An Introduction to Pidgins and Creoles.* Cambridge, UK: Cambridge Univ. Press

Hymes D, ed. 1971. *Pidginization and Creolization of Languages.* Cambridge, UK: Cambridge Univ. Press

Johnson K. 1994. *Ideology and practice of Deaf goodbyes.* PhD thesis. Univ. Calif., Los Angeles

Johnson RE. 1991. Sign language, culture, and community in a traditional Yucatec Maya village. *Sign Lang. Stud.* 73:461–74

Johnson RE, Erting C. 1989. Ethnicity and socialization in a classroom for Deaf children. See Lucas 1989, pp. 41–83

Johnson RE, Liddell S, Erting C. 1989. *Unlocking the curriculum: principles for achieving access in Deaf education. Gallaudet Res. Inst. Work. Pap. 89-3.* Washington, DC.: Gallaudet Univ.

Keating E. 2000. How culture and technology together shape new communicative practices: investigating interactions between Deaf and hearing callers with computer-mediated videotelephone. *Tex. Ling. Forum* 43:99–116

Keating E, Mirus G. 2001. Cross modal conversations: Deaf children and hearing peers at school. *Crossroads of Language, Interaction, and Culture (CLIC) Conf. Proc.* 3:73–90

Kegl J, McWhorter J. 1997. Perspectives on an emerging language. In *Proc. Stanford Child Lang. Res. Forum.* New York: Cambridge Univ. Press. Palo Alto, CA: CSLI. pp. 15–38

Kendon A. 1997. Gesture. *Annu. Rev. Anthropol.* 26:129–61

Kennedy G, Arnold A, Dugdale P, Fahey S, Moskovitz D. 1997. *A Dictionary of New Zealand Sign Language.* Auckland, NZ: Auckland Univ. Press/Bridget Williams

Klima E, Bellugi U. 1979. *The Signs of Language.* Cambridge, MA: Harvard Univ. Press

Kroskrity PV, ed. 2000. *Regimes of Language: Ideologies, Polities, and Identities.* Santa Fe, NM: Sch. Am. Res.

Kyle JG, Woll B. 1985. *Sign Language: the Study of Deaf People and Their Language.* Cambridge, UK: Cambridge Univ. Press

Labov W. 1972. *Sociolinguistic Patterns.* Philadelphia, PA: Univ. Penn. Press

Lane H. 1984. *When the Mind Hears: a History of the Deaf.* New York: Random House

Lane H. 1992. *The Mask of Benevolence: Disabling the Deaf Community.* New York: Knopf

Lane H, Hoffmeister R, Bahan B. 1996. *A Journey into the DEAF-WORLD.* San Diego, CA: DawnSignPress

LeMaster B. 1977. The education of the Deaf: a sub-community in the making. *Kroeber Anthropol. Soc. Pap.*, Vol. 49

LeMaster B. 1983. *Marking ethnic identity in signed conversations.* MA thesis, Univ. Calif., Los Angeles

LeMaster B. 1990. *The maintenance and loss of female and male signs in the Dublin Deaf community.* PhD thesis, Univ. Calif., Los Angeles

LeMaster B. 1997. Sex differences in Irish Sign Language. In *The Life of Language: Papers in Linguistics in Honor of William Bright*, ed. JH Hill, PJ Mistry, L Campbell, pp. 67–85. Berlin: Mouton de Gruyer

LeMaster B. 2002. What difference does difference make? Negotiating gender and generation in Irish Sign Language. In *Gendered Practices in Language*, ed. S Benor, M Rose, D Sharman, J Sweetland, Q Zhang. Stanford, CA: CSLI. In press

LeMaster BA, Monaghan LF. 2002. Sign languages. In *A Companion to Linguistic Anthropology*, ed. A Duranti. Malden, MA: Blackwell. In press

Liddell S, Johnson RE. 1989. American Sign Language: the phonological base. *Sign Lang. Stud.* 64:195–278

Lucas C, ed. 1989. *The Sociolinguistics of the Deaf Community.* San Diego, CA: Academic

Lucas C, Bayley R, Valli C, eds. 2001. *Sociolinguistic Variation in American Sign*

Language. Washington, DC: Gallaudet Univ. Press

Lucas C, Valli C. 1989. Language contact in the American Deaf community. See Lucas 1989, pp. 11–40

Lucy JA. 1992a. *Grammatical Categories and Cognition: a Case Study of the Linguistic Relativity Hypothesis*. Cambridge, UK: Cambridge Univ. Press

Lucy JA. 1992b. *Language Diversity and Thought: a Reformulation of the Linguistic Relativity Hypothesis*. Cambridge, UK: Cambridge Univ. Press

Lucy JA. 1995 [1985]. Whorf's view of linguistic mediation of thought. Originally in *Semiotic Mediation*, ed. E Mertz, R Parmentier, pp. 143–60. See Blount 1995, pp. 415–38

Lucy JA. 2000. Systems of nominal classification: a concluding discussion. In *Systems of Nominal Classification*, ed. G Senft, pp. 326–40. Cambridge, UK: Cambridge Univ. Press

Markowicz H, Woodward JC. 1982 [1978]. Language and the maintenance of ethnic boundaries in the Deaf community. In *How You Gonna to Get to Heaven If You Can't Talk With Jesus: On Depathologizing Deafness*, ed. J Woodward, pp. 3–9. Silver Spring, MD: TJ

McNeill D. 1992. *Hand and Mind*. Chicago: Univ. Chicago Press

Mead M. 1928. *Coming of Age in Somoa: a Psychological Study of Primitive Youth for Western Civilization*. New York: William Morrow

Meath-Lang B. 1996. Cultural and language diversity in the curriculum: towards reflective practice. See Parasnis 1996, pp. 160–70

Messing LS, Campbell R. 1999. *Gesture, Speech and Sign*. Oxford, UK: Oxford Univ. Press

Monaghan LF. 1991. The founding of two Deaf churches: the interplay of Deaf and Christian identities. *Sign Lang. Stud.* 73:431–52

Monaghan LF. 1996. *Signing, oralism and the development of the New Zealand deaf community: an ethnography and history of language ideologies*. PhD thesis, Univ. Calif. Los Angeles

Monaghan LF. 2001. Signing. See Duranti 2001, pp. 223–26

Monaghan LF. 2003. A world's eye view: Deaf cultures in global perspective. See Monaghan et al. 2003

Monaghan LF, Nakamura K, Schmaling C, Turner GH. 2003. *Many Ways to be Deaf*. Washington, DC: Gallaudet Univ. Press. In press

Morford J. 1996. Insights to language from the study of gesture: a review of research on the gestural communication of non-signing Deaf people. *Lang. Commun.* 16(2):165–78

Mottez M. 1993. *Languages, Loyalty, and Identity in Creole Language Situations*. Los Angeles: CAAS

Nakamura K. 2001. *Deaf identities, sign language, and minority social movements politics in modern Japan (1868–2000)*. PhD thesis, Yale Univ.

Nakamura K. 2003. U-turns, 'Deaf shock,' and the hard of hearing: Japanese Deaf identities at the borderlands. See Monaghan et al. 2003

Ochs E. 1988. *Culture and Language Development: Language Acquisition and Language Socialization in a Somoan Village*. Cambridge, UK: Cambridge Univ. Press

Padden C. 1980. The Deaf community and the culture of Deaf people. See Baker & Battison 1980, pp. 89–103

Padden C. 1996a. From the cultural to the bicultural: the modern Deaf community. See Parasnis 1996, pp. 79–98

Padden C. 1996b. Early bilingual lives of Deaf children. See Parasnis 1996, pp. 99–116

Padden C. 2001. Deaf. See Duranti 2001, pp. 52–55

Padden C, Humphries T. 1988. *Deaf in America: Voices from a Culture*. Cambridge, MA: Harvard Univ. Press

Paramount Pictures. 1992. *Children of a Lesser God*. Film.

Parasnis I, ed. 1996. *Cultural and Language Diversity and the Deaf Experience*. Cambridge, UK: Cambridge Univ. Press

Paredes A, Bauman R, eds. 1972. *Toward New*

Perspectives in Folklore. Austin: Univ. Texas Press

Plann S. 1997. *A Silent Minority: Deaf Education in Spain 1550–1835*. Berkeley: Univ. Calif. Press

Polich LG. 1998. *Social agency and Deaf communities: a Nicaraguan case study*. PhD thesis. Univ. Texas, Austin

Polich LG. 2000. Orality: another language ideology. *Proc. VIIth Ann. [1999] SALSA Conf.*, Austin, TX

Preston P. 1994. *Mother Father Deaf: Living Between Sound and Silence*. Cambridge, MA: Harvard Univ. Press

Pursglove M, Komarova A. 2003. The changing world of the Russian Deaf community. See Monaghan et al. 2003

Pyers J. 2001. *Three stages in the understanding of false belief in Nicaraguan signers: the interaction of social experience, language emergence, and conceptual development*. Presented at Ann. Meet. Jean Piaget Soc., 31st, May 31–June 2, Berkeley, CA

Reilly C. 1995. *A Deaf way of education: interaction among children in a Thai boarding school*. PhD thesis, Univ. Maryland

Rumsey A. 2001. Orality. See Duranti 2001, pp. 165–67

Sacks O. 1989. *Seeing Voices*. Berkeley, CA: Univ. Calif. Press

Schein J. 1992. *At Home Among Strangers*. Washington, DC: Gallaudet Univ. Press

Schermer G. 1985. Analysis of natural discourse of deaf adults in the Netherlands: observations on Dutch Sign Language. In *Proc. Third Int. Symp. Sign Lang. Res.*, ed. W Stokoe, V Volterra, pp. 281–88. Silver Spring, MD: Linstok

Schieffelin BB. 1990. *The Give and Take of Everyday Life: Language Socialization of Kaluli Children*. Cambridge, UK: Cambridge Univ. Press

Schieffelin BB, Woolard K, Kroskrity PV. 1998. *Language Ideologies: Practice and Theory*. Oxford: Oxford Univ. Press.

Schmaling C. 2003. A for apple: the impact of Western education and ASL on the Deaf community in Kano State, Northern Nigeria. See Monaghan et al. 2003

Senghas A. 1995. *Children's contribution to the birth of Nicaraguan Sign Language*. PhD thesis. Mass. Inst. Technol., Cambridge, MA

Senghas A. 2001. *The effects of language acquisition on the development of NSL: how minds mold a language*. Presented at Annu. Meet. Jean Piaget Soc., 31st, Berkeley, CA

Senghas A, Coppola M. 2001. Children creating language: how Nicaraguan Sign Language acquired spatial grammar. *Psychol. Sci.* 12(4):323–28

Senghas A, Coppola M, Newport E, Supalla T. 1997. Argument structure in Nicaraguan Sign Language: the emergence of grammatical devices. *Proc. Boston Univ. Conf. Lang. Dev.*, 21:550–61. Boston: Cascadilla

Senghas RJ. 1997. *An 'unspeakable, unwriteable' language: Deaf identity, language and personhood among the first cohorts of Nicaraguan Signers*. PhD thesis. Univ. Rochester, New York

Senghas RJ. 2003. New ways to be Deaf in Nicaragua: changes in language, personhood and community. See Monaghan et al. 2003

Senghas RJ, Kegl J. 1994. Social considerations in the emergence of *Idioma de Signos Nicaragüense* (Nicaraguan Sign Language). *Signpost* 7(1):40–45

Senghas RJ, Kegl J, Senghas A. 1994. *Creation through contact: the emergence of a Nicaraguan Deaf community*. Presented at 2nd Int. Conf. Deaf History, Hamburg, Germany

Senghas RJ, Senghas A, Pyers J. 2001. *The emergence of Nicaraguan Sign Language: questions of development, acquisition, and evolution*. Presented at Annu. Meet. Jean Piaget Soc., 31st, May 31–June 2, Berkeley, CA

Silverstein M. 2000. Whorfianism and the linguistic imagination of nationality. See Kroskrity 2000, pp. 85–138

Siple P, Fischer S, eds. 1991. *Theoretical Issues in Sign Language Research:* Vol. 2, *Psychology*. Chicago: Univ. Chicago Press

Slobin DI, Hoiting N, Anthony M, Biederman Y, Kuntze M, et al. 1999. Sign language transcription at the morphological level: the Berkeley Transcription System (BTS). Report to European Sci. Found., London Intersign Workshop on Acquisition, 4–6 September
Slobin DI, Hoiting N, Anthony M, Biederman Y, Kuntze M, et al. 2000. *A cognitive/functional perspective on the acquisition of 'classifiers'*. Presented at Classifier Constructions in Sign Lang., April 14–16, La Jolla, CA
Sokolov JL, Snow C, eds. 1994. *Handbook of Research in Language Development Using CHILDES*. Hillsdale, NJ: Lawrence Erlbaum
Stokoe WC. 1980. Sign language structure. *Annu. Rev. Anthropol.* 9:365–90
Stokoe WC, Casterline DC, Croneberg CG. 1965. *A Dictionary of American Sign Language on Linguistic Principles*. Silver Spring, MD: Linstok
Stone JB. 1996. Minority empowerment and the education of Deaf people. See Parasnis 1996, pp. 171–80
Trechtor S, Bucholtz M. 2001. Introduction: white noise: bringing language in whiteness studies. *J. Ling. Anthropol.* 11(1):3–21
Tylor EB. 1878. *Researches into the Early History of Mankind and the Development of Early Civilization*. London: Murray
Van Cleve JV, ed. 1987. *Gallaudet Encyclopedia of Deaf People and Deafness*. Three vols. New York: McGraw-Hill
Van Cleve JV, Crouch BA. 1989. *A Place of Their Own: Creating the Deaf Community in America*. Washington, DC: Gallaudet Univ. Press
Volterra V, Erting CJ, eds. 1994. *From Gesture to Language in Hearing and Deaf Children*. Washington, DC: Gallaudet Univ. Press
Washabaugh W. 1981. Sign language in its social context. *Annu. Rev. Anthropol.* 10:237–52
Washabaugh W. 1986. *Five Fingers for Survival*. Ann Arbor, MI: Karoma
Whorf BL. 1995 [1941]. The relation of habitual thought and behavior to language. Originally in *Language, Culture, and Personality, Essays in Memory of Sapir*, ed. L Spier, AI Hallowell, SS Newman, pp. 75–93. See Blount 1995, pp. 64–84
Wilcox S. 1989. *American Deaf Culture: an Anthology*. Silver Spring, MD: Linstok
Wolf ER. 1982. *Europe and the People Without History*. Berkeley: Univ. Calif. Press
Woodward JC. 1972. Implications for sociolinguistic research among the Deaf. *Sign Lang. Stud.* 1:1–7
Woodward JC. 1976. Black southern signing. *Lang. Soc.* 5:211–18
Woodward JC. 1982. *How You Gonna Get to Heaven if You Can't Talk with Jesus: On Depathologizing Deafness*. Silver Spring, MD: TJ
Woodward JC. 2003. Sign languages and Deaf identities in Thailand and Viet Nam. See Monaghan et al. 2003
Woodward JC, DeSantis S. 1977a. Negative incorporation in French and American Sign Language. *Lang. Soc.* 6(3):379–88
Woodward JC, DeSantis S. 1977b. Two to one it happens: dynamic phonology in two sign languages. *Sign Lang. Stud.* 17:329–46
Woolard K, Schieffelin BB. 1994. Language ideology. *Annu. Rev. Anthropol.* 25:55–82
Woll B, Sutton-Spence R, Elton F. 2001. Multilingualism: the global approach to sign languages. In *The Sociolinguistics of Sign Languages*, ed. C Lucas, pp. 8–32. Cambridge, UK: Cambridge Univ. Press
Wrigley O. 1996. *The Politics of Deafness*. Washington, DC: Gallaudet Univ. Press

Annu. Rev. Anthropol. 2002. 31:99–119
doi: 10.1146/annurev.anthro.32.032702.131011

First published online as a Review in Advance on May 10, 2002

THE ANTHROPOLOGY OF FOOD AND EATING

Sidney W. Mintz[1] and Christine M. Du Bois[2]
[1]Anthropology Department, Emeritus, The Johns Hopkins University, Baltimore, Maryland 21218; email: SWMintz@aol.com
[2]Department of International Health, School of Hygiene and Public Health, The Johns Hopkins University, Baltimore, Maryland 21205; email: cmdubois@alumni.princeton.edu

Key Words commensality, meals, cooking, cuisine, food insecurity

■ **Abstract** The study of food and eating has a long history in anthropology, beginning in the nineteenth century with Garrick Mallery and William Robertson Smith. This review notes landmark studies prior to the 1980s, sketching the history of the subfield. We concentrate primarily, however, on works published after 1984. We contend that the study of food and eating is important both for its own sake since food is utterly essential to human existence (and often insufficiently available) and because the subfield has proved valuable for debating and advancing anthropological theory and research methods. Food studies have illuminated broad societal processes such as political-economic value-creation, symbolic value-creation, and the social construction of memory. Such studies have also proved an important arena for debating the relative merits of cultural and historical materialism vs. structuralist or symbolic explanations for human behavior, and for refining our understanding of variation in informants' responses to ethnographic questions. Seven subsections examine classic food ethnographies: single commodities and substances; food and social change; food insecurity; eating and ritual; eating and identities; and instructional materials. The richest, most extensive anthropological work among these subtopics has focused on food insecurity, eating and ritual, and eating and identities. For topics whose anthropological coverage has not been extensive (e.g., book-length studies of single commodities, or works on the industrialization of food systems), useful publications from sister disciplines—primarily sociology and history—are discussed.

INTRODUCTION

Writing more than twenty years ago, Professor Joseph Epstein tells us:

> [T]en years ago I should have said that any fuss about food was too great, but I grow older and food has become more important to me. . . . [J]udging from the space given to it in the media, the great number of cookbooks and restaurant guides published annually, the conversations of friends—it is very nearly topic number one. Restaurants today are talked about with the kind of excitement that ten years ago was expended on movies. Kitchen technology—blenders,

> grinders, vegetable steamers, microwave ovens, and the rest—arouses something akin to the interest once reserved for cars. . . . The time may be exactly right to hit the best-seller lists with a killer who disposes of his victims in a Cuisinart (Aristides 1978, pp. 157–58).

But what Professor Epstein was witnessing turned out to be only the first swallow, so to speak. Since then, food has become even more important to everybody, anthropologists included.

Of course anthropologists have been interested in food for a long time. Garrick Mallery's paper, "Manners and meals" (1888), appeared in Volume 1, No. 3, of the *American Anthropologist.* William Robertson Smith's *Lectures on the Religion of the Semites* (1889) contains an important chapter on food. Frank Hamilton Cushing's little monograph on Zuñi breadstuffs (1920) and Franz Boas's exhaustive treatment of Kwakiutl salmon recipes (1921) are other examples of early work. (Though these last two seemed like mere fact collecting to some, Helen Codere's paper on Boas's salmon recipes (1957) showed just how much could be learned about social organization and hierarchy by carefully reading about how to cook a salmon.)

In a more recent era, Claude Lévi-Strauss (e.g., 1965) and, in his wake, Mary Douglas (1966) made important contributions to a structuralist vision of food and eating. But Jack Goody's book *Cooking, Cuisine, and Class: A Study in Comparative Sociology* (1982) seemed to mark a turning point. Since then, as the world that anthropologists chose to study became different, so has their work on food and eating. The anthropological study of food today has matured enough to serve as a vehicle for examining large and varied problems of theory and research methods.

In theory building, food systems have been used to illuminate broad societal processes such as political-economic value-creation (Mintz 1985), symbolic value-creation (Munn 1986), and the social construction of memory (Sutton 2001). Food studies have been a vital arena in which to debate the relative merits of cultural materialism vs. structuralist or symbolic explanations for human behavior (M. Harris 1998 [1985]; Simoons 1994, 1998; Gade 1999). In addition, food avoidance research has continued to refine theories about the relationship between cultural and biological evolution (Aunger 1994b).

Examinations of the relationships between food supplies and seasonal rituals of conflict (Dirks 1988), food supplies and the frequency of war (Ember & Ember 1994), and food resource periodicity and cooperativeness (Poggie 1995)—while by no means devoid of methodological problems—suggest the utility of the Human Relations Area Files for comparative cross-cultural research. The reasons for intracultural variation in informants' responses, and their implications for data interpretation, have been examined with reference both to hot-cold classifications of foods (Boster & Weller 1990) and to food avoidances (Aunger 1994a). Food systems have also been used to examine tensions between elicited taxonomies and the categories people use in everyday life (Nichter 1986, Wassmann 1993).

Our work here had to take into account nearly two decades of research since Messer's *ARA* review (1984). Serious coverage of the whole field was impractical.

We decided to use just seven headings to define our scope. This coverage omits many worthy sources, even within those headings: classic food ethnographies; single commodities and substances; food and social change; food insecurity; eating and ritual; eating and identities; and instructional materials. We had to neglect closely related topics, such as food in prehistory; biological aspects of eating (nutritional anthropology and food in medical anthropology); infant feeding and weaning (see Van Esterik in this volume); cannibalism (on kuru, see Lindenbaum 2001); and substances causing major psychoactive changes.

Except in our food insecurity section, we set aside works dealing only with food production and not with its consumption. On the one hand, the literature on agriculture in developing countries is extensive and requires separate review; on the other, the social science of food production in industrialized contexts is scant (Murcott 1999a). Our focus on works that postdate Messer's review of similar themes heavily favors anthropology, but unity of theme mattered more in some instances than did disciplinary boundaries.

In addition to the specific sources discussed below, scholars benefit from general reference works including theoretical analyses of social scientific approaches to eating (Murcott 1988, Wood 1995), literature reviews (Messer 1984), compilations of syllabi and bibliographies (Lieberman & Sorensen 1997; Dirks 2002), encyclopedias of food (Davidson 1999, Katz 2002, Kiple & Ornelas 2000), and general histories of food habits (e.g., Toussaint-Samat 1992, Flandrin & Montanari 1999; for surveys of the historical literature on specific European countries, see Teuteberg 1992). Journals oriented to the social life of food include: *Gastronomica*, *Petits Propos Culinaires*, *Food & Foodways*, and *Digest: An Interdisciplinary Study of Food and Foodways*; they are complemented by numerous journals in the subfield of nutritional anthropology (see Messer 1984, p. 207 for a partial listing). Internet sources on agriculture and food (e.g., Agricultural Network Information Center 2000, U.N. Food and Agriculture Organization 2001, U.S. Department of Agriculture 2001), which often yield far more information than first meets the eye, offer statistical data, details of policies and programs, bibliographies, and links to other websites. Among relevant conferences, the Oxford Symposia publish useful proceedings (see R. Harris 1996).

CLASSIC ETHNOGRAPHIES

Comprehensive, anthropological monographs on food systems are lamentably rare. Audrey Richards's (1939) *Land, Labour and Diet in Northern Rhodesia* still remains the model for the field; she and an interdisciplinary team examined food production, preparation, exchange, preferences, symbolism, consumption, and nutritional consequences. Moore & Vaughan have restudied food systems in the region where Richards worked (1994), combining history with ethnography in an analysis that is both broad and richly detailed—a worthy successor to Richards's work. Taken as a pair, Ikpe's history of food systems in Nigeria (1994) and Anigbo's ethnography of commensality among the Igbo (1987) provide similar breadth.

Trankell's culinary ethnography of the Thai Yong of Thailand (1995) lacks historical depth, yet still combines examination of food production, local categorization, preparation, gender dynamics, consumption patterns, and rituals.

More specifically focused ethnographies include: Weismantel's examination of gender and political economy as expressed through food in the Ecuadorian Andes (1988); Kahn's analysis of food, gender identities, and social values in Papua New Guinea (1986); Whitehead's study of gender hierarchy and food sharing rules, also in Papua New Guinea (2000); Mahias's work on culinary beliefs and practices among the Jains of Delhi (1985); Kanafani's finely textured study of the visual, olfactory, and gustatory aesthetics of food preparation and consumption in the United Arab Emirates (1983); and Sutton's extended meditation on how culinary memories help define the identities and social lives of Greeks living on the island of Kalymnos (2001).

These monographs are complemented by several collections of essays dealing with foodways in specific regions: Peru (Weston 1992), the United States (Brown & Mussell 1984, Humphrey & Humphrey 1988), Africa (Devisch et al. 1995; Froment et al. 1996), the Middle East (Zubaida & Tapper 1994), Britain (Murcott 1983, 1998), South Asia (Khare & Rao 1986), Oceania and Southeast Asia (Manderson 1986), and Oceania alone (Kahn & Sexton 1988, N. Pollock 1992). All except Pollock's book on Oceania are anthologies; all cover multiple topics, including food in regional history; food preparation, taboos, and preferences; food and identities; and culinary symbolism.

Scattered among a wide variety of social-scientific journals and anthologies dealing primarily with issues other than food are many valuable ethnographic essays on food systems; we cannot begin to mention them all. We should note, however, the debates among those who study hunter-gatherers over optimal foraging theory, a behavioral-ecological model which posits that people adopt food strategies maximizing their caloric intake per unit of time, with the caloric *costs* of those food strategies taken into account. The theory itself has been propounded (Kaplan & Hill 1985) and contested (Thomas 1992), as have its implications for the study of hunters' motivations for food-sharing (Hawkes 1991, Bliege Bird & Bird 1997, Wood & Hill 2000).

In-depth studies of food systems remind us of the pervasive role of food in human life. Next to breathing, eating is perhaps the most essential of all human activities, and one with which much of social life is entwined. It is hoped that more anthropologists will accord food the central place in their ethnographies that it occupies in human existence.

SINGLE COMMODITIES AND SUBSTANCES

Anthropologists have been writing papers about single substances—food sources, plants, animals, and foods made from them—for a long time. Probably the first substantial work in English devoted to a single such theme was R. N. Salaman's *History and Social Influence of the Potato* (1949). His book dealt with the potato's origins, domestication, worldwide diffusion, and political fate in European life. Since that time many other such books have appeared—on drugs hard and soft, sugar, rhubarb, salt, codfish, capsicums, etc. Many are histories, general or botanical, others economic; it is striking that so few are by anthropologists.

Such works generally incline toward treating the subject mostly in terms of itself; using it to illuminate broader processes; or developing the theme in specific relation to cuisine. Smith on the tomato (1994), Willard on saffron (2001), Jenkins on bananas (2000), and Kurlansky on salt (2002) focus principally on their subject; all make use of history. Anthropologists such as Warman on maize (1988), Ohnuki-Tierney on rice (1993), and Mintz on sucrose (1985) are historical in orientation but try to relate each subject to wider fields of explanation. Two books by anthropologists on a food animal, the guinea pig (Morales 1995, Archetti 1997 [1992]), are quite similar in content. Though perhaps less detailed ethnographically, Archetti's is theoretically richer. Both authors take globalization and the world market into account; both note the spread of the *cuy* as a food source outside the Andes; both treat the guinea pig as a device through which to discuss cultural and social change. Long-Solís's (1986) study of capsicum in Mexico comes early in the succession of such studies. Rare enough to merit mention is Malagón's edited volume on marzipan (1990), which includes anthropological contributions. S. Coe & M. Coe's study of chocolate (1996) successfully combines archaeology and ethnography.

The Quincentenary stimulated much interest in foods that travel. Viola & Margolis (1991), Foster & Cordell (1992), and Long (1996), among many others, produced rich collections on food and diffusion that included work by many anthropologists. The late Sophie Coe's fine book on New World cuisine (1994) also stands out. Though not linked to 1492, the volume edited by Plotnicov & Scaglion (1999) contains, among others, papers on New World capsicums, cassava, the potato and tomato, and sweet potatoes, as well as sugar and coffee, and it stresses plant diffusion.

Fiddes's (1991) approach to meat reopened a subject that had previously held the attention of Sahlins (1976), Ross (1980), and M. Harris (1998 [1985]), among others. Orlove (1997) eloquently addresses the issue of universal vs. contingent meanings for meat by looking at a food riot.

Anthropological articles on single substances are so copious that only a few can be noted here. Messer's nuanced study of potato use in Europe (1997) considers obstacles to and benefits of the spread and assimilation of new food items. Gade, a geographer, raises useful questions with his study of broad beans in Quebec (1994) about how foods gain a foothold in specific settings. Y. Lockwood & W. Lockwood (2000a) consider Finnish-American dairy foods in an Oxford food symposium dedicated entirely to milk; Bestor (1999, 2001) reveals the links of Tokyo's wholesale tuna market to the world outside.

Murcott (1999b) argues for a redefinition of the social construction of food by looking at the history of milk and poultry regulation/definition in the United Kingdom. Gade's examination (1999) of the absence of milking in the Andes recalls Simoons's treatment of the fava bean and favism (1998)—cases of foods people eat sparingly, with unease, or not at all. Somewhat different is McIntosh (2000), who links a temporary decline in U.S. egg consumption to a food scare. Taking a longer historical view, Brandes (1992) looks at maize avoidance and fear of pellagra in Europe, while Leach (2001) explains how a good herb can acquire a bad reputation. Neither "taboo" nor "prohibition" covers these papers; each is a different view of the perception of food.

FOOD AND SOCIAL CHANGE

The effects of broad societal changes on eating patterns, and vice versa, are of growing interest to ethnographers. In-depth food ethnographies that include discussion of social change are covered in our "Classic Ethnographies" section above. In addition, the relevant literature includes both general collections of essays (Harris & Ross 1987, Pelto & Vargas 1992, Macbeth 1997, Lentz 1999, Wu & Tan 2001, Cwiertka & Walraven 2002) and other research exploring the culinary effects of the Soviet collapse; other changes in intergroup relations within societies; mass production of foods; biotechnology; movements of peoples; increasing globalization of foods themselves; and war. These themes are dealt with in turn.

Ethnographic literature on post-Soviet dietary patterns is limited but promising. Çaglar addresses changes in the marketing of Turkish fast-food in Germany after the fall of the Berlin Wall (Çaglar 1999), whereas Ziker discusses food sharing and the moral code of aboriginal peoples in post-Soviet Siberia (Ziker 1998). Chatwin explores extensively the transformation of foodways in the Republic of Georgia, detailing the social, political, and economic context (Chatwin 1997).

Other food shifts are associated with a variety of economic and political changes, such as male out-migration, interclass rivalry and imitation, and market integration. Lentz's edited collection of essays explores several such themes (Lentz 1999). Mayer similarly delineates how changing caste relations are reflected in Indian village foodways (Mayer 1996). Jing's edited volume explores how government policies and social transformations in China have affected dietary habits, particularly of children (2000). Historians, too, have examined how broad social processes have led to culinary change (Mennell 1985, Levenstein 1993), and conversely, how food processing problems, such as massive, natural food poisonings (Matossian 1989), may have fostered social change.

Anthropological work on how the industrialization of food production and distribution has affected dietary patterns is scant. Mintz pioneered in this area with a historical study of sugar production and consumption (Mintz 1985). Anthropologists have also explored the interplay between the requirements of capitalists and consumers in Trinidad's sweet drink industry (D. Miller 1997) and the reaction to industrialized consumption patterns among adherents of Italy's "slow food" movement (Leitch 2000). Historians, rural sociologists, and communications theorists have also taken up the challenge of studying dietary patterns under industrialized capitalism, examining the relationship between food industries and the U.S.

counterculture (Belasco 1989), contestation in the organic foods movement (Campbell & Liepins 2001), food industries and the incorporation of ethnic cuisines (Belasco 1987), the refinement of packaging to entice consumption (Hine 1995), the role of modern advertising and marketing in dietary change (Cwiertka 2000), and the "mad cow" crisis (Ratzan 1998; for an anthropological review of literature on this crisis, see Lindenbaum 2001).

The interactions among the technologies of food production and processing, the physical characteristics of new foods, and consumer responses to new foods are critical determinants of dietary change, as Leach illustrates with historical examples (Leach 1999). In the contemporary period, capitalized agriculture has produced genetically engineered foods, provoking consumer reactions—particularly in Europe—that sorely merit further social-scientific examination (Murcott 1999a, 2001). For histories of agricultural biotechnology's social contexts, see Kloppenburg 1988 and Purdue 2000; for contrasting perspectives on the globalization of such technology, see Levidow 2001 and Buctuanon 2001.

Anthropologists have more commonly recognized peoples on the move—migrants, refugees, and colonizers—as agents of dietary change. Thus, Lockwood & Lockwood explore changes in the foodways of Detroit's Arab community, where not only the foods of the larger society, but also the cuisines of different ethnic groups within the community have inspired dietary shifts (Lockwood & Lockwood 2000b). By contrast, Goody's examination of Chinese migrant food focuses not on their diets, but rather on their influences on diets in the countries to which they move (Goody 1998; see also Çaglar 1999). Wilk examines the complex culinary reactions of Belizeans to colonialism, class differentiation, and modernity (Wilk 1999). Tackling colonialism from a different angle, Dennett & Connell and their commentators have stirred up debate over the effects of acculturation on the diets of aboriginal peoples (Dennett & Connell 1988).

Not only do peoples move across the globe, so also do foods (see D. Miller 1997, Long 1996, and our section "Single Commodities and Substances" above). Sobal provides a useful review of the globalization of food production and transport, drawing on the work of sociologists, political economists, demographers, and other theorists (Sobal 1999; see also McMichael 1995). Focusing by contrast on consumption, Tam explains how the eclectic, international eating style of the residents of Hong Kong helps them construct their paradoxically local identities (Tam 2001). Also studying Asia, Watson has produced a fine edited volume about the varied reactions to McDonald's of consumers in five different societies (Watson 1997).

Finally, the role of war in dietary change must not be overlooked. The following section notes the relationship between war and food insecurity. War as an agent of dietary change has also been researched by anthropologists Vargas (with physician Casillas) (1992), Mintz (1996), and Du Bois (2001), and by food historians Cwiertka (2002), Bentley (1998), Tanner (1999), and Ikpe (1994), among others. In general, however, we argue that the role of war—and the roles of many kinds of social changes—has been relatively neglected in food studies. These are areas ripe for research.

FOOD INSECURITY

Johan Pottier argues that anthropology is threatened not by "a crisis of representation, but by a problem of relevance" (1999, p. 7; emphasis in original). Anthropologists can move beyond sometimes sterile metatheoretical debates either by contributing cultural understanding to nutritional interventions (e.g., Cortes et al. 2001) or by addressing the aching, urgent problem of food insecurity (or both). Those interested in world hunger will find area-studies journals useful, along with the *IDS Bulletin*, *World Development*, *Development and Change*, the *Journal of Peasant Studies*, *Food Policy*, and *Disasters*, among many others.

Pottier has written a masterful, extended review of anthropological work on the problem of food insecurity (1999). He focuses on the social backgrounds behind food insecurity and the projects meant to alleviate it, richly exploring such varied topics as intrahousehold allocation of resources, gender inequality, peasants' risk management, effects of the Green Revolution, rural class polarization, local agricultural knowledge and meanings, constraints on small food marketers, loss of genetic diversity, and effective famine intervention. Pottier repeatedly questions conventional wisdom, suggesting avenues for detailed research in specific locales: Are intrahousehold allocations actually skewed? Is gender-separated farming always in the best interests of women? To what extent have capitalistic relations of agriculture evolved? Has the introduction of modern, scientific crops actually reduced genetic diversity? When should local famine-relief initiatives be prioritized over state initiatives? And so on.

Pottier's book is complemented by development analyst Stephen Devereux's *Theories of Famine* (1993), which explores both the weaknesses and contributions of several major theories about the causes of famine (see also de Waal 1989, which offers an ethnographic critique of standard Western definitions of famine).

Studies dealing with malnutrition among older children and adults (for young children's nutritional issues, see Van Esterik in this volume) identify a variety of reasons for food insecurity. Scheper-Hughes's wrenching ethnography of hunger in northeast Brazil lays the blame squarely on political-economic inequality (1992). Other sources explore powerful links between hunger and war, or ethnic conflict (e.g., Macrae & Zwi 1994, Chatwin 1997, Messer et al. 1998, Ogden 2000, Ikpe 1994), noting that "at the close of the 20th century, greatly enhanced capacity to anticipate and address natural disasters means that serious [acute, mass] food emergencies are almost always due to violent conflict and other human actions" (Pinstrup-Anderson, quoted in Messer et al. 1998, p. v). Still other studies find that infectious epidemics can lead to food insecurity because the most economically active individuals fall ill and networks of social exchange break down (Mtika 2001)—or the converse, that severe food shortages can lead to overcrowding and unsanitary conditions, exposing vast numbers to death from infectious diseases (de Waal 1989).

Many anthropological works on food insecurity focus on Africa. Shipton provides a valuable review for the pre-1990 literature (Shipton 1990). Notable studies have examined the difficulties in feeding African cities (Guyer 1987), African food systems in times of crisis (ecological and land tenure problems, coping mechanisms, and strategies for increasing food security—Huss-Ashmore & Katz 1989/1990), the effects of economic structural adjustment programs on African women farmers (Gladwin 1991; see also Ikpe 1994), and the value of symbolic analyses in understanding the dynamics of food insecurity (Devisch et al. 1995). Studies examining food insecurity and disease in Africa have already been noted (de Waal 1989, Mtika 2001).

More general collections of essays, covering not only Africa but also other regions, likewise address numerous topics, including food policy and development strategies (McMillan & Harlow 1991), indigenous responses to fluctuations in food supplies (including case studies in Afghanistan—de Garine & Harrison 1988), and the relationships of women farmers to agricultural commercialization (Spring 2000). Nutritional anthropologists have undertaken research on food insecurity in the United States (see Himmelgreen et al. 2000). Literature on the hotly debated issue of whether and when food is unequally distributed within households in South Asia (to the detriment of females) is ably reviewed by B. Miller (1997).

EATING AND RITUAL

Ethnographers have found multiple entry points for the study of how humans connect food to rituals, symbols, and belief systems. Food is used to comment on the sacred and to reenact venerated stories (e.g., see the francophone research on Islamic ritual sacrifice—Brisebarre 1998, Bonte et al. 1999, Kanafani-Zahar 1999). In consecrated contexts, food "binds" people to their faiths through "powerful links between food and memory" (Feeley-Harnik 1995; see Sutton 2001). Sometimes the food itself is sacred through its association with supernatural beings and processes (Bloch 1985, Feeley-Harnik 1994); the research on Hinduism is particularly rich in this regard (Singer 1984, Khare 1992, Toomey 1994).

Not only do ritual meals connect participants to invisible beings (e.g., Brown 1995), but they also perform critical social functions. Eating in ritual contexts can reaffirm or transform relationships with visible others (Munn 1986, Murphy 1986, Buitelaar 1993, Feeley-Harnik 1994, Brown 1995)—even when participants in a ritual meal bring very different religious understandings to the event (Beatty 1999). Rituals and beliefs surrounding food can also powerfully reinforce religious and ethnic boundaries (see, e.g., Mahias 1985, Bahloul 1989, Fabre-Vassas 1997).

Among the fundamental questions scholars can ask in this area are how human beliefs and rituals delineate what counts as food, and conversely, how humans use food in delineating what counts as ritual or proper belief. Addressing the first question, geographer Frederick Simoons has produced extensive studies of food taboos (1994, 1998). Simoons argues (against cultural materialist interpretations, such as M. Harris 1987, Katz 1987) that belief systems and their attendant rituals are the causal factors behind food taboos. For example, he contests the view of Katz (1987) and others that the ban against fava bean consumption among the ancient followers of Pythagoras can appropriately be invoked to support a "biocultural evolutionary" theory (Katz 1987, p. 134) of food choice. Rather than evolving as a response to any medical dangers of fava bean consumption, according to Simoons the ban on fava beans sprang from "powerful magico-religious motives" (1998, p. 215). In a related vein, Vialles's structuralist ethnography of French slaughterhouses (1994) examines how ritual and beliefs work to transform taboo items (carcasses) into food (meat) (see also Whitehead 2000 for a cogent social-relations interpretation of taboos).

The second question—how people use the act of eating as a vehicle for ritual—includes the study of food etiquette (Cooper 1986) and how such etiquette is implemented to express and create spirituality. J. Anderson's study of the religious dimensions of the Japanese tea ceremony (1991), and Curran's study of bodily discipline in the food rituals of American nuns (1989) exemplify this approach.

The invocation of deeply held values and beliefs through ritual foods has been analyzed in a variety of settings. Feeley-Harnik details the profound—and in its era, shocking—transformation of biblical symbolism among early Israelite Christians, particularly in the celebration of the Eucharist (1994). Brandes examines the relationship between sugar and Mexican rituals for the Day of the Dead, questioning the extent of these rituals' historical continuities with Aztec practices (1997). By contrast, Weismantel argues that Andean Indian practices of eating and drinking during religious fiestas do have indigenous roots, reflecting Inca beliefs about feasting as a way of nourishing the dead (1991; on food continuities and their transformations, see also Bahloul 1989, Khan 1994).

Ironically, the relationship between eating and the sacred also provides fodder for carnivalesque, ritualized anti-ritual. Kugelmass's essay on an ethnically Jewish restaurant in Manhattan that intentionally subverts the Jewish dietary laws, to comic effect, offers a fascinating example of such a process (1990).

The humor in the restaurant Kugelmass describes depends on a rich symbolic context even as it pokes fun at it. But one can argue that sometimes food rituals are not laden with symbolic meaning. Charsley contends that to his British informants, wedding cakes symbolize little more than weddings themselves (1992). He adds that what little evolution there has been in the meaning of the cake has been driven by technical changes in the cake's materiality.

Less extreme materialists have posited that primary functions of food rituals are material, even as symbolism surrounding them abounds. Following in the footsteps of Rappaport, more recent works have examined ritual as a mechanism for maintaining ecological balance in local environments and/or for redistributing food (M. Harris 1987, Voss 1987). Similarly, many scholars point out that food rituals and taboos that practitioners understand at least partly in symbolic terms often serve either to reinforce (Tapper & Tapper 1986, M. Harris 1987, Aunger 1994b, Fabre-Vassas 1997, Whitehead 2000) or to question (Lindenbaum 1986) hierarchical power relations or access to material goods. Rituals and taboos can also create divisions of labor and economic niches—sometimes even to the benefit of groups despised because of their contamination with "polluted" foodstuffs (M. Harris 1987). In all such analyses, symbolism surrounding food is evaluated as fundamentally in the service of ecological, nutritive, or political-economic ends. Such approaches can contrast with the view that meaning is a powerful human need in and of itself (Giobellina Brumana 1988)—an importance it shares with food, with which it is constantly intertwined.

EATING AND IDENTITIES

Like all culturally defined material substances used in the creation and maintenance of social relationships, food serves both to solidify group membership and to set groups apart. The works noted here deal with how food functions in social allocation, in terms of ethnicity, race, nationality, class, and (less precisely) individuality and gender. Caplan (1997, pp. 1–31) offers a useful introduction to this broad theme.

Ethnicity is born of acknowledged difference and works through contrast. Hence an ethnic cuisine is associated with a geographically and/or historically defined eating community (e.g., Lockwood & Lockwood 2000a). But ethnicity, like nationhood, is also imagined (Murcott 1996)—and associated cuisines may be imagined, too. Once imagined, such cuisines provide added concreteness to the idea of national or ethnic identity. Talking and writing about ethnic or national food can then add to a cuisine's conceptual solidity and coherence. Thus, Ferguson (1998) uses Bourdieu's "cultural field" to claim that discourse really defined French cuisine. This argument fits well, as does Cwiertka's "metacuisine" (1999), with Trubek's study (2000) of how French cuisine was created, and it brings to mind Appadurai's classic paper (1988) on how to create a national cuisine; Pilcher (1998) provides a fine example of how it happens.

Gender does not differ from these other devices of social allocation: its relationship to food and eating is at least as real as food's relationship to the construction of nationhood, ethnicity, and race. Complicating these other distinctions is the part played by class or social position. Weismantel (1989) provides an excellent case in which nationality, ethnicity, class, and gender all intermesh in food habits.

James (1994) counterposes local identity to globalization, suggesting how the global may actually reestablish the local, rather than supplant it. Tuchman & Levine (1993) analyze the urban U.S. Jewish love affair with Chinese food, throwing light on both groups. Two rare little volumes on Vietnamese food and identity (Poulain 1997, Vol. I & II) provide a brief overview of that national cuisine. Kwon & Lee (1995) do a bit of the same for Korea. Finally, Noguchi (1994), Allison (1991), and Fieldhouse (1995, pp. 215–33) together provide a nice example of how lunch—and lunch boxes—can become part of national identity.

So swiftly has the literature on food and gender grown that it could properly merit an article of its own. Relevant work published since 1984 touches on intrafamilial food allocation, familial division of labor, obesity, ethnicity, fasting, sexual identity, and many other subjects. The Counihan-Kaplan anthology (1998) provides an introduction to gender as a basis of social allocation in foodways. Kahn (1986) made a valuable early contribution to our understanding of institutionalized gender differences and their connections to food (see also Munn 1986, Whitehead

2000); Counihan's collected papers (1999) are also useful. Julier's view that food and gender is a subject tackled primarily by female authors (Julier 1999) is convincing. Van Esterik (1999) discusses gender and the right to food; McIntosh & Zey (1989) discuss woman's role as gatekeeper. D. Pollock (1985), Jansen (1997), and Flynn (1999) provide three contrastive cases of the relation of food to sexual identity.

INSTRUCTIONAL MATERIALS

The torrent of new courses on the anthropology of food has been accompanied by a flood of books, syllabi, and films about food. We can document only some of those resources, beginning with works dealing with the foods of one (very populous) society that has been better researched than most others.

When the late K.C. Chang edited the volume *Food in China* (1977), it was a trend-setting achievement in two ways: a serious analytical and historical collection on Chinese cuisine by scholars, the first of its kind in English; and a joint effort, which helped to establish a precedent in food studies. Soon more Chinese food books, as opposed to cook books, appeared, by anthropologist Eugene Anderson (1988) and geographer Frederick Simoons (1991). Additional recent collections relevant to the study of Asian cuisine include: Jun Jing's *Feeding China's Little Emperors* (2000), David Wu & Tan Chee-beng's *Changing Chinese Foodways in Asia* (2001), and Katarzyna Cwiertka & Boudewijn Walraven's *Asian Food: The Global and the Local* (2002). A course on Chinese cuisine could make good use of these sources.

The multiplication of food anthologies without a regional focus is striking. Included are sociologist Anne Murcott's *The Sociology of Food and Eating* (1983); Barbara Harriss-White & Sir Raymond Hoffenberg's *Food* (1994); and Arien Mack's *Food: Nature and Culture* (1998). Volumes by anthropologists include Carola Lentz's *Changing Food Habits* (1999); Harris & Ross's (1987) rich anthology—24 contributions on food and evolution; Carole Counihan & Steven Kaplan's *Food and Gender* (1998); Leonard Plotnicov & Richard Scaglion's *Consequences of Cultivar Diffusion* (1999); and Marie-Claire Bataille-Benguigui & Françoise Cousin's *Cuisines: reflet des sociétés* (1996). Helen Macbeth's *Food Preferences and Taste* (1997) and Martin Schaffner's *Brot, brei und was dazugehört* (1992) are two other nonanthropological anthologies, the first mostly sociological, the second mostly historical; both contain some contributions by anthropologists. The same is true of Wiessner & Schiefenhövel's *Food and the Status Quest* (1996) and Hladik et al.'s *Tropical Forests, People and Food* (1993); both contain socially, culturally, and biologically oriented essays.

We asked a student of anthropology to examine the place of food in anthropology textbooks from the 1920s to the 1990s. Her findings suggest that food had become a much more concrete and important subject by the late 1950s. In post-1955 texts, one or more chapters might be devoted to food, especially food production, often in connection with subsistence levels, and some slant toward an evolutionary treatment of society. By the 1980s, however, textbooks on the anthropology of food as such begin to appear (Farb & Armelagos 1980, MacClancy 1992). The textbook by Bryant et al. (1985) links nutrition and anthropology closely, as does the anthology edited by Sharman et al. (1991). The readers by Counihan & van Esterik (1997) and by Goodman et al. (2000) are entitled *Food and Culture*, and *Nutritional Anthropology*; their contents overlap.

Lieberman & Sorensen (1997) have edited an invaluable collection of syllabi for courses in nutritional anthropology, including a list of useful films, now available in PDF format from the Council on Nutritional Anthropology of the American Anthropological Association. The welter of food-related materials provides prospective course planners with ample material, but the courses themselves appear to be more clearly organized within nutritional anthropology than otherwise.

It appears, though, that sociologists have done even more than anthropologists. Among the many textbooks on the sociology of food, we should mention Mennell et al. (1992), Fieldhouse (1995), Whit (1995), McIntosh (1996), Fine et al. (1996), and Beardsworth & Keil (1997). It seems likely that there will be more textbooks and readers yet to come.

CONCLUDING REMARKS

The staggering increase in the scale of food literature—inside and outside anthropology—makes bibliographic coverage challenging, a challenge compounded by the close intertwining of food and eating with so many other subjects. We posit that three major trends this last quarter century or so have influenced this growth: globalization; the general affluence of Western societies and their growing cosmopolitanism; and the inclusivist tendencies of U.S. society, which spurs even disciplines (and professions, such as journalism and business) without anthropology's strong inclusivist ethic to consider cross-cultural variations in foodways. A vast literature on food and globalization has appeared. Philosophers ponder whether they are exploiting the Third World by eating its foods. Culinary competence in the West declines at almost the same rate as discrimination in taste rises. Social scientists have examined the eating habits of Westerners in terms of ethnic group, region, religion, and much else—though relatively little, it seems, in terms of class (but see Roseberry 1996). Much remains to be done in exploring foodways in other areas of the world. In this setting, anthropologists are in a good position to make useful contributions to the development of policy in regard to health and nutrition, food inspection, the relation of food to specific cultures, world hunger, and other subjects. By and large, though, they have not taken full advantage of this opportunity.

ACKNOWLEDGMENTS

Although we are quite appreciative, we are unable to thank here all the colleagues who sent us suggestions, vitas, syllabi, and copies of their work. We do wish, however, to thank two students: Amy Delamaide and Jomo Smith.

The *Annual Review of Anthropology* is online at http://anthro.annualreviews.org

LITERATURE CITED

Agric. Netw. Inf. Cent. 2000. http://www.agnic.org

Allison A. 1991. Japanese mothers and *obentos*: the lunch-box as ideological state apparatus. *Anthropol. Q.* 64(4):195–208

Anderson EN. 1988. *The Food of China*. New Haven, CT: Yale Univ. Press

Anderson J. 1991. *An Introduction to Japanese Tea Ritual*. Albany: State Univ. N.Y. Press

Anigbo OA. 1987. *Commensality and Human Relationship Among the Igbo*. Nsukka: Univ. Nigeria Press

Appadurai A. 1988. How to make a national cuisine: cookbooks in contemporary India. *Comp. Stud. Soc. Hist.* 30(1):3–24

Archetti E. 1997 (1992). *Guinea-Pigs: Food, Symbol, and Conflict of Knowledge in Ecuador*. Oxford: Berg

Aristides [Epstein J]. 1978. Foodstuff and nonsense. *Am. Scholar* 47(2):157–63

Aunger R. 1994a. Sources of variation in ethnographic interview data: food avoidances in the Ituri Forest, Zaire. *Ethnology* 33(1):65–99

Aunger R. 1994b. Are food avoidances maladaptive in the Ituri Forest of Zaire? *J. Anthropol. Res.* 50:277–310

Bahloul J. 1989. From a Muslim banquet to a Jewish seder: foodways and ethnicity among North African Jews. In *Jews Among Arabs: Contacts and Boundaries*, ed. MR Cohen, AL Udovitch, pp. 85–96. Princeton, NJ: Darwin

Bataille Benguigui M, Cousin F, eds. 1996. *Cuisines: Reflets des Sociétés*. Paris: Éd. Sépia, Musée de l'Homme

Beardsworth A, Keil T. 1997. *Sociology on the Menu: an Invitation to the Study of Food and Society*. London: Routledge

Beatty A. 1999. *Varieties of Javanese Religion: an Anthropological Account*. Cambridge, UK: Cambridge Univ. Press

Belasco WJ. 1987. Ethnic fast foods: the corporate melting pot. *Food Foodways* 2:1–30

Belasco WJ. 1989. *Appetite for Change: How the Counterculture Took on the Food Industry, 1966–1988*. New York: Pantheon

Bentley A. 1998. *Eating for Victory: Food Rationing and the Politics of Domesticity*. Urbana: Univ. Ill. Press

Bestor TC. 1999. Wholesale sushi: culture and commodity in Tokyo's tuna market. In *Theorizing the City*, ed. S Low, pp. 201–42. New Brunswick, NJ: Rutgers Univ. Press

Bestor TC. 2001. Supply-side sushi: commodity, market, and the global city. *Am. Anthropol.* 103(1):76–95

Bliege Bird R, Bird D. 1997. Delayed reciprocity and tolerated theft. *Curr. Anthropol.* 38 (1):49–78

Bloch M. 1985. Almost eating the ancestors. *Man* (n.s.) 20:631–46

Boas F. 1921. *Ethnology of the Kwakiutl*. 35th Annu. Rep. Bur. Am. Ethnol. Washington, DC: US GPO

Bonte P, Brisebarre A, Gokalp A, eds. 1999. *Sacrifices en Islam: Espaces et Temps d'un Rituel*. Paris: Éd. CNRS

Boster JS, Weller SC. 1990. Cognitive and contextual variation in hot-cold classification. *Am. Anthropol.* 92:171–79

Brandes S. 1992. Maize as a culinary mystery. *Ethnology* 31:331–36

Brandes S. 1997. Sugar, colonialism, and death: on the origins of Mexico's Day of the Dead. *Comp. Stud. Soc. Hist.* 39(2):270–99

Brisebarre A, ed. 1998. *La Fête du Mouton: Un Sacrifice Musulman dans l'Espace Urbain*. Paris: Éd. CNRS

Brown KM. 1995. Serving the spirits: the ritual economy of Haitian Vodou. In *Sacred Arts of Haitian Vodou*, ed. DJ Cosentino, pp. 205–23. Los Angeles: UCLA Fowler Mus. Cult. Hist.

Brown LK, Mussell K, eds. 1984. *Ethnic and Regional Foodways in the United States: the Performance of Group Identity*. Knoxville: Univ. Tenn. Press

Bryant CA, Courtney A, Markesbery BA, DeWalt KM. 1985. *The Cultural Feast: an Introduction to Food and Society*. St. Paul, MN: West

Buctuanon EM. 2001. Globalization of biotechnology: the agglomeration of dispersed knowledge and information and its implications for the political economy of technology in developing countries. *New Genet. Soc.* 20(1):26–41

Buitelaar M. 1993. *Fasting and Feasting in Morocco: Women's Participation in Ramadan*. Oxford: Berg

Çaglar AS. 1999. *McDöner: döner kebap* and the social positioning struggle of German Turks. See Lentz 1999, pp. 209–30

Campbell H, Liepins R. 2001. Naming organics: understanding organic standards in New Zealand as a discursive field. *Sociol. Rural.* 41(1):21–39

Caplan P. 1997. Approaches to the study of food, health and identity. In *Food, Health and Identity*, ed. P Caplan, pp. 1–31. London/New York: Routledge

Chang KC. 1977. *Food in China*. New Haven, CT: Yale Univ. Press

Charsley SR. 1992. *Wedding Cakes and Cultural History*. New York: Routledge

Chatwin ME. 1997. *Socio-Cultural Transformation and Foodways in the Republic of Georgia*. Commack, NY: Nova Sci.

Codere H. 1957. Kwakiutl society: rank and class. *Am. Anthropol.* 59(3):473–86

Coe SD. 1994. *America's First Cuisines*. Austin: Univ. Tex. Press

Coe SD, Coe MD. 1996. *The True History of Chocolate*. London: Thames & Hudson

Cooper E. 1986. Chinese table manners: you are *how* you eat. *Hum. Organ.* 45(2):179–84

Cortes LM, Gittelsohn J, Alfred J, Palafox NA. 2001. Formative research to inform intervention development for diabetes prevention in the Republic of the Marshall Islands. *Health Educ. Behav.* 28(6):696–715

Counihan CM. 1999. *The Anthropology of Food and Body: Gender, Meaning, and Power*. New York: Routledge

Counihan CM, Kaplan SL, eds. 1998. *Food and Gender: Identity and Power*. Amsterdam, The Neth.: Harwood Acad.

Counihan CM, Van Esterik P, eds. 1997. *Food and Culture: a Reader*. New York/London: Routledge

Curran P. 1989. *Grace Before Meals: Food Ritual and Body Discipline in Convent Culture*. Urbana: Univ. Ill. Press

Cushing FH. 1920. Zuñi breadstuffs. *Indian Notes and Monographs*, 8. New York: Mus. Am. Indian, Heye Found.

Cwiertka KJ. 1999. *The making of modern culinary tradition in Japan*. PhD thesis. Univ. Leiden

Cwiertka KJ. 2000. From Yokohama to Amsterdam: Meidi-Ya and dietary change in modern Japan. *Japanstudien* 12:45–63

Cwiertka KJ. 2002. Popularising a military diet in wartime and postwar Japan. *Asian Anthropol.* 1(1). In press

Cwiertka KJ, Walraven B, eds. 2002. *Asian Food: the Global and the Local*. Surrey, UK: Curzon

Davidson A, ed. 1999. *The Oxford Companion to Food*. Oxford: Oxford Univ. Press

de Garine I, Harrison GA, eds. 1988. *Coping with Uncertainty in Food Supply*. Oxford: Clarendon

Dennett G, Connell J. 1988. Acculturation and health in the highlands of Papua New Guinea: dissent on diversity, diets, and development. *Curr. Anthropol.* 29(2):273–99

Devereux S. 1993. *Theories of Famine*. New York: Harvester Wheatsheaf

Devisch R, de Boeck F, Jonckers D, eds. 1995. *Alimentations, Traditions, et Développements en Afrique Intertropicale*. Paris: Éd. L'Harmattan

de Waal A. 1989. *Famine that Kills: Darfur, Sudan, 1984–1985*. Oxford: Clarendon

Dirks R. 1988. Annual rituals of conflict. *Am. Anthropol.* 90:856–70

Dirks R. 2002. Resources for the anthropological study of food habits. http://lilt.ilstu.edu/rtdirks

Douglas M. 1966. *Purity and Danger*. New York: Praeger

Du Bois CM. 2001. A specific legume case:

history of soy and soy protein products in the USA. http://www.jhsph.edu/environment/CLF_conferences/Dietary_DuBois.html

Ember M, Ember CR. 1994. Prescriptions for peace: policy implications of cross-cultural research on war and interpersonal violence. *Cross-Cult. Res.* 28(4):343–50

Fabre-Vassas C. 1997. *The Singular Beast: Jews, Christians, and the Pig.* New York: Columbia Univ. Press

Farb P, Armelagos G. 1980. *Consuming Passions: the Anthropology of Eating.* Boston: Houghton-Mifflin

Feeley-Harnik G. 1994. *The Lord's Table: the Meaning of Food in Early Judaism and Christianity.* Washington, DC: Smithson. Inst. 2nd ed.

Feeley-Harnik G. 1995. Religion and food: an anthropological perspective. *J. Am. Acad. Relig.* 63(3):565–82

Ferguson PP. 1998. A cultural field in the making: gastronomy in 19th- century France. *Am. J. Sociol.* 104(3):597–641

Fiddes N. 1991. *Meat: a Natural Symbol.* London: Routledge

Fieldhouse P. 1995. *Food and Nutrition: Customs and Culture.* London: Chapman & Hall. 2nd ed.

Fine B, Heasman M, Wright J. 1996. *Consumption in the Age of Affluence: the World of Food.* London: Routledge

Flandrin JL, Montanari M, eds. 1999. *Food: a Culinary History from Antiquity to the Present.* New York: Columbia Univ. Press

Flynn KC. 1999. Food, gender and survival among street adults in Mwanza, Tanzania. *Food Foodways* 8(3):175–201

Foster N, Cordell LS, eds. 1992. *Chilies to Chocolate: Food the Americas Gave the World.* Tucson: Univ. Ariz. Press

Froment A, de Garine I, Binam Bikoi C, Loung JF, eds. 1996. *Bien Manger et Bien Vivre: Anthropologie Alimentaire et Développement en Afrique Intertropicale: Du Biologique au Social.* Paris: L'Harmattan Orstom

Gade DW. 1994. Environment, culture and diffusion: the broad bean in Quebec. *Cah. Géogr. Québec* 38(104):137–50

Gade DW. 1999. *Nature and Culture in the Andes.* Madison: Univ. Wis. Press

Giobellina Brumana F. 1988. La comida de santo en el candomble. *Am. Indígena* 48(3): 605–17

Gladwin CH, ed. 1991. *Structural Adjustment and African Women Farmers.* Gainesville: Univ. Fla. Press

Goodman AH, Dufour DL, Pelto GH, eds. 2000. *Nutritional Anthropology: Biocultural Perspectives on Food and Nutrition.* Mountain View, CA: Mayfield

Goody J. 1982. *Cooking, Cuisine and Class: a Study in Comparative Sociology.* Cambridge, UK: Cambridge Univ. Press

Goody J. 1998. The globalisation of Chinese food. In *Food and Love: a Cultural History of East and West*, pp. 161–71. London: Verso

Guyer J, ed. 1987. *Feeding African Cities: Studies in Regional Social History.* Bloomington: Ind. Univ. Press

Harris M. 1987. Foodways: historical overview and theoretical prolegomenon. See Harris & Ross 1987, pp. 57–90

Harris M. 1998 [1985]. *Good to Eat: Riddles of Food and Culture.* Prospect Heights, IL: Waveland. 2nd ed.

Harris M, Ross EB, eds. 1987. *Food and Evolution: Toward a Theory of Human Food Habits.* Phila.: Temple Univ. Press

Harris R. 1996. *An Index to the Proceedings of the Oxford Symposium on Food and Cookery, 1981–1994.* Devon, UK: Prospect

Harriss-White B, Hoffenberg R, eds. 1994. *Food: Interdisciplinary Perspectives.* Oxford: Blackwell

Hawkes K. 1991. Showing off: tests of an hypothesis about men's foraging goals. *Ethol. Sociobiol.* 2:29–54

Himmelgreen DA, Pérez-Escamilla R, Segura-Millán S, Peng YK, Gonzalez A, et al. 2000. Food insecurity among low-income Hispanics in Hartford, Connecticut: implications for public health policy. *Hum. Organ.* 59(3):334–42

Hine T. 1995. *The Total Package: the Secret History and Hidden Meanings of Boxes,*

Bottles, Cans, and Other Persuasive Containers. Boston: Back Bay

Hladik CM, Hladik A, Linares OF, Pagezy H, Semply A, Hadley M. 1993. *Tropical Forests, People and Food*. Paris: UNESCO

Humphrey TC, Humphrey LT, eds. 1988. *'We Gather Together': Food and Festival in American Life*. Ann Arbor: UMI Res.

Huss-Ashmore R, Katz SH, eds. 1989/1990. *African Food Systems in Crisis*, Vols. I, II. New York: Gordon & Breach

Ikpe EB. 1994. *Food and Society in Nigeria: a History of Food Customs, Food Economy and Cultural Change, 1900–1989*. Stuttgart: Franz Steiner Verlag

James A. 1994. Cuisiner les livres: identités globales ou locales dans les cultures. *Anthropol. Soc.* 18(3):39–56

Jansen W. 1997. Gender identity and the rituals of food in a Jordanian community. *Food Foodways* 7(2):87–117

Jenkins VS. 2000. *Bananas: an American History*. Washington, DC: Smithson. Inst.

Jing J, ed. 2000. *Feeding China's Little Emperors: Food, Children, and Social Change*. Stanford, CA: Stanford Univ. Press

Julier AP. 1999. Hiding gender and race in the discourse of commercial food consumption. Presented at Annu. Meet. Assoc. Stud. Food Soc., Toronto

Kahn M. 1986. *Always Hungry, Never Greedy: Food and the Expression of Gender in a Melanesian Society*. Cambridge, UK: Cambridge Univ. Press

Kahn M, Sexton L, eds. 1988. *Continuity and Change in Pacific Foodways*, special issue *Food Foodways* 3(1–2)

Kanafani A. 1983. *Aesthetics and Ritual in the United Arab Emirates*. Lebanon: Am. Univ. Beirut

Kanafani-Zahar A. 1999. *Le Mouton et le Mûrier: Rituel du Sacrifice dans la Montagne Libanaise*. Paris: Presses Univ. France

Kaplan H, Hill K. 1985. Food sharing among Ache foragers: tests of explanatory hypotheses. *Curr. Anthropol.* 26:223–46

Katz SH. 1987. Fava bean consumption: a case for the co-evolution of genes and culture. See Harris & Ross 1987, pp. 133–59

Katz SH, ed. 2002. *The Scribner Encyclopedia of Food*. New York: Scribner's

Khan A. 1994. *Juthaa* in Trinidad: food, pollution, and hierarchy in a Caribbean diaspora community. *Am. Ethnol.* 21(2):245–69

Khare RS, ed. 1992. *The Eternal Food: Gastronomic Ideas and Experiences of Hindus and Buddhists*. Albany: State Univ. N.Y. Press

Khare RS, Rao MSA, eds. 1986. *Aspects in South Asia Food Systems: Food, Society and Culture*. Durham: Carolina Acad.

Kiple K, Ornelas K, eds. 2000. *The Cambridge World History of Food*. Cambridge, UK: Cambridge Univ. Press

Kloppenburg JR. 1988. *First the Seed: the Political Economy of Plant Biotechnology, 1492–2000*. Cambridge, UK: Cambridge Univ. Press

Kugelmass J. 1990. Green bagels: an essay on food, nostalgia, and the carnivalesque. *YIVO Annu.* 19:57–80

Kurlansky M. 2002. *Salt: a World History*. New York: Walker

Kwon SSY, Lee CH, eds. 1995. The wisdom of Korean food. *Korean Am. Stud.* Bull. 6

Leach HM. 1999. Food processing technology: its role in inhibiting or promoting change in staple foods. In *The Prehistory of Food*, ed. C Gosden, J Hather, pp. 129–38. London: Routledge

Leach HM. 2001. Rehabilitating 'the stinkinge herbe': a case study of culinary prejudice. *Gastronomica* 1(2):10–15

Leitch A. 2000. The social life of *lardo*: slow food in fast times. *Asia Pac. J. Anthropol.* 1: 103–18

Lentz C, ed. 1999. *Changing Food Habits: Case Studies from Africa, South America, and Europe*. Amsterdam: Harwood Acad.

Levenstein H. 1993. *Paradox of Plenty: a Social History of Eating in Modern America*. Oxford: Oxford Univ. Press

Levidow L. 2001. Utilitarian bioethics?: market fetishism in the GM crops debate. *New Genet. Soc.* 20(1):75–84

Lévi-Strauss C. 1965. Le triangle culinaire. *L'Arc* 26:19–29

Lieberman LS, Sorensen MV, eds. 1997. SNAC II: Syllabi for Courses in Nutritional Anthropology. 2nd ed. http://www.aaanet.org/cna/index.htm

Lindenbaum S. 1986. Rice and wheat: the meaning of food in Bangladesh. See Khare & Rao 1986, pp. 253–76

Lindenbaum S. 2001. Kuru, prions, and human affairs: thinking about epidemics. *Annu. Rev. Anthropol.* 30:363–85

Lockwood WG, Lockwood YR. 2000a. Finnish American milk products in the northwoods. In *Milk: Beyond Dairy*, ed. H Walker. *Proc. Oxford Symp. Food Cookery 1999*, pp. 232–39

Lockwood WG, Lockwood YR. 2000b. Continuity and adaptation in Arab American foodways. In *Arab Detroit: From Margin to Mainstream*, ed. N Abraham, A Shryock, pp. 515–59. Detroit: Wayne State Univ. Press

Long J, ed. 1996. *Conquista y Comida: Consecuencias del Encuentro de Dos Mundos.* Mexico City: Univ. Nacional Autónoma México

Long-Solís J. 1986. *Capsicum y Cultura: La Historia del Chilli.* México: Fondo Cultura Econ.

Macbeth H, ed. 1997. *Food Preferences and Taste: Continuity and Change.* Providence, RI: Berghahn

MacClancy J. 1992. *Consuming Culture.* New York: Holt & Co

Mack A, ed. 1998. Food: nature and culture. *Soc. Res.* 66(1):3–428 (Special issue)

Macrae J, Zwi A, eds. 1994. *War & Hunger: Rethinking International Responses to Complex Emergencies.* London: Zed

Mahias MC. 1985. *Délivrance et Convivialité: le Système Culinaire des Jaina.* Paris: Ed. Maison Sci. l'Homme

Malagón J. 1990. *Historia y Leyenda del Mazapán.* México: San Angel Ed.

Mallery G. 1888. Manners and meals. *Am. Anthropol.* 1(3):193–207

Manderson L, ed. 1986. *Shared Wealth and Symbol: Food, Culture, and Society in Oceania and Southeast Asia.* New York: Cambridge Univ. Press

Matossian MK. 1989. *Poisons of the Past: Molds, Epidemics, and History.* New Haven, CT: Yale Univ. Press

Mayer A. 1996. Caste in an Indian village: change and continuity 1954–1992. In *Caste Today*, ed. CJ Fuller, pp. 32–64. Delhi: Oxford Univ. Press

McIntosh WA. 1996. *Sociologies of Food and Nutrition.* London: Plenum

McIntosh WA. 2000. The symbolization of eggs in American culture: a sociologic analysis. *J. Am. Coll. Nutr.* 19(5):S532–39

McIntosh WA, Zey M. 1989. Women as gatekeepers of food consumption: a sociological critique. *Food Foodways* 3(4):317–32

McMichael P, ed. 1995. *Food and Agrarian Orders in the World-Economy.* Westport, CT: Greenwood

McMillan DE, Harlow J, eds. 1991. *Anthropology and Food Policy: Human Dimensions of Food Policy in Africa and Latin America.* Athens: Univ. Ga. Press

Mennell S. 1985. *All Manners of Food: Eating and Taste in England and France from the Middle Ages to the Present.* Oxford: Blackwell

Mennell S, Murcott A, van Otterloo AH. 1992. *The Sociology of Food: Eating, Diet and Culture.* London: Sage

Messer E. 1984. Anthropological perspectives on diet. *Annu. Rev. Anthropol.* 13:205–49

Messer E. 1997. Three centuries of changing European taste for the potato. See Macbeth 1997, pp. 101–14

Messer E, Cohen MJ, D'Costa J. 1998. *Food From Peace: Breaking the Links Between Conflict and Hunger.* Washington, DC: Int. Food Policy Res. Inst.

Miller BD. 1997. Social class, gender, and intrahousehold food allocations to children in South Asia. *Soc. Sci. Med.* 44(11):1685–95

Miller D. 1997. *Capitalism: an Ethnographic Approach.* New York: Berg

Mintz SW. 1985. *Sweetness and Power: the Place of Sugar in Modern History.* New York: Penguin

Mintz SW. 1996. *Tasting Food, Tasting Freedom*. Boston: Beacon

Moore H, Vaughan M. 1994. *Cutting Down Trees: Gender, Nutrition, and Agricultural Change in the Northern Province of Zambia, 1890–1990*. Portsmouth, NH: Heinemann

Morales E. 1995. *The Guinea Pig: Healing, Food, and Ritual in the Andes*. Tucson: Univ. Ariz. Press

Mtika MM. 2001. The AIDS epidemic in Malawi and its threat to household food security. *Hum. Organ.* 60(2):178–88

Munn ND. 1986. *The Fame of Gawa: a Symbolic Study of Value Transformation in a Massim (Papua New Guinea) Society*. Cambridge, UK: Cambridge Univ. Press

Murcott A, ed. 1983. *The Sociology of Food and Eating*. Aldershot, Hants, UK: Gower

Murcott A. 1988. Sociological and social anthropological approaches to food and eating. *World Rev. Nutr. Diet.* 55:1–40

Murcott A. 1996. Food as an expression of identity. In *The Future of the National State: Essays on Cultural Pluralism and Political Integration*, ed. S Gustafsson, L Lewin, pp. 49–77. Stockholm: Nerenius & Santerus

Murcott A, ed. 1998. *'The Nation's Diet': the Social Science of Food Choice*. London: Longman

Murcott A. 1999a. 'Not science but PR': GM food and the makings of a considered sociology. *Soc. Res. Online* 4(3)

Murcott A. 1999b. Scarcity in abundance: food and non-food. *Soc. Res.* 66(1):305–39

Murcott A. 2001. Public beliefs about GM foods: more on the makings of a considered sociology. *Med. Anthropol. Q.* 15(1):1–11

Murphy CPH. 1986. Piety and honor: the meaning of Muslim feasts in Old Delhi. See Khare & Rao 1986, pp. 85–120

Nichter M. 1986. Modes of food classification and the diet-health contingency: a South Indian case study. See Khare & Rao 1986, pp. 185–222

Noguchi P. 1994. Savor slowly: *EKIBEN*–the fast food of high-speed Japan. *Ethnology* 33(4):317–30

Ogden K. 2000. Coping strategies developed as a result of social structure and conflict: Kosovo in the 1990s. *Disasters* 24(2):117–32

Ohnuki-Tierney E. 1993. *Rice as Self: Japanese Identities Through Time*. Princeton, NJ: Princeton Univ. Press

Orlove BS. 1997. Meat and strength: the moral economy of a food riot. *Cult. Anthropol.* 12(2):234–68

Pelto GH, Vargas LA, eds. 1992. *Perspectives on Dietary Change: Studies in Nutrition and Society–Ecol. Food Nutr.* 27(3–4):1–335 (Special issue)

Pilcher JM. 1998. *¡Que Vivan los Tamales!* Albuquerque: Univ. N.M. Press

Pillsbury R. 1998. *No Foreign Food: the American Diet in Time and Place*. Boulder, CO: Westview

Plotnicov L, Scaglion R, eds. 1999. *Consequences of Cultivar Diffusion. Ethnol. Monogr. 17*. Pittsburgh, PA: Univ. Pittsburgh Press

Poggie JJ. 1995. Food resource periodicity and cooperation values: a cross-cultural consideration. *Cross-Cult. Res.* 29(3):276–96

Pollock DK. 1985. Food and sexual identity among the Culina. *Food Foodways* 1(1):25–42

Pollock N. 1992. *These Roots Remain: Food Habits in Islands of the Central and Eastern Pacific*. Laie, Hawaii: Inst. Polyn. Stud.

Pottier J. 1999. *Anthropology of Food: the Social Dynamics of Food Security*. Malden, MA: Blackwell

Poulain JP, ed. 1997. *Eating And Drinking Habits And Cultural Identity (I) and (II). Vietnam. Stud.* (n.s.) 55(3):5–190, 55(4):5–251

Purdue DA. 2000. *Anti-GenetiX: the Emergence of the Anti-GM Movement*. Aldershot, UK: Ashgate

Ratzan SC, ed. 1998. *The Mad Cow Crisis: Health and the Public Good*. New York: N.Y. Univ. Press

Richards AI. 1939. *Land, Labour, and Diet in Northern Rhodesia: an Economic Study of the Bemba Tribe*. London: Oxford Univ. Press

Roseberry W. 1996. The rise of yuppie coffees

and the reimagination of class in the United States. *Am. Anthropol.* 98(4):762–75
Ross EB. 1980. Patterns of diet and forces of production: an economic and ecological history of the ascendancy of beef in the United States. In *Beyond the Myths of Culture: Essays in Cultural Materialism*, ed. E Ross, pp. 181–225. San Francisco: Academic
Sahlins M. 1976. *Culture and Practical Reason.* Chicago, IL: Univ. Chicago Press
Salaman RN. 1949. *History and Social Influence of the Potato.* Cambridge, UK: Cambridge Univ. Press
Schaffner M, ed. 1992. *Brot, Brei und Was Dazugehört.* Zürich: Chronos Verlag
Scheper-Hughes N. 1992. *Death Without Weeping: the Violence of Everyday Life in Brazil.* Berkeley: Univ. Calif. Press
Sharman A, Theophano J, Curtis K, Messer E, eds. 1991. *Diet and Domestic Life in Society.* Phila.: Temple Univ. Press
Shipton P. 1990. African famines and food security: anthropological perspectives. *Annu. Rev. Anthropol.* 19:353–94
Simoons FJ. 1991. *Food in China: a Cultural and Historical Inquiry.* Boston: CRC
Simoons FJ. 1994. *Eat Not This Flesh: Food Avoidances from Prehistory to the Present.* Madison: Univ. Wis. Press. 2nd ed.
Simoons FJ. 1998. *Plants of Life, Plants of Death.* Madison: Univ. Wis. Press
Singer EA. 1984. Conversion through foodways enculturation: the meaning of eating in an American Hindu sect. See Brown & Mussell 1984, pp. 195–214
Smith AF. 1994. *The Tomato in America: Early History, Culture and Cookery.* Columbia: Univ. S. Carolina Press
Smith WR. 1889. *Lectures on the Religion of the Semites.* New York: Appleton
Sobal J. 1999. Food system globalization, eating transformations, and nutrition transitions. In *Food in Global History*, ed. R Grew, pp. 171-93. Boulder, CO: Westview
Spring A, ed. 2000. *Women Farmers and Commercial Ventures: Increasing Food Security in Developing Countries.* Boulder, CO: Rienner
Sutton D. 2001. *Remembrance of Repasts: an Anthropology of Food and Memory.* Oxford: Berg
Tam SM. 2001. Lost and found?: reconstructing Hong Kong identity in the idiosyncrasy and syncretism of *yumcha*. See Wu & Tan 2001, pp. 49–70
Tanner J. 1999. The rationing system, food policy, and nutritional science during the Second World War: a comparative view of Switzerland. See Lentz 1999, pp. 211–42
Tapper R, Tapper N. 1986. 'Eat this, it'll do you a power of good': food and commensality among Durrani Pashtuns. *Am. Ethnol.* 13(1):62–79
Teuteberg HJ, ed. 1992. *European Food History: a Research Review.* New York: Leicester Univ. Press
Thomas B. 1992. The Utah school of evolutionary ecology: a cost-benefit and materialist-functional veneer of superstructure. *Dialect. Anthropol.* 17:413–28
Toomey P. 1994. *Food from the Mouth of Krishna: Feasts and Festivities in a North Indian Pilgrimage Centre.* Delhi: Hindustan
Toussaint-Samat M. 1992. *A History of Food.* Cambridge, MA: Blackwell
Trankell IB. 1995. *Cooking, Care, and Domestication: a Culinary Ethnography of the Tai Yong, Northern Thailand.* Sweden: Uppsala Univ. Press
Trubek AB. 2000. *Haute Cuisine: How the French Invented the Culinary Profession.* Phila.: Univ. Penn. Press
Tuchman G, Levine HG. 1993. New York Jews and Chinese food: the social construction of an ethnic pattern. *J. Contemp. Ethnog.* 22(3):362–407
UN Food Agric. Organ. 2001. http://www.fao.org
US Dep. Agric. 2001. http://www.usda.gov, http://usda.mannlib.cornell.edu
Van Esterik P. 1999. Right to food; right to feed; right to be fed: the intersection of women's rights and the right to food. *Agric. Hum. Values* 16:225–32
Vargas LA, Casillas LE. 1992. Diet and

foodways in Mexico City. See Pelto & Vargas 1992, pp. 235–47
Vialles N. 1994. *Animal to Edible*. Cambridge, UK: Cambridge Univ. Press
Viola HJ, Margolis C, eds. 1991. *Seeds of Change: Five Hundred Years Since Columbus*. Washington, DC: Smithson. Inst.
Voss J. 1987. The politics of pork and the rituals of rice: redistributive feasting and commodity circulation in northern Luzon, Philippines. In *Beyond the New Economic Anthropology*, ed. J Clammer, pp. 121–41. New York: Macmillan
Warman A. 1988. *La Historia de un Bastardo: Maíz y Capitalismo*. Mexico City: Fondo Cultura Econ.
Wassmann J. 1993. When actions speak louder than words: the classification of food among the Yupno of Papua New Guinea. *Q. Newslett. Lab. Comp. Hum. Cogn.* 15(1):30–40
Watson JL, ed. 1997. *Golden Arches East: McDonald's in East Asia*. Stanford, CA: Stanford Univ. Press
Weismantel MJ. 1988. *Food, Gender, and Poverty in the Ecuadorian Andes*. Phila.: Univ. Penn. Press
Weismantel MJ. 1989. The children cry for bread: hegemony and the transformation of consumption. In *The Social Economy of Consumption*, ed. HJ Rutz, BS Orlove, pp. 85–100. Lanham, MD: Univ. Press Am.
Weismantel MJ. 1991. Maize beer and Andean social transformations: drunken Indians, bread babies, and chosen women. *MLN* 106(4):861–79
Weston RO, ed. 1992. *Cultura, Identidad, y Cocina en el Perú*. Peru: Univ. San Martín de Porres
Whit WC. 1995. *Food and Society: a Sociological Approach*. Dix Hills, NY: General Hall
Whitehead H. 2000. *Food Rules: Hunting, Sharing, and Tabooing Game in Papua New Guinea*. Ann Arbor: Univ. Mich. Press
Wiessner P, Schiefenhövel W, eds. 1996. *Food and the Status Quest: an Interdisciplinary Perspective*. Providence, RI: Berghahn
Wilk RR. 1999. 'Real Belizean food': building local identity in the transnational Caribbean. *Am. Anthropol.* 101(2):244–55
Willard P. 2001. *Saffron*. Boston: Beacon
Wood B, Hill K. 2000. A test of the 'showing-off' hypothesis with Ache hunters. *Curr. Anthropol.* 41(1):124–25
Wood RC. 1995. *The Sociology of the Meal*. Edinburgh: Edinburgh Univ. Press
Wu DYH, Tan CB, eds. 2001. *Changing Chinese Foodways in Asia*. Hong Kong: Chinese Univ. Press
Ziker JP. 1998. Kinship and exchange among the Dolgan and Nganasan of Northern Siberia. *Res. Econ. Anthropol.* 19:191–238
Zubaida S, Tapper R, eds. 1994. *Culinary Cultures of the Middle East*. London: Tauris

Annu. Rev. Anthropol. 2002. 31:121–45
doi: 10.1146/annurev.anthro.31.032902.105935

First published online as a Review in Advance on May 7, 2002

DISCOURSE FORMS AND PROCESSES IN INDIGENOUS LOWLAND SOUTH AMERICA: An Areal-Typological Perspective

Christine Beier, Lev Michael, and Joel Sherzer
Department of Anthropology, University of Texas at Austin, Austin, Texas 78712-1086; email: cmbeier@mail.utexas.edu; lmichael@mail.utexas.edu; jsherzer@mail.utexas.edu

Key Words Amazonia, language change, linguistic area, discourse area, ethnography of speaking

■ **Abstract** In indigenous lowland South America there are several discourse forms and processes that are shared by groups of people of distinct genetic linguistic affiliations; this leads us to posit this large region, which we label greater Amazonia, as a discourse area, a concept that parallels the notion of linguistic area. The discourse forms and processes we examine are ceremonial dialogue, dialogical performance, templatic ratifying, echo speech, ceremonial greeting, ritual wailing, evidentiality, speech reporting practices, parallelism, special languages, and shamanistic language use. We hypothesize that in lowland South America, discourse is the matrix for linguistic diffusion, i.e., that linguistic areas emerge within discourse areas. What we propose then is a discourse-centered approach to language change and history, parallel to a discourse-centered approach to language structure and use. Our survey includes a plea for a careful archiving of recorded and written materials dealing with lowland South American discourse.

INTRODUCTION

This review presents an overview of discourse forms and processes in indigenous lowland South America from an areal-typological perspective. The areal-typological approach to language complements the body of scholarship on genetic relationships among languages and provides another view of history particularly appropriate to indigenous South America. The areal-typological perspective assumes contact between groups within geographic areas and across genetic language boundaries and assumes that intergroup social contact can lead to language change. The growing body of scholarship on South American discourse provides a basis for extending the areal-typological approach to the realm of discourse. This leads us to propose that a significant part of indigenous lowland South America is a discourse area, a region in which particular discourse forms and processes become shared owing to their diffusion between societies.

In the overview presented here, we outline the areas of research that support this view and suggest a number of avenues for future research from within this perspective. Research on discourse processes in indigenous lowland South America is entering an exciting new phase, owing to the growth of interest in discourse on the part of Latin American scholars and the development of new research tools that promise to make discourse-oriented research considerably easier. At present, several web-based archives are being developed that have the potential to profoundly change the nature of discourse-oriented research concerning indigenous Latin American languages and societies. One of the first archives now online, the Archive of the Indigenous Languages of Latin America (AILLA; http://www.ailla.org), will enable researchers and members of indigenous communities to archive and access both audio and textual data of naturally occurring discourse. Data of this sort have previously been very difficult to make available and to share. The centralization of these data, combined with the ease of searching and accessing them through a resource such as AILLA, promises to increase the comparative research carried out on indigenous Latin American discourse and areal-typological research in particular. Similar projects focusing on indigenous languages of Mexico and Venezuela are being planned, and the Max Planck Institute for Psycholinguistics is developing an archive for the DOBES project (http://www.mpi.nl/DOBES), a documentation project for endangered languages, which will include materials from indigenous Latin American languages.

This review of current knowledge of discourse forms and processes from an areal-typological perspective allows us to evaluate the current state of research on this topic, which in turn informs our recommendations for the most fruitful areas for future investigation.

THE CONCEPT OF DISCOURSE

In this review, we use the term discourse to refer to actual instances of language use and the patterning of these instances of language use into systems of communicative practice, including such types of organization as speech genres, participation frameworks, and the poetics of verbal performance.

As such, our use of the term discourse is distinct from Foucault's notion of the term and distinct from the use of the term by many linguists to refer to grammatical organization above the level of the sentence. The Foucauldian use of the term is considerably broader than our own, encompassing not only communicative practice, but also systems of social and political practice more generally, as well as the ideological systems that animate these wide fields of practice. The conventional linguistic use of the term refers to aspects of discourse that can be abstracted from considerations of social interaction and organization. Our use of the term discourse is consistent with the meaning this term has come to have in linguistic anthropology.

AREAL-TYPOLOGICAL LINGUISTICS IN INDIGENOUS LOWLAND SOUTH AMERICA

The areal-typological approach to language is one of two major ways in which relations between and among languages are investigated, the other of which is the genetic approach. The genetic approach is animated by the hypothesis that languages display systematic similarities because they are the result of a historical process of differentiation of a single ancestral language into multiple descendant languages. The assumption of the paramount importance of such genetic differentiation in historical processes of linguistic change has been so prevalent that, by and large, the term historical linguistics has been synonymous with the genetic hypothesis.

Many scholars, however, recognize that processes involving contact between speakers in different speech communities and of different languages must be taken into account to gain a full understanding of processes of language change and how languages are related to one another. In this latter approach, it is assumed that linguistic features of one language may be adopted by speakers of another language under circumstances of intense interaction. It is with this diffusionist perspective that the areal-typological approach to language is most commonly tied. An areal-typological approach combines a concern with typology—the classification of linguistic features in terms of descriptive categories or features dictated by a particular theoretical framework—and a concern with how such features are distributed among speech communities or languages in a particular geographical area (see Figure 1).

The recognition that genetic relationships are not the only relationships that can obtain between languages enables linguists to better understand the role of non-genetic diachronic processes in language change. Likewise, an areal-typological perspective can provide anthropologists with data that speak to the history and nature of intergroup interactions; this is especially valuable in lowland South America where other historical data, such as archaeological and written records, are scant if available at all. Areal-typological approaches thus provide an antidote to seeing indigenous groups as both isolated and ahistoric.

Areal-typological approaches to discourse allow anthropologists to see a region's large-scale patterns, which provide a valuable complementary view to the detailed, focused ethnographies of particular indigenous groups. Also, because discourse forms appear to diffuse much more quickly and easily than grammatical features (see below), they provide complementary evidence to grammatical data for understanding historical interactions between indigenous groups. At the same time, the high social salience of discourse may provide evidence about the nature of intercultural interactions that grammatical evidence does not.

Areal-typological studies of indigenous languages in Latin America have been carried out in Mesoamerica (Campbell et al. 1986), in South America (Aikhenvald 1999, Aikhenvald & Dixon 1998, Derbyshire & Payne 1990, Derbyshire & Pullum 1986, Klein 1992, Migliazza 1985, David Payne 1990, Doris Payne 1990, Seki

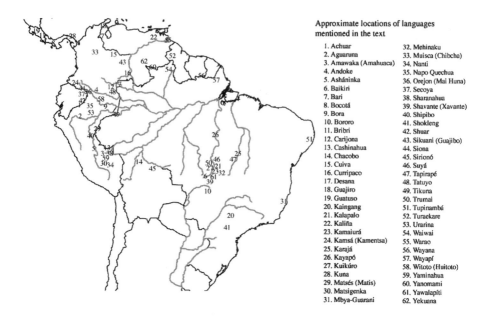

Figure 1 Approximate locations of languages mentioned in the text.

1999), and in the intermediate area between the two (Constenla Umaña 1991). A review and synthesis of areal-typological studies in the Americas is provided in Campbell 1997, which includes a listing of proposed linguistic areas. Areal-typological research to date has concentrated on the grammatical features of language. In this chapter, we take the notion of the linguistic area and extend it to the realm of discourse. Specifically, we propose the existence of a discourse area centered on the Amazon Basin, encompassing several adjacent regions in which discourse forms and processes are shared.

AREAL TYPOLOGY AND DISCOURSE IN INDIGENOUS LOWLAND SOUTH AMERICA

In this review we have chosen an areal-typological approach to discourse as a means to indicate large-scale patterns of similarity and difference in discourse practices among indigenous societies in lowland South America and as a way of synthesizing the research of many different scholars on discourse practices. For several reasons, this approach requires us to be at times tentative, and at other times suggestive; throughout the review, we are motivated by our goal to encourage a new perspective on discourse, to stimulate the further spinning out of the theoretical threads we draw together here, and most importantly, to encourage new research to pursue the empirical questions we raise.

Unlike typological studies addressing formal grammatical features, no commonly recognized theoretical or descriptive framework exists for the comparison of discourse forms and processes. We proceed then, by using particular discourse forms, such as ceremonial dialogue, that have caught the attention of scholars working in indigenous South America as the starting point for comparing and contrasting discourse forms across the continent. When possible, we suggest groupings of discourse forms and processes that bear resemblance to one another and axes of variation that can be used to organize the diversity of discourse forms we see.

Areally, we are presented with a different challenge: the uneven geographical distribution of discourse-oriented research in indigenous South America. Certain areas of the continent (e.g., the upper Xingu region) and certain indigenous groups (e.g., Achuar) have been the focus of thorough investigation by linguists and anthropologists; however, about many indigenous groups and large areas, we know little or nothing. Synthetic studies that map areal distributions of discourse forms and processes are relatively rare (Fock 1963; Urban 1986, 1988).

We write this review in large measure to encourage empirical and theoretical work to remedy these lacunae in our understanding of indigenous South American discourse.

The Greater Amazonian Discourse Area

In this review of discourse-related scholarship, we focus our attention on an area centered on the Amazon Basin and embracing several adjacent areas. This focus is linked to a proposal: that this area constitutes a discourse area. By this we mean that this region constitutes an area in which diverse cultural groups have come historically to share discursive practices through processes of intercultural contact and interaction.

This proposal is founded on two sets of facts. First, we observe in this area the widespread presence of a set of discourse forms and processes that cut across genetic linguistic families; and second, that many of these forms and processes intersect, overlap, and co-occur with one another in particular genres or in particular discourse settings, which suggests a high level of sociocultural salience and interconnectedness for these discourse forms and processes within lowland South America. Widespread forms in this discourse area include dialogical discourse forms of various kinds, including ceremonial dialogues, dialogical performances of verbal art, and marked dialogicality in everyday interactions, and they also include a focus on the epistemic status of utterances, manifested as a grammaticalized evidentiality system or through discursive evidential practices. In addition to these discourse processes and traits, which we discuss at length below, evidence from studies of narrative reveals distributions of themes and motifs that support the idea that this area is one in which discourse forms and processes share affinities that they do not share with discourse processes outside this area (Margery 1997).

The sources we review in this paper suggest a discourse area centering on the Amazon basin, including, in the north, the Orinoco basin, the Guianas, and the Isthmus region; to the east, the Araguaia basin; and to the south, the upper Paraguay and Paraná basins. For ease of reference, we refer to this region as the greater Amazonian discourse area. By the use of this term we signal that the discourse area under question specifically excludes the Andean region and the southern lowlands of South America, including the Chaco and Patagonian regions.

We are not making claims here for a Greater Amazonian linguistic area, which would require that formal linguistic features be common to this area. The empirical status of the Amazon Basin and surrounding areas as a unified linguistic area is controversial, with some scholars supporting linguistic areas that coincide significantly with the discourse area proposed here (Aikhenvald & Dixon 1998, Derbyshire & Pullum 1986, Derbyshire & Payne 1990), whereas others propose smaller areas, or areas that decompose this larger region into smaller ones (Constenla Umaña 1991, Klein 1992, Migliazza 1985). Thus the discourse area we propose may cross the boundary of at least two possible linguistic areas. Below, we discuss our hypothesis regarding the relationship of discourse areas to linguistic areas.

Though the northern and western boundaries of this discourse area are reasonably well defined (the Chibchan languages of Costa Rica in the north and the Andean edge of the Amazon, Orinoco, and Paraguay basins in the west), the southern and eastern boundaries are less certain, owing to our relative ignorance about the discourse processes found in indigenous groups of these areas. Furthermore, it is possible—even likely—that the pre-Columbian extent of the Greater Amazonian discourse area was larger than it is today. It is probable, for example, that the indigenous groups living east of the Araguaia basin, all the way to the Brazilian coast (e.g., Tupinambá), employed discourse features that we identify with the Greater Amazonian discourse area (e.g., ritual wailing, see below). However, the indigenous peoples of this eastern region, like those of the southern periphery of Greater Amazonia, were the earliest and most brutally affected by disease, slavery, and deliberate genocide. Similar comments can be made about the Caribbean region, about which our knowledge of pre-Columbian indigenous discourse forms is so limited that we can only speculate as to whether or not the discourse practices of indigenous groups of this region were related to those of the Amazon Basin.

Our present knowledge of discourse subareas within the Greater Amazonian discourse area includes evidence that the upper Xingu area of central Brazil and the Vaupes region of the northwestern Brazilian/Columbian border form discourse subareas (see below).

AN OVERVIEW OF SCHOLARSHIP ON INDIGENOUS LOWLAND SOUTH AMERICAN DISCOURSE

The body of research most relevant to this review is the work of scholars in the ethnography of speaking and discourse-centered approach to culture traditions. Some works in these traditions seek to describe, typologize, and analyze the major speech genres in the indigenous societies being studied (Juncosa 2000 for Shuar;

Sherzer 1983 for Kuna), whereas other studies focus on a single speech genre or a set of closely related genres (e.g., Basso 1995 for Kalapalo; Franchetto 1997 for Kuikúro; Gnerre 1986 for Shuar; Graham 1995 for Xavante; Maia 1997 for Karajá; Urban 1991 for Shokleng), or on the analysis of a set of performances or texts (Hendricks 1993 for Shuar).

A central concern in this tradition has been with the structures, significance, and social dynamics of the performance of verbal art, including Sherzer 1990, 1987, 1986 for Kuna; Severi 1990 for Kuna; Briggs 1990 for Warao; McDowell 1994 for Kamsá; Hill 1993 for Wakuénai; Constenla Umaña 2000 for Guatuso; de Gerdes 2000 for Kuna; Graham 2000 for Shavante; Hendricks 1993 for Shuar; Beier 2001 for Nanti; Basso 1985, 1987, 1995 for Kalapalo; Franchetto 1997 for Kuikúro; Maia 1997 for Karajá; and Jara 1989 for Turaekare. Like most work in the ethnography of speaking tradition, this research focuses on the analysis of indigenous language texts derived from audio recordings, informed by detailed ethnographic research. This body of research is discussed in greater detail below.

In the 1990s, a concern emerged to extend these ethnographic approaches to include interaction between indigenous societies and nonindigenous populations. This has included an interest in understanding how indigenous discourse is implicated in resistance to nation-state hegemony (Hill 1990); how discourse in indigenous societies is involved in the maintenance and contestation of community (McDowell 1990); and how discourse is implicated in asymmetrical relationships in these societies (Kane 1990).

Merging at times with the ethnography of speaking and discourse-centered approaches is the field of ethnopoetics. Research in that field characteristically focuses on aspects of poetic structure in indigenous verbal art forms (Constenla Umaña 1996 for Chibchan languages; Constenla Umaña 2000 for Guatuso; Franchetto 1989 for Kuikúro; Seeger 1986 for Suyá; Uzendoski 1999 for Napo Quechua), but increasingly, ethnopoetic studies are given sophisticated ethnographic contextualizations (Briggs 2000 for Warao; Graham 1986 for Shavante; Jara 1989 for Turukaere; Maia 1997 for Karajá; Sherzer 1990 for Kuna).

It is important to note that there are scholars working outside the ethnography of speaking tradition that have developed parallel concerns with the ethnographic contextualization of discourse forms studied as actual instances of communicative action (Agerkop 1989 for Kaliña, Wayana, and Turaekare; Reichel-Dolmatoff 1996 for Desana; Taylor & Chau 1983 for Achuar). These scholars similarly base their analyses on a combination of carefully transcribed indigenous language texts and ethnographic research.

Though the discourse-centered and ethnographically contextualized work just discussed is the focus of this chapter, there are other scholarly traditions touching on discourse that are relevant to our concerns, including studies of narrative and myth and of pragmatics.

Any discussion of discourse-related research in lowland South America must also acknowledge the importance of studies of myth. The collection of myths in textual form by missionaries, travelers, and ethnographers was already a venerable practice by the time that Claude Lévi-Strauss' structural studies of South American myth (Lévi-Strauss 1969) made the study of mythology a central concern for several generations of anthropologists and folklorists working in lowland South America. Well into the 1980s, structuralist studies of myth remained dominant (e.g., Weiss 1983 for Asháninka; Magaña & Jara 1983 for Kaliña; Bastien & Olson 1984 for Wayapí; Balzano 1984 for Chacobo; Magaña 1989 for Wayana; Roe 1991a for Shipibo; Cipoletti 1987 for Siona and Secoya; Escribano 2000 for Muisca (Chibcha); Vázquez 1991 for Sirionó; Roe 1991b for Waiwai.) The vast majority of this research, although based on discourse circulating in indigenous communities, was ultimately unconcerned with myths as instances of communicative activity in particular social and cultural contexts. In this tradition, even the textual organization of myths was of modest interest, thereby eliding issues of ethnopoetics as well as those of ethnography.

In the 1980s and into the early 1990s, however, studies of myth in lowland South America began to change in several ways that aligned them more closely with ethnographic approaches to discourse. These included increasing interest in transcribed indigenous language texts [e.g., Bellier 1983, 1987 for Orejon (Mai Huna); Queixalos 1985 for Sikuani; Margery 1990 for Bocotá; Robayo 1989 for Carijona] and attempts to understand myths as manifestations of or commentary on cultural themes (Dean 1994 for Urarina; Renard-Casevitz 1991 for Matsigenka; Sturm 1991 for Mbya-Guarani; Guss 1991 for Yekuana; Perrin 1987 for Guajiro). By the 1990s, the trend away from structuralist decontextualized understandings of myth extended in one direction as attempts to understand how myths served as discursive arenas of contestation within a culture, and extended in another direction as fields of resistance or accommodation to the hegemonic powers of nation states and their elites (Langdon 1991 for Siona; Hendricks 1990 for Shuar; Hill 1990 for Wakuénai; Howe 1994 for Kuna; Hugh-Jones 1988; Jara 1993 for Bribri; Reeve 1988 for Arapaco; Hill & Wright 1988 for Shipibo; Silverblatt 1988 for Kayapó).

Structuralist approaches were not the only early approaches to myth. Another, principally folkloristic, interest in myth and narrative flourished under the rubric of indigenous literature. A principal concern in this tradition involved the areal distribution of folktale motifs. Many scattered texts have been brought together in the edited series from the University of California, Los Angeles (UCLA) (Wilbert 1970 for Warao; Wilbert & Simoneau 1978 for Ge; Wilbert & Simoneau 1983 for Bororo; Wilbert et al. 1986 for Guajiro; Wilbert & Simoneau 1990a for Yaruro; Wilbert & Simoneau 1990b for Yanomami; Wilbert & Simoneau 1991 for Cuiva; Wilbert & Simoneau 1992 for Sikuani). The texts in these volumes are overwhelmingly prose recountings of indigenous myths and narratives in English. In contrast, two journals in which a significant number of indigenous literature texts have been published over the past 15 years, the *Latin American Indigenous Literatures Journal* and especially *Amerindia*, have typically included indigenous language versions of the published texts.

Text collections of a folkloristic nature have become increasingly common in Latin America. Some of this work includes transcribed and translated indigenous texts (Hidalgo 1997 for Bribri; Margery 1990 for Bocotá; Juajibioy Chindoy 1989 for Kamsá; McDowell 1989, 2000 for Kamsa and Ingano; Rueda & Tankamash 1983 for Achuar), whereas others are Spanish prose recountings in a novelistic style (Ochoa Siguas 1999 for Bora; Hidalgo 1997 for Bribri; Kuyoteka Jikomui & Restrepo Gonzalez 1997 for Witoto). Some work in this tradition bears increasing resemblance to scholarship in the ethnopoetic tradition as it engages with indigenous language texts and extends its analysis beyond that of motifs (Margery 1991 for Bocotá; Jara 1991 for Bribri).

As this overview attests, discourse-related research in indigenous lowland South America has overwhelmingly focused on artistic and highly performative aspects of discourse including myths, performances of verbal art, songs, and oratory, although some researchers also make reference to everyday discourse practices (Sherzer 1983 for Kuna; Briggs 1993a,b for Warao; Müller 1990 for Assurini; Orlandi et al. 1991). In recent years some researchers have begun to turn their attention to the more quotidian aspects of discourse, long the domain of pragmatics, conversational analysis, and certain styles of discourse analysis focusing on global languages. This work includes interest in discourse referentiality (Clemente de Souza 1997 for Baikiri), pragmatic principles of utterance structure (Clemente de Souza 1991 for Baikiri; Soares 1991 for Tikuna), and the pragmatics of reported speech (Michael 2001a,b for Nanti).

A significant development that crosscuts the areas of discourse-related research and writing discussed so far is the emergence in the 1980s of literary authors, anthropologists, and linguists from lowland South American indigenous groups often writing in their own languages. These authors and scholars produce works in areas as diverse as fiction, poetry, and oral tradition (Jusayú 1989 for Wayuu [Guajiro]; Kungiler 1997 and http://dulenega.nativeweb.org for Kuna), discourse-based linguistics (Juajibioy Chindoy 1989 for Kamsá [Kamentsa]), studies of myth (Rueda & Tankamash 1983 for Shuar; Kuyoteca Jifikomui & Restrepo González 1997 for Witoto), and collections of oral history and cultural commentary (Vyjkág & Toral 1997 for Kaingang). Critical works on indigenous literature are already appearing (Ferrer & Rodríguez 1998, Vázquez 1999).

We add a final observation here that in addition to works focused explicitly on discourse, numerous ethnographies provide glimpses of the wealth of discourse processes in indigenous lowland South American societies. These glimpses suggest diverse avenues for research to add to the growing body of descriptive and analytical work in the linguistic anthropology of lowland South America.

TYPOLOGICAL PERSPECTIVES ON DISCOURSE IN GREATER AMAZONIA

We begin our areal-typological discussion of discourse forms and processes with those that have been the focus of extensive research within particular ethnographic contexts and that have also been previously considered from areal and typological perspectives. This discussion examines widespread processes of dialogicality, which include forms such as ceremonial dialogue, dialogical performance, templatic ratifying, and echo speech; ceremonial greeting; ritual wailing; evidentiality; and speech reporting practices.

Dialogicality

In speaking of the prevalence of dialogicality in lowland indigenous South America, we are referring specifically to the pervasiveness of dialogical discourse forms that are relatively fixed in structure and are usually associated with particular discourse contexts. We refer to these dialogical discourse forms as templatic dialogicality.

The discourse forms and processes that have received the greatest comparative attention by scholars of indigenous lowland South America are those classified as ceremonial dialogue (Fock 1963, Rivière 1971, Urban 1986). In addition, linguists and anthropologists have observed many other forms of discursive interaction that are significantly dialogical in nature and may bear substantial interactional resemblance to ceremonial dialogues. These highly structured dialogical interactions are perhaps the most widespread and socially significant areal discourse feature of lowland indigenous South America. In this section we propose a preliminary typological framework for their analysis and classification and discuss aspects of the areal distribution of dialogical discourse forms.

It is useful to understand dialogical discourse forms along three classificatory axes: verbal form, interactional framework, and sociocultural salience. These axes are, of course, applicable to all discourse, but in the case of context-dependent structured dialogical interaction, verbal form and interactional framework are constrained in certain ways to yield what we term templatic dialogicality. Specifically, templatic dialogical discourse forms are characterized by an interactional framework in which the discursive roles of the participants are quite delimited (e.g., with one person serving as a principal speaker and the other as responder) and which frequently assigns to those roles certain discursive resources and disallows others (e.g., preferences for highly allusive or parallelistic speech, or special, possibly esoteric, languages).

Templatic dialogicality can have different sociocultural salience in different societies, so that in one society (e.g., Shokleng), templatic dialogical discourse forms are highly ceremonial, whereas among other societies (e.g., Nanti), they are minimally ceremonial, if at all. Similarly, templatic dialogicality is employed for myth-tellings in certain societies (Shokleng, Kalapalo, Kuna); for greetings in others (Achuar); and for reports of important news or the giving of important instructions in others (Nanti).

Likewise, interactional frameworks can vary considerably, from the rigid chanting chief-and-responder framework of the Kuna, to the framework of Achuar ceremonial greetings in which the two interactants exchange roles of principal speaker and responder in the course of the interaction. Finally, verbal form can vary from the syllable-by-syllable alternation between speakers found in certain verbal art forms among the Shokleng, to alternations between long sequences of chanted utterances (e.g., Nanti).

Among the various forms of dialogical performance described for indigenous lowland South America are dialogical myth performance for Shokleng (Urban 1991), *xarintaa* chanting for Nanti (Beier 2001), *kamarataka* chanting for Curripaco (Journet 2000), and dialogical performance of formal narratives throughout the Chibchan area (Constenla Umaña 1996, Pereira 1983).

Forms of templatic ratifying, in which the responder interjects minimal utterances at expected points during the speech of the principal speaker are described for Kuna, in which the responder overlaps the final vowel of the principal speaker (Sherzer 1983); in the Kalapalo "what-saying" in narratives (Basso 1985, 1987); in the *oho-karï* or "yes saying" for Waiwai (Fock 1963).

Another form of dialogic interaction reported for Amazonian societies is echo speech, in which an individual who is being addressed repeats the utterances of the principal speaker in whole or in part, without interrupting the speaker's turn at talk. Among the Nanti of southeastern Peru, for example, recipients of an engaging narrative will frequently repeat large portions of the narrative in an undertone while it is being told, with a delay of roughly one half a second. Extensive echoing is also frequent in Nanti interactions of substantial political and social importance, and some degree of echoing is common in everyday interactions. Sorenson (1972, pp. 83–84) describes a very similar phenomenon among the indigenous groups of the Vaupes region; he indicates that echo speech is "a formal conversational device indicating understanding, assent, and respect." According to Sorenson, the completeness of echoing is related to the formality of the interactional setting, with more formal settings calling forth more complete echoing of another's speech. It is interesting that Gnerre has described a mixed echo speech and ratifying pattern within dialogical performances in Achuar and Shuar discourse (1986), bringing together in one interaction elements of all the processes discussed above.

The above typological framework for dialogicality is intended to serve primarily as a descriptive and heuristic one for the early stages of typological research; we fully expect it to be superceded by a finer and more empirically founded typology as research advances. Likewise, fully assessing the areal distribution of these traits is a matter that awaits future research.

In closing our discussion of dialogicality, it is important to note that scholars working in indigenous communities have observed dramatic shifts in indigenous discourse forms as these societies come more and more under the influence of literate and monologic models for speech production (see Gnerre 1986, Sherzer 1994).

Ceremonial Greeting

Highly marked and elaborated greeting processes are widespread in lowland indigenous South America. Characteristics of these greetings include the use of templatic dialogicality, the use of special vocal channels, marked use of the body, and use of prolonged silence. It is not uncommon for ceremonial greetings to be reserved for individuals with special status or for greetings after prolonged absences.

Ceremonial dialogic greetings are usually chanted and involve special, often metaphorical, vocabulary and patterned overlap in voices. Among the Kuna and Shuar, a series of questions on the part of one greeter is punctuated by regular, largely nonreferential ratifications by the second; then follows a series of answers by the second greeter, punctuated with regular ratifications by the first (Sherzer 1983, 1990; Gnerre 1986). Dialogic greetings have also been documented among the Yanomami (Lizot 1994, 2000).

Ceremonial greetings need not be principally verbal but can be constituted through body comportment and kinesics (Erickson 2000 for Chacobo; Basso 2000 for Kalapalo; Kensinger 1995 for Cashinahua; Galvis 1995 for Bari). In some societies, socially marked greetings are in fact indicated through careful avoidance or minimization of speech (Erickson 2000 for Matsés [Matis]); Sherzer 1999 for Kuna; L. Michael & C. Beier, personal observation for Nanti; Huxley & Capa 1964 for Amawaka [Amahuaca]).

The use of special vocal channels in ceremonial greetings is also noted, such as crying or wailing greetings described among the Tupinambá and the Tapirapé of Brazil (Baldus 1970 for Tupinambá; Wagley 1977 for Tapirapé; Kensinger 1995 for Cashinahua; Siskind 1973 for Sharanahua; Galvão 1996 for Kamaiurá). A falsetto voice is used among some Yaminahua groups of Peru (Michael & Beier, personal observation).

In a recent work, Erickson suggests that the presence of ceremonial greetings in a society is reflective of hierarchical forms of social organization and that ceremonial greetings are not employed in more egalitarian societies (Erikson 2000). Urban has observed that ceremonial dialogical greetings appear to be associated with societies in which relations between subgroups are marked with potential conflict (Urban 1991).

Ritual Wailing

Though forms of ritual wailing have been identified throughout indigenous South America, ritual wailing has been described most extensively for Brazil, beginning with the observations by sixteenth- and seventeenth-century travelers of the "welcome of tears" performed by the now-extinct Tupinambá groups of coastal Brazil (Baldus 1970, Wagley 1977). Styles of ritual wailing have also been described in detail for the Tapirapé (Wagley 1977), the Shokleng and Bororo (Urban 1988), the Shavante (Graham 1986), the Warao (Briggs 1993c); and the Karajá (Maia 1997).

Using recorded data from the Shokleng, Shavante, and Bororo, Urban (1988) discusses, from a comparative perspective, ritual wailing in Amerindian Brazil. Urban first addresses the similarities in form that originally led to the notion of ritual wailing in the anthropological literature; these styles share "sound shape features with crying" and occur "in contexts that include those associated with sadness" (Urban 1988, p. 385). Noting the cultural specificity of each group's form of ritual wailing, Urban analyzes the common semiotic function of wailing across these cultures and proposes the following commonalities: "(1) the existence of a musical line, marked by a characteristic intonational contour and rhythmic structure; (2) the use of various icons of crying; and (3) the absence of an actual addressee, which renders the ritual wailing an overtly monologic or expressive device..." (Urban 1988, p. 386).

In identifying these core features, Urban's work provides an excellent point of departure for building an areal typology of ritual wailing across indigenous lowland South America. These features allow us to identify forms of ritual wailing described but not identified as such in existing ethnographies; for example, Siskind describes circumstances in which Sharanahuan women wail or weep (Siskind 1973); and Sherzer describes tuneful weeping and lament performed by Kuna women in the presence of death (Sherzer 1983).

Evidential Systems in Discourse

Evidentiality, or the grammatical marking of the epistemological status and basis of utterances, has been proposed as an areal feature of languages of the Amazon basin and adjacent areas (Aikhenvald & Dixon 1998). The possibility that evidentiality is an areal feature is significant in two ways for future areal-typological studies of discourse.

First, the discursive use of evidential systems is empirically and theoretically nontrivial (Hill & Irvine 1993), requiring an account of how evidentials are actually employed in talk. Thus, though a language may possess a quotative marker, which is nominally obligatory, the circumstances of its use in actual communicative interaction remains uncertain. In Nanti, for example, an inferential knowledge marker is not used for certain knowledge claims that, strictly speaking, are inferential but are locally considered to be sound knowledge (Michael 2001a,b). Thus, though a grammatical marker exists to convey a particular evidential status, the assessment of which knowledge claims in discourse have that particular evidential status is not a grammatical fact but rather a culturally mediated assessment that no doubt also reflects immediate communicative needs and contextual factors (Gomez-Imbert 1986 for Tatuyo). The widespread existence of grammaticalized systems of evidentiality in indigenous lowland South America therefore calls for ethnographic studies that examine their use in discourse and interaction.

Second, studies suggest that evidential systems can also be realized primarily through discursive, nongrammatical processes. Nanti speakers evince great concern about the epistemological status of knowledge claims in discourse, distinguishing among knowledge claims based on direct experience, those based on inference and partial knowledge, and those based on information obtained through talk with others (Michael 2001a,b). Nanti discourse can be said to have an evidential system in that the epistemological status of any knowledge claim can be determined, but only knowledge claims based on inference or partial knowledge are marked morphologically by the use of a clitic /-ka/. Knowledge claims based on information gained through talk are marked by the use of direct quotation, which is consequently an important feature of everyday Nanti discourse, and knowledge claims that are based on direct experience are unmarked. These facts raise an intriguing possibility: that a prominent concern with epistemological matters is an areal cultural feature, which in some cases becomes grammaticalized as part of the morphological system of the language and in other cases manifests as a discursive evidential system (Aikhenvald & Dixon 1998).

Speech Reporting Practices

Speech reporting practices in indigenous societies in lowland South America display several features that are not widely documented in other areas of the world and that may constitute areal features of speech reporting practices. One candidate areal feature is the predominant use of reported speech to represent human agency and subjectivity in discourse. In societies where this is the case, communication about the agency or subjectivity of individuals does not rely on direct reference to mental or emotional states and processes, such as beliefs or decisions but instead typically involves reporting the speech of the individuals in question.

In describing the use of reported speech among the Kalapalo, a Carib group of the Upper Xingu area, Basso notes that the motives, attitudes, and emotions of individuals in Kalapalo stories are "realized through their quoted speech, rather than through labels or a narrator's more direct description of feelings and motives" (Basso 1995, p. 295; Basso 1986). Striking parallels can be found in the speech reporting practices of the Nanti, an Arawak group of southeastern Peru (Michael 2001a,b). In interactions among Nanti individuals, discussions of human agency and subjectivity by direct references to notions such as beliefs, decisions, or attitudes are very rarely made, as are references to speech acts like orders or requests. Instead, Nanti individuals predominantly report the speech of others (or themselves) that manifests a belief, indicates a decision, or constitutes a request.

Relatively few detailed ethnographic studies examine the use of reported speech in lowland South American discourse, and it is therefore notable that these studies have found two societies on opposite peripheries of the Amazon Basin in which reported speech has similar roles. Several formalistic studies of discourse also suggest similar uses of reported speech in other societies (Larson 1978 for Aguaruna; Kerr 1976 for Cuiva; Waltz 1976 for Andoke).

The social and strategic uses of reported speech constitute another dimension for the comparison and typological classification of speech reporting practices. It has been observed that in some societies, reported speech is employed to distance utterances from the speaker (Sherzer 1983 for Kuna), contributing to the authoritative status of utterances, whereas in other societies, reported speech is employed to unambiguously associate utterances with specific speakers (Michael 2001b for Nanti), thereby situating and qualifying knowledge claims.

AREALLY SIGNIFICANT DISCOURSE FORMS AND PROCESSES IN GREATER AMAZONIA

We now turn to a discussion of discourse forms and processes whose unique manifestations throughout lowland South America have been the focus of descriptive research, but which remain to be studied comparatively. These include parallelism, special languages, and shamanistic language use.

Parallelism

Parallelism is typically understood as the patterned repetition of some discursive unit, such as a poetic line or a clause. The pattern relies on alternation of some element of the discursive unit between repeated instances of the discursive unit. Possible alternations include those that are lexical, phonological, morphological, or intonational. In paradigmatic cases, the alternation is minimal, so that there is only a single difference between the repeated discourse units along whatever axis of alternation is relevant.

Although parallelism is likely a poetic device found throughout human discourse, extensive and pervasive parallelism is especially characteristic of ritual speaking and chanting in the greater Amazonian discourse area. It is also likely that areally unique forms of parallelism are employed in this area.

A widespread form of parallelism in lowland South America, syntactic frame repetition with semantic field alternation, consists of the repetition of a poetic line or clause with the alternation of a single lexical item in the same syntactic position between the repeated lines. The alternation consists of different lexical items from a particular semantic field, such as body parts, color terms, shapes, or kinds of action.

Though it is common for parallelism of this sort to operate between successive lines, parallelism may also operate between discourse units that are separated from each other. This form of parallelism sometimes serves to mark large-scale units in a stretch of discourse, like a stanza or an episode.

Other forms of parallelism found in indigenous lowland South American discourse include syntactic frame repetition with zero alternation in which a lexical item, phrase, or clause is deleted; unit repetition with intonation contour alternation; and nonreferential morpheme alternation with identical lexical roots.

Another form of structural parallelism is found in Curripaco (Journet 2000) and Nanti verbal art, in which parallelism is not created by syntactic, lexical, or morphological similarities between lines, but rather by prosodic resemblances. Nanti *xarintaa* chanting, a form of extemporaneous verbal art performed during weekly feasts, consists of chanted lines in which lexical items can vary freely, but for which the matrix prosodic pattern is relatively fixed. Performers alter the prosodic characteristics of lexical items to match the matrix prosodic pattern through processes of truncation, lengthening, syllable duplication, and affixation of nonreferential morphemes (Beier 2001). Parallelism is omnipresent in Chibchan oral literature, including the use of *difrasismos*, in which two-way lexical alternations serve to signify a third semantically nontransparent entity, reminiscent of certain poetic forms in the Mesoamerican area (Constenla Umaña 1996).

It is important to note that parallelism is not restricted to monological discourse forms in which alternations occur between discourse units repeated by a single speaker; it can also occur in dialogical discourse forms where parallelistic effects are achieved through the distinct discursive contributions of two interactants (Beier 2001 for Nanti; Journet 2000 for Curripaco; Urban 1991 for Shokleng).

Special Languages

Special languages are varieties of language that differ from everyday, ordinary language in their phonology, morphology, syntax, semantics, lexicon, discourse form, and/or modality; they are used in particular social and cultural contexts, particularly in play and in ritual. Specialized vocabulary, perhaps the most common feature of special languages, often differs from everyday vocabulary in that it is esoteric—that is, not known to nonspecialists—and may rely heavily on metaphor. Special vocabulary may include archaisms or borrowings whose referential meaning may or may not be known to the specialist. Common social contexts for the use of special languages include political discourse, curing practices, and life-cycle rituals such as puberty rites and funerary rites (Basso 1973 for Kalapalo; Beier 2001 for Nanti; Botero Verswyvel 1987 for Kogi; Cervantes Gamboa 1990 for Bribri; Constenla Umaña 1990 for Bribri; Constenla Umaña 1996 for Chibchan languages; Franchetto 1983, 2000 for Kuikúro; Gregor 1977 for Mehinaku; Migliazza 1972 for Yanomami; Monod Bequelin 1975 for Trumai; Seeger 1987 for Suyá; Sherzer 1983 for Kuna).

Shamanism and Language

In many societies in indigenous lowland South America, specific discourse forms are often associated with curing practices, divination, prophecy, and forms of magic (Bidou & Perrin 1988). The individuals who engage in this communication are often labeled shamans by scholars. Though no systematic comparative or areal-typological study of shamanic discourse exists, a considerable body of work focusing on, or making reference to, shamanic discursive practice does exist (Buchillet 1990).

Shamanic discourse frequently involves the use of special languages and is often unintelligible to nonspecialists; it is also common for shamans to use marked vocal channels, such as chanting, singing, whispering, or blowing (Baer 1994 for Matsigenka; Buchillet 1992 for Desana; Siskind 1973 for Sharanahua; Sherzer 1983, 1988 for Kuna; Seeger 1987 for Suyá; Cipolletti 1988 for Secoya; Bidou 1988 for Tatuyo; Perrin 1988 for Guajiro; Bellier 1988 for Orejon [Mai Huna]). An understanding of the typological dimensions of shamanistic language use in indigenous lowland South America awaits systematic comparative study.

DISCOURSE AREAS AND LINGUISTIC AREAS

Areal-typological approaches to discourse may serve to illuminate the processes by which linguistic areas are formed. Though scholars have always assumed that borrowing processes of some type are responsible for the genesis of linguistic areas, the mechanisms of this borrowing process have remained unclear. Evidence from certain areas of Amazonia strongly suggests that the formation of linguistic areas may be mediated through the formation of discourse areas. The social context for the sharing of discourse forms and processes is that throughout the area under discussion, from the period of our earliest knowledge up to the present day, there is much travel, bilingualism, intermarriage, and trade. In this view, linguistically distinct cultural groups in a given area come into contact and begin to interact intensely, borrowing discourse forms and processes from one another, such as myths, songs, and even entire ceremonies. Subsequently, phonological, morphological, syntactic, and/or semantic features embedded in these borrowed discourse forms begin to surface in the grammar of the group that has borrowed the discourse forms. In this picture, the sharing of discourse forms, which can be motivated on political and cultural grounds, mediates the borrowing of grammatical forms.

An excellent example of this process seems to be found among the indigenous groups of the upper Xingu region. This region is particularly interesting for purposes of research into language contact because only 10 of the 17 indigenous groups in the area have lived there for more than a century, and many of these have not resided in the region for more than a few centuries (Seki 1999). The origin of the upper Xingu area as a culture area has been dated to the late eighteenth or early nineteenth century (Heckenberger 1996). As either a discourse or linguistic area, then, the upper Xingu area is quite young, and the diachronic processes leading to the formation of such an area are still very active.

The ethnographic and linguistic research carried out in the Upper Xingu region since the 1950s provides a substantial preliminary base of data with which to investigate this question. These data indicate that there has been substantial borrowing of discourse forms related to ceremonial practices, public performances of verbal art, and chiefly oratory (Basso 1973, 1995 for Kalapalo; Monod Bequelin 1975 for Trumai; Seki 1999 for Kamaiurá; Franchetto 2000 for Kuikúro; Seeger 1987 for Suyá).

Seki has recently proposed that the upper Xingu region is an incipient linguistic area and that Xinguan languages share several features not present in languages to which they are genetically related (Seki 1999). What we find in the Upper Xingu region, then, is the substantial diffusion of a number of discourse forms related to ceremonial practice and verbal art, a process that has been underway in the region for at least 50 years, if not in some cases much longer, accompanied by the diffusion of a small number of linguistic features. Discourse diffusion appears to have thus preceded linguistic diffusion. Similarly, more discourse forms appear to have spread between indigenous groups in the Upper Xingu area than between linguistic groups. This makes plausible the hypothesis that the diffusion of discourse forms are the primary means of diffusion of language-related phenomena, including strictly linguistic forms. In short, linguistic forms are diffused by means of the discourse forms that contain them, which can subsequently become adopted into everyday speech.

The Upper Xingu is an excellent laboratory for studying the diachronic processes of discourse area formation, linguistic area formation, and the link between the two. Given the burgeoning interest among researchers in discourse, in Latin America and elsewhere, we can likely look forward to many revealing findings about these topics.

Another region in which a relationship between linguistic area and discourse area can be hypothesized is the Içana-Vaupes basin of the Brazilian-Columbian border, which has already been proposed as a linguistic area by Aikhenvald (1999). Observations by researchers (Sorenson 1972, Chernela 1993) suggest to us the presence of widely shared discourse forms and processes that strongly merit attention.

A VIEW TO THE FUTURE

We close with a summary of our suggestions for future research, in light of the overview and synthesis this review has offered. First and foremost, there is a need for more linguistic anthropological fieldwork. Indigenous lowland South American discourse forms are presently endangered for many sociopolitical reasons. In addition to documenting these unique forms of human expression, the commitment and interest linguistic anthropologists show toward indigenous discourse forms bring a much-needed alternative perspective on the value of indigenous discourse to communities by and large discouraged to continue using indigenous forms of communication.

Second, renewed efforts are needed to make available existing data from lowland South American discourse to other researchers and indigenous language speakers. Over the five decades that anthropologists and linguists have worked with recording technology, vast quantities of irreplaceable data have been gathered and only a fraction of it has been analyzed or published. In most cases, these data are extremely vulnerable to physical deterioration or loss. With the recent development of innovative digital archiving technology such as is offered by the Archive of the Indigenous Languages of Latin America (AILLA, http://www.ailla.org), scholars interested in indigenous lowland South American discourse can now ensure both the preservation and the accessibility of their data corpuses. In addition, online language archives provide researchers with a means to fulfill their obligation to make their data available to the originating communities.

In the course of preparing this chapter, it became increasingly apparent that important and high-quality research focused on indigenous lowland South America has been carried out by scholars across several continents and in many countries, but that this research has frequently been published in ways that limit its circulation and access to it. Thus, a scholarly infrastructure for comparative and typological studies of indigenous discourse is still in its incipient stages. It can be hoped that online archives like AILLA can serve a role in facilitating the exchange and sharing of scholarly studies and discourse data, thereby bringing together the work of the many dedicated scholars now examining indigenous discourse forms and processes in South America.

Third, there is a great need to align existing terminologies and frameworks in order to allow for cross-cultural comparisons in more systematic ways. Without a concerted collaborative effort to generate consistent and robust typologies, valuable insights on indigenous discourse, and on the greater Amazon discourse area more specifically, will be missed. Without erasing or diminishing the merit of diverse schools of description and analysis, efforts to map between terminologies and frameworks will enable the kinds of comparative and systematic research that we are calling for here.

And lastly, there is a need for new comparative and synthetic research drawing from the wealth of disparate data on indigenous lowland South American discourse forms and processes—research which takes as its point of departure an areal-typological perspective informed by the various arguments put forth in this chapter. It is our hope that this review has offered the reader a new and broader perspective on both the remarkable range of creative forms found in indigenous lowland South America and on the patterns found within them that speak to the intricate web of human relationships formed over time in greater Amazonia.

ACKNOWLEDGMENT

We would like to thank Adolfo Constenla Umaña for insightful discussions with us on the topic of this paper.

The *Annual Review of Anthropology* is online at http://anthro.annualreviews.org

LITERATURE CITED

Agerkop T. 1989. Some remarks on Guiana Amerindian song style. *Lat. Am. Indian Lit. J.* 5:31–42

Aikhenvald A. 1999. Areal diffusion and language contact in the Içana-Vaupes basin, north-west Amazonia. See Dixon & Aikhenvald 1999, pp. 385–416

Aikhenvald A, Dixon RMW. 1998. Evidentials and areal typology: a case study from Amazonia. *Lang. Sci.* 20:241–57

Baer G. 1994. *Cosmología y shamanismo de los Matsiguenga (Perú Oriental).* Quito, Ecuador: Ed. Abya-Yala. 389 pp.

Baldus H. 1970. *Tapirapé: Tribo Tupi no Brasil Central.* São Paulo: Nac./EDUSP

Balzano S. 1984. Káko, a cultural hero of the Chacobos. *Lat. Am. Indian Lit. J.* 8:26–34

Basso EB. 1973. *The Kalapalo Indians of Central Brazil.* New York: Holt, Rinehart & Winston. 157 pp.

Basso EB. 1985. *A Musical View of the Universe: Kalapalo Myth and Ritual Performance.* Philadelphia: Univ. Penn. Press. 343 pp.

Basso EB. 1986. Quoted dialogues in Kalapalo narrative discourse. See Sherzer & Urban 1986, pp. 119–68

Basso EB. 1987. *In Favor of Deceit: a Study of Tricksters in an Amazonian Society.* Tucson: Univ. Ariz. Press. 376 pp.

Basso EB. 1995. *The Last Cannibals: a South American Oral History.* Austin: Univ. Tex. Press. 319 pp.

Basso EB. 2000. Dialogues and body techniques in Kalapalo affinal activity. See Monod Becquelin & Erikson 2000, pp. 183–95

Basso EB, Sherzer J, eds. 1990. *Las Culturas Nativas Latinoamericanas a Través de su Discurso: Ponencias del Simposio del 46o Congreso Internacional de Americanistas, Amsterdam, julio de 1988.* Quito, Ecuador: Abya-Yala/MLAL. 418 pp.

Bastien J, Olson G. 1984. Ayã folktales of the Wayapî Indians. *Lat. Am. Indian Lit. J.* 8:1–12

Beier C. 2001. *Creating community: feasting among the Nantis of Peruvian Amazonia.* MA thesis. Univ. Tex. Austin. 226 pp.

Bellier I. 1983. Hetu kone kii hã: histoire de hetu kone, myth Mai Huna (Pérou). *Amerindia* 8:181–216

Bellier I. 1987. La création noyée: Maineno cherche ses femmes. *Amerindia* 12:133–54

Bellier I. 1988. Cantos de yage y Mecedoras Mai Huna (Amazonía peruana). See Bidou & Perrin 1988, pp. 127–50

Bidou P. 1988. Sintaxis y eficacia del discurso chamánico (Amazonia Colombiana). See Bidou & Perrin 1988, pp. 35–48

Bidou P, Perrin M, eds. 1988. *Lenguaje y Palabras Chamánicas*. Quito, Ecuador: Ed. Abya-Yala. 186 pp.

Botero Verswyvel S. 1987. Indígenas de la Sierra Nevada de Santa Marta. In *Introducción a la Colombia Amerindia*, ed. S Botero Verswyvel, pp. 39–49. Bogotá: Inst. Colombiano de Antropología Bogotá

Briggs C. 1990. Diversidad metapragmática en el arte verbal: poesía, imaginación e interacción en los estilos narativos Warao. See Basso & Sherzer 1990, pp. 135–74

Briggs C. 1993a. Generic versus metapragmatic dimensions of Warao narratives: who regiments performance? In *Reflexive Language: Reported Speech and Metapragmatics*, ed. JA Lucy. Cambridge, UK: Cambridge Univ. Press

Briggs C. 1993b. Linguistic ideologies and the naturalization of power in Warao discourse. *Pragmatics* 2:387–404

Briggs C. 1993c. Personal sentiments and polyphonic voices in Warao women's ritual wailing: music and poetics in a critical and collective discourse. *Am. Anthropol.* 95:929–57

Briggs C. 2000. Emergence of the non-indigenous peoples. See Sammons & Sherzer 2000, pp. 174–96

Buchillet D. 1990. Los poderes del hablar: terapia y agresión chamánica entre los indios Desana del Vaupes brasilero. See Basso & Sherzer 1990, pp. 319–54

Buchillet D. 1992. Nobody is there to hear: Desana therapeutic incantations. In *Portals of Power: Shamanism in South America*, ed. EJ Matteson Langdon, G Baer, pp. 211–30. Albuquerque: Univ. N.M. Press

Campbell L. 1997. *American Indian Languages: the Historical Linguistics of Native America*. New York: Oxford Univ. Press. 512 pp.

Campbell L, Kaufman T, Smith-Stark TC. 1986. Meso-America as a linguistic area. *Language* 62:530–70

Cervantes Gamboa L. 1990. *Sulàr: playing for the dead. A study of Bribri funerary chants as speech acts*. MA thesis. State Univ. New York, Albany

Chernela JM. 1993. *The Wanano Indians of the Brazilian Amazon: a Sense of Space*. Austin: Univ. Tex. Press. 185 pp.

Cipolleti M. 1987. The visit to the realm of the dead in the Ecuadorian mythology of the Siona and Secoya. *Lat. Am. Indian Lit. J.* 3:127–56

Cipolleti M. 1988. El animalito doméstico quedo hecho cenizas: aspectos del lenguaje shamánico Secoya. See Bidou & Perrin 1988, pp. 9–34

Clemente de Souza TC. 1991. Perspectivas de análise do discurso numa língua indígena, o Bakairi (carib). In *Discurso Indígena: a Materialidade da Língua e o Movimento da Identidade*, ed. EP Orlandi. Campinas, Brasil: Editora Unicamp

Clemente de Souza TC. 1997. Referencialidade e enunuação em Bakairi (Carib). In *Actas de las III Jornadas de Lingüística Aborigen*, ed. A Gerzenstein, pp. 319–28. Buenos Aires, Argentina: Faculdad Filosofía y Letras

Constenla Umaña A. 1990. The language of Bribri ritual songs. *Lat. Am. Indian Lit. J.* 6:14–35

Constenla Umaña A. 1991. *Las Lenguas del Área Intermedia: Introducción a su Estudio Areal*. San José, Costa Rica: Editorial Univ. Costa Rica. 216 pp.

Constenla Umaña A. 1996. *Poesía Tradicional Indígena Costarricense*. San José, Costa Rica: Editorial Univ. Costa Rica. 279 pp.

Constenla Umaña A. 2000. Colúrinhé: a Guatuso traditional narrative. See Sammons & Sherzer 2000, pp. 125–40

Dean B. 1994. The poetics of creation: Urarina cosmogony amd historical consciousness. *Lat. Am. Indian Lit. J.* 10:22–45

de Gerdes ML. 2000. The life story of Grandmother Elida: Kuna personal narratives as verbal art. See Sammons & Sherzer 2000, pp. 158–73

Derbyshire D, Payne DL. 1990. Noun classification systems of Amazonian languages. In *Amazonian Linguistics: Studies in Lowland South American Languages*, ed. DL Payne, pp. 243–71. Austin: Univ. Tex. Press

Derbyshire D, Pullum G. 1986. Introduction. In *Handbook of Amazonian Languages*, ed. D Derbyshire, G Pullum, pp. 1–28. Berlin: Mouton de Gruyter

Dixon RMW, Aikhenvald A, eds. 1999. *The Amazonian Languages*. Cambridge, UK: Cambridge Univ. Press. 446 pp.

Erikson P. 2000. Dialogues à vif... Note sur les salutations en Amazonie. See Monod Becquelin & Erikson 2000, pp. 115–38

Escribano M. 2000. *Cinco Mitos de la Literatura Oral Mhuysqa o Chibcha: Primer Análisis Hacia el Enigma de la Lengua Mhuysqa*. Santafé de Bogotá: [s.n.]. 186 pp.

Ferrer G, Rodríguez Y. 1998. *Etnoliteratura Wayuu: Estudios Críticos y Selección de Textos*. Barranquilla, Colombia: Fondo Publ. Univ. Atlántico. 182 pp.

Fock N. 1963. *Waiwai: Religion and Society of an Amazonian Tribe*. Copenhagen: Nat. Mus. Denmark. 316 pp.

Franchetto B. 1983. A fala do chefe: um genero de fala kuikúro. *Cadernos Estud. Linguíst. (Campinas, Brazil)* 4:45–72

Franchetto B. 1989. Forma e significado na poética oral kuikúro. *Amerindia* 14:83–118

Franchetto B. 1997. Tolo kuikúru: diga cantando o que não pode ser dito falando. *Invenção do Brasil*. Revista Muséu Descobrimento. Ministério da Cultura, pp. 57–64

Franchetto B. 2000. Rencontres rituelles dans le Haut-Xingu: la parole du chef. See Monod Becquelin & Erikson 2000, pp. 481–509

Galvão E. 1996. *Diários de campo entre os Tenetehara, Kaioá e índios do Xingú*. Rio de Janeiro: Editora UFRJ, Museu Indio/FUNAI

Galvis H. 1995. *Somos Bari*. Bogota: Editorial Presencia Ltda

Gnerre M. 1986. The decline of dialogue: ceremonial and mythological discourse among the Shuar and Acuar of eastern Ecuador. See Sherzer & Urban 1986, pp. 307–41

Gomez-Imbert E. 1986. Conocemiento y verdad en tatuyo. *Rev. Antropología (Bogota)* 1–2:117–25

Graham LR. 1986. Three modes of Shavante vocal expression: wailing, collective singing, and political oratory. See Sherzer & Urban 1986, pp. 83–118

Graham LR. 1995. *Performing Dreams: Discourses of Immortality among the Xavante of Central Brazil*. Austin: Univ. Tex. Press

Graham LR. 2000. The one who created the sea: tellings, meanings, and intertextuality in the translation of Xavante narrative. See Sammons & Sherzer 2000, pp. 252–71

Gregor T. 1977. *Mehinaku: The Drama of Daily Life in a Brazilian Indian Village*. Chicago: Univ. Chicago Press. 382 pp.

Guss D. 1991. All things made: myths of the origins of artifacts. See Preuss 1991, pp. 111–16

Heckenberger M. 1996. *War and peace in the shadow of empire: sociopolitical change in the Upper Xingu of Southeastern Amazonia, AD 1400–2000*. PhD thesis. Univ. of Pittsburg, Penn.

Hendriks J. 1990. La manipulación del tiempo en una sociedad Amazónica: género y evento entre los Shuar. See Basso & Sherzer 1990, pp. 47–70

Hendriks J. 1993. *To Drink of Death. The Narrative of a Shuar Warrior*. Tucson: Univ. Ariz. Press

Hidalgo M. 1997. La figura de Sibö como "trickster" en tres textos Bribris. See Preuss 1997, pp. 151–58

Hill JD. 1990. El mito, la música, y la historia: transformaciones poéticas del discurso narrativo en una sociedad amazónica. See Basso & Sherzer 1990, pp. 71–88

Hill JD. 1993. *Keepers of the Sacred Chants: the Poetics of Ritual Power in an Amazonian Society*. Tucson: Univ. Ariz. Press. 245 pp.

Hill JD, Wright R. 1988. The Josho Nahuanbo

are all wet and undercooked: Shipibo views of the whiteman and Inca in myth, legend, and history. In *Rethinking History and Myth: Indigenous South American Perspectives on the Past*, ed. JD Hill. Urbana: Univ. Ill. Press

Hill JH, Irvine JT. 1993. *Responsibility and Evidence in Oral Discourse*. New York: Cambridge Univ. Press. 316 pp.

Howe J. 1994. Sound heard in the distance: poetry and metaphor in Kuna struggle for autonomy. *Lat. Am. Indian Lit. J.* 10:1–21

Hugh-Jones S. 1988. The gun and the bow: myths of the white man and Indian. *Homme* 18:138–55

Huxley M, Capa C. 1964. *Farewell to Eden*. New York: Harper & Row

Jara CV. 1991. Estructura causal de una narración Bribri. See Preuss 1991, pp. 11–14

Jara CV. 1993. *I ttè Historias Bribris*. San José, Costa Rica: Editorial Univ. Costa Rica. 230 pp.

Jara F. 1989. Alemi songs of the turaekare of southern Surinam. *Lat. Am. Indian Lit. J.* 5: 4–12

Journet N. 2000. Dialogues chantés chez les Curripaco de río Negro: un genre métaphorique. See Monod Becquelin & Erikson 2000, pp. 139–64

Juajibioy Chindoy A. 1989. *Relatos Ancestrales del Folclor Comëntsá*. Colombia: Fund. Interamericana. 304 pp.

Juncosa JE. 2000. *Etnografía de la Comunicación Verbal Shuar*. Quito, Ecuador: Ed. Abya-Yala. 178 pp.

Jusayú MA. 1989. *Takü'jala = Lo que he Contado*. Caracas: Univ. Católica Andrés Bello Cent. Leng. Indígenas. 109 pp.

Kane S. 1990. La experiencia contra el mito: una mujer emberá (chocó) y el patriarcado. See Basso & Sherzer 1990, pp. 235–56

Kensinger K. 1995. *How Real People Ought to Live*. Prospect Heights, IL: Waveland

Kerr I. 1976. The centrality of dialogue in Cuiva discourse structure. In *Discourse Grammar: Studies in Indigenous Languages of Colombia, Panama and Ecuador*, ed. RE Longacre, pp. 133–73. Dallas, TX: Summer Inst. Linguist.

Klein H. 1992. South American languages. In *Oxford International Encyclopedia of Linguistics*, ed. W Bright, pp. 31–25. New York: Oxford Univ. Press

Kungiler I. 1997. *Yar Burba, Anmar Burba = Espiritu de Tierra, Nuestro Espiritu: Dulegaya-Castellano*. Panama: Congreso General Cultura Kuna. 115 pp.

Kuyoteca Jifikomui A, Restrepo González D. 1997. *Mitología Uitota: Contada por un Aron+, "Gente de Avispa."* Medellín, Colombia: Editorial Lealón. 796 pp.

Langdon EJ. 1991. When the tapir is anaconda: women and power among the Siona. *Lat. Am. Indian Lit. J.* 7:5–20

Larson ML. 1978. *The Functions of Reported Speech in Discourse*. Arlington, TX: Summer Inst. Linguist. 421 pp.

Lévi-Strauss C. 1969. *The Raw and the Cooked*. New York: Harper & Row

Lizot J. 1994. Words in the night: the ceremonial dialogue. One expression of peaceful relationships among the Yanomami. In *The Anthropology of Peace and Non-Violence*, ed. L Sponsel, T Gregor, pp. 213–37. London: Lynne Rienner

Lizot J. 2000. De l'interprétation des dialogues. See Monod Becquelin & Erikson 2000, pp. 165–82

Magaña E. 1989. The old-head woman and penis man: two Wayana narratives. *Lat. Am. Indian Lit. J.* 5:15–30

Magaña E, Jara F. 1983. Star myths of the Kaliña (Carib). *Lat. Am. Indian Lit. J.* 7:20–37

Maia M. 1997. Poética oral Karayá: los ibrhuky. In *Actas de las III Jornadas de Lingüística Aborigen*, ed. M Censabella, JP Viegas, pp. 435–42. Buenos Aires, Argentina: Facultad Filosofía y Letras

Margery E. 1990. The tar-baby motif in a Bocotá tale "blísgi sigabá gule" ("The opposum and the agouti"). *Lat. Am. Indian Lit. J.* 6(1):1–13

Margery E. 1991. Directrices temáticas de la narrativa oral Bocotá (dialecto de chiriqui). See Preuss 1991, pp. 3–10

Margery E. 1997. Sobre el desarrollo y la

distribución geográfica del motivo de "la misteriosa ama de casa" (N831.1) en la tradición oral indoamericana. See Preuss 1997, pp. 159–80
McDowell JH. 1989. *Sayings of the Ancestors: the Spiritual Life of the Sibundoy Indians*. Lexington: Univ. Press Ky. 206 pp.
McDowell JH. 1990. Construir la comunidad Kamsá por medio del lenguage ritual. See Basso & Sherzer 1990, pp. 297–318
McDowell JH. 1994. *So Wise Were Our Elders: Mythic Narratives of the Kamsá*. Lexington: Univ. Press Ky. 285 pp.
McDowell JH. 2000. Collaborative ethnopoetics: a view from the Sibundoy Valley. See Sammons & Sherzer 2000, pp. 211–32
Michael L. 2001a. *Knowledge, Experience, and Reported Speech in an Amazonian Society: the Nanti of Southeastern Peru*. Presented at Symp. About Language and Society, Austin. Austin, TX
Michael L. 2001b. *Ari ixanti: speech reporting practices among the Nanti of the Peruvian Amazon*. MA thesis. Univ. Texas, Austin. 216 pp.
Migliazza EC. 1972. *Yanomama grammar and intelligibility*. PhD thesis. Indiana Univ. Bloomington. 458 pp.
Migliazza EC. 1985. Languages of the Orinoco-Amazon region: current status. In *South American Indian Languages: Retrospect and Prospect*, ed. H Klein, L Stark, pp. 17–139. Austin: Univ. Tex. Press
Monod Becquelin A. 1975. *La Pratique Linguistique des Indiens Trumai: Haut-xingu, Mato Grosso, Bresil*. Paris: SELAF. 252 pp.
Monod Becquelin A, Erikson P, eds. 2000. *Les Rituels du Dialogue: Promenades Ethnolinguistiques en Terre Amérindiennes*. Nanterre: Société d'ethnologie. 608 pp.
Müller R. 1990. Contexto histórico, reproducción social y noción de representación entre los Assurini del Xingú: el análisis del discurso en el estudio de las sociedades indígenas. See Basso & Sherzer 1990, pp. 395–416
Ochoa Siguas N. 1999. *Niimúhe: Tradición Oral de los Bora de la Amazonía Peruana*. Lima, Perú: Centr. Amazónico de Antropología y Aplicación Práctica: Banco Central de Reserva del Perú. 309 pp.
Orlandi EP, Soares MF, de Souza TCC. 1991. *Discurso Indígena: a Materialidade da Língua e o Movimento da Identidade*. Campinas, Brasil: Editora da Unicamp. 138 pp.
Payne David L. 1990. Some widespread grammatical forms in South American languages. See Doris L Payne 1990a, pp. 75–87
Payne Doris L, ed. 1990a. *Amazonian Linguistics: Studies in Lowland South American Languages*. Austin: Univ. Tex. Press
Payne Doris L. 1990b. Morphological characteristics of lowland South American languages. See Doris L Payne 1990a, pp. 213–41
Pereira F. 1983. Narraciones de Francisco Pereira. *Tradición Oral Indígena Costarricense* 1:11–50
Perrin M. 1987. *The Way of the Dead Indians: Guajiro Myths and Symbols*. Austin: Univ. Tex. Press. 195 pp.
Perrin M. 1988. Formas de comunicación chamánica: el ejemplo guajiro (Venezuela y Colombia). See Bidou & Perrin 1988, pp. 61–80
Preuss MH. 1991. *Past, Present, and Future: Selected Studies on Latin American Indian Literatures: Including the VIII International Symposium*. Culver City, CA: Labyrinthos, 186 pp.
Preuss MH. 1997. *Latin American Indian Literatures: Messages and Meanings: Papers from the Twelfth Annual Symposium, Latin American Indian Literatures Association*. Lancaster, CA: Labyrinthos, 218 pp.
Queixalos F. 1985. Maduedani, héroe cultural Sikuani. *Amerindia* 10:93–126
Reeve M-E. 1988. Righting history in the northwest Amazon: myth, structure, and history in an Arapaco narrative. In *Rethinking History and Myth: Indigenous South American Perspectives on the Past*, ed. JD Hill, n.p. Urbana: Univ. Ill. Press
Reichel-Dolmatoff G. 1996. *Yuruparí: Studies of an Amazonian Foundation Myth*. Cambridge, MA: Harvard Univ. Cent. Stud. World Religions. 300 pp.

Renard-Casevitz FM. 1991. *Le Banquet Masqué: Une Mythologie de l'Étranger chez les Indiens Matsiguenga*. Paris: Lierre Coudrier Distribution Eadiff. 280 pp.

Rivière P. 1971. The political structure of the Trio indians as manifested in a system of ceremonial dialogue. In *The Translation of Culture*, ed. T Beidelman, pp. 293–311. London: Tavistock

Robayo C. 1989. En faisante une rame: texte Carijona. *Amerindia* 14:189–99

Roe P. 1991a. Panó hüetsa nëtë: the armadillo as scaly discoverer of the lower world in Shipibo and lowland South Amerindian perspective. *Lat. Am. Indian Lit. J.* 7:20–72

Roe P. 1991b. Gifts of the birds: avian protocultural donors and ogres in Waiwai mythology. See Preuss 1991, pp. 89–110

Rueda MV, Tankamash R. 1983. *Setenta "Mitos Shuar."* Quito, Ecuador: Mundo Shuar. 289 pp.

Sammons K, Sherzer J, eds. 2000. *Translating Native Latin American Verbal Art: Ethnopoetics and Ethnography of Speaking*. Washington, DC: Smithson. Inst. Press. 309 pp.

Seeger A. 1986. Oratory is spoken, myth is told, and song is sung, but they are all music to my ears. See Sherzer & Urban 1986, pp. 59–82

Seeger A. 1987. *Why Suyá Sing: a Musical Anthropology of an Amazonian People*. Cambridge, UK: Cambridge Univ. Press. 147 pp.

Seki L. 1999. The Upper Xingu as an incipient linguistic area. See Dixon & Aikhenvald 1999, pp. 417–30

Sherzer J. 1983. *Kuna Ways of Speaking: an Ethnographic Perspective*. Austin: Univ. Tex. Press. 260 pp.

Sherzer J. 1986. The report of a Kuna curing specialist: the poetics and rhetoric of an oral performance. See Sherzer & Urban 1986, pp. 169–212

Sherzer J. 1987. Poetic structuring of Kuna discourse: the line. In *Native American Discourse: Poetics and Rhetoric*, ed. J Sherzer, AC Woodbury, pp. 103–39. Cambridge, UK: Cambridge Univ. Press

Sherzer J. 1988. Arte verbal de los cantos shamanisticos Cuna. See Bidou & Perrin 1988, pp. 49–60

Sherzer J. 1990. *Verbal Art in San Blas: Kuna Culture Through its Discourse*. Cambridge UK: Cambridge Univ. Press. 281 pp.

Sherzer J. 1994. The Kuna and Colombus. *Am. Anthropol.* 96:902–24

Sherzer J. 1999. Ceremonial dialogic greetings among the Kuna indians of Panama. *J. Pragmatics* 31:453–70

Sherzer J, Urban G, eds. 1986. *Native South American Discourse*. New York: Mouton de Gruyter. 347 pp.

Silverblatt I. 1988. History, myth, and social consciousness among the Kayapó of central Brazil. In *Rethinking History and Myth: Indigenous South American Perspectives on the Past*, ed. JD Hill. Urbana: Univ. Ill. Press

Siskind J. 1973. *To Hunt in the Morning*. New York: Oxford Univ. Press. 214 pp.

Soares MF. 1991. Aspectos suprassegmentais e discurso em Tikuna. In *Discurso Indígena: a Materialidade da Língua e o Movimento da Identidade*, ed. EP Orlandi, n.p. Campinas, Brasil: Editora da Unicamp

Sorensen AP Jr. 1972. Multilingualism in the northwest Amazon. In *Sociolinguistics: Selected Readings*, ed. JB Pride, J Holmes, pp. 78–93. New York: Penguin

Sturm F. 1991. Ontological categories implicit in the Mbya Guarani creation myth. See Preuss 1991, pp. 117–22

Taylor A, Chau E. 1983. Jivaroan magical songs: Achuar anent of connubial love. *Amerindia* 8:87–128

Urban G. 1986. Ceremonial dialogues in South America. *Am. Anthropol.* 88:371–86

Urban G. 1988. Ritual wailing in Amerindian Brazil. *Am. Anthropol.* 90(2):385–400

Urban G. 1991. *A Discourse-Centered Approach to Culture: Native South American Myths and Rituals*. Austin: Univ. Tex. Press. 215 pp.

Urban G, Sherzer J. 1988. The linguistic anthropology of native South America. *Annu. Rev. Anthropol.* 17:283–307

Uzendoski MA. 1999. Twins and becoming

jaguars: verse analysis of a Napo Quichua myth. *Anthropol. Linguist.* 41:431–61

Vázquez JA. 1991. The Sirionó myth of the moon: reconstruction and interpretation. See Preuss 1991, pp. 129–48

Vázquez JA. 1999. *Literaturas Indígenas de América: Introducción a su Estudio*. Buenos Aires: Editorial Almagesto. 260 pp.

Vyjkág A, Toral A. 1997. *Eg Jamen Ky Mu: Textos Kanhgag*. Brasilia: APBKG: Dka Austria: MEC: PNUD. 190 pp.

Wagley C. 1977. *Welcome of Tears: the Tapirapé Indians of Central Brazil*. New York: Oxford Univ. Press

Waltz NE. 1976. Discourse functions of Guanano sentence and paragraph. In *Discourse Grammar: Studies in Indigenous Languages of Colombia, Panama and Ecuador*, ed. RE Longacre, pp. 21–145. Dallas, TX: Summer Inst. Linguist.

Weiss G. 1983. The sun god and the jaguars. *Lat. Am. Indian Lit. J.* 7:1–12

Wilbert J, ed. 1970. *Folk Literature of the Warao Indians*. Los Angeles: Univ. Calif. Latin Am. Cent.

Wilbert J, Simoneau K, eds. 1978. *Folk Literature of the Ge Indians*. Los Angeles: Univ. Calif. Latin Am. Cent.

Wilbert J, Simoneau K, eds. 1983. *Folk Literature of the Bororo Indians*. Los Angeles: Univ. Calif. Latin Am. Cent.

Wilbert J, Simoneau K, eds. 1990a. *Folk Literature of the Yaruro Indians*. Los Angeles: Univ. Calif. Latin Am. Cent.

Wilbert J, Simoneau K, eds. 1990b. *Folk Literature of the Yanomami Indians*. Los Angeles: Univ. Calif. Latin Am. Cent.

Wilbert J, Simoneau K, eds. 1991. *Folk Literature of the Cuiva Indians*. Los Angeles: Univ. Calif. Latin Am. Cent.

Wilbert J, Simoneau K, eds. 1992. *Folk Literature of the Sikuani Indians*. Los Angeles: Univ. Calif. Latin Am. Cent.

Wilbert J, Simoneau K, Perrin M, eds. 1986. *Folk Literature of the Guajiro Indians*. Los Angeles: Univ. Calif. Latin Am. Cent.

Annu. Rev. Anthropol. 2002. 31:147–71
doi: 10.1146/annurev.anthro.31.040402.085359

First published online as a Review in Advance on May 7, 2002

STREET CHILDREN, HUMAN RIGHTS, AND PUBLIC HEALTH: A Critique and Future Directions

Catherine Panter-Brick
Department of Anthropology, University of Durham, Durham, UK;
email: Catherine.Panter-Brick@durham.ac.uk

Key Words homeless, youth, homelessness, risk, resilience, poverty, ethics, childhood

■ **Abstract** This review presents a critique of the academic and welfare literature on street children in developing countries, with supporting evidence from studies of homelessness in industrialized nations. The turn of the twenty-first century has seen a sea change of perspective in studies concerning street youth. This review examines five stark criticisms of the category "street child" and of research that focuses on the identifying characteristics of a street lifestyle rather than on the children themselves and the depth or diversity of their actual experiences. Second, it relates the change of approach to a powerful human rights discourse—the legal and conceptual framework provided by the United Nations Convention on the Rights of the Child—which emphasizes children's rights as citizens and recognizes their capabilities to enact change in their own lives. Finally, this article examines literature focusing specifically on the risks to health associated with street or homeless lifestyles. Risk assessment that assigns street children to a category "at risk" should not overshadow helpful analytical approaches focusing on children's resiliency and long-term career life prospects. This review thus highlights some of the challenging academic and practical questions that have been raised regarding current understandings of street children.

INTRODUCTION: A SHIFT OF PERSPECTIVE

The presence of children living on the street has elicited emotive public concern, been given considerable media coverage, and in the late twentieth century, has become a matter of priority for national and international child welfare organizations. Publications in both academic and welfare literature have emphasized the sheer scale of the worldwide problem, have sought to explain the root causes of this phenomenon, have summarized the identifying characteristics of street children worldwide, and have documented the dire consequences of a street lifestyle for children's health and development. Titles such as *A Growing Urban Tragedy* (Agnelli 1986), *Causes and Characteristics of the Street Child Phenomenon* (le Roux & Smith 1998), and *Homelessness is not Healthy for Children* (Wright 1990) capture the essence of such concern.

The turn of the twenty-first century has seen a sea change in most of the writing concerning street youth. The term street children itself has almost disappeared from the welfare and analytical literature, which now uses different appellations to refer to street children and other underprivileged groups. Children themselves, of course, are still on the streets, easily visible in the great majority of urban centers. What has been called the global or "worldwide phenomenon of street children" (le Roux 1996) has neither vanished from sight nor effectively been solved. However, current perspectives tend not to demarcate street children so radically from other poor children in urban centers or to conceptualize the homeless in isolation from other groups of children facing adversity. Welfare agencies now talk of "urban children at risk" (Kapadia 1997), which conceptualizes street children as one of a number of groups most at risk and requiring urgent attention. There is accumulated evidence that children move fluidly on and off the streets and that the street does not represent the sum total of their social networks or experiences. A dialogue between academics and welfare practitioners has also been instigated to broaden the insights gained by people working with different categories of unaccompanied, institutionalized, abused, refugee, street, or working children (Boyden & Mann 2000).

In essence, the change in perspective reflects a shift of attention from the street as the primary focus of concern (as an unacceptable or unhealthy environment for children) to the children themselves (paying close attention to the diversity of their actual experiences and their own strategies for coping with adversity). Current work tends to examine the lives of street children in light of more general analyses of poverty, social exclusion, coping strategies, vulnerability and resilience in adversity.

This review begins with a critique of the category "street child," highlighting the problems generated by the categorization of children based on the apparent characteristics of a street lifestyle. It then relates the change of approach to the powerful human rights discourse—the legal and conceptual framework provided by the United Nations Convention on the Rights of the Child—and to new directions in research emphasizing children's own capabilities in coping with adversity. Finally, it examines literature focused specifically on risks to health in the context of street or homeless lifestyles. In short, this review highlights some of the challenging intellectual and practical questions raised by asking who are street children, how their rights might be safeguarded, and why they are a group at risk.

IDENTIFYING STREET CHILDREN: FIVE CRITICISMS

Deceptively simple, the term street child has proved problematic. A basic definition of the term is "a homeless or neglected child who lives chiefly in the streets" (*Oxford Dictionary*). The statement emphasizes two peculiarities about street children: the *place* they occupy (the streets) and the absence of proper contacts or *links* with adults in the family home and in society. This encapsulates much of the thinking behind studies of street children in the 1980s. Such work was concerned with establishing the hallmarks of a street lifestyle and the characteristics of street children in terms of their use of public spaces and their links with family and public institutions.

Recent literature has argued that the appellation "street children" is problematic for several reasons. First, it is a generic term that obscures the heterogeneity in children's actual circumstances. Second, it does not correspond to the ways many children relate their own experiences or to the reality of their movements on and off the street. Third, it is imbued with pejorative or pitying connotations. Fourth, it deflects attention from the broader population of children affected by poverty and social exclusion. Indeed, "street children" is a construct that reflects various social and political agendas. These are strong criticisms, which go some way toward explaining why "street children" is a difficult working concept and why other terms of reference or appellations have emerged in recent analytical literature.

A Generic Term Obscuring Differences in Children's Circumstances

The first difficulty, the need to recognize that street children are not a homogeneous group but experience very different circumstances and lifestyles, was already obvious more than 20 years ago. Welfare agencies, in particular UNICEF and Save the Children, have reworked their definition of street children many times, finding it difficult to devise meaningful statements about these children as people, to define various categories of street life, and more recently, to identify appropriate categories of "at risk" children (Panter-Brick 2001a).

In the words of Raffaelli & Larson (1999, p. 1): "The term street youth, or street children ... conceals enormous variation in the experiences of youngsters who share the common condition of being 'out of place' in street environments, spending their lives largely outside the spheres typically considered appropriate for children, such as home, school, and recreational settings." The individuals concerned are all minors under 18 years of age, but from a broad age spectrum including teenage and near-teen youth as well as children as young as 5 (and sometimes, also the infants of homeless parents).

An early consensual definition of street children, formulated in 1983 by the Inter-NGO Programme for Street Children and Street Youth, stated: "Street children are those for whom the street (in the widest sense of the word: i.e., unoccupied dwellings, wasteland, etc....) more than their family has become their real home, a situation in which there is no protection, supervision or direction from responsible adults" (Ennew 1994, p. 15). The United Nations adopted the phrasing: "any boy or girl ... for whom the street in the widest sense of the word ... has become his or her habitual abode and/or source of livelihood, and who is inadequately protected, supervised, or directed by responsible adults." For Save the Children Fund, "a street child is any minor who is without a permanent home or adequate protection" (UNESCO 1995, p. 286). There are three important elements in these definitions: the time children spend on the street, the street as a source of livelihood, and the lack of protection and care from adults (le Roux & Smith 1998).

Several terms in these definitions, however, have led to confusion. What is meant by home, family, protection, and a "responsible" adult? Such terms are conceptualized differently across cultures (Hecht 1998). Indeed adult-child relationships may be premised upon a radically different understanding of "normal" childhood. There are communities facing significant poverty where children are the prime caretakers of incapacitated adults and the prime income earners in the household, such that relationships of care, protection, and provision flow from the child to the adult rather than from the adult to the child (Boyden & Mann 2000). Being homeless is also variously rendered across cultures, as *desamparado* (defenceless, unprotected) in Latin America, *furosha* (floating) in Japan, and *khate* (rag-picker) in Nepal. These terms evoke disaffiliation, transience, and marginal economic work, rather than notions of lack of home or abode (Desjarlais 1996).

It has also been difficult to uphold the typology of children "*of* the street" and "*on* the street," established by UNICEF to differentiate street-based or home-based street children. The distinction here is between children *of* the street—who have a family accessible to them but make the streets their home–and child workers *on* the street—who return at night to their families. This terminology was promoted world-wide (*de la calle/en la calle* in Spanish; *de la rue/dans la rue* in French), but in practice it was found unsatisfactory as children themselves defied these generalizations. Many children sleep both at home and on the streets, and they also spend significant periods of time in residential institutions like orphanages, refuges, or correctional establishments. Other distinctions have been made between abandoned and abandoning street children in the Third World (Felsman 1984), or between runaway and throwaway homeless adolescents in the West, according to the degree of family involvement, the amount of deviant behavior (Cosgrove 1990), or a range of sociological characteristics (Lusk 1992). These and other labels, such as children "without family contact" or "abandoned," lack precision and have been used ad hoc rather than analytically (Felsman 1984, Glauser 1990, Panter-Brick 2000).

Today, the focus on discrete categories of street lifestyles has fallen into disuse. Efforts to devise a suitable definition and an appropriate typology of street children represented the first steps toward a useful conceptual framework to think about the children in question. A classification of children is still useful, as long as it is understood that categories are neither discrete nor necessarily homogeneous, and that they may not always coincide with children's own views about their lives. It is with these important provisos that current research makes distinctions between street and working children (Ennew 1994, Barker & Knaul 1991), between street-living and street-working children (Consortium for Street Children 1998), between family-based street workers and independent street workers, or between homeless and working youth (Raffaelli 1999), distinctions that essentially uphold the original UNICEF typology. The category of street children may be "impossibly constructed" (Ennew 2000, p. 171), but there are few practical alternatives available—beyond local terms—to refer to these particular groups of children.

Inadequate Representations of Children's Experiences

A second criticism leveled at earlier studies of street children is that a simple focus on the street tends to promote a unidimensional account of children's lives, which does not do justice to children's actual behaviors and wider social networks.

In his study of Brazilian children, for example, Hecht (1998) asked the question: "How do the children who sleep on the street speak of themselves?" Most interestingly, he sought to explain why some youth describe themselves as street children when their siblings, who lead very similar lives, do not. When does a child consider him or herself a street child? Hecht argued that in the context of Northeast Brazil, the difference of identity hinges on the child's relationship to a mother figure: a street child is one who has abandoned his mother and left the right track. The point is not whether children are *on* or *off* the streets, but how they see themselves in relation to their family and society at large. In his words, some children "work in the street, dance in the street, beg in the street, sleep in the street, but the street is the venue for their actions not the essence of their character" (Hecht 1998, p. 103). Hecht's comparative inquiry of children in poor neighborhoods (*favelas*) is an account of how children interpret for themselves their home and their street lives, which gives a much broader context to their activities and social networks.

Most recent studies agree that portrayals of street children cannot be reduced to a one or two dimensional focus on the street environment, defining the children's existence solely with reference to a physical and/or social dimension (permanence in the street and contacts with responsible adults). Lucchini (1997), for instance, elaborated seven dimensions of a child-street system. In addition to spatial, temporal, and social elements, he considered that dynamic behavior (types of activities), self-identification, motivation vis-à-vis street life, and gender-structured differential access to street environments. This approach served to highlight some striking differences in the life circumstances and negotiated identities of street children in Brazil, Uruguay, and Mexico.

A Stigmatizing Label

The term "street children" has powerful emotional overtones. Common public responses are pity and hostility (Aptekar 1988), with street children perceived as victims or villains. Ironically, the term "street children" itself was widely adopted by international agencies in an attempt to avoid negative connotations for children who had been known as street urchins, vagrants, *gamines*, rag-pickers, glue-sniffers, street Arabs, or vagrants (Williams 1993).

It has been argued that the label street children, now so emotionally charged, does little to serve the interests of the children in question. Consider this statement: "The term has a stigmatising effect, since the child is, as it were, allocated to the street and to delinquent behaviour. The term neither gives consideration to the experience or testimony of the children in question nor to other facets of their identity, which do not necessarily have any relevance to the street. Thus it becomes a cause of discrimination of the children and triggers or strengthens negative social reactions" (Invernizzi 2001, p. 79). In brief, the label "contributes to a social reaction towards them" (p. 81). Even programs of intervention for street children can result in their discrimination and stigmatization.

This social reaction leads to stereotypes related to gender, ethnicity, and age; for instance, that all street girls are prostitutes (Lucchini 1994, p. 6) and street boys junkies, and that younger children should be pitied but teenagers, especially dark-skinned ones, should be feared (Huggins & de Castro 1996). It also lumps together the homeless, a highly visible but minority group, with home-based street-workers. Thus authors writing on street children (*meninos de rua* in Portuguese, *niños de la calle* in Spanish, *enfants de la rue* in French) will declare that they find the use of this generic term questionable—but retain it for lack of useful alternatives (Invernizzi 2001). Street children themselves may reject it as a pejorative label or conversely endorse it in order to define their shared identity (Baker 1997, p. 145–65, Kilbride et al. 2000).

Limited Viewpoint and Limited Action

Finally, a significant argument in some of the literature is that a focus on street children—easily represented as the symbol of child poverty and social exclusion—concentrates attention toward only the most visible tip of a huge iceberg. "As a target group for policy makers, street children have hijacked the urban agenda . . . to the detriment of other groups of disadvantaged urban children" (Ennew 2000, p. 169). Rizzini et al. (1999, p. 3) also argued: "a focus on street children—however well-intentioned—deflects attention from the broader population of low income children and youth in poverty. . . . Most children's programs [in Brazil] have directed their attention to a relatively small number of children and youth in the most dire situations." These authors find compelling reasons for changing policy and program attention in Brazil from street children to all children, with interventions giving social and developmental support "to all children and not just those who face specific risks, such as the risk of being abandoned or abused" (p. 3).

Focusing attention on street children can thus lead agencies to overlook or ignore the much larger problem of urban—and rural—poverty. For Lane (1998, p. 18), however, the distinction between "those that are at greatest risk of taking to street life and those who live in poverty is central to effective prevention strategies": not all disadvantaged children take to the streets, and those who do are most likely to slip though the nets of broad-based community interventions.

The public discourse on street children as victims of violence—particularly in Colombia, Guatemala, Brazil, and Honduras—has also distracted attention from the issue of widespread poverty and violence affecting children who live at home, and the "quiet, private death that is hunger and disease" (Hecht 1998, p. 146). Indeed there are radically different understandings of violence linked to distinct social groups, reflecting distinct constructions of childhood (Márquez

1999, p. 216–18). Such arguments highlight that international, national, and local action on behalf of specific groups of children in adversity (street youth, abandoned children, child laborers, sex workers) closely reflects the construction and management of a social and political issue.

A Social and Political Issue

It has been argued that both the street children issue and the "homelessness problem" are constructs deftly manipulated to reflect the various agendas and interests of stakeholders such as the welfare agencies. For instance, very large estimates of the number of children in the street are produced to draw attention to the need for the agency's work. At best, these estimates rest upon largely elastic and nebulous definitions of homeless and working children. At worst, they are made up. The "arithmetic is as symbolic as the children involved" (Ennew 2000, p. 170).

Many publications on street children impress upon their readership the sheer magnitude of the problem. The talk is of numbers, and the numbers cited are huge. Thus 100 million youth are said to be growing up in the streets of urban centers world-wide (UNICEF 1989, cited in Campos 1994). Other estimates have 170 million living on the street (Pinto et al. 1994), or give a range for street children of 30 to 170 million (United Nations 1986, quoted in Barker & Knaul 1991). In Brazil alone, UNICEF estimated in the late 1980s that 7 million youth spent most of their time and/or slept on the street, and this figure readily came to designate homeless children. Hecht (1998, p. 101) suggests the true number of homeless children in Brazil is less than 1% of that figure. The estimate of 7 million in Brazil is certainly an overstatement (Barker & Knaul 1991).

Estimates will vary, of course, in relation to how a mobile population of children is counted and, most importantly, exactly who is considered for inclusion, because the term street children has different meanings in different regions. For example, in the Philippines, it denotes those who "spend most of their time on the streets yet who maintain some regular contact with a family" (UNESCO 1995, p. 117). In contrast, it may denote more strictly those children who at night have no parental home to go to. Thus the estimates of welfare agencies are not always concerned with the same children. Ennew (1994) states categorically: "Neither UNICEF nor the ILO [International Labour Organization] can give reliable or verifiable figures for the number of working children worldwide, including street children. A basic reason for the lack of accurate figures is that no one can agree on definitions. [Numbers] are often cited at the beginning of reports and descriptions of street and working children, but they have no validity or basis in fact" (p. 32).

The definition of homeless youth in industrialized countries is also elastic and can include those who sleep rough, live in shelters, squat, or double up with other families, encompassing the "literally homeless" and the "precariously housed" (Glasser & Bridgman 1999, Chamberlain & Johnson 2001). In Great Britain, Hutson & Liddiard (1994) have argued that estimates of homeless youth tend to be not only inflated by welfare agencies to legitimate their role, but also minimized by bureaucratic institutions to sidestep legal or financial responsibilities. In brief, the statistics are problematic: They reflect the particular agendas of organizations that collect them, and they are part of the construction and the management of homelessness as a social issue (Hutson & Liddiard 1994).

Summary

The term street children is problematic. It serves to highlight a set of working and living conditions that diverge from accepted norms about children. Thus street children are those who occupy the public spaces of urban centers and whose activities are largely unsupervised by adults, which leads people to view them as different from other children. However, research has convincingly shown that it is important to move beyond a sole focus on the street and that there is more to the lives of children than what is revealed by ad hoc categorizations based on the criteria of physical location, social neglect, and economic activity.

HUMAN RIGHTS AND THE BEST INTERESTS OF CHILDREN

The United Nations Convention on the Rights of the Child (1989), which came into force in September 1990, has had a huge impact in defining conceptual frameworks and humanitarian concerns regarding children in adversity. The Convention asserted a number of rights for children worldwide, formulated basic principles to be applied, and created a legal obligation to put these rights and principles into practice. Concern for children in difficult circumstances was no longer a matter of humanitarian and charitable concern, but now is a legal responsibility falling on a state as party to the Convention. The Convention listed the areas where the rights and interests of children must be taken into account—for example, separation from parents, freedom of expression, health, education and employment—and enunciated that in all actions concerning children, "the best interest of the child shall be a prime consideration" (Article 3.1). This universal mandate was carefully worded to formulate a clear principle to empower intervention while leaving room for some flexibility and cultural interpretation (Alston 1994, Van Bueren 1998, Panter-Brick 2000).

Recent publications concerning street children have explicitly referred to children's rights and their best interests as advocated in the Convention. For instance, The Consortium for Street Children produced *The Human Rights of Street and Working Children*, devised as a practical manual for implementing the Convention (Byrne 1998). UNICEF's *Implementation Handbook for the Convention*, which adopted a wider brief, considered those who live and work on the street under the heading of "children deprived of their family environment" (UNICEF 1998). To these rights enshrined in international law, Ennew (1995) added some important yet unwritten rights for children outside society and "normal" childhood. These include the right for street children not be labeled, to be correctly researched and counted, to work and have their own support systems respected, the rights to privacy and respect for their individuality (including sexuality), and the right to be protected from exploitation by the media, activists, or fundraisers (through an exaggeration of children's weaknesses and vulnerability).

A Change of Emphasis from "Needs" to "Rights"

The Convention heralded a change in the prevailing discourse regarding street children and, more generally, children facing adversity. The emphasis moved significantly from highlighting the *needs* of vulnerable children to defending their *rights* as citizens.

Earls & Carlson (1999, p. 72) expressed this change of approach forcefully: "In recent years, the entire concept of childhood has been reconstructed . . . Children are citizens . . . The idea that they are simply immature creatures whose needs must be met by parents or other charitably inclined adults is becoming obsolete. As citizens, children have rights that entitle them to the resources required to protect and promote their development." Street children, however, are socially excluded, an exclusion that begins with lack of access to birth certificates and registration documents, lack of stability of residence, proper education, and health care: This group of children is deprived of citizenship rights. Advocacy on their behalf has therefore featured lobbying for inclusion of children's rights at the national level (for example, in the Brazilian Constitution; Rizzini 1994, pp. 96–97, Klees et al. 2000, pp. 92–95).

Yet the concept of "the child in need" still permeates "the everyday vocabulary" of social work (Woodhead 1990, p. 60). This construct draws a credible veil over any uncertainty or possible disagreement regarding which action might work in the "best interests" of children (p. 62). It is easily taken for granted and applied indiscriminately to all children facing difficult circumstances. There are several reasons why this approach is unsatisfactory (Moss et al. 2000). First, the problem to be addressed is defined "as essentially individual and psychological, not social and structural" (p. 244). Second, the child is "classified as coming from an abnormal family and is constructed, through the language used, as deficient (having a need), weak (being needy), and a subject of charity" (p. 245).

The discourse about children's rights is revolutionary, yet one must tread carefully. The notion that children as individuals have inalienable human rights must be negotiated with the notion of group and family rights (giving children duties and responsibilities toward their elders) prevailing in many non-Western cultures (Alston 1994, Goonesekere 1998, Montgomery 2001, p. 82–85). The notion that minors have rights usually raises questions regarding their developmental and social maturity: To respect or condone a child's choice to live on the streets, to grow up with peers rather than with a family, to work for an income, and to have sex is for many a morally unsatisfactory position. Should the rights discourse be tempered with a measured consideration of children's capabilities—an appreciation of children as individuals with specific competences and maturity, able to discern and adopt those behaviors that, realistically, will improve their quality of life? To make rights contingent upon capacity is, however, problematic—especially where children are concerned, when adults remain the all-powerful adjudicators of their competences (Freeman 1996).

Children as Agents of Change and Capable of Participation

Another significant shift of emphasis, grounded in the UN Convention, was to recognize that promoting the best interests of children is not just a matter of protecting and providing for them, but of listening to them and fostering child participation. There is a careful balance to be struck between the three broad categories of rights in the Convention: rights to protection, provision, and participation. Adults are wont to emphasize the first two, being reluctant to let street children grasp participatory rights—other than by accident (Ennew 2000, p. 176). The third set of rights recognizes that children are "agents of change in their own lives" (Myers 1988, p. 137), which demands that adults recognize that children have agency and manifest social competency (shaping their lives for themselves). This drives the ethics of a program for research or intervention toward necessary consultation and child participation.

It has been forcefully argued that a portrayal of children as "vulnerable, incompetent and relatively powerless in society" (Morrow & Richards 1996, p. 90) is deeply problematic. To present street children as helpless victims of social discrimination does little to recognize their remarkable initiative and ingenuity in coping with difficult circumstances (Ennew 1994, Panter-Brick 2001a). For this reason, research has shifted emphasis from portrayals of vulnerability and dependency to a discussion of children's coping strategies in the face of adversity: It may be more helpful to identify the factors that help children cope with adversity than to emphasize the problems in their circumstances (Felsman 1989, Engle et al. 1996, Boyden et al. 1998). Thus, several discourses about street children compete for attention. One is journalistic, descriptive, and atheoretical, targeted to mass audiences; another is research-focused and aims to promote critical understanding and to influence effective policy development (Blunt 1994, p. 258). Stark images of children's vulnerabilities (Portrait 1) coexist with a more dignified portrayal of their lives (Portrait 2).

Portrayals of street children (as victims, villains, dependents, or deviants) also have an impact on types of intervention (Ennew 1994). Interventions focused on "rescuing" children from the streets by placing them back at school or with the family have generally not provided lasting solutions because they tend to ignore children's own views and all that they have already accomplished for themselves. As stressed in a Save The Children publication, street and working children are not "objects of concern but people. They are vulnerable but not incapable. They need respect, not pity" (Ennew 1994, p. 35). The key to research and project design has changed to working with children rather than for them, thus giving prime importance to child participation.

The development of interactive and participatory research methods has hinged upon the realization that children have social agency and competency and are capable of making informed decisions about their lives and of expressing views and aspirations that may differ from the views held by adults (Ennew 1994; Johnson et al. 1995, 1998; Hutchby & Moran-Ellis 1998). The call has been for novel ways of conducting research with children, ways that would prioritize their own perspectives and allow for their participation in the design and implementation of

Portrait 1 Columbia's street children "considered disposable" by hired killers. Photograph by Gilles Peress/Magnum, reproduced in *The Independent, 30 January 1994*: Marginalization, destitution, ill-health.

research objectives (Connolly & Ennew 1996, Johnson et al. 1998). These have included participation of the children themselves in the research process, not just as informants but as researchers, conducting interviews, taking photographs, or shooting videos of their world and of one another. It has also led to new approaches for advocacy—a social mobilization of street and working children at grassroots levels culminating in their participation, even ownership, of national and international forums in which children's rights issues were debated (Swift 1997).

These child-centered approaches do not, however, evade the issue of ethical concerns: involving children as participants rather than subjects raises its own set of ethical problems. The ethics of social research with children are not limited to securing informed consent and respecting children's views: They extend to appropriate ways of collecting, interpreting, and disseminating—without distortion—findings. They are complicated by the disparities in power and status between adults and children and by a consideration of age-related competence (Morrow & Richards 1996). And as Hecht noted for research in Northeast Brazil, there are considerable ethical challenges when working with street youth who lead very violent and vulnerable lives; many of these challenges are wholly unanticipated (Hecht 2000).

Portrait 2 India's railway children at Villupuram station in Tamil Nadu. Photograph by David Maidment/The Railway Children, reproduced in the *Streets Apart Magazine, February* 2001: Friendship, social ease.

Summary

Work with street children has turned away from a discourse that categorized them as children in need and emphasized their weaknesses and dependency, in favor of highlighting children's own voices as citizens and their capabilities as agents of change. This reveals a shift in the fundamental assumptions made about children (as active participants rather than underage dependents), which itself brought about fresh approaches regarding appropriate methods for research and interventions on behalf of children. Let us now turn to examine another kind of discourse, one that designates street children as an at risk category.

"AT RISK" CHILDREN AND PUBLIC HEALTH CONCERNS

In current welfare literature, street children are a category of "children at risk." This phrase has replaced the one "children in need" and even taken over UNICEF's appellations "children in especially difficult circumstances" abbreviated as CEDC (Kapadia 1997), and "children in need of special protection" abbreviated as CNSP. Indeed in recent literature the generic category "urban children at risk" tends to replace the terms street and working children (Valentin 1999). But this term of reference may also be ambiguous, analytically unhelpful, stigmatizing for children, and manipulated to serve socio-political agendas. Is "risk" another one of these catch-all phrases that proves under close examination to be an unsatisfactory construct? It does raise the question: "at risk of what?"

The Risk Factors and At Risk Discourse

Given the difficulties that beset earlier categorizations of children *on* and *of* the streets, Hutz & Koller (1999, p. 61) suggested that "perhaps a more appropriate way of classifying street children would be in terms of the risks to which they were exposed" (contact with gangs, use of drugs, school abandonment, inadequate parental guidance) "and the protective factors available to them" (school, supportive social networks, caring adults). These authors noted, however, that risk assessment in research with street children is a particularly complex issue.

In public health, risk factors are variables that predispose an individual to ill-health; the assessment of risk proceeds from a statistical measurement of those factors shown to affect health and well-being. In the case of street children, such risk factors include poverty, family dysfunction, ethnicity, gender, age, education, disability, work experience, and stability of residence. However, it is tempting to generalize from a statistical (and largely empirical) statement regarding specific risk factors to a qualitative (and collective) categorization of the children in question. The quantitative approach to risk—a matter of ordering reality (rendering it into calculable form)—leads to a qualitative assessment of individuals as falling within at risk categories (Dean 1999, pp. 143–44). Thus a statistical statement (being at high or low risk in a specified context) translates into a normative statement—a global narrative regarding groups of children—regardless of context.

This leads to unhelpful assumptions of generalized vulnerability and represents a further instance of categorical thinking about children.

Moreover, although risk factors are based on the calculable, at risk discourses evoke the incalculable—a perception of fear or danger. Particularly when it comes to children, risk anxiety is focused on those who come under public scrutiny, fall outside accepted social boundaries, and are perceived as an endangered or a dangerous group. Risk management in relation to such children is fueled by risk anxiety, honed by "a climate of heightened risk awareness" and the construct of childhood as a protected state in which children should lead safe and carefree lives (Jackson & Scott 1999, p. 87). In discourses about children, there is not only "a growing consciousness of children *at risk*" but also "a growing sense of children themselves as *the risk* ... as people out of place and excess populations to be eliminated" or controlled (Stephens 1995, p. 13). Views about risk thus present an ambivalence in referring to groups who are especially vulnerable but also to groups who explicitly disturb or violate established social norms. It is precisely because street children are so visibly "out of place," many of them living a life of "inchoate rebellion" (Scheper-Hughes & Hoffman 1998, p. 383) and self-destruction characterized by violence, sexual exploitation, illiteracy, and haphazard nutrition, that they are the focus of intense concern—whereas their peers in urban centers, living at home in great poverty in slum and squatter settlements, are not.

Specific Risks to Health: Street Children Relative to Their Peers

Categorical statements about street children being *the most* at risk of negative physical, mental, and developmental outcomes abound in the literature. One striking example of the often polemical stance adopted regarding the health outcomes of a street existence is provided by de la Barra who claimed: "Being poor is itself a health hazard; worse, however, is being urban and poor. Much worse is being poor, urban, and a child. But worst of all is being a street child in an urban environment" (de la Barra 1998, p. 46). As for homelessness, Wright (1990b, p. 62) maintained: "it is hard to conceive of a socially defined 'risk factor' that is of greater consequence for a person's physical wellbeing." Over and above poverty, a homeless existence would expose "persons of all genders and ages" to a characteristic package of disorders (Wright 1990a, p. 84; 1991) identifiable "everywhere" across cultural contexts (Wright & Kaminsky 1993, p. 282). Indeed, by emphasizing the debilitating aspects of street life, most studies have brought street children to prominence as "a category of children whose life circumstances place them at physical and psychosocial risk" (Veale et al. 2000, p. 131).

However, the assessment of risk is problematic because the statistics collected from street children are often suspect in their validity and reliability. Many studies feature samples that are small, ill-defined, or unrepresentative of the homeless or street child population. They also lack in rigor for want of appropriate comparison groups: Homeless street children tend to be compared with Western middle class children, the gold standard of childhood, rather than with local groups of poor, home-based children who arguably represent a more realistic lifestyle alternative for children in the streets (Panter-Brick 2001b). Moreover, there are few comprehensive overviews of the literature, which includes unpublished academic theses, government reports, and advocacy materials, despite some attempts to produce a compilation of studies by topics or geographical areas (see Mermet 1997, Ennew & Milne 1997, Invernizzi 2001). This makes it particularly difficult to distinguish the risks attributed to homelessness or street life from those associated with socioeconomic disadvantage (Holden 1995, Panter-Brick 2001b). Indeed, one review of the health problems of U.S. homeless children asked whether "it is appropriate to focus exclusively on homelessness as a marker of risk" given that homelessness is "one event along the continuum of a child's experience of poverty" (Ziesemer et al. 1994). And if homelessness is "simply the most visible and exaggerated manifestation of chronic poverty, then broader policy questions must be raised" (Molnar et al. 1990, p. 120).

In terms of physical health, some studies—explicitly designed to compare homeless with home-based children—have challenged the assumption that "all street children are pitiful, pale and thin, malnourished" (Gross et al. 1996). They have highlighted the fact that street children had higher, albeit irregular, income than home-based children and relied on networks of solidarity and care within their peer group to buffer themselves against shortfalls. Indeed one paper concluded bluntly that even in Latin America, "street children fare no worse than other children from similar backgrounds" (Scanlon et al. 1998). A review of the evidence to date (drawing from studies in Honduras, Indonesia, Nepal, Ethiopia, and the United States) concludes that it is not possible to uphold facile generalizations about the health outcomes of street children that would easily demarcate them from other poor children (Panter-Brick 2001b). The results of comparative studies are in any case difficult to interpret, because the health status of individuals included in a sample may reflect selective migration onto the street and/or a bias in favor of those who successfully remain on the street (Panter-Brick et al. 1996).

In terms of mental health, criticisms have also been made of the view that street children necessarily suffer from negative developmental outcomes. Felsman and Aptekar are two authors who argue quite strongly that the majority of street children they have studied (mostly in Colombia) were "clearly without pathology" (Aptekar 1991, p. 328), displayed better mental health than poor counterparts (Felsman 1981), and showed a high level of self-management (Aptekar 1988). Other studies make similar claims (deSouza et al. 1995, Monteiro et al. 1998, review by Raffaelli 1999). One set of authors concluded: "Rather than being the most victimized, the most destitute, the most psychologically vulnerable group of children, street children may be resilient and display creative coping strategies for growing up in difficult environments" (Veale et al. 2000, p. 137). Attention is here paid to street-wise behaviors and remarkable survival skills, which cannot however be equated with invulnerability or mature emotional development (see Kilbride et al. 2000, pp. 6–7). There is also evidence of an habituation to stressful events, which extends to a downregulation of the physiological responses associated with stress. In two studies using the hormone cortisol as a sensitive marker of anxiety and psychosocial arousal, average cortisol levels for homeless street children were similar to those of middle class children in Nepal (Panter-Brick 2001b) and to those of home-based street workers in Ethiopia (Dobrowolska & Panter-Brick 1998).

In terms of engaging in drug-taking, survival sex, and HIV-risk behavior, studies overwhelmingly ascribe street youth, and street girls particularly, to an at risk category (Scanlon et al. 1998). But as with the measurement of mental health through psychiatric and psychological morbidity, the assessment of drug-taking and sexual health is fraught with significant methodological problems. Mere use of questionnaire data, without triangulation with other methods, is suspect and provides limited cross-sectional information (Ennew & Milne 1997, Hutz & Koller 1999). Few surveys include the screening of home-based and street-based youth for markers of sexually transmitted infections (Porto et al. 1994, Pinto et al. 1994), nor do they corroborate self-reports for common infections (Panter-Brick et al. 2001). Nonetheless, Raffaelli's review (1999, p. 20) concluded that the weight of studies leaves little doubt that homeless youth are at higher risk of abusive sexual relationships and of sexually transmitted infections than are their peers. HIV in particular poses a dramatic challenge in Africa due to the magnitude of the AIDS epidemic and war-related instability (UNICEF 2001), although to date very little research has been conducted on war, HIV-risks, and street children (Inverzinni 2001, p. 92).

Finally, because many street youth live harsh and violent lives (Childhope 1991; Scheper-Hughes & Hoffman 1994; Human Rights Watch 1996, 1997; Márquez 1999; Berman 2000; Hecht 2000), risks to health include death from violent trauma, suicide, accidents, and murder; however, few survival statistics have ever been published (Raffaelli 1999, p. 18; Huggins & Mesquita 2000). Those deaths represent a brutal end to pervasive social marginalization. Social exclusion is also reflected in the risk of educational failure and poor cognitive performance—although street life can offer opportunities for nonstandard education (Donald & Swart-Kruger 1994, Blunt 1994).

Substantial evidence thus supports the view that street children are a category at risk, but there is also disagreement with a discourse that sets the characteristics of street life in global terms, associating the worst health outcomes with street children by ascription. Specific risks to health need to be rigorously investigated, and not overgeneralized to cover all aspects of health—physical health, mental health, sexual health—which constitute different benchmarks for risk assessment. Otherwise research and public health concerns are in danger of being led by a normative view of at risk categories and marred by a lack of conceptual clarity, rather than focused on the critical appraisal of what constitutes risk. This is true to the extent that the literature on street children is guilty of "systematically ignor[ing] its own findings in favour of predetermined conclusions grounded in Northern, middle class mores" (Bar-On 1997, p. 63).

As Sibert (2000) wisely indicated, what public health professionals would really like to know is whether homeless street children are "uniquely disadvantaged or whether they form one end of the spectrum of poor children" with respect to risks to health. To achieve this, research on children in adversity needs to be quite extensively overhauled. As emphasized by Holden et al. (1995, p. 176) for the United States, "research on children in poverty has already shifted from comparisons between children in low-income and middle-income families to in-depth analyses of processes mediating poverty's influences on developmental and health outcomes . . . [To] understand why some homeless children display a host of [mental] health problems and why others survive and succeed, attention should be focused on variations within homeless populations." What is important to future research are the factors of risk and resilience that shape the long-term coping strategies of individual children, by developing their competence for negotiating high risk situations.

Resilience and Long-Term Career Perspectives

Influential research has argued that a helpful counterpart to the risk discourse is to focus attention on the resilience of children who manage to negotiate extremely difficult circumstances. As Rutter (1987, 2001) explained, resilience is the term used to describe the positive pole of individual differences in responses to stress and adversity. Rutter further emphasized that in the field of psychiatric risk research, there has been a shift of focus not only "from vulnerability to resilience, but also from risk *variables* to the process of *negotiating* risk situations" (1987, p. 316). This represents a useful approach—one that is not constrained by categorical thinking but centers on identifying the protective factors that help individuals cope with adversity.

Research on resilience is by no means simple (Richman & Fraser 2001). In 1990, Rutter (1990, pp. 182–83) made a critically important argument: Research will gain very little if it confines itself to a mechanistic search for protective factors as those sets of *variables* that will predict resiliency with fair consistency (namely, personality features, family cohesion, and external support systems). Instead, it must appraise the developmental and contextual *processes* by which some individuals manage to negotiate adversity (why and how they maintain self-esteem and self-efficacy; how they managed to have effective social networks). It is wrong to assume that vulnerability or protection lies in the variable (e.g., social support) per se, rather than in the active role taken by individuals under adversity: Resilience is a reflection of an individual's agency.

It is also crucial, but obviously difficult, to appraise how protective factors may work in interaction with each other, to investigate their relative importance over a lifetime, and finally to confirm their relevance across different cultures. The majority of risk research remains based on comparison groups within a cross-sectional design (Neiman 1988). The overwhelming body of work on resilience concerns itself with industrialized countries, such that little information exists on children and adversity in other contexts (Boyden & Mann 2000). Significantly, cross-cultural studies on street youth may not support unilateral conclusions regarding gender differences in coping with a long-term existence on the street, despite the argument that girls are at higher risk of negative outcomes than their male peers (Raffaelli et al. 2000).

Current work with street children sees further studies on developmental vulnerability and resilience to be fundamental to both research and practical intervention. For street children present us with a "central and pervasive" paradox—"with evidence of developmental risk and vulnerability on the one hand and of resourcefulness, adaptability, and coping on the other" (Donald & Swart-Kruger 1994, p. 169). Indeed, researchers have been fascinated by both positive and negative aspects of their lives and personalities: Barker & Knaul (1991) describe them as "both needy and bold, exploited but street-smart entrepeneurs." For Felsman, the paradox is that *gamines* in Colombia stand "at the intersection of human strength and vulnerability" (Felsman 1989, p. 56). These and other authors agree that the best approach is not to generalize over what common factors in street lifestyles lead to at risk situations, but to ask a different order of questions. A pertinent issue relates to how key developmental stressors "combine to produce actual, not just putative, developmental vulnerability" (Donald & Swart-Kruger 1994, p. 173); in many cases, it is the combination of multiple stressors rather than the experience of any single factor that defines an individual's vulnerability.

Arguably, the concept of a street or homeless career—or the notion of street children having fluid careers—is another fruitful analytic device for moving the literature beyond its habitual snap shot descriptions of children, because it calls for data giving both time-depth and contextual information. The concept of career, used by Goffman (1961) and Becker (1973) in their studies of social deviance, can help appraise for street children the long-term outcomes of social experiences and negotiated identities (Visano 1990, p. 142). For the homeless, self-perceptions and social experiences are the bedrock of career outcomes, as shown in the United Kingdom by Hutson & Liddiard (1994, p. 124) and in Nepal by Baker & Panter-Brick (2000).

It should not surprise anyone to find that the outcomes of homeless careers will differ by cultural context. In Northeast Brazil, Hecht (1998) reported that prison, insanity, or death were the common expectations of life for street children, while also in Brazil, Vasconcelos (quoted in Raffaelli 1999) thus summarized the stark prospects for street girls: They "disappear. They are arrested or they die. They die from venereal diseases, they are sent to mental institutions, they die from abortion, or in childbirth, or they kill themselves." By contrast, in Nepal, Baker (1998) documented that homeless children could achieve stable employment, marriage and families of their own (see also Baker & Panter-Brick 2000). It is not even well established why there are street children in certain cultures and not in others (Aptekar 1994, p. 195), given the paucity of comparative research linking global to local analyses (see however Mickelson 2000b contrasting the "clean streets" of Cuba with street existence in Brazil and the United States). And while poverty and family dysfunction are ubiquitous causes for homelessness (Glasser & Bridgman 1999), poverty or abuse cannot be held as sole explanations for street children leaving home—when their siblings (and the majority of children) do not (Aptekar

1988, Aptekar 1991, p. 343). An ethnographic focus on the careers of street children in comparison with their peers might help to achieve a more fine-grained understanding of such issues.

Careers are also profoundly influenced by ethnicity (Huggins & de Castro 1996), gender (Barker & Knaul 2000), and disability, as well as age (Aptekar 1988). Moreover, street life is often able to offer payoffs in the short-term, while compromising individuals in the long run (Richter 1991). As Gregori (2000) noted, how Brazilian street children circulate in social spaces and negotiate with a range of institutions is marked by their status as legal minors; when they reach the age of majority, they face a difficult transformation of identity as the institutional support for minors falls away. A career perspective may be a way of articulating more cogently how rights articulate with risks for specific individuals, and how individuals themselves interpret the risks they face, the behavioral choices they make, and the social marginalization they experience.

Summary

Public health concerns for children "at risk" come with several important caveats. First, the risk discourse is helpful if one uses it less as a tool to categorize children and more as a tool to formulate questions of specific importance about children. For instance, one should ask not only what particular aspects of street lifestyles put children's health at risk, but also what processes enable children to cope with adversity. To turn the emphasis of risk on its head, how does one "support the social and cultural expressions of resilience and coping in ways that effectively support children's wellbeing" (Boyden & Mann 2000)? The concept of resilience, found useful in emphasizing a situational and developmental perspective and in departing from earlier vocabularies of marginality, does need to be better articulated in actual research with children. Second, research questions must move beyond the search for a package of risk variables and seek instead comparative and longitudinal information on children's career outcomes in order to appraise their different capabilities to face adversity. In this way, the concepts of risk and resilience would help to provide an overarching view of children whose rights are being jeopardized, moving forward the literature that previously tended to compartmentalize thinking about street children but that now seeks to consider this particular group alongside other groups of underprivileged children.

FUTURE DIRECTIONS

Current studies are careful to contextualize research on homeless street and working children. They have grown increasingly weary of a discourse that categorizes these youngsters as children in need, setting the characteristics of street life in global terms. Some of the shortcomings of categorical thinking also apply to the catch-all phrase "children at risk," although this term has emerged in the literature to usefully broaden the research on how children face adversity. Significantly for the contribution to be made by anthropology, current studies also increasingly seek to look at the circumstances of children as they themselves perceive them.

Specific directions for future research have been suggested in the literature. These would include moving the prime focus of investigation to the families of the children at large rather than focusing solely on individual children (Raffaelli 1997, p. 96). It would include a culturally sensitive understanding of the risk and protective factors that shape children's lives (Campos et al. 1994) in a more explicit developmental perspective. A greater effort should be made to analyze more convincingly the reasons for variation in the life histories of individual children and to relate differences by age, gender, ethnicity, or social support to the range of structural constraints operating at the macro-level. It is also necessary to be better informed about children's vulnerabilities, capabilities, and resilience, if these concepts are indeed significant for the lives of children. One still knows relatively little about how interventions fostering children's agency and participation can be implemented at ground level and translated into practical benefits for them. What is certainly required is a more sophisticated understanding of children's departure from the streets and long-term career outcomes, rather than the habitual focus of attention on the causes of their arrival or existence on the streets.

This highlights how research with street children can further our understanding of childhood adversity and urban social exclusion. Indeed a measure of the true worth of current academic and applied research is reflected in how our conceptual understandings of children under adversity continue to change. Work with street children significantly contributes to theories of agency and competency and of risk and resilience, the development of effective participatory methods, and the effective advocacy for children's rights. It also informs contemporary research on street ethnography and social exclusion in the context of urban poverty (Mingione 1999, Gigengack & van Gelder 2000).

NOTES AND ACKNOWLEDGMENTS

Useful contact points for information on street children are the Consortium for Street Children http://www.streetchildren.org.uk, the European Network on Street Children Worldwide http://www.enscw.org, and Save the Children http://www.savethechildren.org.uk. I thank Jo Boyden, Tobias Hecht, Jill Korbin, Heather Montgomery, and Marie Wernham for very useful comments on drafts of this paper.

The *Annual Review of Anthropology* is online at http://anthro.annualreviews.org

LITERATURE CITED

Agnelli S. 1986. *Street Children—A Growing Urban Tragedy.* London: Weidenfeld & Nicolson.

Alston P. 1994. The best interests principle: towards a reconciliation of culture and human rights. In *The Best Interests of the Child*, ed. P Alston, pp. 1–25. Oxford: Clarendon

Aptekar L. 1988. *Street Children of Cali.* Durham/London: Duke Univ. Press

Aptekar L. 1991. Are Colombian street children

neglected? The contributions of ethnographic and ethnohistorical approaches to the study of children. *Anthropol. Educ. Q.* 22: 326–49

Aptekar L. 1994. Street children in the developing world: a review of their condition. *Cross-Cult. Res.* 28(Aug):195–224

Baker R. 1998. *Negotiating identities: a study of the lives of street children in Nepal.* Dep. Anthropol., Univ. Durham, UK

Baker R, Panter-Brick C. 2000. A comparative perspective on children's 'careers' and abandonment in Nepal. In *Abandoned Children*, ed. C Panter-Brick, MT Smith, pp. 161–81. Cambridge, UK: Cambridge Univ. Press

Barker G, Knaul F. 1991. *Exploited Entrepreneurs: Street and Working Children in Developing Countries.* New York: Childhope-USA

Barker G, Knaul F. 2000. *Urban Girls—Empowerment in Especially Difficult Circumstances.* London: Intermediate Technol. Publ.

Bar-On A. 1997. Criminalising survival: images and reality of street children. *J. Soc. Policy* 26(1):63–78

Becker H. 1973. *Outsiders: Studies in the Sociology of Deviance.* New York: Free Press

Berman L. 2000. Surviving on the streets of Java. *Discourse Soc.* 112:149–74

Blunt A. 1994. Street children and their education: a challenge for urban educators. In *Education in Urban Areas: Cross-National Dimensions*, ed. N Stromquist, pp. 237–61. Westport, CT Praeger

Boyden J, Ling B, Myers W. 1998. *What Works for Working Children.* London: Kingsley

Boyden J, Mann G. 2000. *Children's risk, resilience and coping in extreme situations.* Oxford, UK Background paper to the Consultation on Children in Adversity. 9–12 September 2000

Byrne I. 1998. *The Human Rights of Street and Working Children.* London: Intermediate Technol. Publ.

Campos R, Raffaelli M, Ude W, Greco M, Ruff A, et al. 1994. Social networks and daily activities of street youth in Belo Horizonte, Brazil. *Child Dev.* 65:319–30

Chamberlain C, Johnson G. 2001. The debate about homelessness. *Aust. J. Soc. Issues* 361: 35–50

Childhope. 1991. *Fact Sheet on Violence Against Street Children.* New York: Childhope

Connolly M, Ennew J. 1996. Introduction—Children out of place. *Childhood—A Global J. Child Res.* 32:131–45

Consortium For Street Children. 1998. *Prevention of Street Migration: Resource Pack.* London: Consortium for Street Children, UK

Cosgrove JG. 1990. Towards a working definition of street children. *Int. Soc. Work* 33:185–92

Dean M. 1999. Risk, calculable and incalculable. In *Risk and Sociocultural Theory: New Directions and Perspectives*, ed. D Lupton, pp. 131–59. Cambridge, UK: Cambridge Univ. Press

de la Barra X. 1998. Poverty: the main cause of ill health in urban children. *Health Educ. Behav.* 251:46–59

DeSouza E, Koller S, Hiutz C, Forster L. 1995. Preventing depression among Brazilian street children. *Int. J. Psychol.* 292:261–65

Dobrowolska H, Panter-Brick C. 1998. How much does lifestyle matter? Growth status and cortisol variation in Ethiopian children. *Soc. Biol. Hum. Affairs* 631:11–21

Donald D, Swart-Kruger J. 1994. The South African street child: developmental implications. *S. Afr. J. Psychol.* 244:169–74

Earls F, Carlson M. 1999. Children at the margin of society: research and practice. *New Dir. Child Adoles. Dev.* 85(Fall)

Engle P, Castle S, Menon P. 1996. Child development: vulnerability and resilience. *Soc. Sci. Med.* 43(5):621–35

Ennew J. 1994. *Street and Working Children—A Guide to Planning.* London: Save the Children

Ennew J. 1995. Outside childhood: street children's rights. In *The Handbook of Children's Rights: Comparative Policy and Practice*, ed. B Franklin, pp. 201–14. London/New York: Routledge

Ennew J. 2000. Why the Convention is not

about street children. *Revisiting Children's Rights: 10 Years of the UN Convention on the Rights of the Child*, ed. D Fottrell, pp. 169–82. The Hague/Boston: Kluwer Law Int.

Ennew J, Milne B. 1997. *Methods of Research with Street and Working Children: An Annotated Bibliography*. Stockholm: Sweden, Radda Barnen

Felsman JK. 1984. Abandoned children: a reconsideration. *Children Today* 13:13–18

Felsman K. 1981. Street urchins of Columbia. *Nat. Hist.* (Apr):41–48

Felsman KJ. 1989. Resiliency in context: children coping in extreme circumstances. In *The Child in Our Times: Studies in the Development of Resiliency*, ed. T Dugan, R Coles, pp. 56–80. New York: Brunner/Mazel

Freeman M. 1996. The moral status of children. In *Understanding Children's Rights*, ed. E Verhellen, pp. 9–23. Belgium: Univ. Ghent

Gigengack R, van Gelder P. 2000. Contemporary street ethnography: different experiences, perspectives and methods. *Focaal* 36: 7–14

Glasser I, Bridgman R. 1999. *Braving the Street: The Anthropology of Homelessness*. Oxford, UK: Berghahn

Glauser B. 1990. Street children: deconstructing a construct. In *Constructing and Reconstructing Childhood: Contemporary Issues in the Sociological Study of Childhood*, ed. A James, A Prout, pp. 138–56. London: Falmer

Goffman E. 1988 [1961]. *Asylums: Essays on the Social Situation of Mental Patients and Other Inmates*. Harmondsworth, UK: Penguin

Goonesekere S. 1998. Children, law and justice: a south Asian perspective. New Dehli: Sage

Gregori MF. 2000. *Viraçāo: Experiencias de Meninos nas Ruas*. São Paulo: Companhia das Letras

Gross R, Landfried B, Herman S. 1996. Height and weight as a reflection of the nutritional situation of school-aged children working and living in the streets of Jakarta. *Soc. Sci. Med.* 434:453–58

Hecht T. 1998. *At Home in the Street: Street Children of Northeast Brazil*. Cambridge, UK: Cambridge Univ. Press

Hecht T. 2000. Street ethnography: some notes on studying and being studied. *Focaal* 36:69–76

Holden E, Horton L, Danseco E. 1995. The mental health of homeless children. *Clin. Psychol. Sci. Practice* 2(2):165–78

Huggins M, de Castro M. 1996. Exclusion, civic invisibility and impunity as explanations for youth murders in Brazil. *Childhood* 3(1):77–98

Huggins M, Mesquita M. 2000. Civic invisibility, marginality, and moral exclusion: the murders of street youth in Brazil. See Mickelson 2000a, pp. 257–68

Human Rights Watch. 1996. *Police Abuse and Killings of Street Children in India*. New York: Human Rights Watch

Human Rights Watch. 1997. *Guatemala's Forgotten Children—Police Violence and Abuses in Detention*. New York: Human Rights Watch

Hutchby I, Moran-Ellis J, eds. 1998. *Children and Social Competence: Arenas of Action*. London: Falmer

Hutson S, Liddiard M. 1994. *Youth Homelessness—The Construction of a Social Issue*. London: Macmillan

Hutz C, Koller S. 1999. Methodological and ethical issues in research with street children. *New Dir. Child Adoles. Dev.* 85(Fall)

Invernizzi A. 2001. *Street Children in Africa, Asia and Eastern Europe—Annotated Bibliography (StraBenkinder in Afrika, Asien und Osteuropa—Eine kommentierte Bibliographie)*. Bonn: Deutsche Kommission Justitie et Pax

Jackson S, Scott S. 1999. Risk anxiety and the social construction of childhood. In *Risk and Sociocultural Theory*, ed. D Lupton, pp. 86–107. Cambridge, UK: Cambridge Univ. Press

Johnson V, Hill J, Ivan-Smith E. 1995. *Listening to Smaller Voices: Children in an Environment of Change*. London: Actionaid

Johnson V, Ivan-Smith E, Gordon G, Pridmore P, Scott P. 1998. *Stepping Forward: Children and Young People's Participation in the Development Process.* London: Intermediate Technol. Publ.

Kapadia K. 1997. Children at risk in urban areas in India: a review. *SCARO Briefing paper No.6.* Kathmandu: *Save the Children (UK)* South and Central Asia Reg. Office

Kilbride P, Suda C, Njeru E. 2000. *Street Children in Kenya—Voices of Children in Search of a Childhood.* Westport, CT: Bergin & Garvey

Klees S, Rizzini I, Dewees A. 2000. A new paradigm for social change: social movements and the transformation of policy for street and working children in Brazil. See Mickelson 2000a, pp. 79–98

Lane A. 1998. Identifying and responding to the high risk population: JUCONI's prevention programme. In *Prevention of Street Migration: Resource Pack*, pp. 18–25. London: Consortium for Street Children

le Roux J. 1996. The worldwide phenomenon of street children: conceptual analysis. *Adolescence* 31(124):965–71

le Roux J, Smith C. 1998a. Causes and characteristics of the street child phenomenon: a global perspective. *Adolescence* 33(131): 683–88

le Roux J, Smith C. 1998b. Is the street child phenomenon synonymous with deviant behavior? *Adolescence* 33(132):915–25

Lucchini R. 1994. *The Street Girl—Prostitution, Family and Drug.* Fribourg, Switzerland: Univ. Fribourg Press

Lucchini R. 1997. *Deviance and Street Children in Latin America: the Limits of a Functionalist Approach.* Fribourg, Switzerland: Univ. Fribourg Press

Lusk MW. 1992. Street children of Rio de Janeiro. *Int. Soc. Work* 35:293–305

Márquez P. 1999. *The Street Is My Home: Youth and Violence in Caracas.* Stanford, CA: Stanford Univ. Press

Mermet J. 1997. *Bibliography on Street Children.* Geneva: Henry Durant Inst. www.geocities.com/joelmermet/streetchildren.html

Mickelson R. 2000a. *Children on the Streets of the Americas—Homelessness, Education and Globalization in the United States, Brazil and Cuba.* New York: Routledge

Mickelson R. 2000b. Globalization, childhood poverty, and education in the Americas. See Mickelson 2000a, pp. 11–39

Mingione E. 1999. The excluded and the homeless: the social construction of the fight against poverty in Europe. In *Urban Poverty and the Underclass: a Reader*, ed. E Mingone, pp. 83–104. Oxford: Blackwell

Molnar J, Rath W, Klein TP. 1990. Constantly compromised: the impact of homelessness on children. *J. Soc. Issues* 46(4):109–24

Monteiro J, Campos M, Dollinger S. 1998. An autophotographic study of poverty, collective orientation, and identity among street children. *J. School Psychol.* 138(3):403–6

Montgomery H. 2001. Imposing rights? A case study of child prostitution in Thailand. In *Culture and Rights: Anthopological Perspectives*, ed. J Cowan, M Dembour, R Wilson, pp. 80–101. Cambridge, UK: Cambridge Univ. Press

Morrow V, Richards M. 1996. The ethics of social research with children: an overview. *Children Soc.* 10:90–105

Moss P, Dillon J, Statham J. 2000. The 'child in need' and 'the rich child': discourses, constructions and practice. *Crit. Soc. Policy* 20(2):233–54

Myers WE. 1988. Alternative services for street children: the Brazilian approach. In *Combating Child Labour*, ed. A Beqeule, J Boyden, pp. 125–43. Geneva, Switzerland: Int. Labour Org.

Neiman L. 1988. A critical review of resiliency literature and its relevance to homeless children. *Children's Environ. Q.* 5(1):17–25

Panter-Brick C. 2000. Nobody's children? A reconsideration of child abandonment. In *Abandoned Children*, ed. C Panter-Brick, MT Smith, pp. 1–26. Cambridge, UK: Cambridge Univ. Press

Panter-Brick C. 2001a. Street children: cultural concerns. In *International Encyclopedia of the Social and Behavioral Sciences*, ed. NJ Smelser, PB Baltes, 22:15154–57. Oxford: Elsevier

Panter-Brick C. 2001b. Street children and their peers: perspectives on homelessness, poverty, and health. In *Children and Anthropology: Perspectives for the 21st Century*, ed. H Schwartzman, pp. 83–97. Westport, Connecticut: Bergin & Garvey

Panter-Brick C, Lunn P, Baker R, Todd A. 2001. Elevated acute-phase protein in stunted Nepali children reporting low morbidity: different rural and urban profiles. *Br. J. Nutr.* 85:125–31

Panter-Brick C, Todd A, Baker R. 1996. Growth status of homeless Nepali boys: Do they differ from rural and urban controls? *Soc. Sci. Med.* 43(4):441–51

Pinto J, Ruff A, Paiva J, Antunes C, Adams I, et al. 1994. HIV risk behavior and medical status of underprivileged youth in Belo Horizonte, Brazil. *J. Adoles. Health* 15:179–85

Porto S, Cardoso D, Queiroz D, Rosa H, Andrade A, et al. 1994. Prevalence and risk factors for HBV infection among street youth in central Brazil. *J. Adoles. Health* 15:577–81

Raffaelli M. 1999. Homeless and working street youth in Latin America: a developmental review. *Interam. J. Psychol.* 33(2):7–28

Raffaelli M. 2000. Gender diffierences in Brazilian street youth's family circumstances and experiences on the street. *Child Abuse & Neglect* 24(11):1431–41

Raffaelli M, Larson R, eds. 1999. *Homeless and Working Youth Around the World: Exploring Developmental Issues.* San Francisco: Jossey-Bass

Richman JM, Fraser MW. 2001. Resilience in childhood: the role of risk and protection. See Richman & Fraser 2001, pp. 1–12

Richman JM, Fraser MW, eds. 2001. *The Context of Youth Violence: Resilience, Risk, and Protection.* Westport: Praeger

Richter L. 1991. South African street children: comparisons with Anglo-American runaways. In *Contemporary Issues in Cross-Cultural Psychology*, ed. N Bleichrodt, P Drenth, pp. 96–109. Amsterdam: Swets & Zeitlinger

Rizzini I, Barker G, Cassaniga N. 1999. *From Street Children to all Children: Improving the Opportunities of Low Income Urban Children and Youth in Brazil.* Rio de Janeiro, Brazil: Ctr. Res. on Childhood—CESPI

Rizzini I, Rizzini I, Munoz-Vargas M. 1994. Brazil: a new concept of childhood. In *Urban Children in Distress: Global Predicaments and Innovative Strategies*, ed. C Blanc, pp. 55–99. Reading, Berkshire: Gordon & Breach

Rutter M. 1987. *Psychosocial Resilience and Protective Mechanisms. Am. J. Orthopsychiatr.* 57(3):316–31

Rutter M. 1990. Psychosocial resilience and protective mechanisms. In *Risk and Protective Factors in the Development of Psychopathy*, ed. J Rolf, pp. 181–214. Cambridge: Cambridge Univ. Press

Rutter M. 2001. Psychosocial adversity: risk, resilience and recovery. See Richman & Fraser 2001, pp. 13–41

Scanlon T, Tomkins A, Lynch M, Scanlon F. 1998. Street children in Latin America. *Br. J. Nutr.* 31623(May):1596–1600

Scheper-Hughes N, Hoffman D. 1994. Kids out of place. *NACLA Report on the Americas* XXVII(6):16–23

Scheper-Hughes N, Hoffman D. 1998. Brazilian apartheid: street kids and the struggle for urban space. In *Small Wars—The Cultural Politics of Childhood*, ed. N Scheper-Hughes, N Sargent, pp. 352–88. Berkeley: Univ. Calif. Press

Sibert J. 2000. Book review of "Homeless Children: Problems and Needs" edited by Vostanis P, Cumella S 1999. *Arch. Dis. Child* 82(Mar):272

Stephens S. 1995. Children and the politics of culture in late capitalism. In *Children and the Politics of Culture*, ed. S Stephens, pp. 3–48. Princeton, NJ: Princeton Univ. Press

Swift A. 1997. *Children for Social Change—Education for Citizenship of Street and Working Children in Brazil.* Nottingham, UK: Educ. Heretics Press

UNESCO. 1995. *Working with Street Children: Selected Case-Studies from Africa, Asia and Latin America.* Paris: UNESCO

UNICEF. 1998. *Implementation Handbook for*

the Convention on the Rights of the Child. New York/Geneva: United Nations Children's Fund

UNICEF. 2001. *We the Children: End-Decade Review of the Follow-Up to the World Summit for Children.* New York/Geneva: United Nations Children Fund

Valentin K. 1999. Notions of risk applied to urban children in Nepal. *ETNOFOOR* XII1: 89–99

van Bueren G. 1998. Children's rights: balancing traditional values and cultural plurality. In *Children's Rights and Traditional Values*, ed. G Douglas, L Sebba, pp. 15–30. Aldershot, UK: Dartmouth

Veale A, Taylor M, Linehan C. 2000. Psychological perspectives of 'abandoned' and 'abandoning' street children. In *Abandoned Children*, ed. C Panter-Brick, MT Smith, pp. 131–45. Cambridge, UK: Cambridge Univ. Press

Visano L. 1990. The socialization of street children: the development and transformation of identities. *Sociol. Stud. Child Dev.* 3:139–61

Williams C. 1993. Who are street children? A hierarchy of street use and appropriate responses. *Child Abuse & Neglect* 17:831–41

Woodhead M. 1990. Psychology and the cultural construction of children's needs. In *Constructing and Reconstructing Childhood: Contemporary Issues in the Sociological Study of Childhood*, ed. A James, A Prout, pp. 60–77. London: Falmer

Wright J. 1990a. Homelessness is not healthy for children and other living things. *Child Youth Serv.* 14(1):65–88

Wright J. 1990b. Poor people, poor health: the health status of the homeless. *J. Soc. Issues* 46(4):49–64

Wright J. 1991. Children in and of the streets: health, social policy, and the homeless young. *Am. J. Dis. Children* 145(May):516–19

Wright J, Kaminsky D. 1993. Health and social conditions of street children in Honduras. *Am. J. Dis. Child.* 147:279–83

Ziesemer C, Marcoux L, Marwell BE. 1994. Homeless children: Are they different from other low-income children? *Soc. Work* 39(6): 658–68

Annu. Rev. Anthropol. 2002. 31:173–87
doi: 10.1146/annurev.anthro.31.040402.085347

First published online as a Review in Advance on May 16, 2002

RELIGION IN SOUTH ASIA

Peter van der Veer
Research Centre for Religion and Society, University of Amsterdam, Amsterdam, The Netherlands 1012 DK; email: vanderveer@pscw.uva.nl

Key Words postcolonial studies, state formation, public sphere, transnationalism

■ **Abstract** This article examines the study of religions of South Asia, in particular of India, from the angle of postcolonial criticism. It argues that the study of state formation provides a crucial perspective for the unraveling of the multiple transformations of religion in the colonial and postcolonial public sphere. The colonial state cannot be studied in isolation from the global framework of imperial interactions between metropole and colony, in which colonial and national modernity is produced. Such a study depends on a postcolonial critique of the very category of "religion" while acknowledging the centrality of that category in colonial and postcolonial politics. The transformation of the public sphere in South Asia shows the increasing importance of religious movements and of the political use of religious images in new communication technologies. One of the most important trends in the present era is the attempt to create a homogenous religious community, not only within the national territorial space, but also in a transnational space. Such attempts offer a violent confrontation with "the Other," however defined.

INTRODUCTION

The history of the colonial state is crucial for the anthropological understanding of postcolonial religious formations in South Asia. Postcolonial studies, combining history and anthropology, have contributed much to this area of study, which emerged fully in the 1980s (Cohn 1987, Mathur 2000). Influenced by Foucault (1979) and Said (1979), a major argument is that orientalism as a form of knowledge is central to the control and governance of the Orient (Inden 1990, Breckenridge & van der Veer 1993). Orientalism gives religion a privileged status as the foremost site of essentialized difference between the religious East and the secular West (Dumont 1980). The orientalist privileging of religion is not based simply upon an acknowledgement of the importance of religious institutions in the colonies of the subcontinent; rather, it is directly dependent on modern understandings of religion related to the nationalization of religion and its new location in the public sphere.

Religion became crucial in the transformation of the public spheres in British India and in the postcolonial nation-states of India, Pakistan, and Bangladesh as well as Sri Lanka. Many of the leading political parties and social movements mobilize people around religious issues. A relatively new element is that, especially since the 1960s, transnational migration from South Asia to Europe and the United States has brought a crucial transnational element to these forms of mobilization.

The interpretation of religion in South Asia thus requires an understanding of colonial modernity, of the postcolonial transformation of the public sphere, of religious forms of social mobilization, and of the dialectics between nationalism and transnationalism.

COLONIAL RELIGION

A major debate in the writing of the history of British India is about the importance of colonial rule for the transformation of Indian society. One historical school of thought portrays colonial rule not as an imposition but as an Indian project or as a form of dialogue between the Indians and the British (Bayly 1988, 1998). A Marxist permutation of this view with more emphasis on historical logic than on agency is that of Washbrook (1988), who argues that "colonialism was the logical outcome of South Asia's own history of capitalist development."

Another school of thought emphasizes colonial knowledge and power, and colonialism as a cultural project of control. As Cohn put it, "the conquest of India was the conquest of knowledge" (1996, p. 16). The argument is that colonial rule existed and technologies of knowledge [or, as Ludden (1993) has called it, "orientalist empiricism"] were crucial in the formation of the cultural categories through which Indian realities were understood both by the natives and by the British. Cohn (1987) has famously shown the importance of the census operations on understandings of caste, tribe, and religious community in the development of a politics of numbers. Appadurai (1981) has demonstrated the ways in which the colonial administration of temples was central to colonial governmentality. Dirks (1987) has argued that under colonialism an understanding of caste was developed that enabled the British to dismantle a previous power structure, to make it into "a hollow crown." This kind of work has influenced scholarship on Sri Lanka (Scott 1994, 1999) and Nepal (Ortner 1989) more than it has scholarship on Pakistan and Bangladesh.

Some of the differences in these positions can be traced to the use of the tropes of internality and externality as signifying a structure of mutual exclusivity. The colonial state is portrayed as an external global power formation, originating outside of India, whereas Indian subjects are seen as native agency, internal to India. Another way of looking at this is that the imperial encounters between India and Britain produced an imperial modernity both in India and in Britain, in which these tropes of internality and externality should be taken not as foundational grounds of scholarly discussion, but rather as the shifting grounds of imperial discourse itself (Suleri 1992; Viswanathan 1989, 1998; van der Veer 2001). Religion can be taken as a particularly apt site for this dynamic of power and knowledge.

Asad (1993) has pointed out that the universalization of the concept of "religion" is closely related to the coming of modernity in Europe and to the

European expansion over the world. This raises the broad historical question of the ways in which a modern Western understanding of religion has become dominant and has been applied as a universal concept (Balagangadhara 1994). The project of modernization, which is crucial to the spread of colonial power over the world, has provided new conceptual frameworks in which both the colonizing and the colonized understand themselves and their actions.

The above perspective should not, however, be taken as arguing that the traditions labeled as religion in the nineteenth century are invented, although Hinduism is in fact a good candidate for the claim that it is an invented tradition (Dalmia & von Stietencron 1995, Thapar 1989). Hindu traditions are not invented but are now understood as Hinduism and as Hindu religion. It has often been noted how difficult it is to speak of a religion called Hinduism. The term Hindu is derived from Sanskrit *sindhu* and refers to the people who live near the great river Indus. *Al-Hind* is an early Arabic term used by Muslims who settled in this region. Hindu is thus a term used by outsiders to speak about this region and its population. Later the term Hindustan, again a geographical designation, came into vogue. The term used in the early period of European expansion into India is *gentoo* (Latin: gentiles) or heathen. It was European Orientalism of the eighteenth century that gradually systematized knowledge about the people of India and their various beliefs and practices into an integrated, coherent religion called Hinduism. This was part of a larger, empirical enterprise to map India and its inhabitants, an enterprise framed in metropolitan theoretical concerns. It is often asserted that Hinduism, as such, does not exist, but that there is instead a great variety of heterogeneous practices of a devotional and ritual nature as well as of metaphysical schools that were lumped together under the foreign term Hinduism in the early nineteenth century. Such an assertion contains some truth, but it is exaggerated because these practices and doctrines do belong together as a tradition, although they are not unified by a central authority (Lorenzen 1999, Dube 1998). Moreover, in this regard, Hinduism is not an exception but is similar to other religions in South Asia, such as Islam, Sikhism, and Buddhism (Asad 1986, Oberoi 1994, Gombrich & Obeyesekere 1988).

Revivalist movements, like the Arya Samaj, discovered in Hinduism a monotheistic God, a Book, and congregational worship. This was a substantial transformation of a set of polytheistic traditions with a great variety of scriptures, none of which is really dominant, and domestic and temple worship that is seldom congregational. What these movements wanted to create was a modern Hinduism that would be respectable in the eyes of the world (monotheistic and text-based) and that could be the basis for a morality of acting in the secular world as in Mohandas Gandhi's use of the Bhagavad-Gita as the foundational text for social work. Similar transformations took place in Islam, Sikhism, and Buddhism (Metcalf 1982, Fox 1985, Oberoi 1994, Obeyesekere 1995, Roberts 1997).

If one accepts Asad's argument that religion itself is a modern category, one has to realize that it is applied to Christianity as much as it is applied to Hinduism. The difference, however—and that remains crucial—is that Christianity, at least from Kant onward, is portrayed as the rational religion of Western modernity, whereas

Hinduism is mystified as Oriental wisdom or irrationality (Halbfass 1988, King 1999). It is in the field of historical interaction, established by imperial expansion, that the category of religion receives its significance. One could therefore argue that the modern category of religion was constructed in imperial encounters during the Western expansion and that it transformed both Christianity and other religions such as Hinduism and Islam. Modern forms of knowledge and power are indispensable in the self-understanding of missionaries, reformers, and state officials alike and thus they are the very subject of our historical understanding. The colonial state is crucial for the history of the nineteenth and twentieth centuries, and the debate about it is so bitter because postcolonial questions about religion and politics are tied up with colonial history. There is no "pure" indigenous society that responds to the "purely" external force of the colonial state. The categories of modernity for colonizer and colonized alike are formed in the imperial encounter itself and thus cannot be understood in terms of the imposition of modern concepts on a traditional society that resists this imposition in its own moral languages. The transformation of these moral languages is at issue. Some argue that the colonial expansion entails resistance in the form of peasant insurgence embedded in the ritual beliefs and practices of indigenous society (Guha 1997, Hardiman 1987), but such an argument may place peasants outside of the history of modernity. Others argue in terms of a dialogue between colonizer and colonized (Irschick 1994), but the term dialogue ignores power inequalities in communication.

Although we need to go beyond the study of the colonial state by examining movements and forms of communication that are not sponsored by the state, it is also important to reflect upon the nature of our historical information. The study of Indian religious history has a number of problems that demand conceptual reflection and cannot be solved by simply collecting more factual evidence. The idea that there is a corpus of texts, a dead, inert body that contains answers to everything we want to ask, called the archive, is obviously a fiction. However eager and industrious we are, however much we know the relevant languages, the archive first has to be located, and it has its politics and its history (Amin 1995, Dirks 2001). The archive is not in fact dead, but alive. In research on religious orders one does not find many documents, and the existing documents often refer to landed property, to the building of temples, to patronage. These documents are held in temples, mosques, khanqas, gurdwaras, and they are used and framed in relation to claims in the present. What remains entirely outside of this is the documentation of the history of itinerant monks and faqirs. Even the other textual evidence—devotional literature, songs in praise of God, theological arguments—does not give much clue to those who are footloose. Devotional literature, moreover, has one major difficulty, namely the complete ideological negation of history. Even in its genealogical accounts of the succession of abbots, such literature is hagiographical and miraculous rather than historical (van der Veer 1988, Pinch 1996, Ewing 1997, Carrithers & Humphrey 1991, Lorenzen 1995).

To some extent the answer to these troubles is oral history (Ortner 1989, Amin 1995, Mayaram 1997). One can find out in the ethnographic present what the tensions and fissures are in a social configuration, such as a monastic order or a priestly caste (Parry 1994). Moreover, participants often answer questions in a historical way. This can be done in a quasimythological fashion—"this has been the case since the time of Rama"—but also in a quite specific way in case there are events that people themselves have witnessed. Controversy can lead to the writing of pamphlets that give us the opportunity to read documentary evidence against ethnographic evidence in the reconstruction of a social configuration. A major difficulty, however, is to reconstruct long-term history with the help of oral history (Geertz 1980, Schulte Nordholt 1991, Comaroff & Comaroff 1992). Ethnography helps us to understand a social configuration and thus to make certain historical conjectures, but this can only be a first step. The work done by the doyen of Indian sociology, G. S. Ghurye (1953), on Indian *sadhus* is still extremely useful, both as an ethnographic snapshot and as an exercise in historical conjecture, but there is very little terra firma here. Similarly, in the most important historical and political debate in India over the last twenty years, the Babar Mosque controversy, it is striking that the historical evidence is so slim and that oral history plays such an important role (van der Veer 1988, Gopal 1993). This explains the importance of the colonial archive. Archives are products of state centralization of management and control, and the modern state places empirical evidence squarely at its service. Much of precolonial and extracolonial evidence is framed and given significance in the colonial archive so that metaphors of internality and externality are of little use in describing the colonial intervention.

MODERN RELIGION: THE PUBLIC SPHERE

One finds in modern religions the development of an informed religious public. A number of recent studies show how important religion is for the creation of the public sphere (Hefner 2000, Eickelman & Anderson 1999). This may come as a surprise to those who accept Habermas's understanding of the rise of the public sphere. In his seminal work Habermas (1989) argued that, in the eighteenth century, private individuals assembled into a public body began to discuss openly and critically the exercise of political power by the state. These citizens had free access to information and expressed their opinion in a rational and domination-free manner. Crucial to this development was the emergence and expansion of a market for newspapers and other printed materials, as was the rise of the bourgeoisie, which is why Habermas spoke of the bourgeois public sphere. These bourgeois turn out to be secular liberals rather than religious radicals. Habermas's analysis of the Enlightenment tradition belongs, at the theoretical level, very much to a discourse of modern, European self-representation (Calhoun 1994, van der Veer & Lehmann 1999). A striking element in this self-representation is the neglect of religious public opinion because it cannot be regarded as rational and critical. The productive side of Habermas's argument, however, is his focus on the sociology of the public sphere: both the discursive possibilities of critical debate and the tendency of the public sphere to expand and allow a growing number of participants. The notions of "publicity," "the public," and "public opinion," captured by Habermas's concept of "the public sphere," are important and can be used for comparative purposes if we are not constrained by Habermas's secularist perspective.

One finds a new configuration in the modern nation-state that allows citizens to follow different religions without immediately raising the question of political loyalty. Loyalty to one's king and state follows not from one's religious affiliation, but from one's national identity, of which religion is one ingredient among others. Nationalism replaces religion in this regard, and one can come to nationalism via a variety of religious affiliations. Another way of expressing this is that in the modern era religions are nationalized. Separation of church and state does not lead to the decline of the social and political importance of religion (Madan 1997). With the rise of the nation-state an enormous shift occurred in what religion means. Religion produces the secular as much as vice versa, but this interaction can be understood only in the context of the emergence of nationalism in the nineteenth century. In India religious neutrality of the colonial state left the public sphere open for missionary activities of Christian organizations. A great number of Hindu, Muslim, and Sikh organizations emerged to resist the Christian missionary project. This dialectic of aggressive missionization and Hindu resistance contributed to the formation of a public sphere in British India in the nineteenth century that was not at all secular. Secularity and religion receive particular historical meanings in this atmosphere of debate, however. The administration and upkeep of Hindu temples and rituals fell to newly emergent elites, which used the British legal apparatus to create a new, corporate Hinduism that was fully modern (Thapar 1985). These elites were interested not only in controlling Hindu institutions, which especially in South India were quite powerful and immediately connected to political control; they also had a reformist agenda concerning religious education, ritual action, and customs that is crucial even today (Fuller 1984).

The colonial state attempted not to interfere with native religions; it also did much to disavow any connection to the missionary project and to Christianity as such (Viswanathan 1989). One can indeed speak of a definite secularity of the British state in India that was much stronger than in Britain itself. The British considered a sharp separation of church and state essential to their ability to govern India. Their attempts to develop a neutral religious policy in a society in which religious institutions played an important political role could not be anything but ambivalent. In the management of both South Indian Hindu temples and North Indian Sikh and Muslim shrines, the colonial government remained involved, despite all efforts to remain neutral (Pressler 1987, Gilmartin 1988, Oberoi 1994). Nevertheless, externality and neutrality became the tropes of a state that tried to project itself as playing the role of a transcendent arbiter in a country divided along religious lines. Again, however, this did not contribute to a secular atmosphere in society. Indian religions were transformed in opposition to the state, and religion became more important in the emergent public sphere. As in Britain, religion was transformed and molded in a national form, but that form defined itself in opposition to the colonizing state. The denial of participation in the political institutions of the colony led Indians to develop an alternative set of institutions of a jointly political and religious nature. Indians did not conceive the colonial state as neutral and secular, but rather as fundamentally Christian (Kumar 1998). Similarly, popular conceptions of British rule, as evident in the Cow Protection Movement of the 1880s, portrayed it as of an alien, Christian nature. When in 1888 the North-Western Provincial High Court decreed that the cow was not a sacred object and thus did not have to be protected by the state, the decision galvanized the movement not only against Muslims, but also against rule by Christian "cow-eaters" (Freitag 1989). When the state started to use religion among its census categories, it came itself to be understood in religious categories. Although the legitimizing rituals and discourses of the colonial state were those of development, progress, and evolution and meant to be secular, they could indeed easily be understood as essentially Christian. The response both the state and the missionary societies provoked was also decidedly religious. Hindu and Islamic forms of modernism led to the establishment of modern Hindu and Muslim schools, universities, and hospitals, superseding or marginalizing precolonial forms of education. Far from having a secularizing influence on Indian society, the modernizing project of the secular colonial state in fact gave modern religion a strong new impulse.

The development of a public sphere of debate, petitions, and pamphlets is in Habermas's view the privilege of a literate, bourgeois public. In the later part of the nineteenth century this public sphere, according to Habermas, deteriorated into democratic mass politics, in which critical debate is replaced by agitation. Habermas raises the important issue of elites versus the masses. A number of studies explore whether we can speak of a rise of a bourgeoisie in nineteenth-century India or, more fundamentally, whether the category bourgeoisie is significant in a society stratified by caste and not by class (Chakrabarty 2000, Fuller 1997). I would think that the category is appropriate and that it is signaled by the emergence of a literate group of businessmen, educators, and administrators whose careers show the geographical range of imperial business. It is the spread of education, the improvement of transport, and the modern need for mobility that make this possible. The fact that caste endogamy is still practiced does not mean that this is not a bourgeoisie, but it is a bourgeoisie fractured as in many parts of the modern world by ethnic and religious bonds. According to Chakrabarty (2000), the formation of the bourgeois individual has been incomplete in India because one does not find an interiorized, private self reflected in autobiographies, novels, diaries, and such. This kind of formation of the self does belong to a particular Western history, of which Protestant Christianity is one of the most important sources. This does not mean that there are no Hindu or Muslim individuals with private selves and public personae, but that the discursive sources of the self are different. Nevertheless, there are a number of technologies of the self, like modern education, novel writing, autobiographies, newspapers, and modern art that emerged in India in the nineteenth century as they did in

Britain. Similarly, technologies of public debate, such as pamphlets, petitions, and newspapers, but also processions in public arenas, emerged in India as carriers of public opinion outside of the older patterns of elite patronage and influence.

Chatterjee (1993) has argued for the rise in India of another kind of private and public distinction under colonial rule. This is a division of the world of social institutions and practices into two domains—the material and the spiritual. The private sphere of the household is the site of spirituality and has to be protected against colonial materialism, in Chatterjee's analysis. However, the modern notion of spirituality that comes up in the imperial encounter between Britain and India is not opposed to materialist science at all. Hindu nationalists claim that science is part of India's spiritual heritage, and they find support among Britain's theosophists and spiritualists (Prakash 1999, van der Veer 2001). Moreover, reform of the household, female education, and transformation of marriage practices are precisely the subjects of public debate (Chandra 1998).

The rise of mass politics, of a politics of numbers both in the metropole and in the colony, transformed the public sphere in major ways at the end of the nineteenth and beginning of the twentieth century. In the absence of democratic participation, mass politics led in India to the development of mass agitation in the form of political rituals like Tilak's Ganapati festival in Maharashtra (Hansen 2001). It also led to the representation of Hinduism as a majority religion and Islam and Christianity as minority religions. In the context of a politics of numbers, questions of untouchability, of Dravidianism, of Sufi syncretism took on new meanings. In that context, the religious history of modern India has to deal with Ambedkar and his politics of conversion (Viswanathan 1998, Dirks 2001), with E.V. Ramaswamy or Periyar and his politics of anti-Brahmanism, with Muhammad Ilyas and his politics of internal Islamic conversion, with Gandhi and his politics of Hindu inclusivism.

Religious Movements in the Public Sphere

Crucial in the modern public sphere in South Asia are religious movements that have their origin in the colonial period or are successors of those movements. The most important among them want to unify and homogenize the religious community. As such they respond to what they perceive as the assault by the "pseudo-secular" state and attempts at conversion by other religious communities. In all these movements both clerics and intellectuals, trained in secular institutions, play a dominant role. Striking is the position of leadership in militancy and interethnic violence taken by Buddhist monks in Sri Lanka (Tambiah 1992), Muslim clerics in Pakistan (Nasr 1994, 2000), and Hindu monks in India (van der Veer 1994, McKean 1996). Among Hindu movements most attention has been given to organizations connected to political violence, such as the Rasthriya Swayamsevak Sangh and the Shiv Sena (Ludden 1996; Hansen 1999, 2001). Among Muslim movements both the Tablighi Jama'at, an avowedly apolitical movement, and the radically political Jama'at-i-Islami have been subjects of study. The Tablighi Jama'at and the Visva Hindu Parishad, an offshoot of the Rasthriya Swayamsevak Sangh, are more directly involved in religious issues of belief and conversion.

The Tablighi Jama'at is an internal missionary movement among Muslims, founded in north India in the 1920s (Metcalf 1993, 1996; Masud 2000; Sikand 1998; Troll 1994). Associated with the famous seminary of Deoband, it is focused much less on learning and much more on simple preaching (Metcalf 1982). Its origins are only understandable in the colonial context in which a politics of numbers and communal competition made it essential for both Hindu and Muslim movements to strengthen their ranks and numbers. Hindu purification movements tried to "invite back" and re-convert Muslim communities that had recognizable Hindu customs. Movements like the Tablighi Jama'at tried to counteract this by asking such communities to reform their practices and become "good Muslims." Like the Jehova's Witnesses they go in small groups from community to community to invite Muslims to join them and perform the simplest Islamic tasks, such as going regularly to the mosque and reading the Qur'an. Annually there are gatherings, some of which, such as the ones in Raiwind in Pakistan and Tong in Bangladesh, are the largest gatherings of Muslims (some two million) in the world outside the hajj. Research on the Tablighis is difficult because, contrary to many Islamist movements, they put no value in media such as books and pamphlets and certainly not in video- or audiotapes in spreading their message. They have some official publications such as transcripts of lectures delivered by leading Tablighis, mostly containing simple, short, edifying stories. There are also some hagiographies of the founder of the movement, Muhammad Ilyas, and some other leading figures. This kind of literature is fundamentally antihistorical. Like the stories of the behavior of the Prophet and his companions, they have value only as models for behavior. History is regarded as a worldly pursuit that simply distracts from ritual observance. The focus is not on reading, but on ritual observance. Communication between activists is largely oral and letters are destroyed after being read. The movement is definitely secretive in the way it communicates its way of organizing. Striking is the focus on individual, behavioral change connected with creation of an unmediated public sphere of huge gatherings and people taking time off to go in groups. Tablighi Jama'at is a kind of pietistic quietism that wants to change the world (and make it a place controlled by Islamic Law) by transforming the self.

To what extent does the Tablighi Jama'at belong to the public sphere and provide a space for criticism of the state? The answer is ambiguous because the Tablighis explicitly do not want to be of this world and explicitly do not want to be political. Still, the movement's stress on personal matters such as Islamic dress and education brings it into direct confrontation with the agenda of the secular nation-state that cannot refrain from intervening in the ways communities organize their lives (for examples in Europe, see Gerholm & Lithman 1988, Nielsen 1995, Kepel 1997). When Tablighis immigrate into Western societies, they cannot fail to come into conflict with secular arrangements in schools and so on. Integration into secular societies is the opposite of what this movement wants to achieve. Their personal jihad may be less overtly political than the jihad of Islamist groups, but within the conditions of modern state formation it is still of great political significance. The Tablighi Jama'at is the largest transnational Islamic movement in the world. Thanks to its universalist message it can escape from the claims of national societies and play a significant role in providing models for migrant communities. The studies collected in Masud's volume show how Tablighis cope with the different circumstances in Canada, South Africa, Morocco, France, Belgium, and Germany. By existing in a transnational space, these migrants can create a sphere of their own that is relatively independent of their daily breadwinning activities. This sphere offers them a dignity and routine that is unavailable in the leisure activities offered by the host societies. It allows for a moral condemnation of the state without taking any political responsibility.

The Visva Hindu Parishad (VHP), or World Hindu Council, is of much more recent origin than the Tablighi Jama'at. It is an initiative taken in 1964 to "unite the Hindus" worldwide in order to recapture the Indian state from the secularists who "dominated" it and to prevent conversions from the Hindu fold to Islam. An important role is played by the Rashtriya Swayamsevak Sangh (RSS), a militant organization that emerged in the 1920s and has been continuously involved in communal violence against Muslims (Hansen 1999). The ideology of the VHP is not much different from other Hindu Unity movements over the century. It expresses the need to reassert Hindu dignity and pride in the face of alleged attempts of the state to secularize society and appease the Muslim community. However, its organization is innovative. Its secular leadership, which derives from the RSS, depends on decisions taken in a public debate among religious leaders in what is called a Parliament of Hindu Religion. The Parliament convenes in one of the big Hindu bathing festivals, the latest being the Kumbh Mela in February 2000 in Allahabad, where more than 20 million pilgrims and monks convened for a holy dip in the Ganges. The tone in these meetings is highly critical and demands a change in the policies of the government toward the Hindu community. The Parliament of Hindu Religion sees itself as an alternative to parliamentary politics in Delhi. Its organization, depending on changing alliances between religious leaders, is very unclear and secretive. The political role of the VHP is indirect but very important because its campaigns have led to electoral successes of the allied political party, the Bharatiya Janata Party (BJP), which dominates the current Indian government.

The VHP had its first success in a context very similar to the one in which the Tablighi Jama'at had originated: the context of mass conversion as part of a politics of numbers and communal competition. After the oil crisis of 1973 there had been an explosion of allegations and violence centering on the idea that conversions to Islam, by necessity, had to have been induced by oil money. The most important of such conflicts related to Meenakshipuram, a South Indian village in which an untouchable community converted to Islam in 1981. The VHP successfully mobilized the minority syndrome of the Hindu majority and saw its following increase to the extent that it could mobilize support for the far-reaching attack on the Babar Mosque in Ayodhya that was destroyed in 1992.

Hindu movements like the VHP, the Swaminarayan Movement, and Muslim movements like the Tablighi Jama'at are prime agents in globalization (Williams 1984, 1988; Vertovec & Peach 1997; van der Veer 1995; Werbner 1999). A Hindu guru can be called successful only if he is supported by Hindu followers abroad. These networks are enabled by constant air travel, but also increasingly by digital religion: websites where one can "click a deity." The focus of these global movements is on the family. The struggle of migrants is to reproduce their religious culture in a foreign environment (Blank 2001). The fear is often that the children will lose all touch with the culture of the parents and thus, in some sense, be lost to them. The globalization of production and consumption, including the flexibility and mobility of labor, is addressed by religious movements and is a major element in their politics of belonging. The idea that migrants are rootless because they are highly mobile misunderstands the imaginary nature of roots. To have roots requires a lot of work for the imagination (dreamwork). One element of that dreamwork is that pride in one's nation of origin is important in the construction of self-esteem in the place of immigration (Appadurai 1996, van der Veer 1995).

Media and the Public Sphere

Another important element in the transformation of the public sphere is the development of communication technologies. Viewing (darshan) is a central medium of worship and communication in Hindu devotion. The viewing of a divine image brings one into the presence of the supernatural. Certainly some images are more powerful than others, so much so that Hindus go on long pilgrimages to be in the presence of divine power (van der Veer 1988, Fuller 1992, Parry 1994). Also time is important in this regard: Some spaces are more powerful at some moments. This would entail a certain localization of sacred power that is also found in Islam (Werbner & Basu 1998), but the mechanical reproduction of pictures of deities in Hinduism, of "god posters"—compounded by film and television images, all available on videocassettes—allows for an increasing mobility of sacred power (Babb & Wadley 1995). Especially the broadcasting of the great Hindu epics, Ramayana and Mahabharata, by Indian state-run television has enabled the appropriation of a Hindu visual regime at the popular level in a new political language in the public sphere. This is not to argue that the televised epics have replaced older forms of dramatic performance of these traditions, but that they have created new audiences and new arguments (Lutgendorf 1990). This transformation of the visual register in the public sphere is immediately connected to transformations in the literary and linguistic register (Haq 1999, Rai 2001, Ramaswamy 1997). In South India the connection between populist politics and cinematic performance in the public sphere has been long-standing (Dickey 1994) and has been extended to national television and Bollywood cinema. A number of recent studies have shown the importance of the new media for religious politics in India and Pakistan (Rajagopal 2001, Mankekar 1999, Akhtar 2000). One of the challenges of religious movements today is to appropriate visual imagery in a market saturated with cable television broadcasting fashion shows, advertising, music clips. The VHP, for instance, is able to capture both a peasant audience in rural India and an urban middle-class audience by carrying its message in campaigns that involve the traversing of the country by motorized processions and by simultaneous packaging in video messages and websites. The use of religious symbolism in its campaigns is incredibly astute (Ludden 1996, McKean 1996), informed by the long Bollywood tradition of cinematic melodrama. An important aspect of this is its syncretism, the creation of a unified, national religion that can bridge the gaps between the various strands that make up the Hindu tradition. Not only is this new religious unity excellent for use outside of India, it is in fact created in a transnational space in which transnational migrants contribute to the transformation of religion at home.

CONCLUSION

The study of religion in South Asia requires an understanding of the colonial histories that were formative for the postcolonial nation-state. At the same time it is crucial to understand that nation-states are formed in a global context and that the current transformations of the nation-state under regimes of globalization show not only departures, but also continuities. Religion is one of the defining elements in the politics of belonging and identity in modern South Asia. The social movements and media that communicate religious beliefs and practices and socialize new generations in them are as little confined to South Asia as South Asians themselves. The violent conflicts between Hindus and Muslims, between high castes and dalits, between Shi'as and Sunnis, between Buddhists and Hindus are also not regional, but increasingly global. The study of South Asian religions is thus forced to combine historical awareness, conceptual acuity, and spatial mobility.

LITERATURE CITED

Akhtar RS. 2000. *Media, Religion and Politics in Pakistan*. Karachi: Oxford Univ. Press

Amin S. 1995. *Event, Metaphor, Memory: Chauri Chaura, 1922–1992*. Delhi: Oxford Univ. Press

Appadurai A. 1981. *Worship and Conflict under Colonial Rule: a South Indian Case*. Cambridge, UK: Cambridge Univ. Press

Appadurai A. 1996. *Modernity at Large: Cultural Dimensions of Globalization*. Minneapolis: Univ. Minn. Press

Asad T. 1986. *The Idea of an Anthropology of Islam*. Occas. Pap. Ser. Washington, DC: Georgetown Univ. Cent. Contemp. Arab Stud.

Asad T. 1993. *Genealogies of Religion: Discipline and Reasons of Power in Christianity and Islam*. Baltimore, MD: Johns Hopkins Univ. Press

Babb LA, Wadley SS, eds. 1995. *Media and the Transformation of Religion in South Asia*. Delhi: Motilal Banarsidass

Balagangadhara SN. 1994. *The Heathen in His Blindness... Asia, the West and the Dynamic of Religion*. Leiden: Brill

Bayly CA. 1988. *Indian Society and the Making of the British Empire*. Cambridge, UK: Cambridge Univ. Press

Bayly CA. 1998. *Origins of Nationality in South Asia: Patriotism and Ethical Government in the Making of North India*. Delhi: Oxford Univ. Press

Blank J. 2001. *Mullahs on the Mainframe: Islam and Modernity among the Daudi Bohras.* Chicago: Chicago Univ. Press

Breckenridge CA, van der Veer P, eds. 1993. *Orientalism and the Postcolonial Predicament: Perspectives on South Asia.* Philadelphia: Univ. Penn. Press

Calhoun C, ed. 1994. *Habermas and the Public Sphere.* Cambridge, MA: MIT Press

Carrithers M, Humphrey C, eds. 1991. *The Assembly of Listeners: Jains in Society.* Cambridge, UK: Cambridge Univ. Press

Chandra S. 1998. *Enslaved Daughters: Colonialism, Law and Women's Rights.* Delhi: Oxford Univ. Press

Chakrabarty D. 2000. *Provincializing Europe: Postcolonial Thought and Historical Difference.* Princeton, NJ: Princeton Univ. Press

Chatterjee P. 1993. *The Nation and its Fragments: Colonial and Postcolonial Histories.* Princeton, NJ: Princeton Univ. Press

Cohn BS. 1987. *An Anthropologist Among the Historians and Other Essays.* Delhi: Oxford Univ. Press

Cohn BS. 1996. *Colonialism and Its Forms of Knowledge.* Princeton, NJ: Princeton Univ. Press

Comaroff J, Comaroff J. 1992. *Ethnography and the Historical Imagination.* Boulder, CO: Westview

Dalmia V, von Stietencron H, eds. 1995. *Representing Hinduism: the Construction of Religious Traditions and National Identity.* New Delhi: Sage

Dickey S. 1994. *Cinema and the Urban Poor in South India.* Cambridge, UK: Cambridge Univ. Press

Dirks N. 1993. *The Hollow Crown: Ethnohistory of an Indian Kingdom.* Ann Arbor: Univ. Mich. Press

Dirks N. 2001. *Castes of Mind: Colonialism and the Making of Modern India.* Princeton, NJ: Princeton Univ. Press

Dube S. 1998. *Untouchable Pasts: Religion, Identity, and Power among a Central Indian Community, 1780–1950.* Albany: State Univ. NY Press

Dumont L. 1980. *Homo Hierarchicus: the Caste System and its Implications.* Chicago: Univ. Chicago Press

Eickelman D, Anderson J, eds. 1999. *New Media in the Muslim World: the Emerging Public Sphere.* Bloomington: Indiana Univ. Press

Ewing K. 1997. *Arguing Sainthood: Modernity, Psychoanalysis and Islam.* Durham, NC: Duke Univ. Press

Foucault M. 1979. *Discipline and Punish.* New York: Vintage

Fox RG. 1985. *Lions of the Punjab: Culture in the Making.* Berkeley: Univ. Calif. Press

Freitag SB. 1989. *Collective Action and Community: Public Arenas and the Emergence of Communalism in North India.* Berkeley: Univ. Calif. Press

Fuller CJ. 1984. *Servants of the Goddess: the Priests of a South Indian Temple.* Cambridge, UK: Cambridge Univ. Press

Fuller CJ. 1992. *The Camphor Flame: Popular Hinduism and Society in India.* Princeton, NJ: Princeton Univ. Press

Fuller CJ, ed. 1997. *Caste Today.* Delhi: Oxford Univ. Press

Geertz C. 1980. *The Theatre State in Nineteenth-Century Bali.* Princeton, NJ: Princeton Univ. Press

Gerholm T, Lithman Y, eds. 1988. *The New Islamic Presence in Western Europe.* London: Mansell

Ghurye GS. 1953. *Indian Sadhus.* Bombay: Popular Prakashan

Gilmartin D. 1988. *Empire and Islam: Punjab and the Making of Pakistan.* Berkeley: Univ. Calif. Press

Gombrich R, Obeyesekere G. 1988. *Buddhism Transformed: Religious Change in Sri Lanka.* Princeton, NJ: Princeton Univ. Press

Gopal S, ed. 1993. *Anatomy of a Confrontation: Ayodhya and the Rise of Communal Politics in India.* London: Zed

Guha R. 1997. *Dominance Without Hegemony: History and Power in Colonial India.* Cambridge, MA: Harvard Univ. Press

Habermas J. 1989. *The Structural Transformation of the Public Sphere.* Cambridge, MA: MIT Press

Halbfass W. 1988. *India and Europe: an Essay*

in Understanding. Albany: State Univ. NY Press

Hansen TB. 1999. *The Saffron Wave: Democracy and Hindu Nationalism in Modern India*. Princeton, NJ: Princeton Univ. Press

Hansen TB. 2001. *Wages of Violence: Naming and Identity in Postcolonial Bombay*. Princeton, NJ: Princeton Univ. Press

Haq M. 1999. From piety to romance: Islam-oriented texts in Bangladesh. See Eickelman & Anderson 1999, pp. 133–62

Hardiman D. 1987. *The Coming of Devi: Adivasi Assertion in Western India*. Delhi: Oxford Univ. Press

Hefner R. 2000. *Civil Islam: Muslims and Democratization in Indonesia*. Princeton, NJ: Princeton Univ. Press

Inden R. 1990. *Imagining India*. London: Blackwell

Irschick E. 1994. *Dialogue and History*. Berkeley: Univ. Calif. Press

Kepel G. 1997. *Allah in the West: Islamic Movements in America and Europe*. Cambridge, UK: Cambridge Univ. Press

King C. 1999. *Orientalism and Religion: Postcolonial Theory, India and 'The Mystic East.'* Delhi: Oxford Univ. Press

Kumar N. 1998. Sanskrit Pandits and the modernization of Sanskrit education in the nineteenth to twentieth centuries. In *Swami Vivekananda and the Modernization of Hinduism*, ed. W Radice, pp. 36–61. Delhi: Oxford Univ. Press

Lorenzen D, ed. 1995. *Bhakti Religion in North India: Community Identity and Political Action*. Albany: State Univ. NY Press

Lorenzen D. 1999. Who invented Hinduism? *Comp. Stud. Soc. Hist.* 41:630–59

Ludden D. 1993. Orientalist empiricism: transformations of colonial knowledge. See Breckenridge & van der Veer 1993, pp. 250–79

Ludden D, ed. 1996. *Contesting the Nation: Religion, Community, and the Politics of Democracy in India*. Philadelphia: Univ. Penn. Press

Lutgendorf P. 1990. Ramayan: the video. *Drama Rev.* 4:127–76

Madan TN. 1997. *Modern Myth, Locked Minds. Secularism and Fundamentalism in India*. Delhi: Oxford Univ. Press

Mankekar P. 1999. *Screening Culture, Viewing Politics: an Ethnography of Television, Womanhood and Nation in Postcolonial India*. Durham, NC: Duke Univ. Press

Masud MK, ed. 2000. *Travellers in Faith: Studies of the Tablighi Jama'at as a Transnational Islamic Movement for Faith Renewal*. Leiden: Brill

Mathur S. 2000. History and anthropology in South Asia: rethinking the archive. *Annu. Rev. Anthropol.* 29:89–106

Mayaram S. 1997. *Resisting Regimes: Myth, Memory and the Shaping of a Muslim Identity*. Oxford, UK: Oxford Univ. Press

McKean L. 1996. *Divine Enterprise: Gurus and the Hindu Nationalist Movement*. Chicago: Univ. Chicago Press

Metcalf B. 1982. *Islamic Revival in British India: Deoband 1860–1900*. Princeton, NJ: Princeton Univ. Press

Metcalf B. 1993. Living Hadith in the Tablighi Jama'at. *J. Asian Stud.* 52(3):584–608

Metcalf B, ed. 1996. *Making Muslim Space in North America and Europe*. Berkeley: Univ. Calif. Press

Nasr SVR. 1994. *The Vanguard of the Islamic Revolution: the Jama'at-I Islami of Pakistan*. Berkeley: Univ. Calif. Press

Nasr SVR. 2000. The rise of Sunni militancy in Pakistan: the changing role of Islamism and the Ulama in society and politics. *Mod. Asian Stud.* 34(1):139–80

Nielsen J. 1995. *Muslims in Western Europe*. Edinburgh: Edinburgh Univ. Press

Oberoi HS. 1994. *The Construction of Religious Boundaries: Culture, Identity, and Diversity in the Sikh Tradition*. Chicago: Univ. Chicago Press

Obeyesekere G. 1995. Buddhism, nationhood, and cultural identity: a question of fundamentals. In *Fundamentalisms Comprehended*, ed. M Marty, R Appleby, pp. 34–65. Chicago: Univ. Chicago Press

Ortner S. 1989. *High Religion; A Cultural and Political History of Sherpa Buddhism*. Princeton, NJ: Princeton Univ. Press

Parry J. 1994. *Death in Banaras*. Cambridge, UK: Cambridge Univ. Press

Pinch W. 1996. *Peasants and Monks in British India*. Berkeley: Univ. Calif. Press

Prakash G. 1999. *Another Reason: Science and the Imagination of Modern India*. Princeton, NJ: Princeton Univ. Press

Pressler F. 1987. *Religion Under Bureaucracy: Policy and Administration for Hindu Temples in South India*. Cambridge, UK: Cambridge Univ. Press

Rai A. 2001. *Hindi Nationalism*. Delhi: Orient Longman

Rajagopal A. 2001. *Politics after Television: Hindu Nationalism and the Reshaping of the Public in India*. Cambridge, UK: Cambridge Univ. Press

Ramaswamy S. 1997. *Passions of the Tongue: Language Devotion in Tamil India, 1891–1970*. Berkeley: Univ. Calif. Press

Roberts M. 1997. For humanity. For the Sinhalese. Dharmapala as crusading boat. *J. Asian Stud.* 56(4):1006–1032

Said E. 1978. *Orientalism*. London: Routledge

Schulte Nordholt H. 1991. *State, Village and Ritual in Bali: a Historical Perspective*. Amsterdam: Free Univ. Press

Scott D. 1994. *Formations of Ritual: Colonial and Anthropological Discourses on the Sinhala Yaktovil*. Minneapolis: Univ. Minn. Press

Scott D. 1999. *Refashioning Futures: Criticism after Postcoloniality*. Princeton, NJ: Princeton Univ. Press

Sikand YS. 1998. The origins and growth of the Tablighi Jama'at. *Islam and Christian-Muslim Relations* 9(2):171–92

Suleri S. 1992. *The Rhetoric of English India*. Chicago: Univ. Chicago Press

Tambiah SJ. 1992. *Buddhism Betrayed: Religion, Politics and Violence in Sri Lanka*. Chicago: Univ. Chicago Press

Thapar R. 1985. Syndicated Moksha. *Seminar*, Sept., pp. 14–22

Thapar R. 1989. Imagined religious communities? Ancient history and the modern search for a Hindu identity. *Mod. Asian Stud.* 23:209–31

Troll C. 1994. Two conceptions of Da'wa in India: Jama'at Islami and Tabligh Jama'at. *Arch. Sci. Soc. Relig.* 87:115–33

van der Veer P. 1988. *Gods on Earth: the Management of Religious Experience and Identity in a North Indian Pilgrimage Center*. London: Athlone

van der Veer P. 1994. *Religious Nationalism: Hindus and Muslims in India*. Berkeley: Univ. Calif. Press

van der Veer P, ed. 1995. *Nation and Migration: the Politics of Space in the South Asian Diaspora*. Philadelphia: Univ. Penn. Press

van der Veer P. 2001. *Imperial Encounters: Religion and Modernity in India and Britain*. Princeton, NJ: Princeton Univ. Press

van der Veer P, Lehmann J, eds. 1999. *Nation and Religion: Perspectives on Europe and Asia*. Princeton, NJ: Princeton Univ. Press

Vertovec S, Peach C. 1997. *Islam in Europe: the Politics of Religion and Community*. London: Macmillan

Viswanathan G. 1989. *Masks of Conquest: Literary Study and British Rule in India*. New York: Columbia Univ. Press

Viswanathan G. 1998. *Outside the Fold: Conversion, Modernity and Belief*. Princeton, NJ: Princeton Univ. Press

Washbrook D. 1988. Progress and problems: South Asian economic and social history, c. 1720–1860. *Mod. Asian Stud.* 22.1:74–96

Werbner P. 1999. Global pathways: working class cosmopolitans and the creation of transnational networks. *Soc. Anthropol.* 7(1):17–35

Werbner P, Basu H, eds. 1998. *Embodying Charisma: Modernity, Locality and the Performance of Emotion in Sufi Cults*. London: Routledge

Williams R. 1984. *A New Face of Hinduism: the Swaṃinarayan Religion*. Cambridge, UK: Cambridge Univ. Press

Williams R. 1988. *Religions of Immigrants from India and Pakistan: New Threads in the American Tapestry*. Cambridge, UK: Cambridge Univ. Press

Annu. Rev. Anthropol. 2002. 31:189–209
doi: 10.1146/annurev.anthro.31.040402.085424

First published online as a Review in Advance on May 16, 2002

THE POLITICS OF ARCHAEOLOGY IN AFRICA

Nick Shepherd
Centre for African Studies, University of Cape Town, Private Bag, Rondebosch 7700, South Africa; email: shepherd@humanities.uct.ac.za

Key Words colonialism, postcolonialism, nationalism, apartheid, construction of knowledge

■ **Abstract** "Africa is various," writes Kwame Anthony Appiah in defiance of the Eurocentric myth of a unitary and unchanging continent. The politics of archaeology in Africa has been no less marked by variety. Yet, underlying this multiplicity of historical experience are a number of common themes and ideas. This review traces the engagement between archaeology and politics in Africa through an exploration of these common themes: first, as a colonial science in the context of European conquest and the subjugation of African people and territories; second, in the context of colonial administration and the growth of settler populations; third, in the context of resistance to colonialism and a developing African nationalism; and fourth, in a postcolonial context, among whose challenges have been the growing illicit trade in antiquities originating in Africa, and (in the past two decades) the decline in direct funding for departments of archaeology in universities and museums.

INTRODUCTION: A NOTE ON METHOD

"Africa is various," writes Kwame Anthony Appiah (1992) in defiance of the Eurocentric myth of a unitary and unchanging continent. The politics of archaeology in Africa has been no less marked by variety. From the *savants* who accompanied Napoleon's army of conquest in Egypt to the fiercely nationalist archaeologists of Africa's independence, from the overtly colonialist agendas of early researchers to contemporary debates over human origins and racial diversification, and from projects of excavation aimed at uncovering the glories of indigenous states to those aimed at recalling the horrors of slavery, archaeologists have been implicated directly in political struggles and debates. As we might expect from a discipline that takes as its province of concern nothing less than the narrative of human origins and the coming into being of culture and society, such sites of political identification span the range of issues of race, culture, and identity, and have placed archaeologically constructed knowledge in relation to phenomena of colonialism, nationalism, apartheid, slavery, and neocolonialism.

Yet, for all of this web of political association and implication, references to the politics of archaeology in Africa are remarkably few and far between. In fact, as a subject for a review essay "the politics of archaeology in Africa" hardly exists—or if it does, it sits beneath the horizon of visibility of normal academic methods. The reasons for this are interesting but lie outside of the purview of this article. Briefly put, they have to do, in the first place, with the nature of the colonial sciences at large, heavily invested as they were in a particular version of naturalized knowledge. In the second place, the reasons have to do with the influence of the new archaeology. In its concern to remake archaeology as a positivist science, it had specifically rejected the notion that knowledge is constructed within cultural, political, and economic contexts. More recently, one of the central concerns of postprocessual archaeologies has been to show the "constructedness"—and by extension, the inescapably political nature—of archaeological work, writing, and practice (Bapty & Yates 1990, Hodder 1994, Shanks & Tilley 1987a,b).

From a methodological point of view this has entailed, on my part, a heavier hand than is usual for a review article of this nature, in that the major work has entailed what can best be described as reading *through* texts to arrive at their buried political content and context. In general, the works reviewed here fall into three categories. The first group are works that are not recognized by their authors as being political in nature, but that reveal aspects of the social, economic, and intellectual contexts of archaeological practice or that reveal details that, with hindsight, appear political. The second category are works commenting on issues—for example, the illicit trade in African antiquities or the crisis of resources in African archaeology—which I understand to be political in nature. The third category consists of the small number of works dealing directly with the politics of archaeological practice. These, in turn, fall into two groups. The first are works dealing with intradisciplinary politics, such as competition for resources, access to research opportunities, and contested research agendas. The second are works dealing with broader political contexts, for example, the implication of archaeology in projects of memory and identity, processes of nation-building, bids for reparations or retribution, and so on.

With some important exceptions, most of this final category of works are more recent and have tended to be found in a small number of key sites. The *African Archaeological Review* has through the 1990s provided an important forum for discussing the politics of archaeological practice. A key work in what follows is Robertshaw's impressive volume (1990a), which remains the most comprehensive drawing-together of the historiography of African archaeology to date. A disproportionate amount of what follows is focused on the archaeology of Southern Africa, for three reasons. First, this is the region with which I am most familiar. Because a comprehensive account is impossible in a short review of this nature, some more specific kind of focus is inevitable. The second reason is that Southern Africa has one of the best-documented traditions of archaeological practice on the continent. The third is that this has been a particularly acute site of political contestation. In the mid-1980s events in South Africa pitched the world archaeology movement into a crisis that split the International Union of Prehistoric and Protohistoric Sciences (IUPPS). To the extent that Southern Africa has functioned as a microcosm and a development *in extremis* of the politics of archaeology in Africa, it forms an appropriate case study.

POINTS OF REFERENCE

Given the poorly mapped nature of the terrain, it seems advisable to establish some cardinal points at the outset. I adopt—with reservations—Trigger's useful typology of forms of archaeological practice. Trigger (1984) divides the disciplinary field into a number of "alternative archaeologies," each determined by its position in and orientation toward a global division of wealth and power. The particular world historical processes he identifies as being determining in this regard are those of nationalism, colonialism, and imperialism. Each gives rise to a kind of archaeological practice, in its shadow, which replicates its dominant relations, shares its distinctive features, and repeats its style of operation and practice.

Thus nationalist archaeologies tend to glorify a national past and encourage a spirit of unity and cooperation. Colonialist archaeologies tend to denigrate native societies by representing them as static and lacking in the initiative to develop without external stimuli. In this way they attempt to legitimate various colonial projects. Imperialist archaeologies are archaeologies "with a world mission." They aim to influence the development of archaeology far beyond the borders of countries in which they arise. Historically, imperialist archaeologies have been associated with a handful of states that have enjoyed a disproportionate political and economic influence. In the case of the development of archaeology in Africa, these have been the states of Europe with colonial holdings on the continent. Beginning in the 1960s, the United States has emerged as the dominant metropolitan influence on archaeology in Africa, especially in the more high-profile fields (human origins research, Egyptology, the development of state societies in West Africa).

Trigger's typology has been taken up and reasserted by archaeologists working within Africa (Hall 1990, Holl 1990, Shepherd 1998) and has also been challenged (Deacon 1990, Kense 1990, Robertshaw 1990b). Trigger has, himself, reiterated his typology of forms in the specific context of the development of archaeology in Africa (1990). European archaeology has recently focused on nationalism as a formative context in the development of the discipline in Europe (Atkinson et al. 1996, Diaz-Andreu & Champion 1996, Kohl & Fawcett 1995). In the case of African archaeology, I understand colonialism and its associated processes to provide the dominant formative contexts in the development of the discipline, while at the same time recognizing nationalism as a moving force in anticolonial and postcolonial archaeologies.

As to the place of archaeology within a broader project of knowledge construction, inasfar as archaeology took place in colonial contexts, a substantial body of literature has been collected under the heading of postcolonial studies (Bhabha 1994, Said 1978, Said 1993, Spivak 1987). For the purposes of this review I take some points of reference from the work of Mary Louise Pratt. Pratt (1992) establishes the origins of this project of knowledge construction in a post-Linnaean "systematizing of nature," conducted in terms of "a new kind of Eurocentred planetary consciousness": "Blanketing the surface of the globe, it specified plants and animals in visual terms as discrete entities, subsuming and reassembling then in a finite, totalizing order of European making" (p. 38). This "project of natural history determined many sorts of social and signifying practices," including, eventually, archaeology itself. In order to distinguish it from more direct forms of appropriation, Pratt terms this project the "anti-conquest."

In Pratt's reading, the agents of the anti-conquest, those men of science who followed on the heels of military expeditions in the newly conquered territories, were possessed of a curious innocence. She understands this in terms of the explicit valorization of these new projects of knowledge construction. Armed with the examples of their forebears, and with the light of science in their eyes, they sallied forth to encounter colonial landscapes and native societies. In the case of archaeology, this enabled practitioners to excavate sacred sites, compete for the skeletons of newly deceased indigenous persons, and export the cultural treasures of Africa—all in terms of a normative definition of scientific practice. If, on the one hand, the effect of the anti-conquest was to displace local and indigenous systems of knowledge, on the other hand it served to "underwrite colonial appropriation" (p. 53). Archaeology appears not so much as a neutral means to the "discovery" of pre-existing histories buried in colonial landscapes, as a discipline actively constructing archaeological pasts over and against local and indigenous conceptions of past times.

What are the particular nodes of contestation and points of friction in the disciplinary landscape within which archaeology operates in Africa? In a first approach they appear as follows: First, the archaeology of Africa has, historically, been carried out by non-indigenous practitioners, for whom African landscapes figure as exotic, and African people and cultures figure as "Others." Second, archaeology frequently relies on intrusive methodologies that destroy sites and sacred places in the process of investigation. Third, the field of the past has assumed a special significance for anticolonial and postcolonial movements and commentators. Fourth, excavation is a material practice that involves archaeologists in relations of work and may result in goods of a high intrinsic value, which tend to circulate in parallel networks of exchange. Fifth, archaeology undertakes the investigation of cultural practices and products that may be protected by rites, observances, and cultural values of secrecy and intimacy. Finally, archaeology is part of a broader project of knowledge production that was unequal in its inception and by-and-large remains so today. For an African archaeologist unable to get into the field for lack of spare parts for her vehicle, without access to current journals, and denied advancement because her own political beliefs lie outside of those of the ruling party, archaeology is less a disinterested science than a directly political pursuit tied to rates of exchange, the policies of the International Monetary Fund, and the mechanics of patronage and survival.

ARCHAEOLOGY AND COLONIALISM

Archaeology, both as a discipline and as an idea, was introduced into Africa as part of the process of colonial expansion itself. A curiosity about antecedents and a sense of history as it is represented in the material objects of the past seems to be fairly general to human societies around the world. Pierre de Maret (1990), for example, reports "a devotion to the past" among the majority of sub-Saharan African peoples. This interest extends to the material relics of the past: "oral traditions provide numerous examples of a relationship between material relics of the past and the history of a people" (p. 111). Nevertheless, the particular methodologies, paradigms, procedures, and protocols of reportage and display that make up the discipline of archaeology—as opposed to these informal or folk archaeologies—have their origins in a particular conjunction of historical and intellectual contexts in the societies of northwestern Europe in the eighteenth and nineteenth centuries. These include the Enlightenment, the rise of capitalist production, and not least, colonialism itself. The newly constituted discipline of archaeology figured in a complex nexus: a new valuation of the material object associated with the development of capitalist production; a curiosity about antecedents and a new faith in the scientific method; and an alertness to the diversity of human culture and experience revealed in the course of colonial expansion (Tilley 1990; Trigger 1981, 1989). Its export to other parts of the world took place as part of a more general transfer of goods, technologies, and ideas.

On the ground, in the colonial states in Africa, the relation between colonialism and the development of archaeology could hardly have been more direct. Many of the first archaeological practitioners were themselves employees of the colonial state. Augustin Holl (1990) writes that the earliest research reports dealing with archaeological information on West Africa were published between 1870 and 1900:

> At that time, the colonial powers were engaged in surveying their new territories; powerful expeditions were often organized. Many expeditions headed by army officers crossed the Sahara from the north to the south . . . and from the west to the east, from Dakar to Djibouti. In this process of "pacification," the participants recorded various kinds of information about peoples, languages, customs, geography, geology, traditions and archaeological finds. Thus, it is logical enough that the earliest archaeological reports from West Africa were written by army and medical officers, school teachers and priests. (p. 298)

This was a process in which influence worked in both directions, and Holl notes, "Many of the people who actively participated in colonialism played an important role in the emergence of French archaeology as a self-contained discipline" (p. 298). De Barros (1990) writes of Francophone West Africa in the years 1900–1940: "During this period, archaeology was conducted by colonial administrators, military officers, civil servants and technical personnel (usually geologists). . . . Artefact collections were primarily surface finds obtained during military, scientific and mining expeditions or those accidentally uncovered during various colonial construction projects" (p. 158).

In writing about the archaeology of Central Africa, de Maret (1990) notes, "The Tervuren archives . . . attest to the passion for the collection of lithic artefacts and one is struck by the knowledge of prehistory and its specialist vocabulary shown by the officials of the Independent state, as well as by businessmen, engineers and servicemen" (p. 114). Bernard Fagg, one of the formative figures in Nigerian archaeology, began his career as Assistant District Officer with the Nigerian Administrative Service. His first excavation at Rop Rock Shelter took place in 1944 during his leave from colonial administration (Kense 1990). Finally, Peter Sheppard (1990) titles his account of the development of North African archaeology "Soldiers and Bureaucrats: The Early History of Prehistoric Archaeology in the Maghreb."

Archaeology appears in this context as one of the forms of scientific enquiry that mediated the encounter between the agents of colonialism and audiences back home, and the unfamiliar people, cultures, and territories with which they came into contact. The relation between archaeology and colonialism was the relation between knowledge and power. On the one hand the political and economic processes of colonialism served to open up new territories for inspection; on the other hand, archaeology provided a powerful form of legitimation for the colonial project itself.

DISCIPLINING ARCHAEOLOGY

Beginning in the 1920s—and in some cases, slightly before—archaeology in Africa increasingly fell into the hands of trained professionals working within institutionalized contexts. They brought a sense of order and systematization to archaeology, founded professional bodies, and established the institutional spaces within which the discipline was to be practiced. In 1923 the South African–born archaeologist John Goodwin returned from Cambridge to take up a post at the University of Cape Town. In a series of presentations and publications over the next few years, he proposed a local typology of the Stone Age and an indigenous nomenclature, which have since become standard in sub-Saharan Africa (Goodwin 1958, Goodwin & van Riet Lowe 1929, Malan 1970). In roughly the same period, Louis Leakey began his own research in Kenya.

Yet, if the emergent discipline of archaeology situated its own project close to the centers of colonial power in Africa, then the details of this relation, as well as the position of individual archaeologists, were more complex then a first reading might allow. De Maret (1990), for example, notes that virtually all the archaeologists who worked in the Congo trained at the Free University of Brussels, rather than the traditionally more conservative Catholic University of Louvain: "As this division was not linked to the existence of courses, it seems to indicate that a propensity for African archaeology corresponded to a certain liberal philosophy" (p. 134). It becomes important to specify more closely the positions in which African archaeologists found themselves, as well as the allegiances and ideas that structured their political relationships.

With the professionalization of archaeology in Africa, an important tension emerges between the archaeological metropoles in Europe and their offshoot archaeologies in the colonies. John Goodwin, who himself suffered the divided loyalties of the settler and expatriate, was to have his material whisked away from under his nose by his Cambridge mentor Myles Burkitt, who rushed his own book into print (Burkitt 1928) a year before Goodwin & van Riet Lowe's *The Stone Age Cultures of South Africa*. Philip Tobias (1978) reports that an important sidelight of the first Pan-African Congress on Prehistory, held in Nairobi in 1947, was the visit to the Transvaal of Le Gros Clark, Professor of Anatomy at Oxford, to view the fossil collections. His independent verification of the Australopithecus material opened the door to a reappraisal of the African early hominids and won for Dart, Broom, and others the recognition they had been denied for two decades.

In a much-reported incident at the 1929 meeting of the British Association for the Advancement of Science in Johannesburg, Gertrude Caton Thompson took on settler opinion and the local archaeological establishment by proclaiming the "essentially African" nature of Great Zimbabwe (Hall 1996). Yet, as Hall points out, the grounds on which she did so are instructive. Caton Thompson follows Randall-MacIver in seeing the "Zimbabwe Culture" as not up to much. She writes (1931): "The architecture at Zimbabwe, imitative apparently of a daub prototype, strikes me as essentially the product of an infantile mind, a pre-logical mind, a mind which having discovered the way of making or doing a thing goes on childishly repeating the performance regardless of incongruity" (p. 103). Great Zimbabwe could be African because it was insufficiently developed to be European.

Even as they pioneered a new terminology for the Stone Age, Goodwin & van Riet Lowe (1929) remained convinced that they were working in a part of the world that had been an evolutionary cul-de-sac, or as they put it, "a pocket from which nothing tangible returns" (p. 3). In their account, the Sahara acted as a barrier preventing the movement of cultures from south to north, but allowing "higher" cultures to pass from Europe into Africa. This was a period when Goodwin reportedly funded his field trips from his lecturer's salary. Intellectually bold and passionately committed, these archaeologists remain typical of their time, as Deacon (1990) notes, in regarding their archaeological subjects as "helpless recipients of successive waves of innovation from Europe, the font of knowledge and invention" (p. 46).

This precise conjunction, with its mix of paternalism and sentimentality, and its instinctual deference to the metropole, is nicely captured in an editorial from *Antiquity* on "The Training of Archaeologists," reprinted in the *Southern African Archaeological Bulletin* (Goodwin 1947). It begins by drawing attention to the "crying need in the sphere of archaeology all over the world, and particularly to those still quite extensive regions which are under British Government." It talks of the need to create posts in archaeology in the Sudan, Eritrea, Somalia, Kenya, and Nigeria; and of the need to train local practitioners to fill them:

> But one might go even further back, emphasizing the fact that "new" countries are only new to us Europeans; they have had their own history which can only be discovered and recreated by digging and other archaeological techniques, which we can and should teach them. . . . Under proper direction, primitive peoples can do archaeological work. (p. 97)

ARCHAEOLOGY AND NATIONALISM

If colonialist archaeologies frequently denigrated the achievements of native societies, then nationalist archaeologies have tended to do the opposite. A generalized concern with past times has played an important role in nationalist and anticolonial rhetoric and practice in Africa. According to the anti-apartheid activist and articulator of Black Consciousness, Steve Biko (1978), "colonialism is never satisfied with having the native in his grip but, by some strange logic, it must turn to the past and disfigure and distort it" (p. 95). In an essay called "We Blacks," he comments, "A people without a positive history is like a vehicle without an engine" (p. 29). In the words of Chinweizu (1987), "the colonialist history of Africa was composed as a song of disorientation. . . . The false image of Africa it concocted was a paralysing bullet for our souls. If we are to rouse ourselves from the induced paralysis, we have to counter the image, change that song, draw up a correct map" (p. 75).

Frantz Fanon (1967), perhaps the most eloquent of anticolonial writers, comments, "While the politicians situate their action in actual present-day events, men of culture take their stand in the field of history" (p. 168). He writes of "the secret hope of discovering beyond the misery of today, beyond the self-contempt, resignation and abjuration, some very beautiful and splendid era whose existence rehabilitates us both in regard to ourselves and in regard to others" (p. 169).

Perhaps the best archaeological expression of this imperative is to be found in the work of the Senegalese intellectual, Cheikh Anta Diop (1974, 1979, 1981, 1989, 1996). Diop is concerned to claim ancient Egypt for African scholarship and African cultural history. In a more controversial aspect of his work he asserts that the Nile Valley was the point of origin for a range of African peoples, from the Fulani to the Zulu, and he uses archaeological evidence to trace their migration routes. Although the work of Diop has been widely criticized, Martin Hall (1996) writes that it "has been highly effective in demolishing the tenets of colonial histories of Africa" (p. 37). He notes that the recent interest in Martin Bernal's work has served to focus attention back on Negritude historians like Diop (Bernal 1991).

More problematic are those nationalist archaeologies that have cast off all restraints in terms of submitting to a body of evidence. Few sites have been as subject to the claims of competing nationalisms as has Great Zimbabwe. Despite an established body of credible archaeological work at Great Zimbabwe stretching back to the beginning of the century (Caton Thompson 1931, MacIver 1906, Robinson et al. 1961), the period of the Rhodesian Front regime in the 1960s and 1970s saw the resurgence of a settler nationalist historiography, whose cornerstone was the notion of the exotic origins of the site. Garlake (1982) writes, "Several publications appeared branding Zimbabwe's archaeologists as, at best, misguided tools of politically motivated enemies of the state and, more probably, traitorous agents of a world-wide conspiracy of subversion" (p. 11)—most notably works by Bruwer (1965) and Gayre (1972).

Ken Mafuka's short work, *Dzimbahwe; Life and Politics in the Golden Age 1100–1500 AD* (1983), was written as a riposte to a colonialist historiography of Great Zimbabwe. It is methodologically innovative in using oral sources to complement the archaeological evidence; however, this approach is undone when he allows his imagination to take wings. He writes that below the level of the king in the ancient state there was "an almost equal society," bound together by the exchange of gifts. This was "a socialistic spirit at its best" (p. 31). In one passage he is concerned to show "how despite all the hardships associated with such monumental building, the inhabitants of Great Zimbabwe had moments of pleasure. Indeed, it is amazing how the Zimbabweans, with very little material resources, were capable of infinite happiness. They had such a sense of humour that they were capable of deriving laughter from the most barren of circumstances. This is a heritage which should be the envy of the human race" (p. 24).

ARCHAEOLOGY AND APARTHEID

Conventional accounts of the relationship between archaeology and apartheid in South Africa tend to take one of two possible tacks. Either they regard archaeology as fundamentally apolitical in nature and safely distanced from the political facts of apartheid (Deacon 1986, 1990; Sampson 1988); or they paint a picture of the discipline as an unsung partner in the resistance against the regime. For example, in 1986, when the organizers of a meeting of the IUPPS imposed a ban on South African and Namibian participants, Thurston Shaw (Ucko 1990) wrote: "It is sad that this means excluding courageous South Africans who, by their work, have indeed helped to undermine the theoretical basis of apartheid. Such scholars are, as it were, underground resistance fighters" (p. 84).

In fact, the relationship between archaeology and apartheid in South Africa was a good deal more ambiguous than such an account suggests. At the center of this relationship stands a paradox: How a discipline working with politically explosive material could, on the one hand, be generously supported by an authoritarian state whose security it might be understood to threaten; and, on the other hand, how it could be ignored by anti-apartheid activists and African nationalists. For, *contra* Biko and Fanon, the compelling body of archaeological work on precolonial African societies that existed by the early 1970s was bypassed almost in its entirety by liberation movements in South Africa and abroad.

The fortunes of archaeology under apartheid describe an interesting path. In the 1930s and 1940s South African archaeology was established under the political patronage of Jan Smuts, sometime prime minister and head of the more moderate United Party. In 1935 he intervened personally to establish the Bureau of Archaeology, later to become the Archaeological Survey, under the direction of Peter van Riet Lowe. When D. F. Malan's Afrikaner nationalists swept to power in 1948 on an apartheid ticket, the archaeological establishment was wrong-footed. The new government rescinded an invitation initially extended by Smuts to hold the second Pan-African Congress in South Africa. A series of editorials from the period, penned by Goodwin (1950a,b), show how keenly the loss of official patronage was felt: "We have the materials, we have the will, we have the men; we only lack the essential support of our own Government in this particular instance" (p. 2). In crucial respects the discipline, which tended to be Anglophile and keyed into the transnational network of the British Empire, found itself at odds with the parochialism of Afrikaner nationalist politics. In a bitter jibe, Goodwin writes: "There is no further news of the Second Pan-African Congress on Prehistory, due to be held in 1951. Dr L. S. B. Leakey's brilliant inspiration seems to have been well ahead of its times. Perhaps (at the pace of the ox) we shall have reached an adequate cultural level in 2051 AD, to follow Kenya's brave lead" (p. 42).

Lean years followed. Goodwin died in 1959 and was replaced by Ray Inskeep in what was still the only university-based position in archaeology in the country. Shortly afterwards the Archaeological Survey was closed as a government department. However, in the late 1960s the discipline began a period of exponential growth, linked to increased government spending on museums and universities. Deacon (1990) reports that by 1970 there were six university posts and ten museum posts in archaeology in South Africa, and by 1987 this had risen to a combined total of nearly 60 posts. The re-emergence of archaeology coincided with a period of rapid growth in the South African economy, when an archaeological service was seen as part of the essential cultural apparatus of a modernizing state. Henceforth, the apartheid government would be in the unusual position of generously supporting a discipline whose major work lay in unmasking the extent of black cultural achievement.

In a pair of papers written in the 1980s, Martin Hall (1984, 1990) sets out to address this paradox. He begins with a firm assertion of the inescapably political nature of African archaeology: "In those countries where the archaeology of the colonized is practised by the descendants of the colonizers, the study of the past must have a political dimension" (1984, p. 455). He captures the ambiguously situated position of colonialist archaeology: "while many archaeologists were opposed to the use of history and prehistory for the justification of white nationalistic policies, most are probably also opposed to black nationalism, which threatens existing social and economic orders and therefore the institutions from which archaeological research is conducted" (1984, p. 462). He suggests that successive researchers accommodated this contradiction in one of two ways: "by avoiding the contested ground and researching less controversial periods of antiquity, or by retreating into highly technical analysis which effectively excluded all but the acolytes of the profession" (1990, p. 63). Thus, for example, John Schofield formulated and used typological categories that "were sanitized by numeration; labels such as "NC2D," "ST1," and "NT1" were hardly likely to affront the settler consciousness" (1990, p. 64). Contemporary Iron Age studies in South Africa saw "the tight parcelling of archaeological information in a technical form that made it unintelligible beyond the profession." In place of the technically difficult and deliberately obscure archaeological material, the Black Consciousness movement resorted to "an abstract, utopian vision of the precolonial past" (1990, p. 73).

In the postapartheid period these ambiguities have translated into something of a crisis of purpose in South African archaeology. Writing in the late 1990s,

Hall (1997) reports that "at the very time they should be expanding their horizons, museums are facing unprecedented budget cuts.... Fewer students than ever before are choosing courses in archaeology at South African universities, and fewer still are electing to major in the subject.... Fewer archaeologists than ever before are applying for research grants from government agencies" (p. 6).

THE CRISIS OF RESOURCES IN AFRICAN ARCHAEOLOGY

For many African countries, the sense of optimism that accompanied independence and the two development decades of the 1960s and 1970s gave way to increasing indebtedness and despondency in the 1980s and, in the 1990s, a sense of active crisis. Colin Leys (1994) notes that per capita incomes have been falling at a rate of over 2% a year since 1980, "and there is no obvious prospect that this will be reversed in the foreseeable future" (p. 34). Africa's debt is now the highest in the world as a proportion of GDP. Over the past two decades the social and economic crises attendant on the catastrophic HIV/AIDS pandemic have been added to the list of the continent's burdens (Medical Research Council 2001).

For the practice of archaeology in Africa this has been felt as a crisis of resources. After a hopeful start in the 1960s and 1970s, the past decade has seen the shrinking of indigenous archaeologies in Africa. Merrick Posnansky (1993) documents the "collapse" of West African archaeology following the economic downturn of the late 1970s and early 1980s. The decade of the 1960s dawned as an era of hope and pride: "Universities, museums, ministries of culture, and antiquities services figured strongly in the development plans of the newly emerging states." In Nigeria "every state scrambled to have both a university and a museum" (p. 143). In the early 1970s several departments of archaeology in Nigeria were conducting research and training, and there was a flourishing department in Ghana, with smaller research units in Abidjan and Dakar. The collapse that followed as national funds were withdrawn was traumatic:

> Archaeologists in Ghana and Nigeria lost their capacity to travel into the field. Projects could rarely be sustained. Key faculty, both African and expatriate, sought jobs outside the country, and graduates sent for overseas training never returned.... Opportunities for long-term student participation in field research dissipated. Few books came into the libraries and virtually none arrived in university bookstores. (p. 148)

In Ghana, salaries declined to one fiftieth of their 1960s levels in real terms. In Benin, salaries for archaeologists were up to six months in arrears.

Over the past decade the *African Archaeological Review* has performed a useful service in opening its pages to accounts by African archaeologists of the challenges they face in everyday practice. One of the first of these is Francis Musonda's "African Archaeology: Looking Forward" (1990), written as a companion piece to Thurston Shaw's "African Archaeology: Looking Back and Looking Forward" (1989). Musonda notes of the archaeological scene in Southern Africa:

> Political turbulence, coupled with the depressed world economy, has played a major part in the decline of archaeological activity. The "brain drain" syndrome continues unabated. . . . University departments continue to be starved of lecturers and teaching materials, while museums continue to suffer from lack of adequate conservation and storage facilities, and publication of research findings is often granted even less priority. (p. 12)

He quotes a revealing statistic in connection with the lack of direct funding for established researchers in Africa: "Obtaining funding for archaeological projects is one of the most frustrating exercises that a young archaeologist has to undertake . . . More than ninety percent of research funds that have been given to African archaeologists have been disbursed during the course of training" (p. 12). In an editorial headed "Involvement and Relevance" (1990), the editors of the *AAR* underline the significance of this figure: "Dr. Musonda . . . suggests that many of his contemporaries are effectively ignored by overseas sponsors once their post-graduate training is complete. . . . In effect, this is a form of neo-colonial exploitation" (p. 1).

Karega-Munene (1996) reports that archaeologists in Kenya have resorted to moonlighting in the face of declining salaries: "Virtually every archaeologist working in this country holds a full-time job plus one or more part-time jobs" (p. 88). In the same volume, Kusimba reports of "Archaeology in African Museums" (1996) that "Many museum professionals have gone to the university to teach, changed professions, or sought employment in the West. On a recent visit to one museum, I found that many junior museum staff were dealing with the rising inflation by skipping lunch and walking to and from work to their residences" (p. 166).

"CULTURAL PUPPET ON A STRING"

The underdevelopment of indigenous archaeologies in Africa has taken place as a result of more than simply a shortage of cash or the fact that archaeological services are tied to the macro-economic fortunes of the countries in which they operate. Crucially, it has also come about as the result of the lack of control by African archaeologists of research agendas and priorities. Posnansky (1993) notes that foreign-led archaeological expeditions have continued through the period of crisis but have brought their own problems: "All too frequently many of the foreign researchers have been graduate students working with limited funds themselves, using but not always replacing scarce fieldwork equipment and exporting their finds abroad for study" (p. 149). The result is that although "We certainly now know much more about West Africa's past then [sic] we did a quarter of a century ago, we have paid a price in sites not conserved and an awareness by the wrong groups, for the wrong reasons, of the intrinsic value of the cultural patrimony" (p. 150)—a statement that demands careful unpacking.

One of the places to do this is through a key debate that ran in the mid-1990s on the issue of "Who sets the agenda in African archaeology?" The publication of the debate in question is disjointed, but holds up if we follow the issues. At the 1994 meeting of the Society of Africanist Archaeologists (SAFA, formerly known as the Society of Africanist Archaeologists in America) at the University of Indiana, a round-table discussion was held on the topic of "African Archaeology in the 21st Century." One expression of this discussion in print was an exchange published in the *AAR* under the heading of "The Future of African Archaeology," whose chief distinction is the fact that most of the correspondents are based in North America.

A more immediate response was published in the *West African Journal of Archaeology* by Bassey Andah, A. Adande, C. A. Folorunso, and Obare Bagoda (1994), under the heading of "African Archaeology in the 21st Century; Or, Africa, Cultural Puppet on a String?" Their complaint is that a body, which they describe as a "well meaning Africanist association based in the United States, and whose members are mostly Europeans and Americans" (p. 153), should be setting out to chart the future of African archaeology. They write of a "second colonization" in this regard. In a statement that takes us to the nub of the conflict between funding and control, they write: "Yes there is the problem of adequate funding but much more important is the establishment of the right (truly African) cultural perspective as the basis for training all students—Africans and non-Africans who genuinely want to understand Africa as against wanting to impose their own cultural purview on African peoples and materials" (p. 157).

THE WORLD ARCHAEOLOGICAL CONGRESS

At the 1983 meeting of the Southern African Association of Archaeologists in Gaborone, delegates from Mozambique tabled a motion seeking the condemnation by the Association of apartheid and other forms of discrimination (Hall 1990). The apartheid government was at that time sponsoring a covert war against the democratically elected regime in Mozambique. The majority of the delegates at the Association meeting were South African, and although they may have opposed the racial policies of the South African government, "they had little taste for the explicit involvement of their discipline in the political arena" (p. 75). The motion was never put to the vote, and delegates from Mozambique and Zimbabwe resigned from the Association in protest.

This set in motion a series of events that led to the disinviting of South African and Namibian archaeologists from a meeting of the IUPPS scheduled for Southampton in 1986, in line with the academic boycott against the South African regime then in place. The events around the first World Archaeological Congress constitute the most sharply fought political crisis in world archaeology in recent times—and, perhaps appropriately, the issue of contention was the relationship between archaeology and apartheid. The figure at the center of events, Peter Ucko, describes the split that developed in the international body of archaeologists, a split that persists to this day (Ucko 1990). In the event, the principled stand taken by the organizers of the World Archaeological Congress was to be richly exonerated by developments in the early 1990s, and the political transformation in South Africa. In a pleasing turn of the wheel, the fourth World Archaeological Congress was held in Cape Town in 1999.

ETHNOARCHAEOLOGY

For some time, Africa has attracted attention as a site of ethnoarchaeological research, but as we might expect for a continent in which notions of primitiveness and progress have been defined through the processes of colonialism, the field has been sharply divided. Once again, the debate is usefully summarized by the *AAR*. In volume one, John Atherton (1983) writes enthusiastically of what he calls "living archaeology" in Africa. He writes, "In many areas of Africa, Western influence on material culture remains very limited and much information can be gleaned by the participant-observer" (p. 77); and he continues "While information is lost with the passing of each African elder, it is still possible in most parts of Africa to preserve an enormous amount of data pertinent to traditional material culture" (p. 93).

Atherton's paper and others like it prompted an editorial response by David Phillipson (1989). He writes that archaeologists of Africa rightly pay attention to details of the lifestyles and beliefs of contemporary African societies, but herein "lies an insidious danger. . . . The opinions of such scholars are still all too often expressed in terms of a timeless, almost mythical, status quo which ignores the major economic and social changes that have taken place in many parts of Africa during recent decades." This leads them to "present such attempted reconstructions of traditional practices in the present tense, often tied to 'tribal' designations." Phillipson writes that "we should banish the 'ethnographic present' as intangible, misleading and, above all, past" (p. 1).

In an equally trenchant critique of ethnoarchaeology published in the succeeding volume of the *AAR*, E. Kofi Agorsah (1990) notes: "Africa has been designated the laboratory or testing ground for ethnoarchaeological ideas that have been generated elsewhere" (p. 191). He usefully problematizes the notion of ethnicity itself: rather than being a timeless construct, he emphasizes its "fluidity and multidimensionality." He writes that ethnoarchaeology in Africa needs to be "rescued from the obsessive study of only the so-called foraging groups" and should take as its subject "both modern and traditional societies" (p. 203).

PLUNDERING THE PAST

The period of the late 1990s saw the publication of two works with similar titles. Peter Schmidt and Roderick McIntosh's volume, *Plundering Africa's Past* (1996b), is based on the 1993 Carter Lectures at the Centre for African Studies at the University of Florida. Thurston Shaw's paper, "The Contemporary Plundering of Africa's Past" (1997), was originally given as a lecture at the Royal African Society. Shaw writes that "in the last 20 years, in the course of changing fashions in the art world, wealthy European and American collectors have increasingly moved in on the African field and have been prepared to pay fantastic sums for the things they lust after" (p. 1). The two works tell a tale of illegal excavations, the looting of national monuments, the theft of antiquities from museum collections in Africa (often with the complicity of the museum staff), shady deals by collectors in the West, and the gallery owners, antiques journals, and scientific facilities that assist them.

What alarms contributors is that a trade that one associates with nineteenth-century tomb robbers and the depredations of colonial "collectors" shows no signs of abating, but in fact is on the increase. Michel Brent (1996), a journalist who conducted a six-month investigation into the trade, notes the irony "that it is precisely at the moment when the African peoples have begun to acquire their independence—during the 1960s and 1970s—and thus begun to hold their heads high, to hope in the future, that this clandestine traffic of antique objects developed and took on such huge proportions" (p. 76). A further alarming feature is the active involvement of many Africans in the stripping of their patrimony. Schmidt & McIntosh (1996a) write that one of the key "obstacles to developing a local sense of pride and immediate identification with the objects of the past is the absence of a historical imagination that ties the living and sometimes diverse populations to those who came before them" (p. 10). This is matched by a reciprocal problem of representation in the West: "African cultures have never been viewed as animating and informing such objects but simply as the place from which such objects are harvested" (p. 8).

They see these as instances of a larger issue: Who defines cultural heritage?

> What are the power relations that come into play in defining what is culturally important and what is not? What would induce those who feel they are powerless to make the effort to preserve artifacts or sites? (p. 10)

ARCHAEOLOGY AS SPECTACLE

A significant feature of the recontextualization of archaeological practice in Africa in the period roughly coinciding with the development of postprocessual archaeologies in the West has been the emergence of new forms of consumption and display linking explicitly archaeological themes and narratives to dominant forms of representation in theme parks, leisure complexes, and shopping malls. Martin Hall (1995) describes the so-called "Lost City," an ambitious hotel complex with an archaeological theme constructed in the apartheid "homeland" of Boputhatswana. Designed by the California-based resort designers Wimberley, Allison, Tong and Goo, the resort, which has been modeled to resemble an incompletely reconstructed archaeological ruin, represents an interesting conflation of the patina of antiquity with a kind of postmodern glitz.

The scale of the complex is staggering. It has 338 rooms for guests, restaurants, cinemas, a casino, and a "massive water park open to 5000 day trippers." The special effects that form an integral part of the architecture are "imported from Hollywood," and include a nightly volcanic eruption during which the carved stone "Bridge of Time" rumbles and shakes, the eyes of a stone leopard sitting high above the bridge flash, and steam issues from between the rocks nearby. Architectural features include the King's tower, and the "Kong Gates" of the city, surmounted by a stone gorilla.

Hall's attention in the paper is taken by the narrative that frames the hotel complex, and which contextualizes it in a popular imagery of Africa, the "Legend of the Lost City." This is a wholly spurious tale of an ancient civilization founded by a wandering tribe from the North, which is destroyed by an earthquake and rebuilt some "three hundred centuries" later in its present form. Far from being an innocent romantic tale, or "a Californian fantasy," the Legend of the Lost City "is a master narrative that structures a cultural politics of Africa." Hall writes: "The rebirth of the Legend in the glitz and ersatz of the modern pleasure-palace takes the old ideology of colonialism into the twenty-first century" (p. 181).

ARCHAEOLOGY AND DEVELOPMENT

Where do we look to construct a map of the future? There are a number of current issues and debates to which we might look in plotting future trends in the politics of archaeology in Africa. The practice and discourse of heritage resource management have become established in Africa over the past two decades, and a lively debate exists around perceptions of cultural heritage, the management of archaeological collections and resources, and the development of indigenous management models (Abungu & Abungu 1998, Kibunjia 1997, Macamo 1996, Ndoro & Pwiti 2001, Pwiti 1997, Pwiti & Ndoro 1999, van Schalkwyk 1996). African archaeology has tended to be a recipient rather than an initiator of archaeological theory, but this has been challenged by a small but significant number of works (Andah 1995, Andah & Bagodo 1993, Hall 2000, Kinahan 1995, Schmidt 1996). The role played by archaeology in education has long been recognized, and there exists both an established and a recent debate in the field (Esterhuysen & Smith 1998, Gawe & Meli 1990, Hinz 1990, Mazel & Stewart 1987, Nzewunwa 1990, Pwiti 1994, Sinclair 1990, Smith 1983, Wandibba 1990). In Southern Africa, as elsewhere, there has been a turn toward reappraising collection practices involving human body parts and skeletal material (Legassick & Rassool 1999, Morris 1996). An interest in the African past has long been a feature of the politics of the African diaspora (Gates 1999). Recent works have examined the archaeology of the African diaspora (Agorsah 1996) and the special place held by ancient Egypt in the Afrocentric movement (Roth 1998).

However, if there is a single strand that takes us into the future, then it is the notion of development. M. Adebisi Sowunmi (1998) writes of the need for a "human dimension" in African archaeology. The notion of relevance becomes a watchword. If the first stage of a postcolonial African archaeology involved the celebration of indigenous achievement and the bolstering of national pride, then we need to move to a second stage in which we demonstrate the discipline's relevance to development issues. This will involve "a radical enlargement of... [the] paradigm and operational framework" of archaeologists working in Africa (p. 166). A commitment to social ecology and action research, and a new conception of the role of ethnoarchaeology, are seen as routes toward making archaeology "a vehicle for enhancing our quality of life and promoting development and self-reliance" (p. 165).

Fekri Hassan makes a similar point in "African Archaeology: The Call of the Future" (Hassan 1999). African archaeology needs to take its place in a globalized world as "a means to economic development and trans-national education" (p. 393). He writes: "The motivation to study archaeology of many archaeologists working in Africa and elsewhere is grounded in a much deeper level than that of current political agendas.... Objects of the past legitimize and inform the present; they provide a visible, durable cultural map of transient human affairs." Colonialism and the disappointments of the postcolonial era were painful to experience,

> but we must look beyond the agony and the anger to new vistas of actions that cannot wait. We should not build on the ruins, engaging in a futile dialogue with ghosts. We must instead examine our own historical experience in order to chart a new future grounded in a long-term view of the past and situated on human experiences in different contexts. (p. 398)

CONCLUSION: CENTER AND PERIPHERY

The key issue for practitioners in Africa remains the manner in which they negotiate a place in a globalized field of archaeological pursuit. This is not a new imperative, but the continuation of an historically established relation. From its earliest days African archaeology functioned as part of a transnational network of knowledge production and exchange, and from the earliest days the terms of this exchange have been unequal. This remains generally true, whether with regard to the illicit trade in antiquities, the dynamics of publication, and the market in archaeology graduates, or the setting of research agendas and the way in which Africa has figured in a broader politics of representation. The political challenge for archaeologists in Africa lies in posing the kinds of questions, and developing the forms of practice and the kinds of understandings of our own place and purpose, which begin to tilt this relation in the other direction.

ACKNOWLEDGMENTS

Financial support for the preparation of this paper has come from the National Research Foundation (South Africa) and the Research Unit for the Archaeology of Cape Town and is hereby gratefully acknowledged. Martin Hall has been a consistently inspirational source of comment. I have benefitted from the exemplary research assistance of Janine Dunlop.

The *Annual Review of Anthropology* is online at http://anthro.annualreviews.org

LITERATURE CITED

African Archaeological Review. 1990. Editorial: involvement and relevance. *Afr. Archaeol. Rev.* 8:1–2

Abungu G, Abungu L. 1998. Saving the past in Kenya: urban and monument conservation. *Afr. Archaeol. Rev.* 15:221–24

Agorsah EK. 1990. Ethnoarchaeology: the search for a self-corrective approach to the study of a past human behaviour. *Afr. Archaeol. Rev.* 8:189–208

Agorsah EK. 1996. The archaeology of the African diaspora. *Afr. Archaeol. Rev.* 13:221–24

Andah BW. 1995. The theory and practice of

Afican archaeology: a critical reflection. *W. Afr. J. Archaeol.* 25:89–111

Andah BW, Adande A, Folorunso CA, Bagodo O. 1994. African archaeology in the 21st century; or, Africa, cultural puppet on a string? *W. Afr. J. Archaeol.* 24:152–59

Andah BW, Bagodo O. 1993. Research and theory in archaeology since the 1960s: an assessment of the African especially West African scene. *W. Afr. J. Archaeol.* 22:1–23

Appiah KA. 1992. *In My Father's House: Africa in the Philosophy of Culture*. London: Methuen

Atherton JH. 1983. Ethnoarchaeology in Africa. *Afr. Archaeol. Rev.* 1:75–104

Atkinson JA, Banks I, O'Sullivan J, eds. 1996. *Nationalism and Archaeology; Scottish Archaeological Forum*. Glasgow: Cruithne

Bapty I, Yates T, eds. 1990. *Archaeology after Structuralism: Post-Structuralism and the Practice of Archaeology*. London: Routledge

Bernal M. 1991. *Black Athena: the Afroasiatic Roots of Classical Civilization*. London: Free Association Books

Bhabha HK. 1994. *The Location of Culture*. London: Routledge

Biko S, Stubbs A. 1978. *I Write What I Like*. London: Rowerdean

Brent M. 1996. A view inside the illicit trade in African antiquities. See Schmidt & McIntosch 1996, pp. 63–78

Bruwer A. 1965. *Zimbabwe: Rhodesia's Ancient Greatness*. Johannesburg: Heartland

Burkitt M. 1928. *South Africa's Past in Stone and Paint*. Cambridge: Cambridge Univ. Press

Caton Thompson G. 1931. *The Zimbabwe Culture: Ruins and Reactions*. Oxford: Clarendon

Chinweizu. 1987. *Decolonizing the African Mind*. Lagos: Pero

De Barros P. 1990. Changing paradigms, goals and methods in the archaeology of Francophone West Africa. In *A History of African Archaeology*, ed. P Robertshaw, pp. 155–72. London: James Currey

De Maret P. 1990. Phases and facies in the archaeology of Central Africa. See Robertshaw 1990a, pp. 109–134

Deacon J. 1986. Editorial. *S. Afr. Archaeol. Bull.* 41:4

Deacon J. 1990. Weaving the fabric of Stone Age research in Southern Africa. See Robertshaw 1990a, pp. 39–58

Diaz-Andreu M, Champion TC. 1996. Nationalism and archaeology in Europe: an introduction. In *Nationalism and Archaeology in Europe*, ed. M Diaz-Andreu, TC Champion, pp. 1–23. London: Univ. College London Press

Diop CA. 1974. *The African Origin of Civilization: Myth or Reality*. Chicago: Lawrence Hill

Diop CA. 1979. *Nations, Negres et Culture*. Paris: Presence Africaine

Diop CA. 1981. Origin of the ancient Egyptians. In *UNESCO General History of Africa II: Ancient Civilizations of Africa*, ed. G Mokhtar, pp. 27–57. Berkeley: Univ. Calif./ Heinemann

Diop CA. 1989. *The Cultural Unity of Black Africa: the Domains of Patriarchy and of Matriarchy in Classical Antiquity*. London: Karnak House

Diop CA. 1996. *Towards the African Renaissance: Essays in African Culture and Development 1946–1960*. London: Karnak House

Esterhuysen A, Smith J. 1998. Evolution: the forbidden word? *S. Afr. Archaeol. Bull.* 53: 135–37

Fanon F. 1967. *The Wretched of the Earth*. Harmondsworth: Penguin Books

Garlake PS. 1982. Prehistory and ideology in Zimbabwe. *Africa* 52:1–19

Gates HL. 1999. *Wonders of the African World*. New York: Knopf

Gawe S, Meli F. 1990. The missing past in South African history. See Stone & Mackenzie 1990, pp. 99–108

Gayre R. 1972. *The Origins of the Zimbabwe Civilization*. Salisbury: Galaxie

Goodwin AJH. 1947. Editorial: the training of archaeologists. *S. Afr. Archaeol. Bull.* 2:97

Goodwin AJH. 1950a. Editorial notes and news. *S. Afr. Archaeol. Bull.* 5:1–3

Goodwin AJH. 1950b. Editorial notes and news. *S. Afr. Archaeol. Bull.* 5:41–42

Goodwin AJH. 1958. Formative years of our prehistoric terminology. *S. Afr. Archaeol. Bull.* 13:25–33

Goodwin AJH, van Riet Lowe P. 1929. *The Stone Age Cultures of South Africa.* Cape Town: Trustees S. Afr. Mus.

Hall M. 1984. The burden of tribalism: the social context of Southern African Iron Age studies. *Am. Antiquity* 49:455–67

Hall M. 1990. 'Hidden history': Iron Age archaeology in Southern Africa. See Robertshaw 1990a, pp. 59–77

Hall M. 1995. The legend of the Lost City; or, the man with golden balls. *J. S. Afr. Stud.* 21: 179–99

Hall M. 1996. *Archaeology Africa.* Cape Town: David Philip. ix, 277 pp.

Hall M. 1997. The transformations and future of South African archaeology. *WAC News: the World Archaeol. Cong. Newsl.* 5:5–6

Hall M. 2000. *Archaeology and the Modern World; Colonial Transcripts in South Africa and the Chesapeake.* London: Routledge

Hassan FA. 1999. African archaeology; the call of the future. *Afr. Affairs* 98:393–406

Hinz MO. 1990. The right to a past: Namibian history and the struggle for national liberation. See Stone & Mackenzie 1990, pp. 61–67

Hodder I. 1994. *Reading the Past: Current Approaches to Interpretation in Archaeology.* Cambridge: Cambridge Univ. Press

Holl A. 1990. West African archaeology: colonialism and nationalism. See Robertshaw 1990a, pp. 296–308

Karega-Munene. 1996. The future of archaeology in Kenya. *Afr. Archaeol. Rev.* 13:87–90

Kense FJ. 1990. Archaeology in Anglophone West Africa. See Robertshaw 1990a, pp. 135–54

Kibunjia M. 1997. The management of archaeological collections and resources in Africa. *Afr. Archaeol. Rev.* 14:137–41

Kinahan J. 1995. Theory, practice and criticism in the history of Namibian archaeology. In *Theory in Archaeology*, ed. PJ Ucko, pp. 76–95. London: Routledge

Kohl PL, Fawcett CP. 1995. *Nationalism, Politics, and the Practice of Archaeology.* New York: Cambridge Univ. Press. xi, 329 pp.

Kusimba CM. 1996. Archaeology in African museums. *Afr. Archaeol. Rev.* 13:165–70

Legassick M, Rassool C. 1999. *Skeletons in the Cupboard: Museums and the Incipient Trade in Human Remains, 1907–1917.* Belville, Cape Town: Univ. Western Cape

Leys C. 1994. Confronting the African tragedy. *New Left Rev.* 211:33–47

Macamo SL. 1996. The problems of conservation of archaeological sites in Mozambique. See Pwiti & Soper 1996, pp. 813–16

MacIver D. 1906. *Mediaeval Rhodesia.* London: Macmillan

Malan BD. 1970. Remarks and reminiscences on the history of archaeology in South Africa. *S. Afr. Archaeol. Bull.* 25:88–92

Mazel AD, Stewart PM. 1987. Meddling with the mind: the treatment of San hunter-gatherers and the origins of South Africa's black population in recent South African history textbooks. *S. Afr. Archaeol. Bull.* 42: 166–70

Medical Research Council. 2001. Medical Research Council Report—The impact of HIV/AIDS on adult mortality in South Africa

Morris AG. 1996. Trophy skulls, museums and the San. In *Miscast: Negotiating the Presence of the Bushmen*, ed. P Skotnes, pp. 67–79. Cape Town: Univ. Cape Town Press

Mufuka K. 1983. *Dzimbahwe: Life and Politics in the Golden Age, 1100–1500.* Harare, Zimbabwe: Harare Publ.

Musonda FB. 1990. African archaeology: looking forward. *Afr. Archael. Rev.* 8:3–22

Ndoro W, Pwiti G. 2001. Heritage management in southern Africa: local, national and international discourse. *Public Archaeol.* 2:21–34

Nzewunwa N. 1990. Archaeology in Nigerian education. See Stone & Mackenzie 1990, pp. 33–42

Phillipson D. 1989. Editorial: the ethnographic present is past. *Afr. Archaeol. Rev.* 7:1

Posnansky M. 1993. Coping with collapse in

the 1990s. See Schmidt & McIntosch 1996b, pp. 143–63

Pratt ML. 1992. Narrating the anti-conquest. In *Imperial Eyes: Travel Writing and Transculturation*, pp. 38–85. London: Routledge

Pwiti G. 1994. Prehistory, archaelogy and education in Zimbabwe. In *The Presented Past: Heritage, Museums and Education*, ed. P Stone, pp. 338–48. London: Routledge

Pwiti G. 1997. Taking African cultural heritage management into the twenty-first century: Zimbabwe's masterplan for cultural heritage management. *Afr. Archaeol. Rev.* 14:81–83

Pwiti G, Ndoro W. 1999. The legacy of colonialism: perceptions of the cultural heritage in Southern Africa, with special reference to Zimbabwe. *Afr. Archaeol. Rev.* 16:143–53

Robertshaw P. 1990a. *A History of African Archaeology*. London: James Currey

Robertshaw P. 1990b. A history of African archaeology: an introduction. See Robertshaw 1990a, pp. 3–12

Robinson KR, Summers R, Whitty A. 1961. Zimbabwe excavations 1958. *Occas. Pap. Natl. Mus. S. Rhodesia* 3

Roth A. 1998. Ancient Egypt in America; claiming the riches. In *Archaeology under Fire: Nationalism, Politics and Heritage in the Eastern Mediterranean and Middle East*, ed. L Meskell, pp. 217–29. London: Routledge

Said E. 1978. *Orientalism*. London: Routledge & Kegan Paul

Said E. 1993. *Culture and Imperialism*. London: Chatto & Windus

Sampson CG. 1988. Practical politics in the wilderness of mirrors: a review article. *S. Afr. Archaeol. Bull.* 43:60–63

Schmidt PR. 1996. Rhythmed time and its archaeological implications. In *Aspects of African Archaeology: Papers from the 10th Congress of the PanAfrican Association for Prehistory and Related Studies*, ed. G Pwiti, R Soper, pp. 655–62. Harare: Univ. Zimbabwe Publ.

Schmidt PR, McIntosch RJ. 1996a. The African past endangered. See Schmidt & McIntosch 1996b, pp. 1–17

Schmidt PR, McIntosh RJ, eds. 1996b. *Plundering Africa's Past*. Bloomington: Indiana Univ. Press

Shanks M, Tilley C. 1987a. *Re-Constructing Archaeology: Theory and Practice*. Cambridge: Cambridge Univ. Press

Shanks M, Tilley C. 1987b. *Social Theory and Archaeology*. Cambridge: Polity

Shaw T. 1989. African archaeology: looking back and looking forward. *Afr. Archaeol. Rev.* 7:3–31

Shaw T. 1997. The contemporary plundering of Africa's past. *Afr. Archaeol. Rev.* 14:1–7

Shepherd N. 1998. *Archaeology and postcolonialism in South Africa: the theory, practice and politics of archaeology after apartheid*. PhD thesis. Univ. Cape Town, South Africa

Sheppard PJ. 1990. Soldiers and bureaucrats: the early history of prehistoric archaeology in the Maghreb. See Robertshaw 1990, pp. 173–88

Sinclair PJ. 1990. The earth is our history book: archaeology in Mozambique. See Stone & Mackenzie 1990, pp. 152–59

Smith AB. 1983. The Hotnot Syndrome: mythmaking in South African school textbooks. *Soc. Dynam.* 9:37–49

Sowunmi MA. 1998. Beyond academic archaeology in Africa: the human dimension. *Afr. Archaeol. Rev.* 15:163–72

Spivak GC. 1987. *In Other Worlds: Essays in Cultural Politics*. London: Methuen

Stone P, Mackenzie R. 1990. *The Excluded Past: Archaeology in Education*. London: Unwin Hyman

Tilley C. 1990. On modernity and archaeological discourse. In *Archaeology after Structuralism: Post-Structuralism and the Practice of Archaeology*, ed. I Bapty, T Yates, pp. 127–52. London: Routledge

Tobias P. 1978. The VIIIth Pan-African Congress on Prehistory, Nairobi, 1977, and the opening of the Louis Leakey Memorial Institute. *S. Afr. Archaeol. Bull.* 33:5–11

Trigger BG. 1981. Anglo-American archaeology. *World Archaeol.* 13:138–55

Trigger BG. 1984. Alternative archaeologies: nationalist, colonialist, imperialist. *Man* 19: 355–70

Trigger BG. 1989. *A History of Archaeological Thought*. Cambridge: Cambridge Univ. Press

Trigger BG. 1990. The history of African archaeology in world perspective. See Robertshaw 1990, pp. 309–19

Ucko P. 1990. *Academic Freedom and Apartheid: the Story of the World Archaeological Congress*. London: Duckworth

van Schalkwyk JA. 1996. The past is not dead: cultural resource management in the new South Africa. See Pwiti & Soper 1996, pp. 849–54

Wandibba S. 1990. Archaeology and education in Kenya. See Stone & Mackenzie 1990, pp. 43–49

Annu. Rev. Anthropol. 2002. 31:211–32
doi: 10.1146/annurev.anthro.31.040402.085407

First published online as a Review in Advance on May 21, 2002

VARIATION IN HUMAN BODY SIZE AND SHAPE

Christopher Ruff
Center for Functional Anatomy and Evolution, Johns Hopkins University School of Medicine, 1830 E. Monument St., Baltimore, Maryland 21205; email: cbruff@jhmi.edu

Key Words hominin, climate, nutrition, growth, adaptation

■ **Abstract** Evolutionary trends in human body form provide important context for interpreting variation among modern populations. Average body mass in living humans is smaller than it was during most of the Pleistocene, possibly owing to technological improvements during the past 50,000 years that no longer favored large body size. Sexual dimorphism in body size reached modern levels at least 150,000 years ago and probably earlier. Geographic variation in both body size and shape in earlier humans paralleled latitudinal clines observed today. Climatic adaptation is the most likely primary cause for these gradients, overlain in more recent populations by nutritional effects on growth. Thus, to distinguish growth disturbances, it is necessary to partition out the (presumably genetic) long-term differences in body form between populations that have resulted from climatic selection. An example is given from a study of Inupiat children, using a new index of body shape to assess relative body mass.

INTRODUCTION

Body size and shape vary considerably among living human populations. Mean body mass (weight) varies by 50% or more, within sex, in a worldwide sampling of populations (Ruff 1994), even if Pygmies are not considered. Mean body height (stature) and breadth (bi-iliac or maximum pelvic breadth) also vary between the same samples, although in different ways. Variation in height is smaller (about 10%) and does not follow any particular geographic trend. Variation in breadth is larger (about 25%) and shows a clear latitudinal gradient. The explanation for this difference, and some other systematic human body shape differences, may lie in basic physiological adaptive mechanisms, as discussed below.

There is abundant evidence that both body size and shape were even more variable among Plio-Pleistocene hominins (e.g., Jungers 1988, Ruff 1991, Aiello 1992, McHenry 1992) and, within geographically dispersed taxa, followed clines that were similar to those found among modern humans (Trinkaus 1981; Ruff & Walker 1993; Ruff 1994; Holliday 1997a,b). General temporal trends in body size are also apparent in the fossil record (e.g., Ruff et al. 1997). An appreciation of such variation among human ancestors is important for several reasons: (*a*) Body size (and within-taxon variation in body size) is related to many other characteristics of a species, including life history parameters, ecology, and social organization (Calder 1984, Schmidt-Nielson 1984); thus, it is often used to predict these traits in fossil taxa [notwithstanding some significant problems in doing so (see Smith 1996)]. (*b*) Body size is the usual "denominator" for assessing key evolutionary trends in the hominin lineage, including changes in relative brain size (encephalization), tooth size (megadontia), bone strength (robusticity), and gut size (Pilbeam & Gould 1974; McHenry 1976, 1984, 1988; Ruff et al. 1993, 1997; Aiello & Wheeler 1995; McHenry & Coffing 2000). (*c*) Differences in body shape have been used as population or taxonomic markers among past hominins and to identify migrational and possible interbreeding events (Trinkaus 1981; Holliday 1997a,b; Duarte et al. 1999; Ruff et al. 2002). (*d*) The body size and shape of earlier humans can serve as effective baselines for assessing more recent temporal or geographic variation, for example, the effects of changes in subsistence strategy and the significance of recent secular trends (Frayer 1984, Tobias 1985, Ruff et al. 1997) (see below). Appreciation of long-standing differences in body form between human populations can help inform decisions regarding the most appropriate methods for assessing the health and nutrition of living individuals. Both absolute measures of body size (height, weight) and relative indices reflecting body shape [body mass index (wt/ht^2)] are often used as standards for evaluating growth and under- and over-nutrition (WHO 1995). To the extent that these characteristics vary systematically in response to factors other than health and nutrition, such standards may not be universally applicable across populations.

EVOLUTIONARY TRENDS IN BODY SIZE

Methodological Considerations

Because body size reconstruction in the fossil record almost always depends on extrapolation from fragmentary remains, it is important to clearly understand the rationale behind different reconstruction methods. A purely statistical approach considers the relationship between body mass (or stature) and skeletal/dental features in a modern reference sample and applies resulting prediction equations to the fossil fragments, perhaps preferring those equations with the smallest estimation errors in the modern sample. The problem with such an approach is that it implicitly assumes equality—proportional and/or functional—between the reference sample and the individual to which it is applied, which may or may not be true. For example, equations for predicting stature from long bone lengths developed in European samples severely overestimate stature in East Africans because of their relatively longer limb-to-trunk lengths (Allbrook 1961). This result is predictable given known systematic differences in limb proportions among modern human populations (Roberts 1978). The same rationale applies to reconstruction of stature in the *Homo erectus* KNM-WT 15000, who also had apparently very long limbs (Ruff & Walker 1993). Another example would be the use of tooth size to predict body mass in the hominin lineage, a common practice in primate paleontology (e.g., Gingerich et al. 1982, Conroy 1987) but one that is obviously biased in this case because of temporal (and probably taxonomic) differences in relative tooth size among hominins (Pilbeam & Gould 1974, McHenry 1984, McHenry & Coffing 2000, Teaford et al. 2002). Another not-so-obvious example is the use of long-bone diaphyseal breadth to predict body mass in hominins, a commonly employed procedure in the past (McHenry 1976, Oleksiak 1986, Rightmire 1986, Hartwig-Scherer 1994). It is evident that long-bone diaphyses change their diameters in response to mechanical loading (Trinkaus et al. 1994) and that Plio-Pleistocene hominins had relatively thicker diaphyses than modern humans (Ruff et al. 1993, 1994; Ruff 1998). Thus, use of diaphyseal cross-sectional dimensions and a modern reference sample will lead to systematic overestimates of body mass in fossil hominins.

These examples illustrate the importance of considering the functional significance of skeletal/dental traits when using them for body size reconstruction. In many cases this will involve their mechanical significance because mechanical factors have such a pervasive influence on skeletal form (see references above). The mechanics of weight-bearing in bipeds, in fact, argues for the use of lower limb-bone dimensions for body mass reconstruction in hominins. Articular dimensions have been shown to be less sensitive to differences in activity level than are diaphyseal breadth dimensions (Ruff et al. 1994, Trinkaus et al. 1994, Lieberman et al. 2001); thus, they should more accurately reflect variations in body mass without the potentially confounding effects of individual behavioral differences. For these reasons, lower limb articular size, and particularly femoral head size (because the femoral head is often preserved and is easily measurable), is an effective predictor of body mass in hominins (Ruff et al. 1991, 1997; McHenry 1992; Grine et al. 1995).

Mechanically based methods for estimating body mass can be distinguished from morphometric methods (Ruff 1994, 2000b) that rely on direct reconstruction of body dimensions from preserved bone dimensions. The latter usually involve estimation of stature or body length, followed by estimation of body mass from stature, assuming some specified relationship between the two (Mathers & Henneberg 1995, Porter 1995). Using a cylindrical model of the human body (Ruff 1991), body mass should be predictable from stature and body (cylinder) breadth. In fact, body mass estimates from stature and bi-iliac breadth in living humans are remarkably good (Ruff 1994, 2000b). It is critical when estimating stature, or bi-iliac breadth (if necessary), to use appropriate modern reference samples, i.e., modern populations with body proportions similar to the specimens being estimated (Holliday & Ruff 1997). Fortunately, strong geographical trends in body shape, as well as information gleaned from more complete specimens, can provide guidance with the more usual fragmentary specimens (Ruff et al. 1993; Ruff & Walker 1993; Trinkaus & Ruff 1999a,b). Body mass estimates from femoral head size and a multiple regression using stature and bi-iliac breadth give similar results, on average, when applied to Pleistocene hominin specimens (Ruff et al. 1997).

General Temporal Trends

Figure 1 shows body mass estimates for individual specimens of Pleistocene *Homo* species derived from regressions on femoral head size and/or bi-iliac breadth and stature (Ruff et al. 1997), mean estimates for other Plio-Pleistocene hominin taxa taken from the literature, mainly McHenry (1992), and modern human sex-specific population means from a worldwide sampling, not including Pygmies (Ruff 1994). All estimates for skeletal/fossil specimens were derived from postcranial elements. The Pleistocene *Homo* specimens include 163 individuals used in a previous analysis (Ruff et al. 1997) plus two recently described Middle Pleistocene specimens from Yinnuishan, China (Rosenberg et al. 1999) and Atapuerca, Spain (Arsuaga et al. 1999). Three other specimens attributed to *Homo habilis sensu stricto* (Olduvai 8 and 36 and KNM-ER 3735), whose body masses were estimated by McHenry (1992), are shown enclosed in parentheses because their attribution to the genus *Homo* has been questioned (Wood & Collard 1999). [Other early *Homo* specimens plotted here, including KNM-ER 3228, 1481, and 1472, are not definitely attributable to any particular species but appear to be most similar in morphology to later *H. ergaster/erectus* rather than *H. habilis sensu stricto* (McHenry 1994b, McHenry & Coffing 2000).] Among the *Homo* specimens, those from higher (above 30°) and lower latitudes are distinguished by different symbols. (All *Australopithecus* specimens are from lower latitudes.) Two dotted lines representing the mean body masses of the modern higher- and lower-latitude samples are plotted for reference. Because of differences in data sampling density, the temporal axis is given in three different scales with break points at 2 million and 100,000 years ago.

Several temporal trends in hominin body mass are apparent from Figure 1. First, there is a marked increase in body size with the appearance of early *Homo* (except *H. habilis sensu stricto*) about 2 million years ago. This contrast between *Homo* and earlier and contemporaneous australopithecines has been previously noted (e.g., McHenry 1994a, Wood & Collard 1999, McHenry & Coffing 2000). The explanation for the increase in body size in *Homo* is not clear but may be related to a commitment to a fully terrestrial lifestyle, inhabitation of more open environments, increased foraging distances, and/or dietary shifts (Foley 1987, Wheeler 1992, McHenry 1994a, Leonard & Robertson 1997, Klein 1999). The lack of such an increase in *H. habilis sensu stricto*, with its attendant behavioral implications, is one argument against the inclusion of this taxon within the genus *Homo* (Wood & Collard 1999).

Second, there is an increase in average body size at about 500,000 years ago, corresponding to the first hominin postcranial remains recovered from higher latitudes. It is well documented that among modern humans body mass is distributed clinally, increasing in higher latitudes (Roberts 1978, Ruff 1994, Katzmarzyk & Leonard 1998), as reflected in the living-human data points in Figure 1. This has been interpreted as an example of Bergmann's Rule (Mayr 1956), which is generally explained as an adaptation to decreased heat loss in colder environments.

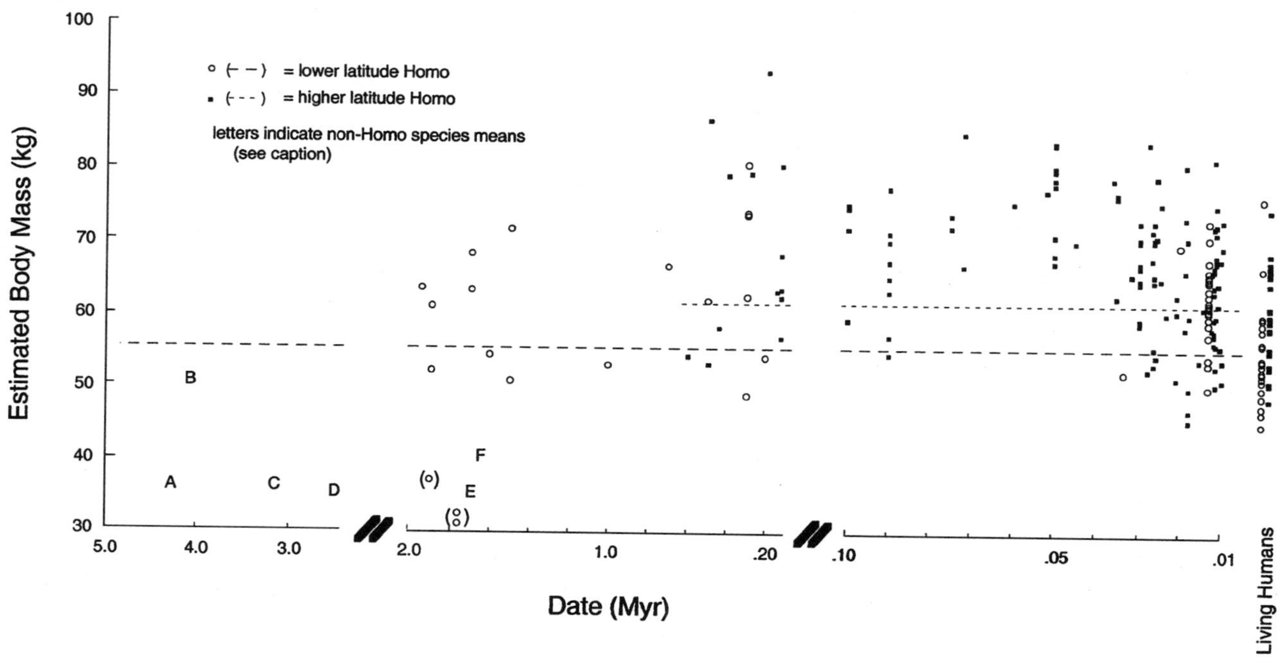

Figure 1 Estimated body mass of Plio-Pleistocene hominins. Letters represent species means of early taxa: *A*, *Ardipithecus ramidus*; *B*, *Australopithecus anamensis*; *C*, *Australopithecus afarensis*; *D*, *Australopithecus africanus*; *E*, *Paranthropus robustus*; *F*, *Paranthropus boisei*. (*A*) Based on similarity in size of humerus to middle of range for *A. afarensis* (White et al. 1994); (*B*) Leakey et al. 1995; (*C–F*): McHenry 1992. Symbols represent individual *Homo* specimens (Ruff et al. 1997, Arsuaga et al. 1999, Rosenberg et al. 1999). Symbols in parentheses are individual *H. habilis sensu stricto* (McHenry 1992). Living humans are sex/population-specific means (Ruff 1994). Open symbols, lower latitude; solid symbols, higher latitude; dotted and dashed lines through living human means for higher and lower latitudes, respectively. Myr, millions of years before present. (Adapted from Ruff 2001, with permission from Elsevier Science.)

Thus, it would be expected that a range expansion into colder climates would increase the average body mass (and total range in body mass) of the genus *Homo*. Body masses for individual Pleistocene *Homo* specimens are generally above the means for living humans from the same latitudinal zones, on the order of 10% higher on average (Ruff et al. 1997). The difference is even greater if only archaic *Homo* specimens (Neandertals and other specimens dated to before 100,000 years ago) are considered: Higher-latitude archaic *Homo* specimens average almost 20% greater in body mass than the means for living higher-latitude populations. This figure may be somewhat inflated by a male preservational bias in the fossil record (Ruff et al. 1997), but even so, it is evident that Middle Pleistocene and early Late Pleistocene humans were significantly larger on average than living humans. A large body size is also consistent with evidence from material culture from this time period, such as very large Middle Pleistocene throwing spears (Thieme 1997).

Third, there is a decline in average body mass beginning about 50,000 years ago. The decline is best demonstrated among higher-latitude samples and is equivalent whether or not archaic humans (Neandertals) are included (Ruff et al. 1997). Lower-latitude samples with body mass estimates are unfortunately rare in the Late Pleistocene. However, similar declines in the Late Pleistocene and early Holocene in other body dimensions, including estimated stature and cranial size, have been demonstrated in many areas of the world, including Europe, the Mediterranean region, sub-Saharan Africa, South Asia, and Australia (Frayer 1980, 1984; Kennedy 1984b; Meiklejohn et al. 1984; Jacobs 1985; Henneberg 1988; Brown 1992; Henneberg & Steyn 1993; Formicola & Giannecchini 1998). The decline continues through the Neolithic, after which it is reversed in European samples. No reversal in this negative trend in size has been reported for lower-latitude samples, except possibly for some very recent increases in some areas over the past few decades (Katzmarzyk & Leonard 1998). As a result, living higher-latitude populations are about as large as terminal Pleistocene samples, whereas living lower-latitude populations are smaller on average than they were 10,000 years ago (Figure 1) (see Ruff et al. 1997).

Several reasons, not mutually exclusive, have been proposed for the Late Pleistocene–Early Holocene decline in human body size (see references above). These include technological improvements that decreased the selective advantage of a larger body (which is also metabolically expensive to maintain), a decline in nutritional quality, climatic factors (adaptation to a warming environment), and reduced gene flow (inbreeding). A reduction in body size has been observed in many, although not all, populations undergoing a transition from a foraging to a food producing economy, especially an intensive agricultural economy (Cohen & Armelagos 1984a). Explanations for this trend usually focus on increases in malnutrition, overcrowding, and spread of infectious diseases. Institution of a class system with resulting social inequities in resource allocation may also be a factor in some populations (Bogin & Keep 1999). However, because body size reduction occurred in many areas of the world prior to the adoption of food production (or where food production was never adopted, i.e., Australia), this factor may be contributory but does not fully explain the trend. Given the timescales involved and the known effects of malnutrition on growth, it seems likely that changes associated with food production were developmental rather than genetic in nature. Recent positive secular trends over the past few hundred years are also most likely to be developmental and related to increased nutritional and overall health levels (Van Wieringen 1986, Eveleth 1994, Stinson 2000). Such positive trends have not been observed in many areas of the world, primarily in lower latitudes that have not enjoyed the same improvements in environment (Malina et al. 1983, Tobias 1985, Pretty et al. 1998). At the same time, the positive secular trend in body size in (mainly) higher-latitude populations may have leveled off over the past few decades (Kimura 1984, Stinson 2000).

One possible explanation for these observations is that the Late Pleistocene reduction in body size was due primarily to genetic factors, possibly reduced selection for large body size in association with technological improvements (Frayer 1984), whereas the succeeding fluctuations (decrease, then, in higher latitudes, increase) in body size in the Holocene were due to environmental effects on growth, e.g., nutrition. Thus, many higher-latitude populations may have recently achieved their maximum "genetic potential" in body size (stature), originally established in the terminal Pleistocene, whereas many lower-latitude populations have not. Additional Late Pleistocene body-mass data from lower-latitude samples would be useful in further testing this hypothesis.

Sexual Dimorphism

Figure 2 shows sexual dimorphism in estimated body mass for early hominin taxa and regional/temporal groupings of *H. sapiens*. Mean male and female body masses for *Australopithecus*, *Paranthropus*, and early *Homo* are from McHenry & Coffing (2000), mean sex-specific body masses for Pleistocene *H. sapiens* are from the data set used in Ruff et al. (1997), and values for individual living human populations ($n = 19$) are from Ruff (1994). The mean sexual dimorphism (male/female) in body mass in the living human populations is about 15%, similar to average figures derived from other living population samples (Stini 1974, McHenry & Coffing 2000). Sexual dimorphism is similar in higher-latitude (mean 15.5%) and lower-latitude (mean 14.7%) living samples ($p > 0.75$, t test). The same is true for the Late Upper Paleolithic sample—the only Pleistocene sample with a sufficient number of individuals from higher and lower latitudes to subdivide in this way—with 16.1% and 15.1% sexual dimorphism for higher and lower latitudes, respectively. Thus, whereas latitude affects average body mass, it appears not to affect sexual dimorphism in body mass in any systematic way. This is the pattern that would be expected if sexual dimorphism in body mass in humans were more influenced by environmental/behavioral factors other than climate per se.

All taxonomic or regional/temporal groupings of *Homo* specimens have levels of body-mass sexual dimorphism comparable to those of modern humans (7%–18%) (Figure 2). In contrast, most earlier and contemporary australopithecines,

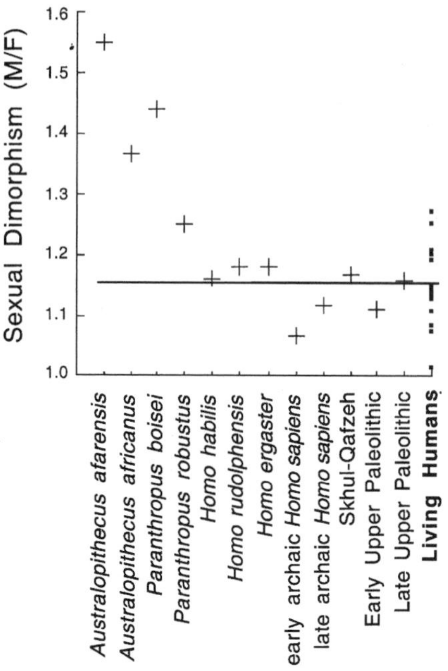

Figure 2 Sexual dimorphism in body mass in hominin taxa or regional/temporal groupings. See text for origin of data. "Early archaic *Homo sapiens*" corresponds to "early Late Pleistocene" in Ruff et al. 1997. Line indicates living human mean.

including *A. afarensis* and *A. africanus*, and *Paranthropus boisei*, show clearly elevated levels of sexual dimorphism (37%–55%). *Paranthropus robustus* is slightly elevated (25%) although just within the range of modern human populations. Some of the estimates for the earlier species are heavily dependent on taxonomic attributions, which can be problematic for isolated postcranial elements; thus, such estimates can change substantially if groups are redefined or additional specimens are added to particular taxa (McHenry 1992, 1994a; McHenry & Coffing 2000). For example, based on newly identified and some reclassified specimens from Swartkrans, South Africa, Susman et al. (2001) estimated body-mass sexual dimorphism to be about 40% in *P. robustus*, equivalent to that in *P. boisei* and *A. africanus* (Figure 2), and even larger in *Homo sp.* from the site, about 80%. This latter figure is similar to earlier estimates of sexual dimorphism in *H. habilis* more broadly defined (*sensu lato*) (McHenry 1992). Another problem in such comparisons is that almost none of the earlier specimens have any associated indicators of sex; thus, sex assignment is made on the basis of size alone (larger = male, smaller = female), often across different sites and temporal ranges, which may exaggerate the degree of estimated dimorphism. In contrast, all of the Late Pleistocene sex assignments shown in Figure 2 for *H. sapiens* are based either on associated pelvic or cranial material or on comparisons within site-specific samples.

Perhaps the most conservative assessment of the data shown in Figure 2 is that sexual dimorphism in body mass definitely reaches modern levels with archaic *Homo sapiens*[1], and very possibly earlier with *H. ergaster/erectus*, but was likely larger in australopithecines and possibly some early species of *Homo*. The behavioral and ecological significance of increased sexual dimorphism in body size in at least some early hominin taxa has been debated (see McHenry 1991, 1992, 1994a; Plavcan & Van Schaik 1997; Plavcan 2001 and references therein). The lack of concurrent marked sexual dimorphism in canine tooth size may imply a social/behavioral system unique among primates (Plavcan & Van Schaik 1997, Plavcan 2001). To the extent that sexual dimorphism in body size reflects social organization, the data for archaic *H. sapiens* indicate that by the Late Pleistocene, at least, patterns of social organization may have been similar to those of modern human foragers. This is concordant with evidence from lower limb bone structure, which indicates a sexual division of labor in archaic *H. sapiens* similar to that of modern hunter-gatherers (Ruff 1987, 2000a).

More recent variations in body-mass sexual dimorphism, not shown in Figure 2, likely reflect more subtle differences in subsistence strategy, diet, and possibly sex-related buffering against the environment (Stini 1974; Frayer 1980, 1984; Meiklejohn et al. 1984; Jacobs 1985; Stinson 1985; Jantz & Jantz 1999). Secular trends in stature over the past few hundred years have been in similar directions for males and females of the same populations (e.g., Meredith 1976, Bogin & Keep 1999), although again with possible subtle differences in magnitude (Jantz & Jantz 1999).

EVOLUTIONARY TRENDS IN BODY SHAPE

There is abundant evidence that many early hominin taxa (australopithecines and *H. habilis sensu stricto*) had basic body proportions that were significantly different from those of modern humans. Upper limbs were large relative to lower limbs, and body breadth (and mass) was large relative to stature (McHenry 1978, Johanson et al. 1987, Leakey et al. 1989, Hartwig-Scherer & Martin 1991, Ruff 1991, Aiello 1992, McHenry & Berger 1998, Asfaw et al. 1999). These differences are probably best accounted for by retained arboreal capabilities combined with the allometric effects of small body size, which itself may be related to locomotor patterns (see above). By 1.5 million years ago body proportions, together with body size, in *H. ergaster/erectus* were well within the range of modern human variation (Ruff & Walker 1993). From this point on, within the *Homo* lineage, a fully terrestrial

[1]The Sima de los Huesos skeletal sample from Atapuerca, Spain, dated to about 200,000 years ago, preserves the remains of many individuals (Arsuaga et al. 1999). Most lower limb remains from the site have not yet been formally described, but a number of acetabular breadths are given in the above reference, some of which have sexually diagnostic regions of the pelvis preserved. The males average 60 mm and the females 52 mm, a 15% difference.

lifestyle can be inferred, with variations in body shape viewed as adaptations to environmental variables other than basic locomotor behavior.

One environmental variable that has long been postulated to influence modern human body shape is climate (see references in Ruff 1994). Relative limb length (Allen's Rule) and body breadth vary systematically with temperature in modern human populations, with those from colder environments having relatively shorter limbs (and shorter distal segments within limbs) and wider bodies than those from warmer environments (Roberts 1978, Trinkaus 1981, Ruff 1994). These clinal variations, and the observed cline in body mass discussed earlier, can all be viewed as part of the same adaptive strategy to reduce body surface area/body mass in colder climates and increase it in warmer climates (Schreider 1964; Ruff 1991, 1994). Of course, body proportions can be affected by other environmental variables as well. For example, relative limb length may increase with improved nutrition and health status (Tanner et al. 1982). However, this factor cannot explain the relatively longer limbs observed in modern tropical populations, most of whom are more nutritionally deprived than higher-latitude populations. Thus, genetic factors (climatic selection) are likely involved (Stinson 2000). Interestingly, there is evidence that body (bi-iliac) breadth is not as affected by nutritional or other developmental influences as limb length proportions, perhaps in part because of stabilizing selection owing to obstetric requirements (Ruff 1994). In terms of climatic adaptation, changes in absolute body breadth will always affect surface area–to–body mass ratios, whereas changes in stature will not (Ruff 1991). Thus, (skeletal) body breadth shows very strong latitudinal trends, whereas stature does not (Ruff 1994).

Where possible to evaluate, body proportions in earlier hominins have been found to follow the same geographic clines as modern humans. Thus, for example, Neandertals have relatively short distal limb segments (Trinkaus 1981) and broad bodies (Ruff 1994), whereas the opposite is true for KNM-WT 15000, a juvenile *H. ergaster/erectus* from East Africa (Ruff & Walker 1993). Furthermore, with the discovery of new fossil specimens over the past several years, it is now apparent that the Neandertal body type is actually part of a broader pattern shared with other higher-latitude archaic *Homo* specimens. These new specimens include the Yinnuishan female, dated to about 280,000 years ago (Rosenberg et al. 1999), and the Atapuerca "Pelvis 1" male, dated to at least 200,000 years ago (Arsuaga et al. 1999). Both specimens preserve enough of the pelvis to allow measurement or accurate estimation of bi-iliac breadth. Yinnuishan also preserves an ulna from which forearm length can be assessed. The Atapuerca Sima de los Huesos remains are all unassociated, but an approximate ulnar length can be calculated from a complete humerus recovered at the same site ("Humerus II") (Carretero et al. 1997). The pairing of the pelvis and humerus is reasonable, because both were at the upper end of the size range represented at the site and so very likely represented large males. Ulna length was calculated from humeral length using a regression formula based on a combined sample of modern East Africans and Pecos Pueblo

Amerindians (Ruff 1995): ulna = 0.873· humerus − 12.4 (r = 0.910, standard error of estimate = 8.4 mm). This is a conservative estimate in terms of testing whether the Atapuerca specimen had relatively short limbs because East Africans have typically tropical proportions (long forearms); using only the Amerindians as a reference sample would produce an ulna length estimate several millimeters shorter.

Figure 3 plots ulna length against bi-iliac breadth for the Yinnuishan and Atapuerca specimens, together with similar data for several other Pleistocene specimens and some modern comparative samples. The modern samples include East African (Ruff 1995) and combined Alaskan Inupiat (Eskimo) and Aleut skeletal samples. Because modern males have relatively longer forearms than females (Trinkaus 1981), sexes are distinguished in the plot.

As expected, the modern tropical sample has much longer forearms relative to body breadth than the high-latitude sample: There is no overlap between same-sex individuals from the two groups. Interestingly, a line indicating equivalent

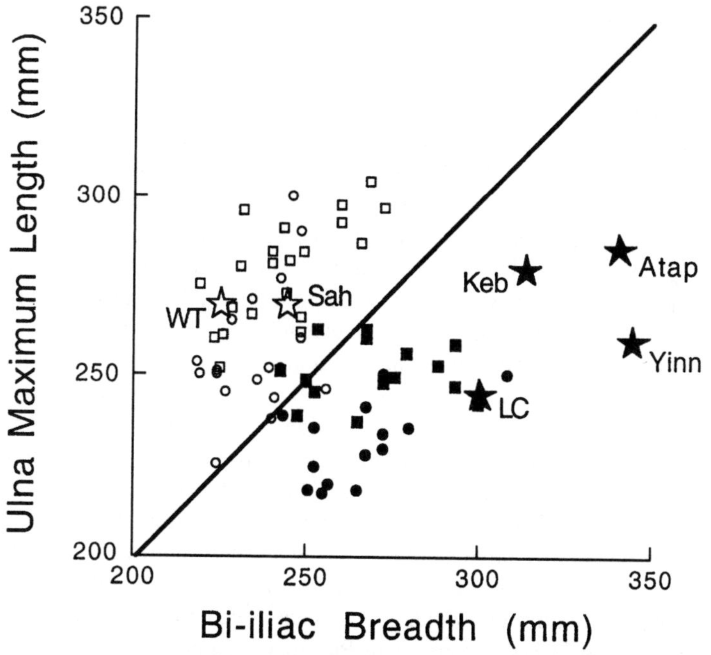

Figure 3 Ulna maximum length against bi-iliac (maximum pelvic) breadth in Pleistocene and modern *Homo*. Open symbols, modern East Africans; filled symbols, modern Eskimos/Aleuts; squares, males; circles, females. Open stars, KNM-WT 15000 and Sahaba 16; filled stars, La Chapelle 1, Kebara 2, Atapuerca "Pelvis 1", Yinnuishan (see text); diagonal line, equivalent ulnar and bi-iliac measures.

ulnar length and bi-iliac breadth, included in the plot, almost perfectly divides the two groups. Multiple analyses of variance (ANOVA) indicate that both sex and latitude have highly significant effects on proportions in the modern samples ($p < 0.0001$). The Yinnuishan and Atapuerca specimens are "hyper-arctic," with very wide bodies and short forearms. Two Neandertals with pelvises sufficiently preserved to measure or estimate bi-iliac breadth [Kebara 2 (Rak & Arensburg 1987) and La Chapelle 1 (Boule 1911, Ruff et al. 1993)] also fall in the high latitude range. (Ulna length for La Chapelle was estimated from its radius length using a formula derived from modern East Africans and Pecos Amerindians: $\text{ulna} = 1.008 \cdot \text{radius} + 16.2$, $r = 0.988$, standard error of estimate = 3.2 mm.) The Atapuerca and La Chapelle specimens are quite similar in proportions, with Yinniushan falling below these two. The extreme proportions of Yinnuishan may be attributable in part to sexual dimorphism: The difference between this female specimen and the Atapuerca and La Chapelle 1 males is about equal to the average difference between modern females and males from the same latitudinal zone (Figure 3). Kebara 2 (also a male) is somewhat less hyper-arctic, reflecting the longer forearms (and possibly somewhat more linear body form) characteristic of Near Eastern as opposed to European Neandertals (Trinkaus 1981, Ruff 1994, Ruff et al. 2002).

Two Pleistocene specimens from tropical regions are also included in Figure 3: KNM-WT 15000, a juvenile male *H. ergaster/erectus* (Walker & Leakey 1993), and Jebel Sahaba 26, a female from a terminal Pleistocene site in Nubia (Wendorf 1968). The juvenile status of KNM-WT 15000 should have relatively little effect on comparisons (Ruff & Walker 1993). Both specimens fall close to the average proportions for sex-matched modern individuals from East Africa.

Thus, the available evidence supports latitudinal clines in body shape in earlier *Homo* similar to those found in modern humans. This in turn suggests a similar physiological mechanism as an explanation, i.e., climatic adaptation. As noted earlier, there are very few available Middle and Early Late Pleistocene specimens from lower latitudes, and none with enough postcranial elements to directly assess body proportions. These would provide very useful comparisons with archaic *Homo* specimens from higher latitudes because the latter show the most extreme examples of apparent adaptation to colder climates. Without this direct contrast it can be argued, for example, that the broad pelvises of higher-latitude archaic *Homo* have more phylogenetic rather than physiological implications (Arsuaga et al. 1999). However, other less direct evidence also supports a latitudinal cline in body shape within the Middle Pleistocene. The complete tibia from Broken Hill, Zambia (E691), is very long, in the Pleistocene equaled in length only by specimens with high crural indices (long tibias relative to femora) (Kennedy 1984a). On the basis of shaft external breadth or cross-sectional properties to length proportions, the Broken Hill tibia and other lower-latitude tibias from the Middle Pleistocene are clearly distinct from the broadly contemporaneous higher-latitude Boxgrove 1 tibia (Stringer et al. 1998, Trinkaus et al. 1999). The most parsimonious explanation is that the Boxgrove specimen had a relatively wide body and short limbs (like

Neandertals, Atapuerca, and Yinnuishan), whereas the lower latitude specimens had relatively narrow bodies and longer limbs (like KNM-WT 15000).

The transition in Europe from Neandertals to "early anatomically modern" (Late Paleolithic) humans 40,000 to 25,000 years ago and subsequent changes in morphology within the latter group, are especially interesting in that they may provide evidence of adaptation following migration to a new climatic zone if these populations were derived from farther south, as suggested by the preponderance of current evidence (Klein 1999). The lack of change between European Early and Late Paleolithic samples in distal-to-proximal limb length proportions (crural and brachial indices) was initially puzzling in this regard because a reduction would have been predicted if climatic adaptation were taking place (Trinkaus 1981). However, more recent work has shown that relative to measures of trunk (vertebral column) height, limb length did decrease significantly within the Upper Paleolithic in Europe, beginning at proportions similar to those of sub-Saharan Africans and ending at proportions similar to those of modern Europeans (Holliday 1997a). Comparisons of long bone lengths to bi-iliac breadths in available European Upper Paleolithic specimens ($n = 15$–19, about a third from the Early Upper Paleolithic) also indicate significant reductions in limb length to body breadth between the Early and Late Upper Paleolithic (unpublished results based on data given in Ruff et al. 1997, supplementary information). Thus, body shape did change significantly in Upper Paleolithic Europeans after exposure to colder climatic conditions, although the change was mosaic in nature, beginning with a general reduction in limb lengths followed by a reduction in distal-to-proximal limb element proportions. The possible significance of this difference in timing has been further explored elsewhere (Ruff et al. 2002).

RELATIVE BODY MASS IN LIVING POPULATIONS

What can the patterns of variation in body size and shape observed in pre-Holocene humans tell us about more recent human variation? If the body size of terminal Late Pleistocene humans does indeed represent a genetic target (or limit) for body size in living humans, then data on such populations, prior to the major changes in diet, social organization, etc., characteristic of the Holocene, could serve as effective baselines for evaluating current body size. As noted earlier, there is evidence that many living populations from developing countries may not be as large as their Pleistocene ancestors. Of course, this does not address the issue of whether maximum potential body size is desirable or not (for a review see Stinson 1992).

Here I concentrate on another issue: how differences in relative body mass, i.e., body shape, between modern populations should be used in health assessment. The above review indicates that body shape varies systematically along latitudinal clines in both modern humans and Pleistocene *Homo*. Nutrition and health status do not seem to explain these trends, which are, however, consistent with climatic adaptation. The temporal depth of such clines and their persistence despite other confounding factors argues that they represent long-standing mechanisms of adaptation within our lineage and are probably at least in part genetically based.[2]

The body mass index (BMI), weight/height^2 (also known as Quetelet's Index), is widely employed in assessing relative under- or over weight status of living individuals and populations (WHO 1995). Standard percentiles for BMI at various ages during childhood and in adults have been developed from U.S. population surveys (WHO 1995). However, questions have been raised concerning the applicability of such standards to other populations, owing to the effects of varying body proportions and lean body mass fraction on the index (Garn et al. 1986) (some of these limitations were also noted in the WHO recommended guidelines cited above). The effects of differences in relative lower limb length (or relative sitting height) on body mass indices have been known for many years (Bardeen 1923).

Arctic populations represent an extreme in modern human body shape variation, with relatively short limbs and wide bodies (see Figure 3). This contributes to their high weight-for-height indices, despite the fact that they do not have increased skinfold thicknesses compared with U.S. standards (Schaefer 1977, Johnston et al. 1982, Jamison 1986). This pattern is apparent among Eskimo (Inupiat and Inuit) children and adults and has led to recommendations that different standards be developed for identifying obesity in these populations (Schaefer 1977, Jamison 1986). One approach would be to develop population-specific weight-for-height standards for such groups. The problems with this approach are that (*a*) it would necessarily rely on a relatively small data set and would not take advantage of the very extensive samples available in large population surveys that allow more secure statistical inferences (e.g., Hamill et al. 1979), and (*b*) results could be confounded by very recent and marked secular changes occurring in some of these groups in diet, lifestyle, and anthropometrics (Schaefer 1970, Jamison et al. 1978).

An alternate approach would be to use a different index of relative weight that is less affected by, or incorporates, variations in body build including relative limb length and relative (skeletal) body breadth. Sitting height is a commonly taken anthropometric measurement that reflects trunk height, i.e., a body length measure that does not include the limbs. Sitting heights of Eskimo children were found to be similar to those of age-matched U.S. whites and blacks, despite large differences in stature (Johnston et al. 1982). Bi-iliac breadth is the best available trunk breadth measurement (see Ruff 1991). As noted above, it also shows strong systematic differences between human populations. The product of trunk height and bi-iliac breadth provides an index of "trunk frame size" (Ruff & Jamison 2002). The ratio of body mass to trunk frame size can then be considered a "trunk frame index" (TFI). Both sitting height and bi-iliac breadth are expressed in cm and body mass in kg; the resulting ratio is multiplied by 1000.

---

[2]Note that this does not imply any close genetic ties between earlier *Homo* species and modern humans from the same geographic regions, but rather the operation of the same adaptational principles to both earlier and more recent populations.

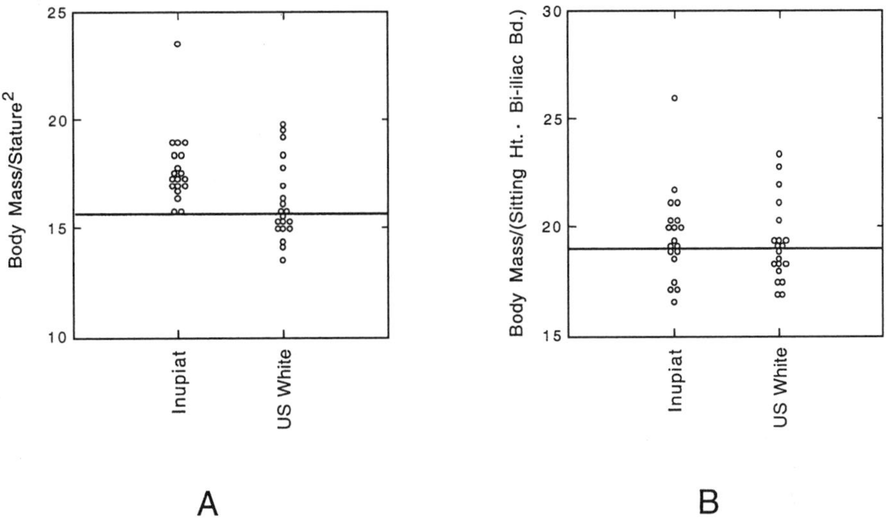

Figure 4 Two body mass indices applied to 9-year-old Inupiat and U.S. white children (see text for derivation of samples). Horizontal lines indicate U.S. white medians. (A) Traditional body mass index (BMI); (B) trunk frame index (TFI).

Figure 4 compares use of the TFI and BMI indices as applied to Inupiat and U.S. white children. The Inupiat data are from northern Alaska and were collected around 1970 by Jamison and colleagues (Jamison 1978, 1986, 1990). Individual raw anthropometric data were obtained courtesy of P.L. Jamison (personal communication). The U.S. white data are from the Denver Growth Study, collected over several decades (McCammon 1970), although all of the measurements included here were taken in the 1950s. Individual data for 20 subjects (10 males and 10 females), followed longitudinally from near birth to late adolescence, were obtained from the study database (R.M. Siervogel, personal communication). An age of 9 years was chosen for comparisons, because it avoids complications owing to differences in timing of the adolescent growth spurt and is an age with little sexual dimorphism in the BMI, allowing pooling of males and females (WHO 1995). (The same similarity between the sexes at this age, within group, was confirmed here for both BMI and TFI.) Anthropometric data were available at this age for 19 Inupiat children (13 females and 6 males, "nonhybrids" only).

BMI is significantly higher in Inupiats than in U.S. whites ($p < 0.01$, t test). In fact, all of the Inupiat children fall above the median BMI for the Denver sample (Figure 4*A*). In contrast, there is no significant difference between Inupiat and U.S. white children for TFI ($p > 0.50$), and the distribution of individual data points, with the exception of one high Inupiat outlier, is very similar in the two groups (Figure 4*B*).

These Inupiat children, like other Eskimo children, do not have large skinfolds. Mean skinfold breadths for 9-year-old boys and girls, respectively, are 8.1 mm and 10.0 mm for triceps and 5.5 mm and 7.1 mm for subscapular [unlike BMI, there is sexual dimorphism for skinfolds at this age (WHO 1995)]. The triceps skinfolds are slightly below, and the subscapular skinfolds slightly above the 50th percentiles for 9-year-olds based on U.S. standards (WHO 1995) or the Denver Growth Study sample (Hansman 1970).

Thus, for the Inupiat sample as a whole, the TFI appears to more faithfully represent relative fatness than does the BMI. The same may be true on an individual basis. The one high outlier for both BMI and TFI is also a high outlier for skinfold values (above the 90th percentile for her age according to the same reference samples), i.e., both indices successfully identified her as overweight relative to direct subcutaneous fat measurements. The next highest BMIs among the Inupiats were from two boys, both above the 85th percentile for their age, the recommended cutoff for "at risk for overweight" (WHO 1995). Interestingly, despite identical BMIs in these boys (18.9), skinfold breadths were high in one (13.0 mm and 9.0 mm for triceps and subscapular, respectively) but not in the other (6.0 mm and 5.0 mm). The individual with the large skinfolds had a relatively high TFI of 21.7—the second highest index in the group—whereas the individual with the moderate skinfolds had a TFI of 20.1, closer to the median of the group (see Figure 4). The identical BMIs but differing TFIs can be attributed to body build differences: The individual with the smaller skinfolds was relatively larger in both bi-iliac breadth and sitting height (>1 sample standard deviation above the other boy for bi-iliac breadth/stature and sitting height/stature). Thus, the BMI tended to overestimate his fatness level, whereas the TFI, which incorporates trunk shape, did not. A noncorrespondence between secular changes in skinfold measurements and BMI has also been noted for Eskimo (Inuit) adults (Leonard 2000), which could be due to similar body shape differences (see Schaefer 1970).

Although this discussion has focused on identification of overweight status in Inupiats, an equally valid question could be posed regarding underweight. As Jamison (1990) has noted, we cannot tell from current weight-for-height data based on U.S. standards where a borderline malnourished Inupiat child would fall. The same reasoning applies, of course, to populations in other areas of the world where malnutrition is severe and that also exhibit apparently intrinsic (genetic) differences in body proportions from U.S. standards, e.g., relatively longer limbs and narrower bodies in lower-latitude populations. Incorporation of such proportional differences into body mass indices should provide more sensitive and less population-biased measures of under- and overweight. The apparent developmental lability of some body proportions, e.g., lower limb length relative to stature (Tanner et al. 1982), does not negate this argument. It is important to recognize such secular trends in skeletal proportions if soft tissue differences are to be distinguished from general body shape changes. For example, Takahashi (1986) found that among Japanese older adolescent and younger adult women, stature had increased more than body mass in the 1970s and early 1980s, which the author attributed primarily to dietary and lifestyle changes resulting from a desire "to be slimmer" and "to keep from getting fat." However, no clear secular trend in skinfold thicknesses could be discerned. The implication is that (skeletal) body breadth did not increase as fast as stature during this time period. In fact, just such a secular trend was found among Japanese-Americans living in Hawaii (Froehlich 1970) as well as in other populations with secular increases in stature (see Ruff 1994 for a discussion). Thus, the inclusion of a body breadth measurement in the Japanese analysis could have provided better discrimination of actual soft tissue changes.

CONCLUSIONS

Both body size and body shape vary systematically in modern humans, and did so in earlier humans as well. Subsequent to the development of full bipedality and prior to the adoption of food production, the most important environmental influences on size and shape were likely climate and technological sophistication. Nutritional and overall health levels may account for an increasing proportion of variation during the Holocene, including very recent secular trends. Differences in body form among modern humans are thus likely to result from an interaction between long-term genetic factors, including climatic adaptation, as well as developmental environment, including diet and disease. In assessing anthropometric variation in living populations, it is important to consider the influence of both kinds of factors in order to distinguish one from the other. Methodologies that incorporate critical dimensions of body form can shed new light on human adaptation in both paleontological and neontological contexts.

ACKNOWLEDGMENTS

I thank Paul Jamison and Roger Siervogel for making available individual data for the Inupiat and Denver Growth Study samples, respectively. Erik Trinkaus and Trent Holliday collaborated heavily in the original compilation of Pleistocene *Homo* body mass data. Thanks also to the various museums and curators who made available specimens and data records in their care, and to Ben Auerbach for his Aleut skeletal data. Original data collection was supported in part by the National Science Foundation and Wenner-Gren Foundation.

The *Annual Review of Anthropology* is online at http://anthro.annualreviews.org

LITERATURE CITED

Aiello LC. 1992. Allometry and the analysis of size and shape in human evolution. *J. Hum. Evol.* 22:127–48

Aiello LC, Wheeler P. 1995. The expensive-tissue hypothesis. *Curr. Anthropol.* 36:199–211

Allbrook D. 1961. The estimation of stature in British and East African males. *J. Forensic Med.* 8:15–28

Arsuaga J-L, Lorenzo C, Carretero J-M, Gracia A, Martinez I, et al. 1999. A complete human pelvis from the Middle Pleistocene of Spain. *Nature* 399:255–58

Asfaw B, White T, Lovejoy O, Latimer B, Simpson S, Suwa G. 1999. *Australopithecus garhi*. A new species of early hominid from Ethiopia. *Science* 284:629–35

Bardeen CR. 1923. General relations of sitting height to stature and of sitting height and stature to weight. *Am. J. Phys. Anthropol.* 6: 355–88

Bogin B, Keep R. 1999. Eight thousand years of economic and political history in Latin America revealed by anthropometry. *Ann. Hum. Biol.* 26:333–51

Boule M. 1911. L'homme fossile de La Chapelle-aux-Saints. *Ann. Paléontol.* 6:111–72

Brown P. 1992. Post-Pleistocene change in Australian Aboriginal tooth size: dental reduction or relative expansion? In *Craniofacial Variation in Pacific Populations*, ed. T Brown, S Molnar, pp. 33–51. Adelaide, Aust.: Anthropol. Genet. Lab., Univ. Adelaide

Calder WA, III. 1984. *Size, Function, and Life History*. Cambridge: Cambridge Univ. Press

Carretero JM, Arsuaga JL, Lorenzo C. 1997. Clavicles, scapulae and humeri from the Sima de los Huesos site (Sierra de Atapuerca, Spain). *J. Hum. Evol.* 33:357–408

Cohen MN, Armelagos GJ. 1984a. Paleopathology at the origins of agriculture: editors' summation. See Cohen & Armelagos 1984b, pp. 585–601

Cohen MN, Armelagos GJ, eds. 1984b. *Paleopathology at the Origins of Agriculture*. Orlando, FL: Academic

Conroy GC. 1987. Problems of body-weight estimation in fossil primates. *Int. J. Primatol.* 8:115–37

Duarte C, Maurício J, Pettitt PB, Souto P, Trinkaus E, et al. 1999. The early Upper Paleolithic modern skeleton from the Abrigo do Lagar Velho (Portugal) and modern human emergence in Iberia. *Proc. Natl. Acad. Sci. USA* 96:7604–9

Eveleth PB. 1994. Secular trends in growth: an indication of changing health status. *Humanbiol. Budapest* 25:193–204

Foley R. 1987. *Another Unique Species: Patterns in Human Evolutionary Ecology*. Harlow, UK: Longman Sci. Tech.

Formicola V, Giannecchini M. 1998. Evolutionary trends of stature in Upper Paleolithic and Mesolithic Europe. *J. Hum. Evol.* 36:319–33

Frayer DW. 1980. Sexual dimorphism and cultural evolution in the late Pleistocene and Holocene of Europe. *J. Hum. Evol.* 9:399–415

Frayer DW. 1984. Biological and cultural change in the European Late Pleistocene and Early Holocene. In *The Origins of Modern Humans: A World Survey of the Fossil Evidence*, ed. FH Smith, F Spencer, pp. 211–50. New York: Wiley-Liss

Froehlich JW. 1970. Migration and the plasticity of physique in the Japanese-Americans of Hawaii. *Am. J. Phys. Anthropol.* 32:429–42

Garn SM, Leonard WR, Hawthorne VM. 1986. Three limitations of the body mass index. *Am. J. Clin. Nutr.* 44:996–97

Gingerich PD, Smith BH, Rosenberg K. 1982. Allometric scaling in the dentition of primates and prediction of body weight from tooth size in fossils. *Am. J. Phys. Anthropol.* 58:81–100

Grine FE, Jungers WL, Tobias PV, Pearson OM. 1995. Fossil *Homo* femur from Berg Aukas, northern Namibia. *Am. J. Phys. Anthropol.* 97:151–85

Hamill PV, Drizd TA, Johnson CL, Reed RB, Roche AF, Moore WM. 1979. Physical growth: National Center for Health Statistics percentiles. *Am. J. Clin. Nutr.* 32:607–29

Hansman C. 1970. Anthropometry and related data, anthropometry skinfold thickness measurements. See McCammon 1970, pp. 103–54

Hartwig-Scherer S. 1994. Body weight prediction in fossil *Homo*. *Cour. Forsch.-Inst. Senckenberg* 171:267–79

Hartwig-Scherer S, Martin RD. 1991. Was

"Lucy" more human than her "child"? Observations on early hominid postcranial skeletons. *J. Hum. Evol.* 21:439–50

Henneberg M. 1988. Decrease of human skull size in the Holocene. *Hum. Biol.* 60:395–405

Henneberg M, Steyn M. 1993. Trends in cranial capacity and cranial index in Subsaharan Africa during the Holocene. *Am. J. Hum. Biol.* 5:473–79

Holliday TW. 1997a. Body proportions in Late Pleistocene Europe and modern human origins. *J. Hum. Evol.* 32:423–47

Holliday TW. 1997b. Postcranial evidence of cold adaptation in European Neandertals. *Am. J. Phys. Anthropol.* 104:245–58

Holliday TW, Ruff CB. 1997. Ecogeographic patterning and stature prediction in fossil hominids: comment on Feldesman and Fountain. *Am. J. Phys. Anthropol.* 103:137–40

Jacobs KH. 1985. Evolution in the postcranial skeleton of Late Glacial and early Postglacial European hominids. *Z. Morphol. Anthropol.* 75:307–26

Jamison PL. 1978. Anthropometric variation. See Jamison et al. 1978, pp. 40–78

Jamison PL. 1986. Growth and development of children as an indicator of the health of arctic populations. *Collegium Anthropol.* 10:179–209

Jamison PL. 1990. Secular trends and the pattern of growth in arctic populations. *Soc. Sci. Med.* 30:751–59

Jamison PL, Zegura SL, Milan FA. 1978. *Eskimos of Northwestern Alaska: A Biological Perspective.* Stroudsberg, PA: Dowden, Hutchinson & Ross

Jantz LM, Jantz RL. 1999. Secular change in long bone length and proportion in the United States, 1800–1970. *Am. J. Phys. Anthropol.* 110:57–67

Johanson DC, Masao FT, Eck GG, White TD, Walter RC, et al. 1987. New partial skeleton of *Homo habilis* from Olduvai Gorge, Tanzania. *Nature* 327:205–9

Johnston FE, Laughlin WS, Harper AB, Ensroth AE. 1982. Physical growth of St. Lawrence Island Eskimos: body size, proportion, and composition. *Am. J. Phys. Anthropol.* 58:397–401

Jungers WL. 1988. Lucy's length: stature reconstruction in *Australopithecus afarensis* (A.L. 288-1) with implications for other small-bodied hominids. *Am. J. Phys. Anthropol.* 76:227–31

Katzmarzyk PT, Leonard WR. 1998. Climatic influences on human body size and proportions: ecological adaptations and secular trends. *Am. J. Phys. Anthropol.* 106:483–503

Kennedy KAR. 1984a. The emergence of *Homo sapiens*: the post-cranial evidence. *Man* 19:94–110

Kennedy KAR. 1984b. Growth, nutrition, and pathology in changing paleodemographic settings in South Asia. See Cohen & Armelagos 1984b, pp. 169–92

Kimura K. 1984. Studies on growth and development in Japan. *Yearb. Phys. Anthropol.* 27:179–214

Klein, RG. 1999. *The Human Career.* Chicago: Univ. Chicago Press

Leakey HG, Feibel CS, McDougall I, Walker A. 1995. New four-million-year-old hominid species from Kanapoi and Allia Bay, Kenya. *Nature* 376:565–71

Leakey RE, Walker A, Ward CV, Grausz HM. 1989. A partial skeleton of a gracile hominid from the Upper Burgi Member of the Koobi Fora Formation, East Lake Turkana, Kenya. In *Hominidae: Proceedings of the 2nd International Congress of Human Paleontology*, ed. G Giacobini, pp. 167–73. Milan: Jaca Book

Leonard WR. 2000. Human nutritional evolution. See Stinson et al. 2000, pp. 295–43

Leonard WR, Robertson ML. 1997. Comparative primate energetics and hominid evolution. *Am. J. Phys. Anthropol.* 102:265–81

Lieberman DE, Devlin MJ, Pearson OM. 2001. Articular area responses to mechanical loading: effects of exercise, age, and skeletal location. *Am. J. Phys. Anthropol.* 116:266–77

Malina RM, Selby HA, Buschang PH, Aronson WL, Wilkinson RG. 1983. Adult stature and age at menarche in Zapotec-speaking communities in the Valley of Oaxaca, Mexico, in a secular perspective. *Am. J. Phys. Anthropol.* 437–49

Mathers K, Henneberg M. 1995. Were we ever that big? Gradual increase in hominid body size over time. *Homo* 46:141–73

Mayr E. 1956. Geographical character gradients and climatic adaptation. *Evolution* 10: 105–8

McCammon RW. 1970. *Human Growth and Development*. Springfield, IL: Thomas

McHenry HM. 1976. Early hominid body weight and encephalization. *Am. J. Phys. Anthropol.* 45:77–84

McHenry HM. 1978. Fore- and hindlimb proportions in Plio-Pleistocene hominids. *Am. J. Phys. Anthropol.* 49:15–22

McHenry HM. 1984. Relative cheek-tooth size in *Australopithecus*. *Am. J. Phys. Anthropol.* 64:297–306

McHenry HM. 1988. New estimates of body weight in early hominids and their significance to encephalization and megadontia in "robust" australopithecines. In *Evolutionary History of the "Robust" Australopithecines*, ed. FE Grine, pp. 133–48. New York: Aldine de Gruyter

McHenry HM. 1991. Sexual dimorphism in *Australopithecus afarensis*. *J. Hum. Evol.* 20: 21–32

McHenry HM. 1992. Body size and proportions in early hominids. *Am. J. Phys. Anthropol.* 87:407–31

McHenry HM. 1994a. Behavioral ecological implications of early hominid body size. *J. Hum. Evol.* 27:77–87

McHenry HM. 1994b. Early hominid postcrania. Phylogeny and function. In *Integrative Paths to the Past* (*Advances in Human Evolution Series* Vol. 2), ed. RS Corruccini, RL Ciochon, pp. 168–251. Englewood Cliffs, NJ: Prentice Hall

McHenry HM, Berger LR. 1998. Body proportions in *Australopithecus afarensis* and *africanus* and the origin of the genus *Homo*. *J. Hum. Evol.* 35:1–22

McHenry HM, Coffing K. 2000. *Australopithecus* to *Homo*: transformations in body and mind. *Annu. Rev. Anthropol.* 29:125–46

Meiklejohn C, Schentag C, Venema A, Key P. 1984. Socioeconomic change and patterns of pathology and variation in the Mesolithic and Neolithic of Western Europe: some suggestions. See Cohen & Armelagos 1984b, pp. 75–100

Meredith HV. 1976. Findings from Asia, Australia, Europe, and North America on secular change in mean height of children, youths, and young adults. *Am. J. Phys. Anthropol.* 44:315–26

Oleksiak DA. 1986. The estimation of body weight for Neanderthals and early anatomically modern humans. *Am. J. Phys. Anthropol.* (Abstr.) 69:248

Pilbeam D, Gould SJ. 1974. Size and scaling in human evolution. *Science* 186:892–901

Plavcan JM. 2001. Sexual dimorphism in primate evolution. *Yearb. Phys. Anthropol.* 44: 25–53

Plavcan JM, Van Schaik CP. 1997. Interpreting hominid behavior on the basis of sexual dimorphism. *J. Hum. Evol.* 32:345–74

Porter AMW. 1995. The body weight of AL 288-1 ("Lucy"): a new approach using estimates of skeletal length and the body mass index. *Int. J. Osteoarchaeol.* 5:203–12

Pretty GL, Henneberg M, Lambert KM, Prokopec M. 1998. Trends in stature in the South Australian Aboriginal Murraylands. *Am. J. Phys. Anthropol.* 106:505–14

Rak Y, Arensburg B. 1987. Kebara 2 neanderthal pelvis: first look at a complete inlet. *Am. J. Phys. Anthropol.* 73:227–31

Rightmire GP. 1986. Body size and encephalization in *Homo erectus*. *Anthropos* 23:139–49

Roberts DF. 1978. *Climate and Human Variability*. Menlo Park, CA: Benjamin-Cummings. 2nd ed.

Rosenberg KR, Lu Z, Ruff CB. 1999. Body size, body proportions and encephalization in the Jinniushan specimen. *Am. J. Phys. Anthropol. Suppl.* (Abstr.) 28:235

Ruff CB. 1987. Sexual dimorphism in human lower limb bone structure: relationship to subsistence strategy and sexual division of labor. *J. Hum. Evol.* 16:391–416

Ruff CB. 1991. Climate, body size and body shape in hominid evolution. *J. Hum. Evol.* 21: 81–105

Ruff CB. 1994. Morphological adaptation to climate in modern and fossil hominids. *Yearb. Phys. Anthropol.* 37:65–107

Ruff CB. 1995. Biomechanics of the hip and birth in early *Homo*. *Am. J. Phys. Anthropol.* 98:527–74

Ruff CB. 1998. Evolution of the hominid hip. In *Primate Locomotion: Recent Advances*, ed. E Strasser, A Rosenberger, H McHenry, J Fleagle, pp. 449–69. Davis, CA: Plenum

Ruff CB. 2000a. Biomechanical analyses of archaeological human skeletal samples. In *Biological Anthropology of the Human Skeleton*, ed. MA Katzenburg, SR Saunders, pp. 71–102. New York: Liss

Ruff CB. 2000b. Prediction of body mass from skeletal frame size in elite athletes. *Am. J. Phys. Anthropol.* 113:507–17

Ruff CB. 2001. Body, evolution of. In *International Encyclopedia of the Social and Behavioral Sciences*, ed. N Smelser, P Baltes, pp. 1274–77. Oxford: Elsevier

Ruff CB, Jamison PJ. 2002. Weight for trunk frame size: an alternative index of fatness in populations of varying body proportions. *Am. J. Phys. Anthropol. Suppl.* 34:134 (Abstr.)

Ruff CB, Scott WW, Liu AY-C. 1991. Articular and diaphyseal remodeling of the proximal femur with changes in body mass in adults. *Am. J. Phys. Anthropol.* 86:397–413

Ruff CB, Trinkaus E, Holliday TW. 1997. Body mass and encephalization in Pleistocene *Homo*. *Nature* 387:173–76

Ruff CB, Trinkaus E, Holliday TW. 2002. Body proportions and size of Lagar Velho 1. In *Portrait of the Artist as a Child. The Gravettian Human Skeleton from the Abrigo do Lagar Velho and its Archaeological Context*, ed. J Zilhão, E Trinkaus. Lisbon: Trabalhos de Arqueologia, Vol. 22. Instituto Portugeês de Arqueologia. In press

Ruff CB, Trinkaus E, Walker A, Larsen CS. 1993. Postcranial robusticity in *Homo*. I. Temporal trends and mechanical interpretation. *Am. J. Phys. Anthropol.* 91:21–53

Ruff CB, Walker A. 1993. Body size and body shape. See Walker & Leakey 1993, pp. 234–65

Ruff CB, Walker A, Trinkaus E. 1994. Postcranial robusticity in *Homo*. III. Ontogeny. *Am. J. Phys. Anthropol.* 93:35–54

Schaefer O. 1970. Pre- and post-natal growth acceleration and increased sugar consumption in Canadian Eskimos. *Can. Med. Assoc. J.* 103:1059–68

Schaefer O. 1977. Are Eskimos more or less obese than other Canadians? A comparison of skinfold thickness and ponderal index in Canadian Eskimos. *Am. J. Clin. Nutr.* 30: 1623–28

Schmidt-Nielson K. 1984. *Scaling: Why is Animal Size So Important?* Cambridge: Cambridge Univ. Press

Schreider E. 1964. Ecological rules, body-heat regulation, and human evolution. *Evolution* 18:1–9

Smith RJ. 1996. Biology and body size in human evolution. Statistical inference misapplied. *Curr. Anthropol.* 37:451–81

Stini WA. 1974. Adaptive strategies of human populations under nutritional stress. In *Biosocial Interrelations in Population Adaptation*, ed. FE Johnston, ES Watts, pp. 19–40. The Hague: Moutan

Stinson S. 1985. Sex differences in environmental sensitivity during growth and development. *Yearb. Phys. Anthropol.* 28:123–47

Stinson S. 1992. Nutritional adaptation. *Annu. Rev. Anthropol.* 21:143–70

Stinson S. 2000. Growth variation: biological and cultural factors. See Stinson et al. 2000, pp. 245–463

Stinson S, Bogin B, Huss-Ashmore R, O'Rourke D, eds. 2000. *Human Biology: an Evolutionary and Biological Approach*. New York: Wiley-Liss

Stringer CB, Trinkaus E, Roberts MB, Parfitt SA, Macphail RI. 1998. The Middle Pleistocene human tibia from Boxgrove. *J. Hum. Evol.* 34:509–47

Susman RL, de Ruiter D, Brain CK. 2001.

Recently identified postcranial remains of *Paranthropus* and early *Homo* from Swartkrans Cave, South Africa. *J. Hum. Evol.* 41: 607–29

Takahashi E. 1986. Secular trend of female body shape in Japan. *Hum. Biol.* 58:293–301

Tanner JM, Hayashi T, Preece MA, Cameron N. 1982. Increase in length of leg relative to trunk in Japanese children and adults from 1957 to 1977: comparison with British and with Japanese Americans. *Ann. Hum. Biol.* 9: 411–23

Teaford MF, Ungar PS, Grine FE. 2002. Paleontological evidence for the diets of African Plio-Pleistocene hominins with special reference to early *Homo*. In *Human Diet: Its Origin and Evolution*, ed. PS Ungar, MF Teaford, pp. 143–66. Westport, CN: Bergin & Garvey

Thieme H. 1997. Lower Palaeolithic hunting spears from Germany. *Nature* 385:807–10

Tobias PV. 1985. The negative secular trend. *J. Hum. Evol.* 14:347–56

Trinkaus E. 1981. Neanderthal limb proportions and cold adaptation. In *Aspects of Human Evolution*, ed. CB Stringer, pp. 187–224. London: Taylor & Francis

Trinkaus E, Churchill SE, Ruff CB. 1994. Postcranial robusticity in *Homo*. II. Humeral bilateral asymmetry and bone plasticity. *Am. J. Phys. Anthropol.* 93:1–34

Trinkaus E, Ruff CB. 1999a. Diaphyseal cross-sectional geometry of Near Eastern Middle Paleolithic humans: the femur. *J. Archaeol. Sci.* 26:409–24

Trinkaus E, Ruff CB. 1999b. Diaphyseal cross-sectional geometry of Near Eastern Middle Paleolithic humans: the tibia. *J. Archaeol. Sci.* 26:1289–300

Trinkaus E, Stringer CB, Ruff CB, Hennessy RJ, Roberts MB, Parfitt SA. 1999. Diaphyseal cross-sectional geometry of the Boxgrove 1 Middle Pleistocene human tibia. *J. Hum. Evol.* 37:1–25

Van Wieringen JC. 1986. Secular growth changes. In *Human Growth: A Comprehensive Treatise*, Vol. 3. *Methodology, Genetic, and Nutritional Effects on Growth*, ed. F Falkner, JM Tanner, pp. 307–31. New York: Plenum. 2nd ed.

Walker A, Leakey R, eds. 1993. *The Nariokotome Homo Erectus Skeleton*. Cambridge, MA: Harvard Univ. Press

Wendorf F. 1968. Site 117: a Nubian Final Paleolithic graveyard near Jebel Sahaba, Sudan. In *The Prehistory of Nubia*, ed. F Wendorf, pp. 2:954–95. Dallas: Southern Methodist Univ. Press

Wheeler PE. 1992. The thermoregulatory advantages of large body size for hominids foraging in savannah environments. *J. Hum. Evol.* 23:351–62

White TD, Suwa G, Asfaw B. 1994. *Australopithecus ramidus*, a new species of early hominid from Aramis, Ethiopia. *Nature* 371: 306–12

WHO. 1995. *Physical Status: The Use and Interpretation of Anthropometry*. Geneva: WHO

Wood BA, Collard M. 1999. The human genus. *Science* 284:65–71

Annu. Rev. Anthropol. 2002. 31:233–55
doi: 10.1146/annurev.anthro.31.040402.085332

First published online as a Review in Advance on May 21, 2002

WEBER AND ANTHROPOLOGY

Charles F. Keyes
Department of Anthropology, University of Washington, Seattle, Washington 98105; email: keyes@u.washington.edu

Key Words interpretive anthropology, developmental history, religion, rationalization, charisma

■ **Abstract** This article is about the influence of the work of the German sociologist Max Weber (1864–1920) on English-speaking anthropologists. Although Weber does not figure prominently in the history of anthropology, his work has, nonetheless, had a profound influence on anthropological methodology and theoretical thinking on the relationship between religion and political economy. The "interpretive anthropology" first developed by Geertz has roots in Weber's "interpretive sociology." Bourdieu's "theory of practice" is also strongly Weberian in character. The anthropological study of religion, and particularly the debate over the foundations of this field between Geertz and Asad, is reconsidered in light of Weber's sociology of religion. His comparative study of the ethics of the world's religions and particularly the "Weber thesis" about the relationship between religion and the development of bourgeois capitalism are shown to have been the foundation for a large body of anthropological research on religion and political economy in societies in which the major world religions have been long established. The essay ends with a suggestion that Weber's work on politics and meaning merits reexamination in light of contemporary anthropological interest, derived from Foucault, in power and knowledge.

INTRODUCTION

David Gellner (2001, p. 1), in his introduction to *The Anthropology of Buddhism and Hinduism: Weberian Themes*, writes, "The conjunction of 'Weber and anthropology' is sufficiently unusual to warrant justification." In this essay I seek both to offer such a justification and to show that whereas there may not be "Weberian anthropology," much anthropological work has been influenced directly or indirectly by the work of Max Weber. Moreover, there are good reasons, I believe, for rethinking Weber's work in light of contemporary anthropological concerns.

This article is about the influence of the work of Max Weber on English-speaking anthropologists. No effort is made here to assess the broader influence of Weber on the social sciences, especially in sociology and political science, where Weber has been and continues to be read more than in anthropology. I also consider only the English translations of Weber's work.

WEBER AND HIS WORK

Max Weber (1864–1920) does not figure in the history of anthropology in the way Durkheim, Freud, or even Marx do because Weber made next to no use of ethnographic (or proto-ethnographic) materials in his work—indeed, few histories of anthropology make any mention of Weber.[1] Weber was trained in economic history, and his very large corpus of work is centrally concerned with historical processes in the great civilizations of the world. His historical sociology has, however, considerable relevance to an anthropology that has become increasingly historically oriented.

If fledgling anthropologists read any of Weber's work today, it is usually *The Protestant Ethic and the Spirit of Capitalism* (Weber 1958a) (hereafter *PESC*). Although the significance of this study cannot be underestimated, it is only one small part of the large corpus of work that Weber produced. *PESC* is part of a three-volume study on the comparative religious ethics of the world religions, the *Gesammelte Aufsätze zur Religionssoziologie* (*Collected Essays in the Sociology of Religion*) (Weber 1922–1923), a work that sets out to answer the question of what role religion in practice (rather than in theology) played in the emergence of capitalism. It begins with an inquiry into the Protestant ethic, which Weber found to have fostered an attitude toward the world—a spirit (*geist*)—that contributed to the rise of bourgeois rational capitalism. It then turns to studies of Hinduism, Buddhism, and Chinese religion to explore why these religious traditions did not foster the same *geist* and to a study of ancient Judaism, in which Weber found the roots of the Protestant ethic. He had also intended to study Islam, but he never completed a sustained examination of this religious tradition, although fragments of it can be found in other parts of his work such as the section of *Economy and Society* concerning law.[2]

The *Gesammelte Aufsätze zur Religionssoziologie* has been translated by different scholars and published piecemeal in English. Weber's introduction to the whole appears as the introduction to *PESC*. His essay "The Protestant Sects and the Spirit of Capitalism" has been published in translation separately (Weber 1958b, pp. 302–22). Two essays comparing the world religions, "The Social Psychology of World Religions" and "Religious Rejections of the World and Their Directions," also have been published separately (Weber 1958b, pp. 267–301, 323–59), and translations of his studies of Chinese religion, Hinduism, Buddhism, and ancient

---

[1]Harris (1968, p. 285) in his monumental history of anthropology dismisses Weber's approach as being "incompatible with historical materialism." Harris sees the Weberian approach as associated with Boasian anthropology, but Stocking (1968) in his historical studies of the Boasian tradition makes no reference to Weber. The histories by Kuper (1973, p. 160) and Eriksen & Nielsen (2001, pp. 32–35) give more positive, but still very brief, assessments of Weber's influence.

[2]B.S. Turner (1974) has attempted to pull these fragments together and to reflect on what a Weberian study of Islam might have looked like.

Judaism have all appeared as separate books (Weber 1951, 1958c, 1952); excerpts from the first two also appear in the collection, *From Max Weber*.

Weber's second monumental work, *Wirtschaft und Gesellschaft* (*Economy and Society*) (hereafter *W&G*) (Weber 1925), has been translated as a whole (Weber 1978), with many parts also published in separate volumes. The opening of this study, which lays out the basis for Weber's "interpretive sociology," has been published separately as *Basic Concepts in Sociology* (Weber 1962). In addition to this work, three other methodological essays not included in *W&G* have been translated in *The Methodology of the Social Sciences* (Weber 1949).

WEBER'S PHILOSOPHY OF HISTORY

Weber, like Marx, operated with a philosophy of history; like Marx, Weber believed that history is progressive. However, Weber differs from Marx in what he saw as leading to progress. Whereas Marx saw progress as a function of humans acting in the world in relation to the forces of production, Weber saw progress as derived from humans giving meaning to the world and their actions. Instead of historical materialism, Weber's philosophy of history is based on the assumption that progress comes through the process of disenchantment that occurs because of rationalization or intellectualization.

Weber was not, however, an idealist; his philosophy of history cannot be reduced to the proposition that "humans think themselves" to progress. He was more sophisticated than the eighteenth-century rationalists because he was aware of the materialist argument. Rationalization occurs with reference to the material conditions (what he called "interest situations") that humans confront. Weber was not interested in ideas per se but in ideas that become practically realized. That is, he was interested in those ways of giving meaning to action within the world that after having been advanced become incorporated into the understandings (culture) by which people orient their lives. In other words, it is not sufficient for an idea to be thought up; it must become the basis for practical action.

There are many passages in Weber's work that have led scholars to see his philosophy of history as entailing a nonmaterialist unilinear evolutionary view of the process of rationalization. Gerth and Mills in their introduction to *From Max Weber* observed that "Weber's view of 'disenchantment' embodies an element of liberalism and of the enlightenment philosophy that construed man's history as a unilinear 'progress' towards moral perfection" (Weber 1958b, p. 51). They went on to note that although Weber expressed a "skeptical aversion" to unilinear evolutionist theories they still "feel justified in holding that a unilinear construction is clearly implied in Weber's idea of the bureaucratic [rationalization] thrust" (p. 51). That this evolutionary thrust was sufficiently marked in Weber's work is manifest in the fact that Parsons (1966) and Bellah (1964) both constructed a nonmaterialist unilinear evolutionary theory based on their interpretation of selected parts of Weber's work.

However, in many other writings Weber adopted a "developmental" view of history (*Entwicklugsgeschichte*) (see Roth 1987, Roth & Schluchter 1979, Schluchter

1981) rather than an evolutionary one. Weber recognized, in his comparative sociology of religion for example, that whereas the impetus to rationalization and intellectualization can be assumed to be universal the processes of rationalization have followed different paths in different societies. As Roth observed, "If there was no deterministic scheme of evolutionary development [for Weber], the only empirical alternative seemed to be the construction of 'type concepts' or socio-historical models and of secular theories of long-range historical transformation" (Roth & Schluchter 1979, p. 195). The rethinking of modernity that has become particularly evident in the wake of the emergence of postmodernism has led some to look again at Weber's work with more emphasis on his development history rather than the evolutionary implications (see the essays in Lash & Whimster 1987 and Turner 1992).

ANTHROPOLOGY'S DISCOVERY OF WEBER

Weber began to be read by English-speaking anthropologists in the post–World War II period when attention was shifted away from the study of primitive societies—that is, the study of the social structures and cultures of small-scale premodern societies—and toward societies that had been radically reshaped by the influences of modern nation-states and the global economy. The first significant influence of Weber on anthropology was in the United States, particularly among anthropologists trained at Harvard, where Parsons had a profound role in the training of those anthropologists who took their degrees in the Department of Social Relations.[3]

Parsons had first made Weber available for English-speaking students in his translation of and introduction to *PESC*, which first appeared in 1930, and especially in *The Structure of Social Action*, first published in 1937 (Parsons 1968). In *The Structure of Social Action* Parsons developed a general theory of social action based on his synthesis of the ideas of the economist Marshall (1842–1924), the economic sociologist Pareto (1848–1923), Durkheim, and Weber. Parson's four

[3]Even in the post-WWII period most British social anthropologists remained wedded to a structural-functionalist orthodoxy that had its roots in the work of Durkheim (Kuper 1973, p. 160). An important exception was Evans-Pritchard, who in his Marrett lecture in 1950 rejected the ahistoricism of structural functionalism (reprinted in Evans-Pritchard 1962, pp. 139–57). In his own effort to historicize what he called the "sociology of religion," Evans-Pritchard found Weber to be relevant. In his *Theories of Primitive Religion* Evans-Pritchard (1965) showed he had read *PESC* as well as other parts of the Weberian comparative study of world religion as translated in the collection *From Max Weber* and *Religion of China* and *Religion of India*. Although he noted that Weber had read little about primitive societies (Evans-Pritchard 1965, p. 117), he advocated that anthropologists emulate Weber's comparative project because "we anthropologists have not made much progress in the sort of relational studies which I believe to be those required and the only ones which are likely to lead us to a vigorous sociology of religion" (Evans-Pritchard 1965, p. 120). Few followed Evans-Pritchard's admonition, and what Weberian influence is found in British anthropology appears mainly to have come via American sources. An important exception is Beidelman (1971).

chapters on Weber (Parsons 1968, pp. 500–94) are based on an extensive reading of much of Weber's work in German.

The Structure of Social Action was required reading for graduate students in the Department of Social Relations, which was founded by Parsons after World War II.[4] In the 1950s and 1960s a number of anthropologists who trained at Harvard in this department came under Parsons' influence.[5] Although Geertz has characterized Parsons as teaching "in his grave and toneless voice" (Geertz 1973, p. 249), he clearly learned much from Parsons. Geertz, together with fellow graduate student Robert Bellah, would emerge as the preeminent interpreter of Weber for anthropology in the 1960s.

FROM INTERPRETIVE SOCIOLOGY TO INTERPRETIVE ANTHROPOLOGY

The publication in 1973 of *The Interpretation of Cultures* by Clifford Geertz inaugurated a new theoretical approach that became known as "interpretive anthropology." Although this approach had its roots partially in the symbolic anthropology that had preceded it (Fischer 1997, p. 263; Fischer 1977), as Geertz made clear in his opening essay, "Thick Description," in *The Interpretation of Cultures*, he drew explicitly on Weber's interpretive sociology (*verstehenden Soziologie*) in formulating his method of "cultural analysis." "Believing, with Max Weber," Geertz wrote, "that man is an animal suspended in webs of significance he himself has spun, I take culture to be those webs, and the analysis of it to be therefore not an experimental science in search of law but an interpretive one in search of meaning" (Geertz 1973, p. 5).

In the methodological section of *Economy and Society*, Weber set forth the basic premise on which his interpretive sociology is predicated:

> Sociology (in the sense in which this highly ambiguous word is used here) is a science concerning itself with the interpretative understanding of social action and thereby with a causal explanation of its course and consequences. We shall speak of 'action' insofar as the acting individual attaches a subjective meaning to his behavior—be it overt or covert, omission or acquiescence. Action is 'social' insofar as its subjective meaning takes account of the behavior of others and is thereby oriented in its course. (Weber 1978, p. 4)

---

[4]I was told about this curricular requirement by the late A.T. Kirsch, long a professor of anthropology at Cornell, who studied in the Social Relations Department at Harvard in the 1960s. Kirsch first introduced me to Weber and to *The Structure of Social Action* when he joined for a year the class in Thai language at Cornell in which I was enrolled as a graduate student. I am very indebted to Kirsch for guiding my first study of Weber.

[5]By no means all trained in anthropology at Harvard during the 1950s and early 1960s fell under Parsons' influence. In the 1950s and 1960s two different departments existed at Harvard in which one could pursue a PhD in anthropology: the Department of Anthropology and the Department of Social Relations. Only some Harvard anthropologists, such as Kluckhohn and DuBois, were sympathetic to Parsons's approach.

Interpretation for Weber was not, as Eldridge (1980, p. 31) observed, "to be confused with psychological reductionism." Rather, interpretation begins with observations of the actions of the individual.

For Weber, the individual is "the sole carrier of meaningful conduct" (Weber 1958b, p. 55). Although he acknowledged that the "organic" approach to the study of society—the approach that based on the work of Durkheim would become dominant for several generations in anthropology—"is convenient for purposes of practical illustration and for provisional orientation." In the end "if its cognitive value is overestimated and its concepts illegitimately 'reified', it can be highly dangerous" (Weber 1978, p. 14–15). Weber was not, however, advocating that the social is only the sum of individual actions; he was no more a behaviorist, as we now use the term, than he was a psychological reductionist. While Weber's approach presumes that individuals act on impulses or motivations, such impulses or motivations are, he argued, manifest in action only through meanings they have acquired from others. In other words, the meaning of actions must be understood by "placing the act in an intelligible and more inclusive context of meaning" (Weber 1978, p. 8).

Our certainty about our interpretation of action is best, he maintained, when there is a clear link perceivable between the ends sought by the actor and the means that the actor has employed "on the basis of the facts of the situation, as experience has accustomed us to interpret them" (Weber 1978, p. 5). This mode of "logical and mathematical" (Weber 1978, p. 5) interpretation can be seen, I suggest, as foreshadowing rational choice theory.

Weber also noted that there are other types of actions that have an emotional or aesthetic quality that do not lend themselves to the rational choice type of interpretation. "Empathetic or appreciative accuracy [of interpretation of this second kind of action] is attained when, through sympathetic participation, we can adequately grasp the emotional context in which the action took place" (Weber 1978, p. 5). There is an inherent rationale for fieldwork, I believe, in the idea of "sympathetic participation."

Although recognizing this second type of action, Weber advocated beginning with an assumption that any action is rationally based (Weber 1978, p. 6). Only by seeing that an action deviates from "a conceptually pure type of rational action" (Weber 1978, p. 6) can affectual factors be brought in to account for the deviation. As Parsons (1968, p. 588) observed in his explication of Weber's theory, only by checking one's interpretation with "reference to a rationally consistent system of concepts" can the interpretive sociologist forestall "an endless succession of 'intuitional judgments' which depart farther and farther from reality."

Geertz followed Weber in making the individual actor central to his methodology: "Nothing is more necessary to comprehending what anthropological interpretation is, and the degree to which it is interpretation, than an exact understanding of what it means—and what it does not mean—to say that our formulations of other peoples' symbols system must be actor-oriented" (Geertz 1973, p. 14).

He differs from Weber in shifting focus from action to symbols. By stressing the symbolic aspect of action, Geertz went on to develop his interpretive approach with reference to Ricoeur's (1971; also see Ricoeur 1976, 1981) "model of the text." "Doing ethnography is like trying to read (in the sense of 'construct a reading of') a manuscript" (Geertz 1973, p. 10). Whereas the model of the text has proven to be useful, it is not adequate for interpreting many types of actions.[6]

BOURDIEU'S THEORY OF PRACTICE AND INTERPRETIVE SOCIOLOGY

Bourdieu's "theory of practice" brought ethnography closer to the interpretive sociology of Weber (Bourdieu 1977; also see Bourdieu 1990). Bourdieu traced his own intellectual genealogy as a movement

> from the anti-individualist philosophy of the Durkheimians to a philosophy of the subject practiced by phenomenologists and existentialists (Sartre, in particular) and later, in the 1960s, to a "philosophy without subject," as Ricoeur, defender of Christian personalism, characterized "structuralism" [that is, Lévi-Strauss], . . . [and] once again towards a philosophy of the subject in the 1980s, with various strands of rational choice theory and "methodological individualism." (Bourdieu 1993, pp. 268–69)

Although Bourdieu did not include Weber in his intellectual genealogy, his references to Weber both in his *Outline of a Theory of Practice* and particularly in his assessment of Weber's sociology of religion (Bourdieu 1987) demonstrate that he was both directly and indirectly influenced by Weber.[7]

To demonstrate the convergence of Bourdieu's theory of practice with Weber's interpretive sociology would require a much more extended discussion than space permits. I would, however, like to discuss how Bourdieu's central concept of *habitus* can be said to exemplify what Weber termed "ideal type" constructs used for interpreting action.

Weber developed his notion of ideal types "to bring order into the chaos of those facts which we have drawn into the field circumscribed by our *interest*" (Weber 1949, p. 105, emphasis in original), that is, to provide the appropriate language for interpreting the actions the observer has observed. An ideal type "is no 'hypothesis' but it offers guidance to the construction of hypotheses. It is not a *description* of reality but it aims to give unambiguous means of expression to such a description"

[6]In making this claim, I am also acknowledging the validity of some of the criticism of my own use of the model of the text (see Keyes 1984, 1986, 1991 and especially Kirsch 1985).
[7]In *Outline of a Theory of Practice*, Bourdieu (1977, pp. 76, 215: note p. 19) referred to Weber's discussion in *Economy and Society* (1978, pp. 319–33) of "custom, convention, and law" and used "interest" in a Weberian manner.

(Weber 1949, p. 90, emphasis in original). Ideal types do not describe reality, nor do they represent anything in reality in a precise one-to-one fashion. They are also not a statistical average or "a formulation of the concrete traits *common* to a class of concrete things, for instance in the sense that having beards is a trait common to men as distinct from women" (Parsons 1968, p. 604, emphasis in original).

> An ideal type is formed by the one-sided *accentuation* of one or more points of view and by the synthesis of a great many diffuse, discrete, more or less present and occasionally absent *concrete individual* phenomena, which are arranged according to those one-sidedly emphasized viewpoints into a unified *analytical* construct (*Gedankenbild*). In its conceptual purity, this mental construct (*Gedankenbild*) cannot be found empirically anywhere in reality. It is a *utopia*. Historical research faces the task of determining in each individual case, the extent to which this ideal-construct approximates to or diverges from reality... When carefully applied, those concepts are particularly useful in research and exposition. (Weber 1949, p. 90, emphasis in original)

An ideal type may, thus, be a model or a generalizing concept or an abstraction from particular historical circumstances.[8] Whatever its logical character, it is a construct developed to make sense out of a chaos of facts or a set of observations of actions.

Bourdieu proposed the concept of *habitus* precisely for this purpose. The appeal of the concept lies in its utility to interpret why people act in certain observable ways. Although these ways seem natural to the person engaged in them, there lies behind them, Bourdieu argued, "dispositions" that are not only explicitly sanctioned in text-like cultural forms such as "wisdom, sayings, commonplaces, ethical precepts" (Bourdieu 1977, p. 77) but are embedded in the structures of space and in social practices whose meaning is implicit.

> The habitus is the universalizing mediation which causes an individual agent's practices, without either explicit reason or signifying intent, to be nonetheless 'sensible' and 'reasonable'. That part of practices which remains obscure in the eyes of their own producers is the aspect by which they are objectively adjusted to other practices and to the structures of which the principle of their production is itself the product. (Bourdieu 1977, p. 79)

The observer who finds Bourdieu's concept of habitus to be useful in rendering as sensible and reasonable the practices (actions) of those for whom their meaning

[8]Weber's own most-extended discussion of ideal types is in the essay, "Objectivity in Social Science and Social Policy" in *The Methodology of the Social Sciences* (Weber 1949). However, there are also many other passages in his other works that discuss ideal types. See Parsons (1968) and Bendix (1960) for guides to Weber's not overly consistent use of the concept.

is obscure has engaged precisely in that methodological move that Weber made central to his interpretive sociology.[9]

Although the label "interpretive anthropology" ceased to have much currency by the 1990s, I suggest that ethnography still remains fundamentally interpretive in the sense that Weber first formulated the interpretive method for his sociology.

WEBER'S SOCIOLOGY OF RELIGION AND THE ANTHROPOLOGICAL STUDY OF RELIGION

Weber's interpretive method is predicated on an assumption that is also fundamental to his theoretical approach. In a passage on "Religious Groups" in *Economy and Society* Weber posited that "the human mind . . . is driven to reflect on ethical and religious questions, driven not by material need but by an *inner compulsion* to understand the world as a meaningful cosmos and to take up a position toward it" (Weber 1963, pp. 116–117, emphasis added).

Whereas much of the meaning that makes possible acting in the world derives from what Weber termed "tradition" (perhaps better formulated in terms of Bourdieu's habitus), there are experiences that render problematic conventional meaning. Parsons, reflecting on such "problems of meaning," observed that

> Weber postulates a basic 'drive' towards meaning and the resolution of these discrepancies on the level of meaning, a drive or tendency which is often held in check by various defensive mechanisms, of which the pre-eminent one here relevant is that of magic. But whatever the situation regarding the effectiveness of this drive, there is a crucial point concerning the *direction* in which this tendency propels the development of culture. This is that the search for grounds of meaning which can resolve the discrepancies must lead to continually more 'ultimate' reference points which are progressively further removed from the levels of common sense experience on which the discrepancies originally arise. The 'explanations,' i.e., solutions to the problems of meaning, must be grounded in increasingly generalized and 'fundamental' philosophical conceptions. (Parsons in Weber 1963, pp. xlvii–xlviii).

"Ultimate" meaning can never be attained through reflection and rationalization; rather, it can come only, Weber argued, through the nonrational acceptance of the dogmatic propositions embedded in the salvation ethic of a religion. Salvation—the

---

[9]It has been suggested to me that I overstate my interpretation of Bourdieu's habitus as an ideal type in Weberian terms. This person notes that for Bourdieu "rules and values exist only in practice. This seems to contrast markedly with the idea of a 'unified analytical construct [that] cannot be found empirically anywhere in reality.'" I still maintain that the comparison is valid and points to the first part of Weber's definition of an ideal type construct as a "synthesis of a great many diffuse, discrete, more or less present and occasionally absent *concrete individual* phenomena." These phenomena for Weber, as for Bourdieu, are manifest in what Weber called "social action" and Bourdieu "practice."

absolute certainty that the cosmos is ultimately meaningful—is more psychological than cognitive. "The quest of *certitudo salutis* itself has . . . been the origin of all psychological drives of a purely religious character" (Weber 1958a, p. 228).

Geertz's (1966; 1973, pp. 87–125) "Religion as a Cultural System" starts with and elaborates on this Weberian position. Asad (1983; 1993, pp. 27–54) has strongly criticized Geertz's approach, and although this was not his intent, his criticism points to some important differences between Geertz and Weber.[10] First, Asad (1993, pp. 30) points to Geertz's (1973, pp. 92) definition of religion as a "system of symbols" as entailing a confusion between symbols as an "aspect of social reality" (what I would term, following Weber, an aspect of social action) and symbols as representations of social reality. Weber, like Asad, saw meaning as embedded in social action, in Asad's (1993, pp. 32) words, being "intrinsically and not temporally connected."

Asad (1993, pp. 28) further criticized Geertz for adopting a modern post-Enlightenment Western view of religion as having an autonomous essence separate from politics. Although this criticism might not be sustainable if one were to take into account Geertz's ethnographic work on Islam in Indonesia and Morocco, the point I want to make here is that Weber certainly would not make such a distinction. In "Religious Rejections of the World and Their Directions," for example, he wrote,

> The widely varying empirical stands which historical religions have taken in the face of political action have been determined by the entanglement of religious organizations in power interests and the struggles for power, by the almost unavoidable collapse of even the highest states of tension with the world in favor of compromises and relativities, by the usefulness and the use of religious organizations for the political taming of the masses and, especially, by the need of the powers-that-be for the religious consecration of their legitimacy. (Weber 1958b, pp. 337–38)

Weber maintained that from time to time in all societies in which religions with rationalized salvation ethics have evolved tensions develop between religious and political institutions:

> Every religiously grounded unworldly love and indeed every ethical religion must, in similar measure and for similar reasons, experience tensions with the sphere of political behavior. This tension appears as soon as a religion has progressed to anything like a status of equality with the sphere of political associations. (Weber 1963, p. 223)

[10]Although Asad shows some familiarity with Weber, he does not draw on him to any significant extent. What is striking, however, is that Asad seeks to push anthropological work in the same direction as Weber. In his introduction to *Genealogies of Religion* he wrote, "I am concerned with how systemacity (including the kind that is essential to what is called capitalism) is apprehended, represented, and used in the contemporary world" (Asad 1993, pp. 7) and "Modern capitalist enterprises and modernizing nation-states are the two most important powers that organize spaces today . . ." (Asad 1993, p. 8).

I disagree with Asad's criticism of Geertz's predication of religion on the experience people encounter with fundamental problems of meaning. Geertz, who in this respect is very much following Weber, formulates these problems as ones in which "chaos—a tumult of events which lack not just interpretations by *interpretability*—threatens to break upon man: at the limits of his analytical capacities, at the limits of his power of endurance, and at the limits of his moral insight. Bafflement, suffering, and a sense of intractable ethical paradox are all, if they become intense enough or are sustained long enough, radical challenges to the proposition that life is comprehensible and that we can, by taking thought, orient ourselves within it—challenges which any religion ... which hopes to persist must attempt somehow to cope" (Geertz 1973, p. 100, emphasis in original). Geertz (1973, pp. 109–10) went on to argue that the experiences of fundamental problems of meaning "drives" people toward "belief" in particular formulations of ultimate meaning that constitute what he calls a "religious perspective." Asad ignored, in his critique of Geertz's discussion of the religious perspective, the central point that "religious belief involves ... a prior acceptance of authority which transforms" the experiences of problems of meaning (Geertz 1973, p. 109). Asad's failure to recognize or unwillingness to accept that problems of meaning, albeit always in particular manifestations, are universal led him to the untenable conclusion that religion, except in "the most vacuous sense," is not "basic to the structure of modern lives" (Asad 1993, p. 49).[11] One wonders how he would approach a study, to take only two presumably very modern societies, of the significance in America of the religious right in politics, the moral debate over abortion, or the proliferation of New Age religions or in Japan of the debate over the visit of a prime minister to a Shinto shrine, the attack on the Tokyo subway of a movement identified as a cult, or the moral debates over the use of organs of deceased persons, and so on. There is now a growing literature that demonstrates well the persistence, resurgence, and transformation of religions in modern societies owing to the fact that although "science and technology, *together* are basic to the structure of modern lives" (Asad 1993, p. 49, emphasis in original), problems of meaning continue to impel people in modern societies towards religion.[12]

"My aim," Asad (1993, p. 54) wrote in the conclusion to his essay, "has been to problematize the idea of an anthropological definition of religion by assigning that endeavor to a particular history of knowledge and power... out of which the modern world has been constructed." This statement could very easily be used to characterize Weber's *Collected Essays in the Sociology of Religion.*

[11]It might seem curious that Asad should, thus, have contributed a most insightful essay on torture to a book entitled *Social Suffering* that is clearly concerned with exploring cross-culturally what Geertz termed the "the sense of intractable ethical paradox" (Asad 1997).

[12]I cannot survey all the relevant literature on this subject but point to only two works that both take up the theme of problems of meaning in modern societies: Keyes et al. (1994) and Kleinman et al. (1997).

Weber sought in this collection to undertake a comparative sociology of the relationship between the major salvation religions of the world (Christianity, Judaism, Hinduism, Buddhism, Chinese religion, and Islam), the political economies of the societies in which large majorities of the populations found the soteriological practices of these religions compelling. Weber was always concerned with the distinctive "developmental history" of each of these religious traditions rather than trying to fit them into a procrustean mold of some essentialized religion.

THE WEBER THESIS AND ANTHROPOLOGICAL STUDIES OF RELIGION AND POLITICAL ECONOMY

Weber's comparative study of world religion was predicated on the premise that orientation toward the world is shaped by the distinctive ethic followers derive from the dogmas about ultimate reality embedded in a particular soteriology. His "thesis," as it came to be known, was that only the ethic derived from Puritanism made possible the development of rational bourgeois capitalism, whereas the ethics of the other great religions served as barriers to this development. In the introduction to his comparative study, which appears in translation as the introduction to the *PESC*, he wrote

> For though the development of economic rationalism is partly dependent on rational technique and law, it is at the same time determined by the ability and disposition of men to adopt certain types of practical rational conduct. When these types have been obstructed by spiritual obstacles, the development of rational economic conduct has also met serious inner resistance. The magical and religious forces, and the ethical ideas of duty based upon them, have in the past always been among the most important formative influences on conduct. In the studies collected here we shall be concerned with these forces. (Weber 1958a, pp. 26–27)

The Weber thesis is not that religious ethics determine whether or not capitalism can develop.

> We have no intention of maintaining such a foolish and doctrinaire thesis as that the spirit of capitalism . . . could only have arisen as the result of certain effects of the Reformation, or even that capitalism as an economic system is a creation of the Reformation . . . . On the contrary, we only wish to ascertain whether and to what extent religious forces have taken part in the qualitative formation and quantitative expansion of that spirit over the world. (Weber 1958a, p. 91)

The Weber thesis has inspired a large body of work on the relationship between religion and economy in the societies in which the dogmas of the major religions of the world have been widely adhered to. Many anthropologists have also taken up this project. However, because their studies have focused on contemporary societies, they have for the most part reformulated Weber's thesis to ask not why in the past did capitalism not emerge in a society with a non-Western religion, but instead how people in such a society today confront the expansion of industrial capitalism from the West.[13]

It is not possible in this short paper to review in detail the anthropological work inspired by the Weber thesis; such should be undertaken in a review of the sociology (including anthropology) of each of the world religions. I only can point the reader toward some selected works that illustrate the contribution of anthropologists to the project begun by Weber.

Although Weber was not able to complete a study of Islamic societies, there have been many studies inspired by the Weber thesis of the relationship between Islam and political economy. Geertz was again at the forefront of this work, having begun his research in Indonesia in a Harvard-MIT project to study the impact of modernization on that society. Geertz's work on Javanese religion and modernization (Geertz 1956; 1960; 1962; 1963; 1965a,b) initiated what has become a major research undertaking not only by Geertz himself, but also by some of Geertz's students and others influenced by him who have worked in Indonesia (e.g., Peacock 1968; Geertz 1984; Hefner 1991, 2000), and also in North Africa (e.g., Geertz 1968; Geertz et al. 1979; Rabinow 1975, 1977; Rosen 1989; Eickelman 1976, 1985; Eickelman & Piscatori 1996), Iran (Fischer 1980), and comparatively (Peacock 1978; Roff 1987; Clammer 1985a, 1996).

Weber's *Religion of China* has inspired a number of works on the relationship between religious values and economy in East Asian societies. Much of this work, beginning with Bellah's study of the religion of the Tokugawa period in Japan (Bellah 1957), has been undertaken by sociologists and historians (e.g., Golzio 1985; Davis 1980, 1989 on Japan; Elvin 1984, Eisenstadt 1985, Hamilton 1985 on China), but a few studies have been done by anthropologists, especially those attempting to understand the marked embrace of capitalism in Taiwan (e.g., Weller 1994, Skoggard 1996a,b) and Japan (Clammer 1997). Bellah's (1965) edited volume, *Religion and Progress in Modern Asia*, has provided a model for other comparative projects on religion and political economic change in East, Southeast, and South Asian societies (Buss 1985b, Clammer 1985b, Keyes et al. 1994, Hefner 1998).

Weber's *Religion of India* (Weber 1958c) "has suffered a strange and undeserved fate," wrote Gellner (2001, p. 19). It is particularly the case among Indianists that the book "has given rise to rather little discussion of the numerous theories it puts forward among the specialists most competent to judge them" (Gellner 2001, p. 19). This neglect has, however, been primarily among Indianists; it is much

[13]Both Peacock & Kirsch (1980, pp. 231–48) and Gellner (2001, Chapter 1) provide good discussions of the Weber thesis as approached by anthropologists.

less characteristic of students of Theravāda Buddhism and society. It is true that the book is marred by "frequent obscurity and inaccuracies in the translation" (Gellner 2001, p. 20) that any student should be aware of.[14] Gellner noted that Sanskritists dismiss the book because it is based on old secondary sources, but the neglect of social scientists seems to be due more to the fact that the work of another scholar, Dumont, has been far more influential. Dumont in his monumental *Homo Hierarchicus: An Essay on the Caste System* (1967, 1970) and his many studies published in *Contributions to Indian Sociology*, clearly set the agenda for the sociology of Hinduism. Although Dumont made few references to Weber, Gellner (2001, p. 41) argues persuasively that he was "the foremost disciple of Weber in the study of South Asia." This is certainly apparent in the work of Madan, the leading Indian anthropologist and long-time editor of *Contributions to Indian Sociology* (Madan 1983, 1994, 1997) (see Buss 1985a, Singer 1985, Schluchter 1984, and especially Kantowsky 1996 for discussion of Weber's *Religion of India*).

The anthropological study of Buddhism and society, or more precisely, the study of religion and society in those countries where Theravāda Buddhism is dominant (Sri Lanka, Burma/Myanmar, Thailand, Cambodia, and Laos) has since the early 1960s, unlike the anthropological studies of Hinduism, been strongly influenced by Weber. Some of this influence can be traced through such scholars as Ames (1964) and Kirsch (1973, 1975, 1982), who were trained at Harvard, or by those such as myself (Keyes 1983a, 1983b, 1990, 1993), who had a close relationship with the "Harvard School." A second strand is associated with Spiro and Nash, two scholars who were at the University of Chicago in the 1950s, where they were strongly influenced by the work on development being undertaken in other departments at Chicago at the time. Both worked in Burma in the late 1950s (see Spiro 1966, 1970; Nash 1965, 1966). Spiro's distinctive synthesis between Weberian and Freudian approaches in his work on Burma markedly shaped the work of his student, Obeyesekere. Whereas Obeyesekere is perhaps better known as a psychological anthropologist, some of his early work on Sri Lankan Buddhism shows a marked Weberian influence (Obeyesekere 1968, 1972), and his more recent work with the well-known textual scholar, Gombrich (Gombrich & Obeyesekere 1989), has made a strong case for the emergence of a "Protestant Buddhism" in Sri Lanka that is conceived of in Weberian terms. Another distinctive Weberian approach to Buddhism and society is manifest in the work of Tambiah. Although first trained in sociology at Cornell, Tambiah, subsequent to having carried out fieldwork in Thailand, came under the influence of Leach at Cambridge. Leach, who had always made economics basic to his ethnographic (as distinct from his later text-based) research, had in his last fieldwork in Sri Lanka focused on the relationship between economy and culture (Leach 1959, 1961). Tambiah (1973, 1976) drew on both Leach's social anthropology and Weber's sociology in a series

[14]Gellner has retranslated a number of passages based on a new German edition of the work (Weber 1996).

of studies of Buddhism and society in Thailand.[15] Tambiah appears to be the primary influence on Gellner (1990, 2001), who has extended the Weberian study of Buddhism and society to the Nepali tradition of Mahayana Buddhism.

This survey certainly does not account for all the work inspired by the Weber thesis, but it should suffice to indicate that the Weberian influence on the anthropological studies of world religions has been quite profound.

RATIONALIZATION AND CHARISMA: SOURCES OF DEVELOPMENTAL CHANGE

As discussed above with reference to Weber's philosophy of history, he saw the drive toward meaning as being a fundamental process in the transformation of the world. This drive manifests itself as rationalization and intellectualization. Through the exercise of the intellect, humans have promoted conscious reflection not only on the world but also on the ideas with which they make sense of the world. Through time such conscious reflection has led to the repudiation of magic, the systematization of meanings under more general principles, and the self-conscious application of rationalized knowledge for action in the world (for good guides to Weber's discussion of rationalization see Roth & Schluchter 1979; Schluchter 1981, 1987; and Roth 1987). Rationalization has often, however, been impeded by habit or by the authority of tradition.

Rationalization is not, however, the only process Weber saw as leading to change. He recognized that humans also act on emotional or affectual impulses and that "in times of psychic, physical, economic, ethical, religious, political stress" (Weber 1958b, p. 245) these impulses may lead individuals to turn to a leader who is neither the holder of an office invested with traditional authority nor an intellectual. The leaders that emerge at such times "have been holders of specific gifts of the body and spirit; and these gifts have been believed to be supernatural, not accessible to everybody" (p. 245). Weber termed the perceived gifts of such individuals *charisma* but used the word "in a completely 'value-neutral' sense" (p. 245) rather than in the specifically Christian sense from which it was derived (On the three types of motivated action—traditional, rational, and charismatic—see Weber 1978, pp. 24–26; also see Gerth and Mills in Weber 1956b, pp. 56–57).

The long debate among anthropologists about "primitive mentality" that began with Lévy-Bruhl (1912, 1922, 1926, 1966) and Boas (1916), continued with Radin (1927, 1953), and culminated with Lévi-Strauss (1966) has some resonance with Weber's theoretical arguments regarding rationalization. The links between this debate and Weber's rationalization have, however, not been explicitly established.

---

[15] I have been critical of Tambiah's work for not being sufficiently historical in the Weberian sense, a criticism that he has rejected (Keyes 1978, 1987; Tambiah 1987). Tambiah (1984) has also contributed to a recent reevaluation of Weber's *Religion of India*.

Rather, those anthropologists who have taken up Weber's project have been concerned with religious reforms that have occurred as a consequence of the challenge posed by contact between cultures. Examples include the "internal conversion" of Balinese religion and of a "primitive" religion that Geertz (1964; 1973, pp. 170–92) and Atkinson (1987) have argued came about because of the requirement imposed by the Indonesian state that all religions be "religions of the book." Other examples include the reformation of Theravāda Buddhism that took place in both Sri Lanka and Thailand because of the challenge of Western culture, including Christianity (Obeyesekere 1972, 1995; Gombrich & Obeyesekere1989; Kirsch 1973; Tambiah 1976). Horton (1975a,b) and Hefner (1993) have both engaged Weber's ideas of rationalization with reference to conversion to Christianity.

In contrast to rationalization, Weber's notion of charisma is probably the most widely used Weberian concept in anthropology.[16] Worsley (1968), in one of the most extended discussions of the concept by an anthropologist, criticized Weber for assuming that charisma was an attribute of personality. In fact, Worsley ended up restating Weber's own position. Worsley wrote that if a "charismatic appeal . . . is to become the basis of collective social actions, [it] needs to be *perceived, invested with meaning*, and *acted upon* by significant others: those who respond to this charismatic appeal" (Worsley 1968, p. xi, emphasis in original). Weber (1956b, p. 246) himself wrote that the claim by someone to charismatic authority "breaks down if his mission is not recognized by those to whom he feels he has been sent." Bourdieu (1987, p. 131) was true to Weber's formulation in admonishing those who use the concept to "dispose once and for all the notion of charisma as a property attaching to the nature of a single individual." The counterpart to charisma might well be said to be *communitas*, the sense of nonhierarchal comradeship that Turner (1969) posited was characteristic of participants in rituals and in religious movements.[17]

A charismatic person, both in its original Christian meaning of charisma and in the ideal typical reformulation that Weber proposed, is always someone who is perceived to have a direct connection with supernatural or sacred power. Charisma is far from being the synonym for popularity that it has become in everyday English usage. The linkage with the supernatural or sacred is always construed according to particular compelling ideas, for example, to whether one has been set apart by virtue of a trip to and from the land of the dead as in classic shamanism (Kracke 1978), whether one manifests the qualities of a Buddhist saint (Keyes 1981b), or

[16]Indicative of this is the inclusion of an article on charisma in a recent dictionary of anthropology (Lindholm 1997). For other general discussions of charisma by anthropologists see Beidelman (1971), Keyes (1981a), and Lewis (1986). I have drawn on only some of the anthropological literature on charisma for illustration rather than attempting a systematic survey of relevant work.

[17]Turner never made this connection himself. He apparently became aware of Weber only after joining the faculty at Cornell in the early 1960s. In *Drama Fields and Metaphors* he made one reference to Weber (V.W. Turner 1974, p. 200) with reference to Peacock & Kirsch's *The Human Direction* (1980).

whether one articulates a new vision that becomes the basis of a new movement or cult (Zablocki 1980, Carter 1990).

Weber conceived of the emergence of charismatic authority as posing a challenge to existing authority based on tradition or on rationalized bureaucracy. Unlike these other forms of authority, charismatic authority in its pure form is always transitory. "The charismatic holder is deserted by his following . . . because pure charisma does not know any 'legitimacy' other than that flowing from personal strength, that is, one which is constantly being proved" (Weber 1958b, p. 248). It is, thus, "the fate of charisma, whenever it comes into the permanent institutions of a community, to give way to powers of tradition or of rational socialization" (Weber 1958b, p. 253). Although always transitory, charisma is never finally domesticated or rationalized (as Weber would say), but erupts from time to time.

Although many, perhaps most, charismatic movements have been what Gluckman (1954) termed "rituals of rebellion," in which a challenge to the social order is followed by a reassertion of that same order, there have been times when charismatic movements have made possible a fundamental rupture in the existing order and have contributed to the establishment of a new, perhaps even more rationalized order. For Weber such charismatic eruptions were central to his theory of developmental history. A number of anthropologists have studied charismatic movements, but most, like Comaroff (1985), have added to our understanding of how such movements are rituals of rebellion rather than how they have contributed to "breakthroughs" (Bellah 1964) to the emergence of new orders. There are a few such studies, however, such as Obeyesekere's (1995) of Angarika Dharmapala (Don David Hewavitarana) (1864–1933), a charismatic Sinhalese Buddhist leader who played a key role in the development of Protestant Buddhism in Sri Lanka.

Weber's theoretical ideas about charisma were formulated as part of a larger effort to think through the question of how noncoercive political authority is established. Other than studies that make reference to charismatic authority, Weber's political sociology has been given little attention by anthropologists. The time may have come for a rediscovery of this part of Weber's contribution to social thought.

RETHINKING WEBER

I have attempted to demonstrate that Weber's influence on anthropology has been more profound and pervasive than might be apparent given the relative paucity of direct references to his work in recent anthropological writings. I also hope to have demonstrated that much can be gained by reading Weber in light of contemporary issues.

Because of the influence of Foucault, many anthropologists have come to recognize the relationship between knowledge (what used to be called culture) and power. This relationship was clearly already explored in many ways by Weber. For example, Weber recognized long before Foucault the role played by discipline in establishing authority over people's actions. "The content of discipline is nothing but the consistently rationalized, methodically trained and exact execution of the received order..." Weber (1956b, p. 253). As Gordon (1987, p. 293) observes,

> There are many respects in which one might compare Michel Foucault's work with that of Max Weber: their studies of forms of domination and techniques of discipline, their concern with what Weber called 'the power of rationality over men', their writings on methodology and intellectual ethics, their interest in Nietzsche—and the effect of that interest on their thought.

Anthropologists could, I believe, gain by rethinking Weber in light of Foucault—and vice versa (Gordon 1987 provides a good starting point for this; also see Turner 1992, especially Chapter 7).

ACKNOWLEDGMENTS

I have not worked with Weber's writings in German and, thus, disclaim any competence as a Weberian scholar. I would like to acknowledge the guidance I have received from Guenther Roth with regard to some problems relating to the translations of Weber's works and in identifying the correspondence of English translations of Weber's work to the original work in German. I would also like to thank the Technical Editor for the Annual Review of Anthropology for useful critical comments even though I did not take them all into account.

The *Annual Review of Anthropology* is online at http://anthro.annualreviews.org

LITERATURE CITED

Ames MM. 1964. Buddhist reformation in Ceylon. *World Buddhism* 12:912; 13:7–10

Asad T. 1983. Anthropological conceptions of religion: reflections on Geertz. *Man J. R. Anthropol. Inst.* 18(2):237–59

Asad T. 1993. *Genealogies of Religion: Discipline and the Reasons of Power in Christianity and Islam*. Baltimore, MD: Johns Hopkins Univ. Press

Asad T. 1997. On torture, or cruel, inhuman, and degrading treatment. See Kleinman et al. 1997, pp. 285–308

Atkinson J. 1987. Religions in dialogue: the construction of a minority religion. *Am. Ethnol.* 10(4):684–96

Beidelman TO. 1971. Nuer priests and prophets: charisma, authority and power among the Nuer. In *The Translation of Culture: Essays to E. E. Evans-Pritchard*, ed. TO Beidelman, pp. 375–416. London: Tavistock

Bellah RN. 1957. *Tokugawa Religion: The Values of Pre-Industrial Japan*. Boston: Beacon

Bellah RN. 1964. Religious evolution. *Am. Soc. Rev.* 29:358–74

Bellah RN, ed. 1965. *Religion and Progress in Modern Asia*. New York: Free Press

Bendix R. 1960. *Max Weber: An Intellectual Portrait*. Garden City, NY: Doubleday

Boas F. 1916. *The Mind of Primitive Man*. New York: Macmillan

Bourdieu P. 1977. *Outline of a Theory of Practice*, transl. R Nice. Cambridge: Cambridge Univ. Press

Bourdieu P. 1987. Legitimation and structured interests in Weber's sociology of religion. See Lash & Whimster 1987, pp. 119–36

Bourdieu P. 1990. *The Logic of Practice*, transl. R Nice. Stanford, CA: Stanford Univ. Press

Bourdieu P. 1993. Concluding remarks: for a sociogenetic understanding of intellectual

works. In *Bourdieu: Critical Perspectives*, ed. C Calhoun, E LiPuma, M Postone, pp. 263–75. Chicago: Univ. Chicago Press
Buss AE, ed. 1985a. *Max Weber in Asian Studies*. Leiden, The Netherlands: Brill
Buss AE. 1985b. Max Weber's contributions to questions of development in modern India. See Buss 1985a, pp. 8–27
Carter LF. 1990. *Charisma and Control in Rajneeshpuram: The Role of Shared Values in the Creation of a Community*. Cambridge: Cambridge Univ. Press
Clammer J. 1985a. Weber and Islam in Southeast Asia. See Buss 1985a, pp. 102–14
Clammer J. 1985b. *Anthropology and Political Economy: Theoretical and Asian Perspectives*. London: Macmillan
Clammer J. 1996. *Values and Development in Southeast Asia*. Selangor Darul Eshan, Malaysia: Pelanduk
Clammer J. 1997. *Contemporary Urban Japan: A Sociology of Consumption*. Oxford/Malden, MA: Blackwell
Comaroff J. 1985. *Body of Power, Spirit of Resistance: The Culture and History of a South African People*. Chicago: Univ. Chicago Press
Davis W. 1980. *Dojo: Magic and Exorcism in Modern Japan*. Stanford, CA: Stanford Univ. Press
Davis W. 1989. Buddhism and the modernization of Japan. *Hist. Relig.* 28(4):304–39
Dumont L. 1967. *Homo Hierarchicus, Essai sur le Système des Castes*. Paris: Gallimard
Dumont L. 1970. *Homo Hierarchicus: The Caste System and Its Implications*, transl. M Sainsbury. Chicago: Univ. Chicago Press
Eickelman D. 1976. *Moroccan Islam: Tradition and Society in a Pilgrimage Center*. Austin: Univ. Texas Press
Eickelman D. 1985. *Knowledge and Power in Morocco: The Education of a Twentieth-Century Notable*. Princeton, NJ: Princeton Univ. Press
Eickelman D, Piscatori J. 1996. *Muslim Politics*. Princeton, NJ: Princeton Univ. Press
Eisenstadt SN. 1985. The worldly transcendentalism and the structuring of the world: Weber's 'Religion of China' and the format of Chinese history and civilization. See Buss 1985a, pp. 46–64
Eldridge JET. 1980. Introductory essay: Max Weber—some comments, problems, and continuities. In *The Interpretation of Social Reality*, ed. JET Eldridge, pp. 9–70. New York: Schocken
Elvin M. 1984. Why China failed to create an endogenous industrial capitalism: a critique of Max Weber's explanation. *Theory Soc.* 13:379–92
Eriksen TH, Nielsen FS. 2001. *A History of Anthropology*. London/Sterling, VA: Pluto
Evans-Pritchard EE. 1962. *Essays in Social Anthropology and Other Essays*. Glencoe, IL: Free Press
Evans-Pritchard EE. 1965. *Theories of Primitive Religion*. Oxford: Clarendon
Fischer MMJ. 1977. Interpretive Anthropology. *Rev. Anthropol.* 4(4):391–404
Fischer MMJ. 1980. *Iran: From Religious Dispute to Revolution*. Cambridge, MA: Harvard Univ. Press
Fischer MMJ. 1997. Interpretive anthropology. In *The Dictionary of Anthropology*, ed. T Barfield, pp. 263–65. Oxford: Blackwell
Geertz C. 1956. Religious belief and economic behavior in a central Javanese town: some preliminary considerations. *Econ. Dev. Cult. Change* 4:134–58
Geertz C. 1960. *The Religion of Java*. Glencoe, IL: Free Press
Geertz C. 1962. Social change and economic modernization in two Indonesian towns: a case in point. In *On the Theory of Social Change*, ed. E Hagen, pp. 385–410. Homewood, IL: Dorsey
Geertz C. 1963. Modernization in a Moslem society: the Indonesian case. *Quest* 39:9–17
Geertz C. 1964. 'Internal conversion' in contemporary Bali. In *Malayan and Indonesian Studies Presented to Sir Richard Winstedt*, ed. J Bastin, R Roolvink, pp. 282–302. Oxford: Oxford Univ. Press
Geertz C. 1965a. *The Social History of an Indonesian Town*. Cambridge, MA: MIT Press

Geertz C. 1965b. Modernization in a Muslim society: the Indonesian case. See Bellah 1965, pp. 93–108

Geertz C. 1966. Religion as a cultural system. In *Anthropological Approaches to the Study of Religion*, ed. Michael Banton, pp. 1–46. London: Tavistock

Geertz C. 1968. *Islam Observed: Religious Development in Morocco and Indonesia*. New Haven, CT: Yale Univ. Press

Geertz C. 1973. *The Interpretation of Cultures: Selected Essays*. New York: Basic Books

Geertz C. 1984. Culture and social change: the Indonesian case. *Man* 19:511–32

Geertz C, Geertz H, Rosen L. 1979. *Meaning and Order in Moroccan Society: Three Essays in Cultural Analysis*. Cambridge: Cambridge Univ. Press

Gellner DN. 1990. Introduction: What is the anthropology of Buddhism about? *J. Anthropol. Soc. Oxford*, spec. issue 21(2):95–112

Gellner DN. 2001. *The Anthropology of Buddhism and Hinduism*. Oxford/New York: Oxford Univ. Press

Gluckman M. 1954. *Rituals of Rebellion in Southeast Africa*. Manchester, UK: Manchester Univ. Press

Golzio K-H. 1985. Max Weber on Japan: the role of the government and the Buddhist sects. See Buss 1985a, pp. 90–101

Gombrich R, Obeyesekere G. 1989. *Buddhism Transformed: Religious Change in Sri Lanka*. Princeton, NJ: Princeton Univ. Press

Gordon C. 1987. The soul of the citizen: Max Weber and Michel Foucault on rationality and government. See Lash & Whimster 1987, pp. 293–316

Hamilton G. 1985. Why no capitalism in China? Negative questions in historical, comparative research. See Buss 1985a, pp. 65–89

Harris M. 1968. *The Rise of Anthropological Theory*. New York: Crowell

Hefner RW. 1991. *The Political Economy of Mountain Java: An Interpretive History*. Berkeley/Los Angeles: Univ. Calif. Press

Hefner RW. 1993. World building and the rationality of conversion. In *Christian Conversion in Cultural Context*, ed. R Hefner, pp. 3–44. Berkeley/Los Angeles: Univ. Calif. Press

Hefner RW, ed. 1998. *Market Cultures: Society and Morality in the New Asian Capitalisms*. Boulder, CO: Westview

Hefner RW. 2000. *Civil Islam: Muslims and Democratization in Indonesia*. Princeton, NJ: Princeton Univ. Press

Horton R. 1975a. On the rationality of conversion. I. *Africa* 45.3:219–35

Horton R. 1975b. On the rationality of conversion. II. *Africa* 45.4:73–99

Kantowsky D, ed. 1996. *Recent Research on Max Weber's Studies of Hinduism*. Munich: Weltforum

Keyes CF. 1978. Structure and history in the study of the relationship between Theravāda Buddhism and political order. *Numen Int. Rev. Hist. Relig.* 25.2:156–70

Keyes CF. 1981a. Charisma: from social life to sacred biography. See Williams 1981, pp. 1–22

Keyes CF. 1981b. Death of two Buddhist saints in Thailand. See Williams 1981, pp. 149–80

Keyes CF. 1983a. The study of popular ideas of karma. In *Karma: An Anthropological Inquiry*, ed. CF Keyes, EV Daniel, pp. 1–24. Berkeley: Univ. Calif. Press

Keyes CF. 1983b. Economic action and Buddhist morality in a Thai village. *J. Asian Stud.* 42.3:851–68

Keyes CF. 1984. Mother or mistress but never a monk: culture of gender and rural women in Buddhist Thailand. *Am. Ethnol.* 11(2):223–41

Keyes CF. 1986. Ambiguous gender: male initiation in a Buddhist society. In *Religion and Gender: Essays on the Complexity of Symbols*, ed. C Bynum, S Harrell, P Richman, pp. 66–96. Boston: Beacon

Keyes CF. 1987. Theravāda Buddhism and its worldly transformations in Thailand: reflections on the work of S.J. Tambiah. *Contrib. Indian Sociol.* 21(1):123–46

Keyes CF. 1990. Buddhist practical morality in a changing agrarian world: a case from northeastern Thailand in *Attitudes Toward Wealth and Poverty in Theravada Buddhism*, ed. DK

Swearer, R Sizemore, pp. 170–89. Columbia: Univ. South Carolina Press

Keyes CF. 1991. The proposed world of the school: Thai villagers entry into a bureaucratic state system. In *Reshaping Local Worlds: Rural Education and Cultural Change in Southeast Asia*, ed. CF Keyes, pp. 87–138. New Haven, CT: Yale Univ. SE Asian Stud.

Keyes CF. 1993. Buddhist economics and Buddhist fundamentalism in Burma and Thailand. In *Remaking the World: Fundamentalist Impact*, ed. M Marty, S Appleby, pp. 367–409. Chicago: Univ. Chicago Press

Keyes CF, Kendall L, Hardacre H, eds. 1994. *Asian Visions of Authority: Religion and the Modern States of East and Southeast Asia*. Honolulu: Univ. Hawaii Press

Kirsch AT. 1973. Modernizing implications of 19th century reforms in the Thai Sangha. *Contrib. Asian Stud.* 8:8–23

Kirsch AT. 1975. Economy, polity, and religion in Thailand. In *Change and Persistence in Thai Society: Homage to Lauriston Sharp*, ed. GW Skinner, AT Kirsch, pp. 172–96. Ithaca, NY: Cornell Univ. Press

Kirsch AT. 1982. Buddhism, sex-roles and the Thai economy. In *Women of Southeast Asia*, ed. P van Esterik, pp. 16–41. DeKalb: Northern Ill. Univ., Cent. Southeast Asian Stud., Monogr. Ser. on Southeast Asia, Occas. Pap. 9

Kirsch AT. 1985. Text and context: Buddhist sex roles/culture of gender revisited. *Am. Ethnol.* 12(2):302–20

Kleinman A, Das V, Lock M, eds. 1997. *Social Suffering*. Berkeley/Los Angeles: Univ. Calif. Press

Kracke W. 1978. *Force and Persuasion: Leadership in an Amazonian Society*. Chicago: Univ. Chicago Press

Kuper A. 1973. *Anthropologists and Anthropology: The British School 1922–1972*. New York: Pica Press

Lash S, Whimster S, eds. 1987. *Max Weber, Rationality, and Modernity*. London: Allen & Unwin

Leach ER. 1959. Hydraulic society in Ceylon. *Past Present* 15:2–25

Leach ER. 1961. *Pul Eliya: A Village in Ceylon*. Cambridge: Cambridge Univ. Press

Lévi-Strauss C. 1966. *The Savage Mind*. Chicago: Univ. Chicago Press

Lévy-Bruhl L. 1912. *Les Fonctions Mentales dans les Sociétés Inférieures*. Paris: Alcan

Lévy-Bruhl L. 1922. *La Mentalité Primitive*. Paris: Libr. Félix Alcan

Lévy-Bruhl L. 1926. *How Natives Think*. Transl. LA Clare. London: Allen & Unwin

Lévy-Bruhl L. 1966. *Primitive Mentality*. Transl. LA Clare. Boston: Beacon

Lewis IM. 1986. *Religion in Context: Cults and Charisma*. Cambridge: Cambridge Univ. Press

Lindholm C. 1997. Charisma. In *The Blackwell Dictionary of Anthropology*, ed. TJ Barfield, pp. 53–54. Oxford: Blackwell

Madan TN. 1983. *Culture and Development*. Delhi: Oxford Univ. Press

Madan TN. 1994. *Pathways: Approaches to the Study of Society in India*. Delhi: Oxford Univ. Press

Madan TN. 1997. *Modern Myths, Locked Minds: Secularism and Fundamentalism in India*. Delhi: Oxford Univ. Press

Nash M. 1965. *The Golden Road to Modernity: Village Life in Contemporary Burma*. New York: Wiley & Sons

Nash M, ed. 1966. *Anthropological Studies in Theravada Buddhism*. New Haven, CT: Yale Univ. SE Asia Stud., Cult. Rep. Ser. No. 13

Obeyesekere G. 1968. Theodicy, sin and salvation in a sociology of Buddhism. In *Dialectic in Practical Religion*, ed. ER Leach, pp. 7–40. Cambridge: Cambridge Univ. Press, Cambridge Pap. Soc. Anthropol., No. 5

Obeyesekere G. 1972. Religious symbolism and political change in Ceylon. In *The Two Wheels of Dhamma*, ed. BL Smith, pp. 58–78. Chambersburg, PA: Am. Acad. Relig.

Obeyesekere G. 1995. On Buddhist identity in Sri Lanka. In *Ethnic Identity: Creation, Conflict, and Accommodation*, ed. G De Vos, L Romanucci-Ross, pp. 222–47. Walnut Creek, CA: Alta Mira. 3rd ed.

Parsons T. 1966. *Societies: Evolutionary and*

Comparative Perspectives. Englewood Cliffs, NJ: Prentice-Hall
Parsons T. 1968 [1937]. *The Structure of Social Action*. New York: Free Press
Peacock JL. 1968. *Rites of Modernization*. Chicago: Univ. Chicago Press
Peacock JL. 1978. *Muslims Puritans: Reformist Psychology in Southeast Asia Islam*. Berkeley/Los Angeles: Univ. Calif. Press
Peacock JL, Kirsch AT. 1980. *The Human Direction: An Evolutionary Approach to Social and Cultural Anthropology*. Englewood Cliffs, NJ: Prentice-Hall. 3rd ed.
Rabinow P. 1975. *Symbolic Domination: Cultural Form and Historical Change in Morocco*. Chicago: Univ. Chicago Press
Rabinow P. 1977. *Reflections on Fieldwork in Morocco*. Berkeley: Univ. Calif. Press
Radin P. 1927. *Primitive Man as Philosopher*. New York/London: Appleton
Radin P. 1953. *The World of Primitive Man*. New York: Schuman
Ricoeur P. 1971. The model of the text: meaningful action considered as a text. *Soc. Res.* 38:529–62
Ricoeur P. 1976. *Interpretation Theory: Discourse and the Surplus of Meaning*. Fort Worth: Texas Christ. Univ. Press
Ricoeur P. 1981. *Hermeneutics and the Human Sciences*. Transl./ed. JB Thompson. Cambridge: Cambridge Univ. Press
Roff WR, ed. 1987. *Islam and the Political Economy of Meaning: Comparative Studies of Muslim Discourse*. London: Croom Helm
Rosen L. 1989. *The Anthropology of Justice: Law As Culture in Islamic Society*. Cambridge/New York: Cambridge Univ. Press
Roth G. 1987. Rationalization in Max Weber's developmental history. See Lash & Whimster 1987, pp. 75–91
Roth G, Schluchter W. 1979. *Max Weber's Vision of History: Ethics and Methods*. Berkeley/Los Angeles: Univ. Calif. Press
Schluchter W. 1981. *The Rise of Western Rationalism: Max Weber's Developmental History*. Berkeley: Univ. Calif. Press
Schluchter W, ed. 1984. *Max Webers Studie über Hinduismus und Buddhismus*. Frankfurt: Suhrkamp
Schluchter W. 1987. Weber's sociology of rationalization and typology of religious rejections of the world. See Lash & Whimster 1987, pp. 92–115
Singer M. 1985. Max Weber and the modernization of India. See Buss 1985a, pp. 28–45
Skoggard IA. 1996a. Inscribing capitalism: belief and ritual in a new Taiwanese religion. In *The Story of Progress*, ed. G Arvastson, M Lindqvist, pp. 13–26. Upsala, Swed.: Acta Univ. Upsaliensis, Stud. Ethnol. Upsaliensia, 17
Skoggard IA. 1996b. *The Indigenous Dynamic in Taiwan's Postwar Development: The Religious and Historical Roots of Entrepreneurship*. Armonk, NY: Sharpe
Spiro ME. 1966. Buddhism and economic action in Burma. *Am. Anthropol.* 68(5):1163–73
Spiro ME. 1970. *Buddhism and Society: A Great Tradition and Its Burmese Vicissitudes*. New York: Harper & Row
Stocking GW Jr. 1968. *Race, Culture and Evolution: Essays in the History of Anthropology*. New York: Free Press
Tambiah SJ. 1973. Buddhism and this-worldly activity. *Mod. Asian Stud.* 7(1):1–20
Tambiah SJ. 1976. *World Conqueror and World Renouncer: A Study of Buddhism and Polity in Thailand against a Historical Background*. Cambridge: Cambridge Univ. Press
Tambiah SJ. 1984. Max Weber's Untersuchung des fruehen Buddhismus: eine Kritik. See Schluchter 1984, pp. 202–46
Tambiah SJ. 1987. At the confluence of anthropology, history, and Indology. *Contrib. Indian Soc.* 21(1):187–216
Turner BS. 1974. *Weber and Islam: A Critical Study*. London/Boston: Routledge & Kegan Paul
Turner BS. 1992. *Max Weber: From History to Modernity*. London: Routledge
Turner VW. 1969. *The Ritual Process: Structure and Anti-Structure*. Chicago: Aldine

Turner VW. 1974. *Dramas, Fields and Metaphors: Symbolic Action in Human Society*. Ithaca, NY: Cornell Univ. Press

Weber M. 1922–1923. *Gesammelte aufsätze zur Religionssoziologie*. 3 vols. Tübingen, Ger.: Mohr

Weber M. 1925. *Wirtschaft und Gesellschaft*. 2 vols. Tübingen, Ger.: Mohr. 2nd ed.

Weber M. 1949. *The Methodology of the Social Sciences*. Transl./ed. EA Shils, HA Finch. New York: Free Press

Weber M. 1951. *The Religion of China: Confucianism and Taoism*. Transl./ed. HH Gerth. New York: Macmillan/London: Collier Macmillan

Weber M. 1952. *Ancient Judaism*. Transl./ed. HH Gerth, D Martindale. Glencoe, IL: Free Press

Weber M. 1958a [1930]. *The Protestant Ethic and the Spirit of Capitalism*. Transl. T Parsons. New York: Scribner's Sons

Weber M. 1958b [1946]. *From Max Weber*. Transl./ed. HH Gerth, CW Mills. New York: Oxford Univ. Press

Weber M. 1958c. *The Religion of India: The Sociology of Hinduism and Buddhism*. Transl./ed. HH Gerth, D Martindale. New York: Free Press

Weber M. 1962. *Basic Concepts in Sociology*. Transl. HP Secher. New York: Citadel

Weber M. 1963. *The Sociology of Religion*. Transl. E Fischoff. Boston: Beacon

Weber M. 1978 [1968]. *Economy and Society: An Outline of Interpretive Sociology*, ed. G Roth, C Wittich. Berkeley/Los Angeles: Univ. Calif. Press

Weber M. 1996. *Die Wirtschaftsethik der Weltreligionen: Hinduismus und Buddhismus, 1916–20*, ed. H Schmidt-Glintzer, K-H Golzio. Tübingen, Ger.: Mohr

Weller RP. 1994. Capitalism, community, and the rise of amoral cults in Taiwan. See Keyes et al. 1994, pp. 141–64

Williams M, ed. 1981. *Charisma and Sacred Biography*. Chico, CA: Scholars Press

Worsley P. 1968. *The Trumpet Shall Sound*. New York: Schocken. 2nd rev. ed.

Zablocki B. 1980. *Alienation and Charisma: A Study of Contemporary American Communes*. New York: Free Press

Annu. Rev. Anthropol. 2002. 31:257–78
doi: 10.1146/annurev.anthro.31.040402.085428

First published online as a Review in Advance on May 21, 2002

CONTEMPORARY TRENDS IN INFANT FEEDING RESEARCH

Penny Van Esterik
Department of Anthropology, York University, M3J1P3, Toronto, Ontario, Canada; email: esterik@yorku.ca

Key Words breastfeeding, complementary feeding, weaning, advocacy, maternal and child health

■ **Abstract** This review examines current research in the subfields of anthropology and related disciplines on the biocultural process of breastfeeding and broader questions of infant and young-child feeding. The themes of sexuality, reproduction, embodiment, and subjective experience are then linked to the problems women who breastfeed face in bottle-feeding cultures. Anthropologists have contributed to policy-relevant debates concerning women's work and scheduling in relation to infant care and exclusive breastfeeding. The extensive ethnographic work on children's transition to consuming household foods demonstrates the need to integrate research on breastfeeding with research on complementary feeding. Current debates around HIV and chemical residues in breastmilk call for a critical examination of the effects of globalization and corporate control on infant feeding practices. The literature shows how the narrow specialty of infant feeding has broad implications for the discipline.

INTRODUCTION

This review examines both the biocultural process of breastfeeding, which intimately connects women's bodies to infants' bodies, and broader questions of infant and young-child feeding, including its relation to sexuality, embodiment, and the important policy issues of women's employment, exclusive breastfeeding, and complementary feeding. The review does not consider the medical literature on the benefits of breastfeeding for child health and growth—topics covered in the 1992 *Annual Review of Anthropology* article by Dettwyler & Fishman.

Those few anthropologists who have researched infant feeding have made a substantial contribution to the subject. Their unique contribution as anthropologists is the examination of the broad context in which infant feeding decisions are made, and the potential for considering both biological and cultural dimensions in a single framework. Breastfeeding is not a discrete behavior but constitutes a range of practices with extraordinary temporal and spatial variation. Paradoxically, the more breastfeeding is valued the more it may be embedded in rules and patterns of interaction unconnected to infant feeding. The more we know about the desirable properties of the product breastmilk, the greater is its potential to be commodified, and the more breastfeeding may become regulated or embedded in coercive practices.

LOCATING INFANT FEEDING RESEARCH

Most research on breastfeeding and infant feeding is not done by anthropologists but by researchers in the areas of health education, international nutrition, clinical nursing, or public health—fields that have had the most influence on policy. Team research by anthropologists and health professionals can build on these disciplinary differences, producing work that interfaces anthropology and epidemiology (Hundt & Forman 1993). The subjects of breasts, breastfeeding, lactation, and child nutrition are all lodged in specialized disciplines, each drawing on distinct theoretical and practical traditions. These disciplines have not traditionally relied on qualitative research. As a result, breastfeeding has not always been seen as a complex process shaped by social and cultural forces interacting with local environmental and political conditions. On the other hand, some health professionals researching infant feeding have been trained in anthropology and make use of qualitative methods and narrative analysis, often without the abstract theoretical framing perceived to be of less relevance to policy makers. Such work frequently has an explicitly applied focus aimed at increasing breastfeeding rates or achieving compliance around complementary feeding.

The Subfields of Anthropology

Edited collections in the past decade (Maher 1992, Stuart-Macadam & Dettwyler 1995) reflect current theoretical and substantive contributions to infant feeding in biological, medical, and sociocultural anthropology. *Breastfeeding: Biocultural Perspectives* examines breastfeeding from a biocultural and evolutionary perspective, integrating "data from diverse fields to present a more holistic view of breastfeeding" (Stuart-Macadam & Dettwyler 1995, p. 1). Maher's edited collection provides cross-cultural examples of breastfeeding in a number of different countries including Tunisia, Italy, Iceland, Iran, and Nepal.

Few ethnographies focus exclusively on infant feeding; however, many of them include accounts about breastfeeding and infant feeding as a way to explore poverty (Scheper-Hughes 1992), fascism and maternity (Whitaker 2000), development (Kwiatkowski 1999), sexuality and social relations (Howard & Millard 1997), and child rearing (Kurtz 1992). These substantial ethnographies demonstrate the ways that breastfeeding is embedded in gender ideologies and systems of household production and consumption in an increasingly globalized economy. Such ethnographies are a reminder of the futility of many short-term interventions designed to "improve" infant feeding practices without also addressing underlying conditions such as poverty or globalization.

The field of linguistics plays only a small role in infant feeding research; however, language use has relevance in at least two ways. First, advocates have noted the biases built into the way breastfeeding is talked about in Euro-American society—the use of a term such as prolonged breastfeeding rather than premature weaning, for example, and the borrowing of concepts from dairying such as residual milk or emptying the breast. These terms have seeped into the way health professionals and mothers understand maternal bodily processes.

Second, potentially valuable insights on language and self-perception might come from analysis of toddlers who can talk about breastfeeding. Stearns (1999, p. 319) notes the code words for breastfeeding California toddlers use to facilitate discrete breastfeeding in public contexts where extended breastfeeding is rare. In Senegal, Mandinka mothers talk their toddlers into weaning (Whittemore & Beverly 1996, p. 56). A pregnant mother from East Bhutan tells the weanling that her milk has "gone bad," assuming the child is talking and understanding (Bohler & Ingstad 1996, p. 1810). Steingraber, an American ecologist and mother, writes: "As soon as they can talk about it, it's time to stop" (2001, p. 267).

Archaeology and biological anthropology often demonstrate complementary approaches to breastfeeding and infant feeding. Archaeologists have examined the processes of lactation and weaning from skeletal material (Sillen & Smith 1984, Blakely 1989, Moggi-Cecchi et al. 1994, Katzenberg et al. 1996). Herring and colleagues (1994, 1998) have developed new methods to study childhood diet in adult skeletons from tooth enamel. Using skeletons from Guatemala, Wright and associates confirmed that children shifted to solid foods such as maize before the age of two while continuing to breastfeed (Wright & Schwarcz 1998).

Biological anthropologists have demonstrated an evolutionary basis for a number of processes related to breastfeeding. These include the hormonal responses that stimulate the contraction of the uterus and the production of milk after birth; the efficient mobilization of maternal fat stores for maintaining lactation; the balance between the underproduction and overproduction of milk; physiological mechanisms to reduce the likelihood of overlapping gestation and lactation; and variation in the age at weaning (Dettwyler 1998, Ellison 2001, Stallings et al. 1998). Research on cosleeping with at least one other person demonstrates advantages for infants, including possible protection against sudden infant death syndrome (SIDS) (McKenna & Bernshaw 1995).

Ellison's evolutionary review of human reproduction (2001) includes a chapter on breastfeeding, "The Elixir of Life." He outlines the constraints on the reproductive success of female mammals, including energy and time constraints not placed on male reproductive success (2001, pp. 167–68), and shows the elegant balance between the costs of lactation, maternal maintenance, and a new pregnancy. Recent clinical research by Daly & Hartmann (1995) explores the distinction between breastmilk storage and breastmilk production. They demonstrate that human milk production is controlled by the infant's appetite, the frequency of milk removal, and a mother's ability to produce milk (Daly & Hartmann 1995, p. 22). In fact, the infant controls the amount of breastmilk consumed (Cohen et al. 1994). Some women can produce more milk than their infants demand. When women raise concerns about breast size in relation to breastfeeding, they are reassured that breast size is poorly correlated with milk production. Daly & Hartmann suggest that larger breasts are in fact capable of storing more milk; mothers with larger milk storage capacity may have more flexibility with regard to their patterns of breastfeeding (1995, p. 32). Research on breast size and symmetry (Manning et al. 1997) is also important for understanding body image.

Even a brief overview of research on infant feeding in anthropology shows that research on breastfeeding in particular and infant feeding in general would benefit from linking the bodies of evidence in the different subfields of anthropology, particularly biological and sociocultural anthropology.

Historical Research

Historical archives have also proven to be rich sources of data on infant feeding. Archival evidence from two Norwegian cities showed the mortality of children not breastfed was three times that of those who were breastfed during the years 1860–1930, and the protective effect on infant survival continued after weaning (Rosenberg 1989, p. 335). The methodological problems in working with historical data are similar to problems reported by ethnographers, including clustering of reports of age of weaning around 3, 6, 9, and 12 months of age and inadequate recording of the distinction between exclusive breastfeeding and mixed feeding.

Treckel's research on breastfeeding and maternal sexuality in colonial America makes use of documents from seventeenth- and eighteenth-century medical authorities to show how changing patterns of breastfeeding reflected changing views about the appropriate roles of women as wives and mothers (1989, p. 25). The humoral theory informed beliefs about the dangers of colostrum and the transformation of menstrual blood into breastmilk. Couples were advised against having sexual relations while women were breastfeeding because "... intercourse encouraged the resumption of menstruation, thereby initiating the transformation of breast milk back into menstrual blood and depriving infants of nourishment" (1989, p. 31). Puritans in particular admonished husbands not to demand a return to sexual relations, which would force their wives to secure wet nurses (1989, p. 33).

Hsiung (1995) reviewed advice on infant feeding from China's Sung dynasty (960–1279). Pediatric texts included practical suggestions about flow, position, regulating times and amounts for feeding, avoiding overfeeding, qualities of breastmilk, the dangers of breastfeeding in bed, and the dietary habits and emotions of mothers and wet nurses. The advice was not sentimental and was devoid of appeals to myth or legend (Hsiung 1995, p. 235).

Parkes (2001) examined milk kinship as a way to establish relations of interdomestic allegiance and tributary patronage in the late nineteenth century in the Hindu Kush of northern Pakistan. The relation between milk siblings and between breastmilk provider and recipient differs from both god-parenting (when no bodily substance is exchanged) and wet nursing (when no permanent relation is established with the family of the wet nurse; cf. Khatib-Chahibi 1992). Islamic shariah law recognizes three alternative relationships established through blood, affinity, and milk. The milk relation is phrased in terms of male proprietorship—milk as paternal substance—rather than milk as conveyor of maternal substance, a refinement of maternal blood, as is common in the Islamic world and in colonial America (Treckel 1989). The practice of milk fosterage can be used as a strategy to evade patrilateral marriage, force community exogamy, obviate suspicions of adultery, and create alliances under conditions of political instability, later eroded by state formation (Parkes 2001, p. 6). Corporate milk kinship where all infants are suckled by all nursing mothers of the community is another means of strengthening tribal unity (Parkes 2001, p. 10). Historical sources provide additional evidence for the temporal variability of infant feeding practices and can be used with ethnographic evidence to suggest potential hypotheses concerning, for example, class differences and health consequences for infants.

THEMES IN INFANT FEEDING RESEARCH

The first three themes in this literature review set out below were selected because they relate to current debates in the social sciences on sexuality, gender, and embodiment, and these themes may provide insight into understanding the Euro-American literature on breastfeeding in bottle-feeding cultures; the remaining topics are more policy-driven and are the specific focus of advocacy work, either by governments and international agencies concerned with child health or by nongovernmental organizations. Where possible, the work of both biological and cultural anthropologists is considered, often within the framework of medical anthropology.

Sexuality and Reproduction

Breastfeeding and infant feeding intersect with sexuality in many ways. Among the Chagga of Tanzania, appropriate sexual behavior connects human reproduction to the fertility of plants and animals. Though rituals celebrate sexuality and the reproductive powers of both men and women, they also require conception to take place at the correct time. For example, if the husband fails to make bridewealth payments or if the wife has not been circumcised, the couple should not start childbearing (Howard & Millard 1997, p. 105). Child malnutrition is attributed to parental sexual misconduct, a sign of ancestral displeasure. Continuing to breastfeed while pregnant is considered particularly dangerous because semen would cause breastmilk to spoil. The importance of postpartum abstinence while breastfeeding illustrates the linkages between food and sex: "Feeding the mouth maintains life, while feeding the vagina during intercourse produces new life .... The proper sequence of feeding must not be altered; that is, one must not have been feeding the vagina of the mother at the same time that she is feeding the mouth of her child" (Howard & Millard 1997, p. 106).

Postpartum sexual abstinence combined with full breastfeeding results in an expected interval of around three years between births and protects mothers from closely spaced pregnancies. Among the Chagga (Howard & Millard 1997), as perhaps in northeast Brazil (Scheper-Hughes 1992), not breastfeeding is a way for a mother to distance herself from a baby who is likely to die or even to hasten its death. The linkages between breastfeeding and postpartum abstinence are also articulated in Zimbabwe around the beliefs that breastmilk is poisoned by intercourse and that a child must be cleansed after drinking "impure, dirty milk" from a pregnant mother by inducing diarrhea and vomiting (Cosminsky et al. 1993, p. 943). In East Bhutan, children who continue breastfeeding when their mothers are pregnant are considered to be "stealing milk" from their siblings (Bohler & Ingstad 1996). These ethnographic accounts provide context for understanding the appeal of bottle feeding using infant formula in the past few decades (Oni 1987, Aborampah 1985).

Although the connection between breastfeeding and lactation amenorrhea has been well established for some time (Agyei 1984 for Papua New Guinea; Jones 1989 for Indonesia), current research by biological anthropologists seeks more information about the mechanism of fertility control. Stallings and colleagues examined prolactin levels among intensively breastfeeding Nepalese mothers and found that elevated prolactin levels across the interval between nursing bouts increase the odds of maintaining lactation amenorrhea (1996, p. 24; 1994). Their ecology-of-breastfeeding studies explore how culturally mediated differences between groups, including daily work patterns and complementary feeding, result in differences in fertility (1998, p. 191). Links between birth intervals and child mortality were also analyzed in Malawi (Manda 1999) and Nepal (Gubhaju 1986).

Research in developing countries stresses the danger of short birth intervals and the importance of postpartum sexual abstinence for spacing births. In North America, the question commonly asked is whether breastfeeding women are more or less interested in resumption of sexual relations compared to women who are not breastfeeding. According to Shibley-Hyde and colleagues (1996), breastfeeding women resume sexual relations later than women who do not breastfeed; however, research in both developing and industrialized countries generally ignores breastfeeding as a subject relevant to sexuality, reproductive health, or women's reproductive rights.

Embodiment and Subjective Experience

Breastfeeding is accomplished by a gendered body. This obvious fact means that women's decisions on how they use their bodies to nurture their children are framed by attitudes toward their bodies and their breasts that may have nothing to do with breastfeeding. These attitudes were formed long before decisions about child feeding arise. The literature on gender and embodiment—particularly as informed by feminist theory—should shed light on how breasts relate to the self. Though breasts figure prominently in feminist literature on embodiment, they are seldom lactating breasts, but excised, augmented, reduced, deformed, and screened breasts (cf. Lupton 1999, Price & Shildrick 1999). As a result, breastfeeding remains undertheorized in both medical anthropology and the embodiment literature (Maher 1992; Carter 1995; Van Esterik 1994; Blum 1993, 1999; Gorham & Andrews 1990).

Breastfeeding heightens awareness of body as self and body boundaries; but meanings assigned to bodies and boundaries are neither universally shared nor unchanging, as A. Wright and colleagues (1993) demonstrate among the Navaho. The fluidity of the boundaries of self and other threatens the integrity of the body/self. Narratives of the experiences of the breastfeeding body are few in number and are primarily written by or about English-speaking women in industrialized societies (Beasley 1998, Schmied & Lupton 2001, Carter 1995, McLean 1990). Rarely is the narrator a male. When Roth published *The Breast* in 1972, the book was ahead of its time in representing the fleshiness of gendering (Shostak 1999, p. 317). How does one think like a breast? The male author becomes a breast—a sign of female identity. He imagines he is the object of voyeuristic display, just as North American women report feeling when they are the subject of the male gaze.

Different parts of the body have been of interest in different historical periods; breasts caught the attention of eighteenth-century medical practitioners. Breasts as visible signs of femininity symbolized women's role in the family and incorporated the assumption that sexual attraction was founded on the breast in a fusion of aesthetic, medical, and social arguments; "The breasts of women not only symbolized the most fundamental social bond, that between mother and child, but they were also the means by which families were made since their beauty elicited the desires of the male for the female" (Jordanova 1999, p. 162).

Research on embodiment and the subjective experience of breastfeeding is deeply Western in its philosophical assumptions. There is great need for more detailed narratives on the experience of self in relation to breastfeeding from non-Western perspectives. Interdisciplinary research in both semiotics and history may provide new perspectives on embodiment and how breastmilk creates social relationships.

Breastfeeding in Bottle-Feeding Cultures

Another research direction, dominated by more sociological and applied approaches, draws attention to attitudes toward breastfeeding in localities where bottle feeding is more common. In North American society, it is not uncommon for women to begin breastfeeding without ever having observed a breastfeeding couple (Millard 1990, p. 212). This is particularly true for teenage mothers (Ineichen et al. 1997, p. 505). Not surprisingly, research on breastfeeding in Euro-American communities where these conditions apply addresses very different questions and is embedded in very different discourses than research in developing countries.

To complicate matters further, infant feeding, and particularly breastfeeding, is a popular topic in the media, where heartfelt discussions of women who wanted to breastfeed but failed are common; a British woman reported "trying breastfeeding just to shut people up" (Murphy 1999, p. 194). Problems such as feeling "tied down" are ranged against more sentimentalized and romanticized accounts of breastfeeding as a sacred trust and natural pleasure. An analysis of British television and print media concluded that the media rarely present a positive image of breastfeeding (Henderson et al. 2000, p. 1196).

Research in Euro-American contexts reveals how breastfeeding has been rendered pathological, the normal medicalized, and the breastfeeding body has been turned into a site of conflict and struggle. In France, where 60% of infants are artificially fed from birth, cultural resistance to breastfeeding reduces women's access to technical and emotional support for breastfeeding (Castro 2000, p. 234). Murphy explores how British women negotiate the charge of maternal deviance when they choose to bottle feed with infant formula instead of to breastfeed (Murphy 1999, p. 189). An important observation from this study is mothers' interpretations of breastfeeding as risky behavior if the mother is stressed or poorly fed; under these conditions mothers argue that bottle feeding becomes the moral and correct choice (Murphy 1999, p. 197). Mothers' concerns about propriety and breastfeeding in public are generally irrelevant in breastfeeding cultures (Beasley 1998). British women distance themselves from immodest breastfeeding behavior, referring to women who display their bodies as exhibitionists—"flashing your flesh ... flicking it out" ... "I know it's natural but it's not very nice for other people" (Murphy 1999, p. 203). Carter's research on working-class women immigrants in the north of England also portrays breastfeeding as a problem, associated with exhaustion, poverty, discomfort, embarrassment, restriction, and authoritarian hospital practices (1995, p. 90).

In North America it is breastfeeding mothers who are told they are violating public morality when they breastfeed in public, not bottle-feeding mothers. Stearns (1999) explores how mothers in Sonoma, California negotiate the act of breastfeeding in front of others—breastfeeding as public performance. In the words of one informant, "Well, I always felt like the biggest accomplishment that you could make (was) if no one even knew you were breastfeeding" (Stearns 1999, p. 313). In Euro-American societies, where breasts are displayed and if necessary improved, women are aware that breastfeeding in public might lead to negative feedback or even legal action, even though legislation decreed that breastfeeding in public is legal behavior and not public nudity (Stearns 1999, pp. 309–12). As a result, the need for a "tricky public performance" mutes somewhat the pleasure of breastfeeding; women breastfeed "with constant vigilance to location, situation and observer" (1999, p. 323), with an eye to not offending or arousing men. Consequently breastfeeding is work that is rendered invisible both by not counting it and by requiring that it be hidden; "to be expected to hide breastfeeding is to hide much of the early work of mothering" (Stearns 1999, p. 323).

Umansky (1998) reviews the American case of a mother charged with "sexual abuse in the first degree, mentioning 'breast to mouth contact' and 'hand to breast contact' when she mentioned inadvertently on a phone hotline her concern about feeling arousal while breastfeeding. The charges were eventually dropped, but the mother was later charged with abuse and neglect. The case reflects ambiguities concerning how mothering and female sexuality intersect with breastfeeding. The evidence against her included breastfeeding the child "beyond apparently a time when that would be necessary," at times sharing her bed with her two–year-old daughter, and taking a rectal temperature from a frontal position (to maintain eye contact and comfort the child) (Umansky 1998, pp. 300–4).

Schmied & Lupton (2001) provide one of the few accounts dealing with ambiguity and resistance to the imperative to breastfeed. Based on interviews with middle-class women from Sydney, Australia, who viewed breastfeeding as a crucial part of their maternal identity, they explore the intensely embodied experience of breastfeeding (2001, p. 239). Whereas some found the experience pleasurable and intimate, others found it unpleasant and disruptive. The fluidity of the boundary between infant and mother can enhance the harmonious embodied experience of breastfeeding or encourage a sense of loss of self and agency. Leaking breasts epitomize the ambiguity of inside and outside and discomfort with the uncontrolled flow of milk. Britton (1998) documents the revulsion British women feel when they experience the letdown reflex, an embodied sensation they were unprepared for and unable to interpret.

Considering the problems many Euro-American women associate with breastfeeding, and how deeply breastfeeding is culturally embedded in body image, it is understandable that some women who choose to bottle feed and not to breastfeed their infants face special challenges. Often they lack social support systems and other resources for breastfeeding or are literally in transition. Migrant workers, refugees (Tuttle & Dewey 1994, Reeves & Dewey 1994, Townsend & Rice 1996), immigrants (de Bocanegra 1998), Native Americans (Houghton & Graybeal 2001, Wright et al. 1993, Martens 1997, Martens & Young 1997), African Americans, and teenage mothers (Peterson & Da Vanzo 1992, Ineichen et al. 1997), among others, have been identified by health professionals as at-risk groups because of their low incidence of breastfeeding (McLorg & Bryant 1989). They thus become targets for interventions by the health care system. The motivation for such research is often to provide advice for improving compliance among particular immigrant groups, for example, South Asian immigrants (Kannan et al. 1999, p. 90), or low-income African Americans (Bronner et al. 1999), assisted, if possible, by anthropologists (who are valued for their facility in eliciting folk beliefs).

Work and Scheduling

In both developing and industrialized countries, women must find ways to integrate infant care and feeding into their daily activities. This is both a scheduling and a resource problem and is deeply affected by gender ideologies. The congruence of breastfeeding with other activities has been examined from different perspectives and demonstrates the many ways women have synchronized their workloads with child care (Nerlove 1974, Levine 1989, Galtry 2000, Draper 1996). Until recently, health professionals in industrial countries assumed breastfeeding and work away from home were incompatible, and researchers looked to employment as a reason for not breastfeeding. Breastfeeding and women's work cannot be examined independently of the economic and political context of maternity entitlements, health insurance, wages, and child-care arrangements.

In North American studies, Gjerdingen & Froberg found that women's readiness to work postpartum was negatively associated with breastfeeding (1991, p. 1401). Killien (1998) found employment patterns were unrelated to parental stress; however, infant feeding was not considered. Western assumptions about the incompatibility of breastfeeding and women's work are easily communicated cross-culturally; for example, the decline in breastfeeding in China has been related to the fact that 90% of urban women of working age are in the labor force. Gottschang's detailed ethnographic research on baby-friendly hospitals in urban China demonstrates how economic reforms and women's status intersect with the dramatic expansion in the infant food market, particularly American-Chinese joint ventures to produce infant formula (Gottschang 2000, pp. 267–78). Pasternak & Ching argue that "the recent development of a milk industry in China has been a response to the breastfeeding decline rather than its cause" (1985, p. 436). Women working in small neighborhood-run collectives breastfeed longer, confirming that type of work is also relevant. Before returning to work, mothers want infants to become accustomed to milk cakes made from grain and soybean (Pasternak & Ching 1985, p. 437). The introduction of complementary foods is part of the strategy that mothers in many societies use to integrate child care with other work (see also Moffat 2001).

Ethnographic work by Panter-Brick spans medical, cultural, and physical anthropology. Her intensive fieldwork in Nepal included keeping a minute-by-minute time record of activities on a sample of Tamang (Tibeto-Burman) and Kami (Indo-Aryan) women throughout the day and in different seasons to see how a mother's workload influences infant feeding or is influenced by infant feeding (1992, p. 137). She found that among the Tamang, duration of and intervals between breastfeeding sessions vary little by season or work context. Infants are carried to work and fed on demand an average of 8.1 minutes at intervals of 87 minutes; women may work slightly shorter hours in the fields when they are breastfeeding. On the other hand, Kami women have lighter workloads and are less mobile, and their infants are often under paternal supervision (1992, pp. 137–40).

Work as an activity and as a microenvironment varies across socioecological contexts and throughout a woman's life. A new direction for research on breastfeeding and women's work explores the influence of sex hormones and stress hormones on work and health outcomes (Panter-Brick & Pollard 1999, pp. 139–41). In developing countries and resource-poor environments, women are unlikely to be able to discontinue subsistence activities when pregnant or lactating. Workloads affect time available for breastfeeding and supplementary feeding. Although women working in a carpet factory in Kathmandu, Nepal supplemented their infants' diet with gruel or milk-based products by three months, the supplementation did not result in early cessation of breastfeeding (Moffat 2001, p. 330). Many studies examine whether working has a negative impact on breastfeeding, but few ask how breastfeeding impacts on work. Thai women who resumed urban office work by six months postpartum cited problems such as decreased productivity, exhaustion, and lack of concentration on work (Yimyam et al. 1999, p. 964). When obstacles such as rigid schedules and expectations of the modern workplace were encountered, no working women quit work in order to breastfeed.

Research on breastfeeding and women's work is used by both breastfeeding advocates and policy makers to develop strategies for improving working conditions for mothers. In June 2000, the International Labour Organization (ILO) adopted a new Maternity Protection Convention (183) and Recommendation (191) giving employed women longer maternity leaves and lactation breaks during the work day, following substantial lobbying by breastfeeding and workers' groups.

Exclusive Breastfeeding

In May 2001, the World Health Assembly passed Resolution 54.2, which confirmed that the optimal length for exclusive breastfeeding is six months (also after substantial lobbying by breastfeeding advocacy groups). Yet research confirms that exclusive breastfeeding for six months is rare in both industrialized and developing countries, in spite of the evidence for its advantages, particularly in resource-poor settings (Obermeyer & Castle 1996, p. 39; Davies-Adetugbo 1997; Guerrero et al. 1999; Nath & Goswami 1997). Elsewhere in Latin America, Perez-Escamilla and colleagues found that women who delivered in hospital wards in Brazil, Honduras, and Mexico with breastfeeding promotion programs were more likely to breastfeed exclusively (1995, p. 2972). Less than 5% of low-income urban mothers in Costa Rica breastfed exclusively at 4 months, although conditions were quite favorable—high feeding frequency, no use of infant formula, and available time (Munoz & Ulate 1991, p. 59). Over half the mothers were using mixed feeding by 15 days. Exclusive breastfeeding was lower among higher-income groups. Women valued breastfeeding highly but not exclusive breastfeeding. To these mothers, exclusive breastfeeding means denying children something mothers or others think they should have.

Exclusive breastfeeding will be particularly hard to implement where supplementary food and drink products are interpreted as good and effective remedies and not as barriers to exclusive breastfeeding. However, peer counseling programs have increased exclusive breastfeeding in many areas. An intervention in Bangladesh (Haider et al. 2000) found peer counselors trained during a 40-hour course were effective in increasing duration of exclusive breastfeeding. The women they helped initiated breastfeeding earlier and were less likely to give prelacteal and postlacteal foods such as honey and mustard oil, often given by family members in keeping with traditional custom. Unfortunately, the project paid the peer counselors, and when the project ended so did the pay; consequently, the counselors stopped counseling mothers (2000, p. 1647).

Although UN agencies put substantial emphasis on exclusive breastfeeding, and clinical and epidemiological research both confirm the benefits, still more detailed ethnographic work would be valuable for understanding the constraints that make exclusive breastfeeding difficult in both developing and industrialized countries.

COMPLEMENTARY FEEDING

Research and policy on breastfeeding is often separated from research and policy on complementary feeding, as if breastfeeding advocates who integrate their work with complementary feeding dilute the message of the importance of exclusive breastfeeding. From the perspective of mothers and households, the two issues must be considered together. The World Health Organization's (WHO) new global strategy to improve child feeding integrates policies on breastfeeding with recommendations for appropriate complementary feeding, and it acknowledges the problem of aggressive marketing of processed complementary foods as well as breastmilk substitutes.

Around six months of age, infants are ready to begin the process of ingesting foods other than breastmilk. In some parts of the world, this process starts long before six months; in other parts of the world, much later (Bentley et al. 1991, Jarosz 1993). The transition is culturally significant, often stressful, and sometimes accompanied by a growth decline between 6 and 18 months of age (Michaelson & Friis 1998, p. 763).

Dettwyler (1998) explores the idea that current infant feeding practices in the United States and elsewhere conflict with underlying evolutionary adaptations. Using primate data and ethnographic sources, she proposes that the natural duration of breastfeeding for humans might be somewhere between 2.5 and 7 years, and she also demonstrates that the duration of breastfeeding directly affects human health over the entire lifespan and not just infant survival.

Weaning refers to both the introduction of food products other than breastmilk and the cessation of breastfeeding (sevrage). Anthropologists have generally chosen to focus on the weaning interval or the weaning process, stressing the multiple transitions involved. The weaning dilemma refers to these difficult, complex trade-offs. Nutritionists and health professionals argue that food provides extra needed nutrients to the growing infant but increases the potential for introducing pathogens (Williams 1991, Martines et al. 1994); to demographers and evolutionary anthropologists, the infant's nutritional needs for breastmilk compete with the mother's nutrient needs for herself and perhaps for starting another pregnancy (Charnov & Berrigan 1993, Rashid & Ulijaszek 1999, Lee 1996); to cultural anthropologists, sevrage also completes the separation begun at birth, ending a special period of bodily intimacy with the mother and introducing a new and separate individual into the household and community.

Transition to Household Foods

The transition to complementary foods presents particular challenges in low-income households (Almedom 1991, Guttman & Zimmerman 2000, Harrison et al.

1993). In periurban Peru, women would return to breastfeeding if children strongly resisted weaning or were in poor health. Mothers would initiate weaning if they had concerns about their own health, including weight loss, and the time commitment of breastfeeding (not the minutes spent feeding the child but the continuous interruption of work tasks) (Marquis et al. 1998, p. 651). Mothers make careful observations of infants' appetite, and infant characteristics may influence their decisions about introducing an item of food or drink into an infant's regular diet (Piwoz et al. 1994, p. 854).

Introducing infant foods involves choices made in the context of environmental constraints, reproductive demands on women, and levels of infant and child mortality (Gray 1996, p. 437). Gray's research with the pastoral Turkana of Kenya explores the adaptiveness of early supplementation with solids in harsh ecological conditions, where there are heavy labor demands on mothers who may also be in poor health and where cow's milk is available. There is a culturally prescribed order for introducing foods to infants beginning with the forced feeding of camel butterfat at a few weeks of age, a practice the author identifies as adaptive because it enhances infant fat storage. Mothers wean their infants with more confidence after the weanling had accepted the taste of blood cooked with milk or porridge (1996, p. 444). Gray argues, "Exclusive breastfeeding in the first 4–6 months confers no health advantage to infants other than immunological effects, which are passed on to the infant regardless of early introduction of non-breast-milk foods" (1996, p. 451), a conclusion that many might challenge.

Tamang (Nepali) mothers often breastfeed their children while they have their meals; thus the breastfeeding infant or toddler is integrated into the system of commensality, joining the mother at the table, so to speak. Tamang toddlers who do not accompany their mothers to work may be fed cold leftovers of hastily prepared maize gruel often contaminated in the heat. These conditions facilitate sevrage (Panter-Brick 1992, pp. 138–39). Mothers in rural Senegal adjust their feeding practices in response to the growth and nutritional status of their infants, giving watery maize gruel to small thin infants as a response to perceived milk insufficiency (Simondon & Simondon 1995, p. 179). But here, as in other communities, the early introduction of complementary foods does not necessarily result in milk insufficiency or sevrage.

Taste is a critical dimension but seldom considered in research on infant feeding. An exception to this is the work of Mennella (1995). Her research confirms that human milk, unlike infant formula, is not a food of invariant flavor but is flavored by ingested compounds such as garlic, mint, vanilla, peppers, and alcohol, to give the infant varying sensory experiences. The past exposure of infants to these flavors in utero may affect their response to the flavors in breastmilk. The sensory attributes of breastmilk may influence the patterning and duration of suckling (1995, p. 41). The opportunity for infants to become familiar with the foods eaten by their mothers is another benefit of breastfeeding. Amniotic fluid, also flavored by the foods consumed by the pregnant woman, acts as a flavor bridge to breastmilk, and breastmilk as a flavor bridge to solid foods (1995, p. 43). In another study, Mennella

& Beauchamp found that infants consumed more cereal when it was mixed with mother's milk than when it was mixed with water (1997, p. 188). Mothers who ate new foods and were not neophobic had infants who consumed more of the cereal/breastmilk mixture, possibly because the infants had been exposed to a wider variety of taste experiences in utero. The research suggests that the process of accustoming an infant to the food and flavor of its culture begins in utero (Mennella & Beauchamp 1997, p. 191).

Overwhelmingly the responsibility of mothers, complementary feeding is time-intensive work. Gryboski (1996) recorded time allocated to breastfeeding and other infant care activities in a Central Javanese village. Her research demonstrates how breastfeeding, complementary feeding, and household provisioning are interconnected. Consider one woman who sold fried bananas in a local market. She brought her daughter with her in order to breastfeed. In addition she received discounted prices on foods purchased for her family from other traders. They also provided extra snacks for her daughter, pampering her in part because of her endearing qualities (Gryboski 1996, p. 213).

Based on local market prices in rural Bangladesh, it would cost at least an additional 21% of the daily wage to provide adequate nutrient intakes for lactating women, but only 8% of the daily wage to provide adequate complementary foods for children (Brown et al. 1993). Nutrition education messages on improving complementary feeding were effective, but those directing women to improve their own diet were not effective (1993, p. 100), as they contradicted cultural assumptions about the sacrificing mother who restricts her own food intake.

These latter two studies are a reminder that understanding child feeding and developing nutrition interventions to improve child feeding require a deep understanding of concepts such as reciprocity, commensality, nurture (Van Esterik 1997), and household meal cycles. Generally, research interests in complementary feeding have shifted to these broader social issues, away from a focus on food prescriptions and proscriptions and the classifications of food suitable for infants (cf. Sukkary-Stolba 1987).

CHALLENGES TO ADVOCACY AND POLICY

"It is said that at night a serpent may crawl surreptitiously into the bedroom where an infant and its nursing mother may be sleeping. When the child awakens from hunger and begins to cry, the serpent suckles the mother's breast and inserts its tail into the infant's mouth. In this manner the serpent draws nourishment from the mother's body at the expense of the infant..." (Brandes 1980, p. 82). This Andalusian folk tale expresses a masculine view of breastmilk as a vulnerable product in short supply and implies a devaluation of the mothers producing it.

Among the squatter settlements and rural villages of Pakistan, breastmilk is regarded as a potential source of destruction as well as nurturance (Mull 1992). Although highly valued, breastmilk is considered susceptible to being tainted by spirits, the evil eye, black magic, the effects of the next pregnancy, and the mother's diet. A woman knows that her breastmilk will be blamed for a child's sickness and death, and if the quality of her breastmilk is questioned, she will have strong incentive to stop breastfeeding until she can have her milk tested for "poison." Both folk healers (who float an insect in the milk) and hospital pathology laboratories (who perform pseudoscientific analyses for "bacteria" and "pus cells") provide these services to address women's anxieties about the quality of their milk (Mull 1992, p. 1286).

There is some congruence between these expressed anxieties about the quality of breastmilk and contemporary concerns about a number of substances that may pass from mother to child through breastmilk. These include HIV and chemical residues. Both subjects require a careful weighing of public health risks and attention to the needs of mothers. In both cases, there are significant information gaps and widely contested claims. For example, we do not know the rate of HIV transmission in exclusively breastfed, formula-fed, and mixed-fed babies, or the mortality rates related to feeding methods in infected and uninfected babies. In the case of chemical residues in breastmilk, we do not know the long-term health consequences for infants and children. Yet public discourse around these subjects has great potential for influencing women's infant-feeding decisions.

HIV/AIDS transmission from mother to child can occur through breastfeeding, although there is a greater chance of transmission during pregnancy and delivery; it is difficult to make a distinction between intrauterine, perinatal, and postnatal transmission. A child breastfeeding from a woman who is HIV-positive has about a 14% risk of infection through breastfeeding (Dunn et al. 1992). Considering communities with a 20% HIV infection rate, only three infants out of 100 are likely to be infected with HIV through breastfeeding, leaving 97 infants who would benefit from breastfeeding. Researchers in South Africa suggest that "it may be more pertinent for health workers to quote a risk of about 5% if breastfeeding is practiced for 6 months . . ." (Coovadia & Coutsoudis 2001, p. 1). For HIV-positive mothers who have chosen to breastfeed or for whom breastfeeding is the only option available (particularly in resource-poor settings where mothers cannot bottle-feed safely), it is possible to support women in their choice to breastfeed and continue effective treatment for them (Castro & Mukherjee 2002); women can be informed of the dangers of mixed feeding and helped to breastfeed exclusively; breast problems can be prevented or treated early, and the use of condoms during intercourse can help avoid further transmission of HIV during the period of lactation (Linkages 1998). Other options include the use of heat-treated expressed breastmilk. In some countries, health care workers are required to advise HIV-positive mothers not to breastfeed, ignoring evidence that exclusive breastfeeding may have as good an outcome as exclusive use of infant formula (Coutsoudis et al. 1999, Coovadia & Coutsoudis 2001). However, no one has been able to show conclusively whether avoiding breastfeeding in low-income, resource-poor settings leads to increased infant survival. Considering that infants in developing countries who are not breastfed have a sixfold greater risk of dying from infectious diseases in the first two months of life than do breastfed infants (WHO 2000), the widespread use of replacement feeding is a questionable solution. Anthropologists already active in AIDS research need to enter these debates and bring a more critical approach to this complex problem.

Similarly, because of widespread chemical contaminants in both rural and urban environments, toxic substances such as polychlorinated biphenyls, dioxins, and heavy metals have been found in samples of breastmilk (Johansen 2000, Guillette et al. 1998). Although more contaminants are passed in utero than through breastmilk, media reports of breastmilk contamination highlight breastfeeding women as the source of contamination rather than the chemical industries (Van Esterik 2001), and demonstrate the extent to which risk discourse is laden with morality (Murphy 2000, p. 321). The unspoken discourse in much of this literature on contaminants in breastmilk is premised on women's bodies—particularly their breasts—as risky environments, sources of problems and impurities. Thus, even complex public health policy issues such as HIV and contaminants in breastmilk need to be linked to considerations of embodiment, power, and gender.

Globalization and Corporate Initiatives

The breastfeeding movement, a single-issue social movement with broad implications for understanding issues of women's reproductive rights, corporatization, poverty, and food security, provides a concrete and easily understood example of how globalization affects infant feeding. It is one of the only advocacy movements to have succeeded in getting an international code that addresses the inappropriate marketing of a consumer product: the International Code for the Marketing of Breastmilk Substitutes, WHO/UNICEF 1981. For those who supported the Nestlé boycott in the 1970s and 1980s or use this example of consumer activism in their teaching (Van Esterik 1989, Pettigrew 1993), updated information can be found on the websites of advocacy groups monitoring code compliance (or lack thereof). Globalization puts these accomplishments at risk through free trade agreements and corporate strategies that undercut national legislation to limit the aggressive promotion of infant feeding products. Other corporate strategies that need to be monitored include the development of genetically modified cow's milk formula made with proteins from human breastmilk. When the female body is valued for its reproductive potential and therefore regulated, women are special targets of commodification (Sharp 2000, p. 293). Who will own the DNA for reproductive products such as breastmilk? Should it be the "life industries" who value human milk proteins more than human milk itself and who have little interest in the women who produce that milk?

CONCLUSION

Although breastfeeding and child feeding remain narrowly specialized domains of inquiry, these subjects raise questions of fundamental importance to the theory and practice of anthropology. The fragmentation of research agendas across subfields and disciplines makes it difficult to address broad questions about the political economy of child feeding. Anthropology has the potential to make explicit the interconnections between social relations, resources, sexuality, embodiment, power, nurturance, and commensality implicated in the challenge of feeding a newborn infant. No other discipline is positioned to ask and answer such fundamental questions about what makes us human.

ACKNOWLEDGMENTS

Many thanks to Debra Pelletier and John Van Esterik whose research assistance made it possible for me to prepare this article while traveling on sabbatical, to the many colleagues who suggested references, and to members of the departments of anthropology at University of Hawaii, Hilo and University of California, Berkeley, who provided refuge and inspiration during the editing process.

The *Annual Review of Anthropology* is online at http://anthro.annualreviews.org

LITERATURE CITED

Aborampah O. 1985. Determinants of breastfeeding and post-partum sexual abstinence: analysis of a sample of Yoruba women, Western Nigeria. *J. Biosoc. Sci.* 17:461–69

Agyei W. 1984. Breastfeeding and sexual abstinence in Papua New Guinea. *J. Biosoc. Sci.* 16:451–61

Almedom AM. 1991. Infant feeding in urban low-income households in Ethiopia: I. The weaning process. *Ecol. Food Nutr.* 25:97–109

Beasley AN. 1998. Breastfeeding and the body politic. *Women's Stud. J.* 14(1):61–82

Bentley ME, Dickin KL, Mebrahtu S, Kayode B, Oni GA, et al. 1991. Development of a nutritionally adequate and culturally appropriate weaning food in Kwara State, Nigeria: an interdisciplinary approach. *Soc. Sci. Med.* 33(10):1103–11

Blakely RJ. 1989. Bone strontium in pregnant and lactating females from archaeological samples. *Am. J. Phys. Anthropol.* 80:173–85

Blum LM. 1993. Mothers, babies, and breastfeeding in late capitalist America: the shifting contexts of feminist theory. *Fem. Stud.* 19(2):290–312

Blum LM. 1999. *At the Breast.* Boston: Beacon

Bohler E, Ingstad B. 1996. The struggle of weaning: factors determining breastfeeding duration in East Bhutan. *Soc. Sci. Med.* 43:1805–15

Brandes S. 1980. *Metaphors of Masculinity: Sex and Status in Andalusian Folklore.* Philadelphia: Univ. Penn. Press

Britton C. 1998. Feeling letdown: an exploration of an embodied sensation associated with breastfeeding. In *The Body in Everyday Life*, ed. S Nettleton, J Watson, pp. 64–81. London: Routledge

Bronner Y, Gross SM, Caulfield L, Bentley ME, Kessler L, et al. 1999. Early introduction of solid foods among urban African-American participants in WIC. *J. Am. Diet. Assoc.* 99:457–62

Brown LV, Rogers BL, Zeitlin MF, Gershoff SN, Huq N, Peterson KE. 1993. Comparison of the costs of compliance with nutrition education messages to improve the diets of Bangladeshi breastfeeding mothers and weaning-age children. *Ecol. Food Nutr.* 30:99–126

Carter P. 1995. *Feminism, Breasts and Breast-Feeding*. New York: St. Martin's Press

Castro A, Marchand-Lucas L. 2000. Does authoritative knowledge in infant feeding nutrition lead to successful breast-feeding? A critical perspective. See Whiteford & Manderson 2000, pp. 233–63

Castro A, Mukherjee J. 2002. The political economy of the prevention of postnatal transmission of HIV. Proc. 14th Int. AIDS Conf. Barcelona, Spain

Charnov EL, Berrigan D. 1993. Why do female primates have such long lifespans and so few babies? or life in the slow lane. *Evol. Anthropol.* 1(6):191–94

Cohen RJ, Brown KH, Canahuati J, Rivera LL, Dewey KG. 1994. Effects of age of introduction of complementary foods on infant breast milk intake, total energy intake and growth: a randomized intervention study in Honduras. *Lancet* 344:288–93

Coovadia HM, Coutsoudis A. 2001. Problems and advances in reducing transmission of HIV-1 through breast-feeding in developing countries. *AIDScience* 1(4):1–10

Cosminsky S, Mhloyi M, Ewbank D. 1993. Child feeding practices in a rural area of Zimbabwe. *Soc. Sci. Med.* 36:937–47

Coutsoudis A, Pillay K, Spooner E, Kuhn L, Coovadia HM. 1999. Influence of infant-feeding patterns on early mother-to-child transmission of HIV-1 in Durban, South Africa: a prospective cohort study. *Lancet* 354:471–85

Daly SE, Hartmann P. 1995. Infant demand and milk supply. Part 1: infant demand and milk production in lactating women. Part 2: the short term control of milk synthesis in lactating women. *J. Hum. Lact.* 11(1):21–37

Davies-Adetugbo AA. 1997. Sociocultural factors and the promotion of exclusive breast-feeding in rural Yoruba communities of Osun State, Nigeria. *Soc. Sci. Med.* 45(1):113–25

de Bocanegra HT. 1998. Breast-feeding in immigrant women: the role of social support and acculturation. *Hisp. J. Behav. Sci.* 20(4):448–68

Dettwyler KA. 1998. Evolutionary medicine and breastfeeding: implications for research and pediatric advice. *David Skomp Disting. Lect. Anthropol. 1998–99*. Indiana Univ., Bloomington

Dettwyler KA, Fishman C. 1992. Infant feeding practices and growth. *Annu. Rev. Anthropol.* 21:171–204

Draper SB. 1996. Breastfeeding as a sustainable resource system. *Am. Anthropol.* 98(2):258–65

Dunn DT, Newell ML, Ades AE, Peckham CS. 1992. Risk of human immunodeficiency virus type 1 transmission through breastfeeding. *Lancet* 340:585–88

Ellison P. 2001. *On Fertile Ground.* London: Harvard Univ. Press

Galtry J. 2000. Extending the "bright line:" feminism, breastfeeding, and the workplace in the United States. *Gender Soc.* 14(2):295–317

Gjerdingen DK, Froberg D. 1991. Predictors of health in new mothers. *Soc. Sci. Med.* 33(12): 1399–1407

Gorham D, Andrews FK. 1990. La Leche League: a feminist perspective. In *Delivering Motherhood*, ed. K Arrup, A Levesque, R Pierson. London: Routledge

Gottschang SZ. 2000. Reforming routines: a baby-friendly hospital in urban China. See Whiteford & Manderson 2000, pp. 265–87

Gray S. 1996. Ecology of weaning among nomadic pastoralists of Kenya: maternal thinking, maternal behaviour and human adaptive strategies. *Hum. Biol.* 68:437–62

Gryboski KL. 1996. Maternal and non-maternal time-allocation to infant care, and care during infant illness in rural Java, Indonesia. *Soc. Sci. Med.* 43(2):209–19

Gubhaju B. 1986. Effect of birth spacing on infant and child mortality in rural Nepal. *J. Biosoc. Sci.* 18:435–47

Guerrero ML, Morrow RC, Calva JJ, Ortega-Gallegos H, Weller SC, et al. 1999. Rapid ethnographic assessment of breastfeeding practices in periurban Mexico City. *Bull. WHO* 77(4):323–36

Guillette EA, Meza MM, Aquilar MG, Soto

AD, Garcia IE. 1998. An anthropological approach to the evaluation of preschool children exposed to pesticides in Mexico. *Environ. Health Perspect.* 106(6):347–53

Guttman N, Zimmerman D. 2000. Low-income mothers' views on breastfeeding. *Soc. Sci. Med.* 50(10):1457–473

Haider R, Ashworth A, Kabir I, Huttly SRA. 2000. Effect of community-based peer counselors on exclusive breastfeeding practices in Dhaka, Bangladesh: a randomised controlled trial. *Lancet* 356:1643–47

Harrison G, Zaghloul S, Galal O, Gabr A. 1993. Breastfeeding and weaning in a poor urban neighbourhood in Cairo, Egypt: maternal beliefs and perceptions. *Soc. Sci. Med.* 36(8):1063–69

Henderson L, Kitzinger J, Green J. 2000. Representing infant feeding: content analysis of British media portrayals of bottle feeding and breastfeeding. *Br. Med. J.* 321(7270):1196

Herring DA, Saunders SR, Katzenberg MA. 1998. Investigating the weaning process in past populations. *Am. J. Phys. Anthropol.* 105(4):425–39

Herring DA, Saunders SR, Katzenberg MA. 1994. Multiple methods for estimating weaning age in a 19th century cemetery sample from Upper Canada. *Am. J. Phys. Anthropol. Suppl.* 18:106 (Abstr.)

Houghton M, Graybeal T. 2001. Breastfeeding practices of Native American mothers participating in WIC. *J. Am. Diet. Assoc.* 101:245–51

Howard M, Millard A. 1997. *Hunger and Shame: Child Malnutrition and Poverty on Mount Kilimanjaro*. New York: Routledge

Hsiung P-C. 1995. To nurse the young: breastfeeding and infant feeding in late imperial China. *J. Fam. Hist.* 20(3):217–39

Hundt GA, Forman MR. 1993. Interfacing anthropology and epidemiology: the Bedouin Arab infant feeding study. *Soc. Sci. Med.* 36(7):957–64

Ineichen B, Pierce M, Lawrenson R. 1997. Teenage mothers as breastfeeders: attitudes and behaviour. *J. Adolesc.* 20:505–9

Jarosz LA. 1993. Liberian practices in feeding infants water, breastmilk and first food. *Ecol. Food Nutr.* 30:221–40

Johansen B. 2000. Pristine no more. The Arctic, where mothers' milk is toxic. *Progressive* 64:27–29

Jones RE. 1989. Breast-feeding and postpartum amenorrhoea in Indonesia. *J. Biosoc. Sci.* 21:83–100

Jordanova L. 1999. Natural facts: a historical perspective on science and sexuality. In *Feminist Theory and the Body. A Reader*, ed. J Price, M Shildrick, pp. 157–68. New York: Routledge

Kannan S, Carruth B, Skinner J. 1999. Cultural influences on infant feeding beliefs of mothers. *J. Am. Diet. Assoc.* 99(1):88–90

Katzenberg MA, Herring DA, Saunders SR. 1996. Weaning and infant mortality: evaluating the skeletal evidence. *Yearb. Phys. Anthropol.* 39:177–99

Khatib-Chahibi J. 1992. Milk kinship in Shi'ite Islamic Iran. See Maher 1992, pp. 109–32

Killien MG. 1998. Postpartum return to work: mothering stress, anxiety, and gratification. *Can. J. Nurs. Res.* 30(3):53–66

Kurtz SN. 1992. *All the Mothers are One*. New York: Columbia Univ. Press

Kwiatkowski L. 1999. *Struggling with Development*. Boulder, CO: Westview

Lee PC. 1996. Meanings of weaning: growth, lactation, and life history. *Evol. Anthropol.* 5(3):87–96

Levine NE. 1989. Women's work and infant feeding: a case from rural Nepal. *Ethnology* 27:231–51

Linkages. 1998. *Frequently Asked Questions on Breastfeeding and HIV/AIDS*. Washington, DC: Linkages

Lupton D. 1999. *Risk and Sociocultural Theory*. New York: Cambridge Univ. Press

Maher V, ed. 1992. *The Anthropology of Breastfeeding: Natural Law or Social Construct*. Oxford: Berg

Manda SO. 1999. Birth intervals, breastfeeding and determinants of childhood mortality in Malawi. *Soc. Sci. Med.* 48:301–12

Manning JT, Scott D, Whitehouse GH, Leinster SJ. 1997. Breast asymmetry and phenotypic quality in women. *Evol. Hum. Behav.* 18: 223–36

Marquis G, Diaz J, Bartolini R, Kanahiro H, Rasmussen K. 1998. Recognizing the reversible nature of child-feeding decisions: breastfeeding, weaning and relactation patterns in a shanty town community of Lima, Peru. *Soc. Sci. Med.* 47:645–56

Martens PJ. 1997. Prenatal infant feeding intent and perceived social support for breastfeeding in Manitoba First Nations communities: a role for health care providers. *Int. J. Circumpolar Health.* 56:104–20

Martens PJ, Young TK. 1997. Determinants of breastfeeding in four Canadian Ojibwa communities: a decision-making model. *Am. J. Hum. Biol.* 9:579–93

Martines JC, Habicht JP, Ashworth A, Kirkwood BR. 1994. Weaning in Southern Brazil: Is there a weanlings dilemma? *J. Nutr.* 124: 1189–98

McKenna J, Bernshaw N. 1995. Breastfeeding and infant-parent co-sleeping as adaptive strategies: Are they protective against SIDS? See Stuart-Macadam & Dettwyler 1995, pp. 265–304

McLean H. 1990. *Women's Experience of Breastfeeding*. Toronto: Univ. Toronto Press

McLorg PA, Bryant CA. 1989. Influence of social network members and health care professionals on infant feeding practices of economically disadvantaged mothers. *Med. Anthropol.* 10(4):265–78

Mennella JA. 1995. Mother's milk: a medium for early flavor experiences. *J. Hum. Lact.* 11(1):39–45

Mennella JA, Beauchamp GK. 1997. Mother's milk enhances the acceptance of cereal during weaning. *Pediatr. Res.* 41(2):188–92

Michaelsen KF, Friis H. 1998. Complementary feeding: a global perspective. *Nutrition* 14: 763–66

Millard A. 1990. The place of the clock in pediatric advice: rationales, cultural themes and impediments to breastfeeding. *Soc. Sci. Med.* 31(2):211–21

Moffat T. 2001. A biocultural investigation of the weanling's dilemma in Kathmandu, Nepal. Do universal recommendations for weaning practices make sense? *J. Biosoc. Sci.* 33:321–38

Moggi-Cecchi J, Pacciani E, Pinto-Cisternas J. 1994. Enamel hypoplasia and age at weaning in 19th-century Florence, Italy. *Am. J. Phys. Anthropol.* 93(3):299–306

Mull D. 1992. Mother's milk and pseudoscientific breastmilk testing in Pakistan. *Soc. Sci. Med.* 34(11):1277–90

Muñoz LM, Ulate E. 1991. Breast-feeding patterns of urban low to middle income women in Costa Rica. *Ecol. Food Nutr.* 25:59–67

Murphy E. 1999. Breast is best: infant feeding decisions and maternal deviance. *Sociol. Health Illn.* 21:187–208

Murphy E. 2000. Risk, responsibility, and rhetoric in infant feeding. *J. Contemp. Ethnog.* 29(3):291–325

Nath D, Goswami G. 1997. Determinants of breastfeeding patterns in an urban society of India. *Hum. Biol.* 69:557–71

Nerlove SB. 1974. Women's workload and infant feeding practices: a relationship with demographic implications. *Ethnology* 13:207–14

Obermeyer CM, Castle S. 1996. Back to nature? historical and cross-cultural perspectives on barriers to optimal breastfeeding. *Med. Anthropol.* 17(1):39–63

Okongwu AF, Mencher JP. 2000. The anthropology of public policy: shifting terrains. *Annu. Rev. Anthropol.* 29:107–24

Oni G. 1987. Breast-feeding patterns in an urban Nigerian community. *J. Biosoc. Sci.* 19: 453–62

Panter-Brick C. 1992. Working mothers in rural Nepal. See Maher 1992, pp. 133–50

Panter-Brick C, Pollard TM. 1999. Work and hormonal variation in subsistence industrial contexts. In *Hormones Health and Behaviour: a Socio-Ecological and Lifespan Perspective*, ed. C Panter-Brick, CM Worthman, pp. 139–83. Cambridge, UK: Cambridge Univ. Press

Parkes P. 2001. Alternative social structures

and foster relation in the Hindu Kush: milk kinship allegiance in former mountain kingdoms of northern Pakistan. *Comp. Stud. Soc. Hist.* 43:4–36

Pasternak B, Ching W. 1985. Breastfeeding decline in urban China: an exploratory study. *Hum. Ecol.* 13(4):433–65

Perez-Escamilla R, Mejia LA, Dewey KG. 1995. Neonatal feeding patterns and reports on insufficient milk among low-income urban Mexican mothers. *Ecol. Food Nutr.* 27: 91–102

Peterson C, Da Vanzo J. 1992. Why are teenagers in the United States less likely to breastfeed than older women? *Demography* 29(3): 431–50

Piwoz E, Black R, de Romana GL, de Kanashiro HC, Brown K. 1994. The relationship between infants' preceding appetite, illness and growth performance and mothers' subsequent feeding practice decisions. *Soc. Sci. Med.* 39(6):851–60

Price J, Shildrick M. 1999. Mapping the colonial body: sexual economies and the state in colonial India. In *Feminist Theory and the Body*, ed. J Price, M Shildrick, pp. 388–98. New York: Routledge

Rashid M, Ulijaszek S. 1999. Daily energy expenditure across the course of lactation among urban Bangladeshi women. *Am. J. Phys. Anthropol.* 110:457–65

Rosenberg M. 1989. Breast-feeding and infant mortality in Norway, 1860–1930. *J. Biosoc. Sci.* 21:335–48

Roth P. 1972. *The Breast*. New York: Vintage

Scheper-Hughes N. 1992. *Death Without Weeping*. Berkeley: Univ. Calif. Press

Schmied V, Lupton D. 2001. Blurring the boundaries: breastfeeding and maternal subjectivity. *Sociol. Health Illn.* 23:234–50

Sharp LA. 2000. The commodification of the body and its parts. *Annu. Rev. Anthropol.* 29: 287–328

Shibley-Hyde J, DeLamater JD, Ashby-Plant E, Byrd JM. 1996. Sexuality during pregnancy and the year postpartum. *J. Sex Res.* 33:143–51

Shostak D. 1999. Return to the breast: the body, the masculine subject and Philip Roth. *Twentieth Century Lit.* 45(3):317–35

Sillen A, Smith P. 1984. Weaning patterns are reflected in strontium-calcium ratios of juvenile skeletons. *J. Archaeol. Sci.* 11:237–45

Simondon KB, Simondon F. 1995. Infant feeding and nutritional status: the dilemma of mothers in rural Senegal. *Eur. J. Clin. Nutr.* 49:179–88

Stallings JF, Worthman CM, Panter-Brick C. 1994. Prolactin levels in nursing Tamang Kami women: effects of nursing practices on lactational amenorrhea. *Am. J. Phys. Anthropol. Suppl.* 18:185–86

Stallings JF, Worthman CM, Panter-Brick C. 1998. Biological and behavioral factors influence group differences in prolactin levels among breastfeeding Nepali women. *Am. J. Hum. Biol.* 10:191–210

Stallings JF, Worthman CM, Panter-Brick C, Coates RJ. 1996. Prolactin response to suckling and maintenance of postpartum amenorrhea among intensively breastfeeding Nepali women. *Endocr. Res.* 22(1):1–28

Stearns CA. 1999. Breastfeeding and the good maternal body. *Gender Soc.* 13(3):308–25

Steingraber S. 2001. *Having Faith: an Ecologist's Journey to Motherhood*. Cambridge, MA: Perseus

Stuart-Macadam P, Dettwyler K, eds. 1995. *Breastfeeding: Bicultural Perspectives*. New York: Aldine de Gruyter

Sukkary-Stolba S. 1987. Food classifications and the diets of young children in rural Egypt. *Soc. Sci. Med.* 25(4):401–4

Townsend K, Rice P. 1996. A baby is born in site 2 camp: pregnancy, birth and confinement among Cambodian refugee women. In *Maternity and Reproductive Health in Asian Societies*, ed. PL Rice, L Manderson, pp. 125–43. Australia: Harwood Acad.

Treckel PA. 1989. Breastfeeding and maternal sexuality in colonial America. *J. Interdiscip. Hist.* 20(1):25–51

Tuttle CR, Dewey KG. 1994. Determinants in infant feeding choices among Southeast Asian immigrants in northern California. *J. Am. Diet. Assoc.* 94(3):282–85

Umansky L. 1998. Breastfeeding in the 1990s: the Karen Carter case and the politics of maternal sexuality. In *Bad Mothers: the Politics of Blame in Twentieth Century America*, ed. M Ladd-Taylor, L Umansky, pp. 299–309. New York: NY Univ. Press

Van Esterik P. 1989. *Beyond the Breast-Bottle Controversy*. New Brunswick, NJ: Rutgers Univ. Press

Van Esterik P. 1994. Breastfeeding and feminism. *Int. J. Gynecol. Obstet.* 47(Suppl.): 41–54

Van Esterik P. 1997. Women and nurture in industrial societies. *Proc. Nutr. Soc.* 56(1B): 335–43

Van Esterik P. 2001. Risks, rights and regulation: communicating about risks and infant feeding. *Work. Pap. World Alliance for Breastfeeding Action, Penang, Malaysia*

Whitaker E. 2000. *Measuring Mamma's Milk: Fascism and the Medicalization of Maternity in Italy*. Ann Arbor: Univ. Mich. Press

Whiteford L, Manderson L, eds. 2000. *Global Health Policy, Local Realities: the Fallacy of the Level Playing Field*. Boulder, CO: Lynne Rienner

Whittemore RD, Beverly EA. 1996. Mandinka mothers and nurslings: power and reproduction. *Med. Anthropol. Q.* 10(1):45–62

WHO Collaborative Study Team. 2000. On the role of breastfeeding in the prevention of infant mortality. Effect of breastfeeding on infant and child mortality due to infectious diseases in less developed countries: a pooled analysis. *Lancet* 355:451–55

Williams W. 1991. Solving the weanling's dilemma: power-flour to fuel the gruel? (Editorial). *Lancet* 338(8767):604–6

Wright AL, Bauer M, Clark C, Morgan F, Begishe K. 1993. Cultural interpretations and intracultural variability in Navajo beliefs about breastfeeding. *Am. Ethnol.* 20(4):781–96

Wright LE, Schwarcz HP. 1998. Stable carbon and oxygen isotopes in human tooth enamel: identifying breastfeeding and weaning in prehistory. *Am. J. Phys. Anthropol.* 106(1): 1–18

Yimyam S, Morrow M, Srisuphan W. 1999. Role conflict and rapid socio-economic change: breastfeeding among employed women in Thailand. *Soc. Sci. Med.* 49(7): 957–65

Annu. Rev. Anthropol. 2002. 31:279–301
doi: 10.1146/annurev.anthro.31.040402.085457

First published online as a Review in Advance on June 4, 2002

THE INTERSECTIONS OF IDENTITY AND POLITICS IN ARCHAEOLOGY

Lynn Meskell
Department of Anthropology, Columbia University, 1200 Amsterdam Avenue, New York, NY 10027; email: lmm64@columbia.edu

Key Words ethnicity, nationalism, gender, diaspora, postcolonialism

■ **Abstract** This paper traces the conjunction of two interrelated epistemic phenomena that have begun to shape the discipline since the early 1990s. The first entails theorizing social identity in past societies: specifically, how social lives are inscribed by the experiences of gender, ethnicity, sexuality, and so on. The other constitutes the rise of a politicized and ethical archaeology that now recognizes its active role in contemporary culture and is enunciated through the discourses of nationalism, sociopolitics, postcolonialism, diaspora, and globalism. Both trends have been tacitly shaped by anthropological and social theory, but they are fundamentally driven by the powerful voices of once marginalized groups and their newfound place in the circles of academic legitimacy. I argue that our disciplinary reticence to embrace the politics of identity, both in our investigations of the past and our imbrications in the present, has much to do with archaeology's lack of reflexivity, both personal and disciplinary, concurrent with its antitheoretical tendencies. The residual force of the latter should not be underestimated, specifically in regard to field practices and the tenacity of academic boundaries.

GETTING PERSONAL

Returning home to Australia in 2000, I was reminded that racism runs riot in the small towns and suburbs of this supposedly young and lucky country. My first recollection is a newspaper clipping, placed prominently, advocating that "white" Australians stop apologizing to Aborigines for the sustained atrocities of colonization and genocide. Australia is largely populated by migrants of British and European descent whose recombinant identities are often privileged over newer foreign arrivals. You can feel how prejudice is enacted, each conversation suffused with deep-seated fears surrounding difference—be it racial, ethnic, cultural, or even sexual. The federal government had just legislated against same-sex couples' or single people's rights to in vitro fertilization (IVF) treatment: It declared that such people exist outside the bounds of the natural family. Dislocation and mis/identification are often foundational in delineating what Irigaray calls the burning question of our time: identity. Put simply, identity refers to the ways in which individuals and collectivities are distinguished in their social relations with other individuals and collectivities (Jenkins 1996, p. 4). In the "social and cultural sciences, what was once called 'identity' in the sense of social, shared sameness is today often discussed with reference to difference. Difference points to the contrastive aspect of identities and thereby emphasizes the implicit condition of plurality" (Sökefeld 1999, pp. 417–18). Self-definition today coalesces around genealogy, heritage, citizenship, and sameness, but underlying that are also diverse and troubling contemporary concerns about disenfranchisement and difference. The constitutive outside, premised on exclusion and otherness, forms the corona of difference through which identities are enunciated. Why has archaeology been reluctant to formulate these topics, to consider them integral to archaeological praxis? The discipline is fundamentally social: social life, social history, social meanings, even social theory. Theoretical time lag and lack of sociopolitical engagement might be justifications for our disciplinary profile; however, the political is always personal.

Archaeology shares with anthropology that specific biographical lens through which certain intellectual strands are prefigured—those that are inflected with our own lifetime experiences and preoccupations. Yet part of the reason for our slow development of identity politics might be the lack of personal narrative, such as the above, and self-reflexive analysis of our own motives and practices. In the past two decades, following the literary turn, anthropologists have produced a surfeit of introspective studies (Clifford 1997, Clifford & Marcus 1986, Geertz 1995, Gupta & Ferguson 1997) and poetics of practice (Ghosh 1992). Presumably archaeologists feel their subjects are dead and buried—as opposed to the conundrums faced by fieldwork with participants—and that they are not implicated in the representation and struggles of living peoples. The ethical dimension of our work is often overlooked or rendered mute by force of scientific objectivity and research agendas. Fieldwork is still shrouded in mystique for ethnographers, whereas it is generally considered mundane in our discipline (Lucas 2001). The tactics of fieldwork, its interventions and ramifications, have only recently been called into question (Fotiadis 1993; Hodder 1998, 1999; Meskell 2001b; Politis 2001). Western academics themselves could be characterized as a highly mobile, rootless group (often by virtue of occupation), who are on the whole analytical and somewhat detached from politics, despite their leftist leanings. Perhaps by getting personal, archaeology has finally entered the contemporary field of debate; Marxist, feminist, indigenous, queer, disenfranchised, and politicized archaeologies are the most transparent examples. In the past 20 years these archaeologies have revitalized the field, made it socially relevant and cross-disciplinary, and given some much-needed heart and soul to an archaeology mired in systems, process, and disembodied external constraints.

In this arena, archaeology as a discipline has something to contribute, other than simply providing ancient fuel to the fire of land claims, ethnic superiority, or historical lineages. Identity issues in archaeology—be they studies of class inequality, gender bias, sexual specificity, politics and nation, heritage representation, or even fundamental topics like selfhood, embodiment, and being—have the capacity to connect our field with other disciplines in academe but more importantly with the wider community at large. Theorizing identity forms a critical nexus in academic discourse bringing together sociologists, anthropologists, political scientists, psychologists, geographers, historians, and philosophers (Jenkins 1996, p. 7). The topic frames a diverse set of intellectual positions from Giddens' (1991) notions of modernity and self-identity, to those surrounding postmodernism and difference (Bauman 1992, Butler 1995, Derrida 1978), to feminist interventions (Butler 1990, 2000; Lennon & Whitford 1994) and the political struggles involved in the global resurgence of nationalist and ethnic tensions (Barth 2000, Cohen 2000). Bauman suggests that identity has come to operate as a verb, rather than a noun, and occupies the ontological status of both a project and a postulate (1996, p. 19). Subjectivity and human agency are also central. Following Foucault (1978, p. xiv), this is not tantamount to a theory of the knowing subject or modern individualism at its extreme but rather moves toward a theory of discursive practices.

REVEALING IDENTITIES IN THE PAST

As demonstrated by the enmeshed themes and evocative studies described below, identities are multiply constructed and revolve around a set of iterative practices that are always in process, despite their material and symbolic substrata. Who we are, what we study, and the questions we ask are not simply trendy polemics of high modernity: These formulations underscore the types of archaeology, the level of political engagement, and the points of connection archaeologists experience. The politics of location is central to our understanding of archaeological subjects and affects us as practitioners today. Part of that locatedness, however, entails evaluating the historicity of our conceptual frameworks and challenging their seemingly natural or foundational constitution. Identity construction and maintenance may have always been salient in the past; taxonomic designations such as ethnicity, gender, or sexuality, for example, may not have existed as the discrete categories we find so familiar (Meskell 1999, 2001a). Many of these domains are now being refigured in contemporary society (Yanagisako & Delaney 1995) and should similarly be interrogated more fully before they are applied to archaeological or historical contexts. If we fail to push these questions further, we risk an elision of difference, conflating ancient and modern experience in the process. What makes questions of identity so intriguing is how specific societies evoked such different responses prompted by categorical differences in their understandings and constructions of social domains.

Archaeology's engagement with identity issues could be described as diffident. If one charts the development of archaeology's commitment to identity and/or politics, as reflected in conference sessions at the Society of American Archeologists meetings, for example, the results demonstrate a relatively recent and gradual growth in interest (see Figure 1). There has been a slippage between the epistemic

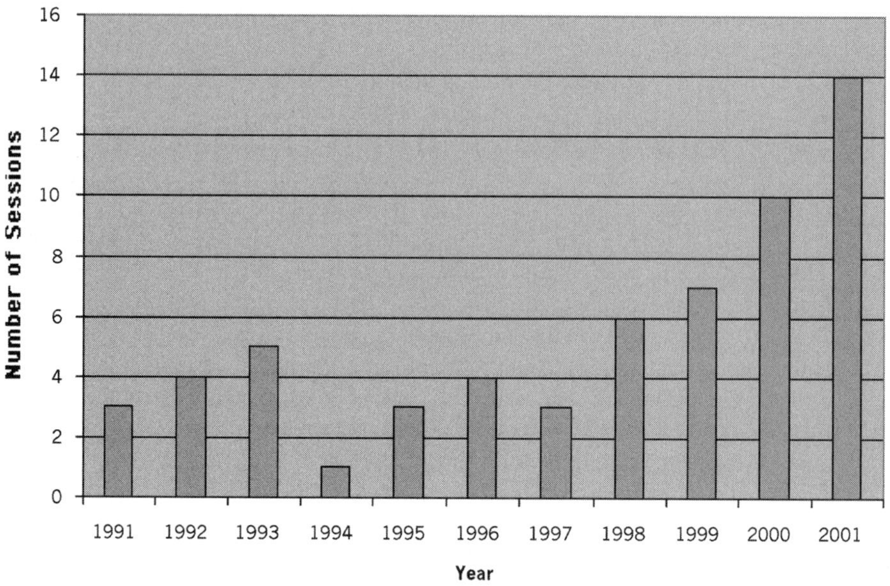

Figure 1 Society of American Archaeologists sessions from 1991 to 2001.

subjects of study and the recognition of context, implication, and connectivity in contemporary settings. Yet as many scholars have argued, archaeology as a discipline was forged in conjunction with the burgeoning national identity and state formation in Europe and elsewhere, in itself a very specific and reductionist construal of identity. However, the particular study of identity in past societies has followed several variant timelines. For example, ethnicity is a category that has sustained interest since the nineteenth century, foregrounded by writers such as Morgan, Kossina, and Childe (Trigger 1989), spurred on by the refashioning of national boundaries, diasporic movements, and ethnic tensions within twentieth-century Europe. We might look to the negative associations of early ethnic studies and their political deployment to explain the subsequent time lag between the first half of the twentieth century and its rather different articulation in very recent scholarship. Additionally, interest in class or status has a longer history than the study of gender or sexuality. Issues of class and status were deemed more relevant to social structure at large, albeit from an unreflexive male perspective. In archaeology, specific vectors of identity reach their own historical moment when the interpretive time and space make it possible—recent interest in sexuality is a salient example—although archaeology has been out of synch with developments elsewhere.

Gender archaeology arrived late on the theoretical scene (Conkey & Spector 1984), first through the lens of first-wave feminist theory (Claassen 1992a, Engelstad 1991) and then by a flurry of substantive case studies outlining women's place in the past (Gero & Conkey 1991; Gibbs 1987; Gilchrist 1991, 1994). Gender remained, and in some circles still remains, the preserve of women, rather than the more dialogic or holistic study of gendered relations, which considers men as gendered beings with a concomitant construction of sexed identity (Knapp 1998, Meskell 1996). Some earlier studies took more radical paths to sexed identity (Yates & Nordbladh 1990); yet they were not seen as representing engendered studies, owing to their lack of explicit focus on women as a monolithic category. The stirrings of a third-wave feminist approach in archaeology were heralded by Elizabeth Brumfiel (1992), although it took several years before these programmatic changes were enacted. Third-wave feminist studies positioned gender as relational to a host of other identity markers such as age, class, ethnicity, sexuality, and so on (Meskell 1999). Its positionality must also be contextualized through other modalities of power such as kinship (Brumfiel 1992, Joyce & Gillespie 2000) and at the nexus of other "naturalized" domains (Meskell 2001a). Identity, in its various manifestations, operates under erasure in the interstices of reversal and emergence and thus cannot be studied in the old ways (Hall 1996, p. 2). This entails interrogating the old taxonomies and categories that we have reified as doxic and impermeable and happily projected across the spatiotemporal divide.

Part of this revisioning has already happened in what is traditionally thought of as gender archaeology. Gender has been instantiated within the wider social context of the life cycle (Gilchrist 2000, Meskell 2002) or linked to age (Moore & Scott 1997), expanding the social milieu, rather than restricted to single-issue polemics. More problematic is the separating out of special categories such as children (e.g., Sofaer-Derevenski 2000), given their particular positioning within recent Western history (Foucault 1978). Instead of falling into the trap of prior gender archaeology, which privileged the female above all other gender constructions, studies of age-related phenomena could be more productively discussed within frameworks of life cycle, life experience, and other constituents of social difference.

After some 15 years of engendered archaeology it is finally possible to interpolate sexuality as a shaping constituent of social life (Schmidt & Voss 2000). Sexuality is key in the formation and lived experience of an individual's identity, and, like gender, it should be integrated into a wider set of social vectors rather than singled out as privileged terrain. The creation of specialty topics, like gender or children, as discursive taxonomic entities has resulted in a predictable ghettoization, whereby the majority of scholars still consider such areas outside their interpretive remit. Sexuality, like gender, should be seen as integral to studies of social life and not simply the preserve of those who feel privileged to speak because of their own construal of sexual difference (Dowson 2000). Moreover, sexuality must be considered in all its variability rather than isolating queer sexualities as the primary locus of study: This again leads to marginalization and leaves categories such as heterosexuality as unproblematized zones. Despite the recent flurry of interest, queer theory and the centrality of Judith Butler have had significant trajectories in archaeology (Claassen 1992b, Joyce 2001, Meskell 1996).

Unlike gender, analyzing wealth and status has always been integral to the archaeological project. Whether in culture historical, processual, or contextual approaches, the study of relationships between elite and nonelite has been key. Yet the degree to which this has coalesced around social identity rather than simply examining exchange, bureaucracy, and power is debatable. Locating those connections in the distant past, however, has not always necessitated or entailed a politicized stance in the present. In fields such as historical archaeology (Hall 2000, Paynter & McGuire 1991) or archaeologies of the recent past (Buchli & Lucas 2001), our findings have sociopolitical valences, and many researchers feel impelled to engage with living communities. Plantation archaeology is a salient example, situated within the larger framework of African-American archaeology—the latter developing out of social, political, and intellectual movements such as black activism, historic preservation legislation, academic interest in ethnicity, and the role of public archaeology (Singleton 1995, p. 122). The focus of study has moved from the identification of slave quarters to more nuanced discussions of power and identity and the complex machinations between plantation owners and their slaves. The archaeology of racism is prefigured in all such discussions, and though there might seem an obvious connection to ethnicity theory, the two should not be conflated (Babson 1990; Orser 1999, p. 666). As Orser warns, whiteness must be denaturalized. Moreover, archaeologists should consider the material dimensions of using whiteness as a source of racial domination, which is inexorably linked to capitalism (Leone 1995). Historical archaeologists are, however, faced with a complex mosaic of racial, ethnic, and class reflections in material culture, which has proven difficult to disentangle. Brackette Williams (1992, p. 611) has questioned how processual archaeologies "can interrogate the culturally 'invisible' that historical processes of contact produced, but which cannot lay claim to cultural autonomy in a manner that allows their creations to be counted in an inventory of 'distinctive culture traits.'" She is similarly concerned that theories of domination and resistance have focused on categories rather than the processes by which production, reification, transformation, or ultimate elimination occur. More recently, such theories have been displaced by multifaceted explanations involving race, class, gender, religion, lineage, and representation (Mullins 1999, Rotman & Nassaney 1997, Russel 1997, Stine 1990, Wall 1999, Wilkie & Bartoy 2000), and the recognition of contemporary sociopolitical relevance. There has been an avid move to include descendants in the participation process and to advocate a wider responsibility and accountability for archaeologists and historians. This also includes important work in the representation and "musealization" of historic sites, such as Colonial Williamsburg, largely investigated by social anthropologists (Castañeda 1996, Handler & Gable 1997).

Historical archaeology has effectively bridged the study of identity issues—past and present. The last decade of scholarship makes the connection across the flow of discourses, as evidenced by a growing scholarship devoted to stewardship and outreach (Franklin 1997; Jameson 1997; McKee 1998; Potter 1992; Singleton 1995, 1999). Exemplary here is Carol McDavid's work (1997, 2000), which focuses on the Levi Jordan Plantation in Brazoria, Texas, and the use of new media technologies for local community outreach involving descendants of both slaves and slave owners. Inspired by pragmatist philosophers such as Rorty and West, she has sensitively negotiated the divide between academic and other worlds, their respective practices, policies, and writings, recentering the role of archaeologists in both cultural and political milieus.

DIASPORIC AND ETHNIC IDENTITIES

The recent articulation of diaspora is an important, albeit late, development in archaeology as a direct offshoot from historical archaeology. Paraphrasing Agorsah (1996, p. 222), the examination of diasporic cultures brings together compelling issues beyond identifying ceramic sequences, namely family, gender, race, and minority communities, and is enmeshed with issues of cultural interaction and transformation, transfers, exchanges, race and power relations, and heritage development. This might be seen as a more theorized extension of archaeology's long-standing interest in migration, though imbued with a more critical stance toward correlating assemblages and enclaves with specific groups. Archaeologists have used the language of diaspora to circumvent the heavily ascriptive associations of ethnicity, while still allowing a discussion of community and identity that crosscuts spatial lines (Goldstein 2000, p. 182). Others have linked archaeological discourse on places and landscapes to some central concerns within diaspora studies, such as migration, displacement, and dislocation (Bender 2001). This has obvious contemporary salience and offers a resonant critique of phenomenological studies of place-making in the past.

Diasporic studies in archaeology have, in themselves, been highly localized. In the Caribbean, a politicized archaeology is being forged through this analytic lens (Haviser 1999, Sued Badillo 1995, Wilkie & Bartoy 2000). Prior to this emergence, few studies sought to document the nexus between archaeology, transnationalism, and political faction. Receptivity to social theory might form one explanation, and in Cuba this was intimately connected to the 1959 revolution and the predominance of Marxism (Davis 1996). Reports on diasporic sites in the Dominican Republic, Jamaica (Agorsah 1999), Brazil (Funari 1995/1996, 1999), and the Americas (Weik 1997) have recently been published. However, the archaeology of the African diaspora still remains confined to studies of New World slavery, despite rich variability in African experience outside Africa, whether in Europe, South Asia, or elsewhere. Suffice to say, archaeologists have lagged behind historians and anthropologists, a delay explained to some degree by a disciplinary reticence toward Islamic archaeology or that of the modern world (Orser 1998, p. 64).

The broader question of identifying ethnicity materially and symbolically extends back to scholars such as Montelius and Childe, through to Hawkes, Piggott, the ethnoarchaeological work of Hodder (1982), processual approaches (Auger et al. 1987, Emberling 1997), and contextual ones (Aldenderfer 1993, Wells 1998).

Yet isolating ethnic specificities has proven to be elusive and potentially teleological in archaeological writing. From this perspective, racial and ethnic studies share a common ontological terrain. As Upton (1996, p. 3) demonstrates, while archaeologists view slave culture as a product of racial experience and a response to the social, economic, legal, and interpersonal conditions of the institution, we have come to expect a particular material resistance. Slaves' artifacts are supposed to be distinctive, and we are suspicious when they are indistinguishable from those of masters. Studies still focus on the articulation of difference in reductive terms by examining ceramics, textiles, architecture, food, burials, etc. Looking for ethnicity mirrors the strategies of gender archaeology, which simply looked for women as discrete and familiar entities. And theories of ethnicity, like those of gender, have moved from a focus on the biological to the social, and from the category to the boundary. The axial ideational, social, and subjective dimensions are lived and potentially porous or changeable, yet often materially invisible. Assuming a specific ethnic identification "must depend on ascription and self-ascription: only in so far as individuals embrace it, are constrained by it, act on it, and experience it will ethnicity make organizational difference" (Barth 1994, p. 12). Manipulation, masking, and passing (Butler 1993, Fanon 1967) are tactics that inhere around difference, problematizing notions of the "real" or "authentic," both socially and materially. Hall (1997, p. 4) reminds us that "identities are constructed within, not outside, discourse" and are "produced in specific historical and institutional sites within specific discursive formations and practices, by specific enunciative strategies." The fluidity and permeability of those identities produce real problems for archaeologists in contexts lacking historical documentation, and even text-aided settings can be complex (Meskell 1999).

Influenced largely by Bourdieu's concept of habitus, Jones' study of ethnicity provides a detailed account of the discipline's engagement and its problematics. She shows that teasing out ethnic difference from the complex fabric of identity more widely is fraught with difficulties if not impossible for many archaeologists. Her definitions are necessarily vague enough to stand for any vector of identity—one could easily replace it here with status or religion:

> Ethnicity is a multidimensional phenomenon constituted in different ways in different social domains. Representations of ethnicity involve the dialectical opposition of situationally relevant cultural practices and historical experiences associated with different cultural traditions. Consequently there is rarely a one-to-one relationship between representations of ethnicity and the entire range of cultural practices and social conditions associated with a particular group. (Jones 1997b, p. 100)

How different is this statement from those made by Childe in works from the 1950s such as *Social Evolution*? This divide characterizes the theoretical impasse archaeologists face. If indeed ethnicity is grounded in the shared subliminal dispositions of social agents and is shaped by practice, how might we approach this? Historically, theorizing ethnicity seems to have either correlated pots with people or written material culture out of the record almost entirely. Other studies took tangential routes to cultural identity in an attempt to move beyond these isomorphic and deterministic studies (Shennan 1994). Some studies argue that not all archaeologists can study ethnicity or that social structures may not indeed correspond to our current classifications, which impels us to revisit anthropological and sociological literatures (Hegmon 1998, p. 274). Archaeology's most compelling studies of ethnicity emanate from historical (Staski 1990, Wall 1999, Woodhouse-Beyer 1999) or ethnohistorical contexts (David et al. 1991, Dietler & Herbich 1998), where diverse sources are inflected with the nuanced valences that represent social complexity. Newer research has moved from ethnicity to crystallize around issues of community, as a more localized perspective on identity (Canuto & Yaeger 2000). In many respects, theorizing ethnicity has not moved far from the position set forward by Hodder two decades ago.

Research into the specificities of ethnic identity and constructions of place lies at the intersection between the two fields of identity politics. On the one hand, investigating ethnicity answers questions about social difference in past societies–on the other hand, in extreme circumstances, it forms a locus for extrapolation to contemporary questions about origins, legitimacy, ownership, and ultimately, rights. That entanglement has singled out ethnicity as the dangerous vector of difference, as opposed to gender or age taxonomies. The latter have not been mobilized by contemporary groups in the same manner and magnitude to instantiate claims of legitimacy, superiority, and territoriality.

ARCHAEOLOGY AND NATIONAL MODERNITIES

Over the past decade we have witnessed a proliferation of studies of archaeology and archaeological narratives in the service of the state. This is, in part, an outgrowth of earlier studies that linked the rise of archaeology with the construction of the modern nation state (McGuire 1992, Patterson 1994, Trigger 1989). Ensuing studies focused more closely on European nation building (Atkinson et al. 1996, Díaz-Andreu & Champion 1996, Graves-Brown et al. 1996), whereas more recent work has brought this into wider global and contemporary perspective (Kohl 1998, Kohl & Fawcett 1995, Meskell 1998, Ucko 1995). Questions of theory in specific countries and the particular relationship between national concerns and theoretical development also emerged as important issues (Hodder 1991, Ucko 1995). Philip Kohl has provided a useful summary of these processes by documenting the development of archaeology in the nineteenth and early twentieth centuries, linking nationalism to considerations of ethnicity and identity. He argues (1998, p. 225) that many cases demonstrate the manipulation of archaeological materials, and though there are sensational examples of this (Hitler's Germany, Mussolini's Italy), I would suggest that many national engagements are more complex, nuanced, and less deterministic in their relationships with the past (e.g., Atatürk in Turkey; see Özdogan 1998). Yet Kohl is correct in stating, following Hobsbawm, that "there are real limits to the invention of tradition" (1998, p. 233). In general, one can argue for a whole series of relationships between nations, regions, and individuals and their respective pasts, and it is dangerous to assume that conscious construction and manipulation are the primary rationales. It is also crucial to provide sociopolitical linkages: The twentieth century was rife with political restructuring and ethnic/religious upheavals (e.g., Balkans, Soviet Union, Israel, India), which sparked relationships with particular historical trajectories, nostalgia, and commemoration, and with the forceful materiality of archaeological remains. National modernities are constructed through dialogic relationships between archaeological materiality and heterogeneous narratives of the past that recursively offer horizons of hybridization. We might question how cultural heritage has been deployed in quests for specific modernities, sometimes at the expense or erasure of others. How do political agendas inhere in monumentalized space?

A surfeit of papers has dealt with the national character of archaeology in European countries (Shnirelman 1995). In the context of France, scholars have discussed a national archaeology rather than a nationalist one (Fleury-Ilett 1993). Here the discursive construction of archaeology is linked to wider developments such as the loss of foreign colonies, sociopolitical change, and the role of collective memory in the shaping of national culture. Identity and unity are foregrounded and monumentalized, especially since the political upheavals of May 1968 (see Demoule 1999; Dietler 1994, 1998; Schnapp 1996). More substantial studies have been undertaken for Germany, specifically its relationship to the Nazi regime (Anthony 1995, Arnold 1990, Marchand 1996) and the divisive effects of the Berlin Wall (Härke 2000, Härke & Wolfram 1993). European scholars have also turned their attention to the deconstruction of field practices, the place of local workers, and remnant colonial hegemonies (Fotiadis 1993; Given 1998; van Dommelen 1997, 1998), reinforcing the suggestion made earlier that trends toward self-reflexivity resonate more strongly outside Americanist archaeology.

Historiographical studies, such as the aforementioned, are certainly less volatile than contemporary encounters or less susceptible to partisan politics or fierce argumentation by different interest groups. Many of these contributions dealt with issues of representation or memorialization, rather than addressing the more pressing concerns over the results of war (Abdi 2001, Naccache 1998), the erasure of heritage (Chapman 1994), the residual effects of colonialism (Chakrabarti 2000, Hall 2000, Loren 2000, Reid 1997, Reid et al. 1997, Trigger 1984), or violence and persecution (Bernbeck & Pollock 1996, Meskell 2000). Although these themes unite many groups across the globe, there has been a notable lack of cross-fertilization between those writing on the topic from Europe, the Caribbean, Latin America, North America, India, and Australia. For instance, there is a growing body of important writing on the politics of archaeology in Latin America, which is more evocative and compelling than much of the literature on Europe (e.g., Mamani Condori 1996, McGuire & Navarrete 1999, Paddayya 1995, Patterson 1995, Politis 1995, Ramos 1994, Vargas Arenas 1995). Chinchilla Mazariegos (1998) has outlined how excavations at Copan shaped the incipient independence of Guatemala, providing the new nation with its own ennobling history, and Higueras (1995) has demonstrated the positive contribution of archaeology to Peruvian national esteem. The iconicity of ancient remains, whether Machu Picchu or Chan Chan, figures prominently in the collective consciousness, yet with little historicity. This places more tacit responsibility on the role of archaeologists, both indigenous and foreign, to promote current findings in the form of museums and community outreach.

More familiar perhaps are the discussions of Mexican archaeology, for which ethnicity, class, and race are crosscut through competing narratives and representations (Bernal 1980, Hyland 1992, Jones 1997a, Patterson 1995). Through displays in the National Museum, "Indianness," past and present, is privileged over other identities. The end result is that Mexicans are presented as Aztecs. Despite the evocative nature of archaeology and its political mobilizations, few archaeologists have seen the potential for linking heritage, national modernity, and tourism (Hyland 1992; Meskell 2000, 2001b). Archaeological monuments lie at a powerful nexus between ethnoscapes and finanscapes and so on. Alternatively, ethnographers have theorized the intersection between performing the past, potent tourist locales, and divergent interest groups (Abu el-Haj 1998, Edensor 1998; but see Odermatt 1996). This conjoins with Herzfeld's (1996) call for more integrated archaeological and ethnographic projects.

Geographically, there are clear imbalances in the scope of literature produced, and this is undoubtedly linked to a perceived receptiveness toward archaeological theory or the place of sociopolitics. For example, only a handful of available studies focus on Southeast Asia (Fawcett 1995, Loofs 1979, Pai 2000, Tong 1995, Tsude 1995, Von Falkenhausen 1995). Few studies have been produced for African countries or, more importantly, by their respective scholars (Andah 1995a,b; Jeppson 1997; Kent 1998; Lewis-Williams 1995; Schmidt 1995), although Peter Ucko has been instrumental in supporting these ventures. From a Sudanese perspective, Elamin (1999, p. 3) argues that cultural identity has recently become a more appealing subject for academics, intellectuals, politicians, and the media to debate. Martin Hall's prolific output has done much to change perceptions about politicization, responsibility, and ethics in the archaeology of South Africa (1992; 1994a,b; 1995). Most recently (2000, p. 160), he has documented Johannesburg's District Six, its destruction and subsequent rise with the success of protest against the apartheid state, teasing apart the transcripts of domination and resistance. His poetics of place and commitment to an archaeology of the recent past have been groundbreaking.

THE COLONIAL QUESTION

Issues of nationalism and archaeology cannot be separated from larger global processes such as colonialism and exploitation. Two decades ago Bruce Trigger brought to the fore a certain frame of political discourse in archaeology. It has taken time to sediment, as this review suggests. Trigger sought to interrogate the history of archaeology (1989), outline the contours of nationalist, colonialist, and imperialist archaeologies from a global perspective (1984), and underscore the social milieus underpinning those discursive productions (1995). As an established scholar, his contribution has had monumental effects in instantiating a responsible and ethical archaeology. In the more recent climate of postprocessual and indigenous archaeologies, scholars have become more politicized and outspoken. Central to this development has been a recognition of the politics of location, both in regard to the effects of colonial hegemonies or transnational tensions, and in terms of our own situated scholarship.

Yet the residual effects of colonialism have occupied distinct trajectories in different countries. There has been an outpouring of literature on Native American issues in the past decade, specifically the problematics of archaeological intervention, reburial and repatriation, representation, the place of Cultural Resource Management and museums, and so on (Dongoske et al. 1997, Echo-Hawk 2000, Goldstein 1992, Goldstein & Kintigh 1990, McGuire 1992, Schmidt & Patterson 1995, Swidler et al. 1997, Thomas 2000). Significantly, the impetus for this shift was initiated by indigenous activists, rather than being an emergent recognition for archaeologists. North American archaeologists were relatively slow in acknowledging the rights of indigenous peoples, especially when compared to legislation on this issue in Australia. They "seem not to have recognized an emergent pressing need to single out Native Americans for attention before such a course of action was imposed upon them by interests which are not naturally sympathetic to archaeological concerns and perhaps even middle-class concerns more generally" (Lilley 2000, p. 113).

Yet the recognition of Native rights in the United States, accompanied by Native American Graves Protection and Repatriation Act (NAGPRA) legislation, has ineluctably entered the slippery terrain of identity politics. On one side, there has been a scientific desire to definitively answer the specificities of ancient identity. Spurred on by a positivist ethos in archaeology that advocated a literal match between artifacts, human remains, and modern people, we have seen the results of manipulation and misuse. Such trends, particularly in the search for ethnic origins, have had a long and ugly history in archaeology, whether in Nazi Germany or more recently with the Saami (e.g., Odner 1985). On the other side, archaeologists of a more theoretical persuasion have spent decades problematizing the connection between ethnicity and artifacts, thus arguing for a more fluid and ongoing constitution of identity. This perspective has been hijacked by high-profile anthropologists who want unrestricted access to studying ancient human remains. Employing the musings of social science as a vehicle for denying indigenous interests, the chair of Anthropology for the American Association for the Advancement of Science has argued (Clark 2001, p. 3):

> Ethnicity, or identity-consciousness, is a fleeting, transient thing—constantly changing, constantly being renegotiated, written on the wind. Anthropologists have known for decades that discrete ethnic groups, rigidly bounded in space

> and time, have no existence beyond a few centuries (and even that is arguable). Too bad this little nugget eluded most American archaeologists.... As the position paper itself makes clear, claims of "pan-Indianness" are insufficient to justify repatriation. Does the archaeology and physical anthropology count for nothing here, or is oral tradition the only thing that matters? ... Sadly, this is what happens when politics takes precedence over disinterested evaluation of the credibility of knowledge claims—in this case, knowledge claims about the human past.

Because a literal identification and correlation has been touted as foundational to the questions of identity posed by NAGPRA, broadly defined as cultural affiliation—a relationship of shared group identity—archaeologists have created a tenuous and spurious connection between positivist assertion and political outcome. Kennewick Man is the most volatile example: Here experts attempt to demonstrate cultural affiliation over some 9000 years with various tribal groups vying for direct descent. NAGPRA's acknowledgment of Native American rights and concerns is not at issue here. Rather, it is the series of foundational claims upon which connections between contemporary communities and ancient cultural property are premised. These claims are dangerous because they are out of synch with everything archaeologists have learned about identity from the work of Gordon Childe onwards. And this is what enables Clark to claim scientific primacy over human remains, at the expense of all other groups—the logical outcome of a positivist argument in today's political climate. Surely a more politically responsible and engaged archaeology can be forged without recourse to such reductionist science. With the recognition that other communities and groups have equally legitimate claims to stewardship, the resolution of such disagreements requires a clear understanding of the different standpoints, structures of power, and politics involved (Patterson 1999). There has to be an epistemic shift, entailing the legitimation of other discourses, rather than simply returning to something called science that privileges the desire for certain knowledge at all costs. "Cultural affiliation" and "cultural patrimony" are separate in the language of NAGPRA, but they still reside within a Western scientific purview, as evinced by Clark, which has yet to be fully interrogated. Within this system, however, one could argue that emphasis should be placed on the patrimonial relationship, which acknowledges that Native peoples can show traditional or historic continuity of connection instead of linear descent. Rather than trying to quantify past and present identities in the face of significant methodological hurdles, it may prove more fitting to argue that specific groups constitute appropriate custodians because they have traditionally, or historically, legitimate cultural or spiritual responsibility for the cultural property at hand. This places more importance on living groups and reconciliation in the wake of colonization, rather than attributing salience entirely to the archaeological record; thus my earlier point returns that our subjects are not always dead.

A more liberal position toward indigenous issues has been central in Australian prehistory for many years (Attwood & Arnold 1992, Hemming 2000, Langford 1983, Meehan 1995, Moser 1995, Pardoe 1990). Ian Lilley (2000, p. 109) has compared Australian legislation with that of other settler societies such as New Zealand, Canada, and South Africa where indigenous claims are prioritized over those of all other interested parties. This stands in contradistinction to the United States, where many publics and multiple interests are acknowledged. Lilley believes that archaeologists and their institutional politics have been very different in the United States as compared to the aforementioned Commonwealth countries, a situation tacitly linked to nation-building. He contends that "in Australia, if not Canada or New Zealand, most archaeologists share a pervasive, middle-class, postcolonialist view that our country cannot be considered a 'whole' nation in the eyes of important others unless we achieve reconciliation with the continent's indigenous populations" (2000, p. 113; see also Pokotylo & Guppy 1999). Despite the progressive Australian legislature, racism runs deep, not only in terms of aboriginal peoples but in terms of other immigrants, such as the Chinese, who accompanied white colonists into Australia. Given disturbing developments in recent political history—staging racism against Asians in parliament and the media—the entwined histories of the nation's peoples have again come under scrutiny (Lydon 2000). But the penumbra of shame still haunts Australia, despite attempts by the federal government to distance past atrocities from present situations: Repudiation cannot simply be followed by loss of memory.

Colonialism, a topic of long-standing interest (Bhabha 1994, Chambers & Curti 1996, Dirks 1992, Thomas 1999), has also been revitalized through the incursion of postcolonial theory in archaeology (see Gosden 1999). Archaeologists are now pursuing notions of hybridity and creolization in the construction of material culture and social identity (Loren 2000; van Dommelen 1997, p. 309), moving between notions of blended or reworked articulations and the hard realities of repression. Though such studies make claims about past life experiences, they are also redolent of contemporary struggles and oppressions. This is powerfully evidenced in the resurgence of interest in South Asian archaeology, in terms of religious factionalism, transnational tensions, and the colonial legacy (Chakrabarti 1997, 2000; Coningham & Lewer 2000a,b; Lahiri 2000; Paddayya 1995). Much of this discussion has been mobilized around the destruction of the Ayodhya mosque in 1992 (Bernbeck & Pollock 1996, Mandal 1993, Rao 1994). Archaeological data have been deployed by opposing sides to prioritize specific historical moments and foci in the site's history, rather than constructing more encompassing narratives that would account for multiple identifications within a wider religious landscape (Shaw 2000, pp. 698–99). The multiplicity of religious traditions and connections might be accommodated within more plural and consensual histories, and this is where archaeology's role may indeed be emancipatory. Though sentiment ran high at the 1994 World Archaeology Congress meetings in Delhi, there has been little follow up given the rash of continued violence and destruction of religious sites across India. The fixity of monumentalized space is shot through with contingent histories and multivalent narratives, and though archaeologists can grapple with heuristic and ethical agendas, we cannot hope to police or monopolize the interpretive borders.

CONCLUSIONS

At the nexus of identity and politics lies the crucial terrain of ethics (Lynott & Wylie 2000, Vitelli 1996). Part of our problem rests with the illusion that the subjects of our research are dead and buried, literally, and that our "scientific" research goals are paramount. It has taken time to convince archaeologists that ours is a subjective enterprise that is far from agenda-free. And though some have been active in critiquing the metanarratives of Western scholarship, the micronarratives of scientific method often go unchecked (Scham 2001). Recently, our role in national arenas has fueled some rather outmoded and pointless arguing over relativism. Here the recognition of subjectivity has been grossly caricatured as an "anything goes" mentalité, ultimately leading to nihilism and fascism (see Lampeter Archaeology Workshop 1997). Despite the difficulties in reconciling archaeology's role in national constructions, most scholars now affirm that the active nature of material culture precludes static readings of the past and that identity construction itself is a fluid, fractured, and ongoing set of processes.

But what sets archaeology apart from other disciplines seeking to represent the nation or culture, such as history or anthropology, is its materiality. The residues of the past are often monumentalized and inescapable in daily life. Individually, the past is memory—collectively, it is history. Both are constructs entangled with identity issues. Though history and memory are imagined, this does not mean that they are imaginary (Jenkins 1996, p. 28). According to Lowenthal (1985, p. 245) "history and memory usually come in the guise of stories which the mind must purposefully filter; physical relics remain directly available to our senses. This existential concreteness explains their evocative appeal." Archaeological materials could be said to operate in thirdspace (Soja 2000), a dialectical position that recursively shapes individuals and is continually shaped by us. Their multivalency and plasticity also result in "a diversity of icons" (Higueras 1995, p. 399) that are prefigured in society through their residual nature. And though archaeological remains iconically signify materiality, identity formation is alternately fluid—the material and the immaterial in constant dialogue. Identification is always a process of articulation or suturing, rather than a subsumption (Hall 1996, p. 3): It is neither essentialist nor foundational, but strategic and positional. Meaning and identity must be construed as projects, sometimes grounded, other times contingent, but always ongoing.

It might prove productive to maneuver between levels of disciplinary engagement the lived experience of social identity and the wider political setting of archaeological praxis: Both entail issues of power and difference, be it national, racial, ethnic, religious, sexual, gender, class, and so on. Part of that engagement necessarily entails getting personal and rendering transparent our own motivations for pursuing different archaeologies. Constitutive identities are performed and iterated though the discourses of sameness and difference, as I outlined through the example of Australian racial and sexual politics. Archaeology has traditionally separated out studies of our dead subjects from the field's contemporary valences;

yet the two domains emerged in tandem and are epistemically interlaced. Although slow to take root, owing to the intransigence of positivistic thinking, archaeologies of identity, past and present, represent one of the most significant growth areas in our discipline. They represent our contemporary engagement with other fields and audiences and fulfill part of our ethical responsibility as public figures charged with the trusteeship of the past (Bender 1998, Scham 1998). The increase in the number of presentations and publications and the diverse perspectives represented in the last decade are an encouraging hallmark of the discipline's integrity and theoretical maturation. It may be some time before we parallel the sophistication of our sister disciplines, but the progression over the last decade has been exponential and promises to lead archaeology toward assuming a more engaged place in the social sciences and toward other publics.

ACKNOWLEDGMENTS

For their thoughtful comments and suggestions I would like to thank Alex Bauer, Emma Blake, Michael Fotiadis, Chris Gosden, Rosemary Joyce, Jonathan Last, Ian Lilley, Carol McDavid, Randy McGuire, Stephanie Moser, Matt Palus, Bob Paynter, Gustavo Politis, Bob Preucel, Uzma Rizvi, and Sandra Scham. I am indebted to Ian Hodder and Ian Lilley for their ongoing conversations and helpful challenges with regard to the more volatile issues where identity and politics intersect. Special thanks to Matt Palus who prepared the SAA chart.

The *Annual Review of Anthropology* is online at http://anthro.annualreviews.org

LITERATURE CITED

Abdi K. 2001. Nationalism, politics, and the development of archaeology in Iran. *Am. J. Archaeol.* 105:51–76

Abu el-Haj N. 1998. Translating truths: nationalism, the practice of archaeology, and the remaking of past and present in contemporary Jerusalem. *Am. Ethnol.* 25:166–88

Agorsah EK. 1996. The archaeology of the African diaspora. *Afr. Archaeol. Rev.* 13:221–24

Agorsah EK. 1999. Ethnoarchaeological consideration of social relationship and settlement patterning among Africans in the Caribbean diaspora. In *African Sites Archaeology in the Caribbean*, ed. JB Hauser, pp. 38–64. Princeton, NJ: Diener

Aldenderfer MS, ed. 1993. *Domestic Architecture, Ethnicity and Complementarity in the South-Central Andes*. Iowa City: Univ. Iowa Press

Andah BW. 1995a. European encumbrances to the development of relevant theory in African archaeology. See Ucko 1995, pp. 96–109

Andah BW. 1995b. Studying African societies in cultural context. See Schmidt & Patterson 1995, pp. 149–81

Anthony D. 1995. Nazi and eco-feminist prehistories: counter points in Indo-European archaeology. See Kohl & Fawcett 1995, pp. 82–96

Arnold B. 1990. The past as propaganda: totalitarian archaeology in Nazi Germany. *Antiquity* 64:464–78

Atkinson JA, Banks I, O'Sullivan J, eds. 1996. *Nationalism and Archaeology*. Glasgow, UK: Cruithne

Attwood B, Arnold J, eds. 1992. *Power, Knowledge and Aborigines*. Bundoora, Aust.: La Trobe Univ. Press

Auger R, Glass MF, MacEachern S, McCartney PH, eds. 1987. *Ethnicity and Culture*. Calgary, Can.: Archaeol. Assoc. Univ. Calgary

Babson DW. 1990. Archaeology of racism and ethnicity on Southern plantations. *Hist. Archaeol.* 24:20–28

Barth F. 1994. Enduring and emerging issues in the analysis of ethnicity. In *The Anthropology of Ethnicity*, ed. H Vermeulen, C Grovers, pp. 11–32. Amsterdam: Het Spinhuis

Barth F. 2000. Boundaries and connections. In *Signifying Identities: Anthropological Perspectives on Boundaries and Contested Values*, ed. AP Cohen, pp. 17–36. London: Routledge

Bauman Z. 1992. *Intimations of Postmodernity*. London: Routledge

Bauman Z. 1996. From pilgrim to tourist—or a short history of identity. In *Questions of Identity*, ed. S Hall, P du Gay, pp. 18–34. London: Sage

Bender B. 1998. *Stonehenge: Making Space*. Oxford: Berg

Bender B. 2001. Landscapes on the move. *J. Soc. Archaeol.* 1:75–89

Bernal I. 1980. *A History of Mexican Archaeology*. London: Thames & Hudson

Bernbeck R, Pollock S. 1996. Ayodhya, archaeology, and identity. *Curr. Anthropol.* 37:138–42

Bhabha HK. 1994. *The Location of Culture*. London: Routledge

Bond GC, Gilliam A, eds. 1994. *Social Construction of the Past: Representation as Power*. London: Routledge

Brumfiel EM. 1992. Distinguished lecture in archaeology: breaking and entering the ecosystem—gender, class, and faction steal the show. *Am. Anthropol.* 94:551–67

Buchli V, Lucas G, eds. 2001. *Archaeologies of the Contemporary Past*. London: Routledge

Butler J. 1990. *Gender Trouble: Feminism and the Subversion of Identity*. New York: Routledge

Butler J. 1993. *Bodies that Matter: On the Discursive Limits of "Sex."* New York: Routledge

Butler J. 1995. Contingent foundations: feminism and the question of "postmodernism." In *Feminist Contentions: a Philosophical Exchange*, ed. S Benhabib, J Butler, J Cornell, N Fraser, L Nicholson, pp. 35–57. New York: Routledge

Butler J. 2000. *Antigone's Claim: Kinship Between Life and Death*. New York: Columbia Univ. Press

Canuto MA, Yaeger J, eds. 2000. *The Archaeology of Communities: a New World Perspective*. London: Routledge

Castañeda Q. 1996. *In the Museum of Maya Culture: Touring Chichén Itzá*. Minneapolis: Univ. Minn. Press

Chakrabarti DK. 1997. *Colonial Indology: Sociopolitics of the Ancient Indian Past*. New Delhi: Munshiram Manoharlal

Chakrabarti DK. 2000. Colonial Indology and identity. *Antiquity* 74:667–71

Chambers I, Curti L, eds. 1996. *The Post-Colonial Question*. London: Routledge

Chapman J. 1994. Destruction of a common heritage: the archaeology of war in Croatia, Bosnia and Hercegovina. *Antiquity* 68:120–26

Chinchilla Mazariegos O. 1998. Archaeology and nationalism in Guatemala at the time of independence. *Antiquity* 72:376–86

Claassen C, ed. 1992a. *Exploring Gender Through Archaeology: Selected Papers from the 1991 Boone Conference*. Madison, WI: Prehistory Press

Claassen C. 1992b. Questioning gender: an introduction. See Claassen 1992a, pp. 1–9

Clark GA. 2001. Letter to the Editor. In *Society for American Archaeology: Archaeological Record*, p. 3

Clifford J. 1997. Spatial practices: fieldwork, travel, and the disciplining of anthropology. In *Anthropological Locations: Boundaries and Grounds of a Field Science*, ed. A Gupta, J Ferguson, pp. 185–222. Berkeley: Univ. Calif. Press

Clifford J, Marcus GE, eds. 1986. *Writing*

Culture: the Poetics of Ethnography. Berkeley: Univ. Calif. Press

Cohen A. 2000. *Signifying Identities: Anthropological Perspectives on Boundaries and Contested Values*. London: Routledge

Conkey MW, Spector JD. 1984. Archaeology and the study of gender. *Adv. Archaeol. Meth. Theory* 7:1–38

Coningham R, Lewer N. 2000a. Archaeology and identity in south Asia—interpretations and consequences. *Antiquity* 74:664–67

Coningham R, Lewer N. 2000b. The Vijayan colonization and the archaeology of identity in Sri Lanka. *Antiquity* 74:707–12

David N, Gavua K, MacEachern AS, Sterner J. 1991. Ethnicity and material culture in north Cameroon. *Can. J. Archaeol.* 15:171–77

Davis DD. 1996. Revolutionary archaeology in Cuba. *J. Archaeol. Method Theory* 3:159–88

Demoule J. 1999. Ethnicity, culture and identity: French archaeologists and historians. *Antiquity* 73:190–98

Derrida J. 1978. *Writing and Difference*. Chicago: Univ. Chicago Press

Díaz-Andreu M, Champion T. 1996. *Nationalism and Archaeology in Europe*. London: Univ. College London Press

Dietler M. 1994. "Our ancestors the Gauls": archaeology, ethnic nationalism, and the manipulation of Celtic identity in modern Europe. *Am. Anthropol.* 96:584–605

Dietler M. 1998. A tale of three sites: the monumentalization of Celtic Oppida and the politics of collective memory and identity. *World Archaeol.* 30:72–89

Dietler M, Herbich I. 1998. Habitus, techniques, style: an integrated approach to the social understanding of material culture and boundaries. In *The Archaeology of Social Boundaries*, ed. MT Stark, pp. 232–63. Washington/London: Smithson. Inst. Press

Dirks N, ed. 1992. *Colonialism and Culture*. Ann Arbor: Univ. Mich. Press

Dongoske KE, Yeatts M, Anyon R, Ferguson TJ. 1997. Archaeological cultures and cultural affiliation: Hopi and Zuni perspectives in the American southwest. *Am. Antiq.* 62:600–8

Dowson TA, ed. 2000. *World Archaeology: Queer Archaeologies*, 32:2. London: Routledge

Echo-Hawk RC. 2000. Ancient history in the New World: integrating oral traditions and the archaeological record in deep time. *Am. Antiq.* 65:267–90

Edensor T. 1998. *Tourists at the Taj: Performance and Meaning at a Symbolic Site*. New York: Routledge

Elamin YM. 1999. Archaeology and modern Sudanese cultural identity. *Afr. Archaeol. Rev.* 16:1–3

Emberling G. 1997. Ethnicity in complex societies: archaeological perspectives. *J. Archaeol. Res.* 5:295–344

Engelstad E. 1991. Images of power and contradiction: feminist theory and post-processual archaeology. *Antiquity* 65:502–14

Fanon F. 1967. *Black Skin White Masks*. New York: Grove

Fawcett C. 1995. Nationalism and postwar Japanese archaeology. See Kohl & Fawcett 1995, pp. 232–46

Fleury-Ilett B. 1993. Identity of France: the archaeological interaction. *J. Eur. Archaeol.* 1: 169–80

Fotiadis M. 1993. Regions of the imagination: archaeologists, local people, and the archaeological record in fieldwork, Greece. *J. Eur. Archaeol.* 1:151–70

Foucault M. 1978. *The History of Sexuality*. London: Routledge

Franklin M. 1997. "Power to the people": sociopolitics and the archaeology of black Americans. *Hist. Archaeol.* 31:36–50

Funari PPA. 1995/1996. A "república de Palmares" e a arqueologia da Serra da Barriga. *Revista USP* 28:6–13

Funari PPA. 1999. Etnicidad, identidad y cultura material: un estudio del cimarrón Palmares, Brasil, Siglo XVII. In *Sed Non Saciata: Teoría Social en la Arqueología Latinoamericana Contemporánea*, ed. A Zarankin, F Acuto, pp. 77–96. Buenos Aires: Ediciones del Tridente

Geertz C. 1995. *After the Fact: Two Countries, Four Decades, One Anthropologist*. Cambridge, MA: Harvard Univ. Press

Gero JM, Conkey MW, eds. 1991. *Engendering Archaeology: Women and Prehistory*. Oxford: Blackwell

Ghosh A. 1992. *In an Antique Land*. London: Granta

Gibbs L. 1987. Identifying gender in the archaeological record: a contextual study. In *The Archaeology of Contextual Meanings*, ed. I Hodder, pp. 79–89. Cambridge, UK: Cambridge Univ. Press

Giddens A. 1991. *Modernity and Self-Identity: Self and Society in the Late Modern Age*. Cambridge, UK: Polity

Gilchrist R. 1991. Women's archaeology? Political feminism, gender theory and historical revision. *Antiquity* 65:495–501

Gilchrist R. 1994. *Gender and Material Culture: the Archaeology of Religious Women*. London: Routledge

Gilchrist R, ed. 2000. *World Archaeology: Lifecycles*, Vol. 31. London: Routledge

Given M. 1998. Inventing the Eteocypriots: imperialist archaeology and the manipulation of ethnic identity. *J. Mediterr. Archaeol.* 11:3–29

Goldstein L. 1992. The potential for future relationships between archaeologists and Native Americans. In *Quandaries and Quests: Visions of Archaeology's Future*, ed. L Wandsnider, pp. 59–71. Carbondale: South. Ill. Univ.

Goldstein L, Kintigh K. 1990. Ethics and the reburial controversy. *Am. Antiq.* 55:585–91

Goldstein PS. 2000. Communities without borders: the vertical archipelago and diaspora in the southern Andes. See Canuto & Yaeger 2000, pp. 182–209

Gosden C. 1999. *Anthropology and Archaeology: a Changing Relationship*. London: Routledge

Graves-Brown P, Jones S, Gamble C, eds. 1996. *Cultural Identity and Archaeology: the Construction of European Communities*. London: Routledge

Gupta A, Ferguson J, eds. 1997. *Anthropological Locations: Boundaries and Grounds of a Field Science*. Berkeley: Univ. Calif. Press

Hall JM. 1997. *Ethnic Identity in Greek Antiquity*. Cambridge, UK: Univ. Cambridge Press

Hall M. 1992. Small things and the mobile, conflictual fusion of power, fear, and desire. In *The Art and Mystery of Historical Archaeology*, ed. A Yentsch, M Beaudry, pp. 373–99. Boca Raton, FL: CRC Press

Hall M. 1994a. Lifting the veil of popular history: archaeology and politics in urban Cape Town. See Bond & Gilliam 1994, pp. 176–84

Hall M. 1994b. The secret lives of houses: women and gables in the eighteenth-century Cape. *Soc. Dyn.* 20:1–48

Hall M. 1995. Great Zimbabwe and the lost city. See Ucko 1995, pp. 28–45

Hall M. 2000. *Archaeology and the Modern World: Colonial Transcripts in South Africa and the Chesapeake*. London: Routledge

Hall S. 1996. Introduction: Who needs 'identity'? In *Questions of Identity*, ed. S Hall, P du Gay, pp. 1–17. London: Sage

Handler R, Gable E. 1997. *The New History in an Old Museum: Creating the Past at Colonial Williamsburg*. Durham, NC: Duke Univ. Press

Härke H, ed. 2000. *Archaeology, Ideology and Society: the German Experience*. Frankfurt: Lang

Härke H, Wolfram S. 1993. The power of the past. *Curr. Anthropol.* 34:182–84

Haviser JB, ed. 1999. *African Sites: Archaeology in the Caribbean*. Princeton, NJ: Wiener

Hegmon M. 1998. Technology, style, and social practices: archaeological approaches. In *The Archaeology of Social Boundaries*, ed. MT Stark, pp. 264–79. Washington/London: Smithson. Inst. Press

Helskog K, Olsen B, eds. 1995. *Perceiving Rock Art: Social and Political Perspectives*. Oslo: Inst. Comp. Res. Hum. Cult.

Hemming S. 2000. Ngarrendjeri burials as cultural sites: indigenous heritage issues in Australia. *World Archaeol. Bull.* 11:58–66

Herzfeld M. 1996. Monumental indifference? *Archaeol. Dialogues* 3:120–23

Higueras A. 1995. Archaeological research in Peru: its contribution to national identity and to the Peruvian public. *J. Steward Anthropol. Soc.* 23:391–407

Hodder I. 1982. *Symbols in Action.* Cambridge, UK: Cambridge Univ. Press

Hodder I, ed. 1991. *Archaeological Theory in Europe: the Last Three Decades.* London: Routledge

Hodder I. 1998. The past and passion and play: Çatalhöyük as a site of conflict in the construction of multiple pasts. See Meskell 1998, pp. 124–39

Hodder I. 1999. *The Archaeological Process: an Introduction.* Oxford: Blackwell

Hyland J. 1992. Archaeological meditations of the Conquest and constructions of Mexican national identity. *Kroeber Anthropol. Soc. Pap.* 73–74:92–114

Jameson JH Jr, ed. 1997. *Presenting Archaeology to the Public: Digging for Truths.* Walnut Creek, CA: AltaMira

Jenkins R. 1996. *Social Identity.* London: Routledge

Jeppson PL. 1997. "Leveling the playing field" in the contested territory of the South African past: a "public" versus a "people's" form of historical archaeology outreach. *Hist. Archaeol.* 31:65–83

Jones L. 1997a. Conquests of the imagination: Maya-Mexican polarity and the story of Chichén Itzá. *Am. Anthropol.* 99:275–90

Jones S. 1997b. *The Archaeology of Ethnicity: Constructing Identities in the Past and Present.* London: Routledge

Joyce RA. 2001. *Gender and Power in Prehispanic Mesoamerica.* Austin: Univ. Tex. Press

Joyce RA, Gillespie SD, eds. 2000. *Beyond Kinship: Social and Material Reproduction in House Societies.* Philadelphia: Univ. Penn. Press

Kent S, ed. 1998. *Gender in African Prehistory.* Walnut Creek, CA: AltaMira

Knapp AB. 1998. Who's come a long way, baby? Masculinist approaches to a gendered archaeology. *Archaeol. Dialogues* 5:91–106

Kohl PL. 1998. Nationalism and archaeology: on the constructions of nations and the reconstructions of the remote past. *Annu. Rev. Anthropol.* 27:223–46

Kohl PL, Fawcett C, eds. 1995. *Nationalism, Politics and the Practice of Archaeology.* Cambridge, UK: Cambridge Univ. Press

Lahiri N. 2000. Archaeology and identity in colonial India. *Antiquity* 74:687–92

Lampeter Archaeology Workshop. 1997. Relativism, objectivity and the politics of the past. *Archaeol. Dialogues* 4(2):164–84

Langford R. 1983. The anthropology and Aboriginal history of Hindmarsh Island, Adelaide. *Aust. Archaeol.* 16:1–16

Lennon K, Whitford M, eds. 1994. *Knowing the Difference: Feminist Perspectives in Epistemology.* London: Routledge. 300 pp.

Leone MP. 1995. A historical archaeology of capitalism. *Am. Anthropol.* 97:251–68

Lewis-Williams JD. 1995. Some aspects of rock art research in the politics of present-day South Africa. See Helskog & Olsen 1995, pp. 317–37

Lilley I, ed. 2000. *Native Title and the Transformation of Archaeology in the Postcolonial World.* Sydney: Univ. Sydney

Loofs HHE. 1979. Recent archaeological discoveries in Vietnam and their social implications. *Hong Kong Archaeol. Soc. J.* 8:99–104

Loren DD. 2000. The intersections of colonial policy and colonial practice: creolization on the eighteenth-century Louisiana/Texas frontier. *Hist. Archaeol.* 34:85–98

Lowenthal D. 1985. *The Past Is a Foreign Country.* Cambridge, UK: Cambridge Univ. Press

Lucas G. 2001. *Critical Approaches to Fieldwork: Contemporary and Historical Archaeological Practice.* London: Routledge

Lydon J. 2000. The disturbing history of Sydney's Rocks, the 'birthplace of a nation'. *World Archaeol. Bull.* 11:94–109

Lynott MJ, Wylie A, eds. 2000. *Ethics in American Archaeology.* Washington, DC: Soc. Am. Archaeol.

Mamani Condori C. 1996. History and prehistory in Bolivia: What about the Indians? In *Contemporary Archaeology in Theory: a Reader*, ed. RW Preucel, I Hodder, pp. 632–45. Oxford: Blackwell

Mandal D. 1993. *Ayodhya: Archaeology After Demolition*. New Delhi: Orient Longman
Marchand S. 1996. *Down with Olympus: Archaeology and Philhellenism in Germany 1750–1970*. Princeton, NJ: Princeton Univ. Press
McDavid C. 1997. Descendants, decisions, and power: the public interpretation of the archaeology of the Levi Jordan Plantation. *Hist. Archaeol.* 31:114–31
McDavid C. 2000. Archaeology as cultural critique: pragmatism and the archaeology of a southern United States plantation. In *Philosophy and Archaeological Practice: Perspectives for the 21st Century*, ed. C Holtorf, H Karlsson, pp. 221–39. Göteborg: Bricoleur
McGuire RH. 1992. Archaeology and the first Americans. *Am. Anthropol.* 94:816–36
McGuire RH, Navarrete R. 1999. Entre motocicletas y fusiles: las arqueologías radicales anglosajona y latinoamericana. *Bol. Antropol. Am.* 34:89–110
McKee L. 1998. Some thoughts on the past, present, and future of the archaeology of the African diaspora. *Afr. Am. Archaeol.* 21:1, 3–7
Meehan B. 1995. Aboriginal views on the management of rock art sites in Australia. See Helskog & Olsen 1995, pp. 295–316
Meskell LM. 1996. The somatisation of archaeology: institutions, discourses, corporeality. *Nor. Archaeol. Rev.* 29:1–16
Meskell LM, ed. 1998. *Archaeology Under Fire: Nationalism, Politics and Heritage in the Eastern Mediterranean and Middle East*. London: Routledge
Meskell LM. 1999. *Archaeologies of Social Life: Age, Sex, Class etc. in Ancient Egypt*. Oxford: Blackwell
Meskell LM. 2000. *Sites of violence: terrorism, tourism and heritage in the archaeological present*. Presented at Am. Anthropol. Assoc., San Francisco
Meskell LM. 2001a. Archaeologies of identity. In *Archaeological Theory: Breaking the Boundaries*, ed. I Hodder, pp. 187–213. Cambridge, UK: Polity
Meskell LM. 2001b. The practice and politics of archaeology in Egypt. In *Ethics and Anthropology: Facing Future Issues in Human Biology, Globalism, and Cultural Property*, ed. A-M Cantwell, E Friedlander, ML Tram, pp. 146–69. New York: Ann. NY Acad. Sci.
Meskell LM. 2002. *Private Life in New Kingdom Egypt*. Princeton, NJ: Princeton Univ. Press
Moore J, Scott E, eds. 1997. *Invisible People and Processes: Writing Gender and Childhood into European Archaeology*. London: Leicester Univ. Press
Moser S. 1995. The 'Aboriginalization' of Australian archaeology. See Ucko 1995, pp. 150–77
Mullins PR. 1999. *Race and Affluence: an Archaeology of African America and Consumer Culture*. New York: Kluwer Acad./Plenum
Naccache AFH. 1998. Beirut's memoryside: hear no evil, see no evil. See Meskell 1998, pp. 140–58
Odermatt P. 1996. Built heritage and the politics of (re)presentation: local reactions to the appropriation of the monumental past in Sardinia. *Archaeol. Dialogues* 3:95–136
Odner K. 1985. Saamis (Lapps), Finns and Scandinavians in history and prehistory. Ethnic origins and ethnic process in Fenno-Scandinavia (and comments). *Nor. Archaeol. Rev.* 18:135
Orser CEJ. 1998. The archaeology of the African diaspora. *Annu. Rev. Anthropol.* 27:63–82
Orser CEJ. 1999. The challenge of race to American historical archaeology. *Am. Anthropol.* 100:661–68
Özdogan M. 1998. Ideology and archaeology in Turkey. See Meskell 1998, pp. 111–23
Paddayya K. 1995. Theoretical perspectives in Indian archaeology. See Ucko 1995, pp. 110–49
Pai H. 2000. *Constructing "Korean" Origins: a Critical Review of Archaeology, Historiography, and Racial Myth in Korean State-Formation Theories*. Cambridge, MA: Harvard Univ. Asia Cent./Harvard Univ. Press
Pardoe C. 1990. Sharing the past: Aboriginal

influence on archaeological practice, a case study from New South Wales. *Aborig. Hist.* 14:208–23

Patterson TC. 1994. *Toward a Social History of Archaeology in the United States*. New York: Harcourt Brace

Patterson TC. 1995. Archaeology, history, *Indigenismo*, and the state in Peru and Mexico. See Schmidt & Patterson 1995, pp. 69–85

Patterson TC. 1999. The political economy of archaeology in the United States. *Annu. Rev. Anthropol.* 28:155–74

Paynter R, McGuire RH. 1991. The archaeology of inequality: material culture, domination, and resistance. In *The Archaeology of Inequality*, ed. RH McGuire, R Paynter, pp. 1–27. Oxford: Blackwell

Pokotylo D, Guppy N. 1999. Public opinion and archaeological heritage: views from outside the profession. *Am. Antiq.* 64:400–16

Politis G. 1995. The socio-politics of the development of archaeology in Hispanic South America. See Ucko 1995, pp. 197–235

Politis G. 2001. On archaeological praxis, gender bias and indigenous peoples in South America. *J. Soc. Archaeol.* 1:90–107

Potter PB Jr. 1992. Critical archaeology: in the ground and on the street. *Hist. Archaeol.* 26:117–29

Ramos A. 1994. From Eden to limbo: the construction of indigenism in Brazil. See Bond & Gilliam 1994, pp. 74–88

Rao N. 1994. Interpreting silences: symbol and history in the case of Ram Janmabhoomi/Babri Masjid. See Bond & Gilliam 1994, pp. 154–64

Reid A, Lane P, Segobye A, Borjeson L, Mathibidi N, Sekgarametso P. 1997. Tswana architecture and responses to colonialism. *World Archaeol.* 28:370–92

Reid DM. 1997. Nationalizing the pharaonic past: Egyptology, imperialism and nationalism, 1922–1952. In *Rethinking Nationalism in the Arab Middle East*, ed. J Jankowski, I Gershoni, pp. 127–49. New York: Columbia Univ. Press

Rotman DL, Nassaney MS. 1997. Class, gender, and the built environment: deriving social relations from cultural landscapes in southwest Michigan. *Hist. Archaeol.* 31:42–62

Russel AE. 1997. Material culture and African-American spirituality at the Hermitage. *Hist. Archaeol.* 31:63–80

Scham SA. 1998. Mediating nationalism and archaeology: a matter of trust? *Am. Anthropol.* 100:301–8

Scham SA. 2001. The archaeology of the disenfranchised. *J. Archaeol. Method Theory* 8(2):183–213

Schmidt PR. 1995. Using archaeology to remake history in Africa. See Schmidt & Patterson 1995, pp. 119–47

Schmidt PR, Patterson TC, eds. 1995. *Making Alternative Histories: the Practice of Archaeology and History in Non-Western Settings*. Santa Fe, NM: Sch. Am. Res. Press

Schmidt RA, Voss BL, eds. 2000. *Archaeologies of Sexuality*. London: Routledge

Schnapp A. 1996. French archaeology: between national identity and cultural identity. In *Nationalism and Archaeology in Europe*, ed. M Díaz-Andreu, T Champion, pp. 48–67. London: Univ. College London Press

Shaw J. 2000. Ayodhya's sacred landscape: ritual memory, politics and archaeological 'fact'. *Antiquity* 74:693–700

Shennan S, ed. 1994. *Archaeological Approaches to Cultural Identity*. London: Routledge

Shnirelman VA. 1995. Alternative prehistory. *J. Eur. Archaeol.* 3:1–20

Singleton TA. 1995. The archaeology of slavery in North America. *Annu. Rev. Anthropol.* 24:119–40

Singleton TA. 1999. *"I, Too, Am American": Archaeological Studies of African-American Life*. Charlottesville: Univ. Press Va.

Sofaer-Derevenski J, ed. 2000. *Children and Material Culture*. London: Routledge

Soja EW. 2000. *Postmetropolis: Critical Studies of Cities and Regions*. Oxford: Blackwell

Sökefeld M. 1999. Debating self, identity, and culture in anthropology. *Curr. Anthropol.* 40:417–47

Staski E. 1990. Studies of ethnicity in North

American historical archaeology. *N. Am. Archaeol.* 11:121–45
Stine LF. 1990. Social inequality and turn-of-the-century farmsteads: issues of class, status, ethnicity, and race. *Hist. Archaeol.* 24:37–49
Sued Badillo J. 1995. The theme of the indigenous in the national projects of the Hispanic Caribbean. See Schmidt & Patterson 1995, pp. 25–46
Swidler N, Dongoske KE, Anyon R, Downer AS, eds. 1997. *Native Americans and Archaeologists: Stepping Stones to Common Ground.* Walnut Creek, CA: AltaMira
Thomas DH. 2000. *Skull Wars: Kennewick Man, Archaeology, and the Battle for Native American Identity.* New York: Basic Books
Thomas N. 1999. *Possessions: Indigenous Art/Colonial Culture.* London: Thames & Hudson
Tong E. 1995. Thirty years of Chinese archaeology (1949–1979). See Kohl & Fawcett 1995, pp. 177–97
Trigger BG. 1984. Alternative archaeologies: nationalist, colonialist, imperialist. *Man* 19: 355–70
Trigger BG. 1989. *A History of Archaeological Thought.* Cambridge, UK: Cambridge Univ. Press
Trigger BG. 1995. Romanticism, nationalism, and archaeology. See Kohl & Fawcett 1995, pp. 263–79
Tsude H. 1995. Archaeological theory in Japan. See Ucko 1995, pp. 298–311
Ucko PJ. 1995. *Theory in Archaeology: a World Perspective.* London: Routledge
Upton D. 1996. Ethnicity, authenticity, and invented traditions. *Hist. Archaeol.* 30:1–7
van Dommelen P. 1997. Colonial constructs: colonialism and archaeology in the Mediterranean. *World Archaeol.* 28:305–23
van Dommelen P. 1998. Between academic doubt and political involvement. *J. Mediterr. Archaeol.* 11:117–21
Vargas Arenas I. 1995. The perception of history and archaeology in Latin America: a theoretical approach. See Schmidt & Patterson 1995, pp. 47–67
Vitelli KD, ed. 1996. *Archaeological Ethics.* Walnut Creek, CA: AltaMira
Von Falkenhausen L. 1995. The regionalist paradigm in Chinese archaeology. See Kohl & Fawcett 1995, pp. 198–217
Wall D. 1999. Examining gender, class and ethnicity in nineteenth-century New York City. *Hist. Archaeol.* 33:102–17
Weik T. 1997. Archaeology of maroon societies in the Americas: resistance, cultural continuity, and transformation in the African diaspora. *Hist. Archaeol.* 31:81–92
Wells PS. 1998. Identity and material culture in the later prehistory of Central Europe. *J. Archaeol. Res.* 6:239–98
Wilkie LA, Bartoy KM. 2000. A critical archaeology revisited. *Curr. Anthropol.* 41:747–77
Williams B. 1992. Of straightening combs, sodium hydroxide, and potassium hydroxide in archaeological and cultural-anthropological analyses of ethnogenesis. *Am. Antiq.* 57:608–12
Woodhouse-Beyer K. 1999. Artels and identities: gender, power, and Russian America. In *Manifesting Power: Gender and the Interpretation of Power in Archaeology*, ed. T Sweely, pp. 129–54. London: Routledge
Workshop LA. 1997. Relativism, objectivity and the politics of the past. *Archaeol. Dialogues* 4:164–84
Yanagisako S, Delaney C. 1995. Naturalizing power. In *Naturalizing Power: Essays in Feminist Cultural Analysis*, ed. S Yanagisako, C Delaney, pp. 1–22. New York: Routledge
Yates T, Nordbladh J. 1990. This perfect body, this virgin text: between sex and gender in archaeology. In *Archaeology After Structuralism*, ed. I Bapty, T Yates, pp. 222–37. London: Routledge

Annu. Rev. Anthropol. 2002. 31:303–21
doi: 10.1146/annurev.anthro.31.040402.085413

First published online as a Review in Advance on June 4, 2002

THE HUMAN Y CHROMOSOME HAPLOGROUP TREE: Nomenclature and Phylogeography of Its Major Divisions

Michael F. Hammer[1,2] and Stephen L. Zegura[1]
[1]Department of Anthropology and [2]Division of Biotechnology, University of Arizona, Tucson, Arizona 85721; email: mhammer@u.arizona.edu

Key Words NRY binary markers, typing recommendations, cladistics, African origin, Siberia

■ **Abstract** In this review we discuss the recent construction of a highly resolved tree of the nonrecombining portion of the Y chromosome (NRY), and the development of a cladistic nomenclatural system to name the resulting haplogroups. This phylogenetic gene tree comprises 18 major haplogroups that are defined by 48 binary polymorphisms. We also present results from a phylogeographic analysis of NRY haplogroups in a global sample of 2007 males, as well as from a regional study focusing on Siberia ($n = 902$). We use the following statistical techniques to explicate our presentation: analysis of molecular variance, multidimensional scaling, comparative measures of genetic diversity, and phylogeography-based frequency distributions. Our global results, based on the 18 major haplogroups, are similar to those from previous analyses employing additional markers and support the hypothesis of an African origin of human NRY diversity. Although Africa exhibits greater divergence among haplogroups, Asia contains the largest number of major haplogroups ($N = 15$). The multidimensional scaling analysis plot indicates that the Americas, Africa, and East Asia are outliers, whereas the rest of the world forms a large central cluster. According to our new global-level analysis of molecular variance, 43% of the total variance of NRY haplogroups is attributable to differences among populations (i.e., $\Phi_{ST} = 0.43$). The Siberian regional analysis of 62 binary markers exhibits nonrandom associations between geographically restricted NRY haplogroups and language families. We conclude with a list of typing recommendations for laboratories that wish to use the Y chromosome as a tool to investigate questions of anthropological interest.

HISTORY OF Y CHROMOSOME MARKERS

The paternally inherited Y chromosome contains the largest nonrecombining block of nucleotides (NRY) in the human genome, recently estimated to be 50 million base pairs (bp) in length and comprising 95% of the entire chromosome

(Bachtrog & Charlesworth 2001, Tilford et al. 2001). Although the first restriction fragment length polymorphisms (RFLPs) on the NRY were not identified until 1985 (Casanova et al. 1985, Lucotte & Ngo 1985), by 2001 two different laboratories had published highly congruent globally based evolutionary trees for the NRY (Underhill et al. 2000, Hammer et al. 2001). After a rather slow start to the search for additional polymorphic sites on the NRY, the past five years have witnessed a veritable data explosion both in terms of number of markers discovered and populations assayed. One of the major reasons for the lack of early progress is that the NRY has a much lower level of polymorphism than any other region of the human genome (International SNP Map Working Group 2001). In fact, by the end of 1996 fewer than 60 NRY polymorphisms had been published, only 11 of which could be genotyped by polymerase chain reaction (PCR) methods. Included among these 11 markers were an ALU insertion, a deletion, and 9 single nucleotide polymorphisms (SNPs) (Hammer 1994, Seielstad et al. 1994, Hammer & Horai 1995, Whitfield et al. 1995, Santos et al. 1995, Jobling et al. 1996, Underhill et al. 1996). In 1997, Underhill and colleagues published 19 new PCR-based polymorphisms found by a novel and efficient mutation detection method known as denaturing high performance liquid chromatography (DHPLC) (Underhill et al. 1997). DHPLC has since been used to discover more than 200 SNPs and small insertions/deletions (indels) on the NRY (Shen et al. 2000, Underhill et al. 2000, Hammer et al. 2001). These types of polymorphisms are particularly useful because of their low rates of parallel and back mutation, which underscore their suitability for identifying stable paternal lineages that can be traced back thousands of years (Karafet et al. 1999, Thomson et al. 2000). Unfortunately, as the number of known polymorphisms increased, so did the number of different systems devised to name the resulting haplogroups. As 2001 comes to a close, there are at least seven different nomenclature systems in use, making it very difficult to compare results from one publication to the next. Our purpose here is twofold: (*a*) to describe the recently published tree of NRY haplogroups and the corresponding nomenclatural system proposed by the Y Chromosome Consortium (YCC 2002), which unifies and supercedes past nomenclatures, and (*b*) to present a phylogeographic analysis of the major NRY haplogroups in a global sample of human males. This should aid anthropological geneticists in the selection and typing of relevant sets of Y chromosome markers in particular populations and will facilitate the efficient accession of information contained in human Y chromosome publications.

Indeed, the haploid Y chromosome (Jegalian & Lahn 2001) has become an extremely important tool in a variety of areas of particular interest to anthropologists, including DNA forensics (Jobling et al. 1997), medical genetics (Jobling & Tyler-Smith 2000), genealogical reconstruction (Jobling 2001), molecular archaeology (Stone et al. 1996), nonhuman primate genetics (Stone et al. 2002), and human evolutionary studies (Hammer & Zegura 1996; Underhill et al. 2000, 2001; Hammer et al. 2001).

CLADISTICS FRAMEWORK FOR A STANDARDIZED NRY NOMENCLATURE SYSTEM

Precise referential terminology is indispensable for successful communication of information in any area of scientific endeavor. Before turning to the Y chromosome, the principal data source for reconstructing the paternal evolutionary history of our species, it is necessary to visit some of the terminological distinctions championed by the Hennigian school of phylogenetic systematics, also known as cladistics (Hennig 1966). These principles and associated definitional framework have been applied during the construction of the recently published Y Chromosome Consortium human Y-chromosome tree (YCC 2002) and were used in the development of the nomenclatural systems devised to accompany and explicate the present and future versions of this evolutionary tree. Figure 1 presents an overview of the partitioning of overall biological similarity into phylogenetically useful and phylogenetically uninformative/deceptive components (Hennig 1966, Sneath & Sokal 1973, Hull 1988). For those interested in pursuing the topic of how to distinguish phylogenetically useful characters in greater depth than the brief discussion provided below, Jolly (2001) has recently published a particularly eloquent and highly instructive (albeit quite sobering) review of the application/misapplication of cladistic methodology to morphological, behavioral, and genetic data sets in primate evolutionary studies.

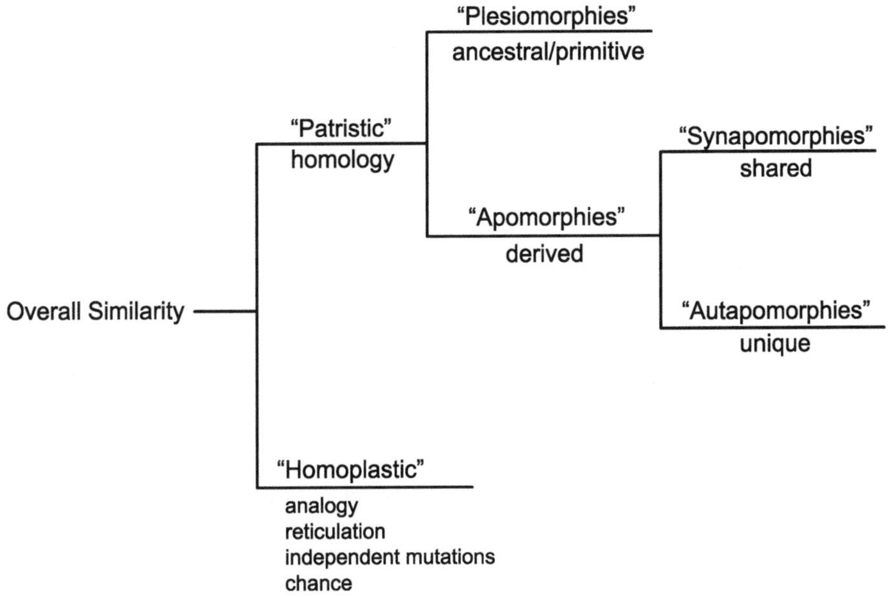

Figure 1 A classification of overall biological similarity. Terms in quotation marks are defined in the text.

Overall phenotypic (phenetic) similarity or genetic similarity can be divided into two major subcategories: (*a*) patristic similarity and (*b*) homoplastic similarity. Patristic similarity involves the correspondence of features due to common ancestry. These are traits that are similar because they are homologous. Homoplastic similarity involves a variety of causes that do not represent inheritance from a common ancestor. An example is evolutionary convergence, wherein unrelated or distantly related evolutionary lines come to resemble one another in certain traits because of similar adaptations to similar environmental pressures. Here, similarity in appearance and/or function occurs for reasons other than common ancestry and these traits are said to be analogous rather than homologous. Other situations leading to character homoplasy include reticulation (gene flow), independent (parallel and back) mutations, chance, incorrect character polarity assessment in terms of ancestral versus derived status of a trait, and other data matrix-associated errors.

Patristic similarity can be further subdivided into ancestral and derived. Traits that exhibit ancestral, retained, or primitive homologies are called plesiomorphies or symplesiomorphies when shared between or among taxa. Derived homologous traits are called apomorphies. The final subdivision in Hennig's system takes derived homologous traits and separates them into shared derived traits called synapomorphies and uniquely derived traits called autapomorphies. It is crucial to understand that apomorphy and plesiomorphy are relative concepts that depend on the comparative framework of analysis. The same character (trait) can be a synapomorphy in one context or a symplesiomorphy in another depending on the outgroups and/or the taxonomic category levels used (Hennig 1966).

In general, only apomorphies are deemed to be useful for phylogenetic reconstruction by proponents of Hennigian methods. Autopomorphies are employed to define new taxa, whereas synapomorphies (i.e., shared, derived homologies) are the exclusive source of information for assessing the evolutionary relationships among taxa. Hennig based this methodology on the assumption that genealogical descent with modification (i.e., Darwin's definition of evolution) is the process responsible for producing organic diversity. In actual practice, cladists classify by inferred branching patterns. They attempt to recover phylogenetic (genealogical) relationships among groups of organisms and produce classifications that exactly reflect those genealogical relationships (Wiley 1981). Thus, the processes of phylogenetic (historical) reconstruction and classification are not separated. Character evolution permits the reconstruction of character phylogenies. Concordant character phylogenies are then used as the basis for deducing the pattern of taxic evolution. Character analysis is, therefore, the key step in a cladistic analysis.

The human Y-chromosome tree presented and discussed below is actually a single gene (character/trait) tree because the lack of recombination within the NRY means that this entire region behaves evolutionarily like a single genetic locus. Each genetic locus has its own evolutionary history, and different population structures and demographic processes can lead to different phylogenetic patterns for these diverse genetic systems. Thus, the human NRY tree, mitochondrial DNA tree, and trees based on different autosomal systems do not necessarily have to be concordant with each other. This makes the phylogenetic inference of our species' true genetic history a difficult (but not impossible) undertaking. It is important to understand that this paper concentrates on character, rather than taxic, evolution.

The biological concept of monophyly is also pertinent to the subsequent explication of how the human Y-chromosome tree was constructed. It is important to note that monophyly is defined differently in phylogenetic systematics and in traditional classical or evolutionary taxonomy. For instance, Mayr (1981) uses the word monophyletic in its original sense as a qualifying adjective of a taxon such that a taxon is monophyletic if all of its members are derived from the nearest common ancestor. A monophyletic group would also include the most recent common ancestor as a member of the group (Ridley 1986). For cladists the term monophyletic becomes a qualifying adjective for descent and is a property of common ancestry and descent. According to this perspective, a monophyletic group is one that contains all and only the descendants of a particular common ancestor (Donoghue 1985). When only some of the descendants of a common ancestor are placed in a group, this group is called paraphyletic by cladists. Paraphyletic groups are usually based on symplesiomorphies or on overall phenetic or genetic similarity. Another nonmonophyletic group is one based on homoplastic similarity. This is called a polyphyletic group and entails multiple common ancestors. Paraphyletic groups abound in evolutionary taxonomy. Polyphyletic groups are more rare; however, the concept of grades (as functional levels of organization) is widely used by evolutionary taxonomists and often encompasses both polyphyletic and paraphyletic entities (Janvier 1984, Wiley 1981). In principle, cladists only recognize monophyletic assemblages when constructing cladograms or phylogenetic trees. Cladograms are essentially synapomorphy distribution schemes. Sister groups (taxa that share a most recent common ancestor) are constructed to depict genealogical descent; cladistic classifications are required to reflect these phylogenetic relationships (Hennig 1966).

The YCC has recently adopted a phylogenetic (cladistics)-based nomenclatural system for the human NRY gene tree in an attempt to standardize how different research groups should refer to the rapidly increasing number of binary polymorphism-defined (see below) paternal lineages in the literature (YCC 2002). These dramatic advances in the resolution of the NRY tree have already resulted in multiple idiosyncratic nomenclatural systems that have hampered communication among NRY researchers and have caused a great deal of confusion for the scientific community at large (including anthropologists). The system explained below is flexible in its ability to assign names at different levels of the phylogenetic hierarchy and can be readily applied to newly discovered marker systems and paternal lineages. Monophyletic groups (i.e., haplogroups) are clearly differentiated from paraphyletic groups (i.e., paragroups), and both the current status as well as the dynamic nature of the human NRY tree should be readily accessible to nonspecialists conversant with basic concepts from cladistics.

MARKERS ON THE NRY

There are several classes of markers on the NRY including microsatellites or short tandem repeats (STRs), minisatellites, insertion/deletion polymorphisms (indels), and single nucleotide polymorphisms (SNPs) (Hammer & Zegura 1996). Microsatellites consist of short tandem arrays of repeat units ranging from 1 to 6 base pairs (bp) in length, whereas minisatellites consist of longer tandem arrays of repeat units ranging in length from 10 to more than 100 bp. Microsatellites and minisatellites can vary in the number of repeat units and/or in the sequence of individual repeat units. Microsatellites (STRs) mutate via a stepwise mutation mechanism (replication slippage) that favors very small (usually one repeat unit) changes in array length. Because their high mutation rates (estimated to be ~0.23%/STR/generation in human pedigrees) (Heyer et al. 1997, Kayser et al. 2000) often lead to situations where two alleles with the same repeat number are not identical by descent (and are, therefore, homoplasies), these markers are not very useful for constructing trees or for inferring the relationships of divergent human populations. Rather, the high heterozygosity of STRs makes them useful for forensic and paternity analysis and for inferring affinities among closely related populations. Studies of more ancient relationships among populations and attempts to reconstruct ancestral relationships among NRY lineages require polymorphisms with lower probabilities of back and parallel mutation (i.e., lower levels of homoplasy) and systems for which the ancestral states can be determined. SNPs and small indels, with mutation rates on the order of $2–4 \times 10^{-8}$/site/generation, are best suited for these purposes. Because these markers are likely to have only two allelic classes segregating in human populations, they are sometimes referred to as binary markers, biallelic markers, or UEPs (unique event polymorphisms). We prefer the term binary markers and use it rather than the other two synonyms.

The NRY has the lowest level of polymorphism of the 24 different human chromosomes (International SNP Map Working Group 2001). Estimates based on sequencing studies show that there is an average of one nucleotide difference per 10,000 bp between two randomly drawn NRY sequences (Whitfield et al. 1995, Shen et al. 2000; M.F. Hammer, unpublished data). This compares with a human whole-genome average rate of one SNP for every 1,000–2,000 bp (International Human Genome Sequencing Consortium 2001, Kruglyak & Nickerson 2001, Venter et al. 2001). Moreover, in human populations there is an over-abundance of rare derived NRY alleles compared with common polymorphisms (i.e., those where the derived allele occurs at a global frequency of $\geq$10%). For example, singleton polymorphisms (i.e., where the derived state is only found on a single Y chromosome) are present at approximately 10 out of every 10,000 bp on the NRY, whereas common polymorphisms are found at a rate of 2 per 10,000 bp (M.F. Hammer, unpublished data). Because of these low rates of polymorphism, a strategy to identify SNPs has been adopted in which several kilobases of DNA on the NRY are sequenced in a small sample of males (e.g., 50–100). SNPs identified in these surveys are then typically genotyped in much larger population samples (e.g., Underhill et al. 2000, Hammer et al. 2001). This strategy circumvents the prohibitive cost and labor required to sequence the same length of DNA in all samples surveyed. The problem with this strategy is that it can result in an ascertainment bias: Polymorphic sites are missed in chromosomes that are genotyped but not sequenced. This means that more emphasis is given to SNPs that happen to be found in the panel of sequenced chromosomes, and to the extent that there is a bias in this representation, there will be a bias in the evolutionary relationships constructed from these data. Fortunately, most of the laboratories that have published SNPs following this strategy have used panels of globally representative Y chromosomes. For example, Underhill et al. (2000) surveyed sequence variation in a panel of 53 samples (13 sub-Saharan Africans, 8 Europeans/Middle Easterners, 22 Asians, 6 Oceanians, and 4 Native Americans), whereas Hammer et al. (2001) surveyed DNA sequences in a panel of 57 males (17 sub-Saharan Africans, 15 Asians, 11 Europeans, 7 Native Americans, and 7 Oceanians). Unfortunately, for regional-scale studies involving populations that are not represented in ascertainment panels for mutation detection experiments, a significant portion of local SNP diversity will be missed. This is a serious problem when assessing the relative amounts of diversity within, and genetic divergence among, local populations, especially because most NRY binary polymorphisms are geographically restricted (Hammer & Zegura 1996, Seielstad et al. 1998, Hammer et al. 2001). We believe that the use of Y-STRs with high mutation rates in combination with Y-SNPs will help to alleviate the effects of these sorts of biases.

NOMENCLATURE AND TERMINOLOGY

The terms haplogroup and haplotype have various, often overlapping definitions in the literature. The YCC (2002) report follows the terminology of de Knijff (2000) in which the term haplogroup refers to NRY lineages defined by binary polymorphisms, whereas the term haplotype is reserved for all sublineages of haplogroups that are defined by variation at STRs on the NRY. Terms such as lineage, basal lineage, sublineage, clade, and subclade all refer to tree branches, often at different hierarchical levels. Mutations labeled with the prefix "M" (standing for mutation) were published by Underhill et al. (2000, 2001), whereas many of the mutations with the prefix "P" (standing for polymorphism) were described by Hammer et al. (1998, 2001). Monophyletic haplogroups are distinguished from lineages that are not defined on the basis of a derived character and which represent underived internal nodes of the haplogroup tree. Such lineages are potentially paraphyletic (i.e., they are comprised of basal lineages and monophyletic subclades). The term paragroup is used to refer to lineages that belong to a clade but not to its subclades. Paragroups are highly sensitive to changes in tree topology, and a given paragroup name may refer to different sets of chromosomes in succeeding versions of the human Y-chromosome tree. In essence, paragroups function much like a plesion (i.e., a plesiomorphic sister group of a monophyletic assemblage) in cladistic analyses that include both extant and fossil taxa (Schwartz et al. 1978, YCC 2002).

Two complementary nomenclatures were proposed in the YCC (2002) report. The first is hierarchical and uses selected aspects of set theory to enable monophyletic clades at all levels to be named unambiguously. Nineteen capital letters (Y, and A–R) are used to identify the major clades and constitute the initial symbols for all subsequent subclade names (Figure 2). Paragroups are distinguished by the addition of a star (*) symbol after the clade designation. Subclades nested within each major haplogroup are named using an alternating alphanumeric system with lower case letters instead of capital letters (once again, paragroups at all levels of the tree are labeled with a * symbol), and the system continues to alternate between numerals and lower case letters until the most terminal branches (i.e., the tip haplogroups) are labeled (see Figure 1 in YCC 2002; also available at http://ycc.biosci.arizona.edu). Thus, the name of each haplogroup contains the information needed to find its location in the tree. The YCC (2002) document recommends that this lineage-based nomenclatural designation be used at least once in any paper dealing with binary polymorphism data on the human NRY.

Alternatively, haplogroups can be named by the mutations that define lineages. This "short-hand" nomenclatural system retains the major haplogroup information (i.e., the 19 capital letters), followed by the name of the terminal mutation that defines a given haplogroup. This system is distinguished from the lineage-based system by including a dash (-) between the capital letter and the mutation name (i.e., capital letter-mutation name; see YCC 2002 for specific examples). Although the adoption of this mutation-based nomenclatural system remains optional, its simplicity and the general familiarity of workers in the Y chromosome field with the widely known "M" and "P" alphanumeric mutational designations lead us to predict that it will become the preferred and most commonly used system.

The YCC (2002) report details the correspondences among seven NRY nomenclatural systems in use before the standardization proposal was published. These previous, and often idiosyncratic, systems were extremely inconsistent (i.e., nonisomorphic) in how they defined haplogroups. Moreover, when there was some consistency between two systems, different names were used for the same haplogroups. Also, all of the human NRY nomenclature schemes published so far have included some unrecognized paraphyletic groupings that can lead to misinterpretations (e.g., when paragroups are thought to be ancestral to descendant haplogroups containing more-derived character states).

THE NRY HAPLOGROUP TREE

The YCC-based tree in Figure 2 was constructed from 237 NRY polymorphisms (YCC 2002). Most of the known binary polymorphisms were typed in a single set of samples (74 male YCC cell lines); however, not all of these markers were variable in the YCC cell line panel. Therefore, additional samples were included to improve the resolution of the phylogeny. For a complete presentation of these marker positions, consult YCC (2002); we show a truncated version of this tree wherein only those markers that define the 18 major haplogroups are listed (Figure 2). Although levels of homoplasy for SNPs are generally much lower than for STRs, there were eight cases of mutational homoplasy at the 237 polymorphic sites. Fortunately, these recurrent mutations were found on different haplogroup backgrounds and, thus, were distinguishable events. This brought the total number of mutational events on the NRY tree to 245. These 245 mutational events gave rise to 153 NRY haplogroups.

To infer the position of the root in the human NRY tree, homologous regions on the NRY of closely related species (e.g., chimpanzees, gorillas, and orangutans) were sequenced whenever possible to determine the ancestral states at human polymorphic sites (YCC 2002). The root of the tree (arrow in Figure 2) falls between a clade defined by the M91 marker and a clade defined by the following set of markers: SRY_{10831a}, M42, M94, and M139. The root falls between haplogroup A and the compound haplogroup BR that encompasses the rest of the tree.

Determining which clades were to receive the highest labeling level was to some extent an arbitrary decision. Clades that were deemed to represent major divisions of human NRY diversity were labeled with single capital letters (YCC 2002). The NRY tree in Figure 2 can be seen as a series of nested monophyletic clades (i.e., a set of lineages related by a shared, derived state at a single site or set of sites) and was drawn as asymmetrically as possible by sorting the descendants of each interior node so that the bottom-most descendant had the greatest number of immediate descendants.

The time to the most recent common ancestral (TMRCA) Y-chromosome and the ages of the mutations defining the major clades on the NRY haplogroup tree have been estimated using the GENETREE program of Bahlo & Griffiths (2000) assuming a random mating population of constant size (Table 1). The TMRCA of ~90,000 years is in agreement with other recent estimates (Thomson et al. 2000).

→

Figure 2 The single most parsimonious tree of 153 haplogroups. The root of the tree is denoted by an arrow. Major haplogroups are labeled with large capital letters and are shaded in boxes except in the cases of *F*, *K*, and *P*, which are shown in open boxes (the entire cladogram is designated haplogroup *Y*). The (*) symbol indicates an internal node on the tree and denotes a paragroup (e.g., *F**, *K**, and *P**; see text for explanation). The length of each branch is proportional to the number of mutations (see key for single mutation unit length). The names of mutations defining the major haplogroups are given along the appropriate branches (mutations within major haplogroups are not shown). The order of phylogenetically equivalent markers shown on each branch is arbitrary. The circles at the ends of some branches denote haplogroups/paragroups present in a regional study of Siberia. Six of these haplogroups/paragroups were present at frequencies ≥10% across Siberia (*shaded circles*), nine were present at frequencies ≤2% (*unshaded circles*), and eight were found in only a single individual (singletons not shown).

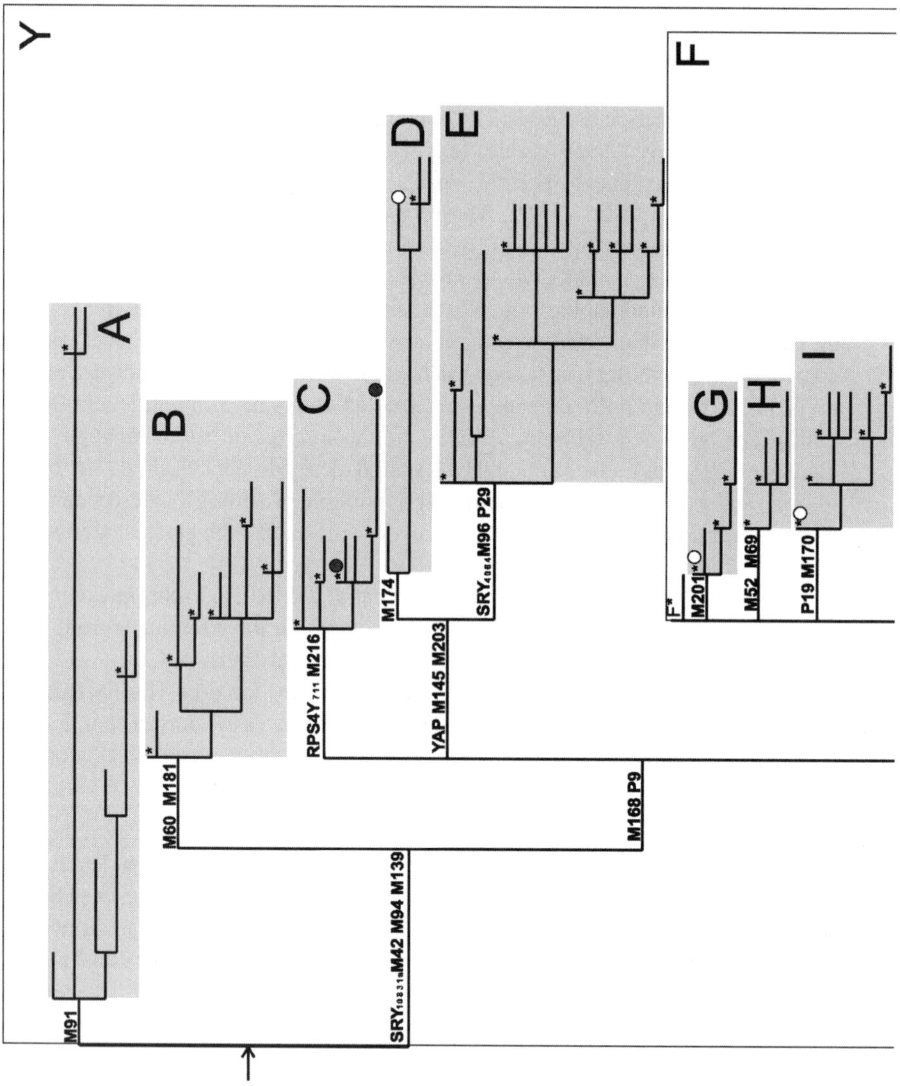
Y
A
B
C
D
E
F
G
H
I
M91
SRY10831a M42 M94 M139
M60 M181
M168 P9
RPS4Y711 M216
YAP M145 M203
M174
SRY4064 M96 P29
F*
M201
M52 M69
P19 M170

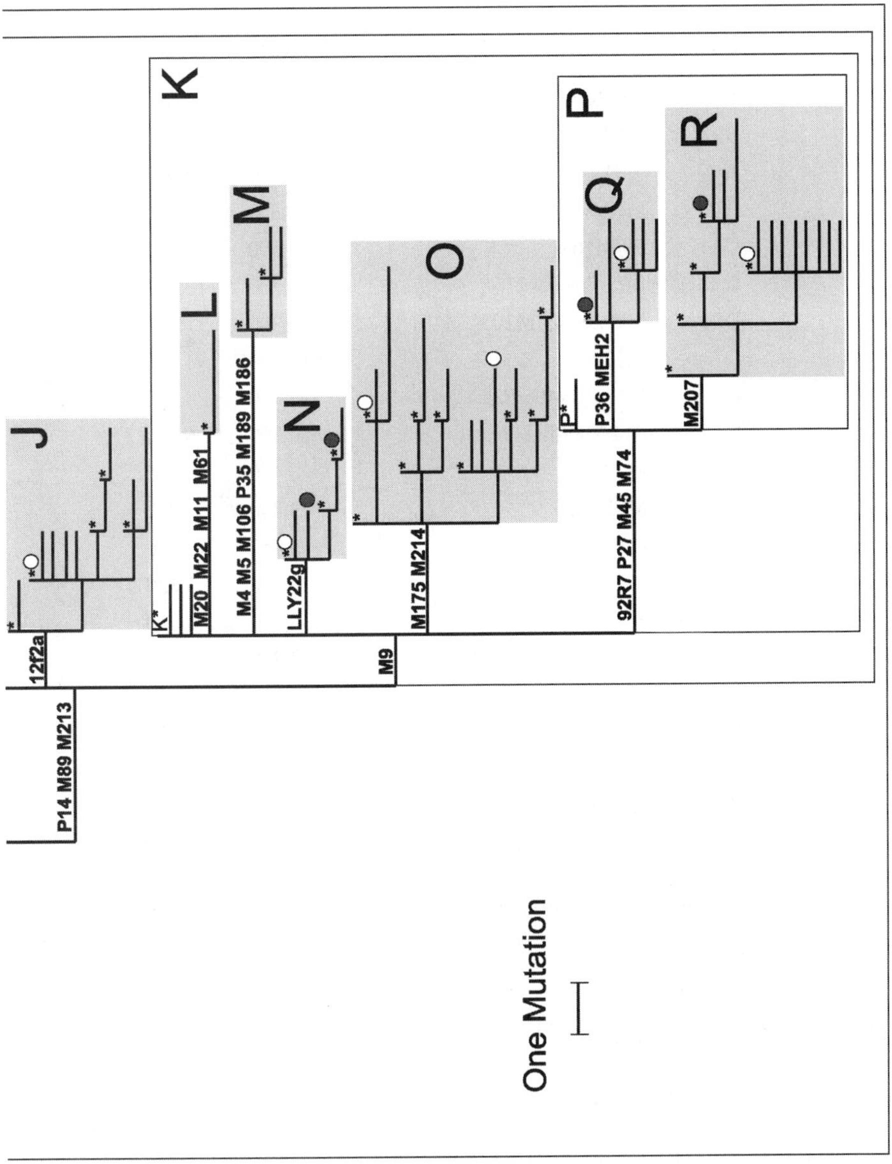
J
12f2a
P14 M89 M213
M9
K
K*
M20 M22 M11 M61
L
M4 M5 M106 P35 M189 M186
M
LLY22g
N
M175 M214
O
P
P*
P36 MEH2
Q
M207
R
92R7 P27 M45 M74
One Mutation

TABLE 1 TMRCA and ages* of mutations defining the major clades of the NRY haplogroup tree

Clade	Mutation(s)	Age (years)	Standard deviation (years)
Y	TMRCA	90,420	20,090
BR	SRY_{10831a}/M42/M94/M139	82,000	17,000
A	M91	42,800	23,000
B	M60/M181	36,800	13,600
CR	P9/M168	68,500	6,030
C	$RPS4Y_{711}$/M216	27,500	10,100
DE	YAP/M145/M203	38,300	7,830
D	M174	13,000	4,700
E	SRY_{4064}/M96/P29	17,400	3,200
F	P14/M89/M213	50,300	6,500
G	M201	6,470	2,990
H	M52/M69	3,850	2,770
I	P19/M170	5,950	2,450
J	12f2a	9,840	3,820
K	M9	35,600	6,010
L	M20/M22/M11/M61	2,910	2,120
M	M4/M5/M106/P35/M189/M186	12,700	7,160
N	LLY22g	8,830	3,170
O	M175/M214	17,500	4,630
P	P27/M45/92R7M74	29,900	4,200
Q	P36/MEH2	17,700	4,820
R	M207	16,300	4,430

*Based on a model of constant population size, $\theta = 14$, and 20 million simulations using GENETREE (Bahlo & Griffiths 2000).

PHYLOGEOGRAPHIC ANALYSIS

In this section, we present an analysis of a set of markers that define the highest clade-level haplogroups in the YCC tree. Many of the 48 markers shown in Figure 3 (see color insert) are phylogenetically equivalent; that is, they define the same clade on the NRY tree. We genotyped the 20 markers shown as red-labeled cross-hatches in Figure 3 and assumed that each of these markers was, indeed, phylogenetically equivalent to the others marking the same branch of the tree. The primer information for these 20 markers, as well as for the other markers on the tree in Figure 3, is available at http://ycc.biosci.arizona.edu (YCC 2002).

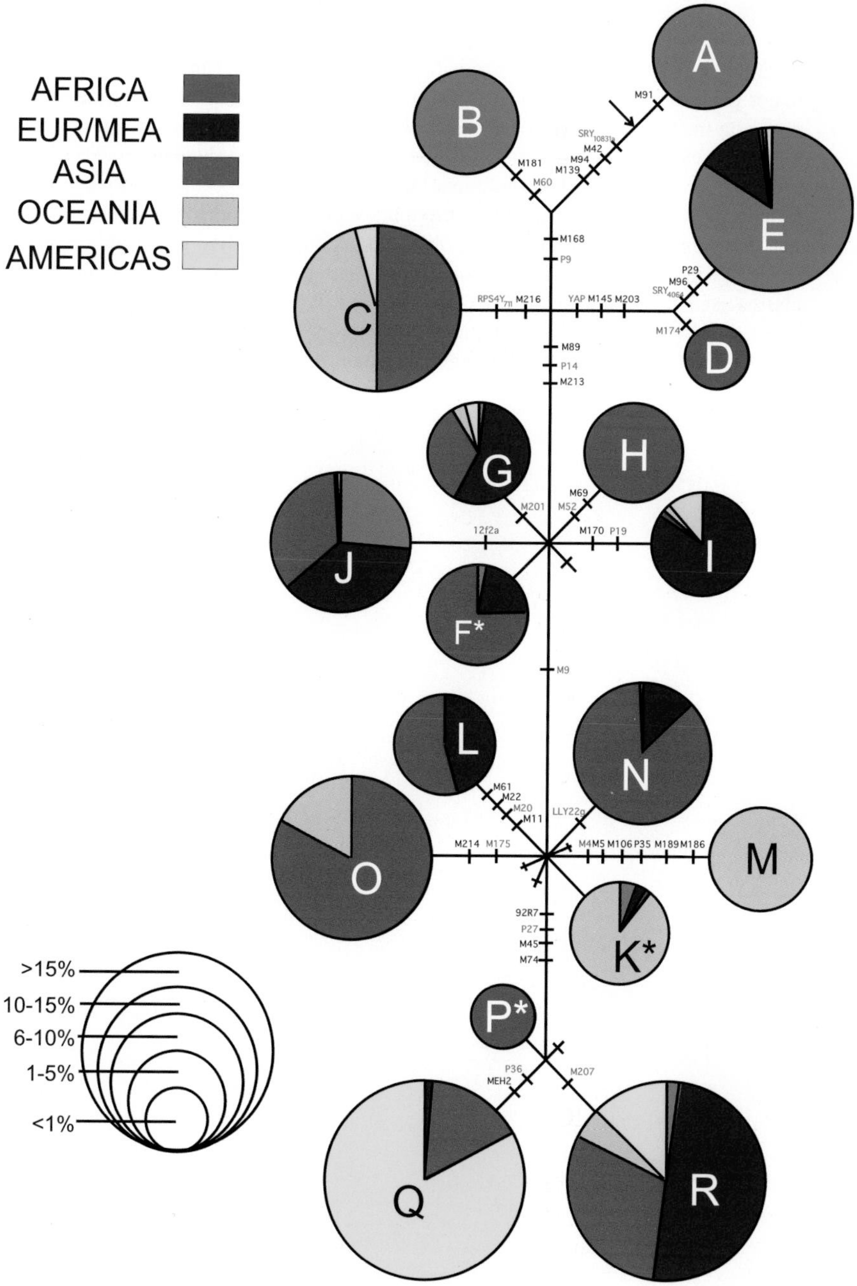

See text page C-2

Figure 3 (page C-1) Evolutionary tree for 18 major NRY haplogroups/paragroups. The root of the tree is denoted by an arrow. Cross-hatches indicate mutational events; the 48 mutational events defining the major haplogroups are labeled by mutation name. Three major paragroups (F*, K*, and P*) are indicated by a (*) symbol and represent internal nodes on the tree. The 20 marker names shown in *red* were typed in the present analysis, while the 28 in *black* represent assumed phylogenetically redundant markers. The five unlabeled cross-hatches represent mutational sites that were not typed and that mark very rare lineages (Underhill et al. 2000); these lineages were assumed to be absent in our survey. Haplogroups/paragroups are color-coded according to five geographic regions (see figure for key). The overall size of each pie chart corresponds to one of five frequency classes (see figure for frequency class key) and represents the frequency of that haplogroup/paragroup in the total sample of 2007 chromosomes. Each pie chart represents the proportion of these global haplogroup/paragroup frequencies associated with each of the five geographic regions.

For Figure 3, we analyzed a total of 2007 males from 40 globally distributed populations. The sample was divided into five major geographic regions: Africa, the Europe/Middle East region, Asia, Oceania, and the Americas. The root of this NRY haplogroup tree is once again indicated by an arrow. Haplogroups A and B are entirely restricted to African populations, while the remainder of the tree is composed of haplogroups/paragroups that are present in as well as outside of Africa or that only occur in non-African locales. This pattern supports the hypothesis of an African origin of human NRY diversity (Hammer et al. 1998, Underhill et al. 2000). Additional region-specific major haplogroups/paragroups include Asia (D, H, and P*) and Oceania (M). Paragroup F* and haplogroups L and N are shared primarily between Asia and the Europe/Middle East region, whereas haplogroup O is shared by Asia and Oceania. Haplogroups G and R are widely shared outside of Africa. Haplogroup J is primarily distributed throughout Africa, the Europe/Middle East region, and Asia, whereas haplogroup I is most often found in the Europe/Middle East region and paragroup K* occurs predominantly within Oceania.

The geographic distribution of the 18 major haplogroups/paragroups (A–R) is shown by continent/region in Figure 4. The number of haplogroups/paragroups by region ranges from 8 in Africa and the Americas to 15 in Asia. Three of the regions are characterized by a predominant haplogroup: E in Africa (60%), R in the Europe/Middle East region (45%), and Q in the Americas (80%). Both the large number of Asian haplogroups/paragroups and their comparatively even distribution underscore the centrality of Asia for human dispersals; an inference supported by a combination of analytical methods (Hammer et al. 2001). Because African populations are characterized by divergent haplogroups (i.e., those differing from one another by many mutations), Africa exhibits greater NRY diversity than other continents when diversity is measured by the mean number of pairwise differences among haplogroups, despite having a smaller number of major haplogroups. For example, the mean pairwise difference ($p \pm$ SE) among African Y chromosomes is 6.6 ± 0.2 compared with values of 5.7 ± 0.2, 5.4 ± 0.2, 5.3 ± 0.1, and 2.1 ± 0.1 for the Europe/Middle East region, Oceania, Asia, and the Americas, respectively. On the other hand, because of the rather even frequencies of Asian NRY haplogroups, Asia exhibits higher levels of haplogroup diversity as measured by Nei's (1987) h statistic ($h \pm$ SE values for Asia and Africa are 0.85 ± 0.00 and 0.60 ± 0.00, respectively).

Some haplogroups contain a great deal more internal diversity than others. For example, haplogroup E has the largest number of sublineages ($n = 22$) and downstream mutational events ($n = 30$) (whereas the mean values of these two parameters for all haplogroups are 9.7 and 12.7, respectively). Haplogroup A has the largest average number of mutations per lineage ($n = 3.1$), whereas haplogroups A–E all have higher than mean numbers of mutations per lineage. Because African populations have haplogroups with greater than average internal diversity, analyses of downstream markers should also underscore the greater mutational divergence within Africa compared with other continents/regions (see Hammer et al. 2001).

Figure 5 shows the results of a multidimensional scaling (MDS) analysis based on Φ_{ST} genetic distances (Excoffier et al. 1992) for 10 geographic groupings. Here,

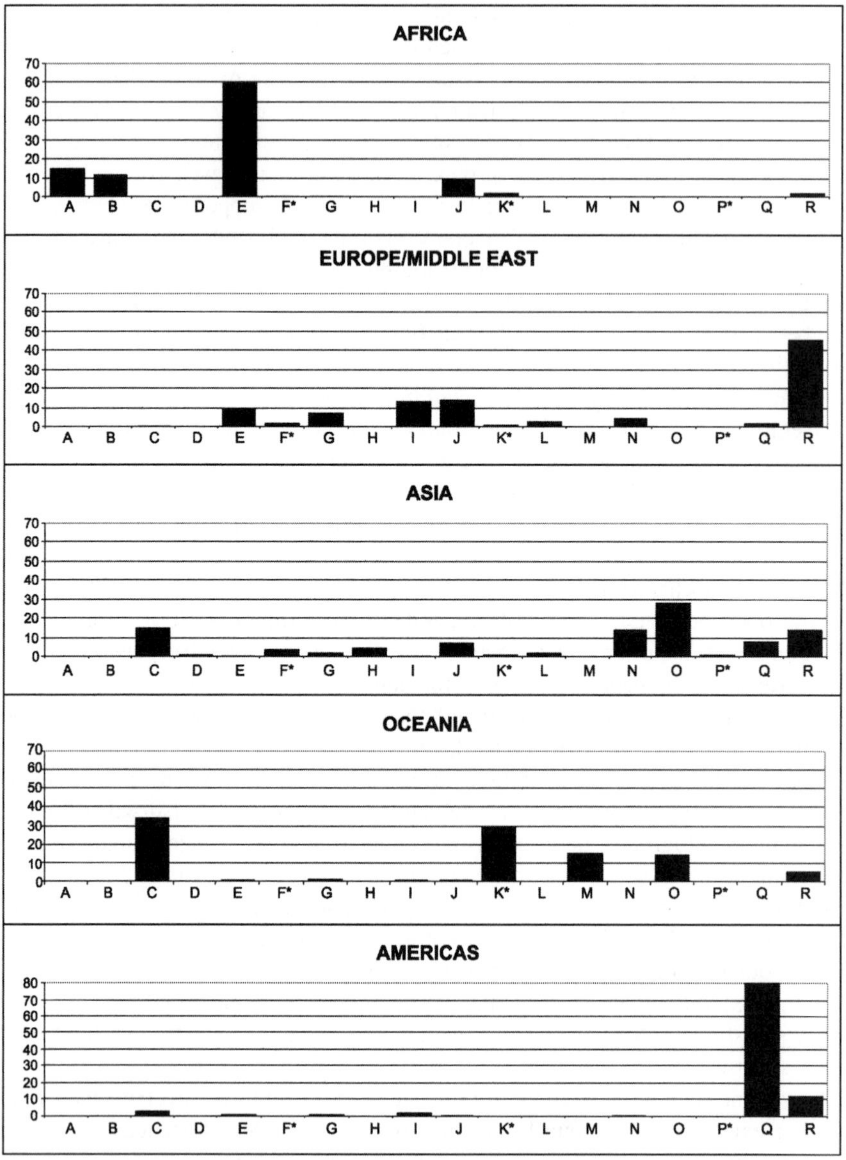

Figure 4 Histogram representations of 18 major NRY haplogroup/paragroup frequencies by geographic region. The frequencies of each haplogroup/paragroup (shown on the y-axis) are based on the following sample sizes for each region: Africa = 374; the Europe/Middle East region = 355; Asia = 672; Oceania = 276; and the Americas = 330. Unfortunately, when haplogroup/paragroup frequencies are close to zero, the corresponding bars are not readily visible. The correct total number of haplogroups/paragroups for each geographic region is as follows: Africa = 8; the Europe/Middle East region = 11, Asia = 15; Oceania = 9; and the Americas = 8.

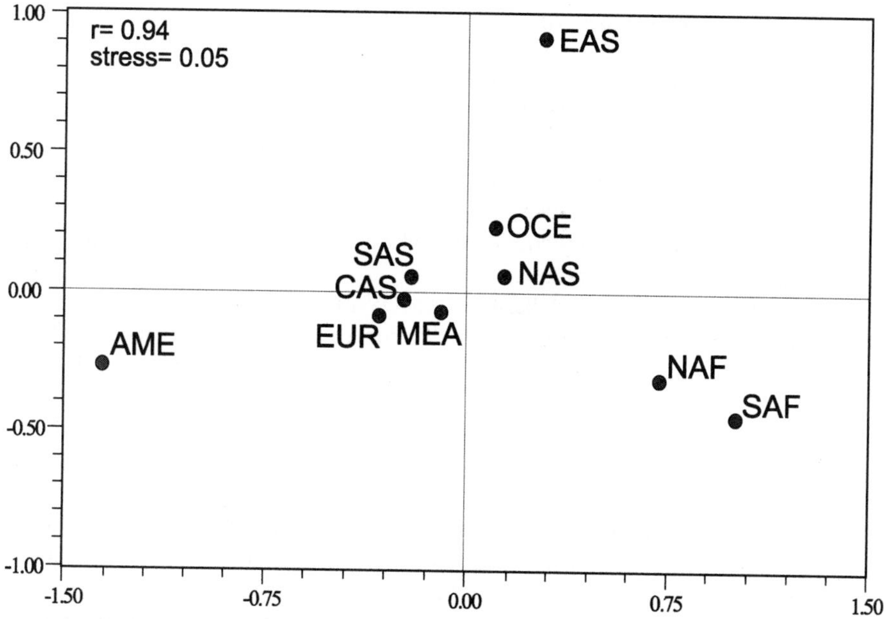

Figure 5 MDS plot of 10 regional populations based on Φ_{ST} genetic distances. SAF = sub-Saharan Africans; NAF = North Africans; EUR = Europeans; MEA = Middle Easterners; SAS = South Asians; CAS = Central Asians; EAS = East Asians; NAS = North Asians; OCE = Oceanians; and AME = Native Americans.

the continent of Africa is divided into sub-Saharan Africa and North Africa; the Europe/Middle East grouping has been separated into two components; and the continent of Asia is divided into East Asia, South Asia, North Asia, and Central Asia. The correlation between the original Φ_{ST} molecular distances calculated by the analysis of molecular variance (AMOVA) (Schneider et al. 2000) and a Euclidean distance matrix derived from this MDS two-dimensional plot was high ($r = 0.94$). The low stress value (0.05) of the MDS plot indicates an especially good fit between the two-dimensional graph and the original distance matrix. The Americas and East Asia occupy extreme outlier positions in Figure 5. North Africa and sub-Saharan Africa form a subcluster that is separated from the rest of the global regions. The remaining six geographic regions form a tight, centrally located cluster reflecting the broad sharing of major haplogroups among most of Eurasia and Oceania. The overall relationships in Figure 5 are reminiscent of the MDS analysis in Hammer et al. (2001), which was based on 43 binary NRY markers typed in 50 human populations encompassing a total of 2858 males. Many of the markers in the Hammer et al. (2001) survey were more derived (i.e., downstream) than in the present study and are therefore not shown in Figure 2.

The major difference between these two MDS plots is the position of East Asia, which is now much more of an outlier than in the Hammer et al. (2001) analysis. This is primarily the consequence of the extremely high frequency of haplogroup O in East Asia. For example, 95% of all the Asian haplogroup O chromosomes are present in East Asia; indeed, more than 78% of all haplogroup O chromosomes in this global sample are from East Asia. Interestingly, haplogroup O is one of the most diverse haplogroups with 18 sublineages and 23 downstream mutational events. In addition to its predominance in East Asia, this haplogroup is also found at moderate frequency in Oceania.

According to our new global-level AMOVA results, 43% of the total variance of NRY haplogroups is attributable to differences among populations (i.e., $\Phi_{ST} = 0.43$). This compares with a Φ_{ST} estimate of 0.36 in our previous global survey (Hammer et al. 2001). This difference in Φ_{ST} values may reflect the fact that here we are typing only those markers that define the major haplogroups, which has resulted in a pattern of less within-group variation, and consequently, a higher Φ_{ST} value.

For the purpose of facilitating comparisons across NRY studies of different global samples, it would be most useful if each laboratory (at a minimum), would type markers defining these same 18 major haplogroups/paragroups. As shown in the next section, choosing markers for regional studies is more challenging because different haplogroups/paragroups predominate in different local populations.

REGIONAL SCALE STUDIES

As an example of a regional study, we discuss our ongoing survey of 902 males from 18 Siberian populations (T. M. Karafet, S. L. Zegura, and M. F. Hammer, unpublished data). In addition to the 20 markers (red-labeled cross-hatches in Figure 3) defining the aforementioned major NRY haplogroups/paragroups, we typed 42 downstream markers. The 23 resulting haplogroups/paragroups fell into 12 of the 18 major haplogroups/paragroups; however, the vast majority (96%) of Siberian Y chromosomes belonged to only 4 of these 18 major clades (N, C, Q, and R) (Figure 2). A phylogeographic analysis of the six haplogroups/paragroups with frequencies $\geq$10% in Siberia (shaded circles in Figure 2) revealed that the two most frequent haplogroups/paragroups were both subclades of haplogroup N: one, with a frequency of 22.7%, was widely distributed within Siberia, whereas the other, with a frequency of 19.7%, had a much more spotty distribution that was highly correlated with language (i.e., 92.0% of the Siberians with this haplogroup were Uralic-speakers). One paragroup and one haplogroup within haplogroup C were concentrated in Altaic-speaking populations scattered across Siberia (accounting for 9.5% and 13.0% of the sampled Siberian Y chromosomes, respectively). The derived state of a mutation (P36) defining haplogroup Q was present in 18.8% of the Siberian Y chromosomes; however, the vast majority of haplogroup Q chromosomes occurred in only two Siberian populations. Finally, a paragroup within haplogroup R with a Siberian frequency of 10.3% was concentrated in the Altai and in some Northwest Siberian populations. Many of the above nonrandom NRY-geography/language family associations in Siberia can lead directly to microevolutionary/historical hypotheses that can be readily tested using other genetic data sets, as well as anthropological data sets derived from linguistics, archaeology, and biological anthropology.

RECOMMENDATIONS FOR TYPING NRY MARKERS

Although between-group variation in Siberia is more extensive than for many other regions of the world (T.M. Karafet, S.L. Zegura, and M.F. Hammer, unpublished data), Siberia's highly nonrandom and geographically restricted distribution of NRY haplogroups is actually typical of many other regions of the world. Thus, we make the following general recommendations: (*a*) for global-scale studies (at a minimum) type markers defining the 18 major haplogroups/paragroups; (*b*) after determining the location of a sample with respect to its position on the tree, no further genotyping is necessary for that sample (note that this commonly adopted hierarchical genotyping protocol means that not every individual will be typed for every marker, and hence, it is possible that some recurrent mutations will remain undetected using this strategy); (*c*) for geographically more restricted studies, in addition to (*a*) and (*b*), specific suites of SNPs need to be chosen that characterize the majority of Y chromosomes in a given geographic region; (*d*) to reduce the ascertainment bias that ensues from using markers discovered in global populations, laboratories should also consider the option of performing new mutation detection studies using samples from their population(s) of interest (note that the additional use of Y-STRs may help to lessen the effects of ascertainment bias); and (*e*) to distinguish truly monophyletic haplogroups from paragroups, it is necessary to type all known mutational sites that mark lineages descending from internal nodes on the haplogroup tree, as well as newly discovered mutational sites that further subdivide the pool of ancestral lineages.

ACKNOWLEDGMENTS

We thank Tatiana Karafet for data analysis, and the following individuals supplied helpful comments on an earlier draft of this manuscript: Mathew Hurles, Tatiana Karafet, Chris Tyler-Smith, and Elizabeth Wood. We also thank Chris Tyler-Smith and Elizabetta Righetti for unpublished information on the LLY22g marker. This work was supported by grants to MH from the National Science Foundation (OPP-9806759), the National Institute of General Medical Sciences (GM53566-06), and the National Institute of Justice (2000-IJ-CX-K006).

The *Annual Review of Anthropology* is online at http://anthro.annualreviews.org

LITERATURE CITED

Bachtrog D, Charlesworth B. 2001. Towards a complete sequence of the human Y chromosome. *Genome Biol.* 2:1016.1–16.5

Bahlo M, Griffiths RC. 2000. Inference from gene trees in a subdivided population. *Theor. Popul. Biol.* 57:79–95

Casanova M, Leroy P, Boucekkine C, Weissenbach J, Bishop C, et al. 1985. A human Y-linked DNA polymorphism and its potential for estimating genetic and evolutionary distance. *Science* 230:1403–6

de Knijff P. 2000. Messages through bottlenecks: on the combined use of slow and fast evolving polymorphic markers on the human Y chromosome. *Am. J. Hum. Genet.* 67:1055–61

Donoghue M. 1985. A critique of the biological species concept and recommendations for a phylogenetic alternative. *Bryologist* 88:172–81

Excoffier L, Smouse PE, Quattro JM. 1992. Analysis of molecular variance inferred from metric distances among DNA haplotypes: application to human mitochondrial DNA restriction data. *Genetics* 131:479–91

Hammer MF. 1994. A recent insertion of an Alu element on the Y chromosome is a useful marker for human population studies. *Mol. Biol. Evol.* 11:749–61

Hammer MF, Horai S. 1995. Y chromosomal DNA variation and the peopling of Japan. *Am. J. Hum. Genet.* 56:951–62

Hammer MF, Karafet T, Rasanayagam A, Wood ET, Altheide TK, et al. 1998. Out of Africa and back again: nested cladistic analysis of human Y chromosome variation. *Mol. Biol. Evol.* 15:427–41

Hammer MF, Karafet TM, Redd AJ, Jarjanazi H, Santachiara-Benerecetti S, et al. 2001. Hierarchical patterns of global human Y-chromosome diversity. *Mol. Biol. Evol.* 18: 1189–203

Hammer MF, Zegura SL. 1996. The role of the Y chromosome in human evolutionary studies. *Evol. Anthropol.* 5:116–34

Hennig W. 1966. *Phylogenetic Systematics.* Urbana: Univ. Illinois. 263 pp.

Heyer E, Puymirat J, Dieltjes P, Bakker E, de Knijff P. 1997. Estimating Y chromosome specific microsatellite mutation frequencies using deep rooting pedigrees. *Hum. Mol. Genet.* 6:799–803

Hull D. 1988. *Science as a Process.* Chicago: Univ. Chicago. 586 pp.

International Human Genome Sequencing Consortium. 2001. Initial sequencing and analysis of the human genome. *Nature* 409:860–921

International SNP Map Working Group. 2001. A map of human genome sequence variation containing 1.42 million single nucleotide polymorphisms. *Nature* 409:928–33

Janvier P. 1984. Cladisitics: theory, purpose, and evolutionary implications. In *Evolutionary Theory: Paths into the Future*, ed. JW Pollard, pp. 39–75. Chichester: Wiley. 271 pp.

Jegalian K, Lahn B. 2001. Why the Y is so weird. *Sci. Am.* 284:56–61

Jobling MA. 2001. In the name of the father: surnames and genetics. *Trends Genet.* 17:353–57

Jobling MA, Pandya A, Tyler-Smith C. 1997. The Y chromosome in forensic analysis and paternity testing. *Int. J. Legal Med.* 110:118–24

Jobling MA, Samara V, Pandya A, Fretwell N, Bernasconi B, et al. 1996. Recurrent duplication and deletion polymorphism on the long arm of the Y chromosome in normal males. *Hum. Mol. Genet.* 5:1767–75

Jolly CJ. 2001. A proper study for mankind: analogies from the Papionin monkeys and their implications for human evolution. *Yrbk. Phys. Anthropol.* 44:177–204

Karafet TM, Zegura SL, Posukh O, Osipova L, Bergen A, et al. 1999. Ancestral Asian source(s) of New World Y-chromosome founder haplotypes. *Am. J. Hum. Genet.* 64: 817–31

Kayser M, Roewer L, Hedman M, Henke L, Henke J, et al. 2000. Characteristics and frequency of germline mutations at microsatellite loci from the human Y chromosome, as revealed by direct observation in father/son pairs. *Am. J. Hum. Genet.* 66:1580–88

Kruglyak L, Nickerson DA. 2001. Variation is the spice of life. *Nat. Genet.* 27:234–36

Lucotte G, Ngo NY. 1985. p49f, a highly polymorphic probe, that detects *Taq*1 RFLPs on the human Y chromosome. *Nucleic Acids. Res.* 13:82–85

Mayr E. 1981. Biological classification: toward a synthesis of opposing methodologies. *Science* 214:510–16

Nei M. 1987. *Molecular Evolutionary Genetics.* New York: Columbia Univ. Press. 512 pp.

Ridley M. 1986. *Evolution and Classification.* London: Longman. 201 pp.

Santos FR, Pena SDJ, Tyler-Smith C. 1995. PCR haplotypes for the human Y chromosome based on alphoid satellite variants and heteroduplex analysis. *Gene* 165:191–98

Schneider S, Kueffer J-M, Roessli D, Excoffier L. 2000. *Arlequin: a Software for Population Genetic Analysis version 2000*. Geneva: Genet. Biom. Lab. 111 pp.

Schwartz JH, Tattersall I, Eldredge N. 1978. Phylogeny and classification of the primates revisited. *Yrbk. Phys. Anthropol.* 21:95–133

Seielstad MT, Hebert JM, Lin AA, Underhill PA, Ibrahim M, et al. 1994. Construction of human Y-chromosomal haplotypes using a new polymorphic A to G transition. *Hum. Mol. Genet.* 3:2159–61

Seielstad MT, Minch E, Cavalli-Sforza LL. 1998. Genetic evidence for a higher female migration rate in humans. *Nat. Genet.* 20:278–80

Shen P, Wang F, Underhill PA, Franco C, Yang WH, et al. 2000. Population genetic implications from sequence variation in four Y chromosome genes. *Proc. Natl. Acad. Sci. USA* 97:7354–59

Sneath PHA, Sokal RR. 1973. *Numerical Taxonomy.* San Francisco: Freeman. 573 pp.

Stone AC, Griffiths RC, Zegura SL, Hammer MF. 2002. High levels of Y-chromosome nucleotide diversity in the genus *Pan. Proc. Natl. Acad. Sci. USA* 99:43–48

Stone AC, Milner G, Paabo S, Stoneking M. 1996. Sex determination of ancient human skeletons using DNA. *Am. J. Phys. Anthropol.* 99:231–38

Thomson R, Pritchard JK, Shen P, Oefner PJ, Feldman MW. 2000. Recent common ancestry of human Y chromosomes: evidence from DNA sequence data. *Proc. Natl. Acad. Sci. USA* 97:7360–65

Tilford CA, Kuroda-Kawaguchi T, Skaletsky H, Rozen S, Brown LG, et al. 2001. A physical map of the human Y chromosome. *Nature* 409:943–45

Underhill PA, Jin L, Lin AA, Mehdi SQ, Jenkins T, et al. 1997. Detection of numerous Y chromosome biallelic polymorphisms by denaturing high-performance liquid chromatography. *Genome Res.* 7:996–1005

Underhill PA, Jin L, Zemans R, Oefner PJ, Cavalli-Sforza LL. 1996. A pre-Columbian Y chromosome-specific transition and its implications for human evolutionary history. *Proc. Natl. Acad. Sci. USA* 93:196–200

Underhill PA, Passarino G, Lin AA, Shen P, Lahr MM, et al. 2001. The phylogeography of Y chromosome binary haplotypes and the origins of modern human populations. *Ann. Hum. Genet.* 65:43–62

Underhill PA, Shen P, Lin AA, Jin L, Passarino G, et al. 2000. Y chromosome sequence variation and the history of human populations. *Nat. Genet.* 26:358–61

Venter JC, Adams MD, Myers EW, Li PW, Mural RJ, et al. 2001. The sequence of the human genome. *Science* 291:1304–51

Whitfield LS, Sulston JE, Goodfellow PN. 1995. Sequence variation of the human Y chromosome. *Nature* 378:379–80

Wiley EO. 1981. *Phylogenetics.* New York: Wiley. 439 pp.

Y Chromosome Consortium (YCC). 2002. A nomenclature system for the tree of Y chromosomal binary haplogroups. *Genome Res.* 12:339–48

Annu. Rev. Anthropol. 2002. 31:323–38
doi: 10.1146/annurev.anthro.31.040402.085403

First published online as a Review in Advance on June 4, 2002

ENERGETICS AND THE EVOLUTION OF THE GENUS *HOMO*

Leslie C. Aiello[1] and Jonathan C. K. Wells[2]
[1]*Department of Anthropology, University College London, Gower Street, London WC1E 6BT; email: L.Aiello@ucl.ac.uk*
[2]*MRC Childhood Nutrition Research Centre, Institute of Child Health, 30 Guilford Street, London WC1N 1EH; email: J.Wells@ich.ucl.ac.uk*

Key Words human evolution, metabolic rate, diet, growth, *Homo erectus*, *Homo ergaster*, australopithecines, brain evolution

■ **Abstract** The genus *Homo* as represented by *Homo ergaster* (= early African *Homo erectus*) is characterized by a pattern of features that is more similar to modern humans than to the earlier and contemporaneous australopithecines and paranthropines. These features include larger relative brain sizes, larger bodies, slower rates of growth and maturation, dedicated bipedal locomotion, and smaller teeth and jaws. These features are phenotypic expressions of a very different lifestyle for the earliest members of the genus *Homo*. This paper considers the energetic correlates of the emergence of the genus *Homo* and suggests that there were three major changes in maintenance energy requirements. First, there was an absolute increase in energy requirements due to greater body size. Second, there was a shift in the relative requirements of the different organs, with increased energy diverted to brain metabolism at the expense of gut tissue, possibly mediated by changes in the proportion of weight comprised of fat. And third, there was a slower rate of childhood growth, offset by higher growth costs during infancy and adolescence. These changes, as well as energetic requirements of reproduction and bipedal locomotion, are considered in a discussion of one of the major transitions in adaptation in human evolution, the appearance of our own genus.

INTRODUCTION

Modern humans are very different than our closest living relatives, the African apes. Among other traits, we have larger brains, walk on two legs, have slower rates of growth and maturation, longer lifespans, a long period of post reproductive life for females, differently shaped bodies, different foraging behaviors, and higher quality diets. These features are all phenotypic expressions of the human life history pattern and reflect the pace and energetic requirements of human life. Humans, as well as all other organisms, are confronted by constraining relationships, or trade-offs, in terms of how energy is invested in either growth, maintenance, activity, or reproduction (Stearns 1992). Natural selection operates very strongly on these trade-offs because of their overall influence on lifetime reproductive success (Wells 2002).

This paper reviews the energetic consequences of the evolution of *Homo*. It identifies the features of the modern human life history pattern that were present at the first appearance of our genus and considers their costs and benefits in relation to adaptive fitness. The assumption underlying this is that features should only be selected for when the cost/benefit ratio is optimal (Ulijazek 1995). Physical and behavioral adaptations seen in our early *Homo* ancestors should minimize their use of energy and optimally balance expenditure to achieve optimal reproductive success.

When the genus *Homo* first appeared is a matter of debate that depends largely on how the genus is defined. Wood & Collard (1999) convincingly argue that *Homo ergaster* (= early African *Homo erectus*), as defined by Wood (1992) and best known from the Turkana basin in Kenya between 1.9 and 1.5 Ma, is the first known species in the genus *Homo. Homo ergaster* is distinguished from earlier possible members of the genus *Homo* such as *H. habilis* (2.3–1.6 Ma) or *H. rudolfensis* (2.4–1.8 Ma) by a complex of skeletal and dental features reflecting a lifestyle that was more similar to that of modern humans than that inferred for earlier and contemporaneous hominins. These skeletal and dental features include a larger body mass, more human-like body proportions, relatively long legs, obligate bipedalism coupled with a limited facility for climbing, relatively small teeth and jaws suggesting major dietary change, and a tendency towards an extended period of growth and development. Although not all anthropologists agree that *Homo ergaster* is the first member of the genus *Homo* (e.g., McHenry & Coffing 2000), this review follows Wood & Collard (1999) and focuses on the energetic consequences of the human-like complex of features that distinguishes *Homo ergaster*.

INCREASED BODY MASS

One of the most obvious and energetically important features of *Homo ergaster* is its significantly larger body mass in comparison to earlier and contemporaneous hominins. The body mass estimates (Table 1) that are commonly accepted in the literature are derived largely from the work of McHenry (1992a,b; 1994) and are determined on the basis of hindlimb joint size (but see Aiello & Wood 1994 and Kappelman 1996 for cranially determined body mass estimates). It is clear from these estimates that *Homo ergaster* is considerably heavier than any of the australopithecines or paranthropines and that females have increased in mass more than males. This means that *Homo ergaster* is not only characterized by a significant size increase but also by a marked reduction in sexual dimorphism (Leonard & Robertson 1997, Aiello & Key 2002).

There is increasing evidence that *Homo ergaster* was occupying a more open (xeric) environment than were the australopithecines and paranthropines (de Menocal 1995, Reed 1997, Sikes 1999). Large body size has a number of advantages in a more open environment including the capacity to exploit broader dietary niches in larger foraging areas, greater mobility and prey size, and increased sociality (Foley 1987). Large body size also permits females to efficiently

TABLE 1 Inferred body mass and daily energy requirements for the hominins

	Sex	Body mass[a]	RMR[b]	DEE[c]	DEE[c] + gestation[d]	DEE[c] + lactation[e]	DEE[f]	DEE[f] + gestation[d]	DEE[f] + lactation[e]
A. afarensis	f	29.3	881.6	1175.3	1469.1	1633.7	1248.1	1560.2	1734.9
	m	44.6	1208.1	1610.6			1740.9		
A. africanus	f	30.2	901.8	1202.3	1502.8	1671.2	1278.4	1598.0	1777.0
	m	40.8	1130.0	1506.6			1622.3		
A. robustus	f	31.9	939.6	1252.7	1565.9	1741.2	1335.1	1668.8	1855.7
	m	40.2	1117.6	1489.9			1603.4		
A. boisei	f	34.0	985.6	1314.0	1642.6	1826.5	1404.2	1755.3	1951.8
	m	48.6	1288.5	1717.8			1863.4		
H. ergaster	f	52.0	1355.5	1807.2	2259.0	2475.8	1966.0	2457.4	2732.7
	m	63.0	1565.3	2086.9			2288.6		
H. sapiens	f	56.8	1448.3	1930.9	2413.6	2664.7	2108.3	2635.4	2930.6
	m	70.0	1694.0	2258.5			2487.8		

[a]Body mass (kg) after McHenry (1992).

[b]RMR (resting metabolic rate) is computed according to the Kleiber equation (Kleiber 1932, 1961) RMR $= 70\ W^{0.75}$, where W = body mass (kg).

[c]Daily energy requirements (kcal d^{-1}) $= 93.3\ W^{0.75}$ (Key & Ross 1999).

[d]Daily energy requirements during gestation = DEE*1.25 (Aiello & Key 2002).

[e]Daily energy requirements during lactation = DEE*1.39 for the australopithecines and paranthropines, = DEE*1.37 for *Homo ergaster*, and = DEE*1.38 for *Homo sapiens* (Aiello & Key 2002).

[f]Daily energy requirements (DEE) $= 86.0\ W^{0.792}$ (Leonard & Robertson 1997). Note that this equation produces daily energy requirements that are between 6%–10% higher than those produced by the Aiello & Key (2002) equation (DEE[3]). The daily energy requirements during gestation and lactation are correspondingly elevated. See text for explanation.

carry their children to an older age and increased mass (Kramer 1998). Coupled with the taller and more linear physique of *Homo ergaster*, there are also physiological advantages in relation to thermoregulation and water budgets (Ruff 1991; Wheeler 1992, 1993). These physiological advantages may have been particularly important to pregnant females because of their increased susceptibility to heat stress as the result of their increased weight for height as the pregnancy developed (J. C. K. Wells, submitted). A recent analysis found that 10% of the between population variability in modern human birth weight could be attributed to thermal load, after taking confounding factors into account (Wells & Cole 2002). It would benefit both mothers and their unborn children to maximize their thermoregulatory advantage. In modern humans, hot weather mothers are smaller, gain less weight, and are less fat than cold weather mothers. Further modeling is needed to demonstrate the net thermoregulatory advantage of the larger body mass coupled with the more linear physique of *Homo ergaster* in comparison to the lighter but squatter australopithecines. It is, however, highly probable that the *Homo ergaster* body form provided a net thermoregulatory advantage in the relatively xeric conditions of the African Plio-Pleistocene.

One major disadvantage of larger body size in *Homo ergaster* is the increased energetic burden it represents and the correspondingly increased dietary requirements necessary to fuel the increased energy demands. The extra maintenance metabolic requirements of this weight gain can be calculated using Kleiber's standard formula for the relationship between body mass and resting metabolic rate (RMR). RMR is the amount of energy utilized by an inactive organism under thermal neutral conditions (Durnin & Passmore 1967), and in the following formula W = body mass (kg) and RMR = kcal/d^{-1} (Kleiber 1932, 1961):

$$\mathrm{RMR} = 70\ \mathrm{W}^{0.75}.$$

The resting metabolic requirements of *Homo ergaster* would have been 39% higher than for *Australopithecus afarensis* (30% higher for males and 54% higher for females) (Table 1).

DIETARY IMPLICATIONS OF INCREASED ENERGY EXPENDITURE

The larger body size in *Homo* implies a corresponding increase in either the daily amount of food or the quality of the food eaten in order to satisfy the increased energy needs. If *Homo ergaster* ate the same type of diet as the smaller bodied australopithecines, this would imply a significant alteration in the activity budget where feeding time would have to be increased in proportion to the extra calories required by the larger body mass. Even if this had been possible and *Homo ergaster* could have balanced time needed for traveling, socializing, and resting against the necessarily increased feeding time, it is unlikely that they adopted this strategy. *Homo ergaster* jaws and teeth are reduced in size, which suggests a major dietary shift away from more fibrous and more difficult to masticate foods (Walker & Leakey 1993, Wood & Aiello 1998). Equally, the trunk proportions in *Homo ergaster* suggest a relatively small gut that is compatible with a higher quality and more easily digested diet (Aiello & Wheeler 1995). The more open xeric habitat occupied by *Homo ergaster* would also offer different dietary opportunities.

It is probable that meat comprised a greater proportion of the *Homo ergaster* diet than it did for the earlier and contemporaneous australopithecines and paranthropines (Aiello & Wheeler 1995). However, it is unlikely that meat by itself would have met the increased energy requirements of *Homo ergaster*. It is clear from analyses of modern people that humans are incapable of metabolizing sufficient protein to meet more than 50% of their energy needs (Speth & Spielmann 1983, Speth 1989). Those modern people who rely more heavily on animal-based resources also rely heavily on fat for the remainder of their energy requirements.

For a number of reasons such a diet would have been unlikely for *Homo ergaster*. The specific dynamic action, the rise in metabolism or heat production resulting from ingestion of food, is very high for protein. If modern people such as the Eskimos for whom 90% of caloric needs are met by meat and fat are anything to go by, such a diet would elevate RMR by 13%–33%, with significant implications for thermoregulation in a hot open country environment. This also means that they would have had to eat correspondingly more meat to satisfy their basic energy requirements. A high meat diet also demands increased water intake, and this is an unlikely strategy to adopt in a hot open environment (Speth & Spielmann 1983). Furthermore, wild African ungulates have a relatively low fat content (Speth & Spielmann 1983, Speth 1989), and modern African hunters and gatherers such as the San or Hadza who rely heavily on meat during the dry season also rely on cultural means to recover maximum fat from the carcasses—a strategy that would not have been available to the early hominins.

Meat protein is easier to digest than plant protein and even with a limited amount of fat would still have been a valuable source of essential amino and fatty acids, fat soluble vitamins, and minerals (Milton 1999). It would satisfy nutritional requirements with a lower dietary bulk. This would allow increased reliance on plants of lower overall nutritive quality but high carbohydrate content, such as underground storage organs, to provide the majority of the energy to fuel their larger bodies. Carbohydrates also have a protein sparing advantage over dietary supplementation with fat. In situations of calorie restriction such as might be expected during the dry season on the African savanna, a diet supplemented with carbohydrates is more efficient than one supplemented by fat in sparing limited protein from being metabolized for energy and thereby restricts the availability of the limited essential nutrients and amino acids derived from that protein (Speth & Spielmann 1983).

An added advantage of including meat in the diet is the high methionine content of animal protein (Milton 1999). This would provide an adequate supply of sulfur-containing amino acids that are necessary for the detoxification of toxic (cyanogenetic) plant foods. Milton (1999) also points out that infants need dietary protein consisting of 37% of its weight in essential amino acids (compared to 15% in adults) and that animal protein would have been a valuable component of weaning foods.

Homo ergaster would undoubtedly have made use of a variety of other food resources such as invertebrates (e.g., termites) or nuts, seeds, honey, etc. However, increased reliance on mammalian meat and fat would have altered the basic balance between dietary quality and dietary bulk and would be consistent with the assumptions of the expensive tissue hypothesis (ETH) (Aiello & Wheeler 1995) and also the work of Barton (1992), which suggests that for our body sizes, humans eat less bulk than nonhuman primates. The diet of *Homo ergaster* was therefore not an australopithecine diet with added meat, but involved a change in the proportions and type of both animal and vegetable foods (Leonard & Robertson 1992, 1994).

WHAT RMR IS ACTUALLY MEASURING—THE ROLE OF EXPENSIVE TISSUES AND ADIPOSE TISSUE

Overall RMR is the sum total of the RMR of the tissues that compose the body. Organ tissues tend to be of high metabolic rate per unit mass whereas muscle and adipose tissue is of substantially lower metabolic cost. There is considerable variation across species and during ontogeny. For example, in adult humans the brain takes up approximately 20% of the total RMR of the individual, whereas in other primates it takes up 8%–9% (Holliday 1986, Mink et al. 1981). There is also considerable variation in the size of other organ masses across species (Stahl 1965).

The differential contribution of tissues to total body RMR is the basis of the ETH for the co-evolution of brain size, gut size, and diet in human evolution (Aiello & Wheeler 1995, Aiello 1997, Aiello et al. 2001). Prior to the publication of the ETH, there was considerable puzzlement over the apparent lack of correlation between relative brain size and relative RMR across mammals (e.g., Leonard & Robertson 1994). Humans have a RMR predicted by the Kleiber equation, but have a significantly larger brain size that would be expected to considerably elevate human RMR (Leonard & Robertson 1994, Aiello & Wheeler 1995). Aiello & Wheeler (1995) demonstrated that the metabolic costs of the relatively large and energy-expensive human brain were balanced by a corresponding reduction of the size of the equally expensive human gut. Diet quality in primates is significantly correlated with relative brain size (Leonard & Robertson 1994) but also determines the relative size of the gut. The higher the quality of the diet the smaller and simpler is the gut. It is probable that the well-known relationship between diet quality and relative brain size is explained, at least in part, by the energy sparing consequences of the relatively smaller gut. Aiello & Wheeler (1995) also suggest that the change in the size and shape of the thorax and pelvis between australopithecines and *Homo ergaster* reflects a reduction in the size of the gut in *Homo ergaster*.

It is important to remember that this does not negate other possible relationships between diet quality and brain size such as the importance of essential fatty and amino acids, vitamins, and minerals (Broadhurst et al. 1998, Horrobin 1998, Milton 1999) or the role of a high quality diet in supporting maternal nutrition during gestation and especially lactation (Martin 1996, Leonard & Robertson 1994). It is also important to remember that the hypothesis is not necessarily weakened by the fact that there is no universal correlation between relative brain size and relative gut size across mammals. Brain size does not make up a significant component of total body RMR in many other animals as it does in humans and therefore is not a limiting factor. The emerging field of ecophysiology also clearly demonstrates that animals as varied as snakes, birds, and mammals manipulate their RMRs through differential size of other expensive tissues to meet varying environmental or lifehistory challenges (Aiello et al. 2001).

Changes in the expensive tissues are also not the only potential source of changes in the constituents of the human RMR. A further hypothesis, to our knowledge not considered previously, is that the increased adiposity of later *Homo* species has partially concealed an increase in RMR of *Homo sapiens*. Reconstruction of hominin energy stores is well nigh impossible due to the poor preservation of soft tissue in the fossil record. Data on body fatness of nonhuman apes is sparse, and body composition is rarely considered when addressing the relationship between body size and metabolic rate. Although orangutans, like humans, appear to have the capacity to store fat in the abdomen (Zihlman & McFarland 2000), wild-living individuals from most contemporary primate species have percentage body fat lower than the 26%–28% of a well nourished woman or than the 14% of a man (Forbes 1987, Rutenberg et al. 1987, McFarland 1997). Even in populations inhabiting harsh environments, body fatness in women is around 20% (Lawrence et al. 1987).

In modern humans, both fat mass and fat-free mass contribute to total RMR. Based on 104 normal women, the relative contribution of fat mass (FM) and fat-free mass (FFM) is:

$$\mathrm{RMR} = \mathrm{k}_1\ \mathrm{FM} + \mathrm{k}_2\ \mathrm{FFM},$$

where values for k_1 and k_2 are 0.31 and 1.35 Joules s^{-1} kg^{-1}, respectively (Garby et al. 1988). These values increase to 0.96 and 2.14 Joules s^{-1} kg^{-1} at moderate activity levels, indicating that the relative metabolic cost of fat stores rises with the level of activity. The contribution of FM to RMR is attributed to the energy requirements of adipose tissue (Simonsen et al. 1994).

A change in the relative contributions of fat mass and fat-free mass to body mass confounds between-species energetic comparisons on a per kg body weight basis. In this instance, the greater fatness of humans suggests that, relative to nonhuman primates, RMR per unit fat-free mass of *Homo sapiens* has increased. Such an increase would suggest that rather than increased brain costs being fully offset by reduced gut costs, they may in part remain, concealed by the low-cost requirements of increased adipose tissue.

A higher maintenance expenditure of energy than expected on the basis of body size implies that humans must either compensate on expenditure energy on non-basal functions such as physical activity or obtain increased food resources. In general, higher resting energy requirements are predicted to be favored when food supply is abundant (Mueller & Diamond 2001). This may not be the case in hominin evolution; however, an alternative strategy for supporting high maintenance expenditure is the preservation of energy as fat in order to overcome fluctuations in food availability.

We do not know when hominins began to become fat, although Pond (1997) demonstrates that the distribution of fat deposits is similar in many mammals, including humans. In her opinion, bipedal posture is important in the distribution of human fat and, for example, the groin deposits in other mammals are extended in humans to form a continuous layer from pelvis to knee. Because the details of the anatomy and distribution of adipose tissue in living apes remain largely unknown, it is not possible to say when the unique features of human adipose tissue evolved (Pond 1991, 1997).

The ability to accumulate fat would be of enormous value in the more seasonal open environments occupied by *Homo ergaster*. Horrobin (2001) notes a kilogram of fat provides around 9000 calories, enough to survive reasonably well for 4–6 days (assuming consumption of 1500–2500 kcal d^{-1}). Although famine conditions may have been relatively rare in hominin evolution, less extreme fluctuations in food availability may have been relatively common. Contemporary Gambian farmers experience successive hunger and harvest seasons in which the highest energy expenditure on subsistence is required in the season of lowest food availability (Lawrence et al. 1987). Gambian women accommodate these seasonal stresses through highly flexible fat stores, and may gain or lose up to 4 kg of fat depending on the ability of energy intake to satisfy requirements (Lawrence et al. 1987). The ability to accommodate seasonal variation in food supply through physiological adaptation contrasts with the alterations of group size and structure that characterize closely related species such as chimpanzees, although orangutans also store fat to buffer against seasonal food supply fluctuations (Knott 1997).

Accumulation of fat to buffer seasonal stresses may therefore have been a crucial factor in the survival of *Homo ergaster* as compared to other hominin lines, and may have influenced group structure and sociality as well as energy balance per se. This hypothesis is particularly interesting given the faster reproductive turnover of human versus ape females and the proposed role of grandmothers in feeding older dependent offspring, implying a greater need to preserve group structure over time (see below).

The significance of energy stores for female reproductive fitness is also supported by observations of a reduced ability to conceive (Frisch & Macarthur 1974) and a higher rate of miscarriage in thin women, consistent with the life history theory prediction that unpredictable environments should favor maintaining parental survival probability at the expense of reproductive investment (Hirschfield & Tinkle 1975).

MORE ON THE ENERGETIC COSTS OF THE BRAIN

There is more in relation to the energetic costs of the brain than the relationship between relatively large brain and the energy balance of the adult individual. The increased brain costs of later hominin species are particularly significant in early life, when brain weight is a higher proportion of total body mass and takes up to 60%–70% of total energy requirements in the individual (Holliday 1986). Modern human infants and children have an elevated RMR throughout ontogeny that undoubtedly supports the higher energy demands of the proportionally large brain as well as the costs of growth (see below). Foley & Lee (1991) have calculated the human brain to increase energy requirements by 8.7% relative to *Pan* during the first 18 months postpartum.

Aiello and colleagues (2001) have suggested that the payoff between the size of the brain and gut may be particularly important to the child's energy balance after it is weaned and before it has acquired the necessary skills to acquire food for itself. However, increased energy intake is not the only strategy for meeting the costs of a larger brain, and during childhood the alternative strategy of reduced growth is observed.

A comparison of modern humans and *Pan* indicates that whereas growth in weight up to 2 years is relatively similar, for the ensuing 10 years *Pan* grows at a significantly faster rate (Ulijaszek 1995). Subsequently, this pattern is reversed, with growth in *Pan* slowing and mature size attained by about 12 years, whereas humans maintain and even increase their childhood growth rate during an adolescent growth spurt that continues to about 18 years.

The total energy cost of tissue growth is relatively constant between primate species, regardless of whether the weight gain comprises fat or lean tissue (Roberts & Young 1988). Further, given that much of the weight gain represents water, it is possible to ascribe a final cost of 4.5 kcal g^{-1} of tissue gain (FAO/WHO/UNU 1985). Growth costs, averaged over the first 10 years can therefore be calculated as 57 kcal d^{-1} and 44 kcal d^{-1} in male and female *Pan*, but only 27 kcal d^{-1} in both sexes in modern humans. In the following 8 years, the contrast is reversed, with *Pan* costs averaging 11 kcal d^{-1} in both sexes, and human costs being 42 kcal d^{-1} in both sexes.

This comparison indicates that the energy costs of growth are divided into three periods, with the most vulnerable childhood period protected by a slower growth rate. The initial growth period is funded directly through maternal metabolism (see also Martin 1996), whereas the final period is funded by the independent offspring when the ability to compete against adult conspecifics is improved (Jansen & van Schaik 1993).

Foley & Lee (1991) use the increased costs of brain growth to infer the likely evolution of slowed growth rate across hominin taxa. They suggest that with the evolution of *Homo* the burden becomes sufficiently severe to benefit from slower growth. Consistent with this prediction of the importance of brain size for growth rate, growth in *Homo ergaster*, with a brain size two-thirds of that of average modern humans, appears not to be slowed to the degree present in *Homo sapiens* (Dean et al. 2001).

Furthermore, slowed growth is a general feature of highly social species such as primates and carnivores (Bogin & Smith 1996). However, the association between slowed growth and sociality need not necessarily be attributed only to increased costs of brain growth. In social species, weaned offspring may remain partially dependent on the mother for food during the juvenile period, and selection may have favored slowed childhood growth in humans in order to protect maternal total fitness at the expense of fitness of individual offspring (Wells 2002). Thus parent-offspring conflict as well as increased energy requirements for brain growth may have favored slower growth during human childhood.

THE ENERGETIC COSTS OF LOCOMOTION

Homo ergaster was not only significantly larger than the australopithecines and paranthropines, but also had significantly longer legs in relation to its body mass. This has further ramifications for energy turnover. The majority of the literature on bipedalism and energetics has been concerned with the energetic advantage of human bipedalism over primate quadrupedalism. It has been well established that, at maximum running speed, human bipedalism is twice as expensive energetically than estimated for a quadrupedal mammal of the same body mass (Taylor et al. 1970, Fedak & Seeherman 1979) and that human walking is energetically much more efficient that human running (Fedak et al. 1974). At an average walking speed of 4.5 km h^{-1}, human bipedalism is slightly more efficient than is quadrupedalism in the average mammal (Rodman & McHenry 1980). Both bipedalism and quadrupedalism are equally as expensive in chimpanzees (Taylor & Rowntree 1973), and at average walking speeds the chimpanzee consumes 150% more energy (g^{-1} km^{-1}) than does a similarly sized quadruped (Rodman & McHenry 1980).

This means that if the proto-hominin was energetically equivalent to a modern chimpanzee there would have been considerable energy savings through adoption of bipedalism, particularly if a large proportion of time was spent moving on the ground (Foley & Elton 1998). Foley (1992) calculated that at the same body mass a bipedal hominin would have been able to travel up to 11 km for the same level of energy expenditure as a chimpanzee would use over a 4-km distance. At a larger body size, bipedal hominins were likely to have been more energy efficient than chimpanzees, to the extent that a 53-kg hominin would have been able to travel 14 km, while a 57-kg hominin would have been able to travel 13 km. This would have allowed a greater foraging area. Similarly, using data on the energetics of modern human locomotion, Leonard & Robertson (1995) calculate that the energy savings for females would have been considerably greater than that for males, an important conclusion in relation to the high-energy demand of gestation and lactation (see below).

These estimates assume that bipedalism in hominins was as efficient as that in modern humans. However, it has generally been assumed that the relatively long legs in *Homo ergaster* gave it an advantage over the shorter-legged australopithecines and paranthropines (e.g., Jungers 1982, 1991; McHenry1991; Webb 1996). Kramer (1999) and Kramer & Eck (2000) convincingly demonstrates that although long legs allow an individual to take fewer steps to cover a given distance and thereby reduce energy, long legs also are heavier and require more energy to move. The mass-specific mechanical power (W kg^{-1}) required to move australopithecine lower limbs (specifically AL 288-1, *Australopithecus afarensis*) is considerably less than in modern humans, whereas the cost of transport (J kg^{-1} m^{-1}) is virtually identical (Kramer 1999). The main disadvantage of australopithecine short legs would be a reduced walking speed, and on this basis Kramer & Eck (2000) calculate that the daily range of AL 288-1 would have been between 20%–40% smaller than for a modern human.

The advantage of bipedalism appears to be energy savings at walking speeds, whereas the advantage of relatively long *Homo* legs would have been the potential for a significantly increased daily range. Put simply, *Homo* could have moved faster at an energetically advantageous walking speed than would have been possible for the australopithecines. The cost of locomotion, however, is still proportional to body mass and distance covered. This brings up the issue of the daily energy expenditure (DEE) of the hominins.

DAILY ENERGY EXPENDITURE (DEE)

In spite of the fact that bipedalism is more efficient than primate quadrupedalism, Leonard & Robertson (1997) have established that human hunter-gatherers have substantially higher daily energy requirements than would be expected for a primate of our body mass. Their analysis is based on time-budget data from the literature, and DEE was computed by summing the caloric needs for maintenance (i.e., sleeping) and daily activities. Data for nonhuman primates were converted to caloric costs using the energetic models derived from Coelho (Coelho 1974, Coelho et al. 1979) and those for humans (!Kung and Ache) using models from the World Health Organization (FAO/WHO/UNU 1985). Their analysis results in a positive relationship between DEE and body mass ($DEE = 86.0\ W^{0.793}$, where W = body mass in kilograms), although the relationship is isometric when humans are excluded from the analysis (Key & Ross 1999, Aiello & Key 2002). Based on the inferred body mass of *Homo ergaster*, Leonard & Robertson suggest that its DEE would be between 40% and 85% greater than that of the australopithecines (see also Table 1). The higher percentage increase (80%–85%) is based on the assumption that *Homo ergaster* had human-like and not chimpanzee-like ranging behavior.

Leondard & Robertson (1997) also demonstrate that relative energy expenditure and day ranges are positively correlated with diet quality across primates, including humans. The relationship between diet quality and increased energy levels is also consistent with the observation that primates with higher diet quality have higher levels of social activity (Milton 1999).

SPECULATIONS ON THE RELATIONSHIP BETWEEN ENERGETICS AND THE EVOLUTION OF HUMAN SOCIAL ORGANIZATION

A further effect of the increased size of *Homo ergaster* mothers and hence offspring would have been the greater energy requirements during gestation and lactation. Gestation increases DEE by 20%–30% in mammals (Gittleman & Thompson 1988) and lactation by at least 37%–39% in primates (Oftedal 1984, Aiello & Key 2002). Aiello & Key (2002) demonstrate that the DEE for a lactating *Homo ergaster* female is about 45% higher than for a lactating australopithecine or paranthropine and almost 100% higher than for a nonlactating and nongestating smaller-bodied hominin (Table 1). They argue that the resulting high per offspring energy costs could have been considerably reduced by decreasing the interbirth interval, with the additional benefit of increasing the number of offspring per mother. A faster reproductive schedule reduces the most expensive part of reproduction, lactation, although the benefit would be countered by a smaller increase in the energy required to support dependent offspring. Interbirth intervals have been estimated at around 4 years in gorillas, 5.5 years in wild chimpanzees, and 8 years in orangutans (Galdikas & Wood 1990), considerably longer than in most contemporary hunter-gatherer societies (Sear et al. 2000, Aiello & Key 2002).

Even taking into account this improved efficiency of reproduction in *Homo*, Aiello & Key (2002) argue that the increased requirements could only have been attained through a radical shift in foraging strategy involving the dietary changes highlighted earlier in this paper including increased exploitation of both animal products and underground storage organs (O'Connell et al. 1999, Wrangham et al. 1999).

An important aspect of this is that the energetic costs of feeding dependent offspring need not be met only by the mother. Hawkes and colleagues (1997a,b; 1998) have proposed the grandmother hypothesis, whereby postmenopausal women contribute to the parenting of their daughter's offspring. An increased level of paternal care, possibly mediated by changes in the stability of the parental pair bond, represents another potential source of energy for parental investment (Key 1998, 1999; Key & Aiello 1999, 2000; Kaplan et al. 2000). A recent analysis of data from the Gambia provided support for the grandmother hypothesis, showing that maternal grandmothers had a significant effect on offspring height (Sear et al. 2000). In contrast, the effect of paternal grandfathers and male kin on child height was negligible. An alternative and simpler hypothesis is that the cost of supporting offspring is reduced when there are several dependent offspring simultaneously (Peccei 2001), although the principal energetic costs of growth and maintenance are predicted to be minimally affected by such a strategy (Aiello & Key 2002).

SUMMARY

In summary, the emergence of *Homo* is characterized by three changes in maintenance energy requirements: (*a*) an absolute increase, due to greater body size; (*b*) a shift in the relative requirements of different organs, with increased energy diverted to brain metabolism at the expense of gut tissue, possibly mediated by changes in the proportion of weight comprised of fat; and (*c*) a slower rate of childhood growth, offset by higher growth costs during infancy and adolescence when faster growth rates are more viable. These direct changes then impose significant knock-on costs, including increased costs of reproduction, and also must be viewed in the context of the inferred changes in foraging strategy for *Homo ergaster*, which would have involved larger daily ranges and correspondingly elevated locomotor costs. Collectively, these increased costs are predicted to have been met by adaptations in energy stores, reproductive schedule, social interaction, changes in body form and leg length, and in foraging strategies that were modified by some form of economic division of labor. Of particular interest, given the contemporary increase in obesity, is the increased tendency to store fat as a buffer between high energy turnover and variable food supply.

ACKNOWLEDGMENTS

We would like to thank Tim Cole, Cathy Key, Kristin Hawkes, and Peter Wheeler for numerous and invaluable discussions during the development of the ideas presented in this paper.

The *Annual Review of Anthropology* is online at http://anthro.annualreviews.org

LITERATURE CITED

Aiello LC. 1997. Brains and guts in human evolution: the expensive tissue hypothesis. *Braz. J. Genet.* 20:141–48

Aiello LC, Bates N, Joffe T. 2001. In defense of the expensive tissue hypothesis. In *Evolutionary Anatomy of the Primate Cerebral Cortex*, ed. D Falk, K Gibson, pp. 57–78. Cambridge: Cambridge Univ. Press

Aiello LC, Key C. 2002. The energetic consequences of being a *Homo erectus* female. *Am. J. Hum. Biol.* 14:In press

Aiello LC, Wheeler P. 1995. The expensive tissue hypothesis: the brain and digestive system in human and primate evolution. *Curr. Anthropol.* 36:199–221

Aiello LC, Wood BA. 1994. Cranial variables as predictors of hominine body mass. *Am. J. Phys. Anthropol.* 95:409–26

Barton RA. 1992. Allometry of food intake in free-ranging anthropoid primates. *Folia Primatol.* 58:56–59

Bogin B, Smith BH. 1996. Evolution of the human life cycle. *Am. J. Hum. Biol.* 8:703–16

Broadhurst CL, Cunnane SC, Crawford MA. 1998. Rift Valley lake fish and shellfish provided brain-specific nutrition for early *Homo*. *Br. J. Nutr.* 7:3–21

Coelho AM. 1974. Socio-bioenergetics and sexual dimorphism in primates. *Primates* 15: 263–69

Coelho AM, Bramblett CA, Quick LB. 1979. Activity patterns in howler and spider monkeys: an application of socio-bioenergetic methods. In *Primate Ecology and Human Origins*, ed. IS Bernstein, EO Smith, pp. 175–200. New York/London: Garland STPM

Dean C, Leakey MG, Reid D, Schrenk F, Schwartz GT, et al. 2001. Growth processes in teeth distinguish modern humans from *Homo erectus* and earlier hominins. *Nature* 414:628–31

de Menocal PB. 1995. Plio-Pleistocene African climate. *Science* 270:53–59

Durnin JVGA, Passmore R. 1967. *Energy, Work and Leisure*. London: Heinemann. 166 pp.

FAO/WHO/UNU. 1985. Energy and protein requirements. *WHO Tech. Rep. Ser.* 724. Geneva: WHO

Fedak MA, Pinshow B, Schmidt-Nielsen K. 1974. Energetic cost of bipedal running. *Am. J. Physiol.* 227:1038–44

Fedak MA, Seeherman AJ. 1979. Reappraisal of energetics of locomotion shows identical costs in bipeds and quadrupeds including ostrich and horse. *Nature* 282:713–16

Foley RA. 1987. *Another Unique Species: Patterns in Human Evolutionary Ecology*. Harlow: Longman Sci. Tech.

Foley RA. 1992. Evolutionary ecology of fossil hominids. In *Evolutionary Ecology and Human Behavior*, ed. EA Smith, B Winterhalder, pp. 131–64. Chicago: Aldine de Gruyter

Foley RA, Elton S. 1998. Time and energy: the ecological context for the evolution of bipedalism. In *Primate Locomotion*, ed. E Strasser, J Fleagle, A Rosenberger, H

McHenry, pp. 419–33. New York/London: Plenum

Foley RA, Lee PC. 1991. Ecology and energetics of encephalisation in hominid evolution. *Philos. Trans. R. Soc. London Ser. B* 334:223–32

Forbes GB. 1987. *Human Body Composition: Growth, Aging, Nutrition and Activity*. New York: Springer-Verlag. 350 pp.

Frisch RE, McArthur JW. 1974. Menstrual cycles; fatness as a determinant of minimum weight for height necessary for their maintenance or onset. *Science* 185:949–51

Galdikas BMF, Wood JW. 1990. Birth spacing patterns in humans and apes. *Am. J. Phys. Anthropol.* 83:185–91

Garby L, Garrow JS, Jørgensen B, Lammert O, Madsen K, et al. 1988. Relation between energy expenditure and body composition in man: specific energy expenditure in vivo of fat and fat-free tissue. *Eur. J. Clin. Nutr.* 42:301–5

Gittleman JL, Thompson DS. 1988. Energy allocation in mammalian reproduction. *Am. Zool.* 28:863–75

Hawkes K, O'Connell JF, Blurton Jones NG. 1997a. Menopause: evolutionary causes, fossil and archaeological consequences. *J. Hum. Evol.* 32:A8–9 (Abstr.)

Hawkes K, O'Connell JF, Blurton Jones NG. 1997b. Hadza women's time allocation, offspring provisioning, and the evolution of long post-menopausal lifespans. *Curr. Anthropol.* 38:551–77

Hawkes K, O'Connell JF, Blurton-Jones NG, Alvarez H, Charnov EL. 1998. Grandmothering, menopause, and the evolution of human life histories. *Proc. Natl. Acad. Sci. USA* 95:1336–39

Hirschfield MF, Tinkle DW. 1975. Natural selection and the evolution of reproductive effort. *Proc. Natl. Acad. Sci. USA* 72:2227–31

Holliday MA. 1986. Body composition and energy needs during growth. In *Human Growth: A Comprehensive Treatise*, ed. F Falkner, JM Tanner, 2:101–7. New York: Plenum. 2nd ed.

Horrobin DF. 1998. Schizophrenia: the illness that made us human. *Med. Hypotheses* 50: 269–88

Horrobin DF. 2001. *The Madness of Adam and Eve*. London: Bantam. 275 pp.

Janson CH, van Schaik CP. 1993. Ecological risk aversion in juvenile primates: slow and steady wins the race. In *Juvenile Primates: Life History, Development and Behaviour*, ed. ME Pereira, LA Fairbanks, pp. 57–74. Oxford: Oxford Univ. Press

Jungers WL. 1982. Lucy's limbs, skeletal allometry and locomotion in *Australopithecus africanus*. *Nature* 297:676–78

Jungers WL. 1991. A pygmy perspective on body size and shape in *Australopithecus afarensis* (AL 288-1, 'Lucy'). In *Origines de la Bipedie chez les* Hominides, ed. Y Coppens, B Senut, pp. 215–24. Paris: Editions Centre Natl. Rech. Sci.

Kaplan H, Hill K, Lancaster J, Hurtado AM. 2000. A theory of human life history evolution: diet, intelligence, and longevity. *Evol. Anthropol.* 9:156–85

Kappelman J. 1996. The evolution of body mass and relative brain size in fossil hominids. *J. Hum. Evol.* 30:243–76

Key CA. 1998. *Cooperation, paternal care and the evolution of hominid social groups*. Doctoral diss. Dep. Anthropol., Univ. Coll. London/Univ. London

Key CA. 1999. Non-reciprocal altruism and the evolution of paternal care. In *Proceedings of Genetic Algorithms and Evolutionary Computation Conference (GECCO-99)*, ed. W Banzhaf, J Daida, AE Eiben, MH Garzon, V Honavar, M Jakiela, RE Smith, 2:1313–20. San Francisco: Morgan-Kaufman

Key CA, Aiello LC. 1999. The evolution of social organization. In *The Evolution of Culture*, ed. RIM Dunbar, C Knight, C Power, pp. 15–33. Edinburgh: Edinburgh Univ. Press

Key CA, Aiello LC. 2000. A prisoner's dilemma model of the evolution of paternal care. *Folia Primatol.* 71:77–92

Key CA, Ross C. 1999. Sex differences in energy expenditure in non-human primates. *Proc. R. Soc. London Ser. B* 266:2479–85

Kleiber M. 1932. Body size and metabolism. *Hilgardia* 6:315–53

Kleiber M. 1961. *The Fire of Life: An Introduction to Animal Energetics*. Huntington, NY: Krieger

Knott CD. 1997. The effects of changes in food availability on diet, activity and hormonal patterns in wild Bornean orangutans. *Am. J. Phys. Anthropol. (Suppl.)* 24:145

Kramer PA. 1998. The costs of human locomotion: maternal investment in child transport. *Am. J. Phys. Anthropol.* 107:71–85

Kramer PA. 1999. Modelling the locomotor energetics of extinct hominids. *J. Exp. Biol.* 202:2807–18

Kramer PA, Eck GG. 2000. Locomotor energetics and leg length in hominid bipedality. *J. Hum. Evol.* 38:651–66

Lawrence M, Coward WA, Lawrence F, Cole TJ, Whitehead RG. 1987. Fat gain during pregnancy in rural African women: the effect of season and dietary status. *Am. J. Clin. Nutr.* 45:1442–50

Leonard WR, Robertson ML. 1992. Nutritional requirements and human evolution: a bioenergetics model. *Am. J. Hum. Biol.* 4:179–95

Leonard WR, Robertson ML. 1994. Evolutionary perspectives on human nutrition: the influence of brain and body size on diet and metabolism. *Am. J. Hum. Biol.* 6:77–88

Leonard WR, Robertson ML. 1995. Energetic efficiency of human bipedality. *Am. J. Phys. Anthropol.* 97:335–38

Leonard WR, Robertson ML. 1997. Comparative primate energetics and hominid evolution. *Am. J. Phys. Anthropol.* 102:265–81

Martin RD. 1996. Scaling of the mammalian brain: the maternal energy hypothesis. *News Physiol. Sci.* 11:149–56

McFarland R. 1997. Female primates: fat or fit? In *The Evolving Female*, ed. ME Morbeck, A Galloway, AL Zihlman, pp. 163–75. Princeton: Princeton Univ. Press

McHenry HM. 1991. Femoral lengths and stature in Plio-Pleistocene hominids. *Am. J. Phys. Anthropol.* 85:149–58

McHenry HM. 1992a. Body size and proportions in early hominids. *Am. J. Phys. Anthropol.* 87:407–31

McHenry HM. 1992b. How big were early homnids? *Evol. Anthropol.* 1:15–19

McHenry HM. 1994. Behavioral ecological implications of early hominid body size. *J. Hum. Evol.* 27:77–87

McHenry HM, Coffing K. 2000. *Australopithecus* to *Homo*: transformations in body and mind. *Annu. Rev. Anthropol.* 29:125–46

Milton K. 1999. A hypothesis to explain the role of meat-eating in human evolution. *Evol. Anthropol.* 8:11–21

Mink JW, Blumenschine RJ, Adams DB. 1981. Ratio of central nervous system to body metabolism in vertebrates: its constancy and functional basis. *Am. J. Physiol. Regul. Integr. Comp. Physiol.* 241:R203–12

Mueller P, Diamond J. 2001. Metabolic rate and environmental productivity: well-provisioned animals evolved to run and idle fast. *Proc. Natl. Acad. Sci. USA* 98:12550–54

O'Connell JF, Hawkes K, Blurton Jones NGB. 1999. Grandmothering and the evolution of *Homo erectus*. *J. Hum. Evol.* 36:461–85

Oftedal TO. 1984. Milk composition, milk yield and energy output at peak lactation: a comparative review. *Symp. Zool. Soc. London* 51:33–85

Peccei JS. 2001. Menopause: adaptation or epiphenomenona? *Evol. Anthropol.* 10:43–57

Pond C. 1991. Adipose tissue in human evolution. In *The Aquatic Ape: Fact or Fiction*?, ed. M Roede, J Wind, JM Patrick, V Reynolds, pp. 193–220. London: Souvenir

Pond C. 1997. The biological origins of adipose tissue in humans. In *The Evolving Female*, ed. ME Morbeck, A Galloway, AL Zihlman, pp. 147–62. Princeton: Princeton Univ. Press

Reed KE. 1997. Early hominid evolution and ecological change through the African Plio-Pleistocene. *J. Hum. Evol.* 32:289–322

Roberts SB, Young VR. 1988. Energy costs of fat and protein deposition in the human infant. *Am. J. Clin. Nutr.* 48:951–55

Rodman PS, McHenry HM. 1980. Bioenergetics and the origin of hominid bipedalism. *Am. J. Phys. Anthropol.* 52:103–6

Ruff CB. 1991. Climate and body shape in hominid evolution. *J. Hum. Evol.* 21:81–105

Rutenberg GW, Coehlo AM Jr, Lewis DS, Carey KD, Gill HC Jr. 1987. Body composition in baboons: evaluating a morphometric method. *Am. J. Primatol.* 12:275–85

Sear R, Mace R, McGregor IA. 2000. Maternal grandmothers improve nutritional status and survival of children in rural Gambia. *Proc. R. Soc. London Ser. B* 267:1641–47

Sikes NE. 1999. Plio-Pleistocene floral context and habitat preferences of sympatric hominid species in East Africa. In *African Biogeography, Climate Change, and Human Evolution*, ed. T Bromage, F Schrenk, pp. 301–15. Oxford: Oxford Univ. Press

Simonsen L, Bulow J, Madsen J. 1994. Adipose tissue metabolism in humans determined by vein catheterization and microdialysis techniques. *Am. J. Physiol. Endocrinol. Metab.* 266:E357–65

Speth JD. 1989. Early hominid hunting and scavenging: the role of meat as an energy source. *J. Hum. Evol.* 18:329–43

Speth JD, Spielmann KA. 1983. Energy source, protein metabolism, and hunter-gatherer subsistence strategies. *J. Anthropol. Archaeol.* 2:1–31

Stahl WR. 1965. Organ weights in primates and other mammals. *Science* 150:1039–42

Stearns SC. 1992. *The Evolution of Life Histories.* Oxford: Oxford Univ. Press

Taylor CR, Rowntree VJ. 1973. Running on two or four legs: which consumes more energy? *Science* 179:186–87

Taylor CR, Schmidt-Nielsen K, Raab JL. 1970. Scaling of energetic cost of running to body size in mammals. *Am. J. Physiol.* 219:1104–7

Ulijaszek SJ. 1995. Energetics and human evolution. In *Human Energetics in Biological Anthropology*, ed. SJ Ulijaszek, pp. 166–75. Cambridge: Cambridge Univ. Press

Walker A, Leakey R, eds. 1993. *The Nariokotome Homo erectus Skeleton.* Cambridge, MA: Harvard Univ. Press

Webb D. 1996. Maximum walking speed and lower limb length in hominids. *Am. J. Phys. Anthropol.* 101:515–25

Wells JCK. 2002. Thermal environment and human birth weight. *J. Theor. Biol.* 214:413–25

Wells JCK, Cole TJ. 2002. Birth weight and environmental heat load: a between-population analysis. *Am. J. Phys. Anthropol.* In press

Wheeler PE. 1992. The thermoregulatory advantages of large body size for hominids foraging in savanna environments. *J. Hum. Evol.* 23:351–62

Wheeler PE. 1993. The influence of stature and body form on hominid energy and water budgets: a comparison of *Australopithecus* and early *Homo*. *J. Hum. Evol.* 24:13–28

Wood B. 1992. Origin and evolution of the genus *Homo*. *Nature* 355:783–90

Wood B, Aiello LC. 1998. Taxonomic and functional implications of mandibular scaling in early hominins. *Am. J. Phys. Anthropol.* 105:523–38

Wood B, Collard M. 1999. The human genus. *Science* 284:65–71

Wrangham RW, Jones JH, Laden G, Pilbeam D, Conklin-Brittain N. 1999. The raw and the stolen: cooling and the ecology of human origins. *Curr. Anthropol.* 5:567–94

Zihlman AL, McFarland RK. 2000. Body mass in lowland gorillas: a quantitative analysis. *Am. J. Phys. Anthropol.* 113:61–78

Annu. Rev. Anthropol. 2002. 31:339–61
doi: 10.1146/annurev.anthro.31.040402.085352

First published online as a Review in Advance on June 12, 2002

LANGUAGE SOCIALIZATION: Reproduction and Continuity, Transformation and Change

Paul B. Garrett[1] and Patricia Baquedano-López[2]

[1]*Department of Anthropology, Temple University, Philadelphia, Pennsylvania 19122; email: paul.garrett@temple.edu*

[2]*Graduate School of Education, University of California, Berkeley, Berkeley, California 94720; email: pbl@uclink.berkeley.edu*

Key Words language acquisition, cultural reproduction, childhood development, lifespan, learning

■ **Abstract** While continuing to uphold the major aims set out in the first generation of language socialization studies, recent research examines the particularities of language socialization processes as they unfold in institutional contexts and in a wide variety of linguistically and culturally heterogeneous settings characterized by bilingualism, multilingualism, code-switching, language shift, syncretism, and other phenomena associated with contact between languages and cultures. Meanwhile new areas of analytic focus such as morality, narrative, and ideologies of language have proven highly productive. In the two decades since its earliest formulation, the language socialization paradigm has proven coherent and flexible enough not merely to endure, but to adapt, to rise to these new theoretical and methodological challenges, and to grow. The sources and directions of that growth are the focus of this review.

INTRODUCTION

Socialization, broadly defined, is the process through which a child or other novice acquires the knowledge, orientations, and practices that enable him or her to participate effectively and appropriately in the social life of a particular community. This process—really a set of densely interrelated processes—is realized to a great extent through the use of language, the primary symbolic medium through which cultural knowledge is communicated and instantiated, negotiated and contested, reproduced and transformed.

Taking this latter observation as its point of departure, language socialization research is concerned with how children and other novices are socialized through the use of language as well as how they are socialized to use language (Ochs & Schieffelin 1984). The first *Annual Review of Anthropology* article on the topic of language socialization appeared in 1986, not long after the language socialization research paradigm's initial formulation in the early 1980s. That review (Schieffelin

& Ochs 1986a) continues to serve as an important programmatic statement that complements others published by the same authors at about the same time (Ochs & Schieffelin 1984, Schieffelin & Ochs 1986b). This review seeks to pick up where the 1986 review left off by charting important new directions that language socialization research has taken during the past 16 years.

Despite various lacunae that remain to be addressed and areas of inquiry that demand further development (Goodwin 1997, Hirschfeld 1999), the study of first language acquisition, child development, and other aspects of childhood and children's social worlds has gradually assumed a prominent place in anthropology (though not yet as prominent a place as it occupies in psychology) (Bloom 1998, Bugental & Goodnow 1998). Language socialization research has been a driving force in this positive trend. The study of language socialization encompasses more than language acquisition and child development, however; although it has certain clear affinities with approaches taken in such fields as developmental psychology and psycholinguistics, it differs from them in its strongly ethnographic orientation and its explicit attention to the ways in which culture influences all aspects of human development as a lifelong process, of which language acquisition is only one (albeit a crucial one to which many others are closely linked). Over the past 16 years the language socialization paradigm has been revisited and in various ways further elaborated by its originators (Ochs 1988, 1990, 1993; Ochs & Schieffelin 1989, 1995; Schieffelin 1990, 1994; Schieffelin & Ochs 1996); it has likewise benefited from the ongoing work of other scholars who made significant contributions to its early formulation and development (e.g., Clancy 1999, Corsaro & Miller 1992, Miller 1994, Watson-Gegeo 1992, Watson-Gegeo & Gegeo 1999). Meanwhile the paradigm has been taken up avidly by a new generation of researchers (e.g., Baquedano-López 2000, Cook 1996, de León 1998, Fader 2001, Field 2001, Fung 1999, Garrett 1999, He 2001, Jacobs-Huey 1999, Jacoby 1998, Meek 2001, Moore 1999, Paugh 2001, Riley 2001, Rymes 2001) and has influenced the ongoing research programs of more established scholars (e.g., Brown 1998, Budwig 2001, Mertz 1996, Sperry & Sperry 2000, Zentella 1997). Studies carried out in Mayan communities of southern Mexico (Brown 1998; de León 1998; Haviland 1998; Pye 1986, 1992) have begun to provide an areal concentration heretofore unseen in language socialization research, as well as a solid empirical basis for current and future comparative work (very much in keeping with the paradigm's broader aims).

Most of the pioneering studies of language socialization—for present purposes, those featured in Schieffelin & Ochs (1986a,b)—were conducted in small-scale societies. The few early studies that were conducted in larger-scale societies such as the United States and Japan tended to focus on relatively homogeneous monolingual communities (an important exception being Heath 1983). More recent and currently ongoing studies uphold the major areas of concern identified in the first generation of language socialization research while also directing attention to the particularities of language socialization processes as they unfold within sociolinguistically and culturally heterogeneous settings characterized by bilingualism and multilingualism, code-switching, language shift, syncretism, and other phenomena associated with contact between two or more languages and cultures. These studies have been (and in many cases continue to be) carried out in postcolonial settings (Garrett 1999, Moore 2002, Paugh 2001, Sidnell 1997), dependencies with ties to distant metropoles (Riley 2001), indigenous communities situated within the geopolitical boundaries of large, heterogeneous nation-states (Field 2001, Meek 2001), and urban and diasporic communities in the United States (Baquedano-López 2000, Bhimji 2002, Fader 2001, González 2001, Needham 1996, Smith-Hefner 1999). Another large group of studies focuses on language socialization in institutional environments, such as schools and workplaces, that are characterized by complex relationships to the larger communities and societies in which they are embedded (Dunn 1999b, He 2001, Jacobs-Huey 1999, Jacoby 1998, Rymes 2001, Senghas 2002).

Such diverse settings as these have presented new theoretical and methodological challenges for language socialization research, as they have for ethnography and anthropology more generally in recent decades. In the years since its initial formulation, the language socialization paradigm has proven robust, coherent, and flexible enough not merely to endure, but to rise to these new challenges, to adapt, and to grow. The sources and directions of that continuing growth are the focus of this review.

AIMS AND ORIENTATIONS

Language socialization research draws on anthropological, (socio)linguistic, sociological, and psychological approaches to human development, seeking a maximally holistic and integrative perspective. It examines how young children and other novices, through interactions with older and/or more experienced persons, acquire the knowledge and practices that are necessary for them to function as, and be regarded as, competent members of their communities. Language socialization research takes a longitudinal approach, documenting these processes over the course of developmental time. It is ethnographic in orientation, in that it relates these individual developmental processes to the sociocultural contexts in which they are embedded. Finally, it is cross-cultural in perspective, recognizing that while there are universal biological and psychological components to these processes, cultural factors, which vary considerably from one time and place to another, condition and substantially influence how these processes unfold.

As linguistic anthropologists have long recognized, local values, ideologies, patterns of social organization, and cultural preferences are inscribed in everyday discourse and social interactions, making it possible to discern and investigate the relationships between everyday linguistic and discursive practices and broader social structures and systems of cultural meaning such as mythologies, kinship systems, and patterns of exchange and reciprocity. This is perhaps nowhere more clearly seen than in caregiver-child interactions, which were the main focus of the earliest language socialization studies (Schieffelin & Ochs 1986b). As young children interact with their caregivers in socializing activities, they acquire linguistic and social skills as well as a culturally specific world view. They learn to recognize, negotiate, index, and co-construct diverse types of meaningful social contexts, making it possible for them to engage with others under an increasingly broad range of circumstances and to expand their social horizons by taking on new roles and statuses. In learning how to speak, they also learn how to think, how to comport themselves, and even how to feel and how to express (or otherwise manage) those feelings. As a developmental process, then, language acquisition is far more than a matter of a child learning to produce well-formed referential utterances; it also entails learning how to use language in socially appropriate ways to co-construct meaningful social contexts and to engage with others in culturally relevant meaning-making activities.

Firmly grounded in ethnographic methodology and informed by social theory, the language socialization approach takes all of this into account while availing itself of descriptive and analytic concepts developed in formal linguistics, sociolinguistics, developmental psycholinguistics, and related disciplines. This dual focus on linguistic form and sociocultural context allows the language socialization researcher to integrate micro and macro levels of investigation in such a way that close analysis of naturalistic interactions among individuals provides empirically grounded access to broader issues of sociocultural reproduction and transformation. This has proved to be one of the paradigm's greatest strengths, allowing researchers to capture continuity as well as change in language and culture alike. In recent work it has provided an effective means of investigating language shift, cultural revival movements, and other sociocultural transformations that operate on multiple levels, from the family and household to the state (Crago et al. 1993; Fader 2000; Field 2001; Garrett 1999, 2000; Kulick 1992; Meek 2001; Paugh 2001; Riley 2001).

METHODOLOGICAL TRENDS

The combined ethnographic rigor and cross-disciplinary character of language socialization research has provided an empirically driven approach to linguistic and social theory–building as well as outward linkages to key issues in contemporary social science inquiry. The theories and methods of discourse analysis and conversation analysis, for example, have provided effective means of capturing the moment-to-moment deployment of talk in interaction and have offered analytic access to the ways in which social relations (including caregiver-child and novice-expert relations) are maintained, contested, and transformed across a variety of socializing interactions such as professional education (Duff et al. 2000, Jacobs-Huey 1998, Jacoby & Gonzales 1991, Mertz 1996, Ochs & Jacoby 1998), counseling encounters (He & Keating 1991), schooling (Baquedano-López 1997, 1998, 2000; Duff 1993; Gutiérrez et al. 1995, 1999; Moore 1999; Rymes 2001; Zentella 1997), and family interactions (Bhimji 1997, Capps & Ochs 1995, McKee et al. 1991, Ochs & Taylor 1992, Pease-Alvarez & Vásquez 1994, Vásquez et al.

1994). New technologies have also had an impact on data collection and analysis; the availability of increasingly sophisticated digital audio-video recording equipment and software has made possible significant advances in the study of gesture and nonverbal behavior (de León 1998; Goodwin 1995, 2000; Haviland 1998), for example, and has enabled researchers to accomplish unprecedented micro-level analyses of both verbal and nonverbal aspects of human interaction.

This attention to linguistic detail has not precluded attention to the historicized subject as language socialization researchers have sought to make visible the ideologies and power relations that underlie socializing interactions (Baquedano-López 1997, 2000; Rymes 2001; Schieffelin 1996, 2000). Traditional ethnography, as the study of a single cultural or linguistic group, has in some cases given way to multi-site ethnographies that attempt to capture cultural and linguistic movement across time and space. For example, the study of literacy practices in Western Samoa in the 1980s (Ochs 1988) has been rendered more sociopolitically acute through comparison to literacy practices among Samoans living in Southern California (Duranti et al. 1995); in the latter locale, a particular learning tool, a syllabary (introduced by Western missionaries in Samoa in order to teach English), now serves as a link to Samoan worldviews and culture. Jacobs-Huey (1998, 1999, 2001) follows the language socialization practices of cosmetology schools from Oakland to Los Angeles to Charleston, South Carolina, revealing similarities and differences in African-American women's professional discourse and membership in a historicized community of practice.

THE ROUTINE AND THE EVERYDAY

One of the most significant contributions of language socialization research is the insight it has yielded into everyday life—the mundane activities and interactions in which ordinary individuals participate, constituting the warp and woof of human sociality. The focus of language socialization research on socializing routines—recurrent, situated activities that provide structured opportunities for children to engage with caregivers and other community members—has been highly productive. This focus can be traced to the paradigm's roots in ethnomethodology (Heritage 1987) and its assumption that much of the cultural knowledge that underlies everyday interactions is tacit, i.e., part of practical consciousness but not discursive consciousness (Giddens 1979) and hence not ordinarily reflected upon or spoken about. Close analysis of the routine and the everyday allows the researcher to make inferences about the "background" knowledge that guides and organizes all social activity but is rarely articulated. Socializing activities are one of the few contexts in which, for the benefit of a child or other novice, such knowledge may be discursively elaborated. The language socialization approach stresses that the routine, however mundane and everyday in character, must also be regarded as an achievement (Schegloff 1986)—the contingent, co-constructed product of sequentially organized communicative acts, both verbal and nonverbal. These communicative acts are finely guided by preferences, orientations, and dispositions that are social in origin and culturally specific in nature, while at the same time they are interest-laden and are creatively and strategically deployed by individuals. Inspired by phenomenological approaches to interaction, language socialization research highlights the open-ended, negotiated, sometimes contested character of the routine and thus recognizes that it contains the potential for innovation and change. Such a dual perspective on the routine—as socially structured and hence enduring, but also as situated, contextually grounded, and emergent in character—has been elucidated in social theory of recent decades through such notions as "habitus" (Bourdieu 1980), stressing the embodied, dispositional, generative character of everyday practice, and "duality of structure" (Giddens 1979), stressing the recursive, mutually constitutive nature of the relationship between social structure and individual agency. While centrally concerned with the reproduction of social structures and of the practices that produce them and are produced by them, these theoretical perspectives also take fully into account the potential for change; as Giddens (1979, p. 128) notes, "Routinisation implies '*ethnomethodological continuity*' more than reproduction of the empirical content of practices" (emphasis in original).

PRACTICES AND ACTIVITIES

As suggested above, practice theory was a crucial element in the language socialization research paradigm's formulation, providing a strong but flexible framework for its routine-based and activity-based analytic approaches. As such, it strongly complements socioculturally oriented theories of learning developed by the sociohistorical school of Soviet psychology, particularly in the work of Vygotsky, Luria, and Leont'ev (Wertsch 1985), which in turn has stimulated much recent theory-building by anthropologists and researchers in related disciplines (Chaiklin & Lave 1993, Engeström 1987, Lave & Wenger 1991, Rogoff 1990, Wenger 1998).

Practice-based approaches to language-in-use (and communicative behavior more generally) draw on certain key working assumptions that have always guided language socialization research. One assumption is that although languages exhibit internal structures and principles that are uniquely linguistic in nature, language is not a self-contained system impervious to the social worlds of its speakers; on the contrary, it is thoroughly interpenetrated by those worlds (Hanks 1996). While speakers are always constrained to some extent by formal and conventional properties of their languages, those properties are to a great extent precipitates of language usage in socially and historically particular settings (Bakhtin 1986, Ochs et al. 1996b); and as Bakhtin notes, the individual speaker/author, while never free of the conventional aspects of language, can nevertheless exercise a considerable degree of creativity—much like Lévi-Strauss's *bricoleur*—by actively appropriating and manipulating pre-existing forms (from phonemes and morphemes to discourses and genres) to suit his or her own expressive and social ends.

Another, related assumption is that language, like culture, is extrinsic to any given individual speaker-agent and comprises more information than any individual can know or acquire; consequently, there is variation among individuals, variation which is socially structured and is at the same time a wellspring of ongoing social dynamics (Schieffelin 1990). As Hanks (1996, p. 229) observes, in order for two or more persons "to communicate, at whatever level of effectiveness, it is neither sufficient nor necessary that they 'share' the same grammar. What they must share, to a variable degree, is the ability to orient themselves verbally, perceptually, and physically to each other and to their social worlds." Language socialization research is fundamentally concerned with how children and other novices develop their abilities to achieve just such mutuality of orientation with others.

To this end, the activity (Chaiklin & Lave 1993, Engeström 1987) is a crucial unit of analysis in language socialization research, allowing the researcher to examine how novices and more experienced persons engage each other in emergent, situated interactions (many but not all of which are routinized and recurrent to some degree). Within these co-constructed interactions, participants co-operatively instantiate cultural knowledge through practices as well as through emotions and affective stances (Clancy 1999, Schieffelin 1990) and moral and normative evaluations (Briggs 1998, Fader 2000, Fung 1999, Rydstrom 2001, Smith-Hefner 1999). From the researcher's perspective, activities are not pre-existing objects of inquiry, but neither are they merely a product of theoretical or analytic perspective; activities provide the raw materials of empirical analysis and serve as windows on underlying principles of social organization and cultural orientation. Methodologically, a focus on activities demands that the researcher be attentive to the larger sociocultural framework in which they are embedded and from which they derive their significance for participants. Such an analytic focus also prevents undue emphasis on either the child/novice (as learner or acquirer) or the more experienced person(s) (as source of "input"), emphasizing instead their mutual alignment and engagement as an emergent phenomenon that is at once structured and structuring, socially organized and socially organizing (Ochs 2000).

COMPETENCE REVISITED

Strongly rooted in the ethnography of communication, language socialization research takes a more comprehensive view of competence than does linguistics or developmental psycholinguistics (two other fields in which the notion of competence is often encountered). Language socialization research is concerned with the "microgenesis" (Schieffelin & Ochs 1996) of communicative competence, which involves much more than linguistic competence in the generativist sense (or even in the broader developmental pragmatic sense); it also involves the practical knowledge that is needed in order to use language as a social tool, to engage in talk as an activity (Wertsch 1985), and to co-construct meaningful interactive contexts. In short, language socialization research is concerned with all of the knowledge and practices that one needs in order to function as—and, crucially, to be regarded by others as—a competent member of (or participant in) a particular community or communities, however broadly or narrowly defined.

Certain questions arise from this broad notion of competence. How is competence assessed and evaluated, and by whom? What are the consequences of such assessments? How might evaluations of competence be negotiated and contested? The notion of bidirectionality in socialization—that is, the idea that novices are not just passive recipients, but have the potential to socialize experts (Rogoff 1990, 1993; Schieffelin & Ochs 1986a; Vygotsky 1978)—calls attention to the fact that the novice (even a very young child) brings to every interaction some degree of competence, some type of knowledge and/or expertise. Children and other novices actively use their developing knowledge not just to co-construct but sometimes to resist and reframe their participation in socializing interactions (Bhimji 1997, 2002; Capps & Ochs 1995; Jacoby & Gonzales 1991; Ochs & Capps 2001; Ochs et al. 1989; Rymes 1996). Children may in fact be the experts themselves in some areas; this is seen, for example, when children introduce their elders to new technologies and resources (e.g., computers and the Internet), or when immigrant adults with limited second-language proficiency rely on their children to mediate and broker their relationships with persons and institutions outside the household or immediate community.

These and related considerations call for a notion of competence that takes into account the inherent heterogeneity of culture and the cross-cutting dimensions of power and identity that partially structure and organize that heterogeneity. Child and adolescent peer group–based studies (Goodwin 1990, Hewitt 1986, Rampton 1995b, Sheldon 1998, Thorne 1993) suggest that competence is largely a matter of participating effectively—of deploying linguistic and other communicative resources (e.g., athletic and game-playing skills, as demonstrated through embodied actions) in ways that enable one to locate oneself strategically and flexibly with respect to currently ongoing interactions and activities as well as group boundaries and the identities (gender, ethnic, racial, etc.), often fluid and shifting, that they index. Analytic focus on participation frameworks (Goodwin 1990, de León 1998) provides insight into how individuals use both talk and embodied action to signal to one another what kinds of interactive contexts or activities they are enacting at a given moment and how they expect (or hope) others will respond; those responses can in turn provide insight into competence as locally constituted, transforming the notion of competence from abstract and static to empirically grounded and dynamic.

PROBLEMATIZING THE COMMUNITY

Language socialization research presupposes ongoing dynamic changes in the child or novice's relationship to some group or groups, which are typically conceptualized as communities. The notion of community has a long and problematic history in anthropology and the other social sciences, much like the notions of culture and language (which, not coincidentally, are almost always invoked as central considerations in defining it). Agreement as to how the notion of community should be defined theoretically and implemented methodologically remains elusive, despite apparently widespread consensus that some such working concept is virtually indispensable. These difficulties and controversies derive in part from ongoing debates in anthropology, sociology, and related disciplines over certain long-standing antinomies—structure/agency, structure/history, subjectivity/objectivity, synchrony/diachrony—that prominent social theorists such as Bourdieu and Giddens have identified as the greatest stumbling blocks of the social sciences and have sought to transcend. Partly in response to these theoretical developments, there has been a broad-based shift of analytic and theoretical focus in the social sciences (as well as in the humanities, e.g., history and literary criticism) from the group or collectivity to the individual agent—or more accurately, there has been increased attention to dialectical tensions between the individual and the group, and to the situated, dynamic nature of that relationship. There has likewise been greater acknowledgment of heterogeneity and increased attention to the multiple cross-cutting divisions and tensions (if not conflicts) that inhere in any group or community. Pratt (1987) has eloquently critiqued the "utopian" character of a prevailing "linguistics of community" which, despite oft-proclaimed rejections of Saussurean, Chomskyan, and other formalist models, nevertheless persists (semi-covertly) in upholding and reproducing "the centrifugal, homogenising tendencies of western thinking" about languages and communities of speakers. Significantly, Pratt points out that such tendencies are particularly problematic for the study of ludic activity, intimacy, nurturance, and socialization, all of which are routinely excluded from theories that continue to fixate on "normal" and "straightforward" modes of communication and interaction. She goes on to note that it is scholarship in precisely these areas, including language socialization research, that is doing the most to challenge and overcome the problems that she outlines.

Although it does not necessarily allow one to evade all of the pitfalls that Pratt identifies, one of the most attractive models of community for language socialization researchers and others in recent years has been the "community of practice"—or better, communities of practice, since the model presupposes that every individual participates in multiple such communities, during the course of his/her lifetime and likewise at any given point in time (Lave & Wenger 1991, Wenger 1998). As part of a general social theory of learning, a practice-based approach to community offers a number of advantages. It seeks to address explicitly the theoretical tensions between group and individual agent that are generated by such pairings as structure and agency, collectivity and subjectivity, power and meaning, practice (as socially constituted ways of engaging with the world) and identity (as a function of the mutual constitution of group and self). It defines community not in terms of geography, language(s) spoken, or broad presupposed social categories such as race or ethnicity, but in terms of mutual social and interactive engagement. A community of practice is thus defined neither in terms of membership alone nor practices alone, but in relational terms that link the two. One implication of this is that the boundaries of community (insofar as such can be said to exist) must be conceptualized as fuzzy and relatively permeable. Individual changes in status and competence—e.g., from "legitimate peripheral participation" (Lave & Wenger

1991) to mastery and/or full participation—can be closely tracked with attention to subtle variations in degrees and forms of engagement (de León 1998).

The communities of practice model presumes the existence of diversity in any group and admits the possibility of dynamic, shifting patterns of participation in multiple (often overlapping) communities. Older notions of community have become increasingly problematic due to the diminishing relevance of certain kinds of social and geographic boundaries (e.g., those associated with the territoriality of the nation-state) and frames of social reference (e.g., nationality and race; the heightened relevance of ethnicity in many contemporary situations cannot be discounted, however). Communities studied in current language socialization research may cut across or straddle the traditional boundaries of ethnicities, nation-states, regions, etc.; researchers need ways of dealing with the challenges presented, for example, by border communities and transnational social phenomena (González 2001, Needham 2001, Vásquez et al. 1994). More than ever before, researchers must be attentive to the ways in which individuals (as opposed to groups) draw on language and other semiotic resources at their disposal to construct and index their multiple, multifaceted, shifting identities (Fader 2000; Ochs 1990, 1993; Rampton 1995a,b; Rymes 2001; Zentella 1997).

SOCIALIZATION ACROSS THE LIFESPAN

Language socialization has always been regarded as a lifelong process (Schieffelin & Ochs 1986a). Although most early studies focused on interactions involving young children, the lifelong nature of socialization was explicitly acknowledged through attention to the agency of the child and the reciprocal, dialectical nature of socialization processes; even a preverbal infant can be regarded as socializing others into such roles as mother, older sibling, etc. Language socialization researchers have therefore avoided treating children's development as a teleological, unilinear progression toward a static adult status (Goodwin 1997), recognizing that adults likewise continue to be socialized into new roles, statuses, and practices.

Various recent studies have focused on language socialization later in the life cycle: in middle childhood (Baquedano-López 2000, Goodwin 1990, Sheldon 1998, Thorne 1993, Zentella 1997), adolescence (Rampton 1995a,b; Rymes 2001), and early to middle adulthood (Capps & Ochs 1995, Dunn 1999b, Jacoby & Gonzales 1991). A few studies combine a cross-sectional perspective with the more characteristic longitudinal approach in order to capture a sense of the typical and/or normative developmental trajectory in a particular community (Fader 2000, Zentella 1997); such approaches offer the added benefit of capturing change at the community level. Very little research thus far has focused on late adulthood, but the topic is certainly open for exploration; it seems especially likely to attract interest in the near future in the United States and other societies in which the average lifespan is increasing and in which aging is now associated with an increasing variety of residence patterns, institutional contexts, lifestyles, and activities. Goodwin's (2000) studies of interactions involving persons affected by aphasia suggest some possible directions that such research might take.

Studies of adolescents have tended to focus on their construction and negotiation of social identities and on the formation of identity-based social groupings in which gender, class, ethnicity, and other salient categories are constituted and indexed through both discursive and nondiscursive practices (Eckert & McConnell-Ginet 1995, Mendoza-Denton 1996, Rymes 2001). Significantly, the socialization processes in question occur largely within the peer groups that characteristically take form in schools and other institutional contexts in which youth in industrialized and postindustrial societies spend significant portions of their time. Adolescents are not seen as simply trying on and gradually assuming ready-made adult roles and identities; both within and across peer groups, adolescents may in fact directly challenge and contest the racial/ethnic stereotypes and other semiotica of identity (whether positively or negatively valenced) that prevail in society at large (Hewitt 1986; Leap 1993; Rampton 1995a,b).

A significant number of studies published since the middle of the last decade examine the language socialization of adult novices. Some of these studies make clear that speakers' verbal repertoires may continue to develop well into the adult years, as when adults must master new registers or speech styles associated with work and professional life and expanding social horizons, or new discursive and performative genres, which may be either spoken or written (Dunn 1999a,b). Adults likewise become socialized into new roles, statuses, and identities associated with education and training (Jacobs-Huey 1998, 1999; Mertz 1996, 1998; Philips 1982), work and professional life (Jacoby 1998, Levine & Moreland 1991, Wenger 1998), immigration, religious conversion and other significant life changes (Duff et al. 2000, Schieffelin 2000), and transgendered identity (Kulick 1998). Recent studies of narrative and discursive practices focus attention on ways in which adults interpret past events and experiences while coping with ongoing challenges and projecting possible futures (Capps & Ochs 1995, Ochs & Capps 2001); these studies, incidentally, provide an important complement to studies of children's narrative construction of self (Miller et al. 1990). Such reworkings, reconfigurations, and transformations of adult subjectivities typically involve entry into pre-existing communities (Jacoby 1998, Jacoby & Gonzales 1991), but in some cases they may involve the emergence of entirely new communities and codes, as in the emergence of new Deaf communities and new sign languages (see Senghas & Monaghan 2002, this volume)—even new conceptions of personhood, as seen in the recent emergence of a Deaf community in Nicaragua (Senghas 1997, 2002). On a similar scale, linguistic and cultural systems may be pervasively affected by sustained contact between disparate world views, cosmologies, technologies, and ideologies of language, as seen in Schieffelin's (1996, 2000) ongoing work on the introduction of literacy among the Kaluli by Christian missionaries.

BILINGUAL AND MULTILINGUAL SOCIALIZATION

Numerous recent language socialization studies have been carried out in bilingual and multilingual settings, and in others characterized by significant linguistic variation (e.g., creole settings). The coexistence of two or more codes within a particular community, whatever the sociohistorical circumstances that have given rise to them or brought them into contact, is rarely a neutral or unproblematic state of affairs; it tends to be a focal point of cultural elaboration and social conflict with complex linkages to other, equally contested issues. Language differences (either real or perceived) may map onto and index, or may be used to constitute and reinforce, the boundaries of other social categories and divisions based on such notions as ethnicity, nationality, race, class, gender, religiosity, and generation (Irvine & Gal 2000). As children are socialized to use language and to engage in specific communicative practices, they are also socialized, from their earliest years, into knowledge of these intimately related issues and culturally preferred ways of dealing with them (Bhimji 2002, Fader 2000, Field 2001, Garrett 1999, Meek 2001, Paugh 2001, Riley 2001). Ochs's (1985, 1988) work on language socialization in Western Samoa set an important precedent for more recent studies. The Samoan language has distinct registers, and Ochs shows that Samoan children acquire knowledge of the indexical and pragmatic features of particular grammatical and lexical forms from an early age; register differentiation and the hierarchical character of Samoan society thus directly influence the course of Samoan children's language acquisition. In another landmark study, Kulick (1992) investigates a case of ongoing language shift in Papua New Guinea in which children whose elders are bi- or multilingual are acquiring only one language, Tok Pisin. Kulick shows how macrosociological changes (such as those that typically fall under the rubric of "modernization") may be interpreted by individuals in ways that have direct bearing on daily practices, including language socialization practices. He goes on to demonstrate that this can yield unintended, unforeseen consequences, including some as profound and far-reaching as the rapid decline of a people's vernacular. Several subsequent studies conducted in bi- and multilingual settings also focus on processes of language change and shift (Field 2001; Garrett 1999, 2000; Meek 2001; Paugh 2001; Riley 2001); others emphasize such issues as the maintenance and contestation of community boundaries (Fader 2001) and the construction of ethnic and cultural identity (Baquedano-López 2000, Bhimji 2002, He 2002, Smith-Hefner 1999, Zentella 1997).

Multilingual individuals, even young children, may be in a position to renegotiate, challenge, or transcend the existing social categories that are constituted and indexed by the codes and communicative practices at their disposal. Children and their caregivers in these settings must therefore be regarded as agents with the potential to transform language as well as the cultural systems of meaning that it so thoroughly interpenetrates. In some cases, changing practices lead to the "loss" or transformation of existing codes (Garrett 2000, Paugh 2001, Riley 2001); in others, language socialization practices are centrally involved in shaping notions of ethnicity, cultural identity, morality, and personhood (Baquedano-López 2000, Fader 2000, He 2002, Paugh 2001, Smith-Hefner 1999), and thus in (re)constituting and (re)defining communities. Current language socialization studies are concerned with examining these broader social processes as well as the ways in which individuals assert and negotiate their sometimes shifting identities within these heterogeneous contexts.

LITERACY SOCIALIZATION

Attention to the centrality of language in cultural reproduction and transformation has influenced our understanding of language as a mediating tool in literacy development. Broadly conceived, literacy is a culturally organized act of control over certain forms of language (Barton 1994, Besnier 1995, Gee 1991, Heath 1983). The focus on the activity as a unit of analysis in language socialization studies has contributed to the ways in which literacy learning is identified, described, and analyzed. This focus has produced descriptions of socializing interactions around literacy events, i.e., communicative events in which literacy plays a central role (Heath 1983); bedtime story reading, for example, constitutes a literacy event within certain groups in the United States. The situated practice of reading is constituted in part by the ways in which bedtime reading is socially organized—who reads to whom, what is being read, the time and place of the event (Barton 1994). Literacy practices are thus inherently social, reflecting the cultural knowledge and expectations that participants bring to bear on the literacy event.

Language socialization research on literacy has revealed continuities as well as discontinuities between the literacy practices of homes or local communities and those of schools. The discontinuities may have important social and cognitive consequences for children and other newcomers to mainstream formal education. This has been supported by empirical work that has documented gains in learning and participation when students engage in activities that draw on their home and community literacy and language repertoires (Gutiérrez et al. 1995, 1997; Lee 1993; Michaels 1991; Pease-Alvarez & Vásquez 1994). We have also come to understand that for some groups the literacy practices of the home correspond to those of the school, facilitating the transition between home and school contexts. Activities such as the reading of bedtime stories (Heath 1983) and communal family mealtime conversations among white middle-class families (Ochs & Taylor 1992, Taylor 1995) promote specific problem-solving skills and a particular scientific orientation that prepares children for the acquisition of the skills endorsed in school.

A growing body of discourse analytic studies has informed our understanding of the acquisition and uses of literacy across a broad range of institutional contexts including schools (Budwig 2001, Larson 1995, Gutiérrez et al. 1999, Poole 1989, Rymes 1997), after-school programs (Gutiérrez et al. 2001, Needham 1996), religious instruction (Baquedano-López 1997, 1998, 2000; Duranti et al. 1995; Fader 2000, 2001; Schieffelin 1996), and physics laboratories (Ochs et al. 1996a). As these studies suggest, literacy practices are never neutral; rather, they are political acts and are invariably tied to larger sociohistorical processes that have bearing on ongoing social relations (Collins 1995).

THE SELF IN THE SOCIAL, EMOTIONAL, AND MORAL WORLD

Across communities, novices are expected to recognize and display emotions in culturally defined ways and according to local norms and preferences (e.g., as internal or external responses to events). Affect is linguistically mediated and permeates talk, infusing words with emotional orientations (Besnier 1990, Ochs 1986, Ochs & Schieffelin 1989, Schieffelin & Ochs 1986b). A number of studies have focused on the analysis of discrete affect-encoding particles that speakers use to position themselves in relation to a local moral order (Clancy 1999, Cook 1996, Schieffelin & Ochs 1986b); other studies, taking a somewhat broader perspective, examine how language is used in the construction and transformation of the moral order (Meek 2001, Smith-Hefner 1999). In both perspectives, the language used to encode emotions forms the basis for the socialization of morality, that is, the social sanctioning or rejection of actions (one's own as well as those of others).

The development of personhood and of the self through language is intricately related to moral ways of acting and being in the social world (Field 2001, Fung 1999, Rydstrom 2001). Recent language socialization studies locate the use of affective language in the construction of a moral order across contexts ranging from family interactions (Briggs 1998, Capps & Ochs 1995, de León 1998, Fader 2000, Ochs & Taylor 1992, Ochs et al. 1992, Taylor 1995) to the playground (Goodwin 1990, 1995) to schools (Baquedano-López 1997, 1998, 2000; Ochs & Capps 2001; Rymes 2001). By investigating the ways in which participants in everyday routines learn to internalize and express emotion and to make sense of the moral order that they are actively constructing with others, these studies reveal that notions of morality are negotiated through linguistically mediated understandings of daily life and events and of one's place in the world, both as an individual and as part of a collectivity.

A significant contribution of the language socialization paradigm has been its problematization of the relationship among the individual, the group, and the social order. This has given rise to a large body of research on the construction of identity in which participants' roles in interaction are conceptualized as dynamic collaborative achievements (Ochs 1993). In the course of a given interaction, participants may use language to index aspects of their co-constructed, contingent, fluid identities with respect to gender (Fader 2000, 2001; Farris 1991; Jacobs-Huey 2001; Kulick 1998; Sheldon 1998), culture, race, and ethnicity (Baquedano-López 1997, Cheng & Kuo 2000, Cook 1996, Lo 1997, Ou & McAdoo 1999, Zentella 1997), age (Briggs 1998, Budwig 2001, Clancy 1999, de León 1998), institutions (Duff et al. 2000, He & Keating 1991, Moore 1999, Rymes 2001), and professions (Jacobs-Huey 1998, 1999; Jacoby 1998). Attention to the ways in which both experts and novices use linguistic and interactional resources during the course of socializing activities enables language socialization researchers to observe and describe the emergent identities of novices as they become competent members of their communities. These resources are also employed in the sanctioning, rejection, or contestation of those identities by more expert others.

NARRATIVE SOCIALIZATION

Narrative is a primordial tool of socialization. Stories of personal experience are told from present perspectives, creating present experiences for both narrator and audience (Duranti & Brenneis 1986, Ochs & Capps 1996). People tell their stories in a search for coherence and authenticity of the self and also as a means of positioning the self in relation to others (Ochs & Capps 2001). The narrative is often a site of multiple socializing activities (Michaels 1991; Miller 1994; Miller et al. 1997; Ochs 1994, 1997). In their study of dinnertime narratives, Ochs et al. (1992) explain that when family members tell narratives in which they directly quote an argument or a complaint, these narratives serve more than one intention; besides relating events, narrative tellers are also constructing discursive acts and positioning themselves and others in a moral order (Ochs et al. 1989, 1992; Rymes 1996; Taylor 1995). Narrative thus focuses on particular protagonists and events while situating tellers and their audiences within a web of cultural and moral expectations, ideologies, and meanings (which are not necessarily shared by all members of the group).

The narrative process often extends beyond the boundaries of the here and now to embrace people and places in a historical and cultural past. Narrative thus creates more or less shared understandings of membership, collectivity, and community among participants. Collective narratives tend to reify existing ideologies, but they can also constitute resistance to dominant master narratives (Baquedano-López 1997, 2000; Duff 1993). Collective narratives tell the experiences of a group and constitute ways of encoding and sharing collective experience; recitation and recollection of a group's historical events are a means through which the past is made relevant to present-day concerns. Duff's (1993) ethnographic study of educational discourse in the context of history lessons at three Hungarian-English secondary schools focuses on the structure and transformation of a recitational exercise, *felelés*, which is used to describe historical change; Duff reveals that the changing structure of lessons is linked to political changes of the late 1980s, including the rejection of Soviet-era policies and ideologies. As this study illustrates, collective narratives organize the diverse and changing experiences of the collectivity and can be used to normalize as well as to contest interpretations of those experiences.

IDEOLOGIES OF LANGUAGE

Language socialization research has been deeply influenced by the literature on ideologies of language that has taken shape alongside it—in tandem with it, in many respects—over the past two decades (Schieffelin et al. 1998, Silverstein 1979, Woolard & Schieffelin 1994). Cultural belief systems about language and its relationship to other aspects of social life have always been a focus of language socialization research; Schieffelin's early work, for example, explored the relationship of Kaluli ideas about the nature of language to ethnotheories of language acquisition as a developmental process (Feld & Schieffelin 1981, Schieffelin 1983).

More recent work on ideologies of language has enabled language socialization researchers to sharpen this focus. Among the contributions of this body of work is its attention to variation—its explicit recognition of the fact that ideologies are not uniform within any given social group, but rather are multiple, situated, and "interested," i.e., rooted in individual experiences of the social order that vary with class, age, gender, etc. Ideologies of language are often sites of contestation over language itself as well as over a host of other issues that may or may not be transparently linked to language.

Language ideologies tend to come to the fore in multilingual settings (Ochs & Schieffelin 1995). At the most general level, notions of what language itself is, and of its relation to cultural and individual identity, vary considerably across communities—and sometimes within the same community, since in most cases where two or more languages are in contact, an equal number of cultural traditions likewise coexist and mutually influence one another. Normative and prescriptive imperatives, though they may originate far outside the local context, are enacted (and sometimes reinterpreted, syncretically or otherwise) at local levels (Riley 2001). Local notions of what counts as a language, of who counts as a speaker, and of what can (and cannot) be done with (and done to) particular languages vary considerably; also of interest are widely differing attitudes toward code-switching and matters of language "purity." These and other aspects of language ideology inform and organize everyday practices, which in turn engender specific linguistic and sociocultural outcomes—often unforeseen outcomes, which may then go partially or wholly unrecognized (or misrecognized) by those whose actions and practices are bringing them about. This is often true in cases of language attrition and shift—adults may assume that the local, "traditional" language will continue to be reproduced across the generations, just as it "always has," when in fact they are now socializing their own children in such a way that the children are not acquiring full command of the language (Field 1999, Garrett 1999, Kulick 1992, Meek 2001, Paugh 2001, Schieffelin 1994). In still other settings, language may be used to constitute social categories and to delineate or reinforce the boundaries thereof (Fader 2000, Needham 2001). Some recent studies document self-conscious (but still very much ideologically informed) efforts toward language maintenance or revival. In these cases, the link between language and community or culture tends to be explicitly foregrounded; those involved in these efforts see themselves as preserving community and "tradition" (or "culture," or "heritage") as well as language. But despite such cultivated awareness of (certain aspects of) the relationship between language and culture, these efforts too can lead to unforeseen and unexpected outcomes; processes variously conceived as preservation, revival, standardization, etc. tend to be deeply transformative (Garrett 2000, Paugh 2001, Riley 2001).

In these and other regards, language socialization researchers are finding that ideologies of language intersect in complex and interesting ways with local notions of cultural and group identity, nationhood, personhood, childhood, and language acquisition as a developmental process. While the specific language socialization practices motivated by these intermeshing systems of ideas and beliefs are always a central concern, these studies stress the inherent dynamism and mutability of language socialization, as a locus of reproduction as well as change, by exploring the channels of mutual influence linking ideology, practice, and outcome.

CONCLUSION

Ochs (2000, p. 231) has recently sounded a cautionary note by commenting that a tendency toward certain types of generalizations that has sometimes manifested itself in language socialization research can "have several undesirable effects: for one thing, cultures are essentialized, and variation in communicative practices within communities is underemphasized." Left unchecked, the result of such a tendency is that "[o]ur accounts also seem like fixed cameos, members and communities enslaved by convention and frozen in time rather than fluid and changing over the course of a generation, a life, and even a single social encounter." Clearly Ochs's point is well taken, by language socialization researchers and indeed by all anthropologists. Based on this review of recent work, we suggest that language socialization researchers are keenly aware of, and attentive to, these potential pitfalls and are assiduously and creatively exploring new ways of addressing them. Meanwhile they are taking the paradigm in exciting new directions by infusing it with new theoretical insights developed in anthropology and other disciplines, and by exploring the potential benefits of using new models and methods, venturing into new fieldwork settings, and identifying productive new areas of analytic focus. Processes of language socialization always involve reproduction—of language as formal system, of social structures, and of cultural knowledge and practices. While these processes and their intricate interrelationships remain a central concern of current language socialization research, recent studies also emphasize that language socialization is central to—and in some cases a driving force in—dynamic processes of transformation and change.

The *Annual Review of Anthropology* is online at http://anthro.annualreviews.org

LITERATURE CITED

Bakhtin MM. 1986. *Speech Genres and Other Late Essays*. Austin: Univ. Tex. Press

Baquedano-López P. 1997. Creating social identities through *doctrina* narratives. *Issues Appl. Linguist.* 8(1):27–45

Baquedano-López P. 1998. *Language socialization of Mexican children in a Los Angeles Catholic parish*. PhD thesis. Univ. Calif., Los Angeles

Baquedano-López P. 2000. Narrating community in *Doctrina* classes. *Narrat. Inq.* 10(2):1–24

Barton D. 1994. *Literacy: an Introduction to the Ecology of Written Language*. Oxford: Blackwell

Besnier N. 1990. Language and affect. *Annu. Rev. Anthropol.* 19:419–51

Besnier N. 1995. *Literacy, Emotion, and Authority: Reading and Writing on a Polynesian Atoll*. Cambridge: Cambridge Univ. Press

Bhimji F. 1997. *¡Mueve la almohada! ¡Levante la cara!* (Move the pillow! Lift your head!): an analysis of correction talk in Mexican and

Central American parent-child interaction. *Issues Appl. Linguist.* 8(2):133–45

Bhimji F. 2002. "Dile *family*"*: socializing language skills with directives in three Mexican families in South Central Los Angeles.* PhD thesis. Univ. Calif., Los Angeles

Bloom L. 1998. Language acquisition in its developmental context. In *Handbook of Child Psychology*, ed. W Damon, D Kuhn, RS Siegler, 2:309–70. New York: Wiley

Bourdieu P. 1980. *The Logic of Practice.* Stanford, CA: Stanford Univ. Press

Briggs J. 1998. *Inuit Morality Play: the Emotional Education of a Three-Year-Old.* New Haven, CT: Yale Univ. Press

Brown P. 1998. Conversational structure and language acquisition: the role of repetition in Tzeltal. *J. Linguist. Anthropol.* 8(2):197–221

Budwig N. 2001. Language socialization and children's entry into schooling (preface to special issue). *Early Educ. Dev.* 12(3):295–302

Bugental DB, Goodnow JJ. 1998. Socialization processes. In *Handbook of Child Psychology*, ed. W Damon, N Eisenberg, 3:389–462. New York: Wiley

Capps L, Ochs E. 1995. *Constructing Panic: the Discourse of Agoraphobia.* Cambridge, MA: Harvard Univ. Press

Chaiklin S, Lave J, eds. 1993. *Understanding Practice: Perspectives on Activity and Context.* Cambridge, UK: Cambridge Univ. Press

Cheng S, Kuo W. 2000. Family socialization of ethnic identity among Chinese American pre-adolescents. *J. Comp. Family Stud.* 31(4):463–84

Clancy P. 1999. The socialization of affect in Japanese mother-child conversation. *J. Pragmat.* 31(11):1397–421

Collins J. 1995. Literacy and literacies. *Annu. Rev. Anthropol.* 24:75–93

Cook HM. 1996. Japanese language socialization: indexing the modes of self. *Discourse Process.* 22(2):171–97

Corsaro WA, Miller PJ, eds. 1992. *Interpretive Approaches to Children's Socialization.* San Francisco: Jossey-Bass

Crago MB, Annahatak B, Ningiuruvik L. 1993. Changing patterns of language socialization in Inuit homes. *Anthropol. Educ. Q.* 24(3):205–23

de León L. 1998. The emergent participant: interactive patterns in the socialization of Tzotzil (Mayan) infants. *J. Linguist. Anthropol.* 8(2):131–61

Duff P. 1993. *Changing times, changing minds: language socialization in Hungarian English schools.* PhD thesis. Univ. Calif., Los Angeles

Duff PA, Wong P, Early M. 2000. Learning language for work and life: the linguistic socialization of immigrant Canadians seeking careers in healthcare. *Can. Mod. Lang. Rev./La Rev. Can. Lang. Vivantes* 57(1):9–57

Dunn CD. 1999a. Toward the study of communicative development as a life-span process. *Anthropol. Educ. Q.* 30(4):451–54

Dunn CD. 1999b. Coming of age in Japan: language ideology and the acquisition of formal speech registers. In *Language and Ideology: Selected Papers from the Sixth International Pragmatics Conference*, ed. J Verschueren, 1:89–97. Antwerp: Int. Pragmat. Assoc.

Duranti A, Brenneis D. 1986. The audience as co-author. *Text* 6(3):239–347

Duranti A, Ochs E, Ta'ase E. 1995. Change and tradition in literacy instruction in a Samoan American community. *Educ. Found.* Fall:57–74

Eckert P, McConnell-Ginet S. 1995. Constructing meaning, constructing selves: snapshots of language, gender, and class from Belten High. In *Gender Articulated: Language and the Socially Constructed Self*, ed. K Hall, M Bucholtz, pp. 469–507. New York: Routledge

Engeström YE. 1987. *Learning by Expanding: an Activity-Theoretical Approach to Developmental Research.* Helsinki: Orienta-Konsultit

Fader A. 2000. *Morality, gender, and language: socialization practices in a Hasidic community.* PhD thesis. New York Univ.

Fader A. 2001. Literacy, bilingualism and

gender in a Hasidic community. *Linguist. Educ.* 12(3):261–83

Farris C. 1991. Gender of child discourse: same-sex peer socialization through language use in a Taiwanese preschool. *J. Linguist. Anthropol.* 1(2):198–224

Feld S, Schieffelin BB. 1996 [1981]. Hard words: a functional basis for Kaluli discourse. In *The Matrix of Language: Contemporary Linguistic Anthropology*, ed. D Brenneis, R Macaulay, pp. 56–73. Boulder, CO: Westview

Field M. 1999. *Maintenance of indigenous ways of speaking despite language shift: language socialization in a Navajo preschool.* PhD thesis. Univ. Calif., Santa Barbara

Field M. 2001. Triadic directives in Navajo language socialization. *Lang. Soc.* 30(2):249–63

Fung H. 1999. Becoming a moral child: the socialization of shame among young Chinese children. *Ethnos* 27(2):180–209

Garrett PB. 1999. *Language socialization, convergence, and shift in St. Lucia, West Indies.* PhD thesis. New York Univ.

Garrett PB. 2000. "High" Kwéyòl: the emergence of a formal creole register in St. Lucia. In *Language Change and Language Contact in Pidgins and Creoles*, ed. J McWhorter, pp. 63–101. Amsterdam: Benjamins

Gee J. 1991. What is literacy? In *Rewriting Literacy: Culture and the Discourse of the Other*, ed. C Mitchell, K Weiler, pp. 3–11. Westport, CT: Bergin & Garvey

Giddens A. 1979. *Central Problems in Social Theory: Action, Structure, and Contradiction in Social Analysis.* Berkeley: Univ. Calif. Press

González N. 2001. *I Am My Language: Discourses of Women and Children in the Borderlands.* Tucson: Univ. Ariz. Press

Goodwin C. 2000. Gesture, aphasia and interaction. In *Language and Gesture*, ed. D McNeill, pp. 84–98. New York: Cambridge Univ. Press

Goodwin MH. 1990. *He-Said-She-Said: Talk as Social Organization Among Black Children.* Bloomington: Indiana Univ. Press

Goodwin MH. 1995. Co-construction in girls' hopscotch. *Res. Lang. Soc. Interact.* 28(3):261–82

Goodwin MH. 1997. Children's linguistic and social worlds: the knowns and unknowns. *Anthropol. Newsl.* 38(4):1, 4–5

Gutiérrez K, Baquedano-López P, Alvarez H. 2001. Using hybridity to build literacy in urban classrooms. In *The Best for Our Children: Latina/Latino Voices in Literacy*, ed. M Reyes, J Halcón, pp. 122–41. New York: Teachers Coll. Press

Gutiérrez K, Baquedano-López P, Alvarez H, Chiu M. 1999. Building a culture of collaboration through hybrid language practices. *Theory Pract.* 38(2):87–93

Gutiérrez K, Baquedano-López P, Turner MG. 1997. Putting language back into the Language Arts: when the radical middle meets the Third Space. *Lang. Arts* 74(5):368–78

Gutiérrez K, Rymes B, Larson J. 1995. Script, counterscript, and underlife in the classroom: James Brown versus Brown v. Board of Education. *Harvard Educ. Rev.* 65(3):445–71

Hanks WF. 1996. *Language and Communicative Practices.* Boulder, CO: Westview

Haviland J. 1998. Early pointing gestures in Zincantán. *J. Linguist. Anthropol.* 8(2):162–96

He AW. 2001. The language of ambiguity: practices in Chinese heritage language classes. *Discourse Stud.* 3(1):75–96

He AW. 2002. Speaking variedly: socialization of speech roles in Chinese heritage language classes. In *Language Socialization and Bilingualism*, ed. R Baley, S Schecter. Clevedon, UK: Multilingual Matters. In press

He AW, Keating E. 1991. Counselor and student at talk: a case study. *Issues Appl. Linguist.* 2(2):183–209

Heath SB. 1983. *Ways with Words: Language, Life, and Work in Communities and in Classrooms.* Cambridge, UK: Cambridge Univ. Press

Heritage J. 1987. Ethnomethodology. In *Social Theory Today*, ed. A Giddens, JH Turner, pp. 224–51. Cambridge, UK: Polity

Hewitt R. 1986. *White Talk, Black Talk:*

Inter-Racial Friendship and Communication Amongst Adolescents. Cambridge, UK: Cambridge Univ. Press

Hirschfeld LA. 1999. *L'enfant terrible*: anthropology and its aversion to children. *Etnofoor* 12(1):5–26

Irvine JT, Gal S. 2000. Language ideology and linguistic differentiation. In *Regimes of Language: Ideologies, Polities, and Identities*, ed. PV Kroskrity, pp. 35–83. Santa Fe, NM: Sch. Am. Res. Press

Jacobs-Huey L. 1998. "We are just like doctors, we heal sick hair": cultural and professional discourses of hair and identity in a black hair care seminar. In *SALSA V: Proc. 5th Annu. Symp. Lang. Soc. at Austin*, ed. MC Chalasani, J Grocer, P Haney, pp. 213–23. Austin: Tex. Linguist. Forum

Jacobs-Huey L. 1999. *Becoming cosmetologists: language socialization and identity in an African American beauty college*. PhD thesis. Univ. Calif., Los Angeles

Jacobs-Huey L. 2001. Epistemological deliberations: constructing and contesting knowledge in women's cross-cultural hair testimonies. In *EnGendering Rationalities*, ed. N Tuana, S Morgen, pp. 335–59. Albany: State Univ. NY Press

Jacoby S. 1998. *Science as performance: socializing scientific discourse through physics conference talk rehearsals*. PhD thesis. Univ. Calif., Los Angeles

Jacoby S, Gonzales P. 1991. The constitution of expert-novice in scientific discourse. *Issues Appl. Linguist.* 2:149–81

Kulick D. 1992. *Language Shift and Cultural Reproduction: Socialization, Self, and Syncretism in a Papua New Guinean Village*. Cambridge, UK: Cambridge Univ. Press

Kulick D. 1998. *Travesti: Sex, Gender, and Culture Among Brazilian Transgendered Prostitutes*. Chicago: Univ. Chicago Press

Larson J. 1995. *Talk matters: knowledge distribution among novice writers in kindergarten*. PhD thesis. Univ. Calif., Los Angeles

Lave J, Wenger E. 1991. *Situated Learning: Legitimate Peripheral Participation*. Cambridge, UK: Cambridge Univ. Press

Leap WL. 1993. Learning gay culture in "a desert of nothing": language as a resource in gender socialization. *High Sch. J.* 77(1-2):122–32

Lee C. 1993. *Signifying as a Scaffold for Literacy Interpretation: the Pedagogical Implications of an African-American Discourse Genre*. Urbana: Natl. Counc. Teach. Engl.

Levine JM, Moreland RL. 1991. Culture and socialization in work groups. In *Perspectives on Socially Shared Cognition*, ed. LB Resnick, JM Levine, SD Teasley, pp. 257–82. Washington, DC: Am. Psychol. Assoc.

Lo A. 1997. Heteroglossia and the construction of Asian-American identities. *Issues Appl. Linguist.* 8(1):47–65

McKee RL, Johnson K, Marbury N. 1991. Attention-getting strategies of deaf children at the dinner table. *Issues Appl. Linguist.* 2(2):239–68

Meek BA. 2001. *Kaska language socialization, acquisition and shift*. PhD thesis. Univ. Ariz., Tucson

Mendoza-Denton N. 1996. 'Muy macha': gender and ideology in gang girls' discourse about makeup. *Ethnos* 61:47–63

Mertz E. 1996. Recontextualization as socialization: text and pragmatics in the law school classroom. In *Natural Histories of Discourse*, ed. M Silverstein, G Urban, pp. 229–49. Chicago: Univ. Chicago Press

Mertz E. 1998. Linguistic ideology and praxis in U.S. law school classrooms. See Schieffelin et al. 1998, pp. 149–62

Michaels S. 1991. The dismantling of narrative. In *Developing Narrative Structure*, ed. A McCabe, C Peterson, pp. 303–51. Hillsdale, NJ: Erlbaum

Miller P. 1994. Narrative practices: their role in socialization and self-construction. In *The Remembering Self: Construction and Accuracy in the Self-Narrative*, ed. U Neisser, R Fivush, pp. 158–79. Cambridge, UK: Cambridge Univ. Press

Miller PJ, Potts R, Fung H, Hoogstra L, Mintz J. 1990. Narrative practices and the social construction of self in childhood. *Am. Ethnol.* 17(2):292–311

Miller PJ, Wiley AR, Fung H, Liang C-H. 1997. Personal storytelling as a medium of socialization in Chinese-American families. *Child Dev.* 68(3):557–68

Moore LC. 1999. Language socialization research and French language education in Africa: a Cameroonian case study. *Can. Mod. Lang. Rev./La Rev. Can. Lang. Vivantes* 56(2):329–50

Moore LC. 2002. Language mixing at home and school in a multilingual community (Mandara Mountains, Cameroon). In *Georgetown Univ. Round Table on Languages and Linguistics 2000: Linguistics, Language, and the Professions: Education, Journalism, Law, Medicine, and Technology*, ed. JE Alatis, H Hamilton, A-H Tan. Washington, DC: Georgetown Univ. Press

Needham S. 1996. *Literacy, learning and language ideology: intracommunity variation in Khmer literacy instruction.* PhD thesis. Univ. Calif., Los Angeles

Needham S. 2001. "How can you be Cambodian if you don't speak Khmer?" Language, literacy, and education in a Cambodian "rhetoric of distinction." In *Negotiating Transnationalism: Selected Papers on Refugees and Immigrants*, ed. M Hopkins, N Wellmeier, pp. 123–41. Arlington, VA: Am. Anthropol. Assoc.

Ochs E. 1985. Variation and error: a sociolinguistic study of language acquisition in Samoa. In *The Crosslinguistic Study of Language Acquisition*, ed. D Slobin, 1:783–838. Hillsdale, NJ: Erlbaum

Ochs E. 1986. From feelings to grammar. See Schieffelin & Ochs 1986b, pp. 251–72

Ochs E. 1988. *Culture and Language Development: Language Acquisition and Socialization in a Samoan Village.* New York: Cambridge Univ. Press

Ochs E. 1990. Indexicality and socialization. In *Cultural Psychology: Essays on Comparative Human Development*, ed. JW Stigler, RA Shweder, GH Herdt, pp. 287–308. New York: Cambridge Univ. Press

Ochs E. 1993. Constructing social identity: a language socialization perspective. *Res. Lang. Soc. Interact.* 26(3):287–306

Ochs E. 1994. Stories that step into the future. In *Perspectives on Register: Situating Register Variation within Sociolinguistics*, ed. E Finnegan, D Biber, pp. 106–35. Oxford: Oxford Univ. Press

Ochs E. 1997. Narrative. In *Discourse as Structure and Process*, ed. T van Dijk, pp. 185–207. Thousand Oaks, CA: Sage

Ochs E. 2000. Socialization. *J. Linguist. Anthropol.* 9(1-2):230–33

Ochs E, Capps L. 1996. Narrating the self. *Annu. Rev. Anthropol.* 25:19–43

Ochs E, Capps L. 2001. *Living Narrative: Creating Lives in Everyday Storytelling.* Cambridge, MA: Harvard Univ. Press

Ochs E, Gonzales P, Jacoby S. 1996a. "When I come down I'm in the domain state": grammar and graphic representation in the interpretive activity of physicists. See Ochs et al. 1996b, pp. 328–69

Ochs E, Jacoby S. 1998. Down to the wire: the cultural clock of physicists and the discourse of consensus. *Lang. Soc.* 26(4):479–505

Ochs E, Schegloff EA, Thompson SA, eds. 1996b. *Interaction and Grammar.* New York: Cambridge Univ. Press

Ochs E, Schieffelin BB. 1984. Language acquisition and socialization: three developmental stories and their implications. In *Culture Theory: Essays in Mind, Self and Emotion*, ed. RA Shweder, RA LeVine, pp. 276–320. New York: Cambridge Univ. Press

Ochs E, Schieffelin BB. 1989. Language has a heart. *Text* 9(1):7–25

Ochs E, Schieffelin BB. 1995. The impact of language socialization on grammatical development. In *The Handbook of Child Language*, ed. P Fletcher, B MacWhinney, pp. 73–94. Oxford: Blackwell

Ochs E, Smith R, Taylor C. 1989. Detective stories at dinnertime: problem-solving through co-narration. *Cult. Dyn.* 2:238–57

Ochs E, Taylor C. 1992. Family narrative as political activity. *Discourse Soc.* 3(2):301–40

Ochs E, Taylor C, Rudolph D, Smith R. 1992.

Story-telling as a theory-building activity. *Discourse Process.* 15(1):37–72
Ou Y, McAdoo HP. 1999. The ethnic socialization of Chinese American children. In *Family Ethnicity: Strength in Diversity*, ed. HP McAdoo, pp. 252–76. Thousand Oaks, CA: Sage
Paugh AL. 2001. *"Creole day is every day": language socialization, shift, and ideologies in Dominica, West Indies.* PhD thesis. New York Univ.
Pease-Alvarez L, Vásquez O. 1994. Language socialization in ethnic minority communities. In *Educating Second Language Children: the Whole Child, the Whole Curriculum, the Whole Community*, ed. F Genesee, pp. 82–102. Cambridge, UK: Cambridge Univ. Press
Philips SU. 1988 [1982]. The language socialization of lawyers: acquiring the "cant." In *Doing the Ethnography of Schooling: Educational Anthropology in Action*, ed. G Spindler, pp. 176–209. Prospect Heights, IL: Waveland
Poole D. 1989. *Everyday testing as language socialization: a study of the quiz review.* PhD thesis. Univ. South. Calif.
Pratt ML. 1987. Linguistic utopias. In *The Linguistics of Writing: Arguments between Language and Literature*, ed. N Fabb, D Attridge, A Durant, C MacCabe, pp. 48–66. Manchester, UK: Manchester Univ. Press
Pye C. 1986. Quiche' Mayan speech to children. *J. Child Lang.* 13:85–100
Pye C. 1992. The acquisition of K'iche' Mayan. In *The Cross-Linguistic Study of Language Acquisition*, ed. DI Slobin, pp. 221–308. Hillsdale, NJ: Erlbaum
Rampton B. 1995a. Language crossing and the problematisation of ethnicity and socialisation. *Pragmatics* 5(4):485–513
Rampton B. 1995b. *Crossing: Language and Ethnicity Among Adolescents.* London: Longman
Riley KC. 2001. *The emergence of dialogic identities: transforming heteroglossia in the Marquesas, F.P.* PhD thesis. City Univ. New York
Rogoff B. 1990. *Apprenticeship in Thinking: Cognitive Development in Social Context.* New York: Oxford Univ. Press
Rogoff B. 1993. Children's guided participation and participatory appropriation in sociocultural activity. In *Development in Context: Acting and Thinking in Specific Environments*, ed. R Wozniak, K Fischer, pp. 121–53. Hillsdale, NJ: Erlbaum
Rydstrom H. 2001. Like a white piece of paper: embodiment and the moral upbringing of Vietnamese children. *Ethnos* 66(3):394–413
Rymes B. 1996. Naming as social practice: the case of Little Creeper from Diamond Street. *Lang. Soc.* 25(2):237–60
Rymes B. 1997. Second language socialization: a new approach to second language acquisition research. *J. Intensiv. Engl. Stud.* 11:143–55
Rymes B. 2001. *Conversational Borderlands: Language and Identity in an Urban Alternative High School.* New York: Teachers Coll.
Schegloff EA. 1986. The routine as achievement. *Hum. Stud.* 9:111–51
Schieffelin BB. 1983. Talking like birds: sound play in a cultural perspective. In *Acquiring Conversational Competence*, ed. E Ochs, BB Schieffelin, pp. 177–84. London: Routledge & Kegan Paul
Schieffelin BB. 1990. *The Give and Take of Everyday Life: Language Socialization of Kaluli Children.* New York: Cambridge Univ. Press
Schieffelin BB. 1994. Code-switching and language socialization: some probable relationships. In *Pragmatics: From Theory to Practice*, ed. LE Hewett, RM Sonnenmeier, JF Duchan, pp. 20–42. Englewood Cliffs, NJ: Prentice Hall
Schieffelin BB. 1996. Creating evidence: making sense of written words in Bosavi. See Ochs et al. 1996b, pp. 435–60
Schieffelin BB. 2000. Introducing Kaluli literacy: a chronology of influences. In *Regimes of Language: Ideologies, Polities, and Identities*, ed. PV Kroskrity, pp. 293–327. Santa Fe, NM: Sch. Am. Res. Press

Schieffelin BB, Ochs E. 1986a. Language socialization. *Annu. Rev. Anthropol.* 15:163–91

Schieffelin BB, Ochs E, eds. 1986b. *Language Socialization Across Cultures.* New York: Cambridge Univ. Press

Schieffelin BB, Ochs E. 1996. The microgenesis of competence: methodology in language socialization. In *Social Interaction, Social Context, and Language*, ed. DI Slobin, J Gerhardt, A Kyratzis, J Guo, pp. 251–64. Mahwah, NJ: Erlbaum

Schieffelin BB, Woolard KA, Kroskrity PV, eds. 1998. *Language Ideologies: Practice and Theory.* New York: Oxford Univ. Press

Senghas RJ. 1997. *An "unspeakable, unwriteable" language: Deaf identity, language and personhood among the first cohorts of Nicaraguan signers.* PhD thesis. Univ. Rochester

Senghas RJ. 2003. New ways to be Deaf in Nicaragua: changes in language, personhood, and community. In *Many Ways to be Deaf*, ed. L Monaghan, K Nakamura, C Schmaling, GH Turner. Washington, DC: Gallaudet Univ. Press

Senghas RJ, Monaghan L. 2002. Signs of their times: Deaf communities and the culture of language. *Annu. Rev. Anthropol.* 31:69–97

Sheldon A. 1998. Talking power: girls, gender enculturation and discourse. In *Gender and Discourse*, ed. R Wodak, pp. 225–44. Thousand Oaks, CA: Sage

Sidnell J. 1997. Organizing social and spatial location: elicitations in Indo-Guyanese village talk. *J. Linguist. Anthropol.* 7(2):143–65

Silverstein M. 1979. Language structure and linguistic ideology. In *The Elements: a Parasession on Linguistic Units and Levels*, ed. PR Clyne, WF Hanks, CL Hofbauer, pp. 193–247. Chicago: Chicago Linguist. Soc.

Smith-Hefner NJ. 1999. *Khmer American: Identity and Moral Education in a Diasporic Community.* Berkeley: Univ. Calif. Press

Sperry L, Sperry D. 2000. Verbal and nonverbal contributions to early representation: evidence from African American toddlers. In *Communication: an Arena of Development*, ed. N Budwig, I Uzgiris, J Wertsch, pp. 143–65. Stamford, CT: Ablex

Taylor C. 1995. You think it was a fight? Co-constructing (the struggle for) meaning, face, and family in everyday narrative activity. *Res. Lang. Soc. Interact.* 28(3):283–317

Thorne B. 1993. *Gender Play: Girls and Boys in School.* New Brunswick, NJ: Rutgers Univ. Press

Vásquez O, Pease-Alvarez L, Shannon S, Moll L. 1994. *Pushing Boundaries: Language and Culture in a Mexicano Community.* Cambridge, UK: Cambridge Univ. Press

Vygotsky LS. 1978. *Mind in Society: the Development of Higher Psychological Processes.* Cambridge, MA: Harvard Univ. Press

Watson-Gegeo KA. 1992. Thick explanation in the ethnographic study of child socialization: a longitudinal study of the problem of schooling for Kwara'ae (Solomon Islands) children. In *Interpretive Approaches to Children's Socialization*, ed. WA Corsaro, PJ Miller, pp. 51–66. San Francisco: Jossey-Bass

Watson-Gegeo K, Gegeo DW. 1999. (Re)modeling culture in Kwara'ae: the role of discourse in children's cognitive development. *Discourse Stud.* 1(2):227–45

Wenger E. 1998. *Communities of Practice: Learning, Meaning, and Identity.* Cambridge, UK: Cambridge Univ. Press

Wertsch JV. 1985. *Culture, Communication and Cognition: Vygotskian Perspectives.* Cambridge, UK: Cambridge Univ. Press

Woolard KA, Schieffelin BB. 1994. Language ideology. *Annu. Rev. Anthropol.* 23:55–82

Zentella AC. 1997. *Growing Up Bilingual: Puerto Rican Children in New York.* Malden, MA: Blackwell

Annu. Rev. Anthropol. 2002. 31:363–93
doi: 10.1146/annurev.anthro.31.040402.085416

First published online as a Review in Advance on June 14, 2002

The Upper Paleolithic Revolution

Ofer Bar-Yosef
Harvard University, Department of Anthropology, Peabody Museum, Cambridge, Massachusetts, 02138; email: obaryos@fas.harvard.edu

Key Words Middle Paleolithic, modern humans

■ **Abstract** The transition from the Middle Paleolithic to the Upper Paleolithic is considered one of the major revolutions in the prehistory of humankind. Explanations of the observable archaeological phenomena in Eurasia, or the lack of such evidence in other regions, include biological arguments (the role of Cro-Magnons and the demise of the Neanderthals), as well as cultural-technological, and environmental arguments. The paper discusses issues of terminological ambiguities, chronological and geographical aspects of change, the emergence of what is viewed as the arch-types of modern forager societies, and the hotly debated and loaded issue of modern behavior. Finally, the various causes for the Upper Paleolithic revolution are enumerated, from the biological through the technocultural that relies on the analogy with the Neolithic revolution.

OPENING REMARKS

Paleolithic archaeology primarily addresses issues of stratigraphy, chronology, object assemblage analysis for defining cultural entities and adaptive strategies, examination of faunal and vegetal components, and site formation processes. Investigations often culminate in a coarse-grained reconstruction of prehistoric lifeways within an evolutionary context. Modern research stresses the necessity of establishing regional sequences and their Pleistocene and Holocene paleo-ecological conditions. Radiometric dates facilitate chronological correlations and the integration of the findings into a continent-wide record. For the Upper Paleolithic, the period under discussion, the combination of radiocarbon, thermoluminescence, and electron spin resonance dating techniques (Wagner 1998) assisted investigators during the past decade in constructing a reasonably coherent global chronology. Large standard deviations in thermoluminescence and electron spin resonance readings, as well as ambiguities concerning the calibration of 14C dates at the range of 40–30 thousand years ago (Ka) (Beck et al. 2001), make it difficult to establish the precise onset of the Upper Paleolithic revolution. However, with the current rapid progress in the use of these techniques one expects much better resolutions in the next decade. The dates in this paper are quoted as B.P. uncalibrated unless otherwise specified.

0084-6570/02/1021-0363$14.00

The term Upper Paleolithic period was coined in Western Europe, the homeland of the discipline of prehistoric archaeology. Historically it designated the time when *Homo sapiens sapiens*, referred to as Cro-Magnons, replaced the European Neanderthals (Bocquet-Appel & Demars 2000). The cultural manifestations of blade-dominated lithic assemblages along with mobile and cave art were seen as the hallmarks of the achievements of the new people. However, even the pioneers of prehistoric research, when the geographic scope of their knowledge expanded beyond Europe, were in doubt, and their queries (Bricker 1976) continue to linger with us today. These are questions regarding (*a*) how long Neanderthals survived in the various regions of Eurasia; (*b*) the identity of the bearers of the prehistoric cultures such as the Chatelperronian, Aurignacian, Gravettian and others and; (*c*) whether prehistoric migrations or climatic changes were the main causes for the cultural changes. These and additional topics are at the forefront of current debates, such as (*a*) whether the transition to the Upper Paleolithic was a major evolutionary event of global dimensions or a gradual transition; (*b*) whether the impetus for the change was biological, cultural, or both; (*c*) whether Upper Paleolithic archaeological manifestations are the markers for the capacity for modern culture; and (*d*) the point in time at which one can interpret the archaeological documents to indicate the emergence of modern behavior.

There is no way to satisfy the entire community of investigators while responding to these queries, because interpretations of the same evidence vary. The following pages provide a survey of the particular traits of the Upper Paleolithic while at the same time examining possibilities for their earlier emergence. Subsequently I present an overview of the terminological jumble, comments on the geographic distribution of Upper Paleolithic entities, the arguments concerning the indications for the capacity for modern behavior, and the potential causes for the Upper Paleolithic revolution.

THE NATURE AND CHARACTERISTICS OF THE UPPER PALEOLITHIC REVOLUTION

The nature of the Upper Paleolithic revolution is at the center of current debates (e.g., White 1982, 1997; Mellars 1989, 1996a, 2000; Straus 1996; Gibson 1996; Bar-Yosef 1998; Zilhao & D'Errico 1999; Wadley 2001; Clark 1997a,b; Klein 1995, 1999; McBrearty & Brooks 2000; Churchill & Smith 2000; Hublin 2000). The variable mosaic of archaeological and human fossil data sets are open to different interpretations. It is generally agreed that the way to identify a revolution is to compare the overall cultural-behavioral and economic system before and after a given point in time. This means we need to compare the Middle Paleolithic (or Middle Stone Age as it is known in Africa) and the Upper Paleolithic (or Late Stone Age). These two archaeologically determined periods are not of equal duration. Whereas the latter is of ~30 Ka duration (~40,000–10,000 years ago), the former lasted from ~250,000 to 40,000 or 30,000 years ago. Hence, the comparison should be limited to the same length of time. To facilitate the identification of the possible roots of Upper Paleolithic behavioral and material manifestations, only the last 30 Ka of the late Middle Paleolithic are taken into account. It is assumed that the period prior to the revolution may disclose silent indications that herald the ensuing changes.

Several scholars view the accumulation of markers for modern behavior as gradual during at least the Upper Pleistocene, if not since earlier times, and therefore conclude that there was no revolution (e.g., McBrearty & Brooks 2000; Clark 1997a,b; Straus 1996). Others view the new innovations and shifts in social structure as appearing first within the late Middle Paleolithic (e.g., Deacon & Deacon 1999; Straus 1996, 2001). However, most researchers agree that the observed cultural and technological traits, as well as the population increase during the Upper Paleolithic, were more rapid and had distinct global effects across Eurasia and Africa when compared with the slow pace of cultural changes during the Middle Paleolithic. Not the least of the human achievements of the Upper Paleolithic were the long-distance exchanges of raw materials and precious items, the occupation of the northern latitudes under periglacial conditions, the colonization of the Americas, and the first steps in coastal navigation and seafaring.

To test the hypothesis that recorded changes during the late Middle Paleolithic foretold the Upper Paleolithic, I proceed by presenting the attributes of the Upper Paleolithic revolution, as enumerated by archaeologists, with comments concerning their uniqueness or their earlier appearance during the Middle Paleolithic. However, most of the documented material components, as well as the inter- and intrasettlement patterns, are derived from Europe and western and northern Asia, whereas fewer cases are known from the sparsely explored east and south Asia or sub-Saharan Africa. Hence, the current picture contains inherent bias. In spite of this, one may notice within the vast continental area of the northern hemisphere that there is a mosaic of cultural expressions (mentioned below), and that the suite of elements often considered typical Upper Paleolithic markers as derived from Western Europe were not shared by all populations.

The list of Upper Paleolithic material components is briefly summarized here:

1. Upper Paleolithic assemblages are considered to present systematic production of prismatic blades, and only rarely is flake production dominant (e.g., Mellars 1989, 1996a; Kozlowski 2000; Kuhn & Bietti 2000; Rigaud 1997). An exception is southeast Asia, where the common late Pleistocene industry is the flake-dominated Hoabinian, and Tasmania, where human occupation began during the Upper Paleolithic. Earlier production of blades, mostly around 250–150 Ka and during the last Interglacial, was reported from Africa, Europe, and Asia (Conard 1990, Révillion & Tuffreau 1994, Bar-Yosef & Kuhn 1999). However, blade production in the Upper Paleolithic evolved into manufacturing bladelets and their shaping into microlithic stone tools of various forms.

2. It was assumed that a high degree of standardization and morphological variability prevails among tool types and differentiates the Upper Paleolithic from the Middle Paleolithic (e.g., Mellars 1989). This observation was often based on the number of types shown on the type lists of Bordes (1961) for the Middle Paleolithic compared with the one composed by de Sonneville-Bordes & Perrot (1953) for the Upper Paleolithic. It should be noted that the two lists were composed on the basis of traditional morphological observations, developed mainly during the first half of the twentieth century in Europe for reporting local assemblages. Numerous types of the Bordesian type list were later shown to be the results of resharpening or consecutive reduction (Dibble 1995, Bisson 2000). In addition, the contention that Mousterian assemblages are poorer in tool types than the Aurignacian in France was recently tested by Grayson & Cole (1998). These authors concluded that the Aurignacian industries are somewhat richer than the Mousterian, but this statement could be due to the differences in the classification systems. Even if this is not the case, there is still no theoretical framework that would enable us to evaluate and explore the meaning of such differences.

   Marks and associates (2001) tackled the issue of standardization among the lithic tool groups, often seen to a higher degree in the Upper than Middle Paleolithic industries. Their analysis, although limited to burins, demonstrated that there is a common level of standardization between both Middle and Upper Paleolithic samples.

   However, in spite of these observations, there is no doubt that relatively rapid shifts (within several centuries or a few thousand years) in core reduction strategies as well as bone and antler tool design occurred during the Upper Paleolithic in various regions. These shifts are interpreted as reflecting changes in style (i.e., transmitting cultural information) and rarely are related to functional needs (e.g., Barton 1997; Close 1989; Sackett 1983, 1991; Conkey & Hastorf 1990; Wobst 1999; Wiessner 1989; Goring-Morris et al. 1998; Jensen 1988; Geneste & Plisson 1993; Guilbaud 1996).

3. The exploitation of bone and antler as raw materials for the production of daily or ritual tools and objects became a common practice in the Upper Paleolithic (Mellars 1989). Whereas these raw materials were common in Middle Paleolithic sites they were generally not exploited. Some proposals to view pre–Upper Paleolithic bone objects as well-made artifacts were dismissed (Villa & D'Errico 2001). The exception is the assemblages of the Howiesons Poort in Klasies River Mouth cave and in particular in Blombos cave (Singer & Wymer 1982, Henshilwood & Sealy 1997, Henshilwood et al. 2001). The Howiesons Poort entity is generally dated to 80–60 Ka and is undoubtedly a unique and isolated cultural phenomenon, stratigraphically and chronologically intercalated between two Middle Stone Age industries without bone tools.

   Another case, with a different evolutionary implication, is the Chatelperronian bone and antler assemblage from Arcy sur Cure (Farizy 1990, 1994;

Mellars et al. 1999; Mellars 2000). Human relics indicate that this assemblage was originally designed by Neanderthals. However, the dates around 38–36 Ka correlate with the early entry of Cro-Magnons into Europe. Hence, this surprising Chatelperronian assemblage may have been the result of transmitted ideas, not necessarily face-to-face acculturation as sometimes proposed.

4. Systematic use of grinding and pounding stone tools began during the Upper Paleolithic. This is best documented where plant food played a major role in the diet such as in the Mediterranean region and Africa (Wright 1992). None of these tools were found in Middle Paleolithic contexts, although the consumption of vegetal substances during the Middle Paleolithic is known, for example, from Levantine sites (Bar-Yosef 2000).
5. Systematic use of body decorations—beads and pendants—made from marine shells, teeth, ivory, and ostrich egg shells are recorded from both Europe and the Levant (e.g., Taborin 1993; White 1993, 1997; Kuhn et al. 2001). These are considered to communicate the self-awareness and identity of the individual as well as the social group. No similar objects, and therefore no clear signs for the identity of the social units, were recorded in Middle Paleolithic contexts. The sole element, which may reflect shared transmission among individuals, was in lithic manufacturing indicated by the *chaînes opératoires*. Similar operational sequences may have delineated human interaction over relatively large geographic territories. These could have been the markers of mating systems, but such a determination requires supportive evidence.
6. Long-distance exchange networks in lithics, raw materials, and marine shells during the Upper Paleolithic reach the order of several hundred kilometers (Gamble 1993, Taborin 1993, Smith 1999, Johnson & Earle 2000). They consistently differ from the much shorter ranges of raw material procurement during the Middle Paleolithic (Conard 2001, Hovers 2001, Marks & Chabai 2001, Richter 2001, Geneste 1988, Féblot-Augustins 1993). Perhaps one of the exceptions is again the Howiesons Poort in South Africa (Deacon & Wurz 1996) because raw material was transported to the site from a long distance.
7. The Upper Paleolithic witnessed the invention of improved hunting tools such as spear throwers, and later bows and arrows and boomerangs (Mulvaney & Kaminga 1999). These devices facilitated targeting animals from longer distances and could have brought higher rates of hunting success. However, hafted spears with Levallois or other Mousterian points were recorded in more than a few instances (Shea 1988; Boëda et al. 1999).
8. Human and animal figurines, decorated and carved bone, antler, ivory and stone objects, and representational abstract and realistic images, either painted or engraved, began to appear in caves, rockshelters, and exposed rocky surfaces by 36 Ka (e.g., Marshack 1972, 1997; Clottes 1997; Conkey et al. 1997; Lewis-Williams 1997; Bahn 1997; Zilhão 1995; Soffer et al. 2000). We

must wonder why western Europe and, in particular, the Franco-Cantabrian region is so different from the rest of the Upper Paleolithic world. It is not the lack of limestone caves or suitable rock surfaces that prevented other social groups or their shamans from leaving behind similar paintings and engravings. Possibly this local flourish had to do with the vagaries and pressures faced by foragers in two major refugia regions at the ends of the inhabited world—Western Europe and Australia—where there are claims for rock art of the same general age. If this explanation has any foundation, we should look for the details of the common behavioral denominators (e.g., Davidson 1997, Lewis-Williams 1991).

Beyond mobile and stationary material elements there are additional components, such as intrasite features including burials, and subsistence strategies, and the extent to which they reflect modern behavior is often debated. These include

- Storage facilities, generally known from northern latitudes where underground freezing kept food edible (Soffer 1985, 1989; Grigor'ev 1993). Storage occurs in Upper Paleolithic sites after the initial phase. None of these structures was recorded in Middle Paleolithic contexts.
- Structured hearths with or without the use of rocks for warmth banking and parching activities were recorded in Upper Paleolithic sites. Variable types of hearths are known from both Middle and Upper Paleolithic contexts, although the use of rocks is almost exclusively documented from contexts of the latter period (Bar-Yosef et al. 1992, Meignen et al. 1989, Rigaud et al. 1999, Pastó et al. 2000).
- Distinct functional spatial organization within habitations and hunting stations such as kitchen areas, butchering space, sleeping grounds, discard zones, and the like are relatively common in Upper Paleolithic sites. Such features are better preserved in the later phases (after 20 Ka), but even the very early Upper Paleolithic sites produced good examples. Among others are Aurignacian contexts in Western and Central Europe (e.g., Svoboda & Siman 1989, Oliva 1993, Harrold 1989, Kuhn 1998, Kozlowski 1999, Otte & Derevianko 2001). These features may reflect the social structure or a particular combination of members of the band, such as a male task group (Binford 1983; Deacon 1992, 1995). This kind of information is rarely available from Middle Paleolithic sites. Among the known examples are Klasies River Mouth and Rose Cottage (South Africa), Kebara, Tor Faraj (Levant), Gibraltar, Abric Romani (Spain), Grotte XVI (France), and others (e.g., Deacon & Wurz 1996, Bar-Yosef et al. 1992, Meignen et al. 1998, Rigaud et al. 1999, Wadely 2001, Barton 2000, Pastó et al. 2000).
- Burials are already known from Middle Paleolithic contexts, and their presence has led to debates concerning two issues. The first was a proposal to view all Middle Paleolithic burials as the result of various natural processes and not as intentional mortuary practices (Gargett 1999). This was shown

not to be the case, especially if data from the Upper Paleolithic (including the later phase known as Epi-Paleolithic) is taken into account (Belfer-Cohen & Hovers 1992, Hovers et al. 2000). The second issue, raised by Chase & Dibble (1987), concerns the symbolic behavior one may expect as part of the funerary acts. The evidence for some grave goods incorporated into Middle Paleolithic burials such as Skhul V, where a wild boar jaw was placed under the arm of the dead, hints at numerous details that we still lack. In addition this and other burials in this site and Qafzeh are all related to the archaic modern humans and thus cannot be taken as the rule for all their contemporaries.

- Potential differences in subsistence activities were also taken into account as differentiating the Middle from the Upper Paleolithic (e.g., Marean 1998, Marean & Assefa 1999). As our knowledge concerning the exploitation of plants is poor, most of the discussions center on the issue of hunting versus scavenging. Briefly, the current evidence clearly demonstrates that both Middle Paleolithic and Upper Paleolithic humans were hunters. There are regional differences between South Africa, the Levant, and Western Europe in the selection of game animals, as well as the techniques employed to hunt, transport whole or partial carcasses, and the like (Klein 1998). In addition, alterations to diet breadth does not necessarily require a change in hunting techniques, as shown by the analysis of late Mousterian contexts in Italy and Israel (Speth in Bar-Yosef et al. 1992, Meignen et al. 1998, Stiner et al. 1999) or in Early Upper Paleolithic contexts in southwest France (Grayson & Delpech 1998). In certain cases it reflects population increases, and in others a change in the environmental conditions that favored one species over another.

In sum, most of the components discussed above are seen as evidence for rapid technological changes, emergence of self-awareness and group identity, increased social diversification, formation of long-distance alliances, the ability to symbolically record information and that these are being the most typical expressions for the capacity of Upper Paleolithic humans for modern culture. The latter term means that the creators and bearers of these cultural traits were most probably the forerunners of historically recorded societies of hunter-gatherers. This also implies that they had modern cognitive capacities, although scholars who study cognitive evolution warn against such a simple conclusion.

THE TERMINOLOGICAL AMBIGUITIES

The history of research provides insight into the current terminological ambiguities. In 1913 Breuil formulated the first synthesis of the Western European Upper Paleolithic. Breuil's scheme, which left an indelible terminological impact, was based on the differences in tool types among stratified assemblages of the rockshelters of southwest France (Breuil 1912, Bricker 1976, Harrold 1991). The earliest entity, overlying the Mousterian, was named the Lower Aurignacian and contained the Chatelperronian-backed curved knives or points. Next was the Middle Aurignacian with carinated and nosed scrapers and rich bone and antler industries, as well as beads and pendants. The last in this sequence was labeled the Upper Aurignacian and contained Gravette points, straight-backed elements made on blades. Younger entities were the Solutrean and the Magdalenian.

In the 1930s Peyrony suggested renaming the Lower Aurignacian through the Upper Aurignacian as Perigordian I–V, because they were all blade-dominated assemblages with backed points. In Peyrony's view one could demonstrate regional continuity. The English literature reserved the term Chatelperronian for the Lower Aurignacian, known today also as Castelperronian (Bordes 1968, Mellars 1989, Djindjian et al. 1999, Gamble 1999). The Middle Aurignacian retained the appellation of Aurignacian culture, and the Late Aurignacian (called Perigordian IV by Peyrony) is better known today as the Gravettian, with its extension into Eastern Europe (e.g., Gamble 1986, Collins 1986, Djindjian et al. 1999).

The focus here is that the Chatelperronian—within which blade production is a distinct phenomenon—was viewed as marking the onset of the Upper Paleolithic. Recognizing the evolutionary meaning of this designation came later. First, the detailed lithic analysis demonstrated its origin in the Late Mousterian of the Acheulian Tradition industry. Second, the discovery of Neanderthal remains in a Chatelperronian layer at St. Cesaire provided the hard evidence for biological continuity concurrent with cultural change within a single population (Lévêque & Vandermeersch 1981). Indeed, the Upper Paleolithic traits of the Chatelperronian, such as the production of curved-backed blades documented in the study of the operational sequence (Pelegrin 1990a,b; Lévêque et al. 1993), the presence of body decorations, and a bone tool assemblage in Arcy sur Cure, are instructive (Farizy 1994). This raises two important issues. First, that the term "transitional industry" can have both biological and cultural implications. Second, when other entities in Europe and Africa are taken into account, Upper Paleolithic industries, identified on the basis of cultural attributes, could have been produced by different populations. Therefore, identifying biologically the people who manufactured the lithic assemblages that form the basis for the cultural definition depends on the discovery of human relics. Without human fossils the correlation between the industries and a particular biological population is tenuous. The case of the Chatelperronian indicates a potential archaeological resolution for other European entities. Owing to the biological and cultural continuity represented by the Chatelperronian, one may suggest that a similar techno-typological continuity between a given Mousterian industry—which on that continent was produced everywhere by Neanderthals—and an industry contemporary with other Upper Paleolithic entities, may be viewed as indicating biological continuity.

This proposal is exemplified by the case of central Europe, where the Szeletian emerges from the Mousterian industries with foliates, while the Bohunician lacks a relationship with all earlier Mousterian industries in the region (e.g., Svoboda & Skrdla 1995, Tostevin 2000). The origins of the Szeletian are not agreed upon by all (Kozlowski 2000), but the possibility that it represents a later adaptation

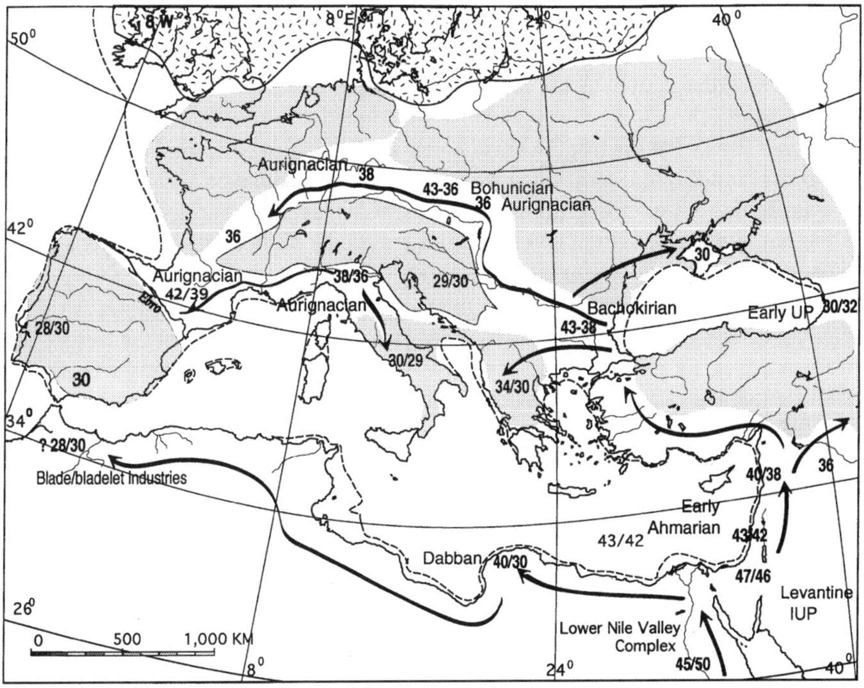

Figure 1 Suggested diffusion/migration of modern humans into Europe and North Africa. The dates (uncalibrated) indicate the early manifestations of Upper Paleolithic industries.

of the Mousterian—at the time when Cro-Magnons were present at the gates of Europe—is probable (Figure 1). The documented penetration of the Szeletian into the extreme north of Europe (Pavlov et al. 2001) may support this view by suggesting that certain innovations, such as improved clothing and means of communication that allowed this incursion into a new environment, were adopted owing to cultural contacts. Similar interpretations may apply to the entities of Jermanowician, Bryndzenian, and Streletskian, all of which are dated to after the first colonization by Initial Upper Paleolithic entities from the east such as the Bachokirian (Kozlowski 2000, Allsworth-Jones 2000). It is therefore best to abandon the term transitional industry, which was extensively employed over the past five decades, and refer to the Early or Initial Upper Paleolithic (Marks 1990) dated entities by local names.

A major ambiguity results from the mixture of lithic assemblage–based definitions and chronological determination with what was probably a new social structure or a new social landscape as represented by certain Upper Paleolithic entities (Gamble 1999). As is shown below, the Upper Paleolithic revolution is a process that most likely began in a core area and expanded by demic-diffusion, migration over long distances, and the transmission of technologies. Hence, in certain regions the Initial Upper Paleolithic assemblages were earlier than in others, and how the people or the technology spread across Africa and Eurasia (except for southeast Asia), is debatable. As mentioned above, gradualists view regional continuities and environmental adaptations as the forces behind the changes, and others employ the molecular, nuclear genetic evidence as well as the currently available radiometric chronology to suggest that migration, contact, and acculturation determined the course of history around 45,000–30,000 years ago (e.g., Cavalli-Sforza et al. 1993, Hublin 2000).

The use and the definition of the term Aurignacian (Kozlowski & Otte 2000, Otte & Kozlowski 2001) is ambiguous. Here again, the impact of the history of the prehistoric research plays a major role. Western European scholars generally agree that the Aurignacian was the first culture of the Cro-Magnons (Gambier 1989, Churchill & Smith 2000). Although the interpretations of the radiometric dates vary (Zilhao & D'Errico 1999), a date of 38 or 36 Ka for the earliest Aurignacian in temperate Europe would mean that the first cultural manifestation of local *H. sapiens sapiens* was a few thousand years later than the onset of the Upper Paleolithic in the Levant (Figure 1). By 36 Ka the Levant had already witnessed the shift from the Emiran (transitional industry) to the Early Ahmarian (Bar-Yosef 2000). This means the Upper Paleolithic began earlier in the eastern Mediterranean and later in Western Europe. A somewhat similar time and geographic trajectory can be drawn eastward across the region of central Asia beyond the Caspian Sea and into northern Asia. If the dates of Kara Bom, a site in the Altai mountains, are accepted at face value, although there are unresolved issues concerning the effects of site-formation processes in this locale, then the shift to Upper Paleolithic was faster in this part of Asia than in Europe (Derevianko 1998, Derevianko et al. 2000, Vasil'ev 1993). In conclusion, the notion that the Aurignacian was the first culture of the Cro-Magnons is therefore false.

The second ambiguity concerning the term Aurignacian relates to the naming of assemblages as Aurignacian on the basis of an insufficient number of attributes. As the definition of this entity was based on a particular suite of stone tools in France, it is expected that not all types will be available wherever the bearers of this industry went. The question is, what are the minimal number of types required to label an assemblage as Aurignacian? The current literature does not provide a detailed definition. The use of one morpho-type, such as the carinated, narrow cores from which bladelets were removed (also known as *rabot* in the French Aurignacian), hardly justifies calling assemblages Aurignacian. This kind of core reduction strategy is known from various geographically and temporally isolated sites such as the 20 Ka Upper Paleolithic layers in the Caucasus and 17–15 Ka Kebaran assemblages in the Levant. However, the presence of the Levantine Aurignacian along the eastern Mediterranean coastal ranges is based on the assemblages that contain carinated nosed scrapers, Dufour bladelets, bone and antler objects (with split based points), and deer-teeth pendants.

In conclusion, whereas the use of traditional classification systems, together with attribute analysis and in particular the study of *chaînes opératoires*, are essential for documenting and reporting the results of excavations and surveys, the naming of the industries should be done carefully. We must avoid hasty, unfounded long-distance correlations that without justification suggest expansions of prehistoric cultures or migrations. Even the alternative view, which advocates that the assemblages are solely expressions of adaptive strategies within a given environment, does not forego the naming of the industries. Once named, we tend to combine those industries that bear the same label in order to create a more complete regional picture of prehistoric lifeways.

A BRIEF SURVEY OF THE GEOGRAPHY OF UPPER PALEOLITHIC ENTITIES

Even a cursory survey of Upper Paleolithic entities in the Old World would reveal their particular characteristics. I do not reiterate the list of early Upper Paleolithic European cultures, which are well described in a rich body of literature (see Gamble 1999 and references therein for an updated survey in English; Djinjian et al. 1999, Straus 1996). Only a few points should be made.

In the interval of 40,000–30,000 radiocarbon years Europe underwent numerous changes. It is still possible that the earliest Aurignacian can be dated to ~42–39 Ka in the sites of El Castillo and Abrerda in northern Spain (Cabrera et al. 1997, Carbonell et al. 2000) and perhaps even in northern Italy (Kuhn & Bietti 2000). Whether or not the earliest dates of the Western European Aurignacian are ~40 Ka or only 38–36 Ka, it seems that this culture was created locally by the Cro-Magnons and later expanded into neighboring regions including the northeast corner of the Mediterranean coastal ranges.

Evidence of the Uluzzian, a derivative of the local Mousterian in southern Italy, and thus a phenomenon similar to the Chatelperronian, was recently found in southern Greece. The latest dates for this entity are around 30 Ka (Kuhn & Bietti 2000, Koumouzelis et al. 2001), indicating contemporaneity with the Aurignacian. However, the Mediterranean Levant (Goring-Morris & Belfer-Cohen 2002) presents an older, complex Upper Paleolithic sequence, which may bear upon the question of where the Upper Paleolithic revolution began. The earliest entity, often referred to as a transitional industry is known from two sites—Ksar 'Akil (Lebanon) and Boker Tachtit (Israel)—and its brief description follows.

The lower levels at Ksar 'Akil (XXIV through XXI/XX) contained a variety of flakes and blades, including a number of elongated Levallois points, obtained by knapping from convergent unidirectional cores. From the early to later levels these gradually shift to a design with parallel edges. Most of the products were obtained by soft rather than by hard hammer (Ohnuma 1988). The typical tool forms were scrapers, chamfered pieces, and burins. The upper levels (XX/XIX through XVI) were characterized by the appearance of blades and bladelets that had been removed from crested bipolar cores with linear and punctiform striking platforms. The tool categories show high frequencies of end scrapers followed by backed pieces. Although not dated directly, by comparing the assemblages with those dated in Kebara (Bar-Yosef et al. 1996), the early phase at Ksar 'Akil is probably around 45–43 Ka.

In the second site, Boker Tachtit (Marks 1993), the refitted nodules uncovered in the lower layers (dated to 47–46 Ka) demonstrate how Levallois points were obtained from bidirectional blade cores. Among the tools, Emireh points (with the bifacial trimming of the butt) suggest that earlier observations by Garrod and Neuville (Garrod & Bate 1937, Neuville 1951) concerning the chrono-stratigraphic position of this point as demarcating the Initial Upper Paleolithic, was correct. In the uppermost layer at Boker Tachtit the core reduction strategy produced regular blades.

The next phase in the Levant, sometimes called Early Ahmarian, dates to ~43–38 Ka (Henry 1995, Bar-Yosef 2000, Bar-Yosef et al. 1996, Goring-Morris & Belfer-Cohen 2002 and references therein). Blank reduction was performed by manipulating cores with one or two platforms, and the major tool groups consist of retouched and backed blades and bladelets that include the El-Wad points. End scrapers are quite common, but burins are rare. Body decorations from that time were discovered in both Ksar 'Akil and Üçagizli (Kuhn et al. 2000).

The early radiometric dates in the Levant and the possible autochtonic shift in the core reduction strategies from the latest Mousterian (such as in Ksar 'Akil) to the Emiran (or the transitional industry) shows that this may have been the first phase of the Upper Paleolithic revolution (Copeland 1975). Although the genetic evidence indicates that the origin of modern humans was in sub-Saharan Africa, it does not tell us where the techno-cultural revolution took place. It could have been in South Africa, East Africa (Ambrose 1998a,b), the Nile Valley (van Peer 1998), or the Levant.

In South Africa, according to current chronologies, the capacity for modern culture appears and disappears in the Howiesons Poort (Deacon & Deacon 1999). Rarely do archaeologists consider population extinctions, but they may have occurred. The next phase, when the combination of traits among the stone tools and the site spatial arrangement indicate modernization is in the late Middle Stone Age ~30 Ka (Wadley 2001). In addition, the shift to the Late Stone Age occurred only around 20 Ka.

In the case of the Kenyan site (Ambrose 1998a,b), whereas the evidence may show early manifestations of body decorations around 40 Ka, the available data do not indicate a primacy over the earlier sites in Eurasia. This could have been the result of ambiguities in dating and the calibration of the dates earlier than 30 Ka (Klein 2001a,b).

In the Levant human fossils from this period are lacking, but it is assumed that the two early entities were the creation of modern humans, as their contexts contain decorative elements crafted from sea shells (Kuhn et al. 2001). The near-modern human skeleton was discovered in Egypt. The quarry site of Taramsa 1, in the mid–Nile Valley, produced a skeleton buried in a sandy deposit, and Middle Paleolithic industry dated it to ~80–50 Ka (Vermeersch et al. 1998). However, the lithics of a later exploitation of the site, dated to 38–37 Ka, demonstrated transitional characteristics similar to the Levantine Initial Upper Paleolithic. These finds may indicate that the shift from the Middle to the Upper Paleolithic in this region—as expected from the genetic evidence and the entire suite of African fossils (Deacon & Deacon 1999; McBrearty & Brooks 2000; Stringer 1998, 2001; Howell 1998)—was produced by modern humans, who originally emerged some 300–100,000 years ago (Harpending et al. 1998).

In most of central and northern Asia, from the Ural Mountains to Mongolia, Upper Paleolithic sites occur (Vasil'ev 1993, Derev'anko 1998). Analysis of the available radiocarbon dates (Kuzmin & Orlova 1998) indicates that the same time trajectory of the expansion of the Upper Paleolithic is recognizable. It first appeared in the western part (Altai mountains) and later in the eastern sector. The typical blade industry had seen a shift toward the production of bladelets from microblade cores around 20–18 Ka. The bearers of this type of industry also exploited the environments of Mongolia and northern China and moved across Beringia to colonize North America (West 1996 and references therein; Goebel et al. 2000).

Information on Upper Paleolithic contexts in southern Asia is relatively flimsy. There are blade-dominated Upper Paleolithic assemblages and they stratigraphically follow the Middle Paleolithic (Murty 1979, Ghosh 1993).

The vast region of Southeast Asia did not witness the shift in knapping techniques. The Hoabinian is generally a flake dominated industry (Allchin 1966; Anderson 1990, 1997). Similar flake industry was uncovered in most sites in southern China that are dated to the time of the Upper Paleolithic. With current knowledge, one can separate the Middle from the Upper Paleolithic only when bone tools are present. The production of blades, and later of microliths, characterizes the very late Pleistocene prior to the emergence of agriculture.

WHAT CONSTITUTES MODERN BEHAVIOR?

The debate concerning the nature of the Upper Paleolithic revolution, which changed the evolutionary course of prehistoric foragers forever, centers on the issue of modern behavior. This is a fuzzy definition, and almost every researcher who has written about the subject arrives at a slightly different list or combination of behavioral attributes. The question is also phrased as, can we see Upper Paleolithic hunting and gathering societies as the ancestors of those known to us from ethno-history?

The list of cultural attributes, features in sites, and intersite relations either as part of one social system or as part of an interaction sphere are all taken into account. However, if one introduces the genetic evidence as Renfrew (1996) did, then from at least 60,000 to 30,000 B.P. our species expanded across the entire Old World and was on its way to the Americas. There are no other subspecies involved, and even if the issue of hybridization with the Neanderthals or any other unnamed groups is not fully resolved, the conclusion is that the Upper Paleolithic revolution reduced the number of human species to one. By comparison to 2.5 million years of evolution, the changes during the Upper Paleolithic had ensuing dramatic effects on world prehistory. All scholars agree that language plays a major role and that it probably evolved in time (Wynn 1991, Trask et al. 1998). Communication facilitated everything from transfer of technologies to long-distance exchange. This in turn had effects on subsistence economy and therefore led to population growth.

Indeed, most researchers agree that the larger the number of archaeological attributes that can be assembled to designate an Upper Paleolithic context, the clearer will be the markers of this human revolution. If we reexamine the list above, we may end up with only a few traits such as distinct intrasite spatial organization, the presence of beads and pendants, and the production of bone and antler tools and objects. Others would only reflect regional variability, important by itself, such as grinding stones and mobile and rock art, but can hardly be employed on a global scale. We should also be ready to accept that the capacity for the modern culture of *H. sapiens sapiens* could have been adopted, even if not for long, by others such as certain groups of Neanderthals in Arcy sur Cure. In the same flexible interpretation of cultural evolution and population demise, we may view the case of the Howeisons Poort as a historically accidental appearance of a somewhat similar combination of material elements to those of the Upper Paleolithic, but it ultimately had no impact on the general trend of human evolution. Only around 50,000–45,000 years ago did the Upper Paleolithic revolution begin. The cause remains a highly debatable subject.

CAUSES OF THE UPPER PALEOLITHIC REVOLUTION

There are primarily three approaches to the study of the causes and the early course of the transition from the Middle to the Upper Paleolithic. There is a wide range of variability among researchers, and this summary is rather schematic.

The first approach suggests that there were gradual cultural changes from the late Middle and the Upper Pleistocene—an accumulation of material and behavioral traits finally leading to the formation of Upper Paleolithic social and cultural constructs. In short, these scholars see no revolution in either Eurasia or in Africa (e.g., Lindly & Clark 1990; Clark 1997a,b; McBrearty & Brooks 2000).

The second approach considers the shift from the Middle to the Upper Paleolithic as taking place more or less contemporaneously in most of the regions of North Asia, the Near East, and Europe. Supporters of this approach are split between those who see the change as accomplished by local populations (i.e., in Europe by the Neanderthals) (Straus 1996, Derev'anko 1998, Otte & Kozlowski 2001) and others who view the final establishment of the Upper Paleolithic as solely an *H. sapiens sapiens* achievement.

The third view stresses the origin of this revolution in a core area and its dispersal by human groups who share the same social system and means of communication and who carry the essential components of the new technology into new territories. Proponents of this model view the cultural revolution as triggered either by a biological change or by techno-typological and socio-economic circumstances. As this approach is currently at the center of heated debates, I begin with the review of the biological aspects.

The main proponent of the need for an additional mutation, a neurological change in the human brain to explain the capacity for modern behavior, is Klein (1995, 1999, 2001a,b). In his view only this change brought about the socio-economic restructuring that is documented in the archaeological records across the continents. His explanation takes into account what was earlier called "Out of Africa 2" (Stringer & Gamble 1993), which posits that modern humans dispersed from Africa some 60,000–50,000 years ago. Hence, according to Klein it was only after 50,000 years ago that humans possessed and expressed the markers of modern behavior.

While colonizing Eurasia and Australia, modern humans most likely gradually replaced the local nonmodern populations such as the Neanderthals. The latter, based on only three ancient DNA samples (Feldhofer cave in Germany, Vindja in Croatia, and Mezmaskaya in the Caucasus, Russia), are known to differ from modern humans (Krings et al. 1997, 2000; Ovchininkov et al. 2000). In addition, current genetic evidence for the modern-day European population indicates that there may not have been mixing between the entering Cro-Magnons and the local population (Semino at al. 2000).

Therefore, although brain volume of 1200–1700 cc was measured among Neanderthal skulls, which is within the range of *H. sapiens sapiens*, it seems that neither the volume nor the calculation of the neocortical ratio (Aiello & Dunbar 1993, Dunbar 1993) disclose the nature of the differences between both human morpho-types. Nor could the limited evolution of the frontal lobe or the role of the location of the sphenoid (D.E. Lieberman 1998). In addition, the definition of Neanderthal fossils outside the classical region of western Europe, such as the Levant, is open to disagreement (Arensburg & Belfer-Cohen 1998, Trinkaus et al. 1998, Rak 1998, Stefan & Trinkaus 1998, Akazawa et al. 1999).

Earlier views on the importance of the position of the larynx in relation to the base of the skull were modified following the realization that archaic modern humans such as those found in the Qafzeh and Skhul caves in Israel could have had the ability to speak like moderns (P. Lieberman 1998).

By reference to contemporary studies of general trends in human brain evolution it was proposed that a complex internal circuitry evolved between the separate sections of the brain, mainly in order to increase efficiency in the social information processing that was essential for survival in variable environments under fluctuating climatic conditions. Among the most effective means would be language, and not surprisingly the emergence of language is seen as a determinant factor. Whether following Chomsky or Pinker in their views of genetically programmed "universal grammar" or "language instinct," the question that remains open is whether it was a one-time biological change or a long building process (Pinker 2000).

This brings us to the issue of the creation of the storage of symbols as suggested by Donald (1991) that leads to the emergence of modernity. In this proposal, as in others, the imagery from the west European Upper Paleolithic arena and the body decorations play a major role. However, as mentioned above, this region differs considerably in its artistic expressions from most other provinces of the Upper Paleolithic world. A similar view is held by Deacon (1997), who sees the appearance of such symbols as occurring within a social system, but not necessarily as the crucial evidence for claiming its correlations with the sudden emergence of language. Along a somewhat similar line of thought, Gibson (1996) suggested that the Upper Paleolithic was a cultural revolution triggered by technological changes among people who long possessed modern neurological and cognitive capacities. However, for Mellars (1989, 1996b), judging from the shift in material components as described above and the appearance of imagery as well as beads and pendants, fully modern language and symbolic expressions emerged at or slightly prior to the Upper Paleolithic.

The efforts to explain the differences between the Middle and Upper Paleolithic manifestations as biologically determined continue with proposals concerning the brain's modularity structure. Mithen (1994, 1996) suggested that Neanderthals had domain-specific intelligence. According to this model, the Neanderthals' domains of intelligence—in which information concerning nature, social interaction, and technology were processed—shared little between them, as opposed to modern human brains, in which all fields of information are coordinated. This modern domain-sharing intelligence could have happened only if the additional neurological change in the brain took place as suggested by Klein (1995, 2001a,b).

Both the second and third approaches above address issues of behavior. Most scholars agree that the material elements (stone, bone, antler technology, exchange, site structure, etc.) and symbolic components (red ochre, mobile imagery, burials) reflect a change in behavior. Some of these tools, techniques, and inferred behaviors, which characterize *H. sapiens sapiens*, are also known from various sites of Middle Paleolithic age, as mentioned above. For example, bone tools are known from the Middle Stone Age Bloombos cave in South Africa and the Chatelperronian contexts of Arcy sur Cure, and intentional burials were practiced both in Europe and the Levant in Mousterian contexts. However, the point to be stressed is that these and other traits such as blade production and the collection of marine shells appear as sporadic phenomena during the late Lower and Middle Paleolithic but become regular cultural components after the Initial Upper Paleolithic from about 45 Ka and during the course of the ensuing millennia.

Using a Marxist approach, Gilman (1984), following a summary of the available evidence at the time of writing, proposed this view: Starting with the stylistic manifestations in the Upper Paleolithic contexts, he stressed that such innovations could only reflect social changes. Gilman accepted the earlier suggestions by Wobst (1976), Conkey (1978), and White (1982) that changes increased corporate solidarity, the development of closed mating systems, and the overall appearance of prehistoric ethnicity (i.e., cultures in the traditional sense). Incorporating these aspects within alliance theory, he proposed that the changes resulted from the developing forces of production. The environmental conditions and cultural processes during the Upper Pleistocene led to a population increase and, hence, further competition between social groups. Restricting the scope of the alliances and increasing group cohesion through ceremonies resulted in more sharing, storage, and technological innovations, and therefore a decrease in subsistence failures. This process would result in further population increase. The pace of the change would be slow, and therefore the Upper Paleolithic revolution occurred over a relatively long period but ended with "significantly qualitative changes" (Gilman 1984, p. 235). Egalitarian foragers, in the course of the changes in the social forces of production, in this model, develop complex social systems. The merit of Gilman's approach is the importance he places on social organization as a demographic pressure that leads to revolution.

The demographic aspects are currently favored by numerous researchers who see a population increase during the late Mousterian. For example, in Europe the impact of the harsh glacial conditions of Oxygen Isotope Stage 4 (OIS 4) on confined territories was probably the cause for a population bottle neck (Richter 2000, Shennan 2001). The ameliorated environmental conditions during OIS 3 (~65–24 Ka) indicate an alternation of warmer and colder periods (van Andel & Tzedakis 1996). This climatic scenario may explain the population growth among Eurasian Mousterian groups as evidence for greater techno-typological variability among the lithic industries as expressing the increase of social intensification (Shennan 2001) as well as the need for widening the diet breadth (e.g., Stiner & Kuhn 1992, Stiner et al. 1999); hence, the authors emphasize the role of climatic fluctuations in what has generally tended to be a socioeconomic model. However, whether the environmental changes in Eurasia caused the onset of the Upper Paleolithic revolution depends on what each investigator views as the course of the social and cultural changes.

In partial accordance with the approach that mixes climatic conditions and the history of social structures, I have suggested elsewhere (Bar-Yosef 1992, 1998) that the models available for explaining the Neolithic revolution could be used in constructing hypotheses for the Upper Paleolithic revolution. One of the main advantages in employing the agricultural revolution is the direct relationship between the Near East and Europe, resembling the geographic spread of the Upper Paleolithic across Europe (Figure 1). In addition, the improved data sets for the transition to the Neolithic, collected from a well-defined region, demonstrate temporal and spatial trajectories. The main points to be learned from the Neolithic revolution are the following:

1. The Neolithic revolution was set in motion by *H. sapiens sapiens*, a single human species, and does not coincide with any biological change. The major shifts in technology—tools (forms and function), tilling the land, food

preparation techniques, domestication of goat, sheep, cattle and pig—that led to major changes in diet as well as living conditions resulted in impacts on human body size, health, and the ability to digest dairy products (Cohen 1989, Durham 1991).

2. Prior to the Neolithic revolution a major increase in population after the Last Glacial Maximum was recorded from numerous regions, as well as shifts in settlement patterns including the emergence of sedentism [~14,500 cal. B.P., a cyclical phenomenon known from earlier Upper Paleolithic sites (Bar-Yosef 2001)]. It seems that the climatic crisis of the Younger Dryas (12,900–11,600 cal. B.P.) affected basic subsistence strategies of the sedentary Natufian population in the Levant (Belfer-Cohen & Bar-Yosef 2000).
3. Alternative food acquisition strategies, such as increased mobility, forced a change in social structure among the Late Natufian people. For example, in the marginal semiarid Sinai Late Natufian groups improved their hunting techniques through the invention of the Harif point, a more efficient arrowhead (Goring-Morris 1991). Hunting, as well as gathering plant food, is reflected in the animal bone assemblages, grinding stones, mortars, and cup-holes. Large collections of marine shells testify to long-range exchanges with both the Red Sea and Mediterranean shores (Bar-Yosef 1991), probably in order to support group alliances.

   The main onset of agricultural activities occurred in the northern Levant. There, people started to cultivate the wild cereals and legumes (Hillman 2000), which were already their basic staple food, along with other seeds, fruits, roots, and game animals in the region since at least 21 Ka cal. B.P. (Kislev et al. 1992). Hence, early farming communities, labeled as Pre-Pottery Neolithic A (PPNA) (~11,600–10,500 cal. B.P.) were established within the Levantine Corridor (Bar-Yosef & Meadow 1995; Cauvin 2000).
4. Population growth is documented in the size of the early (PPNA) villages. It was the consequence of enhanced sedentism, predictable supplies of weaning foodstuffs from cereals, and reliable food resources ensured by storage. Therefore, a longer period of fertility for the better-fed women is expected (e.g., Bentley 1996). Large villages became viable biological units and reduced the need to travel substantial distances to find a mate. The sense of territoriality and ownership grew, sustaining the more complex social alliances and leading to redesigned cosmologies as described by Cauvin (2000).
5. The ongoing process of change once intentional cultivation began continued with the domestication of goat, sheep, cattle, and pig that took place during the Pre-Pottery Neolithic B period (PPNB) in the context of sedentary and semisedentary farmer-hunter villages. Corralling and tending wild animals was initiated in the hilly flanks of the Taurus/Zagros (e.g., Legge 1996, Martin 1999, Hole 1996, Zeder & Hesse 2000), where these animals had been hunted for many millennia by local foragers. It was before the completion of the biological changes, expressed in morphological traits, that goats, cattle, and

other animals were transported by seacrafts to islands such as Cyprus (Vigne et al. 1999).

6. Population increase resulted in active emigration into central Anatolia (9000–8000 cal. B.P.), Thessaly, and the islands of Cyprus (8,600 cal. B.P.), Crete, and others (Ammerman & Cavalli-Sforza 1984, Cavalli-Sforza et al. 1993, van Andel & Runnels 1995, Peltenberg et al. 2001). It is also conceivable that the Nile Delta was colonized by sea at a later date (~8000 cal. B.P.).
7. The dispersal of the new economy, either as a partial or complete "agricultural package," occurred in a few ways. The eastward transmission to the Zagros foothills, from Kurdistan in the north to Khuzistan in the south, probably occurred without major displacements of human communities, but rather by adoption. Evidently, in this area the same microlithic Late Paleolithic tradition lasted into Neolithic times, indicating that the flint knappers were not replaced (Hole 1989, Kozlowski 1999).
8. The spread of the Neolithic economy westward took two paths: one through the Balkans and the Danube river valley and the other through coastal navigation and colonization. It was a long and complicated process, and there are various opinions concerning who were the Near Eastern farmers and where local Mesolithic foragers adopted agriculture through acculturation and imitation (Cherry 1990, Ammerman & Cavalli-Sforza 1984, Renfrew 1987, Zvelebil & Lillie 2000). The eastward expansion of the agricultural package reached the Indus Valley within 2000–1500 years.

In conclusion, the current archaeological, archaeobotanical, and plant genetic evidence confirms that the core area of the Neolithic Revolution lay in the Levantine Corridor—the western wing of the Fertile Crescent. The advantage of this model of the Upper Paleolithic revolution is that it removes the biological factor from the debate and centers instead on a population in an unknown core area that for local reasons (either climatic, social, economic, or all together) generated the initial step in the techno-typological and social revolution. Probably, in contrast to cases such as the Howeisons Poort, this social entity was large, viable, and successful and started spreading relatively fast as colonizers and distributors of new techniques.

CONCLUSION

To avoid misunderstanding I begin with the terminology. Upper Paleolithic, like Neolithic, is a term that designates a time period and not an economy or social structure. These terms were coined before radiometric chronology was available. The Chatelperronian is Upper Paleolithic in age, but it did not result, as we might expect from a so-called transitional culture, in turning into a new socio-economic structure. The origins of the Aurignacian are not rooted in the Chatelperronian but in a different entity that inhabited a region outside western Europe. If we want to retain the term Upper Paleolithic as synonym for the new regime, we should reserve it solely for contexts in which the archaeological sequence demonstrates the transition from the Mousterian or Middle Stone Age to the new entities—those that later evolved into the more recent cultural manifestations of the Upper Paleolithic period, including mobile and rock art, body decorations, and later the microlithic industries. The acceptance of such an approach would sideline discussions about whether Neanderthals had the capacity for modern behavior. Even if they had, most or all of them did not survive beyond 30–29 Ka. The same would be true for North Africa. The Aterian, although produced by some form of modern humans, did not survive, and there is no evidence for a transitional phase in this region. The bearers of the blade-dominated and microlithic industries in this region could have been the descendents of the local Aterian population, but given the genetic evidence, they more likely originated from the same sub-Saharan parent population of all *H. sapiens sapiens* (Wengler 1997).

Figure 1 shows a selection of radiometric dates that indicate an east-west "wave of advance" of the Upper Paleolithic revolution, a term borrowed from Neolithic studies (Ammerman & Cavali-Sforza 1984). As mentioned above, with the progress in field research in central and northern Asia one may expect a similar trajectory. The same accounts for improved dating. Once certain ambiguities concerning the calibration of the dates in the range of 40,000–30,000 years ago are satisfactorily resolved, better maps can be drawn.

Most scholars accept that modern humans came out of Africa. Ideas diverge about the meaning of this movement or movements. Evidently, Australia was colonized some 60,000 years ago, prior to the onset of the Upper Paleolithic revolution. There could be a variety of explanations for the early dispersals. One could suggest an expansion of modern humans from southern Asia into Australia, who were innovative—being on their way to a continent that was still separated from southeast Asia by a 100-km waterway. Hence, the idea that water crafts were constructed, either boats or some sort of raft, has been proposed (Davidson & Noble 1992). Another possible explanation is that modern humans who were already present in the Levant during the Last Interglacial made their way into Asia, and like their contemporaries in Africa and eastern Asia, initiated technological and social changes that enabled them to get to Australia. The lack of evidence from the vast portion of southern Asia hampers better resolutions to this issue.

As mentioned above, there are two views about what modern humans carried with them as they left the African continent. According to those who believe the Upper Paleolithic revolution took place in Africa, modern humans were already equipped with the essential techno-cultural elements that characterize the Upper Paleolithic. These investigators believe the exit was earlier and the increasing population in Eurasia was caused by the incoming moderns from Africa. Each of these hypotheses, whether implicit or explicit, points to a core area in Africa as the source and the cause of the change.

Demographic factors are accepted as the trigger for the change by scholars who interpret the evidence on the basis of regional sequences. According to this view, the

Late Middle Paleolithic incubated the upcoming changes. In Europe the increasing variability of the lithic industries immediately following the harsh conditions of OIS 4 (~75–65 Ka) considerably reduced the habitable areas, decreasing the size of the population and therefore triggering the need for social intensification (Richter 2000). Indeed, during OIS 3 (or the pleniglacial) Neanderthal populations grew. This process is represented by the increasing techno-typological variability among late Mousterian industries and expresses territorial competition that caused the need for change. The new socio-economic structure was achieved by the Upper Paleolithic revolution. This model is similar in its basic ingredients to the Neolithic model presented above. As much as the Neolithic model is not fully adopted by all researchers, neither is the proposal that the population increase in Europe was an independent factor. One thorny issue is why, with competing Neanderthal societies, is there no evidence for the use of some sort of body decoration for self-awareness and group identity?

Ecology plays a minor role in most of the debates. The realization that Neanderthals survived in Europe under various climatic fluctuations in both the temperate and the Mediterranean belts limits the discussion to particular regions, availability of food resources, hunting techniques, etc. In addition, numerous animal bone analyses indicate that the bearers of the Mousterian industries were reasonably successful hunters. The difference could have been between intercept hunting, which required getting close to the target, and the use of spear throwers or bows. It appears that time allocation among Upper Paleolithic hunters was either short by comparison to the Mousterian foragers or that the returns were higher owing to better communication and information storage, as well as improved hunting gear.

The issue of the capacity for modern behavior or modern culture, and the evolution of cognition, will continue to play a major role in the debates on the nature of the Upper Paleolithic revolution and the ensuing cultural changes. From a list of independent attributes it seems that researchers will be willing to settle for particular combinations. Among these the aspects of communication, symbolic expressions for information storage, self awareness and group identity, new hunting tools, and a clearer daily and seasonal spatial organization of activities that reflects an accepted social organization would be the prime components or antecedents to ethno-historically known foraging societies. These were the elementary achievements of the Upper Paleolithic revolution gleaned through the archaeological perspective.

The *Annual Review of Anthropology* is online at http://anthro.annualreviews.org

LITERATURE CITED

Aiello LC, Dunbar RIM. 1993. Neocortex size, group size, and the evolution of language. *Curr. Anthropol.* 34:184–93

Akazawa T, Aoki K, Bar-Yosef O, eds. 1998. *Neandertals and Modern Humans in Western Asia*. New York: Plenum

Akazawa T, Muhesen S, Ishida H, Kondo O, Griggo C. 1999. New discovery of a

Neanderthal child burial from the Dederiyeh Cave in Syria. *Paléorient* 25:129–42

Allchin B. 1966. *The Stone-Tipped Arrow: Late Stone-Age Hunters of the Tropical Old World.* New York: Barnes & Noble. 224 pp.

Allsworth-Jones P. 2000. Dating the transition between Middle and Upper Palaeolithic in Eastern Europe. In *Neanderthals and Modern Humans—Discussing the Transition: Central and Eastern Europe from 50,000-30,000 B.P.*, ed. J Orschiedt, G-C Weniger, pp. 20–29. Mettman, Germany: Neanderthal Mus.

Ambrose SH. 1998a. Chronology of the Later Stone Age and food production in East Africa. *J. Archaeol. Sci.* 25:377–92

Ambrose SH. 1998b. Late Pleistocene human population bottlenecks, volcanic winter, and differentiation of modern humans. *J. Hum. Evol.* 34:623–51

Ammerman AJ, Cavalli-Sforza LL. 1984. *The Neolithic Transition and the Genetics of Populations in Europe.* Princeton, NJ: Princeton Univ. Press. 176 pp.

Anderson DD. 1990. *Lang Rongrien Rockshelter: a Pleistocene-Early Holocene Archaeological Site from Krabi, Southwestern Thailand.* Univ. Mus. Monogr. 71. Philadelphia: Univ. Mus.

Anderson DD. 1997. Cave archaeology in southeast Asia. *Geoarchaeol.: Int. J.* 12:607–38

Arensburg B, Belfer-Cohen A. 1998. Sapiens and Neandertals: rethinking the Levantine Middle Paleolithic hominids. See Akazawa et al. 1998, pp. 311–22

Bahn PG. 1997. *Journey through the Ice Age.* London: Weidenfeld & Nicholson. 240 pp.

Bar-Yosef DE. 1991. Changes in the selection of marine shells from the Natufian to the Neolithic. See Bar-Yosef & Valla 1991, pp. 629–36

Bar-Yosef O. 1992. The role of Western Asia in modern human origins. *Philos. Trans. R. Soc. London Ser. B* 337:193–200

Bar-Yosef O. 1998. On the nature of transitions: the Middle to Upper Palaeolithic and the Neolithic Revolution. *Cambridge Archaeol. J.* 8:141–63

Bar-Yosef O. 2000. The Middle and Early Upper Paleolithic in Southwest Asia and neighboring regions. See Bar-Yosef & Pilbeam 2000, pp. 107–56

Bar-Yosef O. 2001. From sedentary foragers to village hierarchies: the emergence of social institutions. In *The Origin of Human Social Institutions*, ed. G Runciman, pp. 1–38. Oxford: Oxford Univ. Press

Bar-Yosef O, Arnold M, Belfer-Cohen A, Goldberg P, Housley R, et al. 1996. The dating of the Upper Paleolithic layers in Kebara Cave, Mount Carmel. *J. Archaeol. Sci.* 23:297–306

Bar-Yosef O, Kuhn S. 1999. The big deal about blades: laminar technologies and human evolution. *Am. Anthropol.* 101:1–17

Bar-Yosef O, Meadow RH. 1995. The origins of agriculture in the Near East. In *Last Hunters, First Farmers: New Perspectives on the Prehistoric Transition to Agriculture*, ed. TD Price, AB Gebauer, pp. 39–94. Santa Fe, NM: School Am. Res.

Bar-Yosef O, Pilbeam D, eds . 2000. *The Geography of Neandertals and Modern Humans in Europe and the Greater Mediterranean.* Cambridge, MA: Peabody Mus., Harvard Univ.

Bar-Yosef O, Valla FR, eds. 1991. *The Natufian Culture in the Levant.* Ann Arbor, MI: Int. Monogr. Prehistory

Bar-Yosef O, Vandermeersch B, Arensburg B, Belfer-Cohen A, Goldberg P, et al. 1992. The excavations in Kebara Cave, Mount Carmel. *Curr. Anthropol.* 33:497–550

Barton CM. 1997. Stone tools, style, and social identity: an evolutionary perspective on the archaeological record. In *Rediscovering Darwin: Evolutionary Theory and Archaeological Explanation*, ed. CM Barton, GA Clark, pp. 141–56. Washington, DC: Am. Anthropol. Assoc.

Barton N. 2000. Mousterian hearths and shellfish: late Neanderthal activities on Gibraltar. See Stringer et al. 2000, pp. 211–19

Beck JW, Richards DA, Edwards RL,

Silverman BW, Smart PL, et al. 2001. Extremely large variations of atmospheric C14 concentration during the last glacial period. *Science* 292:2453–58

Belfer-Cohen A, Bar-Yosef O. 2000. Early sedentism in the Near East: a bumpy ride to village life. In *Life in Neolithic Farming Communities: Social Organization, Identity, and Differentiation*, ed. I Kuijt, pp. 19–37. New York: Plenum

Belfer-Cohen A, Hovers E. 1992. In the eye of the beholder: Mousterian and Natufian burials in the Levant. *Curr. Anthropol.* 33:463–71

Bentley GR. 1996. How did prehistoric women bear "Man the Hunter"? Reconstructing fertility from the archaeological record. In *Gender and Archaeology*, ed. RP Wright, pp. 23–51. Philadelphia: Univ. Penn. Press

Binford LR. 1983. *In Pursuit of the Past: Decoding the Archaeological Record.* London: Thames & Hudson

Bisson MS. 2000. Nineteenth century tools for twenty-first century archaeology? Why the Middle Paleolithic Typology of François Bordes must be replaced. *J. Archaeol. Method and Theory* 7:1–48

Bocquet-Appel J-P, Demars PY. 2000. Neanderthal contraction and modern human colonization of Europe. *Antiquity* 74:544–52

Boëda E, Geneste JM, Griggo C, Mercier N, Muhesen S, et al. 1999. A Levallois point embedded in the vertebra of a wild ass (Equus africanus): hafting, projectiles and Mousterian hunting weapons. *Antiquity* 73:394–402

Bordes F. 1961. *Typologie du Paléolithique Ancien et Moyen.* Bordeaux, France: Delmas

Bordes F. 1968. *The Old Stone Age.* New York: McGraw-Hill. 255 pp.

Breuil H. 1912. Les subdivisions de Paléolithique Supérieur et leur signification. *Compte rendu de Congrès international d'anthropologie et archéologie préhistorique, Geneva*, pp. 165–238

Bricker HM. 1976. Upper Palaeolithic archaeology. *Annu. Rev. Anthropol.* 5:133–48

Cabrera Valdés V, Hoyos Gómez M, Bernaldo de Quirós Guidotto F. 1997. The Transition from Middle to Upper Paleolithic in the Cave of El Castillo (Cantabria, Spain). See Clark & Willermet 1997, pp. 177–88

Carbonell E, Vaquero M, eds . 1996. *The Last Neandertals, the First Anatomically Modern Humans.* Tarragona, Spain: Univ. Rovira i Virgili

Carbonell E, Vaquero M, Maroto J, Rando JM, Mallol C. 2000. A geographic perspective on the Middle to Upper Paleolithic transition in the Iberian Peninsula. See Bar-Yosef & Pilbeam 2000, pp. 5–34

Cauvin J. 2000. *The Birth of the Gods and the Origins of Agriculture.* Cambridge: Cambridge Univ. Press. 259 pp.

Cavalli-Sforza LL, Menozzi P, Piazza A. 1993. Demic expansions and human evolution. *Science* 259:639–46

Chase PG, Dibble HL. 1987. Middle Paleolithic symbolism: a review of current evidence and interpretations. *J. Anthropol. Archaeol.* 6:263–96

Cherry JF. 1990. The first colonization of the Mediterranean islands: a review of recent research. *J. Mediterr. Archaeol.* 3:145–221

Churchill SE, Smith FH. 2000. Makers of the Early Aurignacian of Europe. *Yearbk. Phys. Anthropol.* 43:61–115

Clark GA, ed. 1991. *Perspectives on the Past: Theoretical Biases in Mediterranean Hunter-Gatherer Research.* Philadelphia: Univ. Penn. Press

Clark GA. 1997a. Through a glass darkly: conceptual issues in modern human origins research. See Clark & Willermet 1997, pp. 60–76

Clark GA. 1997b. The Middle-Upper Paleolithic transition in Europe: an American perspective. *Nor. Archaeol. Rev.* 30:25–53

Clark GA, Willermet CM, eds . 1997. *Conceptual Issues in Modern Human Origins Research.* New York: Aldine de Gruyter

Close AE. 1989. Identifying style in stone artefacts: a case study from the Nile Valley. In *Alternative Approaches to Lithic Analysis*, ed. DO Henry, GH Odell, pp. 3–26. Washington, DC: Am. Anthropol. Assoc.

Clottes J. 1997. Art of the light and art of the depths. See Conkey et al. 1997, pp. 203–16

Cohen MN. 1989. *Health and the Rise of Civilization*. New Haven, CT: Yale Univ. Press

Collins D. 1986. *Palaeolithic Europe: a Theoretical and Systematic Study*. Devon, UK: Clayhanger. 291 pp.

Conard N. 1990. Laminar lithic assemblages from the last interglacial complex in northwestern Europe. *J. Anthropol. Res.* 46:243–62

Conard NJ, ed. 2001. *Settlement Dynamics of the Middle Paleolithic and Middle Stone Age*, Introductory Volume. Tübingen, Ger.: Kerns. 611 pp.

Conkey MW. 1978. Style and information in cultural evolution: toward a predictive model for the Palaeolithic. In *Social Archaeology: Beyond Subsistence and Dating*, ed. CL Redman, MJ Berman, EV Curtin, WT Langhorne Jr, NM Versaggi, JC Wanser, pp. 61–85. New York: Academic

Conkey M, Hastorf C, ed. 1990. *The Uses of Style in Archaeology*. Cambridge: Cambridge Univ. Press. 124 pp.

Conkey MW, Soffer O, Stratmann D, Jablonski NG, ed. 1997. *Beyond Art: Pleistocene Image and Symbol*. San Francisco: Calif. Acad. Sci.

Copeland L. 1975. The Middle and Upper Palaeolithic of Lebanon and Syria in the light of recent research. In *Problems in Prehistory: North Africa and the Levant*, ed. F Wendorf, AE Marks, pp. 317–50. Dallas: SMU Press

Davidson I. 1997. The power of pictures. See Conkey et al. 1997, pp. 125–59

Davidson I, Noble W. 1992. Why the first colonisation of the Australian region is the earliest evidence of modern human behaviour. *Prespect. Archaeol. Oceania* 27:113–19

de Sonneville-Bordes D, Perrot J. 1953. Essai d'adaptation des méthodes statistiques au Paléolithique supérieur: premiers résultats. *Bull. Societé Prehistorique Fr.* 50:323–33

Deacon HJ. 1992. Southern Africa and modern human origins. *Philos. Trans. R. Soc.* 337: 177–83

Deacon HJ. 1995 Two late Pleistocene-Holocene archaeological depositories from the southern Cape, South Africa. *S. Afr. Archaeol. Bull.* 50:121–31

Deacon HJ, Deacon J. 1999. *Human Beginnings in South Africa: Uncovering the Secrets of the Stone Age*. Cape Town, S. Afr./Walnut Creek, CA: Phillips & Altamira. 214 pp.

Deacon HJ, Wurz S. 1996. Klasies River main site, cave 2: a Howiesons Poort occurrence. In *Aspects of African Archaeology*, ed. G Pwiti, R Soper, pp. 213–18. Harare: Univ. Zimbabwe

Deacon T. 1997. *The Symbolic Species: the Co-Evolution of Language and the Brain*. New York: Norton

Derev'anko AP. 1998. *The Palaeolithic of Siberia: New Discoveries and Interpretations*. Urbana: Univ. Illinois Press

Derevianko AP, Petrin VT, Rybin EP. 2000. The Kara-Bom Site and the characteristics of the Middle-Upper Paleolithic Transition in the Altai. *Archaeol. Ethnol. Anthropol. Eurasia* 2:33–52

Dibble HL. 1995. Middle Paleolithic scraper reduction: background, clarification, and review of the evidence to date. *J. Archaeol. Method Theory* 2:299–368

Djindjian F, Kozlowski JK, Otte M. 1999. *Le Paléolithique Supérieur en Europe*. Paris: Colin. 474 pp.

Donald M. 1991. *Origins of the Modern Mind: Three Stages in the Evolution of Culture and Cognition*. Cambridge, MA: Harvard Univ. Press

Dunbar R. 1993. Coevolution of neocortical size, group size and language in humans. *Behav. Brain Sci.* 16:681–735

Durham WH. 1991. *Coevolution: Genes, Culture, and Human Diversity*. Palo Alto, CA: Stanford Univ. Press

Farizy C. 1990. The Transition from Middle to Upper Palaeolithic at Arcy-sur-Cure (Yonne, France): technological, economic and social aspects. In *The Emergence of Modern Humans*, ed. P Mellars, pp. 303–26. Edinburgh: Edinburgh Univ. Press

Farizy C. 1994. Behavioral and cultural changes at the Middle to Upper Paleolithic transition in western Europe. In *Origins of Anatomically Modern Humans*, ed. MH Nitecki, DV Nitecki, pp. 93–100. New York: Plenum

Féblot-Augustins J. 1993. Mobility strategies in the late Middle Palaeolithic of central Europe and western Europe: elements of stability and variability. *J. Anthropol. Archaeol.* 12:211–65

Gambier D. 1989. Fossil hominids from the early Upper Paleolithic (Aurignacian) of France. See Mellars & Stringer 1989, pp. 194–211

Gamble C. 1986. *The Palaeolithic Settlement of Europe*. Cambridge: Cambridge Univ. Press

Gamble C. 1993. Exchange, foraging and local hominid networks. In *Trade and Exchange in Prehistoric Europe*, ed. C Scarre, F Healy, pp. 35–44. Oxford: Oxbow

Gamble C. 1999. *The Paleolithic Societies of Europe*. Cambridge: Cambridge Univ. Press

Gargett RH. 1999. Middle Palaeolithic burial is not a dead issue: the view from Qafzeh, Saint-Césaire, Kebara, Amud, and Dederiyeh. *J. Hum. Evol.* 37:27–90

Garrod DAE, Bate DM. 1937. *The Stone Age of Mount Carmel*. Oxford: Clarendon

Geneste J-M. 1988. Economie des resources lithiques dans le Moustérien du sud-ouest de la France. In *L'Homme Neandertal*. Vol. 6. *La Subsistance*, ed. M Otte, pp. 75–97. Liège, Belgium: ERAUL

Geneste JM, Plisson H. 1993. Hunting technologies and human behavior: lithic analysis of Solutrean shouldered points. See Knecht et al. 1993, pp. 117–36

Ghosh A. 1993. Upper Palaeolithic blade technology: a preliminary analysis of the cores from Mehtakheri (Madhya Pradesh). *Man Environ.* 18:11–19

Gibson K. 1996. The biocultural human brain, seasonal migrations, and the emergence of the Upper Palaeolithic. See Mellars & Gibson 1996, pp. 33–46

Gilman A. 1984. Explaining the Upper Palaeolithic revolution. In *Marxist Perspectives in Archaeology*, ed. E Springs, pp. 220–37. Cambridge: Cambridge Univ. Press

Goebel T, Waters MR, Buvit I, Konstantinov MV, Konstantinov AV. 2000. Studenoe-2 and the origins of microblade technologies in the Transbaikal, Siberia. *Antiquity* 74:567–75

Goring-Morris AN. 1991. The Harifian of the Southern Levant. See Bar-Yosef & Valla 1991, pp. 173–216

Goring-Morris NA, Belfer-Cohen A, eds. 2002. *More than Meets the Eye: Studies on Upper Palaeolithic Diversity in the Near East*. Oxford: Oxbow

Goring-Morris AN, Marder O, Davidzon A, Ibrahim F. 1998. Putting Humpty together again: preliminary observations on refitting studies in the Eastern Mediterranean. In *The Organization of Lithic Technology in Late Glacial and Early Postglacial Europe*, ed. S Milliken, pp. 149–82. Oxford: B.A.R. Int. Ser. 700

Grayson DK, Cole SC. 1998. Stone tool assemblage richness during the Middle and Early Upper Palaeolithic in France. *J. Archaeol. Sci.* 25:927–38

Grayson DK, Delpech F. 1998. Changing diet breadth in the Early Upper Palaeolithic of southwestern France. *J. Archaeol. Sci.* 25: 1119–29

Grigor'ev GP. 1993. The Kostenki-Avdeevo archaeological culture and the Willendorf-Pavlov-Kostenki-Avdeevo cultural unity. In *From Kostenki to Clovis: Upper Paleolithic-Paleo-Indian Adaptations*, ed. O Soffer, ND Praslov, pp. 51–66. New York: Plenum

Guilbaud M. 1996. Psychotechnic analysis and culture change: origins of the Upper Paleolithic as seen through the example of Saint-Césaire. See Carbonell & Vaquero 1996, pp. 337–54

Harpending H, Batzer M, Gurven M, Jorde L, Rogers A, Sherry S. 1998. Genetic traces of ancient demography. *Proc. Natl. Acad. Sci. USA* 95:1961–67

Harris D, ed. 1996. *The Origins and Spread of Agriculture and Pastoralism in Eurasia*. London: UCL Press

Harrold FB. 1989. Mousterian, Chatelperronian and Early Aurignacian in Western Europe: continuity or discontinuity? See Mellars & Stringer 1989, pp. 677–713

Harrold FB. 1991. The elephant and the blind men: paradigms, data gaps, and the Middle-Upper Paleolithic transition in southwestern France. See Clark 1991, pp. 164–82

Henry DO. 1995. *Prehistoric Cultural Ecology and Evolution*. New York: Plenum. 464 pp.

Henshilwood C, Sealy J. 1997. Bone artifacts from the Middle Stone Age at Blombos Cave, Southern Cape, South Africa. *Curr. Anthropol.* 38:890–95

Henshilwood CS, Sealy JC, Yates R, Cruz-Uribe K, Goldberg P, et al. 2001. Blombos Cave, Southern Cape, South Africa: preliminary report on the 1992–1999 excavations of the Middle Stone Age levels. *J. Archaeol. Sci.* 28:421–48

Hillman GC. 2000. Abu Hureyra 1: the Epipalaeolithic. In *Village on the Euphrates: From Foraging to Farming at Abu Hureyra*, ed. AMT Moore, GC Hillman, AJ Legge, pp. 327–99. Oxford: Oxford Univ. Press

Hole F. 1989. A two-part, two-stage model of domestication. In *The Walking Larder*, ed. J Clutton-Brock, pp. 97–104. London: Unwin Hyman

Hole F. 1996. The context of caprine domestication in the Zagros region. See Harris 1996, pp. 263–81

Hovers E. 2001. Territorial behavior in the Middle Paleolithic of the Southern Levant. See Conard 2001, pp. 123–52

Hovers E, Kimbel WH, Rak Y. 2000. Amud 7—still, a burial: response to Gargett. *J. Hum. Evol.* 39:253–60

Howell FC. 1998. Evolutionary implications of altered perspectives on hominine demes and populations in the Later Pleistocene of western Eurasia. See Akazawa et al. 1998, pp. 5–27

Hublin J-J. 2000. Modern-nonmodern hominid interactions: a Mediterranean perspective. See Bar-Yosef & Pilbeam 2000, pp. 157–82

Jensen HJ. 1988. Microdenticulates in the Danish Stone Age: a functional puzzle. In *Industries Lithiques: Tracéologie et Technologie*, ed. S Beyries. Oxford: B.A.R. Int. Ser. 441

Johnson AW, Earle T. 2000. *The Evolution of Human Societies: From Foraging Group to Agrarian State*. Stanford, CA, Stanford Univ. Press

Kislev ME, Nadel D, Carmi I. 1992. Epi-Palaeolithic (19,000 B.P.) cereal and fruit diet at Ohalo II, Sea of Galilee, Israel. *Rev. Palaeobot. Palynol.* 71:161–66

Klein R. 1998. Why anatomically modern people did not disperse from Africa 100,000 years ago. See Akazawa et al. 1998, pp. 509–21

Klein RG. 1995. Anatomy, behavior, and modern human origins. *J. World Prehist.* 9:167–98

Klein RG. 1999. *The Human Career: Human Biological and Cultural Origins*. Chicago: Univ. Chicago Press

Klein RG. 2001a. Southern Africa and modern human origins. *J. Anthropol. Res.* 57:1–16

Klein RG. 20001b. Fully modern humans. In *Archaeology at the Millennium*, ed. GM Feinman, TD Price, pp. 109–35. New York: Plenum

Knecht H, Pike-Tay A, White R, eds. 1993. *Before Lascaux: the Complete Record of the Early Upper Paleolithic*. Boca Raton, FL: CRC Press

Koumouzelis M, Ginter B, Kozlowski JK, Pawlikowski M, Bar-Yosef O, et al. 2001. The Early Upper Palaeolithic in Greece: the excavations in Klisoura Cave. *J. Archaeol. Sci.* 28:515–39

Kozlowski JK. 2000. The problem of cultural continuity between the Middle and the Upper Paleolithic in central and eastern Europe. See Bar-Yosef & Pilbeam 2000, pp. 77–105

Kozlowski JK, Otte M. 2000. The formation of the Aurignacian in Europe. *J. Anthropol. Res.* 56:513–34

Kozlowski SK. 1999. *The Eastern Wing of the Fertile Crescent: Late Prehistory of Greater Mesopotamian Lithic Industries*. Oxford: Archaeopress. 220 pp.

Krings M, Capelli C, Tschentscher F, Geisert H, Meyer S, et al. 2000. A view of Neandertal genetic diversity. *Nat. Genet.* 26:144–49

Krings M, Stone A, Schmitz RW, Krainitzki

H, Stoneking M, Pääbo S. 1997. Neandertal DNA sequences and the origin of modern humans. *Cell* 90:19–30

Kuhn SL. 1998. The economy of lithic raw materials and the economy of food procurement. In *Économie préhistorique:les comportements de subsistance au Paléolithique*, ed. J-P Brugal, L Meignen, M Patou-Mathis, pp. 215–26. Sophia Antipolis, France: Éditions APDCA

Kuhn SL, Bietti A. 2000. The Late Middle and Early Upper Paleolithic in Italy. See Bar-Yosef & Pilbeam 2000, pp. 49–76

Kuhn SL, Stiner MC, Reese DS, Gulec E. 2001. Ornaments of the earliest Upper Paleolithic: new insights from the Levant. *Proc. Natl. Acad. Sci. USA* 98:7641–46

Kuzmin YV, Orlova LA. 1998. Radiocarbon chronology of the Siberian Paleolithic. *J. World Prehist.* 12:1–53

Legge T. 1996. The beginning of caprine domestication in Southwest Asia. See Harris 1996, pp. 238–62

Lévêque F, Backer AM, Guilbaud M, eds. 1993. *Context of a Late Neanderthal*. Madison, Wisc.: Prehistory Press

Lévêque F, Vandermeersch B. 1981. Le néandertalien de Saint-Césaire. *Recherche* 119:242–44

Lewis-Williams JD. 1991. Wrestling with analogy: a methodological dilemma in upper Palaeolithic art research. *Proc. Prehist. Soc.* 57:149–62

Lewis-Williams JD. 1997. Harnessing the brain: vision and shamanism in Upper Paleolithic western Europe. See Conkey et al. 1997, pp. 321–42

Lieberman DE. 1998. Sphenoid shortening and the evolution of modern human cranial shape. *Nature* 393:158–62

Lieberman P. 1998. *Eve Spoke: Human Language and Human Evolution*. New York: Norton. 192 pp.

Lindly JM, Clark GA. 1990. Symbolism and modern human origins. *Curr. Anthropol.* 31: 233–62

Marean CW. 1998. A critique of the evidence for scavenging by Neandertals and early modern humans: new data from Kobeh Cave (Zagros Mountains, Iran) and Die Kelders Cave 1 Layer 10 (South Africa). *J. Hum. Evol.* 35:111–36

Marean CW, Assefa Z. 1999. Zooarcheological evidence for the faunal exploitation behavior of Neandertals and early modern humans. *Evol. Anthropol.* 8:22–37

Marks AE. 1990. The Middle and Upper Palaeolithic of the Near East and the Nile Valley: the problem of cultural transformations. In *The Emergence of Modern Humans*, ed. P Mellars, pp. 56–80. Edinburgh, UK: Univ. Edinburgh Press

Marks AE. 1993. The Early Upper Paleolithic: the view from the Levant. See Knecht et al. 1993, pp. 5–22

Marks AE, Chabai VP. 2001. Constructing "Middle Paleolithic" settlement patterns in Crimea: potentials and limitations. See Conard 2001, pp. 179–204

Marks AE, Hietala HJ, Williams JK. 2001. Tool standardization in the Middle and Upper Palaeolithic: a closer look. *Cambridge Archaeol. J.* 11:17–44

Marshack A. 1972. *The Roots of Civilization; The Cognitive Beginnings of Man's First Art, Symbol, and Notation*. New York: McGraw-Hill. 413 pp.

Marshack A. 1997. Paleolithic image making and symboling in Europe and the Middle East: a comparative review. See Conkey et al. 1997, pp. 53–91

Martin L. 1999. Mammal remains from the Eastern Jordanian Neolithic, and the nature of caprine herding in the steppe. *Paléorient* 25:87–104

McBrearty S, Brooks AS. 2000. The revolution that wasn't: a new interpretation of the origin of modern human behavior. *J. Hum. Evol.* 39:453–563

Meignen L, Bar-Yosef O, Goldberg P. 1989. Les structures de combustion moustériennes de la grotte de Kébara (Mont Carmel, Israël). In *Nature et Fonctions des Foyers Prehistoriques*, ed. M Olive, Y Taborin, pp. 141–46. Nemours, France: APRAIF

Meignen L, Beyries S, Speth J, Bar-Yosef O.

1998. Acquisition, traitement des matières animales et fonction du site au Paléolithique moyen dans la grotte de Kébara (Israël): approche interdisciplinaire. In *Economie Préhistorique:Les Comportements de Subsistance au Paléolithique*, ed. J-P Brugal, L Meignen, M Patou-Matis, pp. 227–42. Sophia Antipolis, France: Editions APDCA

Mellars P. 1989. Technological changes at the Middle-Upper Palaeolithic transition: economic, social and cognitive perspectives. See Mellars & Stringer 1989, pp. 338–65

Mellars P. 1996a. *The Neanderthal Legacy: an Archaeological Perspective from Western Europe*. Princeton, NJ: Princeton Univ. Press

Mellars P. 1996b. Symbolism, language, and the Neanderthal mind. See Mellars & Gibson 1996, pp. 15–32

Mellars P. 2000. Châtelperronian chronology and the case for Neanderthal/modern human 'acculturation' in Western Europe. See Stringer et al. 2000, pp. 33–39

Mellars P, Gibson K, eds. 1996. *Modelling the Early Human Mind*. Cambridge, UK: McDonald Inst. Archaeol. Res.

Mellars P, Otte M, Straus L, Zilhão J, D'Errico F. 1999. The Neanderthal problem continued. CA Forum on Theory in Anthropology. *Curr. Anthropol.* 40:341–64

Mellars P, Stringer C, eds. 1989. *The Human Revolution: Behavioural and Biological Perspectives on the Origins of Modern Humans*. Edinburgh: Edinburgh Univ. Press

Mithen S. 1994. From domain specific to generalized intelligence: a cognitive interpretation of the Middle/Upper Palaeolithic transition. In *The Ancient Mind: Elements of a Cognitive Archaeology*, ed. C Renfrew, E Zubrow, pp. 29–39. Cambridge: Cambridge Univ. Press

Mithen S. 1996. Domain-specific intelligence and the Neanderthal mind. See Mellars & Gibson 1996, pp. 217–29

Mulvaney DJ, Kamminga J. 1999. *Prehistory of Australia*. Washington, DC: Smithson. Inst. Press: Allen & Unwin. 481 pp.

Murty MLK. 1979. Recent research on the Upper Paleolithic phase in India. *J. Field Archaeol.* 6:301–20

Neuville R. 1951. *Le Paléolithique et le Mésolithique de Désert de Judée*. Paris: Masson et Cie

Ohnuma K. 1988. *Ksar Akil, Lebanon: a Technological Study of the Earlier Upper Palaeolithic Levels at Ksar Akil*,Vol. III. *Levels XXV-XIV*. Oxford: B.A.R. Int. Ser. 426

Oliva M. 1993. The Aurignacian in Moravia. See Knecht et al. 1993, pp. 37–56

Orschiedt J, Weniger G-C, eds. 2000. *Neanderthals and Modern Humans—Discussing the Transition: Central and Eastern Europe from 50,000-30,000 B.P.* Mettman, Germany: Neanderthal Mus.

Otte M, Derevianko AP. 2001. The Aurignacian in Altai. *Antiquity* 75:44–48

Otte M, Kozlowski JK. 2001. The transition from the Middle to Upper Paleolithic in North Eurasia. *Archaeol. Ethnol. Anthropol. Eurasia* 3:51–62

Ovchininkov IV, Götherström A, Romanova GP, Kharitonov VM, Lidén K, Goodwin W. 2000. Molecular analysis of Neanderthal DNA from the northern Caucasus. *Nature* 404:490–93

Pastó I, Allué E, Vallverdú J. 2000. Mousterian hearths at Abric Romaní, Catalonia (Spain). See Stringer et al. 2000, pp. 59–67

Pavlov P, Svendsen JI, Indrelid S. 2001. Human presence in the European Arctic nearly 40,000 years ago. *Nature* 413:64–67

Pelegrin J. 1990a. Observations technologiques sur quelques séries du Châtelperronien et du MTA B du Sud-Ouest de la France. Une hypothèse d'evolution. In *Paleolithique Moyen Récent et Paléolithique Supérieur ancien en Europe, Colloque International de Nemours*, ed. C Farizy, pp. 39-42. Nemours, France: APRAIF

Pelegrin J. 1990b. Prehistoric lithic technology: some aspects of research. *Archaeol. Rev. Cambridge* 9:116–25

Peltenburg E, Colledge S, Croft P, Jackson A, McCartney C, Murray MA. 2001. Neolithic dispersals from the Levantine corridor: a Mediterranean perspective. *Levant* 33: 35–64

Pinker S. 2000. *The Language Instinct: How the*

Mind Creates Language. New York: Perennial. 525 pp.

Rak Y. 1998. Does any Mousterian cave present evidence of two hominid species? See Akazawa et al. 1998, pp. 353–66

Renfrew C. 1987. *Archaeology and Language: the Puzzle of Indo-European Origins*. Cambridge: Cambridge Univ. Press. 346 pp.

Renfrew C. 1996. The sapient behaviour paradox: how to test for potential? See Mellars & Gibson 1996, pp. 11–14

Révillion S, Tuffreau A, ed. 1994. *Les industries laminaires au Paléolithique moyen*. Paris: CNRS

Richter J. 2000. Social memory among late Neanderthals. See Orschiedt & Weniger 2000, pp. 123–32

Rigaud J, Simek JF, Thierry G. 1999. Mousterian fires from Grotte XVI (Dordogne, France). *Antiquity* 69:901–12

Rigaud J-P. 1997. Scenarios for the Middle to Upper Paleolithic transition: a European perspective. See Clark & Willermet 1997, pp. 161–67

Sackett JR. 1983. Style and ethnicity in archaeology: the case for isochrestism. See Conkey & Hastrof 1983, pp. 32–43

Sackett JR. 1991. Straight archaeology French style: the phylogenetic paradigm in historic perspective. See Clark 1991, pp. 109–39

Semino O, Passarino G, Oefner PJ, Lin AA, Arbuzova S, et al. 2000. The genetic legacy of Paleolithic *Homo sapiens sapiens* in extant Europeans: a Y chromosome perspective. *Science* 290:1155–59

Shea JJ. 1988. Spear points from the Middle Paleolithic of the Levant. *J. Field Archaeol.* 15:441–50

Shennan S. 2001. Demography and cultural innovation: a model and its implication for the emergence of modern human culture. *Cambridge Archaeol. J.* 11:5–16

Singer R, Wymer JJ. 1982. *The Middle Stone Age at Klasies River Mouth in South Africa*. Chicago: Univ. Chicago Press

Smith ML. 1999. The Role of ordinary goods in premodern exchange. *J. Archaeol. Method Theory* 6(2):109–35

Soffer O. 1985. *The Upper Paleolithic of the Central Russian Plain*. New York: Academic. 539 pp.

Soffer O. 1989. Storage, sedentism and the Eurasian Palaeolithic record. *Antiquity* 63: 719–32

Soffer O, Adovasio JM, Hyland DC. 2000. The "Venus" figurines: textiles, basketry, gender, and status in the Upper Paleolithic. *Curr. Anthropol.* 41:511–37

Svoboda J, Simán K. 1989. The Middle-Upper Paleolithic transition in southeastern Central Europe (Czechoslovakia and Hungary). *J. World Prehist.* 3:283–322

Svoboda J, Skrdla P. 1995. Bohunician technology. In *The Definition and Interpretation of Levallois Technology*, ed. H Dibble, O Bar-Yosef, pp. 432–38. Madison, Wisc.: Prehistory Press

Stefan VH, Trinkaus E. 1998. Discrete trait and morphometric affinities of the Tabun 2 mandible (hu970210). *J. Hum. Evol.* 34(5): 443–68

Stiner MC, Kuhn SL. 1992. Subsistence, technology, and adaptive variation in Middle Paleolithic Italy. *Am. Anthropol.* 94:306–39

Stiner MC, Munro ND, Surovell TA, Tchernov E, Bar-Yosef O. 1999. Paleolithic population growth pulses evidenced by small animal exploitation. *Science* 283:190–94

Straus LG. 1996. Continuity or rupture; convergence or invasion; adaptation or catastrophe; mosaic or monolith: views on the Middle to Upper Paleolithic transition in Iberia. See Carbonell & Vaquero 1996, pp. 203–18

Straus LG. 2001. Africa and Iberia in the Pleistocene. *Quat. Int.* 75:91–102

Stringer C. 1998. Chronological and biogeographic perspectives on later human evolution. See Akazawa et al. 1998, pp. 29–37

Stringer C. 2001. Modern human origins: distinguishing the models. *Afr. Archaeol. Rev.* 18:67–75

Stringer C, Gamble C. 1993. *In Search of the Neanderthals*. London: Thames & Hudson
Stringer CB, Barton RNE, Finlayson JC, eds. 2000. *Neanderthals on the Edge: Papers from a Conference Marking the 150th Anniversary of the Forbes' Quarry Discovery, Gibraltar*. Oxford: Oxbow
Taborin Y. 1993. Shells of the French Aurignacian and Périgordian. See Knecht et al. 1993, pp. 211–28
Tostevin GB. 2000. The Middle to Upper Paleolithic transition from the Levant to Central Europe: *in situ* development or diffusion. See Orschiedt & Weniger 2000, pp. 92–111
Trask L, Tobias PV, Wynn T, Davidson I, Noble W, Mellars P. 1998. The origins of speech. *Cambridge Archaeol. J.* 8:69–94
Trinkaus E, Ruff CB, Churchill SE. 1998. Upper limb versus lower limb loading patterns among Near Eastern Middle Paleolithic hominids. See Akazawa et al. 1998, pp. 391–404
van Andel T, Runnels CN. 1995. The earliest farmers in Europe. *Antiquity* 69:481–500
van Andel TH, Tzedakis PC. 1996. Palaeolithic landscapes of Europe and environs, 150,000-25,000 years ago: an overview. *Quat. Sci. Rev.* 15:481–500
Van Peer P. 1998. The Nile Corridor and the Out-of-Africa model: an examination of the archaeological record. *Curr. Anthropol.* 39: S115–40
Vasil'ev SA. 1993. The Upper Paleolithic of northern Asia. *Curr. Anthropol.* 34:82–92
Vermeersch PM, Paulissen E, Stokes S, Charlier C, Van Peer P, et al. 1998. A Middle Palaeolithic burial of a modern human at Taramsa Hill, Egypt. *Antiquity* 72:475–84
Vigne J-D, Buitenhuis H, Davis S. 1999. Les premiers pas de la domestication animale à l'Ouest de l'Euphrate: Chypre et l'Anatolie Centrale. *Paléorient* 25:49–62
Wadley L. 2001. What is cultural modernity? A general view and a South African perspective from Rose Cottage Cave. *Cambridge Archaeol. J.* 11:201–21
Wagner GA. 1998. *Age Determination of Young Rocks and Artifacts: Physical and Chemical Clocks in Quaternary Geology and Archaeology*. Berlin: Springer Verlag. 466 pp.
Wengler L. 1997. La Transition du Moustérien à l'Atérien. *Anthropologie* 101:448–81
West FH. 1996. *American Beginnings*. Chicago: Univ. Chicago Press
Villa P, d'Errico F. 2001. Bone and ivory points in the Lower and Middle Paleolithic of Europe. *J. Hum. Evol.* 41:69–112
White R. 1993. A technological view of the Castelperronian and Aurignacian body ornaments in France. In *El Origen del Hombre Moderno en el Suroeste de Europea*, ed. V Cabrera Valdés. Madrid: UNED
White R. 1997. Substantial acts: from materials to meaning in Upper Paleolithic representation. See Conkey et al. 1997, pp. 93–121
White RK. 1982. Rethinking the middle/upper paleolithic transition. *Curr. Anthropol.* 23:169–76, 87–92
Wiessner P. 1989. Style and changing relations between the individual and society. In *The Meaning of Things: Material Culture and Symbolic Expression*, ed. I Hodder. London: Unwin Hyman
Wobst MH. 1976. Locational relationship in Palaeolithic society. *J. Hum. Evol.* 5:49–58
Wobst HM. 1999. Style in archaeology or archaeologists in style. In *Material Meanings: Critical Approaches to the Interpretation of Material Culture*, ed. ES Chilton, pp. 118–132. Salt Lake City: Univ. Utah Press
Wright KI. 1992. A classification system for ground stone tools from the prehistoric Levant. *Paléorient* 18:53–81
Wynn T. 1991. Archaeological evidence for modern intelligence. In *The Origins of Human Behavior*, ed. RA Foley. London: Unwin Hyman
Zeder MA, Hesse B. 2000. The initial domestication of goats (Capra hircus) in the Zagros Mountains 10,000 years ago. *Science* 287:2254–57
Zilhão J. 1995. The age of the Coa valley (Portugal) rock-art: validation of archaeological

dating to the Paleolithic and refutation of 'scientific' dating to historic or proto-historic times. *Antiquity* 69:883–901

Zilhão J, D'Errico F. 1999. The chronology and taphonomy of the earliest Aurignacian and its implications for the understanding of Neanderthal extinction. *J. World Prehist.* 13:1–68

Zvelebil M, Lillie M. 2000. Transition to agriculture in eastern Europe. In *Europe's First Farmers*, ed. TD Price, pp. 57–92. Cambridge: Cambridge Univ. Press

Annu. Rev. Anthropol. 2002. 31:395–417
doi: 10.1146/annurev.anthro.31.031902.161108

LABORING IN THE FACTORIES AND IN THE FIELDS

Sutti Ortiz
Emerita Professor, Department of Anthropology, Boston University, 232 Bay State Road, Boston, Massachusetts 02215; email: sortiz@bu.edu

Key Words labor markets, agriculture, industry, labor control, labor segmentation

■ **Abstract** Since 1980, studies of the wage labor process have been centered mostly on three topics: the new international division of labor, control over the labor process, and "flexibilization" of production. Anthropologists have contributed rich studies about modes of control and about how these modes are linked to social relations within the work place and workers' communities of origin. They have explained how and why market segmentation can be a powerful tool of control some of the time, whereas at other times it can enhance tensions. Anthropologists have also contributed by transforming stylized models into models centered on actors with social and class identities and with ambivalent expectations and aspirations. However, they have neglected to integrate their findings with those from the literature on labor migrations and job search. They also have neglected to consistently examine contracts and hiring practices, two major tools of labor control. Although anthropologists have been attentive to paradigms about global restructuring of industries, they have often disregarded an intermediate level of analysis: the relationship of producers and industries to relevant actors in their respective regional labor markets, and how producers and industries structure local labor markets. A spatial portrayal of labor markets will facilitate comparative studies about the impact of industrial restructuring and correct possible biases.

INTRODUCTION

Economic anthropologists have been very concerned with the organization of labor and social relations on the factory floor (Holzberg & Giovannini 1981). By contrast, they have paid little attention to the topic of wage laborers in agriculture; it was the world of peasant producers that fired the imagination of researchers (Kay 2000). The few studies about landless rural laborers have mostly been limited to those who worked on plantations (Mintz 1960, 1979; Knight 1972; Miller 1964) or in mines (Nash 1979, Godoy 1990, Long & Roberts 1984). Even then, these rural laborers have been described by many anthropologists as part-peasants or rural proletarians (Taussig 1977, Giusti-Cordero 1997). The rural-urban divide of the anthropology of the 1960s and early 1970s hampered the formulation of overarching propositions about how the labor process is structured and restructured in industry and agriculture (Kearney 1996).

This review discusses the achievements of the 1980s and 1990s when issues raised in industrial studies began to be incorporated into the analytic framework of rural research. During the late 1970s and 1980s, industrial anthropologists moved beyond the themes of job satisfaction and social relations in the factory to examine wage differences and the labor relations that were generated by the industrial drive for profit. I examine the legacy of that intellectual shift and its reflection in the study of the labor process in agriculture. I also address the impact of insights into the gendering of the labor process gleaned from women's studies. In so doing, I try to bridge the divides between research on rural versus industrial workers and between female and male laborers. I also try to bring together the concerns and viewpoints of social scientists from different parts of the world. I cannot do justice to all of these endeavors, but I hope to contribute to a more global view of the wage-labor process.

THE EMERGENCE OF WAGE-LABOR MARKETS

The development of wage-labor markets remains one of the major unresolved intellectual problems in the social sciences. It is a central analytical issue for Marxist scholars who argue that propertyless laborers can participate in the market sale of their labor only if unencumbered by ties of bondage or slavery. For many Marxists, the freedom to sell one's labor signals a transformation in modes of production from precapitalist to capitalist (Patnaik 1995, Woodiwiss 1987). By contrast, social scientists influenced by a Weberian-Durkheimian tradition are neither concerned with the uneven transformation from unfree to free wage-labor nor with how to situate this within a mode of production framework (Rutledge 1987, Richards 1979, Laliberte & Satzewich 1999). They are interested in studying the labor process itself and the role of institutions and culture in hampering or facilitating that transformation. For institutional economists, degrees of freedom raise questions about the definition of labor markets, varieties of labor market regimes, and the welfare of laborers.

The number of contrasting, complex field studies that have been published in the past 20 years have challenged neat definitions and propositions about the relation between types of labor markets and economic systems. Nevertheless, the debate continues about what constitutes free and unfree labor (Brass 1997a,b, 1999, 2000; Prakash 1997; Breman 1999; Brass & van der Linden 1997). Despite its vitriolic character, the debate has served to alert scholars to issues and questions that must be considered. First, it is not possible to talk about labor market exchange when laborers are legally bonded to their employers (Gonzales 1985, Campi 1991, Guy 1978, Santamaría 1986, Lagos 1992, Teruel de Lagos 1991). Second, in most cases, laborers are not totally free; social obligations, expectations, and economic realities limit their ability to choose work offers and to end their employment. Breman has coined the term neobondage to depict an intermediate state between free and unfree labor in India (Breman 1996). Others prefer to recognize a range of intermediate situations (Amin & van der Linden 1997, Ramachandran 1990,

Morgan 1982). In any case, it is important to specify the forms that bondage takes, the conditions that permit it, and those that make it possible to evade it. Tying laborers with loans can be expensive and ineffective (Gonzales 1985, Carr 1998, Peloso 1999, De Neve 1999).

Third, bondage and other forms of unfree labor may have been a consequence of capitalist expansion, "destined to be deployed either at the core or at the edge of the regional political economy" (Cohen 1987). Bondage allows employers to impose their authority (Brass 1997b, 1999; Brass & van der Linden 1997), though their ability to do so depends on the power and ideology of the state and on the political influence of producers and firms (Hart 1986a, 1989). Fourth, bondage is only one of the many strategies that can be used to reduce labor costs. Often a mix of strategies are used (Ramachandran 1990). The mix reflects perceived economic conditions (e.g., availability of credit and labor) and political conditions. Levy's study of mine labor in South Africa between 1886 and 1906 illustrates the range of political solutions that can be used and how social and political conflicts determined the strategy adopted (Levy 1982).

LABORERS AND LABOR MARKETS

Studies tracing labor migration circuits and the regionalization of agricultural production in Argentina served to relate labor supply enclaves to the dynamics of migration (Forni 1988, Forni et al. 1991, Reboratti 1983, Bendini et al. 1999, Aparicio & Benencia 2001, Giarracca 2000). By including in their study all household members (migrating and stay-at-home), these researchers were able to document that the search for work is not an individual pursuit but an activity structured by family dynamics and by the character of migrants' social networks. It is also structured by capital flows, by producers' management strategies geared to reduce the cost of labor, by government policies, by the cash needs of small producers, and by ecological conditions. Structured labor migrations should be viewed as more than arrows on a map because they regionally link local labor markets (Ortiz 1999). In a recent book, Peck (1996) forcefully argues for the incorporation of a spatial framework in the analysis of labor markets. Hanson & Pratt (1995) suggest that we should consider the relationships between the sites where work is performed and where labor is reproduced. The regionalization of labor markets opens up the possibility for comparative analysis to explain regional variations in the labor process and participation in paid employment (Ortiz 1999). As several anthropologists have pointed out, managerial strategies and forms of contestation reflect the configuration of social and political conditions in the local labor market regime and the relation of the firm to the community (Wells 1996, p.14; Griffith 1993). Peck (1996) adds that a geographic perspective facilitates the identification of the underlying forces behind local variability and uneven development. If we also follow Hanson & Pratt's (1995) recommendation, we can incorporate factors affecting labor supply, such as familial strategies used for survival and the reproduction of the labor force, cyclical social demands for cash, and lines of authority within the domestic and kin group. This perspective is familiar to anthropologists who have been studying labor migrations in U.S. agriculture (Griffith 1993, van der Klei 1985). Anthropologists, however, have been more likely to identify laborers by class membership than by participation in a particular spatially defined market (Stichter 1985); Wells (1996) suggests that we do both.

Labor markets may transcend national political boundaries and cross oceans. Colonial powers engineered flows of forced migrants through taxation, regulation, and coercion. The trade in slave and indentured laborers are two sad examples. But there were also flows of free European laborers (described as "swallows") who received free passage and traveled seasonally to harvest wheat in the Argentine pampas during the late nineteenth and early twentieth centuries (Scobie 1977). During the same period, Europeans were recruited to work in Brazilian coffee plantations (Holloway 1980, Stolcke 1988). Hahamovitch describes the coinciding interests of northern Italian industrialists and New Jersey fruit and vegetable producers (Hahamovitch 1997). Willing to favor northern capitalists, the Italian government shifted the tax burden to the rural south and forced many newly destitute peasants and laborers to emigrate "voluntarily" to the United States. The development of the oil industry and sugar cane production in Venezuela encouraged the immigration of laborers from Colombia, many of whom entered the country illegally (Gomez Jimenez & Días Mesas 1983). In all of these cases, some state intervention was required, at least to permit entry of immigrant laborers. However, states are not always willing to support the interests of their own industrialists. The Colombian state never responded to the plea of coffee growers for cheap foreign laborers. A more dramatic example is Trujillo's manipulation of labor immigrations of Haitians between 1937 and 1950, not as a means of helping sugar cane producers in the Dominican Republic but as a strategy to gain control over the industry (Band 1992, Martinez 1999). Peron's labor legislation did not favor the owners of the sugar mills of northern Argentina, and the sugar mills had to send recruiters to Bolivia to bring back cheap laborers. These laborers did not have work permits; hence they could not demand the fringe benefits of the new labor legislation (Whiteford 1981). Numerous studies by social scientists illustrate the conflicting interests that states must satisfy and their strategic alliances with certain sectors (Bach 1985, Wood & McCoy 1985, Weber 1994, Martin 1996, Hahamovitch 1997); they also illustrate the role that states and dominant elites play in setting the direction of labor migrations.

Capitalist expansion in highly industrialized nations has not only forced and enticed labor to migrate but also has generated pockets of poverty in peripheral countries or peripheral regions that were later tapped as relatively stable sources of cheap labor (Bach 1985, Portes & Walton 1981, Fernandez Kelly 1985). These impoverished regions were forced to bear the costs of "reproducing" future laborers (Brass 1997a; Krissman 1996, 1997; Wolpe 1972; Murray 1981; Beinart 1980; Levy 1982). Burawoy (1976) is often quoted in support of the contention that by externalizing the costs of reproduction of the labor force, capitalists can cheapen labor costs. His thesis, however, is not that simple. In assessing the costs and benefits of a migrant labor supply, Burawoy distinguishes seasonal migrants from longer-term migrants who become a burden to communities during periods of unemployment. He also adds that we have to determine the costs of maintaining the "migrant" system, a point illustrated by Levy (1982) in his description of the role of the state in organizing and subsidizing the migration of "cheap" laborers (see Stichter 1985). Furthermore, we have to establish whether there are mechanisms to perpetuate the renewal of labor in the migrant's home society (Burawoy 1976, pp. 152–53, 181–84). For Burawoy it is not a simple matter of differential costs of living or peasant origins. He leaves open the possibility that "peasantness" does not assume the costs of reproduction but that "peasantness" can be subsidized by seasonal migrations. Though agreeing that the growth of northern capitalism has contributed to transnational migrations of cheap labor, many scholars consider that the historical-structuralist explanation and bipolar division of space is simplistic (Briody 1989, Georges 1990, Martinez 1995) because it fails to capture the range of migratory patterns and the variety of labor regimes (Cohen 1987). The bipolar framework also reflects a northerner's perspective and has underscored labor migration flows between similarly endowed countries (Whiteford 1981): e.g., the migration of fruit harvesters between Chile and Southern Argentina (Bendini et al. 1999, Cerutti & Pita 1999), Bolivia cane cutters to Argentina (Whiteford 1981, Dandler & Madeiros 1988), and Haitian sugar cane workers to the Dominican Republic (Martinez 1995).

Regardless of how far the system of binational labor markets succeeds in cheapening the cost of production, it is likely to survive. Workers from poorer nations will continue to perform most of the less-skilled, lower-paid jobs. Anthropologists need to explore more systematically how industries manage to overcome political boundaries and expand their labor supply sources to generate binational labor markets. They also need to determine how migrant laborers are incorporated into the sociopolitical fabric of the regions they migrate to. What are the laborers' bargaining positions? What contractual relations can they forge? Do they experience a similar exploitation in their home countries and in their new work sites? Griffith (1993) adds that we should also examine the jobs available to these migrants to sustain themselves after the season ends. What are the available strategies for the reproduction of domestic units? Such questions might encourage scholars from different regions to collaborate in using findings from their ongoing research. A methodology for considering such questions can be found in the cited anthropological and sociological literature on labor migrations. A geographic perspective would help to integrate comparative findings with information on labor process, sociopolitical organization, and the configuration of production. The vast literature on labor migrations to and within the United States, only touched on in this review, has already contributed to a clarification of how labor markets are structured. It has elucidated the process of social reproduction of labor, the role of the state, and the unintended consequences of state and industry policies. By placing the migrants, brokers, and employers at the core of their research, anthropologists have traced the source of the unintended consequences.

GLOBAL CAPITAL AND LOCAL LABORERS: THE NEW INTERNATIONAL DIVISION OF LABOR

Poorer and less-industrialized nations are no longer mainly exporters of labor and primary commodities (Fröbel et al. 1980). They also ceased to be sites for "northern" capitalists to invest in plantations. These nations, instead, have become the new sites for investment by international capital searching to lower costs by decentralizing, subcontracting industrial production, as well as by hiring cheaper labor. Many of the overseas factories produce agricultural inputs or processed food. Other factories produce or assemble finished commodities. Because these factories hire local laborers, Fröbel et al. (1980) believe that northern capitalist investments in overseas factories have restructured the labor process. The new international division of labor is the term coined to describe this transformation—an infelicitous term, as Fernandez-Kelly points out (1985). Nevertheless, it caught the attention of anthropologists, in part because many of these new industrial sites (electronic, textile, and clothing factories) engaged women and introduced them to globally standardized labor relations and to a global culture (Nash & Fernandez-Kelly 1983).

The relocation of capital rather than labor is not new. What is new is that the investments are mostly in industry rather than in agriculture and mining. It is hard to tell whether or not this will continue given political and market instability and changes in trade and aid policies.

Since the notion of a new international division of labor was advanced and since the publication of Nash & Fernandez-Kelly's book (1983), a small number of lengthy ethnographies and a plethora of short articles in journals and edited volumes have appeared on the subject. However, these studies do not offer enough information to substantiate the contention that these new industrial sites represent an international restructuring of the labor process; they may just represent a relocation of production. Fernandez-Kelly (1983) lists the key issues that still need to be considered: Why do only some of these new global industries rely on women? Have workers in the North as well as the South lost bargaining power? Does the advanced technology that has been introduced enhance control that capital has over workers? Do the recruitment policies overseas differ from those in the industrial countries? How do textile factories overseas, for example, differ from sweatshops in the United States?

Theorists have alerted us to another development: the restructuring of industry by "flexibilizing" production. For Latin Americanists this restructuring was ominously linked to neoliberal policies intent on dismantling relatively recent protective labor legislation and limiting the power of unions. These scholars recognized that, while flexibilization may humanize the labor process and may enhance the competitiveness of firms, it also has a "dark side" (Lara Flores 1998). The term flexibilizing production condenses several strategies: the substitution of permanent workers with occasional workers; the loosening of job demarcation; the reorganization of work from individual to team work. Thus, it affects permanent workers in the formal industrial sector because they lose stability, seniority, and many fringe benefits, and it affects those agricultural workers who were protected by labor legislation. Wigfield (2001) assumes that flexibilization will affect women more than men, and Lara Flores (1998) believes that it will also affect migrants. Waylen (2000) believes that the transformation has been uneven and that women have sometimes profited. Latin Americanist anthropologists and sociologists have been trying to evaluate the consequences of the flexibilization and neoliberal reforms (Aparicio & Benencia 1999; Bendini et al. 1995, 1999; Neiman & Quaranta 2000; Lara Flores 1995, 1998; Tsakoumagkos & Bendini 2000; Collins & Krippner 1999). At the moment it is difficult to consider their impact separate from the events related to stagnation, fiscal crisis, and unemployment.

CONNECTING LABORERS TO JOBS

Migrating and Searching for Jobs

Labor migration studies have helped to delineate how laborers learn about jobs and search for them by mobilizing kinship and friendship networks (Kameir El Wathig 1988; Borjas & Tienda 1985; Hagan 1994; Breman 1996, pp. 91–92; Fernandes 1997). Kinship networks provide reliable information, whereas networks of friends, coworkers, and patrons serve to open new opportunities (Granovetter 1973, Griffith & Kissam 1995, Krissman 1996, Grey 1996). Fernandes (1997), however, cautions that job search through personal networks also serves to create hierarchies of power within the workforce. However, as networks expand, the links become weaker and affect the quality of the information and the effectiveness of the links. Social networks are most effective when they link migrating job seekers with communities of settled kin or compatriots (Kearney & Nagengast 1989, Krissman 1996, Murphy et al. 2001). When push and pull factors generate sustained circular migrations, the home community becomes a labor supplying sattelite (Portes & Bach 1995, Rothstein 1992, Mines 1981, Piore 1979, Massey et al. 1987). Poultry producers in North Carolina and northern Georgia encouraged satellite relations and even paid a bonus to those workers who brought friends or relatives with them (Griffith 1993).

Urban-Rural Divide

Concern for the plight of migrants has blinded us to the fact that most laborers, even in agriculture, do not work far away from their homes. Only in some industries and regions do seasonal migrants outnumber local residents; California might be a case in point (Martin 1989). Furthermore, we overlook that many of the local agricultural laborers reside in towns and cities and commute daily to work.

The most spectacular case of urban labor mobilization was that of the hop trains that moved families from the dock area in the east end of London to the field in Kent until the mid–twentieth century (Grieco 1996). The urban-rural circulation of labor has also been portrayed for sugar beet fields in the midwestern United

States during the 1920s (Valdes 1991, p. 11), for sugar cane production in northern Argentina until 1990 (Whiteford 1981), for the harvest of coffee in Colombia during the 1980s (Errazuriz 1986, Hataya 1992, Ortiz 1999) and presently in Costa Rica (Tatar 1998). Other relevant examples are to be found in studies about the circulation of labor between seasonal industries, like construction or textiles and farm work (Griffith & Kissam 1995, Breman 1996). To regard these cases as transitional stages in the development of capitalism or as partial proletarianization is to miss an important point. The participation of women in the hop fields of Kent and the grape harvest in Italy was related to the gendered segmentation of labor in the urban sector. The concept of articulation can be used here to understand the linkage of the urban and rural labor markets (Breman 1996; see Pahl 1984).

Labor Contractors

In some cases, a kinsman may be not only a source of information but also a recruiter for a farmer or small producer. These mediators often start as workmen, become supervisors, and are eventually charged with recruiting seasonal laborers (Wells 1996, Griffith 1993). After a few years, they become independent entrepreneurs who structure the regional labor market along lines that favor certain producers. These mediators are paid by the farmers and are not particularly interested in protecting laborers. They often engage in exploitative practices, usually taking advantage of the weak bargaining position of those they recruit (Kurian 1988, Vaupel & Martin 1986, Gonzalez 1985).

However, the market can restrain the power of contractors (Gonzales 1985). In some cases, the state has tried to regulate their operation and protect workers who challenge unfair practices (Stolcke 1988). In other cases, social pressure can prevent labor contractors from systematically exploiting laborers (Breman 1974, Teeringk 1995).

Labor contractors provide a number of services to producers. They can tap vulnerable labor pools, cheapen wages, reduce recruitment costs, and assume responsibility for organizing and supervising tasks (Emerson 1984, Godoy 1990, Ramachandran 1990, Grijns 1992, Simeon 1997). Martin (1988) and Krissman (1996) link the use of labor contractors to the need for linguistic and cultural brokers when hiring immigrants. Griffith & Kissam (Griffith 1993, Griffith & Kissam 1995) associate the use of contractors with the need to provide housing for migrants after farmers closed their labor camps. They also protect the farmer who wants to avoid labor laws (Schaffne 1993, Sosnick 1978, Thomas 1985). Historians, sociologists, and anthropologists have also noted that farmers use contractors when they fear the intrusion of labor unions (Vandeman 1988). Once labor unions are organized and are allowed to set hiring and seniority rules, then labor contractors lose their operating market niche (Martin 1989). All of these explanations describe the rationale for the use of contractors in specific situations, particular regions, and particular industries, but they do not explain why contractors are not always used under similar circumstances (Wells 1996). Vandeman tries to answers this question for the case of California growers by using a transaction cost model (Vandeman 1988, Vandeman et al. 1991). She incorporates two important elements often neglected in the more parsimonious sociological arguments: Labor contractors can be expensive, and they are often more interested in increasing the pace rather than the quality of work. Producers of long-season crops that require laborers to harvest with care are likely to avoid the risk and cost associated with labor contractors. Anthropologists may discover that a transaction cost paradigm is helpful to determine when farmers are likely to use labor recruiters' aid and to examine the dynamics of this relation.

Labor contractors are not always small entrepreneurs who are servants of their clients or who can easily escape the observing eye of the state. Some of them can be merchant-hacendados (Gonzales 1985), private employment agencies (Valdes 1991), or large service firms (Polopoulos & Emerson 1991, Aparicio & Ortiz 2001). They can also be state functionaries (Gonzales 1985).

CONTROLLING THE TRANSACTION AND PERFORMANCE OF LABOR

Accepting a Job and Negotiating Terms of Employment

There are a few descriptions of how laborers and employers connect with each other (Griffith & Kissam 1995, Ortiz 1999, Breman 1985). Nijeholt & Lycklama (1980, pp. 39–42) describe the helplessness of laborers who find jobs through crew leaders. Grieco (1996) recounts the concerns of female crew leaders when responding to letters inviting them to return to the hop fields. She specifies the issues open to bargaining in their letter of acceptance and upon arrival, when they were able to evaluate working conditions in the fields and organize collective demands. Peloso (1999) indicates that while the agent specifies the terms of the contract, the laborers come armed with questions. In contrast, Kim (1997) describes Korean women scanning through factory job announcements that fail to mention the wages paid. Ortiz (1999) contrasts the possibilities for bargaining during and after the harvest. The market power and culture of maquila factories also limits what can be asked when hired (Iglesias Prieto 1997[1985], Fernandez-Kelly 1983). If asking questions is interpreted as disrespect or unruliness, silence should not be read as conformity.

It is important to determine what information is given to the prospective laborer and what negotiating space is allowed. It is also important to clarify if the hiring terms have been negotiated collectively and to what extent they protect each worker when applying for specific jobs in specific places. Citrus harvesters are unable to renegotiate rates—set by collective agreement—as they enter new groves. If the daily earnings are unsuitable, they can only respond with absenteeism. This information helps us in the analysis of what has been called "everyday forms of resistance" (Scott 1985). It allows us to differentiate acts motivated by hiring practices (Thompson 1983) from those related to degrees of exploitation (Turton 1986), and the degrees of workers autonomy and collective solidarity (Toth 1993).

Labor Contracts

In some cases, laborers are asked to sign contracts that may be standardized agreements or specifically designed collective agreements. Morgan (1982, pp. 111–13) describes contracts with 21 clauses written in 1891. However, what often transpires is only a verbal exchange (Cartwright 1991). Nevertheless, employers always specify how the laborer is expected to behave and how the job is to be performed. Thus, it is also important to reflect on how the contract itself is used as a means of control and how it shapes the modes of resistance.

A variety of forms of labor remuneration and contractual conditions have been documented (Morgan 1982). Although variation relates to tasks, Ramachandran (1990) points out that the same task may be paid on a time-rate basis in one region of India and a piece-rate basis in another; differences can occur even within the same village. Such variation in the form of hiring agricultural laborers has been explained by differences in ownership of resources, in the size of the producing unit, in the method of production, in market conditions, in skill requirements, in social organization, in state intervention with labor legislation and monitoring, and in the balance of power between employers and laborers (Ramachandran 1990, Robertson 1987, Collins 1993, Collins & Krippner 1999, Ortiz 1999, Wells 1996). Paying laborers per unit harvested has been one of the favored methods (Morgan 1982) and is also used for other activities, for example: mining (Godoy 1990, Simeon 1997), brick making, diamond cutting, roadwork (Breman 1996), textile production (Lamphere 1987, De Neve 2001), and garment work (Bonacich 1994). It is associated with tasks easily measurable by weight, length, or quantity of discreet units. For employers, it can be advantageous because it allows them to keep the costs of a specific task constant (Martin 1989) while avoiding the cost of waiting and preparation time. It simplifies seasonal recruitment and allows for the hiring of local laborers, regardless of their efficiency (Ortiz 1999). Piece-rate remuneration also stimulates productivity and encourages a competitive spirit (Peña 1997). In mining, it is the system favored by small prospectors because it reduces the costs of careless practices (Godoy 1990). Piece-rate remuneration also has its disadvantages for employers: facilitating absenteeism and shifts in employment when work is slow (Ortiz 2001, Breman 1996, González 1994); contributing to disruptive tensions in the workplace, especially when laborers work in teams (De Neve 2001); and promoting speed at the price of quality. In industries where quality matters, producers have to incur the costs of supervision, bonuses, or other quality incentives (González 1994, Lamphere 1987, Kim 1997, Crisp 1983, Wells 1996, Fernandez-Kelly 1983, Ortiz 2002). Laborers often prefer piece-rate contracts, despite the risk of fluctuating incomes, because they can control how much they earn (Ortiz 1999, Morgan 1982) and because they are at greater liberty to come and go (Gannagé 1986), which is particularly important to illegal immigrants who face the risk of deportation (Wells 1996). Piece rates allow laborers to enhance their earnings by drawing on family labor (Ortiz 1999, Godoy 1990, Simeon 1997) or by hiring underage helpers (Whiteford 1981). In recent years, however, laws have limited the use of child labor in the fields.

Not all harvesting tasks are paid by unit. Day or hourly contracts are more common when labor quality is important, when casual laborers are required to perform different tasks, or when they are hired for an extended period. The payment may be in cash or kind (Ramachandran 1990, Gough 1987, Bardhan & Rudra 1981). Wages reflect market conditions, labor regulations, social status, and fringe benefits or privileges. Loans linked to employment and their potential effect on wages have been the subject of much controversy (Hart 1986b). One of the drawbacks of time-rate payment is its failure to stimulate productivity. One of the solutions is to couple day wages with quotas and bonuses (Kim 1997, Peña 1997, Crisp 1983, Nash 1979).

Long-term employment of day laborers benefits employers who want to invest in training (Collins 1993) and insure the laborer's availability at a moment's notice (Gough 1987). Long-term contracts also offer employers the opportunity to build trust through patronage (Platteau 1995). If patronage is neither viable nor desired, laborers compliance and commitment can be achieved by paying them above the market rate or by offering attractive fringe benefits (Schaffner 1993, Collins & Krippner 1999, Nash 1979). However, laborers hired on a longer-term basis are more costly because they have to be retained during slow production periods. Thus, employers support neoliberal reforms that allow them to shift toward casual labor. The concern of Latin Americanists is that these reforms are dismantling security and fringe benefits, which have been the products of labor struggle.

Laborers are sometimes paid a share of what is produced. Share payments need to be distinguished from sharecropping, though there are similarities between the two systems (Robertson 1987). The share laborer is a member of a crew who neither assumes organizational responsibility nor contributes with inputs other than his own labor (see Bardhan & Rudra 1981). This mode of contracting resolves the problem of cash shortages for employers but at the expense of laborers who have to face fluctuating incomes. Paying laborers with a share of the output may discourage investments because laborers will benefit without contributing to the purchase of new equipment (Doeringer et al. 1986). The complexity and flexibility of share systems has been documented in the literature (Russell 1994; Alexander 1982; Quaranta 2001; Wells 1984, 1996). The effectiveness of this form of remunerating laborers depends on the ability to adjust shares to respond to price or technological changes, the risk of theft (Russell 1994), and the ability of employers and laborers to arrive at a consensus about the fairness of the agreement; otherwise tensions arise and collaboration breaks down (Benencia & Quaranta 2001).

Finally, laborers may also be paid by tasks performed (Grieco 1996, Ortiz 1999, Breman 1996). A labor crew, under the leadership of a parent or a respected member, may bargain a contract, organize the work, and then distribute the payment according to an established practice. Large families with many dependents may benefit from task contracts. They are often preferred because laborers feel more autonomous and can avoid the watchful eye of supervisors. However, unless the crew leader can correctly estimate the time and effort required to complete the task, his coworkers will be underpaid.

Contracts also include clauses about hours of work, rest, privileges, discipline, how the task is to be carried out, benefits, the rights to some resources, and the right to glean (Morgan 1982, Scott 1985, Godoy 1990). Because contracts and hiring encounters initiate the worker into a particular work situation, anthropologists should consistently analyze contracts in their discussions of the labor process.

Controlling or Maneuvering Performance

Some anthropologists and sociologists privilege the term control in their case studies; control implies the power to bend, coerce, or extract labor. In many of these studies, control is conceptualized as a structural consequence of the logic of accumulation of capitalist production, the result of competition and opposition. Gordon et al. (1982) and Braverman (1974) have explored a number of modes of control used by capital: segmenting markets, deskilling tasks, centralizing decisions, and imposing ever new relations of production. Burawoy (1979) and Edwards (1979) add that despotic centralized decisions have contributed to class tensions that eventually were diffused by the bureaucratization of management. Supervisors' control of promotion has served to split work groups (Zavella 1987), shifting workers' attention from collective plight to their own personal aspirations. It is also assumed that with bureaucratization there was a shift in the mode of controlling performance: from the brutal and arbitrary sanctions of foremen to sanctions by rules.

These models of historical changes in the industrial labor process were very influential in defining the direction of labor studies in sociology and to some extent in anthropology. Sociologists and anthropologists have examined some of these propositions in situations that differed considerably from those assumed in the model of regimes portrayed by these theorists (Nash 1985), which revealed the effectiveness and the limitations of the models. Two studies about banana plantations analyze how an ethnically segmented hierarchy of jobs effectively divided the labor force in Panama (Bourgois 1989, 1988) and allowed the Belize banana growers to lower labor costs and diminish class resistance (Moberg 1996, 1997). In the United States and Latin America, farmers and food industries achieved the same goal by consecutively employing ethnically diverse laborers as well as immigrants (Valdes 1991, Griffith 1993, Griffith & Kissam 1995, Fink 1998) or by strategically hiring women, who prefer flexible schedules (Collins 1993, 1995), for certain jobs (Thomas 1985). In many countries, most subaltern jobs in plantations, textile factories, apparel, and electronic industries are reserved for women as employers exploit their socially junior status to pay them lower wages (Ong 1987, 1991; Kurian 1998; Kim 1992; Wolf 1992). The use of this strategy is associated with the marginality of the firms in the market, as well as with the subaltern role that women have in their families and communities. It became strategically opportune in recent years to transfer production to countries or regions where the gendering of roles or the construction of ethnic identities opened pools of cheap and docile laborers (Nash 1985, Fernandez-Kelly 1983). Parry (1999), however, warns us that this strategy can change.

The concentration of labor in industrial plants permits other, sometimes ruthless, forms of manipulating the performance of laborers. The impact of Fordist strategies are described in several case studies (Fink 1998, Kim 1992, Peña 1997). Thomas (1985) describes how large lettuce-growing enterprises have recreated some aspects of machine pacing in the open fields. Managerial bureaucracy explored other forms of coaxing workers to increase productivity: scientific management and Japanese management. Time studies of required body movement led to the setting of standard rates that could be expected from workers and estimated the speed at which the line could be set without incurring costly injuries (Gartman 1986, Crisp 1983, Willson 1993). Some agricultural producers are experimenting with similar strategies to control pace and quality. Lemon producers in Argentina, concerned by fruit damage, have designed and redesigned more efficient stepladders, scissors, and receptacles for fruit. They have also changed the landscape and the distribution of bins to reduce the distanced traveled by harvesters. Computers facilitate record keeping and monitoring of the productivity and performance of each laborer. In large firms, experimenting and record keeping is done in-house by specialized harvest and human relations departments. Smaller producers have managed to achieve the same end by exchanging information and gaining the collaboration of the technical staff in packing enterprises (Ortiz 2002). Modern, commercial agriculture is now adopting forms of control commonly associated with industrial sites to solve the cost of seasonal production. It is hard to attract responsible and efficient laborers and, in many countries, it is expensive to retain them for most of the year.

Taylor's scientific management, however, did not do away with well-entrenched authoritarianism (Crisp 1983, Peña 1997, Fink 1998, Ong 1987, Fernandez-Kelly 1983). In many work sites, authoritarianism remains the main tool used to increase productivity (Kim 1997, Fink 1998, Wolfe 1992). In other smaller settings, paternalism or patronage is used as a means of control (De Neve 2001, Breman 1974, Platteau 1995) or to gain collaboration (Jain 1998). The managerial style of formal sector construction firms in the United States has been quite different, perhaps because of the decentralized nature of the work sites and the skills required. Laborers own most of the small tools they need and have considerable autonomy over decisions that pertain to their safety and to production (Applebaum 1999). Peña also reminds us that, despite the commonality of Fordist and Taylorist practices, not all maquilas are rife with exploitation (Peña 1997). Field studies have demonstrated that the transformation of the managerial and labor control process is more complex than what was suggested by the theoretical models.

It is also clear, from the case studies by anthropologists and sociologists, that tools of control have a double edge. Labor management can also become more intractable when, at their instigation, ethnic antagonism becomes explosive (Moberg 1996, 1997; Bourgois 1988, 1989). Low rates or attempts to lower labor costs by decreasing wage rates or increasing productivity through piece-rate contracts are thwarted by sloppy work, absenteeism, or sabotage (Kar 1984, Ortiz 2001, Fink 1998, Gartman 1986, Lamphere 1987, Palmer 1986). Disagreeable management policies and mangagement monopoly over expertise are also frequently contested in the fields or on the shop floor (Fink 1998, Ong 1987, Torres 1997, Peña 1997). Although these challenges may appear to be carried out by individuals, they often require the collaboration of others: A coworker may vouch that a worker was ill, ignore that a worker is tampering with machinery, or help him/her do it. Sabotage, disrupting operations, and pace slackening serve two purposes: They convey grievance and facilitate more direct collective action, such as stoppages, strikes, and unionization (Asher & Edsforth 1995, Crisp 1983, Peña 1997, Thomas 1985, Fink 1998, Wells 1996). However, employers and management can respond with even more repressive rules generating endemic tensions (Asher & Edsforth 1995).

Employers who expected docility from female laborers and from "factory daughters" were mistaken in their beliefs (Kim 1992, Ong 1987, Wolf 1992). Tiano suggests that when academics talk about the docility of women, they are colluding with a myth promoted by employers (Tiano 1994, p. 19). Women have often questioned their subordination at home, and one would expect them to eventually enact that challenge in the work place. However, it is hard to determine if their challenges are less frequent and less likely to lead to collective protest. In England, women were able to enlist support from coworkers, kin, and community networks (Griecco & Whipp 1986). In the United States, women often organized strikes and have been engaged in industries often associated with male labor (Wertheimer 1977, Lamphere 1987). Confrontational behavior may take the form of what Torres (1997) describes as ironic games, or it may give rise to cultural forms of resistance (Ong 1991). Wolf (1992) argues that to understand the incidence and the forms that protest takes, we also have to examine gender relations in the family and labor relations in the village.

Although Burawoy is often quoted, few anthropologists explore another aspect of his contribution: how management tries to manipulate consent to stimulate the pace of work or the quality of workmanship, and how the social relations on the shop floor contribute to the invisibility of exploitation. Piece rate provides a reward for those willing to compete to avoid tedium (Fernandez-Kelly 1983). Gannagé quotes a garment industry worker explaining that piece work "puts people in the position of being a manufacturer"; another worker explains that "it's a mental thing," "if it goes well, then you feel good" (1986, p. 125). Becerril (1995) describes how Mexican women laboring in the flower industry collude with their employer's equation of femininity with maternity and life-giving source. They become very protective of their plants, yet recognize literally and symbolically the oppressive quality of their work. If collaboration cannot be attained or management is not intent on it, the alternative is to allow disruptive behavior that may deflect or disguise labor-management conflict. De Neve (2001) suggests that teasing, joking, and open conflict between loom workers in Indian textile factories, together with their dependence on patronage, do serve that purpose. Chomsky (1998) makes the same point when she describes the frequent fights among miners in Costa Rica. Bonacich (1994) documents how owners of sweatshops in Los Angeles hired laborers of differing ethnic groups to focus confrontational discourse along ethnic lines rather than on work grievances. Bourgois (1989) makes a similar point.

Torres (1997) undercuts much of what has been said about the politics of consent with several sensible observations: Workers often prefer to accommodate to tasks rather than be coerced; they discern the opportune moment for taking initiative and doing more than asked because it will benefit the foremen or even the owner. Among lemon and coffee harvesters, some did not consider their jobs as being unskilled, as theorists or employers thought, and they took pride in their performance, aware that they also attracted trust. This alerts us to the dangers of interpreting instrumentality, a point illustrated by White's analysis of workers' behavior in two British factories (White 1988). Teasing, carelessness, slowness, and disruptive behavior may be intended to convey a message to pressure an employer or contest policies in the workplace, but it may also be a response to social conditions long in the making and to relations in work settings in the past (Rafel 1992). The same applies to our interpretations of managerial practices. The regulation and the mechanization of some tasks may be intended to improve quality and lower spoilage instead of enhancing control, even when it manages to do both.

The major contribution of anthropologists to the literature on labor control has been to highlight the connection between modes of control, contestation, and confrontation with social realities outside the work place. For example, Moberg (1996, 1997), Bourgeois (1989), and Fink (1998) link hiring policies with the dynamics of ethnic relations and changes in legislation. Wells discusses the complex role of the state and its legal system on class formation and on the ideological dynamics of class relations (Wells 1996). Ong (1987, 1991) relates forms of resistance, in part, to cultural constructions of status and social relations. By including quotes and stories, anthropologists have also humanized propositions and theories about how the contractual exchange and the work experience affect people's freedom and their control of incomes and opportunities. As Parry pointedly remarks, "Labour does not merely respond to the strategy of the employers, its organization is at least in part an independent product of its own ideological and material concerns" (Parry 1999, p. XXII). The same is true of industrialists and farmers.

The *Annual Review of Anthropology* is online at http://anthro.annualreviews.org

LITERATURE CITED

Alexander P. 1982. *Sri Lankan Fisherman: Rural Capitalism and Peasant Society*. Canberra: Aust. Natl. Univ.

Amin S, van der Linden M, eds. 1997. "Peripheral" labour? Studies in the history of partial proletarianization. *Int. Rev. Soc. Hist.*, (*Suppl. 4*). Cambridge, UK: Cambridge Univ. Press

Aparicio S, Benencia R. 1999. Empleo rural en la Argentina: viejos y nuevos actores en el mercado de trabajo. In *Empleo Rural en Tiempos de Flexibilidad*, ed. S Aparicio, R Benencia, pp. 29–76. Buenos Aires: La Colmena

Aparicio S, Benencia R. 2001. Los asalariados rurales en la investigacíon social. In *Antiguos y Nuevos Asalariados en el Agro Argentino*, ed. S Aparicio, R Benencia, pp. 1–14. Buenos Aires: La Colmena

Aparicio S, Ortiz S. 2001. *La globalización y la transformación de la industria citrícola en Tucumán, Argentina*. Paper presented at the XXIII Congress of the Latin Am. Stud. Assoc., Washington, DC

Applebaum H. 1999. *Construction Workers, U.S.A*. Westport, CT: Greenwood

Asher R, Edsforth R, eds. 1995. *Autowork*. Binghampton: State Univ. NY Press

Bach R. 1985. Political framework for international migrations. See Sanderson 1985

Band M. 1992. Sugar and unfree labour: reflection on labour control in the Dominican Republic: 1870–1935. *J. Peasant Stud.* 19:301–25

Bardhan P, Rudra A. 1981. Terms and conditions of labour contracts in agriculture: results of a survey in west Bengal, 1979. *Oxford Bull. Econ. Stat.* 43:89–111

Becerril O. 1995. ¿Como las trabajadoras agrícolas de la flor en México, hacen femenino el proceso del trabajo en el que participan? See Flores 1995, pp.181–93

Beinart W. 1980. Labour migrancy and rural production: Pondoland: 1900–1950. In *Black Villagers in an Industrial Society*, ed. P Mayer, pp. 81–108. Oxford: Oxford Univ. Press

Bendini M, Pescio C, Palomares M. 1995. El mercado del trabajo y los cambios técnicos en la fruticultura Argentina: las trabajadoras en los galpones de empaque de manzanas y peras. See Flores 1995, pp. 49–61

Bendini M, Radonich MM, Steimbreger NG. 1999. Historia de la vulnerabilidad social de los "golondrinas" en la cuenca frutícola de Río Negro. See Bendini & Radonich 1999, pp. 31–51

Bendini MI, Radonich MM, eds. 1999. *De Golondrinas y Otros Migrantes*. Buenos Aires: Editorial La Colmena

Benecia R, Quaranta G. 2001. *Reestructuracíón y contratos de mediería en producciones agropecuarias de la región pampeana Argentina*. Paper presented at the XXIII Congress of Latin Am. Stud. Assoc., Washington, DC, September 6–8

Borjas G, Tienda M. 1985. *Hispanics in the U.S. Economy*. Orlando, FL: Academic

Bourgois P. 1988. Conjugated oppression: class and ethnicity among the Guaymi and Kuna banana workers. *Am. Ethnol.* 15:328–48

Bourgois P. 1989. *Ethnicity at Work: Divided Labor on a Central American Banana Plantation*. Baltimore, MD: John Hopkins Univ. Press

Bonacich E. 1994. Asians in the Los Angeles garment industry. In *The New Asian Immigration in Los Angeles and Global Restructuring*, ed. P Ong, E Bonacich, L Cheng, pp. 137–64. Philadelphia: Temple Univ. Press

Boyd M. 1989. Family and personal networks in migration. *Int. Migration Rev.* 27:638–70

Brass T. 1997a. Some observations on unfree labour, capitalist restructuring and deproletarianization. See Brass & van der Linden 1997, pp. 31–50

Brass T. 1997b. Immobilized workers, footloose theory. *J. Peasant Stud.* 24:337–58

Brass T. 1999. *Towards a Comparative Political Economy of Unfree Labour*. London: Cass

Brass T. 2000. Labour in post-colonial India: a response to Jan Breman. *J. Peasants Stud.* 28:126–46

Brass T, van der Linden M, eds. 1997. *Free and Unfree Labour: the Debate Continues*. New York: Lang

Braverman H. 1974. *Labour and Monopoly Capital: the Degradation of Work in the Twentieth Century*. New York: Mon. Rev.

Breman J. 1974. *Patronage and Exploitation; Changing Agrarian Relations in South Gujarat, India*. Berkeley: Univ. Calif. Press

Breman J. 1985. *Of Peasants, Migrants and Paupers*. Oxford: Clarendon

Breman J. 1996. *Footloose Labour: Working in India's Informal Economy*. Cambridge, UK: Cambridge Univ. Press

Breman J. 1999. The study of industrial labour in India—the informal sector: a concluding review. In *The Worlds of Industrial Labour*, ed. J Parry, J Breman, K Kapadia, pp. 407–32. Thousand Oaks, CA: Sage

Briody EK. 1989. *Household Labor Patterns Among Mexican Americans in South Texas: Buscando Trabajo Seguro*. New York: AMS

Burawoy M. 1976. The functions and reproduction of migrant labor: comparative material from southern Africa and the United States. *Am. J. Sociol.* 81:1050–87

Burawoy M. 1979. *Manufacturing Consent: Changes in the Labor Process Under Monopoly Capitalism*. Chicago: Univ. Chicago Press

Campi D. 1991. Captación y retención de la mano de obra por endeudamiento. El caso de Tucumán en la segunda mitad del siglo XIX. In *Estudios Sobre la Historia de la Industria Azucarera Argentina*, Vol. I, ed. D Campi, pp.179–212. San Miguel de Tucumán: Facultad Economía, Univ. Nac. Tucumán

Carr B. 1998. "Omnipotent and omnipresent"? Labor shortage, worker mobility and employer control in the Cuban sugar industry, 1910–1934. In *Identity and Struggle at the Margins of the Nation-State: the Laboring Peoples of Central America and the Hispanic Caribbean*, ed. A Chomsky, A Lauria-Santiago, pp. 260–92. Durham, NC: Duke Univ. Press

Cartwright J. 1991. *Unequal Bargaining: a Study in Vitiating Factors in the Formation of Contracts*. Oxford: Clarendon

Cerutti A, Pito C. 1999. Cuando los hombres cruzan la cordillera. Los chilenos en el Territorio de Neuquén, 1884–1930. See Bendini & Rodonich 1999, pp. 9–28

Chomsky A. 1998. Laborers and smallholders in Costa Rica's mining communities. In *Identity and Struggle at the Margins of the Nation-State: the Laboring Peoples of Central America and the Hispanic Caribbean*, ed. A Chomsky, A Lauria-Santiago, pp. 169–96. Durham, NC: Duke Univ. Press

Cohen R. 1987. *The New Helots. Migrants and the International Division of Labour*. Brookfield, VT: Avebury

Collins J. 1993. Gender, contracts and wage work: agricultural restructuring in Brazil's São Francisco Valley. *Develop. Change* 24:53–82

Collins J. 1995. Transnational labor process and gender relations: women in fruit and vegetable production in Chile, Brazil and Mexico. *J. Latin Am. Anthropol.* 1:178–99

Collins J, Krippner G. 1999. Permanent labor contracts in agriculture: flexibility and subordination in a new export crop. *Comp. Stud. Soc. Hist.* 41:510–34

Crisp J. 1983. Productivity and protest. Scientific management in the Ghanian gold mines, 1947–1956. In *Struggle for the City: Migrant Labor, Capital and the State in Urban Africa*, ed. F Cooper, pp. 91–139. Beverly Hills, CA: Sage

Dandler J, Madeiros C. 1988. Temporary migrations from Cochabamba, Bolivia to Argentina. In *When Borders Don't Divide: Labor Migrations and Refugee Movements in the Americas*, ed. PR Pessnar, pp. 8–41. New York: Cent. Migr. Stud.

De Neve G. 1999. Asking for and giving Baki: neo-bondage or the interplay of bondage and resistance in the Tamilnadu power-loom industry. In *The Worlds of Industrial Indian Labour*, ed. J Parry, J Breman, K Kapadia, pp. 379–407. Thousand Oaks, CA: Sage

De Neve G. 2001. *Towards an ethnography of the workplace: hierarchy, authority and sociability on the south Indian textile shop floor*. Paper presented at School of African and Asian Studies, University of Sussex, Falmer, Brighton, UK

Doeringer PB, Moss P, Terkla D. 1986. *The New England Fishing Economy: Jobs, Income and Kinship*. Amherst: Univ. Mass. Press

Edwards R. 1979. *Contested Terrain: the Transformation of the Workplace in the Twentieth Century*. New York: Basic Books

Emerson RD, ed. 1984. *Seasonal Agricultural Labor Markets in the United States*. Ames: Iowa Univ. Press

Errazuriz M. 1986. *Cafeteros y Cafetales del Líbano*. Bogotá: Univ. Nac.

Fernandes L. 1997. *Producing Workers: the Politics of Gender, Class and Culture in the Calcutta Jute Mills*. Philadelphia: Univ. Penn. Press

Fernandez-Kelly MP. 1983. *For We are Sold, I and My People: Women and Industry in Mexico Frontier*. Albany: State Univ. NY Press

Fernandez-Kelly MP. 1985. Contemporary production and the new international division of labor. See Sanderson 1985, pp. 206–25

Fink D. 1998. *Cutting into the Meatpacking Line: Workers and Change in the Rural Midwest*. Chapel Hill: Univ. N.C. Press

Flores SML, ed. 1995. *Jornaleras, Temporeras y Bóias Frias: El Rostro Femenino del Mercado del Trabajo Rural en America Latina*. Caracas: Ed. Nueva Sociedad

Forni FB. 1988. Asalariados y campesinos pobres: el recurso familiar y la producción de la mano de obra. *Desarrollo Económico* 28:245–79

Forni F, Benencia R, Neiman G. 1991. *Empleo, Estrategias de Vida y Reproducción. Hogares Rurales en Santiago del Estero*. Buenos Aires: Centr. Estud. Investig. Labor.

Fröbel F, Heinrich J, Kreye O. 1980. *The New International Division of Labour*. Cambridge, UK: Cambridge Univ. Press

Gannagé C. 1986. *Double Day, Double Bind: Women Garment Workers*. Toronto: Women's Press

Gartman D. 1986. *Auto Slavery: the Labor Process in the American Automobile Industry*, 1897–1950. New Brunswick, NJ: Rutgers Univ. Press

Georges E. 1990. *The Making of a Transnational Community: Migration, Development and Cultural Change in the Dominican Republic*. New York: Columbia Univ. Press

Giarracca N, ed. 2000. *Tucumanos y Tucumanas: Zafra, Trabajo, Migraciones e Identidad*. Buenos Aires: La Colmena

Giusti-Cordero JA. 1997. Labour, ecology and history in a Puerto Rican plantation region: "classic" rural proletarians revisited. See Amin & van der Linden 1997, pp. 53–82

Godoy RA. 1990. *Mining and Agriculture in Highland Bolivia: Ecology, History and Commerce Among the Jukumanis*. Tucson: Univ. Ariz. Press

Gómez Jiménez A, Díaz Mesas LM. 1983. *La Moderna Esclavitud: los Indocumentados en Venezuela*. Bogotá: Oveja Negra

González GG. 1994. *Labor and Community: Mexican Citrus Worker Villages in Southern California County, 1900–1950*. Urbana: Univ. Ill. Press

Gonzales MJ. 1985. *Plantation Agriculture and Social Control in Northern Peru, 1875–1933*. Austin: Univ. Tex. Press

Gordon D, Edwards R, Reich M. 1982. *Segmented Work, Divided Workers*. Cambridge, UK: Cambridge Univ. Press

Gough K. 1987. Socio-economic change in southeast India. *J. Contemp. Asia* 17:276–92

Granovetter M. 1973. The strength of weak ties. *Am. J. Sociol.* 78:1360–80

Grey MA. 1996. Patronage, kinship and recruitment of a Lao and Mennonite labor to Storm Lake, Iowa. *Culture Agric.* 18(1):14–18

Grieco M. 1996. *Workers Dilemmas: Recruitment, Reliability and Repeated Exchange: an Analysis of Urban Social Networks and Labour Circulation*. London: Routledge

Grieco M, Whipp R. 1986. Woman and the workplace: gender and control in the workplace. In *Gender and the Labour Process*, ed. D Knight, H Willmott. Brookfield, VT: Gower

Griffith D. 1993. *Jones Minimal: Low-Wage Labor in the United States*. New York: State Univ. NY Press

Griffith D, Kissam E. 1995. *Working Poor: Farmworkers in the United States*. Philadelphia: Temple Univ. Press

Grijns M. 1992. Mediating women: labor brokerage by mandors in West Java. In *Women and Mediation in Indonesia*, ed. S van Bemmelen, pp. 65–87. Leiden: KITLV

Guy DJ. 1978. The rural working class in nineteenth century: forced plantation labor in Tucumán. *Latin Am. Res. Rev.* 13:135–45

Hagan JM. 1994. *Deciding to be Legal: Maya Community in Houston*. Philadelphia: Temple Univ. Press

Hahamovitch C. 1997. *The Fruits of Their Labor. Atlantic Coast Farmworkers and the Making of Migrants Poverty, 1870–1945*. Chapel Hill: Univ. N.C. Press

Hanson S, Pratt G. 1995. *Gender, Work and Space*. New York: Routledge

Hart G. 1986a. *Power, Labour and Livelihood: Process of Change in Rural Java*. Berkeley: Univ. Calif. Press

Hart G. 1986b. Interlocking transactions. Obstacles, precursors or instruments of agrarian capitalism? *J. Dev. Econ.* 23:117–203

Hart G. 1989. Agrarian change in the context of state patronage. In *Agrarian Transformations: Local Processes and the State in Southeast Asia*, ed. G Hart, A Turton, B White, pp. 31–51. Berkeley: Univ. Calf. Press

Hataya N. 1992. Urban-rural linkage of the labor market in a coffee growing zone in Colombia. *Dev. Econ.* 30:63–83

Holloway TH. 1980. "*Immigrants on the Land.*" *Coffee and Society in São Paulo, 1886–1934*. Chapell Hill: Univ. N.C. Press

Holzberg CL, Giovannini MJ. 1981. Anthropology and industry: appraisal and new directions. *Annu. Rev. Anthropol.* 10:317–60

Iglesias Prieto N. 1997 [1985]. *Beautiful Flowers of the Maquiladora. Life Histories of Women Workers in Tijuana*. Austin: Univ. Tex. Press

Jain S. 1998. Gender relations and the plantations system in Assam, India. In *Woman Plantation Workers*, ed. S Jain, R Reddock, pp. 107–29. New York: Berg

Kameir El Wathig M. 1988. *The Political Economy of Labor Migration in Sudan. A Comparative Study of Migrant Workers in an Urban Situation*. Hamburg: Institut für Afrika-Kunde

Kar RK. 1984. Labour patterns and absenteeism: a case study in tea plantations in Assam, India. *Anthropos* 79:13–24

Kay C. 2000. Latin America's agrarian transformation: peasantization and proletarianization. In *Disappearing Peasantries? Rural Labour in Africa, Asia and Latin America*, ed. D Bryceson, C Kay, J Mooij. London: Intermed. Technol.

Kearney M. 1996. *Reconceptualizing the Peasantry. Anthropology in Global Perspective*. Boulder, CO: Westview

Kearney M, Nagengast C. 1989. *Anthropological perspectives on transnational communities in rural California*. Calif. Inst. Rural Studies Work. Group on Farm Labor and Rural Poverty, Work Pap. No. 3

Kim SK. 1992. Women workers and the labor movement in South Korea. In *Anthropology and the Global Factory*, ed. FA Rothstein, ML Blim, pp. 220–38. New York: Bergin & Garvey

Kim SK. 1997. *Class Struggle or Family Struggle? The Lives of Women Factory Workers in South Korea*. Cambridge, UK: Cambridge Univ. Press

Knight R. 1972. *Sugar Plantations and Labor Patterns in the Cauca Valley, Colombia*. Univ. Toronto, Anthropol. Ser. No. 12

Krissman F. 1996. *California agribusiness and Mexican farm workers (1942–1992): a bi-national agricultural system of production/reproduction*. PhD thesis. Univ. Calif., Santa Barbara

Krissman F. 1997. Farm labor systems in California (1769–1994): a case study in historical variations between free and unfree labor. See Brass & van der Linden 1997, pp. 201–38

Kurian R. 1998. Tamil women on Sri Lankan plantation: labour control and patriarchy. In *Women Plantation Workers*, ed. S Jain, R Reddock, pp. 67–89. New York: Berg

Lagos M. 1992. Conformación del Mercado Laboral en la Etapa de Despegue de los Ingenios Azucareros Saltojujeños. In *Estudios Sobre la Historia Industrial Azucarera Argentina*, Vol. II, ed. D Campi, pp. 51–91. San Miguel de Tucumán: Facultad Economía, Univ. Nac. Tucumán

Laliberte R, Satzewich V. 1999. Native migrant labour in the southern Alberta sugar-beet industry: coercion and paternalism in the recruitment of labour. *Can. Rev. Sociol. Anthropol.* 36:65–85

Lamphere L. 1987. *From Working Daughters to Working Mothers: Immigrant Women in a New England Industrial Community*. Ithaca, NY: Cornell Univ. Press

Lara Flores SM. 1995. La femininación del trabajo asalariado en los cultivos de exportación no tradicional en America Latina. In *Jornaleras, Temporeras y Bóias Frias: El Rostro Femenino del Mercado del Trabajo en America Latina*, ed. SM Flores, pp. 13–35. UNRISD. Caracas: NuevaSociedad

Lara Flores SM. 1998. *Nuevas Experiencias Productivas y Nuevas Formas de Organización Flexible del Trabajo en la Agricultura Mexicana.* Mexico City: Juan Pablo

Levy N. 1982. *The Foundations of the South African Cheap Labour System.* London: Routledge, Kegan Paul

Long N, Roberts B. 1984. *Miners, Peasants and Entrepreneurs. Regional Development in the Central Highland of Peru.* Cambridge, UK: Cambridge Univ. Press

Lycklama à Nijeholt G. 1980. *On the Road for Work: Migratory Workers on the East Coast of the United States.* Boston: Martinus Nijhoff

Martin P. 1988. *Harvest of Confusion. Migrant Workers in U.S. Agriculture.* Boulder, CO: Westview

Martin P. 1989. *The California Farm Labor Market.* Calif. Inst. Rural Studies Work. Group on Farm Labor and Rural Poverty, Work. Pap. No. 4

Martin P. 1996. *Promises to Keep: Collective Bargaining in Californian Agriculture.* Ames: Iowa Univ. Press

Martinez S. 1995. *Peripheral Migrants, Haitians and Dominican Republic Sugar Plantations.* Knoxville: Univ. Tenn. Press

Martinez S. 1999. From hidden hand to heavy hand: sugar, the state and labor in Haiti and the Dominican Republic. *Latin Am. Res. Rev.* 34:57–85

Massey DS, Alarcon R, Durand J, Gonzalez H. 1987. *Return to Aztlan: the Social Process of Migration from Western Mexico.* Berkeley: Univ. Calif. Press

Miller S. 1964. *The Hacienda and the Plantation in Northern Peru.* Washington, DC: Dumbarton Oaks

Mines R. 1981. *Developing a Community Tradition of Migration to the United States.* La Jolla, CA: Cen. U.S. Mexican Stud.

Mintz S. 1960. *Workers in the Cane.* New Haven, CT: Yale Univ. Press

Mintz S. 1979. The rural proletariat and problems of the rural proletariat consciousness. In *Peasant and Proletarians: The Struggle of Third World Workers*, ed. R Cohen, PCW Gutkind, P Brazier, pp. 173–98. London: Hutchinson

Moberg M. 1996. Myths that divide: immigrant labor and class segmentation in the Belizean banana industry. *Am. Ethnol.* 23:311–30

Moberg M. 1997. *Myth of Ethnicity and Nation: Immigration, Work and Identity in the Belize Banana Industry.* Knoxville: Univ. Tenn. Press

Morgan DH. 1982. *Harvesters and Harvesting, 1840–1900.* London: Croom Helm

Murphy AD, Blanchard C, Hill JA. 2001. *Latino Workers in the Contemporary South.* Athens: Univ. Ga. Press

Murray C. 1981. *Families Divided: The Impact of Migrant Labour in Lesotho.* Cambridge, UK: Cambridge Univ. Press

Nash J. 1979. *We Eat the Mines and the Mines Eat Us.* New York: Columbia Univ. Press

Nash J. 1985. Segmentation of the work process in the international division of labor. See Sanderson 1985, pp. 253–72

Nash J, Fernandez-Kelly MP, eds. 1983. *Women, Men and the International Division of Labor.* Albany: City Univ. NY Press

Neiman G, Quarantas G. 2000. Reestructuracion de la producción y flexibilidad funcional del trabajo agrícola en la Argentina. *Estud. Trabajo* 6(12):45–71

Ong A. 1987. *Spirit of Resistance and Capitalist Discipline: Factory Women in Malasya.* Albany: State Univ. NY Press

Ong A. 1991. The gender and labor politics of postmodernity. *Annu. Rev. Anthropol.* 20: 279–309

Ortiz S. 1999. *Harvesting Coffee, Bargaining Wages. Rural Labor Markets in Colombia, 1975–1990.* Ann Arbor: Univ. Mich. Press

Ortiz S. 2001. *Bargaining Wages and Controlling Performance. Harvest in Coffee and Citrus.* Paper presented at the Soc. Econ. Anthropol. Annu. Conf., Milwaukee, WI

Ortiz S. 2002. *Harvest Management Response to the Demands of Fresh Fruit Markets*. Paper to be presented at the 2002 Annu. Meet. Soc. Adv. Socio-Economics, Minneapolis, MN

Pahl RE. 1984. *Divisions of Labour*. Oxford: Blackwell

Palmer R. 1986. Working conditions and workers responses on Nayasaland tea estates 1930–1953. *J. African Hist.* 27:105–26

Parry J. 1999. Introduction. In *The Worlds of Indian Labour*, ed. J Parry, J Breman, K Kapadia, pp. IX–XXXVI. Thousand Oaks, CA: Sage

Patnaik U. 1995. On capitalism and agrestic unfreedom. *Int. Rev. Soc. Hist.* 40:77–92

Peck J. 1996. *Work Place: The Social Regulation of Labour Markets*. New York: Guildford

Peloso VC. 1999. *Peasants on Plantations: Subaltern Strategies of Labor Resistance in the Pisco Valley, Peru*. Durham, NC: Duke Univ. Press

Peña DG. 1997. *The Terror of the Machine: Technology, Work, Gender and Ecology on the U.S.-Mexico Border*. Austin: Univ. Tex. Press

Piore M. 1979. *Birds of Passage: Migrant Labor and Industrial Society*. Cambridge, UK: Cambridge Univ. Press

Platteau JP. 1995. A framework for the analysis of evolving patron-client ties in agrarian economies. *World Dev.* 23:767–86

Polopoulus LC, Emerson R. 1991. Entrepreneurship, sanctions and labor contracting. *South. J. Agric. Econ.* 23:57–68

Portes A, Bach RL. 1995. *Latin Journey: Cuban and Mexican Migrants in the U.S.* Berkeley: Univ. Calif. Press

Portes A, Walton J. 1981. *Labor, Class and the International System*. New York: Academic

Prakash G. 1997. Colonialism, capitalism and the discourse on freedom. See Amin & van der Linden 1997

Quaranta G. 2001. Organización del trabajo y trabajadores en la producción lechera de la pampa húmeda bonaerense. In *Antiguos y Nuevos Asalariados en el Agro Argentino*, ed. G Neiman, S Aparicio, R Benencia, pp. 117–37. Buenos Aires: La Colmena

Rafel L. 1992. Rethinking modernity: space and factory discipline in China. *Cult. Anthropol.* 7:93–114

Ramachandran VK. 1990. *Wage Labour and Unfreedom in Agriculture. An Indian Case Study*. Oxford: Clarendon

Rao JM. 1999. Agrarian power and unfree labor. *J. Peasant Stud.* 26:242–62

Reboratti C. 1983. *Peón Golondrina: Cosecha y Migraciones en la Argentina*. Buenos Aires: Cuadernos del CENEP No. 24

Richards A. 1979. The political economy of Gutswirthschaft: a comparative analysis of East Elbian Germany, Egypt and Chile. *Comp. Stud. Soc. Hist.* 21:483–518

Robertson AF. 1987. *The Dynamics of Productive Relations: African Share Contracts in Comparative Perspective*. Cambridge, UK: Cambridge Univ. Press

Rothstein FA. 1992. What happened to the past? Return industrial migrants in Latin America. In *Anthropology and the Global Factory. Studies of the New Industrialization in the Late Twentieth Century*, ed. AF Rothstein, ML Blim, pp. 33–47. New York: Bergin & Garvey

Russell S. 1994. Institutionalizing opportunism: cheating on baby purse seiners in Batangas Bay, Philippines. In *Anthropology and Institutional Economics*, ed. J Acheson, pp. 87–108. Monograph in Economic Anthropology no. 12. Langham, MD: Univ. Press Am.

Rutledge I. 1987. *Cambio Agrario e Integración. El Desarrollo del Capitalismo en Jujuy. 1550–1960*. Buenos Aires: Serie Monográfica, Antropología Social e Historia, Univ. Buenos Aires

Sanderson SE, ed. 1985. *The Americas in the New International Division of Labor*. New York: Holmes & Meier

Santamaría D. 1986. *Azucar y Sociedad en el Noroeste Argentino*. Buenos Aires: IDES

Schaffner JA. 1993. Rural labor legislation and permanent agricultural employment in northeastern Brazil. *World Dev.* 21:705–19

Scobie JR. 1977. *Revolution in the Pampas*. Austin: Univ. Tex. Press

Scott J. 1985. *Weapons of the Weak: Everyday Forms of Peasant Resistance*. New Haven, CT: Yale Univ. Press

Sen S. 1997. Unsettling the household: act VI (of 1901) and the regulation of women migrants in Colonial Bengal. See Amin & van der Linden 1997, pp. 65–87

Simeon D. 1997. Coal and colonialism: production relations in an Indian coalfield, c.1895–1947. See Amin & van der Linden 1997, pp. 83–108

Sosnick SH. 1978. *Hired Hands. Seasonal Farmworkers in the United States*. Santa Barbara, CA: McNally & Loftin West

Stichter S. 1985. *Migrant Laborers*. Cambridge, UK: Cambridge Univ. Press

Stolcke V. 1988. *Coffee Planters, Workers and Wives. Class Conflict and Gender Relations on São Paulo Plantations 1859–1980*. London: Macmillan

Tatar B. 1998. Coffee workers in Buenos Aires, Costa Rica: the daily grind with the seventh death. *Vinculos. Rev. Antropol. Mus. Nac. Costa Rica* 23:58–78

Taussig M. 1977. The evolution of rural wage labour in the Cauca Valley of Colombia 1700–1970. In *Land and Labour in Latin America. Essays in the Development of Agrarian Capitalism in the Nineteenth and Twentieth Century*, ed. K Duncan, I Rutledge, pp. 397–435. Cambridge, UK: Cambridge Univ. Press

Teeringk R. 1995. Migrating and its impact on Khandeshi women in the sugar cane harvest. In *Women and Seasonal Labor Migrations*, ed. L Schenk-Sandbergen, pp. 210–300. New Dehli: Sage

Teruel de Lagos A. 1991. Regulación legal del trabajo en haciendas, ingenios y plantaciones de Caña de Azúcar en la provincia de Jujuy. In *Estudios Sobre la Historia de la Industria Azucarera Argentina*, Vol. I, ed. D Campi, pp. 139–79. San Miguel de Tucumán: Facultad Economía, Univ. Nac. Tucumán

Thomas RJ. 1985. *Citizenship, Gender and Work. Social Organization of Industrial Agriculture*. Stanford, CA: Stanford Univ. Press

Thompson P. 1983. *The Nature of Work*. London: MacMillan

Tiano S. 1994. *Patriarchy on the Line: Labor, Gender and Ideology on the Mexican Maquila Industry*. Philadelphia: Temple Univ. Press

Torres G. 1997. *The Force of Irony: Power in the Everyday Life of Tomato Workers*. Oxford: Berg

Toth J. 1993. Manufacturing consent. "Resistance in peripheral production." *Dialect. Anthropol.* 18:291–335

Tsakoumagkos P, Bendini M. 2000. Modernización agroindustrial y mercado de trabajo. ¿Flexibilización o precarización? El caso de la fruticultura en la cuenca del Río Negro. *Rev. Latinoam. Estud. Trabajo* 6(12):89–113

Turton A. 1986. Patrolling the middle-ground: methodological perspectives on 'everyday peasant resistance.' In *Everyday Forms of Resistance in South-East Asia*, ed. J Scott, BJT Kerkvliet, pp. 36–48. London: Frank Cass

Valdes DN. 1991. *Al Norte: Agricultural Workers in the Great Lake Region, 1917–1970*, Austin: Univ. Tex. Press

Van der Klei JM. 1985. Articulation of modes of production and the beginning of labour migrations among the Diola of Senegal. In *Old Modes of Production and Capitalist Encroachment. Anthropological Explorations in Africa*, ed. W van Binsbergen, P Geschiere, pp. 79–94. London: Routledge & Kegan Paul

Vandeman AM. 1988. *Labor contracting in California agriculture*. PhD dissertation. Univ. Calif., Berkeley

Vandeman AM, Sadoulet E, de Janvry A. 1991. Labor contracting and the theory of contract choice in California agriculture. *Am. J. Agric. Econ.* 67:681–92

Vaupel S, Martin P. 1986. Farm labor contractors. *Calif. Agric.* March–April:12–15

Waylen G. 2000. Gendered political economy and feminist analysis. In *Towards a Gendered Political Economy*, ed. J Cook, J Roberts, G Waylen, pp. 14–38. London: MacMillan

Weber D. 1994. *Dark Sweat, White Gold: California Farm Workers and the New Deal.* Berkeley: Univ. Calif. Press

Wells M. 1984. The resurgence of sharecropping: historical anomaly or political strategy? *Am. J. Sociol.* 90:1–29

Wells M. 1996. *Strawberry Fields. Politics, Class and Work in California Agriculture.* Ithaca, NY: Cornell Univ. Press

Wertheimer BM. 1977. *We Were There. The Story of Working Women in America.* New York: Pantheon

White C. 1988. Why do workers bother? *Crit. Anthropol.* 7(3):51–68

Whiteford S. 1981. *Workers from the North. Plantations, Bolivian Labor and the City in Northern Argentina.* Austin: Univ. Tex. Press

Wigfield A. 2001. *Post-Fordism, Gender and Work.* Burlington, VT: Ashgate

Willson P. 1993. *The Clockwork Factory. Women and Work in Fascist Italy.* Oxford: Clarendon

Wolf DL. 1992. *Factory Daughters. Gender Household Dynamics in Java.* Berkeley: Univ. Calif. Press

Wolpe H. 1972. Capitalism and cheap labour power in South Africa: from segregation to apartheidism. *Econ. Soc.* 1:425–56

Wood CH, McCoy T. 1985. Caribbean cane cutters in Florida: implications for the study of the internationalization of labor. See Sanderson 1985, pp. 125–44

Woodiwiss A. 1987. The discourse on production (Part II): the contract of employment and the emergence of Democratic capitalist law in Britain and the United States. *Econ. Soc.* 16:441–525

Zavella P. 1987. *Women's Work and Chicano Families. Cannery Workers in the Santa Clara Valley.* Ithaca: Cornell Univ. Press

Annu. Rev. Anthropol. 2002. 31:419–47
doi: 10.1146/annurev.anthro.31.040402.085432

First published online as a Review in Advance on June 14, 2002

MIGRANT "ILLEGALITY" AND DEPORTABILITY IN EVERYDAY LIFE

Nicholas P. De Genova
Department of Anthropology and Latina/o Studies, Columbia University, 1130 Amsterdam Avenue, New York, NY 10027; email: npd18@columbia.edu

Key Words undocumented migration/immigration, illegal aliens, law, labor, space, racialization, United States, Mexican/Latin American

■ **Abstract** This article strives to meet two challenges. As a review, it provides a critical discussion of the scholarship concerning undocumented migration, with a special emphasis on ethnographically informed works that foreground significant aspects of the everyday life of undocumented migrants. But another key concern here is to formulate more precisely the theoretical status of migrant "illegality" and deportability in order that further research related to undocumented migration may be conceptualized more rigorously. This review considers the study of migrant "illegality" as an epistemological, methodological, and political problem, in order to then formulate it as a theoretical problem. The article argues that it is insufficient to examine the "illegality" of undocumented migration only in terms of its consequences and that it is necessary also to produce historically informed accounts of the sociopolitical processes of "illegalization" themselves, which can be characterized as the legal production of migrant "illegality."

INTRODUCTION

Illegal immigration has emerged as a generalized fact in virtually all of the wealthiest nation-states (Sassen 1998; 1999, p. 143) as well as in many regional centers of production and consumption (Harris 1995) during the post–World War II era, regardless of the political culture or particular migration policies of any given state. Migrant "illegality" has risen to unprecedented prominence as a "problem" in policy debates and as an object of border policing strategies for states around the world. The literature written in English on migrant "illegality" is predominantly focused on undocumented migration to the United States (cf. Harris 1995) and especially on undocumented Mexican migration. There are, of course, historical reasons for this uneven development in scholarship.

In Europe, "illegal immigration . . . has emerged as a major issue" only "in the last few years" (Sassen 1999, p. 104). By the 1970s, several Western European states—as well as Australia, Canada, Venezuela, and Argentina—were already attempting to "regularize" undocumented migrants by recourse to "legalization" procedures (adjustments of status) and official "amnesties": 12,000 were "legalized" in Belgium in 1974; 15,000 in the Netherlands in 1975; 140,000 in France in 1981; 44,000 in Spain in 1986, and 104,000 more in 1991 (Soysal 1994, p. 132); 15,000 in Australia and 30,000 in Venezuela by the early 1990s (Hagan 1994, p. 174; cf. Meissner et al. 1986). Yet these figures are dwarfed by the 3.2 million undocumented migrants "legalized" in the United States following the 1986 "amnesty." Moreover, the U.S. Border Patrol's apprehension and deportation practices began in the 1920s [contrast this with the case of Japan, where migrant "illegality" was made an object of law only in 1990, as Sassen (1998) points out]. The geographical unevenness of the scholarly literature on undocumented migration reflects its character as a response to real sociopolitical transformations. Predictably, the revision of analytic frameworks and the development of new theoretical perspectives have tended to lag far behind the sheer restlessness of life.

Thus, this essay strives to meet two challenges. As a review essay, it provides a critical discussion of the scholarship on undocumented migration, with a special emphasis on ethnographically informed works that foreground significant aspects of the everyday life of undocumented migrants. Other reviews in this series that have addressed some of the broader themes that frame the specific concern of this essay include Alonso (1994), Alvarez (1995), Kearney (1986, 1995), and Ortiz (this volume). But another key concern here is to formulate more precisely the theoretical status of the themes of migrant "illegality" and deportability in order that further research related to undocumented migration may be conceptualized more rigorously.

THE STUDY OF MIGRANT "ILLEGALITY" AS AN EPISTEMOLOGICAL, METHODOLOGICAL, AND POLITICAL PROBLEM

There is a vast social science literature on so-called "illegal aliens" and "illegal immigration." At the outset, it is worthwhile dwelling for a moment on the terminologies that signal more fundamental analytic categories that operate pervasively in the formulation of the subject at hand. In this essay, the term undocumented will be consistently deployed in place of the category "illegal" as well as other, less obnoxious but not less problematic proxies for it, such as "extra-legal," "unauthorized," "irregular," or "clandestine." Throughout the ensuing text, I deploy quotes in order to denaturalize the reification of this distinction wherever the term "illegality" appears, as well as wherever the terms "legal" or "illegal" modify migration or migrants. Thus, the appearance of quotes around these terms should not be understood to indicate the precise terminology that pertains in any particular nation-state context, or any historically specific instance, or any particular author's usage, so much as a general analytic practice on my part. Likewise, the term "migration" will be consistently deployed here to supplant "immigration." Unless referring specifically to immigration law or policy, I also deploy quotes wherever the terms "immigration" or "immigrant" appear, in order to problematize the implicitly unilinear teleology of these categories (posited always from the standpoint of the migrant-receiving nation-state, in terms of outsiders coming in, presumably to stay). This strategy allows me to problematize the way that U.S. nationalism, in particular, interpellates historically specific migrations in its production of "immigration" and "immigrant" as an essentialized, generic, and singular object, subordinated to that same teleology by which migrants inexorably become permanent settlers and the U.S. nation-state assumes the form of a "promised land"—a self-anointed refuge of liberty and opportunity. [For an expanded treatment of this "immigrant" essentialism and the figure of "the immigrant" as an object of U.S. nationalism, see De Genova (1999, pp. 67–104; n.d.); (cf. Chock 1991 and Honig 1998, 2001)].

The conceptual problems embedded in terminology are symptomatic of deeper problems of intellectual—and ultimately political—orientation. Remarkably, little of this vast scholarship deploys ethnographic methods or other qualitative research techniques to elicit the perspectives and experiences of undocumented migrants themselves, or to evoke the kinds of densely descriptive and textured interpretive representations of everyday life that sociocultural anthropologists tend to relish. If, as Kearney (1986, p. 331) has suggested, the academic home of migration studies was long a murky "back room of demography," where it did not receive much attention from anthropologists, then surely the study of undocumented migration has long been lost in the shuffle somewhere in a corridor between demography, policy studies, and criminology. Indeed, much of the scholarship has been persistently prescriptive, either explicitly promulgating one or another purported "solution" to the putative "problem," or simply deploying the entire arsenal of social scientific objectivities in order to assess the presumed "successes" or "failures" of such legislative strategies or administrative and enforcement tactics. Portes (1978) made this point nearly 25 years ago, and the situation is not drastically different today. As he explained at that time, "The reasons for this emphasis are not difficult to determine. Illegal immigration is one of those issues in which the interests of scholars and government agencies converge. Hence, much of the recent literature aims at an audience composed of decision-makers . . . " (1978, p. 469). The concern of such researchers with policy-relevance, now as then, entails presuppositions through which research is effectively formulated and conducted from the standpoint of the state, with all of its ideological conceits more or less conspicuously smuggled in tow. In contrast, from the standpoint of "the free movement of people," as Harris puts it, "the problem is the state rather than those who are mobile" (Harris 1995, p. 85; cf. Carens 1987). Assuming that undocumented migration is indeed a "problem," that the state genuinely seeks to remedy this situation on behalf of the majority of its citizenry and that the state is capable of actually effecting the recommendations of such studies, "studies which examine the problem within officially pre-established limits [. . .] yield a constrained and impoverished product" (1978, p. 470). "If governmental definitions of reality do not coincide with those of other actors in the system," Whiteford elaborates, "that should not come as a surprise. What does seem surprising is that social scientists . . . share the worldview of the bureaucrats" (1979, p. 134).

"Illegality" (much like citizenship) is a juridical status that entails a social relation to the state; as such, migrant "illegality" is a preeminently political identity. To conduct research related to the undocumented noncitizens of a particular nation-state from the unexamined standpoint of its citizens, then, involves the kind of uncritical ethnocentrism that is, by definition, a perversion of anthropology's putative aims as a distinctive mode of inquiry (De Genova 1999, 2003). There is a still deeper methodological problem, however. It is necessary to distinguish between studying undocumented people, on the one hand, and studying "illegality" and deportability, on the other. The familiar pitfalls by which ethnographic objectification becomes a kind of anthropological pornography—showing it just to show it, as it were—become infinitely more complicated here by the danger that ethnographic disclosure can quite literally become a kind of surveillance, effectively complicit with if not altogether in the service of the state. As Foucault observes, in his characteristic style that so elegantly states the obvious, "the existence of a legal prohibition creates around it a field of illegal practices" (1979, p. 280). In the case of undocumented migrants, the ethnographic documentation and exhibition of such practices can have quite practical consequences and entail certain ethical quandaries and strategic risks at the levels of both research practice and representation.

It is important to clarify that undocumented migrants, as such, do not comprise an objectively or intrinsically self-delimiting domain for anthropological study. As Malkki argues with respect to "refugees," the analytic validity and usefulness of the term undocumented migrants is that it supplies "a broad legal or descriptive rubric" that includes within it a tremendous heterogeneity (Malkki 1995, p. 496; cf. Brennan 1984, Couper 1984). Undocumented migrations are, indeed, preeminently labor migrations (cf. Burawoy 1976; Bustamante 1972, 1976, 1978; Castells 1975; Chavez 1992a, pp. 139–55; Hondagneu-Sotelo 2001; Kearney 1998; Rouse 1995a,b). (Note that the U.S. Border Patrol, from 1925—when it was first created—until 1940, operated under the auspices of the Department of Labor). As such, undocumented migrations would be inconceivable were it not for the value they produce through the diverse services they supply to citizens. "Illegality," then, both theoretically and practically, is a social relation that is fundamentally inseparable from citizenship. Furthermore, concretely, there are no hermetically sealed communities of undocumented migrants. In everyday life, undocumented migrants are invariably engaged in social relations with "legal" migrants as well as citizens, and they commonly live in quite intimate proximity to various categories of "documented" persons—sometimes as spouses, frequently as parents or extended family members (often sharing the same households), as well as neighbors, coworkers, and so on. "On a day-to-day basis, their illegality may be irrelevant to most of their activities, only becoming an issue in certain contexts . . . . Much of the time they are undifferentiated from those around them, but suddenly . . . legal reality is superimposed on daily life" (Coutin 2000, p. 40; cf. Corcoran 1993, pp. 144–51). To conduct research on undocumented migrants as such—conceptualized in isolation—is therefore to perpetrate a rather egregious kind of epistemic violence on the social reality of everyday life for those migrants. Furthermore, by constituting undocumented migrants (the people) as an epistemological and ethnographic "object" of study, social scientists, however unwittingly, become agents in an aspect of the everyday production of those migrants' "illegality"—in effect, accomplices to the discursive power of immigration law. In her ethnography of Sanctuary Movement activists' struggles on behalf of securing refugee status and political asylum for undocumented Central Americans, Coutin (1993) emphasizes the everyday social relations that help to sustain what she calls "alienation" (the process through which individuals come to be defined as "illegal aliens"). "Given the pervasiveness of this system," Coutin (1993, p. 89) contends, "any act that constructs individuals' legal identities has political implications." Notably, in her ethnography of Salvadoran legalization struggles, Coutin is explicit in her characterization of the research as "an ethnography of a legal process rather than of a particular group" (2000, p. 23). There is a need for such research on "illegality" *qua* sociopolitical condition, in contradistinction to research on undocumented migrants *qua* "illegal aliens."

A premier challenge, therefore, is to delineate the historical specificity of contemporary migrations as they have come to be located in the legal (political) economies of particular nation-states. Only by reflecting on the effects of sociolegal, historical contexts on research does it become possible to elaborate a critical anthropological perspective that is not complicit with the naturalization of migrant "illegality." It thus becomes possible for the ethnographic study of undocumented migrations to produce migrant "illegality" as the kind of ethnographic object that can serve the ends of a distinctly anthropological critique of nation-states and their immigration policies, as well as of the broader politics of nationalism, nativism, and citizenship.

What at first appeared to be a merely terminological matter, then, upon more careful consideration, is revealed to be a central epistemological and conceptual problem, with significant methodological ramifications, ethical implications, and political repercussions.

THE STUDY OF MIGRANT "ILLEGALITY" AS A THEORETICAL PROBLEM

Undocumented migrations are, as I have already suggested, preeminently labor migrations, originating in the uniquely restless creative capacity and productive power of people. The undocumented character of such movements draws our critical scrutiny to regimes of immigration law and so demands an analytic account of the law as such, which is itself apprehensible only through a theory of the state. Likewise, the specific character of these movements as labor migrations within a global capitalist economy demands an analysis of the mobility of labor, which itself is only understandable through a critical theoretical consideration of labor and capital as mutually constituting poles of a single, albeit contradictory, social relation.

This review is concerned with the theoretical challenge of denaturalizing migrant "illegality," not merely as a fetish that commands debunking but rather as a determinant (or real) abstraction produced as an effect of the practical materiality of the law. Sassen contends that migrations are not autonomous processes—they "do not just happen; they are produced. And migrations do not involve just any possible combination of countries; they are patterned" (1998, p. 56). This argument applies even more decisively to undocumented migrations: They are not self-generating and random; they are produced and patterned. It is useful here to consider a distinction between that which simply falls outside of any precise legal prohibition and so is beyond the law's purview, on the one hand, and that which is constituted as "illegal," on the other (cf. Heyman & Smart 1999, p. 1). The law defines the parameters of its own operations, engendering the conditions of possibility for "legal" as well as "illegal" practices. "Illegalities" are constituted and regimented by the law—directly, explicitly, in a manner that presumes to be more or less definitive (albeit not without manifold ambiguities and indeterminacies, always manipulable in practice) and with a considerable degree of calculated deliberation. Furthermore, at the risk of sounding tautological, within the context of any given state, the history of legal debate and action concerning "immigration," and the determinant effects so produced by the law comprise, precisely, a history. There is, therefore, a methodological double-emphasis here on the productivity of the law as well as on its historicity.

The recent proliferation and acceleration of transnational migration has involved the global emergence of a variety of sociohistorically distinct undocumented migrations as well as a concomitant variety of sociohistorically particular configurations of migrant "illegality." Demographic perspectives in particular seem stubbornly resistant, if not inherently averse, to assigning the law a primary role in defining the character of migration processes. By recourse to a discourse of demographics influencing the effective operation of law, laws themselves appear to merely provide a neutral framework. Thus, the inequalities generated by the law's apparently uniform application among asymmetrically constituted migrations from distinct sending countries tend to be naturalized. This essay insists on the historical specificity of the distinct configurations of "illegality" that are mutually constituted by particular migrations within the respective immigration regimes of specific nation-states. Hence, this is likewise a call for research that is emphatically concerned with distinct migrations and that repudiates the validity of any claim to the existence of "the" (generic) "immigrant experience"; there simply is no such animal.

The history of immigration law, in any given state, is nothing if not a history of rather intricate and calculated interventions. This should not be understood to suggest that such a calculus is simply derivative of some apparently coherent and unified strategy. Nor should this contention be misconstrued to imply that this history is merely a functional by-product of some presumed (and thus, teleological) structural logic. Both of these analytic frameworks would suggest an externality of structure and struggle, and thus, would fall into the trap of reifying (again) the already fetishized divide between social relations and the objectified forms of their appearance (Bonefeld 1994, 1995; Holloway 1995). That is, by treating the law as effectively definitive, coherent, and complete, such perspectives tend to recapitulate the reification of the state's authority and power, which the state itself propagates. On the contrary, the intricate history of law-making is distinguished above all by the constitutive restlessness and relative incoherence of various strategies, tactics, and compromises that nation-states implement at particular historical moments, precisely to mediate the contradictions immanent in social crises and political struggles, above all, around the subordination of labor (cf. Bonefeld 1994, 1995; Holloway 1994, 1995). Thus, immigration laws serve as instruments to supply and refine the parameters of both discipline and coercion, but this is largely so through the deployment of those laws as tactics. By emphasizing this "tactical" character of the law, it is imperative to recall that tactics that aim to make a disciplined and manageable object of any given social group are conjunctural and can never be assured of the certainty of their realization. These tactics are ensnared in a struggle to subordinate the intractability that is intrinsic to the constitutive role of labor within capital—what Marx described as "a protracted and more or less concealed civil war" (Marx 1976, p. 412 [1867]; cf. Bonefeld 1995, Holloway 1995). If we understand the state to be a particularization of "the political"—which is to say, "the abstraction" [and separation] "of coercion from the immediate process of exploitation" (Holloway 1994, p. 31; cf. Pashukanis 1989, p. 143 [1929])—then it is useful here to underscore that labor plays such a constitutive role not only within capital but also within the capitalist state itself. As Holloway writes, "Once the categories of thought are understood as expressions not of objectified social relations but of the struggle to objectify them, then a whole storm of unpredictability blows through them. Once it is understood that money, capital, the state . . . " [and here I would add, emphatically, the law] " . . . are nothing but the struggle to form, to discipline, to structure what Hegel calls 'the sheer unrest of life,' then it is clear that their development can be understood only as practice, as undetermined struggle" (Holloway 1995, p. 176). It is this appreciation of the law—as undetermined struggle—that I want to bring to bear on how we might apprehend the historicity of immigration law, especially as it has devised for its target those characteristically mobile social formations comprised by labor migrations, particularly the undocumented.

One prominent formulation of the theoretical problem concerning the productivity of the law, and the production of migrant "illegality" in particular, has been derived from Foucault's analysis (1979) of modern power as productive, and specifically, from his discussion of "illegalities" and "the production of delinquency" (1979, pp. 257–92).

Behdad (1998) advances a Foucauldean rendering of U.S.-Mexico border enforcement in terms of discipline, surveillance, and the production of delinquency—emphasizing the critical role that the "illegality" of the undocumented plays for disciplining and othering all noncitizens, and thus for perpetuating monolithic normative notions of national identity for citizens themselves. (Note that Behdad's invocation of the "delinquency" of the undocumented resonates with Bustamante's much earlier [1976] revisionist recourse to the sociological convention of "deviance" as a means for situating social perceptions of the undocumented that culminate in discrimination and subjection to organized control by the state. (By way of contrast, for an unreconstructed deployment of the category of "deviance" with respect to undocumented Irish migrants in the United States, see Corcoran 1993). Unfortunately, however, Behdad refers only superficially to border enforcement practices and otherwise reveals a regrettable disregard for any consideration of the law itself and its historicity in generating the pertinent sociopolitical categories that might substantiate his theoretical insights. Coutin (1993, 1996, 2000) is likewise explicit in her efforts to deploy Foucault's insights for theorizing the relationship between law and migration, but she is considerably more precise than Behdad in her examination of how immigration law produces its subjects. Coutin admirably insists that one must not presuppose the category of "illegal immigration," which itself should be under critical scrutiny, and argues for a consideration of U.S. immigration law's production of "illegality," stressing the power of the law to constitute individuals through its categories of differentiation. Furthermore, Coutin's work (1998, 2000; cf. Coutin & Chock 1995) is quite grounded (both historically and ethnographically) and does indeed provide excellent, detailed, empirical discussions of how immigration law structured the experiences of undocumented Salvadorans who later sought asylum status as refugees.

Coutin's reliance on a Foucauldean conception of power leads to an emphatic interest in understanding immigration law as comprising "*more than* legal codes, government policies, and bureaucratic apparatuses" (1993, p. 88, emphasis added). This orientation proves to be methodologically enabling for Coutin's ethnography of how "a myriad of practices, usually carried out by people who have no connection to the government, produce knowledge that constitutes individuals as citizens, illegal aliens, legal residents, asylees, and so forth" (1993, p. 88). As suggested above, Coutin offers crucial insights into the production of "illegality" in everyday life—precisely where ethnographic approaches can make their greatest contribution. She points to a variety of ways that surveillance in the United States has been increasingly displaced in recent years from immigration authorities, to local police, to other state officials (e.g., clerks in a variety of bureaucratic capacities related to public education, housing, and welfare benefits), to private citizens—from employer verification of the work authorization of migrant workers, to charitable organizations who scrutinize immigration documents as a condition of their social service provisioning, to college admissions and financial aid officers charged with monitoring the legal statuses of prospective students (Coutin 1993, p. 97; cf. Coutin 2000, p. 11; cf. Mahler 1995, p. 161; for an example of an employer complaining that the 1986 U.S. immigration law "forces us [employers] to do the police work for the government . . . to do their surveillance," see Repak 1995, p. 157).

In her work on Salvadoran "legalization" struggles, Coutin—revisiting a point made much earlier, in passing, by Castles & Kosack (1973, p. 105) with regard to undocumented migrant workers in Western Europe—creatively expands her theorization of "illegality" in terms of a consideration of the multiple ways in which the contradiction between undocumented migrants' physical and social presence and their official negation as "illegals" generates "spaces of nonexistence" (Coutin 2000, pp. 27–47). The social space of "illegality" is an erasure of legal personhood—a space of forced invisibility, exclusion, subjugation, and repression that "materializes around [the undocumented] wherever they go" (p. 30) in the form of real effects ranging from hunger to unemployment (or more typically, severe exploitation) to violence to death—that is nonetheless always already confounded by their substantive social personhood. Coutin outlines several dimensions of the nonexistence imposed by migrant "illegality": the delimitation of reality to that which can be documented (Coutin 2000, p. 30; cf. Cintron 1997, pp. 51–60; Mahler 1995, pp. 159–87); the "temporalization of presence," whereby the undocumented come to be qualified or disqualified for adjustments of legal status according to the accumulation of continuous, verifiable (documentable) "illegal" residence (Coutin 2000, p. 31); "legal aconsanguinity," whereby immigration policies nullify the legal legitimacy of certain kinship ties (Coutin 2000, pp. 32–33; cf. Heyman 1991, pp. 197–200); enforced clandestinity (Coutin 2000, p. 33; cf. Chavez 1992a, pp. 157–69; Rouse 1992); the transformation of mundane activities—such as working, driving, or traveling—into illicit acts, related to compounded legal ineligibility (Coutin 2000, p. 33; cf. De Genova 1999, 2003; Heyman 1998b; Mahler 1995); restricted physical mobility, paradoxically effected as a consequence of the initial, unauthorized mobility of undocumented migration, which signifies a measure of captivity and social death (Coutin 2000, pp. 33–34; cf. Corcoran 1993, pp. 151–55; Hagan 1994, pp. 163–64; Patterson 1982; Rouse 1992); and restricted social mobility, related to compounded legal ineligibility (Coutin 2000, p. 34; cf. Jenkins 1978, Portes 1978). Although she does not comment on it, another feature of these conditions of nonexistence that arises in the comments of one of Coutin's undocumented interlocutors is something that might be called an enforced orientation to the present, or in Carter's (1997, p. 196) eloquent phrase, "the revocability of the promise of the future," occasioned by the uncertainties arising from the possibility of deportation, which inhibit the undocumented from making many long-term plans (Coutin 1993, p. 98; cf. Chavez 1992a, pp. 158–65; Hagan 1994, pp. 94, 129, 160), although they nevertheless do inspire various short- and medium-term precautions (Chavez 1992a, p. 164). In all of this, Coutin's contribution to a deeper theorization of everyday life for undocumented migrants is extraordinary and suggests many avenues for further ethnographic inquiry, including the investigation of how the incommensurability of multiple interrelated forms of existence and nonexistence can enable certain evasions and subversions of legal obligations entailed by the putative social contracts from which the undocumented are excluded (Coutin 2000, pp. 43–44), and more generally, may facilitate participation in multiple transnational, political, economic, and social spaces that generate new claims of belonging and formations of citizenship (Coutin 2000, pp. 45–47; cf. Appadurai 1996; Basch et al. 1994; De Genova 1998; Flores & Benmayor 1997; Glick Schiller et al. 1992; Kearney 1991, 1996; Rosaldo 1994, 1997; Rouse 1991, 1992, 1995a; Sassen 1996a, 1996b, 1998; Whiteford 1979).

The requirement for the undocumented to refashion their social status with false "papers" raises more general theoretical questions about legal legibility. "Legalization" required documentation from the undocumented in order to prove continuous unauthorized residence within the space of the U.S. nation-state. A verifiable past became the condition of possibility of a documentable present, which itself would serve as a condition of eligibility for a documented future (cf. Coutin 2000, pp. 49–77). This points toward the more general sociopolitical condition of "the documented" themselves. Republican forms of government have created their citizens in relation to a founding document—a constitution—"and as a result, what had been a concrete relationship between subject and monarch became an abstract linkage between individuals and the law . . . [granting] citizens a *legal* existence in addition to their *physical* existence, a juridical form of being that continues to be affirmed through birth certificates, death certificates, and the like" (Coutin 1993, p. 94, emphasis in original; cf. Marrus 1985).

There is a more general problem of methodological presentism that is common in ethnographic work, however, to which Coutin becomes susceptible. Though her examinations of the revisions in immigration law that transpired during her study are indisputably incisive, Coutin nevertheless largely presupposes the extant U.S. immigration regime that preceded the 1980s and 1990s (the specific period of her research), and thus she does not examine the historical genesis of the contemporary U.S. economy of "legality" and "illegality." As a result of these limitations of historical horizon, coupled with the theoretical orientations that justify them by seeking to transcend an analysis of "legal codes" and "government policies" in favor of a privileging of the more capillary forms of power, Coutin's specific argument about U.S. immigration law's production of "illegality" remains rather too partial. Indeed, though Coutin's work demonstrates that Foucauldean analyses of power are instructive for law as a broad discursive field of signifying practices, it also demonstrates the insufficiencies of such a theoretical approach, in its anemic treatment of the state—not in the reified (structuralist) sense of a fixed institutional matrix, but rather as a site of struggle in itself.

Ultimately, Coutin's analysis of the law, as such, is much more illustrative of the conditions of possibility of "legalization" (the production of "legal" status for migrants/refugees who were previously undocumented) than of the law's actual production of "illegality" (cf. Coutin & Chock 1995). In contrast, Hagan (1994), in her ethnography of "legalization" by undocumented Guatemalan Mayan migrants in the United States, concisely but admirably identifies how the history of revisions in U.S. immigration law, beginning in 1965, has been instrumental in producing Mexican/migrant "illegality" in its contemporary configuration (cf. De Genova 1999, 2003). Not confining her historical horizon to the narrower parameters of her own study, Hagan perceptively identifies how the earlier revised immigration policies actually "generated" the new undocumented influx from Mexico, which came to be socially and politically constructed as a new "social problem" (Hagan 1994, p. 82). In addition to Coutin's (1998, 2000) and Hagan's (1994) studies, there have been other noteworthy ethnographies that have included considerations of undocumented (primarily Central American) migrants' participation in the "legalization" program established by the 1986 U.S. immigration act (Hamilton & Chinchilla 2001, Mahler 1995, Repak 1995, Villar 1999; cf. Baker 1990, 1997; Hagan & Baker 1993). It is nonetheless another matter entirely to study the sociopolitical processes of "illegalization" (cf. Calavita 1982, p. 13; 1998, pp. 531–32, 557; Joppke 1999, pp. 26–31).

Indeed, "illegalizations"—or what I call the legal production of migrant "illegality"—supply the foundational conditions of possibility for these programs, variously called "legalizations," "regularizations," or "amnesty," that institute an official adjustment of status for the undocumented. Every "illegalization" implies the possibility of its own rectification. Once we recognize that undocumented migrations are constituted in order not to physically exclude them but instead, to socially include them under imposed conditions of enforced and protracted vulnerability, it is not difficult to fathom how migrants' endurance of many years of "illegality" can serve as a disciplinary apprenticeship in the subordination of their labor, after which it becomes no longer necessary to prolong the undocumented condition. Furthermore, every "legalization" has an inherently episodic and strictly partial character that never eliminates the field of "illegality" but rather, in concert with the amassing of immense quantities of data for scrutiny by the authorities, simply refines and reconstitutes that field for the ineligible who will remain undocumented along with all subsequent "illegal" arrivals. This kind of rationalization tends to be a rather explicit feature of such "regularizing" operations, as in the 1986 law in the United States (De Genova 1999, 2003; cf. Coutin 2000, p. 16; Mahler 1995, pp. 159–87) as well as the 1972 regulations enacted in France (Castells 1975). Indeed, in this light, "legalizations" are themselves disciplinary and serve as instruments of labor subordination. Here, it is useful to recall both Coutin's point concerning the perceived subversiveness of migrant "illegality" (1993, p. 95; 2000, pp. 43–44) and Behdad's insight into the usefulness of migrant "illegality" as a justification for expanded surveillance against all of the state's subjects (1998, p. 106).

An attempt to incorporate some of the Foucauldean insights into the productivity of power with Gramsci's conception of hegemony as a contingent interlocking of coercion and consent (1971 [1929–1935]), as well as a synthesis of legal anthropological perspectives and critical legal realism, is elaborated by Heyman & Smart (1999). Positing the analytic necessity of coupling law and its evasion and the theoretical challenge of conceiving of states and illegal practices as counterparts, these authors develop a position that resembles my own perspective. They emphasize "the incompleteness of formal states and the unlikelihood that they will master their own and people's 'illegal' maneuvers" (p. 2). In this way, they also critique the totalizing aspects of Foucault's treatment of power and instead favor analyses that foreground the indeterminacy, ambiguity, open-endedness, and duplicity of practices and processes "on both sides of the state/illegal practice nexus" (p. 7). They seek to destabilize the hegemonic claims by which states project their own purportedly definitive authority, integrity, and boundedness, yet without ever relinquishing a focus on the state as such (pp. 10–11). Furthermore, they sustain a combined attention to both the legal formalism that imbues an ideology of the purity of the state's orderliness, sovereignty, and legitimacy, on the one hand, and the empirical messiness that reveals how that ideology "disguises the ambiguous dealings of its agents" (pp. 11–14). Likewise, illegality is not essentialized as deviance, subversion, or the putative subculture of a stigmatized group, but instead, is construed as an option or resource available to diverse groups at particular moments, including elites and state functionaries as well as states themselves (pp. 13, 19). In these respects, Heyman & Smart critically recuperate many of the hallmarks of legal anthropology—an awareness of the play of law in its practical contexts, the persistence of plural and nonlegal modalities, the importance of sociohistorical specificities, and an analytic distinction between legitimacy and legality (p. 8).

It is noteworthy that Heyman & Smart's position marks, in important respects, a considerable theoretical advance from Heyman's earlier work, in which he contends, rather more simplistically, that "states are aggregations of rules . . . and the bureaucratic organizations required to implement these rules; for short, states are rules of the game" (1994, p. 51). Heyman makes a compelling case for ethnography in his insightful work on the U.S. Border Patrol (1995, 1998b) and the ways that de facto policies actually guide law enforcement with respect to the undocumented. He falls prey to a familiar anthropological trap, however, by articulating a theoretical/methodological disinclination to examine law itself, advancing instead a one-sided preference for studying the state "from below," through the ethnography of local enforcement practices (1998b). Clearly, Heyman & Smart's approach—explicitly requiring "that states be viewed 'from below' and 'from within' as much as 'from above'" (1999, p. 15)—is more sophisticated and significantly problematizes the one-sidedness of a complacent anthropological predilection for the view "from below."

In much of his prior work (1991, pp. 40, 197; 1998a, pp. 24–29), Heyman's general orientation to the practices of everyday life, including undocumented migrants' border crossings as well as law enforcement's efforts at apprehension, obstructs his capacity to appraise the larger forces at work in the "illegalization" of migrants who cross the U.S.-Mexico border. Though Heyman discerns the decisive facts in the history of U.S. immigration law since 1965 that would substantiate an account of the legal production of migrant "illegality" in its contemporary formulation, he nonetheless persists in treating undocumented migration as if dramatic revisions of the law had not been instrumental in restructuring it. Heyman argues:

> The migration laws of the United States rely on 'numerical control': numerical targets for finite social types . . . . Yet such numbers mismatch the social process of migration and inclusion into the host society . . . . In real-world migratory situations, people adapt numerical-legal categories to these actual connections when possible, and ignore the law when it does not fit migratory intentions . . . . Unlike numerical control, actual migration is flexible in who enters and how long they stay, and adapts quickly to the actual niches and labor demand (that is, the realities) of U.S. society. As a result, either the migrant network system manipulates the legal system to its own ends . . . or people migrate illegally . . . . If current U.S. migration is disordered, the reordering of immigration sought here simulates, but enriches, the *naturalistic* migration system. (1998a, pp. 28–29; emphasis added)

Here, Heyman problematizes the law's quotas and preferences, but his critique remains at the formal level, suggesting a mere mismatch between legal abstraction and actual migration patterns that he depicts as "naturalistic" and systematic. This is a rather grave example of how the fetishization of "demographics," referred to above, can derail a critical analysis of the law. By naturalizing migration processes themselves, Heyman tends here to naturalize "illegality" and diminish the significance of the historical specificities of the law by characterizing its apparatus of "numerical control" as little more than a symptom of an abstract rationality ill-matched to the "natural" flexibility and opportunism of "real-world" migration scenarios. Again, Heyman & Smart's insistence on the combined examination of illegal practices in concert with the law itself is an immeasurably more promising line of inquiry.

Everyday life for the undocumented has become more and more saturated by the regimes that receiving states impose through immigration laws. Historical scholarship on U.S. immigration law has been recently described as still "a relatively new field" (Lee 1999, p. 86). Nonetheless, recent scholarship on the history of U.S. immigration, naturalization, and citizenship law has begun to demonstrate the extent to which legislation is in fact only one feature of the law. Research on law also requires an investigation of judicial cases and administrative decisions affecting the implementation of admission and deportation procedures, as well as policies regulating access to employment, housing, education, and eligibility for various social welfare benefits (Ancheta 1998, Chang 1999, Fitzgerald 1996, Haney López 1996, Hing 1993, Johnson 1993, Kim 1994, Salyer 1995; cf. Lee 1999). Anthropologists interested in the everyday life of the undocumented need not become legal historians. Yet, with respect to the "illegality" of undocumented migrants, a viable critical scholarship is frankly unthinkable without an informed interrogation of immigration law. However, anthropologists are often insufficiently concerned with, if not sorely negligent of, even the elementary aspects of the legislative history affecting the formulation of "illegality" itself, especially as it pertains to particular migrations. Moreover, when ethnographers make even brief passing mention of immigration law, it is not uncommon to find that crucial details of these legal histories have been woefully misrepresented (e.g., Chavez 1992a, p. 15; Chock 1991, p. 291). Thus, the treatment of "illegality" as an undifferentiated, transhistorical fixture is, sadly, a recurring motif in much of the scholarship on migration (e.g., Passel 1994, Reimers 1985).

THE VISIBILITY OF "ILLEGAL IMMIGRANTS" AND THE INVISIBILITY OF THE LAW

Migrant "illegality" is produced as an effect of the law, but it is also sustained as an effect of a discursive formation (cf. Carter 1997, pp. 129–58). Calling the apparent naturalness of migrant "illegality" into question requires a critique of the ways that the sociospatial presuppositions and conceits of nationalism have significantly shaped the very conceptualization of migration itself and a critique of how scholars have reproduced what Alonso (1994) calls "dominant strategies of spatialization" in the very paradigms that organize academic knowledge (De Genova 1998). It is imperative in a review such as this to clarify that the social science scholarship of undocumented migration is itself often ensnared in this discursive formation of "illegality" (cf. De Genova 1999, 2003).

Indeed, across an extensive, multidisciplinary, social science literature, one encounters a remarkable visibility of "illegal immigrants" swirling enigmatically around the stunning invisibility of the law. Only infrequently does one encounter an explicit discussion of the law, much less the history of its revision and reformulation. When immigration law is addressed directly, a detailed empirical investigation of its actual operations is not provided (e.g., Cardenas 1975, Garcia 1995, Heller 1992, Johnson 1997, Sassen 1990). The material force of law, its instrumentality, its historicity, its productivity of some of the most meaningful and salient parameters of sociopolitical life—all of this seems strangely absent, with rather few exceptions. This entanglement within the fetishism of the law (Pashukanis 1989 [1929]; cf. Collins 1982) tends to characterize even the work of scholars who criticize the disciplinary character of the Border Patrol and the policing of migrant workers' documented or undocumented statuses and who question or frankly reject the dubious distinction between "legal" and "illegal" migrations (e.g., Cockcroft 1986, p. 214; Johnson 1997, pp. 171–74; Mirandé 1987, p. 127). Rather than investigate critically what the law actually accomplishes, much scholarship takes the stated aims of the law, such as deterring undocumented migration, at face-value and hence falls into a naïve empiricism. Many scholars then proceed to evaluate legislation—and specifically, various efforts to restrict undocumented migration—in order to sustain the claim that these legal efforts were somehow not effective or were simply "failures" (e.g., Cornelius 1989, pp. 10–14). Furthermore, there is a subcategory of scholarship that is derivative of this naïve empiricism, whereby the overtly restrictive intent of particular laws is not only taken at face-value, but also supplied with a preemptive apology. Such commentators (e.g., Hondagneu-Sotelo 1994, p. 26) assert that the effects on particular migrations of changes in a state's immigration laws can be somehow presumed to have been inadvertent—unanticipated and thus unintended consequences. This show of "good faith" toward the state, and its underlying belief in the law's transparency, does not even allow for the possibility that the law may have been instrumental in generating parameters of migrant "illegality." Still other researchers (e.g., Reimers 1985, Tienda 1989, Zolberg 1990) do identify crucial aspects of legal histories that result in the expansion or reconstitution of migrant "illegality," only then to persist in treating "illegal immigration" as a transparent and self-evident fact. There is, in short, an unfortunate taken-for-grantedness that bedevils much of this scholarship, resulting from an uncritical reproduction of hegemonic common sense. In the best of cases (e.g., Bach 1978; Burawoy 1976; Calavita 1982; Cockcroft 1986; Coutin 1996, 2000; Kearney 1996, 1998; Portes 1978; Tienda 1989; Zolberg 1990), the explanatory power of the work is dulled, and its critical potential is inhibited; in the worst scholars naturalize the category of "illegality."

The tenuous distinction between "legal" and "illegal" migration, which has become increasingly salient throughout the world, was deployed to stigmatize and regulate mainly Mexican migrant workers in the United States for much of the twentieth century. Indeed, the Annual Reports of the U.S. Immigration and Naturalization Service (INS) long divided statistics for their apprehensions of "deportable aliens" into two discrete categories—Mexicans and All Others. In 1973, for instance, the INS reported that Mexicans literally comprised 99% of all apprehended "deportable aliens" who had entered surreptitiously (Cardenas 1975, p. 86). Selective enforcement of the law—coordinated with seasonal labor demand by U.S. employers (as well as the occasional exigencies of electoral politics)—has long maintained a revolving door policy, whereby mass deportations are concurrent with an overall, large-scale, more or less permanent *im*portation of Mexican migrant labor (Cockroft 1986). One of the consequences of this history of selective border enforcement is that the sociopolitical category "illegal alien" itself—inseparable from a distinct "problem" or "crisis" of governance and sovereignty—has come to be saturated with racialized difference and indeed has long served as a constitutive dimension of the racialized inscription of "Mexicans" in the United States (De Genova 1999, 2003; cf. Ngai 1999, 2003). Although he has rather little to say directly about undocumented migration and the social condition of "illegality," Vélez-Ibáñez (1996) advances the idea of a "commodity identity" for Mexicans in the United States—a concept originally articulated specifically for undocumented Mexican migrants by Bustamante (1978). Vélez-Ibáñez suggests important ways in which the stigmatization of undocumented Mexicans—as a people reducible to the disposability of their labor for a price—has become central to the racialization of all Mexicans/Chicanos and other Latinos (regardless of immigration status or even U.S. citizenship). During the Great Depression, this more plainly racist character of Mexican criminalization became notoriously and abundantly manifest, culminating in the systematic exclusion of Mexican migrants and Chicano (Mexican American) U.S. citizens alike from employment and economic relief, followed by the forcible deportation of at least 415,000 Mexicans and Chicanos and the "voluntary" repatriation of 85,000 more (Balderrama & Rodríguez 1995, Guerin-Gonzáles 1994, Hoffman 1974). People were expelled with no regard to their status as legal residents or U.S. citizens by birth—simply for being "Mexicans." The conjunctures of migrant "illegality," nativism, and racialization should become increasingly prominent in future research (cf. Balibar 1991a,b,c,d; Bosniak 1996, 1997; Chavez 2001; De Genova & Ramos-Zayas 2003; Carter 1997; Perea 1997; Pred 2000; Sanchez 1999; Vila 2000).

Though Mexican migrants are very commonly the implied if not overt focus of mass-mediated, journalistic, as well as scholarly discussions of "illegal aliens" (Chavez 2001, García 1980, Johnson 1997), the genesis of their condition of "illegality" is seldom examined. In my own research, I have sought to interrogate the history of changes in U.S. immigration law through the specific lens of how these revisions—especially the imposition, since 1965, of numerical restrictions on "legal" migration from Western Hemisphere countries—have had a disproportionately deleterious impact on Mexican migrants (De Genova 1999, 2003). In her historical research, Ngai (1999, 2003) makes an analogous argument for the period beginning in the second half of the 1920s, on the basis of substantially different modes of migrant inclusion and exclusion. It is crucial to explore how the U.S. nation-state came to deploy a variety of different tactics at distinct historical moments, to systematically recreate "illegality" in ways that have ever more thoroughly constrained and circumscribed the social predicaments of undocumented migrants.

Mexican scholars of Mexican migration to the United States (publishing primarily in Spanish, but also, to a limited extent, in English; e.g., Bustamante 1972, 1976, 1978) have tended to be much more inclined to approach the topic in terms of the structural features of U.S. capitalism and labor demand and to engage in the kinds of analyses that cast a critical light on "illegalization." Many U.S. scholars (including some Chicanos), however, when not preoccupied with policy-driven questions, more typically have tended to approach the subject through the hegemonic sociological rubric of "settlement" and "assimilation" (cf. De Genova 1999, pp. 19–104; n.d.). (On this score, arguing for Mexican migration as a temporary national economic development opportunity, Gamio 1971 [1930], as a student of Boas and a founder of Mexican Anthropology, is the most prominent exception among Mexican researchers.) Beginning with the very earliest efforts of anthropologists and sociologists to produce social science accounts of Mexican migrants in the United States, the literature has been distinguished by a strikingly disproportionate, seemingly compulsive obsession with "the transition ... from an immigration of temporary laborers to one of settlers" (Clark 1974 [1908], p. 520). In 1911, the Dillingham U.S. Immigration Commission produced its own assessment: "Because of their [Mexicans'] strong attachment to their native land, low intelligence, illiteracy, migratory life, and the possibility of their residence here being discontinued, few become citizens of the United States" (quoted in Weber 1982, p. 24). And further: "While they are not easily assimilated, this is of no very great importance as long as most of them return to their native land. In the case of the Mexican, he is less desirable as a citizen than as a laborer" (quoted in Calavita 1992, p. 180; cf. Reisler 1976a, 1996 [1976b]).

In a significant sense, the themes that revolve around discerning whether or not Mexican migrants to the United States can or will "assimilate," and the variety of ways that this question has been elaborated through the "sojourner"—"settler" binary, have remained quite ubiquitous ever since (e.g., Gamio 1971 [1930]; Bogardus 1970 [1934]; Chavez 1988, 1991, 1992a,b, 1994; Cornelius 1992; Durand & Massey 1992; Hondagneu-Sotelo 1994; Massey 1987; Massey et al. 1987; Massey & Liang 1989; Portes & Bach 1985; Smith 1996; Suárez-Orozco 1998; Rouse 1992; Villar 1990). In his ethnographic monograph, *Shadowed Lives: Undocumented Immigrants in American Society*, Chavez (1992a) explicitly counterposes the analytic categories "migrants" (as "sojourners") and "settlers," as he explains that he "concluded that the important story to be told is that of the transition people undergo as they leave the migrant life and instead settle in the United States" (1992a, p. 4; cf. 1991, Chavez et al. 1989). Chavez then proceeds to invoke an anthropological analogy—the rite of passage—as the organizing theoretical metaphor through which he characterizes the process of migrant "settlement":

> For undocumented migrants, crossing the border is a territorial passage that marks the transition from one way of life to another [. . ..] A territorial passage, like more conventional rites of passage, can be divided into three important phases: *separation* from the known social group or society, *transition* (the 'liminal' phase), and *incorporation* into the new social group or society [. . ..]
>
> [B]y examining practical, everyday experiences, modes of behavior, and knowledge acquired by undocumented immigrants during their territorial passage, we can begin to understand this transition and the problem of the undocumented immigrant's incorporation into the larger society [. . ..]
>
> For some the transition phase begins with crossing the border, but never comes to a close; these people never accumulate enough links of incorporation . . . to allow them to become settlers and feel part of the new society. They remain 'liminals,' outsiders during their stay in the United States, often returning to their country of origin after a relatively brief time [. . ..] However, even individuals who have accumulated a great number of such links may find full incorporation into the new society blocked because of their undocumented status and the larger society's view of them as illegal aliens [. . ..] This observation gives added significance to the questions this book poses [. . ..] How do the experiences of undocumented migrants influence their decision to return home or settle in this country? (Chavez 1992a, pp. 4–6, emphases in original; cf. 1991)

Chavez's schema of the "transition," "settlement," and "incorporation" of undocumented Latinos in their passage from "migrants" to "immigrants," driven by the teleological analogy of "rites of passage" in the life cycles of "individuals," almost perfectly reiterates Park's logic in "Migration and the Marginal Man" (Park 1980[1914/1928]), whereby the migrant is characterized as a "cultural hybrid" moving across the marginal zone between two societies. What seems to matter, above all, to Chavez, is to repudiate the allegation that undocumented Mexican and Central American migrants are mere "sojourners" (cf. 1991, 1994). "Illegality" as such, however, is treated here as little more than a prejudicial perception on the part of citizens toward newcomers that obstructs their integration. With regard to the genesis of "illegality" for these Latino (mainly Mexican) migrants, Chavez (1992a, p. 15) not only recapitulates the dominant mythology of the 1965 U.S. immigration law as a grand liberalization but also goes further by celebrating as "egalitarian" the introduction of a numerical quota for Western Hemisphere migrations—precisely that which, in this reform, was most illiberal and restrictive (and inordinately detrimental for Mexican migration in particular) (De Genova 1999, 2003).

The figure of the "sojourner" has always been gendered as male, and profit from his labor has relied upon exploiting the separation of the (migrant) working man from the woman (and children) who remained "in his native land" in order to defray some of the costs of the reproduction of labor power (Chock 1991, 1995, 1996;

Coutin & Chock 1995; Gonzalez & Fernandez 1979; Hondagneu-Sotelo 1994; Kearney 1986; Rouse 1992; cf. Burawoy 1976; Kearney 1991, 1996, 1998; Ortiz, this volume). What has been insufficiently explored is how the historical production of the racialized figure of "the Mexican," as male "sojourner," has been rendered synonymous with migrant "illegality." This linkage has become more readily visible with the increasing equation of undocumented migrant women with permanent migrant (family) settlement (Chock 1995, 1996; Coutin & Chock 1995; Roberts 1997; cf. Lowe 1996, pp. 159–60). Chock poignantly identifies the pervasive presumption that "a natural relationship between babies and mothers [blurs] lines of rights and responsibilities mapped by the state between two categories of people (citizen and alien)," such that "women's fertility [multiplies] the risk to the nation" (Chock 1995, p. 173).

THE BORDER SPECTACLE

Undocumented migration, and Mexican migration in particular, has been rendered synonymous with the U.S. nation-state's purported "loss of control" of its borders and has supplied the pretext for what has in fact been a continuous intensification of militarized control on the U.S.-Mexico border (Dunn 1996, Jiménez 1992; cf. Andreas 1998; Heyman 1991, 1999; Kearney 1991, 1998). Overstaying a visa—the rather discrete act by which very significant numbers of people become undocumented migrants—is, after all, not terribly dramatic. Hence, it is precisely "the Border" that provides the exemplary theater for staging the spectacle of "the illegal alien" that the law produces. The elusiveness of the law, and its relative invisibility in producing "illegality," requires the spectacle of "enforcement" at the U.S.-Mexico border that renders a racialized migrant "illegality" visible and lends it the commonsensical air of a "natural" fact.

There is a pattern of policing that is critical for the perpetuation of the "revolving door" policy: the great majority of INS apprehensions of "deportable aliens" consist of those who have just surreptitiously crossed the Mexican border, and this has increasingly been the case. These enforcement proclivities and perogatives, and the statistics they produce, have made an extraordinary contribution to the commonplace fallacy that Mexicans account for virtually all "illegal aliens," have served to restage the U.S.-Mexico border as the theater of an enforcement "crisis," and have rendered "Mexican" the distinctive national/racialized name for migrant "illegality." Heyman (1995) describes what he calls "the voluntary-departure complex," whereby "deportable aliens" apprehended at the U.S.-Mexico border (who are, predictably, overwhelmingly Mexican) "are permitted (indeed, encouraged) to waive their rights to a deportation hearing and return to Mexico without lengthy detention, expensive bonding, and trial," and then, upon release in Mexico near the border, "they can and do repeat their attempts to evade border enforcement until they finally succeed in entering" (1995, pp. 266–67). Heyman thus establishes that the U.S. state maximizes arrests and enhances the mass-mediated impression of "border control," while actually negating the efficacy of those apprehensions and facilitating undocumented labor migration. Indeed, undocumented border-crossing has become a staple for journalistic "participant-observation"; see, e.g., Conover 1987; Decker 1994; Dwyer 1994.

The operation of the "revolving door" at the U.S.-Mexico border couples an increasingly militarized spectacle of apprehensions, detentions, and deportations, with the banality of a continuous importation of undocumented migrant labor (Cockcroft 1986). Indeed, Mexican as well as Central American migrants' border-crossing narratives quite often relate experiences of tremendous hardship that are commonly juxtaposed with accounts of easy passage (Chavez 1992a; Davis 1990; De Genova 1999, 2003; Kearney 1991; Martínez 1994; e.g., Guillén 2001, Hart 1997, Pérez 1991). These same narratives are commonly punctuated with accounts of life in the United States that are distinguished by arduous travail and abundant exploitation (De Genova 1999, 2003; Kearney 1991; Mahler 1995; Martínez 1994). The legal production of Mexican (and also Central American) migrant "illegality" requires the spectacle of enforcement at the U.S.-Mexico border for the spatialized difference between the nation-states of the United States and Mexico (and effectively, all of Latin America) to be socially inscribed upon the migrants themselves—embodied in the spatialized (and racialized) status of "illegal alien." The vectors of race and space, therefore, are both crucial in the constitution of the class specificity of Mexican labor migration (De Genova 1999, 2003).

The "illegality" effect of protracted and enduring vulnerability has to be recreated more often than on the occasions of crossing the border. Indeed, the 1986 U.S. legislation, for instance, which instituted for the first time federal sanctions against employers who knowingly hired undocumented workers, was tantamount to an extension of the "revolving door" to the internal labor market of each workplace where undocumented migrants were employed. By establishing an affirmative defense for all employers who could demonstrate that they had complied with the verification procedure—simply by having filled out and kept on file a routine I-9 form attesting to the document check, without any requirement that they determine the legitimacy of documents presented in that verification process—the legislation insulated employers from any penalty. What this meant in practice was that the employer sanction provisions generated a flourishing industry in fraudulent documents, which merely imposed further expenses and greater legal liabilities upon the migrant workers themselves, while supplying protection for employers (Chavez 1992a, pp. 169–71; Cintron 1997, pp. 51–60; Coutin 2000, pp. 49–77; Mahler 1995, pp. 159–87; cf. U.S. Department of Labor 1991, p. 124). It also required a heightening of INS raids on workplaces. Given that inspectors are required to give employers a three-day warning prior to inspections of hiring records, to make it "pragmatically easy" for employers to comply with the letter of the law (Calavita 1992, p. 169), and that, in order to avoid fines associated with infractions, employers typically fire or temporarily discharge workers known to be undocumented prior to a raid—these provisions have primarily served to introduce greater instability into the labor-market experiences of undocumented migrants and to institute an internal "revolving door." What are putatively "employer sanctions," then, have actually functioned to aggravate the migrants' condition of vulnerability and have imposed new penalties upon the undocumented workers themselves (cf. Sassen & Smith 1992).

The "illegalities" of everyday life are often, literally, instantiated by the lack of various forms of state-issued documentation that sanction one's place within or outside the strictures of the law (Cintron 1997, Coutin 2000, Hagan 1994, Mahler 1995). The policing of public spaces outside of the workplace, moreover, serves to discipline undocumented migrants by surveilling their "illegality" and exacerbating their sense of ever-present vulnerability (Chavez 1992a; Coutin 2000; De Genova 1999, 2003; Heyman 1998b; Mahler 1995; Rouse 1992). The lack of a driver's license, for instance, is typically presumed by police in most states in the U.S. to automatically indicate a migrant's more generally undocumented condition (De Genova 1999, 2003; cf. Mahler 1995, pp. 146–47).[1] Such forms of everyday "illegality" are responsible for many undocumented migrants' encounters with everyday forms of surveillance and repression. But there are also those "illegalities" that more generally pertain to the heightened policing directed at the bodies, movements, and spaces of the poor—especially those spatialized as "foreigners" in the United States, Europe, Canada, and Australia and those racialized as not-white in particular (cf. Balibar 1991a,c,d; Calavita 1998; Carter 1997; Haney López 1996; Lowe 1996; Paul 1997; Pred 2000; Satzewich 1991; Saxton 1971). Subjection to quotidian forms of intimidation and harassment reinforces undocumented migrants' vulnerability as a highly exploitable workforce.

Yet the disciplinary operation of an apparatus for the everyday production of migrant "illegality" is never simply intended to achieve the putative goal of deportation. It is deportability, and not deportation per se, that has historically rendered undocumented migrant labor a distinctly disposable commodity. There has never been sufficient funding for the INS to evacuate the United States of undocumented migrants by means of deportations, nor even for the Border Patrol to "hold the line." The INS is neither equipped nor intended to actually keep the undocumented out. The very existence of the enforcement branches of the INS (and the Border Patrol, in particular) is premised upon the continued presence of migrants whose undocumented legal status has long been equated with the disposable (deportable), ultimately "temporary" character of the commodity that is their labor-power. Indeed, although the Border Patrol has, since its inception, defined unauthorized entry as "a continuous offense [that] is not completed . . . until the alien reaches his interior destination," and so defined its jurisdiction as effectively the entire interior (Ngai 2003), INS enforcement efforts have disproportionately targeted the U.S.-Mexico border, sustaining a zone of relatively high tolerance within the interior (Chavez 1992a, Delgado 1993). The true social role of INS enforcement

[1]There are only four states in the United States that issue driver's licenses to any state resident who can pass the driving test, regardless of their legal status; they are North Carolina, Tennessee, Utah, and Virginia (*New York Times*, 4 August 2001).

(and the Border Patrol) is in maintaining the operation of the border as a "revolving door" (Cockcroft 1986), simultaneously implicated in importation as much as deportation (Calavita 1992), and sustaining the border's viability as a filter for the unequal transfer of value (Kearney 1998).

Migrant "illegality" is lived through a palpable sense of deportability, which is to say, the possibility of deportation, the possibility of being removed from the space of the nation-state. There are some significant analogies between migrant deportability and the threat of deportation confronted by denationalized citizens [as, for example, with European Jews and Gypsies under Nazi Germany (Agamben 1998, pp. 126–35, 166–80), or women who were U.S. citizens by birth but denationalized for having married noncitizen men (Bredbenner 1998), or political dissidents under McCarthy-era legislation that still remains in effect in the United States (e.g., Randall 1987; cf. Nathan 1991, pp. 90–108)], but my focus here is the specificity of migrant deportability. What makes deportability so decisive in the legal production of migrant "illegality" and the militarized policing of nation-state borders is that some are deported in order that most may remain (un-deported)—as workers, whose particular migrant status may thus be rendered "illegal." Therefore, migrant "illegality" is a spatialized social condition that is frequently central to the particular ways that migrants are racialized as "illegal aliens" within nation-state spaces, as for example when "Mexicans" are racialized in relation to "American"-ness in the United States (De Genova 1998, 1999, 2003). Moreover, the spatialized condition of "illegality" reproduces the physical borders of nation-states in the everyday life of innumerable places throughout the interiors of the migrant-receiving states. Thus, the legal production of "illegality" as a distinctly spatialized and typically racialized social condition for undocumented migrants provides an apparatus for sustaining their vulnerability and tractability as workers.

CONCLUSION

There is nothing matter-of-fact about the "illegality" of undocumented migrants. As Calavita has argued with respect to immigration law in Spain, "There may be no smoking gun, but there is nonetheless a lot of smoke in the air" (1998, p. 557). "Illegality" is the product of immigration laws—not merely in the abstract sense that without the law, nothing could be construed to be outside of the law; nor simply in the generic sense that immigration law constructs, differentiates, and ranks various categories of "aliens"—but in the more profound sense that the history of deliberate interventions that have revised and reformulated the law has entailed an active process of inclusion through "illegalization."

Undocumented migrant labor has been criminalized as "illegal" and subjected to excessive and extraordinary forms of policing. The undocumented have been denied fundamental human rights and many rudimentary social entitlements, consigned to an uncertain sociopolitical predicament, often with little or no recourse to any semblance of protection from the law. The category "illegal alien" is a profoundly useful and profitable one that effectively serves to create and sustain a legally vulnerable—and hence, relatively tractable and thus "cheap"—reserve of labor. That proposition is quite old; indeed, it is so well established and well documented as to be irrefutable (cf., for example, Burawoy 1976; Bustamante 1972, 1976, 1978; Calavita 1990, 1992; Castells 1975; Cockcroft 1986; Delgado 1993; Galarza 1964; Gamio 1971 [1930]; Gledhill 1998; Grasmuck 1984; Hondagneu-Sotelo 2001; Jenkins 1978; Kearney 1996; Kwong 1997; McWilliams 1949; Piore 1979; Rouse 1995a; Samora 1971; Sassen 1988; Smith 1998; Taylor 1932). A central contention of this review has been that, in and of itself, this important critical insight into the consequences of migrant "illegality" is insufficient insofar as its origin may be left unexamined and thus naturalized. We must go further and examine the fundamental origin of the status "illegal" (and its attendant sociospatial condition of deportability) in the law itself—what I call the legal production of migrant "illegality."

ACKNOWLEDGMENTS

The author would like to express his gratitude and appreciation for the resourcefulness and meticulous attention of Ryan Chaney and Ashley Greene, whose energy and diligence as graduate student research assistants were invaluable in the preparation of this review.

The *Annual Review of Anthropology* is online at http://anthro.annualreviews.org

LITERATURE CITED

Agamben G. 1998. *Homo Sacer: Sovereign Power and Bare Life*. Stanford, CA: Stanford Univ. Press

Alonso AM. 1994. The politics of space, time, and substance: state formation, nationalism, and ethnicity. *Annu. Rev. Anthropol.* 23:379–405

Alvarez RR. 1995. The Mexican-U.S. border: the making of an anthropology of borderlands. *Annu. Rev. Anthropol.* 24:447–70

Ancheta AN. 1998. *Race, Rights, and the Asian American Experience*. New Brunswick, NJ: Rutgers Univ. Press

Andreas P. 1998. The U.S. immigration control offensive: constructing an image of order on the southwest border. See Suárez-Orozco 1998, pp. 343–56

Appadurai A. 1996. *Modernity at Large: Cultural Dimensions of Globalization*. Minneapolis: Univ. Minn. Press

Bach RL. 1978. Mexican immigration and the American state. *Int. Migr. Rev.* 12(4):536–58

Baker SG. 1990. *The Cautious Welcome: the Legalization Programs of the Immigration Reform and Control Act*. Washington, DC: Urban Inst. Press

Baker SG. 1997. The 'Amnesty' aftermath: current policy issues stemming from the legalization programs of the 1986 Immigration Reform and Control Act. *Int. Migr. Rev.* 31(1):5–27

Balderrama FE, Rodríguez R. 1995. *Decade of Betrayal: Mexican Repatriation in the 1930's*. Albuquerque: Univ. N. M. Press

Balibar E. 1991a. Is there a "neo-racism"? See Balibar & Wallerstein 1991, pp. 17–28

Balibar E. 1991b. Racism and nationalism. See Balibar & Wallerstein 1991, pp. 37–67

Balibar E. 1991c. The nation form: history and

ideology. See Balibar & Wallerstein 1991, pp. 86–106
Balibar E. 1991d. Racism and crisis. See Balibar & Wallerstein 1991, pp. 217–27
Balibar E, Wallerstein I, eds. 1991. *Race, Nation, Class: Ambiguous Identities*. New York: Verso
Basch L, Glick Schiller N, Szanton Blanc C. 1994. *Nations Unbound: Transnational Projects, Postcolonial Predicaments, and De-territorialized Nation-States*. Langhorne, PA: Gordon & Breach
Behdad A. 1998. INS and outs: producing delinquency at the border. *Aztlán* 23(1):103–13
Bogardus ES. 1970(1934). *The Mexican in the United States*. San Francisco: R & E Res. Assoc.
Bonefeld W. 1994. *The Recomposition of the British State During the 1980s*. Brookfield, VT: Dartmouth
Bonefeld W. 1995. Capital as subject and the existence of labour. See Bonefeld et al. 1995, pp. 182–212
Bonefeld W, Gunn R, Holloway J, Psychopedis K, eds. 1995. *Emancipating Marx: Open Marxism* 3. East Haven, CT: Pluto
Bosniak LS. 1996. Opposing Prop. 187: undocumented immigrants and the national imagination. *Conn. Law Rev.* 28(3):555–619
Bosniak LS. 1997. "Nativism" the concept: some reflections. See Perea 1997, pp. 279–99
Bredbenner CL. 1998. *A Nationality of Her Own: Women, Marriage, and the Law of Citizenship*. Berkeley, CA: Univ. Calif. Press
Brennan EM. 1984. Irregular migration: policy responses in Africa and Asia. *Int. Migr. Rev.* 18(3):409–25
Burawoy M. 1976. The functions and reproduction of migrant labor: comparative material from southern Africa and the United States. *Am. J. Sociol.* 81(5):1050–87
Bustamante J. 1972. The historical context of undocumented Mexican immigration to the United States. *Aztlán* 3(2):257–78
Bustamante J. 1976. Structural and ideological conditions of Mexican undocumented immigration to the United States. *Am. Behav. Sci.* 19(3):364–76
Bustamante J. 1978. Commodity migrants: structural analysis of Mexican immigration to the United States. In *Views Across the Border: the United States and Mexico*, ed. SR Ross, pp. 183–203. Albuquerque: Univ. N. M. Press
Bustamante JA, Reynolds CW, Hinojosa Ojeda RA, eds. 1992. *U.S.-Mexico Relations: Labor Market Interdependence*. Stanford, CA: Stanford Univ. Press
Calavita K. 1982. *California's "Employer Sanctions": the Case of the Disappearing Law. Res. Rep. Ser. No. 39*. Cent. U.S.-Mex. Stud., Univ. Calif., San Diego
Calavita K. 1990. Employer sanctions violations: toward a dialectical model of white-collar crime. *Law Soc. Rev.* 24(4):1041–69
Calavita K. 1992. *Inside the State: the Bracero Program, Immigration, and the I.N.S.* New York: Routledge
Calavita K. 1998. Immigration, law, and marginalization in a global economy: notes from Spain. *Law Soc. Rev.* 32(3):529–66
Cardenas G. 1975. United States immigration policy toward Mexico: an historical perspective. *Chicano Law Rev.* 2:66–89
Carens JH. 1987. Aliens and citizens: the case for open borders. *Rev. Polit.* 49(2):251–73
Carter DM. 1997. *States of Grace: Senegalese in Italy and the New European Immigration*. Minneapolis: Univ. Minn. Press
Castells M. 1975. Immigrant workers and class struggles in advanced capitalism: the western European experience. *Polit. Soc.* 5:33–66
Castles S, Kosack G. 1973. *Immigrant Workers and Class Structure in Western Europe*. New York: Oxford Univ. Press
Chang RS. 1999. *Disoriented: Asian Americans, Law, and the Nation-State*. New York: N.Y. Univ. Press
Chavez LR. 1988. Settlers and sojourners: the case of Mexicans in the United States. *Hum. Organ.* 47:95–108
Chavez LR. 1991. Outside the imagined community: undocumented settlers and experiences of incorporation. *Am. Ethnol.* 18:257–78
Chavez LR. 1992a. *Shadowed Lives: Undocumented Immigrants in American Society.*

Ft. Worth, TX: Harcourt, Brace, & Jovanovich

Chavez LR. 1992b. Paradise at a cost: the incorporation of undocumented Mexican immigrants into a local level labor market. See Bustamante et al. 1992, pp. 271–301

Chavez LR. 1994. The power of the imagined community: the settlement of undocumented Mexicans and Central Americans in the United States. *Am. Anthropol.* 96(1):52–73

Chavez LR. 2001. *Covering Immigration: Popular Images and the Politics of the Nation.* Berkeley: Univ. Calif. Press

Chavez LR, Flores ET, Lopez-Garza M. 1989. Migrants and settlers: a comparison of undocumented Mexicans and Central Americans. *Front. Norte* 1:49–75

Chock PP. 1991. 'Illegal aliens' and 'opportunity': myth-making in congressional testimony. *Am. Ethnol.* 18(2):279–94

Chock PP. 1995. Ambiguity in policy discourse: congressional talk about immigration. *Policy Sci.* 28:165–84

Chock PP. 1996. No new women: gender, "alien," and "citizen" in the congressional debate on immigration. *PoLAR: Polit. Legal Anthropol. Rev.* 19(1):1–9

Cintron R. 1997. *Angels' Town: Chero Ways, Gang Life, and Rhetorics of the Everyday.* Boston: Beacon

Clark VS. 1974 (1908). *Mexican Labor in the United States* (*U.S. Dep. Commer. Labor Bur. Labor Bull., No. 78*). In *Mexican Labor in the United States*, ed. CE Cortés. New York: Arno

Cockcroft JD. 1986. *Outlaws in the Promised Land: Mexican Immigrant Workers and America's Future.* New York: Grove

Collins H. 1982. *Marxism and Law.* New York: Oxford Univ. Press

Conover T. 1987. *Coyotes: a Journey Through the Secret World of America's Illegal Aliens.* New York: Vintage Books

Corcoran MP. 1993. *Irish Illegals: Transients Between Two Societies.* Westport, CT: Greenwood

Cornelius WA. 1989. Mexican migration to the United States: an introduction. In *Mexican Migration to the United States: Origins, Consequences, and Policy Options*, ed. WA Cornelius, JA Bustamante, pp. 1–24. San Diego: Center for U.S.-Mexican Studies, Univ. Calif.

Cornelius W. 1992. From sojourners to settlers: the changing profile of Mexican immigration to the United States. See Bustamante et al. 1992, pp.155–95

Couper K. 1984. An elusive concept: the changing definition of illegal immigrant in the practice of immigration control in the United Kingdom. *Int. Migr. Rev.* 18(3):437–52

Coutin SB. 1993. *The Culture of Protest: Religious Activism and the U.S. Sanctuary Movement.* Boulder, CO: Westview

Coutin SB. 1996. Differences within accounts of U.S. immigration law. *PoLAR: Polit. Legal Anthropol. Rev.* 19(1):11–20

Coutin SB. 1998. From refugees to immigrants: the legalization strategies of Salvadoran immigrants and activists. *Int. Migr. Rev.* 32(4):901–25

Coutin SB. 2000. *Legalizing Moves: Salvadoran Immigrants' Struggle for U.S. Residency.* Ann Arbor: Univ. Mich. Press

Coutin SB, Chock PP. 1995. "Your friend, the illegal": definition and paradox in newspaper accounts of U.S. immigration reform. *Identities* 2(1–2):123–48

Davis MP. 1990. *Mexican Voices/American Dreams: an Oral History of Mexican Immigration to the United States.* New York: Holt

Decker P. 1994. The Mexican "illegal alien" commute. *Migr. World* 14(3):13–21

De Genova N. 1998. Race, space, and the reinvention of Latin America in Mexican Chicago. *Lat. Am. Perspect.* (Issue 102) 25(5): 91–120

De Genova N. 1999. *Working the boundaries, making the difference: race and space in Mexican Chicago.* PhD thesis. Univ. Chicago. 544 pp.

De Genova N. 2003. *Working the Boundaries: Race, Space, and "Illegality" in Mexican Chicago.* Durham, NC: Duke Univ. Press. In press

De Genova N. n.d. *"The immigrant" as an object of American studies and U.S. nationalism.* Work. Pap. Dep. Anthropol., Columbia Univ.

De Genova N, Ramos-Zayas AY. 2003. *Latino Optics: Racialization and Citizenship Between Mexicans and Puerto Ricans in Chicago.* New York: Routledge. In press

Delgado H. 1993. *New Immigrants, Old Unions: Organizing Undocumented Workers in Los Angeles.* Philadelphia: Temple Univ. Press

Dunn TJ. 1996. *The Militarization of the U.S.-Mexico Border, 1978–1992: Low-Intensity Conflict Doctrine Comes Home.* Austin: Cent. Mex. Am. Stud. Books/Univ. Tex. Press

Durand J, Massey DS. 1992. Mexican migration to the United States: a critical review. *Lat. Am. Res. Rev.* 27(2):3–42

Dwyer A. 1994. *On the Line: Life on the U.S.-Mexican Border.* London: Lat. Am. Bur.

Fitzgerald K. 1996. *Face of the Nation: Immigration, the State, and the National Identity.* Stanford, CA: Stanford Univ. Press

Flores WV, Benmayor R, eds. 1997. *Latino Cultural Citizenship: Claiming Identity, Space, and Rights.* Boston: Beacon

Foucault M. 1979. *Discipline and Punish: the Birth of the Prison.* New York: Random House

Galarza E. 1964. *Merchants of Labor: the Mexican Bracero Story.* Santa Barbara, CA: McNally & Loftin

Gamio M. 1971(1930). *Mexican Immigration to the United States: a Study of Human Migration and Adjustment.* New York: Dover

García JR. 1980. *Operation Wetback: the Mass Deportation of Mexican Undocumented Workers in 1954.* Westport, CT: Greenwood

García RJ. 1995. Critical race theory and proposition 187: the racial politics of immigration law. *Chicano-Latino Law Rev.* 17:118–48

Gledhill J. 1998. The Mexican contribution to restructuring US capitalism: NAFTA as an instrument of flexible accumulation. *Crit. Anthropol.* 18(3):279–96

Glick Schiller N, Basch L, Szanton-Blanc L, eds. 1992. *Towards a Transnational Perspective on Migration. Ann. NY Acad. Sci.* Vol. 645

Gonzalez RM, Fernandez RA. 1979. U.S. imperialism and migration: the effects on Mexican women and families. *Rev. Radic. Polit. Econ.* 11(4):112–23

Gramsci A. 1971 (1929–1935). *Selections from the Prison Notebooks.* New York: International

Grasmuck S. 1984. Immigration, ethnic stratification, and native working-class discipline: comparisons of documented and undocumented Dominicans. *Int. Migr. Rev.* 18(3):692–713

Guerin-Gonzáles C. 1994. *Mexican Workers and American Dreams: Immigration, Repatriation, and California Farm Labor, 1900–1939.* New Brunswick, NJ: Rutgers Univ. Press

Guillén A. 2001. Traveling north: a chronicle of an undocumented journey. *NACLA Rep. Am.* 35(2):36–42

Hagan JM. 1994. *Deciding to be Legal: a Maya Community in Houston.* Philadelphia: Temple Univ. Press

Hagan JM, Baker SG. 1993. Implementing the U.S. legalization program: the influence of immigrant communities and local agencies on immigration policy reform. *Int. Migr. Rev.* 27(3):513–36

Hamilton N, Chinchilla NS. 2001. *Seeking Community in a Global City: Guatemalans and Salvadorans in Los Angeles.* Philadelphia: Temple Univ. Press

Haney López IF. 1996. *White by Law: the Legal Construction of Race.* New York: N.Y. Univ. Press

Harris N. 1995. *The New Untouchables: Immigration and the New World Worker.* New York: Tauris

Hart DW. 1997. *Undocumented in L.A.: an Immigrant's Story.* Wilmington, DE: Scholarly Resourc. Books

Heller T. 1992. Immigration and regulation: historical context and legal reform. In *U.S.-Mexico Relations: Labor Market*

Interdependence, ed. JA Bustamante, CW Reynolds, RA Hinojosa Ojeda, pp. 42–74. Stanford, CA: Stanford Univ. Press

Heyman JMC. 1991. *Life and Labor on the Border: Working People of Northeastern Sonora, Mexico, 1886–1986*. Tucson: Univ. Ariz. Press

Heyman JMC. 1995. Putting power in the anthropology of bureaucracy: the Immigration and Naturalization Service at the Mexico-United States border. *Curr. Anthropol.* 36(2): 261–87

Heyman JMC. 1998a. *Finding a Moral Heart for U.S. Immigration Policy: an Anthropological Perspective. Am. Ethnol. Soc. Monogr. Ser. No. 7*. Arlington, VA: Am. Anthropol. Soc.

Heyman JMC. 1998b. State effects on labor: the INS and undocumented immigrants at the Mexico-United States border. *Crit. Anthropol.* 18(2):157–80

Heyman JMC. 1999. State escalation of force: a Vietnam/US-Mexico border analogy. In *States and Illegal Practices*, ed. JMC Heyman, pp. 285–314. New York: Berg

Heyman JMC, Smart A. 1999. States and illegal practices: an overview. See Heyman 1999, pp. 1–24

Hing BO. 1993. *Making and Remaking Asian America Through Immigration Policy, 1850–1990*. Stanford, CA: Stanford Univ. Press

Hoffman A. 1974. *Unwanted Mexican Americans in the Great Depression: Repatriation Pressures, 1926–1939*. Tucson: Univ. Ariz. Press

Holloway J. 1994. Global capital and the national state. *Cap. Class* 52:23–49

Holloway J. 1995. From scream of refusal to scream of power: the centrality of work. See Bonefeld et al. 1995, pp. 155–81

Hondagneu-Sotelo P. 1994. *Gendered Transitions: Mexican Experiences of Immigration*. Berkeley: Univ. Calif. Press

Hondagneu-Sotelo P. 2001. *Doméstica: Immigrant Workers Cleaning and Caring in the Shadows of Affluence*. Berkeley: Univ. Calif. Press

Honig B. 1998. Immigrant America? how foreignness "solves" democracy's problems. *Soc. Text* 56:1–27

Honig B. 2001. *Democracy and the Foreigner*. Princeton, NJ: Princeton Univ. Press

Jenkins JC. 1978. The demand for immigrant workers: labor scarcity or social control? *Int. Migr. Rev.* 12(4): 514–35

Jiménez M. 1992. War in the borderlands. *NACLA Rep. Am.* 26(1):29–33

Johnson KR. 1993. *Los olvidados*: images of the immigrant, political power of noncitizens, and immigration law and enforcement. *Brigham Young Univ. Law Rev.* 1993(4): 1139–56

Johnson KR. 1997. The new nativism: something old, something new, something borrowed, something blue. See Perea 1997, pp.165–89

Joppke C. 1999. *Immigration and the Nation-State: the United States, Germany, and Great Britain*. New York: Oxford Univ. Press

Kearney M. 1986. From the invisible hand to visible feet: anthropological studies of migration and development *Annu. Rev. Anthropol.* 15:331–61

Kearney M. 1991. Borders and boundaries of states and self at the end of empire. *J. Hist. Sociol.* 4(1):52–74

Kearney M. 1995. The local and the global: the anthropology of globalization and transnationalism. *Annu. Rev. Anthropol.* 24:547–65

Kearney M. 1996. *Reconceptualizing the Peasantry: Anthropology in Global Perspective*. Boulder, CO: Westview

Kearney M. 1998. *Peasants in the fields of value: revisiting rural class differentiation in transnational perspective*. Work. Pap., Dep. Anthropol., Univ. Calif., Riverside

Kim H. 1994. *A Legal History of Asian Americans, 1790–1990*. Westport, CT: Greenwood

Kwong P. 1997. *Forbidden Workers: Illegal Chinese Immigrants and American Labor*. New York: New Press

Lee E. 1999. Immigrants and immigration law: a state of the field assessment. *J. Am. Ethn. Hist.* 18(4):85–114

Lowe L. 1996. *Immigrant Acts: On Asian*

American Cultural Politics. Durham, NC: Duke Univ. Press

Mahler SJ. 1995. *American Dreaming: Immigrant Life on the Margins*. Princeton, NJ: Princeton Univ. Press

Malkki LH. 1995. Refugees and exile: from "refugee studies" to the national order of things. *Annu. Rev. Anthropol.* 24:495–523

Marrus MR. 1985. *The Unwanted: European Refugees in the Twentieth Century*. New York: Oxford Univ. Press

Martínez OJ. 1994. *Border People: Life and Society in the U.S.-Mexico Borderlands*. Tucson: Univ. Ariz. Press

Marx K. 1976 (1867). *Capital: a Critique of Political Economy*, Volume One. New York: Penguin Books

Massey DS. 1987. Understanding Mexican migration to the United States. *Am. J. Sociol.* 92(6):1372–1403

Massey DS, Alarcón R, Durand J, González H. 1987 . *Return to Aztlan: the Social Process of International Migration from Western Mexico*. Berkeley: Univ. Calif. Press

Massey DS, Liang Z. 1989. The long-term consequences of a temporary worker program: the U.S. bracero experience. *Popul. Res. Policy Rev.* 8:199–226

McWilliams C. 1949. *North from Mexico: the Spanish-Speaking People of the United States*. New York: Greenwood

Meissner D, Papademetriou D, North D. 1986. *Legalization of Undocumented Aliens: Lessons from Other Countries*. Washington, DC: Carnegie Endowments Int. Peace

Mirandé A. 1987. *Gringo Justice*. Notre Dame, IN: Univ. Notre Dame Press

Nathan D. 1991. *Women and Other Aliens: Essays from the U.S.-Mexico Border*. El Paso, TX: Cinco Puntos Press

Ngai MM. 1999. The architecture of race in American immigration law: a reexamination of the Immigration Act of 1924. *J. Am. Hist.* 86(1):67–92

Ngai MM. 2003. *Illegal Aliens and Alien Citizens: Immigration Restriction, Race, and Nation, 1924–1965*. Princeton, NJ: Princeton Univ. Press. In press

Ortiz S. 2002. Laboring in the factories and in the fields. *Annu. Rev. Anthropol.* 31:395–417

Park RE. 1980(1914/1928). Migration and the marginal man. In *The Pleasures of Sociology*, ed. LA Coser, pp. 241–47. New York: New Am. Libr.

Pashukanis EB. 1989 (1929). *Law and Marxism: a General Theory Towards a Critique of the Fundamental Juridical Concepts*. Worcester, UK: Pluto

Passel JS. 1994. Illegal migration to the United States—the demographic context. In *Controlling Immigration: a Global Perspective*, ed. WA Cornelius, PL Martin, JF Hollifield, pp. 113–18. Stanford, CA: Stanford Univ. Press

Patterson O. 1982. *Slavery and Social Death: a Comparative Study*. Cambridge, MA: Harvard Univ. Press

Paul K. 1997. *Whitewashing Britain: Race and Citizenship in the Postwar Era*. Ithaca, NY: Cornell Univ. Press

Perea JF, ed. 1997. *Immigrants Out! The New Nativism and the Anti-Immigrant Impulse in the United States*. New York:N.Y.Univ. Press

Pérez RT. 1991. *Diary of an Undocumented Immigrant*. Houston, TX: Arte Público Press

Piore MJ. 1979. *Birds of Passage: Migrant Labor in Industrial Societies*. London: Cambridge Univ. Press

Portes A. 1978. Toward a structural analysis of illegal (undocumented) immigration. *Int. Migr. Rev.* 12 (4):469–84

Portes A, Bach RL. 1985. *Latin Journey: Cuban and Mexican Immigrants in the United States*. Berkeley: Univ. Calif. Press

Pred A. 2000. *Even in Sweden: Racisms, Racialized Spaces, and the Popular Geographical Imagination*. Berkeley: Univ. Calif. Press

Randall M. 1987. Threatened with deportation. *Lat. Am. Perspect.* 14(4):465–80

Reimers DM. 1985. *Still the Golden Door: the Third World Comes to America*. New York: Columbia Univ. Press

Reisler M. 1976a. *By the Sweat of Their Brow: Mexican Immigrant Labor in the United States, 1900–1940*. Westport, CT: Greenwood

Reisler M. 1996 (1976b). Always the laborer, never the citizen: Anglo perceptions of the Mexican immigrant during the 1920's. In *Between Two Worlds: Mexican Immigrants in the United States*, ed. DG Gutiérrez, pp. 23–43. Wilmington, DE: Scholarly Resourc. Books

Repak TA. 1995. *Waiting on Washington: Central American Workers in the Nation's Capital*. Philadelphia: Temple Univ. Press

Roberts DE. 1997. Who may give birth to citizens? reproduction, eugenics, and immigration. See Perea 1997, pp. 205–19

Rosaldo R. 1994. Cultural citizenship and educational democracy. *Cult. Anthropol.* 9(3): 402–11

Rosaldo R. 1997. Cultural citizenship, inequality, and multiculturalism. In *Latino Cultural Citizenship: Claiming Identity, Space, and Rights*, ed. WV Flores, R Benmayor, pp. 27–38. Boston: Beacon

Rouse R. 1991. Mexican migration and the social space of postmodernism. *Diaspora* 1(1): 8–23

Rouse R. 1992. Making sense of settlement: class transformation, cultural struggle, and transnationalism among Mexican migrants in the United States. See Glick Schiller et al. 1992, pp. 25–52

Rouse R. 1995a. Thinking through transnationalism: notes on the cultural politics of class relations in the contemporary United States. *Public Cult.* 7(2):353–402

Rouse R. 1995b. Questions of identity: personhood and collectivity in transnational migration to the United States. *Crit. Anthropol.* 15(4):351–80

Salyer LE. 1995. *Laws Harsh as Tigers: Chinese Immigrants and the Shaping of Modern Immigration Law.* Chapel Hill: Univ. N. C. Press

Samora J. 1971. *Los Mojados: the Wetback Story*. Notre Dame, IN: Univ. Notre Dame Press

Sanchez GJ. 1999. Race, nation, and culture in recent immigration studies. *J. Am. Ethn. Hist.* 18(4):66–84

Sassen S. 1988. *The Mobility of Labor and Capital: a Study in International Investment and Labor Flow*. New York: Cambridge Univ. Press

Sassen S. 1990. U.S. immigration policy toward Mexico in a global economy. In *J. Int. Aff.* 43(2):369–83

Sassen S. 1996a. *Losing Control? Sovereignty in an Age of Globalization*. New York: Columbia Univ. Press

Sassen S. 1996b. Whose city is it? globalization and the formation of new claims. *Public Cult.* 8(2): 205–23

Sassen S. 1998. *Globalization and Its Discontents: Essays on the New Mobility of People and Money*. New York: New Press

Sassen S. 1999. *Guests and Aliens*. New York: New Press

Sassen S, Smith RC. 1992. Post-industrial growth and economic reorganization: their impact on immigrant employment. See Bustamante et al. 1992, pp. 372–93

Satzewich V. 1991. *Racism and the Incorporation of Foreign Labour: Farm Labour Migration to Canada Since 1945*. New York: Routledge

Saxton A. 1971. *The Indispensable Enemy: Labor and the Anti-Chinese Movement in California*. Berkeley, CA: Univ. Calif. Press

Smith RC. 1996. Mexicans in New York: membership and incorporation in a new immigrant community. In *Latinos in New York: Communities in Transition*, ed. G Haslip-Viera, SL Baver, pp. 57–103. Notre Dame, IN: Univ. Notre Dame Press

Smith RC. 1998. Closing the door on undocumented workers. *NACLA Rep. Am.* 31(4): 6–9

Soysal YN. 1994. *Limits of Citizenship: Migrants and Postnational Membership in Europe*. Chicago: Univ. Chicago Press

Suárez-Orozco MM, ed. 1998. *Crossings: Mexican Immigration in Interdisciplinary Perspectives*. Cambridge, MA: David Rockefeller Cent. Ser. Lat. Am. Stud./Harvard Univ. Press

Taylor PS. 1932. *Mexican Labor in the United States. Univ. Calif. Publ. Econ.*, Vol. 7. Berkeley: Univ. Calif. Press

Tienda M. 1989. Looking to the 1990's: Mexican immigration in sociological perspective. In *Mexican Migration to the United States: Origins, Consequences, and Policy Options*, WA Cornelius, JA Bustamante, pp. 109–47. San Diego: Center for U.S.-Mexican Studies, Univ. Calif.

US Dep. Labor. 1991. *Employer Sanctions and U.S. Labor Markets: Final Report*. Washington, DC: Div. Immigr. Policy Res., US Dep. Labor

Vélez-Ibáñez CG. 1996. *Border Visions: Mexican Cultures of the Southwest United States*. Tucson: Univ. Ariz. Press

Vila P. 2000. *Crossing Borders, Reinforcing Borders: Social Categories, Metaphors, and Narrative Identities on the U.S.-Mexico Frontier*. Austin: Univ. Tex. Press

Villar ML. 1990. Rethinking settlement processes: the experience of Mexican undocumented migrants in Chicago. *Urban Anthropol.* 19(1–2):63–79

Villar ML. 1999. The Amnesty reveals intra-ethnic divisions among Mexicans in Chicago. *Urban Anthropol.* 28(1):37–64

Weber DS. 1982. *Anglo views of Mexican immigrants: popular perceptions and neighborhood realities in Chicago, 1900–1940*. PhD thesis. Ohio State Univ. 379 pp.

Whiteford L. 1979. The borderland as an extended community. In *Migration Across Frontiers: Mexico and the United States*, ed. F Camara, RV Kemper, pp. 127–36. Albany, NY: Inst. Mesoam. Stud., SUNY

Zolberg AR. 1990. Reforming the back door: the immigration reform and Control Act of 1986 in historical perspective. In *Immigration Reconsidered: History, Sociology, Politics*, ed. V Yans-McLaughlin, pp. 315–39. New York: Oxford Univ. Press

Annu. Rev. Anthropol. 2002. 31:449–67
doi: 10.1146/annurev.anthro.31.040402.085436

First published online as a Review in Advance on June 14, 2002

THE ANTHROPOLOGY OF ONLINE COMMUNITIES

Samuel M. Wilson and Leighton C. Peterson
Department of Anthropology, The University of Texas at Austin, Austin, Texas 78712; email: s.wilson@mail.utexas.edu; leighton@mail.utexas.edu

Key Words Internet, media, computer-mediated communication, cyberspace, information technology

■ **Abstract** Information and communication technologies based on the Internet have enabled the emergence of new sorts of communities and communicative practices—phenomena worthy of the attention of anthropological researchers. Despite early assessments of the revolutionary nature of the Internet and the enormous transformations it would bring about, the changes have been less dramatic and more embedded in existing practices and power relations of everyday life. This review explores researchers' questions, approaches, and insights within anthropology and some relevant related fields, and it seeks to identify promising new directions for study. The general conclusion is that the technologies comprising the Internet, and all the text and media that exist within it, are in themselves cultural products. Anthropology is thus well suited to the further investigation of these new, and not so new, phenomena.

INTRODUCTION

In the last fifteen years, the growth of the global computer network known as the Internet has facilitated the rapid emergence of online interactions of dispersed groups of people with shared interests. These online groups exhibit a wide range of characteristics and serve a variety of purposes, from small groups engaged in tightly focused discussions of specific topics, to complex created worlds with hundreds of simultaneous participants, to millions of users linked by an interest in markets or exchange networks for goods and information. These new media collectives might be mobilized to further particular political agendas or to bring together dispersed members of familial or ethnic groups, or they might be organized around commodity consumption or multinational corporate interests. This article addresses the phenomenon of Internet-based groups and collectives, generally referred to as online communities. In reviewing anthropological approaches to these groups, we must raise several questions: How have scholars approached online communities and online communication in general? Is the concept of community itself misleading? How are issues of power and access manifested in this arena? And given that the Internet and the communication technologies based upon it—as well as all the texts and other media that exist there—are themselves cultural products, will an anthropological approach to these phenomena necessarily differ from other types of anthropological investigation?

As is the case in other academic disciplines, anthropology's interest in Internet-based social and communicative practices is relatively new, and a coherent anthropological focus or approach has yet to emerge. Despite the early interest in new media and Internet phenomena and an emerging anthropological literature, there have been relatively few ethnographic works on computing and Internet technologies within anthropology. The relative scarcity of mainstream anthropological research on the Internet and computing reflects the fact that anthropology has not played a central role in studies of mass media in the past; anthropologists have positioned media as peripheral to culture (Dickey 1997) or have viewed technology in general as a context for, rather than a central part of, culture (Aronowitz 1996, Hakken 1999, Latour 1992, Pfaffenberger 1992). As a result, much of our understanding of new information and communication technology comes from other disciplines through research into online computer-mediated interactions within the framework of the Internet, whose locus of interaction has been commonly referred to as cyberspace. Nevertheless, anthropologists remain intrigued, as they long have been, by the nexus of culture, science, and technology.

Indeed, anthropology is uniquely suited for the study of socioculturally situated online communication within a rapidly changing context. Anthropological methodologies enable the investigation of cross-cultural, multileveled, and multi-sited phenomena; emerging constructions of individual and collective identity; and the culturally embedded nature of emerging communicative and social practices. Recently there have been calls for an ethnographic approach to the issues of new media, an approach that is timely and indispensable as we begin to theorize the sociocultural implications of new communication technology (DiMaggio et al. 2001, Escobar 1994, Hakken 1999, Kottak 1996, Miller & Slater 2000). The following sections address anthropological and related research dealing with the following broad investigative topics: the ways in which information technology and media are themselves cultural products, the ways that individual and community identities are negotiated on- and offline, and the dynamics of power and access in the context of new communications media.

THE INTERNET REVOLUTION

Through most of the 1980s and 1990s, the conviction was widespread that the growing and evolving communications medium comprising inter-networked computers would enable the rapid and fundamental transformation of social and political orders. Much of the early literature surrounding the Internet regarded the new technology as revolutionary in both its technical innovation and its broad social and political implications (Benedikt 1991, Gore 1991, Negroponte 1995). Early commentators conceived of a "cyberspace" as a monolithic cyberreality, "everywhere yet nowhere, as free-floating as a cloud" (*Economist* 2001, p. 9).

Rheingold's important work *The Virtual Community* anticipated the Internet's "capacity to challenge the existing political hierarchy's monopoly on powerful communications media, and perhaps thus revitalize citizen-based democracy" (Rheingold 1993). Kirshenblatt-Gimblett (1996) argued that electronic communications separate modern and postmodern communication; Poster (1990) discussed the potential of virtual realities in altering our perceptions of reality in a postindustrial world; and Castells (1996) has suggested that information technologies represent a new information age, which is a common perspective among contemporary scholars (Lyon 1988, Webster 1995).

A genre of science fiction known as cyberpunk envisioned even more far-reaching transformations, both utopian and Orwellian, in which much of an individual's social interactions would take place in virtual spaces. Gibson's *Neuromancer* (Gibson 1984) defined and described the idea of cyberspace for a generation of readers. Other works such as Sterling's *Mirrorshades* collection (Sterling 1986) and Stephenson's *Snow Crash* (Stephenson 1992) continued to fuel the popular imagination. These inspired visions resonated in such nonfiction works as Stone's *The War of Desire and Technology at the Close of the Mechanical Age* (Stone 1995), Turkle's *Life on the Screen* (1995), or Dery's *Flame Wars* (Dery 1994) and *Escape Velocity* (Dery 1996). At the beginning of the twenty-first century, however, it appears that the salience of the most extreme of these early revolutionary visions is in decline, overtaken by what Margolis & Resnick (2000) call the "normalization of cyberspace."

As Agre (1999) notes with reference to *Neuromancer*, "Gibson famously defined cyberspace as a space apart from the corporeal world—a hallucination. But the Internet is not growing apart from the world, but to the contrary is increasingly embedded in it." By 2002, for example, the same powerful corporations that control offline news content dominated Internet-based news sources, and they accounted for the vast majority of news-related pages served (http://www.nua.com). Some anthropologists have argued that scholarship has echoed too closely the popular discourse and notions of virtual worlds. Hakken points to uncritical appropriations of the popular rhetoric on technology in much of the scholarly Internet research—rhetoric that has created "multiple, diffuse, disconnected discourses which mirror the hype of popular cyberspace talk" (Hakken 1999).

The disparate approaches to new media and Internet studies also reflect the ephemeral nature of the new media, the often elusive and ambiguous constructions of individual and collective identities mediated by these technologies, and the problem of gaining an ontological footing within rapidly obsolescing technologies. Internet interfaces such as multi-user domains (MUDs), MUD, Object-Oriented (MOOs), and Usenet—media in existence before the World Wide Web that have been the focus for scholarly research—quickly can become irrelevant, especially as increasing numbers of users become connected, beginning their Internet experiences with the latest technologies.

Similarly, the optimistic notion that the Internet would inform and empower individuals worldwide, while subverting existing power structures, may underestimate the power of states to control information access. Although there have been examples of effective use of the Internet by small groups—such as the Zapatista movement's successful use of the Internet to gain support for their cause (http://www.ezln.org) or the survival of Belgrade's web-based Radio B92 in the late 1990s (http://www.b92.net)—in many countries there have been intensive state efforts (of widely varying effectiveness) to regulate and control Internet-based access to information. Among anthropologists, early reactions to visions of online utopia were also skeptical, pointing to issues of class, gender, or race that would impede equal access (Escobar 1994, Gray & Driscoll 1992, Kottak 1996, Pfaffenberger 1988, Robins & Webster 1999), and warned of overly optimistic predictions for egalitarian communication and social change. Others scholars began pointing to the potentially negative effects of continuous virtual experience (Boal 1995, Heim 1993, Kroker & Weinstein 1994), which they feared would lead to further alienation, anomie, and antisocial behavior in postmodern society.

Internet Terminology and Ephemerality

In a newly developing field, terminology presents some problems. The confusion surrounding jargon is compounded by the appropriation of terminology from other academic fields and literary genres, including science fiction and popular culture. For this review, we are reluctant to label or characterize particular technologies or applications with great specificity because they may no longer exist in a few years. At a fundamental level, however, we refer to the infrastructure and uses of the global network of computers, or what is generally defined as the "network of networks" (Uimonen 2001), as the Internet. This substrate supports a number of communication-oriented technologies, including email and the World Wide Web—that is, data in the form of a text and graphic "page" stored on hard drives or web servers, available to anyone running protocol-translating web browser software. In the works we have reviewed, Internet refers to the physical global infrastructure as well as the uses to which the Internet as infrastructure is put, including the World Wide Web, email, and online multiperson interactive spaces such as chat-rooms (DiMaggio et al. 2001, p. 308). Communications or interactions mediated by these applications are often referred to as media, which, following Spitulnik (2001, p. 143), is "best defined by what it is not: face-to-face communication" (cf. Hannerz 1992). Media subcategories include mass media, alternative media, and print media. New media as used in this paper is another subset comprising digital-based electronic media—multimedia CD ROMs, the Internet, and video games.

These definitions are necessarily flexible and open to refinement because both the field and the phenomenon are changing so rapidly. As this review was being written in early 2002, the Internet was changing as rapidly as it had in the preceding decade. Internet traffic was doubling annually, as it had been since about 1994, and the demography of online users was also changing. Until the late 1990s the majority of users were located in the United States and other industrialized nations, but there was a trend toward change. English language use may have been surpassed by other languages in 1999 and as of late 2001, people in the United States and Canada accounted for only about 35% of the estimated 513 million Internet users worldwide (http://www.nua.com/surveys/how_many_online/index.html).

Furthermore, research conducted in the early days of personal computing and Internet access reflects technologies that are physically and semiotically different from subsequent technologies, resulting in an academic dilemma: On one level, we are not talking about the same Internet; on another level, we are talking about similar social processes and practices. In order to address this issue, we are suggesting research that focuses on social processes and emerging communicative practices rather than on specific user technologies. From that beginning, one strategy for research is to explore how and if local users are employing and defining terms such as Internet, cyberspace, and the Web, and to explore "how diversely people experience similar technologies" (Markham 1998, p. 114).

Regardless of the particular media, interface, or application—which will continue to change in the coming years—general categories of communication will persist, including one person-to-one (as in sending an email message), one-to-many (as in publishing a Web page), and many-to-many (participating in a discussion forum). These categories of communication require us to pay attention to the nature of communicative practices and online interactions. The communication technologies that make use of the Internet's infrastructure share some special characteristics. Thus, they offer special possibilities and constraints for communicative practices and social interaction and provide a context for emerging forms of communication.

INFORMATION TECHNOLOGY AS CULTURAL (RE)PRODUCTION

What is missing from new media literature is the link between historically constituted sociocultural practices within and outside of mediated communication and the language practices, social interactions, and ideologies of technology that emerge from new information and communication technologies. In order to address this issue, we should heed those who view Internet spaces and technologies as "continuous with and embedded in other social spaces" that "happen within mundane social structures and relations that they may transform but that they cannot escape" (Miller & Slater 2000, p. 5). For anthropology's contribution to the study of online practices, it may be more productive to follow those who seek to understand the offline social, cultural, and historical processes involved in the global flows of information (Brown & Duguid 2000, Garfinkel 2000) and in the diffusion, development, and acceptance of new technologies (Escobar 1994, Latour 1996, Pfaffenberger 1992, Uimonen 2001, Winston 1998).

Such an approach involves bringing research back from cyberspace and virtual reality into geographical, social spaces, to address a variety of issues such as the ways in which new participants are socialized into online practices; how gendered and racialized identities are negotiated, reproduced, and indexed in online interactions; and how Internet and computing practices are becoming normalized or institutionalized in a variety of contexts. For anthropology and its developing engagement with new media studies, however, the nature of local transformations of and within these new global media should still remain a question for ethnographic research and analysis, and the recursive relationship between virtual and offline interactions cannot be ignored (Marshall 2001). Local responses to Internet technologies will obviously vary, and even constricting spaces open up room for opposing discourses (Gal 1989), unintended consequences (Bourdieu 1977, Giddens 1979), or new dimensions of social change. It is perhaps too soon to make assertions and value judgments about systems and practices that are only beginning to emerge and for which we lack even a shared semantic framework.

Internet as Media

One way to situate computing and Internet practices is to compare them with previously existing media and communication technologies, as new forms of technologically mediated language and human interaction. An anthropological approach that builds upon the work of visual anthropology and the anthropology of mass media, as well as approaches in media and cultural studies, is one such productive vantage point in which to view phenomena of online interactions.

Much of the work on new media has been interdisciplinary, originating many times in communication and media studies, and often called computer-mediated communication (CMC) research. These scholars revealed changing communicative practices online, which were seen to be either limited (Hiltz et al. 1986) or determined (Rice 1987) by the technology. Like much of the early Internet research, this early work reflects the popular rhetoric of the new medium's virtual potentials and tends to position online communication away from other social interactions. More recent investigations of computer-mediated communication explore how online communication can change interactions and how interactions are shaped by local contexts (Cherny 1999). Such studies, however, remain situated in online communication, analyzed through texts generated in chatrooms, news groups, MOOs, and other multi-user domains (MUDs). These interfaces represent but one of many available mediated communication technologies on the Internet, which include pictures and graphics, online verbal communication, and traditional media like television and radio.

We can productively draw from CMC research while drawing anthropological questions to these phenomena and maintaining important distinctions (Morton 2001). CMC research focuses on social process and communicative practice but has been situated within theories and methods dissimilar to anthropology. Some anthropologists claim that media and cultural studies scholars lack a nuanced understanding of ethnography and culture (Ruby 2000)—methods and concepts which they increasing employ—leading to a focus instead on dichotomies of hegemony and resistance, production and reception, and of mass media and alternative media (McEachern 1998). This approach hinders the situated analysis of local cultural and media phenomena. Ginsburg suggests an important locus for anthropological contribution to media studies: To "break up the 'massness' of the media ... by recognizing the complex ways in which people are engaged in processes of making and interpreting media works in relation to their cultural, social, and historical circumstances" (Ginsburg 1994a, p. 8).

In the most-often cited work on the topic, Spitulnik (1993) calls for continuing analyses of power relations, global capital, and the role of subaltern/minority peoples in the emergence of new media processes and products (see also Dickey 1997, Hannerz 1992, Nichols 1994). The term mediascape, coined by Arjun Appadurai (1990), offers one way to describe and situate the role of electronic and print media in "global cultural flows," which are fluid and irregular as they cross global and local boundaries. For Appadurai, mediascape indexes the electronic capabilities of production and dissemination, as well as "the images of the world created by these media" (Appadurai 1990, p. 9). Ginsburg draws from Appadurai to theorize the position of the indigenous media in Australia and argues that a mediascape "helps to establish a more generative discursive space ... which breaks what one might call the fetishizing of the local" (Ginsburg 1994b, p. 366). This model drawn from Appadurai and Ginsburg has many benefits for analyses of Internet communication, as one way to draw cyberspace back into offline processes and practices and a way to incorporate new media practices with other forms of media.

Community

As has been the case for some time in anthropology, community is a difficult focus for study, generally because it seems to imply a false circumscription and coherence. Individuals belong to many communities, bounded to different extents and in varying ways. In some cases the term suggests, as in the community studies of the 1940s and 1950s, that the defined entity was reasonably complete and self-contained. The assessment then [see Foster's (1953) critique of Redfield's (1947) isolated "folk" societies] and more recently (Gupta & Ferguson 1997) has been that an analytical emphasis on a community's boundedness and isolation usually masks significant interactions between the individuals of that community and others, as well as the heterogeneity of the community itself (Appadurai 1991). A more fluid concept of community fits well within ethnographic explorations in multisited situations with complex, spatially diverse communities (Marcus 1995) and translocal sites (Hannerz 1998). Just as Wolf (1982) rejected the conception of cultural groups as "hard and round billiard balls" bouncing off of one another, and Barthes (1992) recognized the asymmetrical, indirect connections that knit communities together, we simply acknowledge that individuals within any community are simultaneously part of other interacting communities, societies, or cultures.

In the case of Internet-mediated communication within a group, constituted around some shared interest or condition, the problem is compounded. Within the scholarly literature on Internet communication, a debate has continued about whether online, virtual, or otherwise computer-mediated communities are real or imagined (Bordieu & Colemen 1991, Calhoun 1991, Markham 1998, Oldenburg 1989, Rheingold 1993, Thomsen et al. 1998). This debate explored whether these sorts of community are too ephemeral to investigate as communities per se, or whether the nature of the communication medium made them somehow quite different from the face-to-face groupings traditionally thought of as communities. Rhinegold (1993) suggested that online communities were replacing public spaces such as pubs and cafés as loci of public social interaction. As Agre observed, "[s]o long as we persist in opposing so-called virtual communities to the face-to-face communities of the mythical opposite extreme, we miss the ways in which real communities of practice employ a whole ecology of media as they think together about the matters that concern them" (Agre 1999, p. 4). Indeed, reference to "communities of practice" (Lave & Wenger 1991, Wenger 1998) or "communities of interest" (Brown & Duguid 1991, Uimonen 2001) shows the wide range of disciplinary interest in the nature of online communities, with similar discussions going on in education, management, cognitive psychology, and other fields (Fernback 1999).

We agree that a focus on interactions that take place online to the exclusion of those that do not is counterproductive. The idea that a community was defined by face-to-face interaction was effectively challenged long ago by scholars of the development of nationalism (Anderson 1983) and transnationalism (Basch et al. 1994, Hannerz 1996). An online/offline conceptual dichotomy [for example Castells' (1996) "network society"] is also counter to the direction taken within recent anthropology, which acknowledges the multiple identities and negotiated roles individuals have within different sociopolitical and cultural contexts. We are not suggesting that this point has been completely overlooked in Internet research, as scholars continue to research the development of online communities within the context of geographical communities (Agre & Schuler 1997, Hamman 2000). Specific case studies such as Kuwaiti women's uses of the Internet for political action (Wheeler 2001), American teenage dating practices in chat rooms (Clark 1998), and a study of the norms and practices of community maintenance in an online lesbian café (Correll 1995) illustrate how offline social roles and existing cultural ideologies are played out, and sometimes exaggerated, in online communication.

We are suggesting, however, that closer attention be given to deconstructing dichotomies of offline and online, real and virtual, and individual and collective. An important part of the research going on, particularly in communications and sociology, involves the new media's potential for online community building and the patterns this process has taken or might take (Agre & Schuler 1997, Caldwell 2000, Correll 1995, Ess & Sudweeks 2001, Jones 1998, Rheingold 1993, Schuler 1996). Our view, and one that seems most consonant with current anthropological theory and practice, is that the distinction of real and imagined or virtual community is not a useful one, and that an anthropological approach is well suited to investigate the continuum of communities, identities, and networks that exist—from the most cohesive to the most diffuse—regardless of the ways in which community members interact.

Identity

Within sociology and psychology, as well as in more popular genres, considerable attention has been given to the idea that virtual spaces allow for fundamentally new constructions of identity: Interactive chatrooms and online spaces were often seen to be gender-neutral, egalitarian spaces. Turkle described online interaction spaces as places where an individual could take on multiple identities in ways never before possible and indeed bring about changes in conventional notions of identity itself (Turkle 1984, 1995). Haraway (1993) conceived of entirely new constructions of individuality based on cyborgs, or hybrids of machine and human. This work had implications for the virtual individual, especially in the realm of sexuality, and deprivileges "nature," sexual reproduction, and identity of the discrete, identifiable self (Haraway 1993). Morse investigated the implications of cyberspace for subjectivity, identity, and presence (Morse 1998). With reference to Peter Steiner's famous New Yorker drawing (Figure 1), online identities were seen to be infinitely malleable.

Of course, identities are negotiated, reproduced, and indexed in a variety of ways in online interactions, and these often cannot be understood without considering the offline context. As Agre (1999) notes, "so long as we focus on the limited areas of the internet where people engage in fantasy play that is intentionally disconnected from their real-world identities, we miss how social and professional identities are continuous across several media, and how people use those several media to develop their identities in ways that carry over to other settings" (Agre 1999, p. 4). Several researchers are exploring the ways in which online interactions are influenced by offline power relations and constructions of identity, which involve the exploration of gender (Brook & Boal 1995, Correll 1995, Dietrich 1997, O'Brien 1999, Wellman & Gulia 1999, Wheeler 2001) and race and racialized discourses (Burkhalter 1999, Ebo 1998, Kolko et al. 2000) in a variety of ways. Scholars have also viewed online identities as directly tied to the notion of credibility, context, and frame in the exploration of real vs. virtual identities (Markham 1998, O'Brian 1999). Nevertheless, this is an area in which a great deal more could be done.

Online groups can also be centered around offline ethnic or national identities, and researchers have explored this issue in a variety of contexts—for example, the ways in which Tongans (Morton 1999, 2002) or Inuit (Christensen 1999) create shared spaces in online interaction. The nature of computer-mediated interactions will not merely recreate offline interactions, and "online groups may be significantly different to their offline communities" (Morton 2001, p. 4), and it is important to consider that an Internet user is not always privileging the same national or ethnic identity in every online interaction. Multiple participatory frames and identities are available and used by a wide variety of Internet users in a wide

"On the Internet, nobody knows you're a dog."

Figure 1 Peter Steiner's drawing from the *New Yorker*, July 5, 1993.

variety of contexts. We are suggesting an approach for research in this area, best termed contextualized identities (rather than performed, negotiated, or contested) to break through the virtual/real dichotomy of online identity.

Communication and Practice

Any investigation into the nature of online communities involves language and communicative practice. The most comprehensive overview of the language of new media is Crystal's (2001) synthesis of emergent communicative practices surrounding the Internet. Crystal states that "if the Internet is a revolution, therefore, it is likely to be a linguistic revolution" (p. x), and notes the importance of language-based research on new media technologies. Using English-language data such as emails, chat room transcriptions, and bulletin board posts, Crystal asserts that new varieties of language are indeed emerging from new technologies, but suggests that cultural and linguistic differences which influence online interactions remain underesearched.

The idea of a speech community is relevant to the study of online communities through interactions between individuals or groups with a variety of sociolinguistic histories, but with shared communicative competence and repertoires. Internet-based speech communities are constructed around socioculturally constituted interactions that, like offline speech communities, "cannot be defined by static physical location" (Morgan 2001). Interacting members of online groups constitute a speech community as they presumably share to some extent communicative practices, beliefs, and norms, since communication would be hindered otherwise. However, much of the research into computer mediated communication has been based exclusively upon the use of varieties of English in text-based interactions, limiting our understanding of this global, multimedia phenomenon. A notable exception is Keating's (2000) research into emergent practices in American Sign Language resulting from Intermet-based video chat relays.

Analyzed through the lens of contemporary approaches in ethnographies of communication, research in multilingual, multisited Internet experiences would contribute to debates in the literature which seeks to position studies of mediated communication and technology in local social and communicative practices (Goodwin 1994; Goodwin 1990; Heath & Luff 2000; Hollan et al. 2000; Keating 2000; Spitulnik 1996, 1998, 2000). Such research might help our understanding of the ways in which speakers incorporate new technologies of communication from existing communicative repertoires, and these technologies influence new and emerging cultural practices. In this sort of investigation, researchers must ask: Where do community members situate computers and other communication and information technologies in their daily lives? How are the tools of new media changing the contexts and frames of communicative practices? Are new forms of communicative competence developing as a consequence of new media tools in offline speech communities? How does technology enhance or displace discourses and practices of tradition? How might new technologies alter novice-expert relations? How do linguistic structures of online interactions affect offline practice?

The emerging framework of distributed cognition (Cole et al. 1997, Hollan et al. 2000, Hutchins 1995, Hutchins & Klausen 1996) has the potential to address these phenomena, moving beyond the initial conceptions of an ungrounded cyberspace and two-dimensional human-computer interactions toward understanding "the emerging dynamic of interaction in a world that contains material and social organization" (Hollan et al. 2000). This framework provides a link between human-computer interaction, the Internet, previously existing media, and social spaces, and it allows anthropologists to address important issues of the social role of technology, the relationship between language and technology, and questions of access to technologies in traditionally marginalized communities.

Power, Ideology, and Access

Particularly within anthropology, some researchers have attempted to relate online experiences within larger contexts of power and broader social hierarchies. They and others have explored the Internet's potential to advance efforts for social justice (Burkhalter 1999, Downing 1989, Downing et al. 2000, Loader 1998). Within nearly all of the foregoing works, the issue of class has played a significant part, as it does in the research of English-Lueck (1998), Kirshenblatt-Gimblett (1996), Merrifield et al. (1997), and Loader (1998). Hakken & Andrews (1993) for example studied the effects of computing technology on class structures in work environments in England. Ethnographers have also explored the social impacts of technology practices in a variety of innovative ways, including Kelty's (2000) research on the impact of (non)regulation of software development and computer use in healthcare organizations.

Our focus in this review has excluded consideration of the digital divide and other kinds of inequality of access to online communication. Of course, the makeup of online communities rests directly upon the constitution of Internet users, i.e., those who have access. We would note, however, that access includes a great deal more than the right of entry to the places where Internet-based equipment is kept. It also involves some knowledge of technology itself, as well as a facility and experience level, not just in a technical sense but in the sense of the social context of Internet-based media and the implications of the technology on a wider scale. Others have argued well that equal access is not achieved simply by installing computers and fast Internet connections in schools and homes (Burbules 1998, Burbules & Callister 2000, Wilson 2000). The material approach will be insufficient "if prospective users do not also have an opportunity to develop the skills and attitudes necessary to take advantage of those resources" (Burbules & Callister 2000, p. 20). For example, Kirshenblatt-Gimblett (1996) argued that users who don't subscribe to the dominant ideologies of language and technology may not be able to have equal access to Internet resources.

In addressing the complex issue of access, we must also touch on ideology: particularly the language contexts surrounding these new media, the ways in which information and communication technologies are used, and the ways in which individuals' ideologies interact with the ideologies inscribed in technology, and how they combine to create new ways of viewing and talking about the world. In more marginalized communities, discourses of technological empowerment have been shown to influence, but not to determine, local perceptions of technology's potential and strategies for its use (Uimonen 2001). Sherry's (2002) research on computers in Navajo work environments revealed a dialectical, sometimes conflicting, relationship between ideologies of technology and the discourses of Navajo tradition. Understanding local discourse and ideologies of media technology is crucial since speakers incorporate new technologies of communication from existing communicative repertoires, which influence new and emerging cultural practices (Hutchins 1995, Keating 2000). These metadiscursive practices have broader implications for participation in new public spheres (Briggs Bauman 1999, Spitulnik 2001), the "social organization of technology" (Keating 2000), and the consequences of shifting spaces for language use and language contact (Crystal 2001). The relationship of ideology to social and linguistic practice is an increasingly important avenue for future research.

ETHICAL CONSIDERATIONS FOR INTERNET RESEARCH

Internet phenomena are leading us to ask new questions, and new media research requires adapting ethnographic methods to new technological environments (Hamman nd, Jacobson 1999, Jones 1999, Markham 1998, Paccagnella 1997, Ruhleder 2000). Within this environment of change, however, we are also in a moment in which the ethical responsibilities of the researcher are far from clear. As Turkle (1995, p. 324) notes, "virtual reality poses a new methodological challenge for the researcher: what to make of online interviews and indeed, whether and how to use them." As Jacobson discusses, when carrying out research online the researcher must be aware of "the identifiability of human subjects, the conceptualization of privacy, difficulties associated with obtaining informed consent, and the applicability of copyright laws" (Jacobson 1999, p. 139; see also Morton 2001, Thomas 1996). As of this writing the American Anthropological Association offers no ethical protocols or standards specific to online interactions in its Code of Ethics (AAA 1998). For some researchers, the statements made in publicly accessible discussion boards or other communication spaces are in the public domain and may thus be freely used by researchers. For others, this is a form of electronic eavesdropping that violates the speaker's expectation of privacy. Our feeling, in keeping with the view that anthropology online is substantially the same as any other sort of anthropological research, is that although the AAA Code of Ethics does not address electronic communication directly, its ethical principles—of showing respect for people under study, of protecting their dignity and best interests, of protecting anonymity or giving proper credit, and of obtaining informed consent—apply online as well as in face-to-face contexts.

CONCLUSION

Although we have concluded that online phenomena share important similarities with other types of human experience and are amenable to relatively conventional anthropological concepts and assumptions, the Internet is still in a period of innovation, experimentation, and rapid change. The ability for groups and individuals to interact at great distances raises interesting questions for those investigating the construction of identity, social interactions, and collective action—political or otherwise. As noted above, the Web has created a new arena for group and individual self-representation, changing the power dynamics of representation for traditionally marginalized groups such as Native Americans within the discourses of popular culture. It is also an exciting moment for those studying changes in communicative practice, as people invent new forms of communication or adapt old ones to new technologies.

The revolutionary claims made for the Internet and the communications media it supports have faded in recent years. The realization has grown that though online communication may happen faster, over larger distances, and may bring about the reformulation of some existing power relationships, the rapid and fundamental transformations of society that some foresaw have not come to pass. Inter-networked computers are cultural products that exist in the social and political worlds within which they were developed, and they are not exempt from the rules and norms of those worlds.

On the other hand, the social uses of the Internet, in the few years of its existence, have been astonishing and almost completely unanticipated by those who began networking computers in the 1960s (Berners-Lee & Fischetti 1999). These new communicative practices and communities very properly demand the attention of anthropologists, not to invent completely new analytical approaches to virtual spaces, but to bring to bear our existing expertise on human communication and culture.

ACKNOWLEDGMENTS

The authors wish to thank Elizabeth Keating, Chris Kelty, Helen Morton, Edward Proctor, John Schaeffer, Joel Sherzer, Pauline Turner Strong, and Paula Uimonen for their comments on earlier drafts of this article.

The *Annual Review of Anthropology* is online at http://anthro.annualreviews.org

LITERATURE CITED

Agre P. 1999. Life after cyberspace. *EASST (Eur. Assoc. Study Sci. Technol.) Rev.* 18:3–5

Agre P, Schuler D. 1997. *Reinventing Technology, Rediscovering Community: Critical Explorations of Computing as a Social Practice*. Greenwich, CT: Ablex

American Anthropological Association. 1998. *Code of Ethics of the American Anthropological Association*. http://www.aaanet.org/committees/ethics/ethcode.htm

Anderson B. 1983. *Imagined Communities: Reflections on the Origin and Spread of Nationalism*. London: Verso

Appadurai A. 1990. Disjuncture and difference in the global cultural economy. *Public Cult.* 2:1–24

Appadurai A. 1991. Global ethnoscapes: notes and queries for a transnational anthropology. In *Recapturing Anthropology: Working in the Present*, ed. RG Fox, pp. 191–210. Santa Fe, NM: Sch. Am. Res. Press

Aronowitz S. 1996. *Technoscience and Cyberculture*. New York: Routledge
Barthes F. 1992. Towards greater naturalism in conceptualizing societies. In *Conceptualizing Society*, ed. A Kuper, pp. 17–33. London/New York: Routledge
Basch L, Schiller NG, Blanc CS. 1994. *Nations Unbound: Transnational Projects, Postcolonial Predicaments, and Deterritorialized Nation-States*. Langhorne, PA: Gordon & Breach
Benedikt M. 1991. Introduction. In *Cyberspace: First Steps*, ed. M Benedikt, pp. 1–25. Cambridge, MA: MIT Press
Berners-Lee T, Fischetti M. 1999. *Weaving the Web: the Original Design and Ultimate Destiny of the World Wide Web by Its Inventor*. San Francisco: Harper
Boal IA. 1995. A flow of monsters: Luddism and virtual technologies. In *Resisting the Virtual Life: the Culture and Politics of Information*, ed. J Brook, IA Boal, pp. 3–15. San Francisco: City Lights
Bourdieu P. 1977. *Outline of a Theory of Practice*. Cambridge: Cambridge Univ. Press
Bordieu P, Colemen JS. 1991. *Social Theory for a Changing Society*. Boulder, CO: Westview
Briggs C, Bauman R. 1999. "The Foundation of All Future Researches": Franz Boas, George Hunt, Native American texts, and the construction of modernity. *Am. Q.* 51:479–528
Brook J, Boal IA. 1995. *Resisting the Virtual Life: the Culture and Politics of Information*. San Francisco: City Lights
Brown JS, Duguid P. 2000. *The Social Life of Information*. Boston: Harvard Bus. Sch. Press
Burbules NC. 1998. Questions of content and questions of access to the Internet. *Access* 17:79–89
Burbules NC, Callister TA. 2000. *Watch IT: the Risks and Promises of Information Technologies for Education*. Boulder, CO: Westview
Burkhalter B. 1999. Reading race online: discovering racial identity in Usenet discussions. In *Communities in Cyberspace*, ed. MA Smith, P Kollock, pp. 60–75. London/New York: Routledge
Caldwell JT, ed. 2000. *Electronic Media and Technoculture*. New Brunswick, NJ: Rutgers Univ. Press
Calhoun C. 1991. Indirect relationships and imagined communities: large-scale social integration and the transformation of everyday life. See Bordieu & Coleman 1991, pp. 95–120
Castells M. 1996. *The Rise of the Network Society*. Cambridge, MA: Blackwell
Cherny L. 1999. *Conversation and Community: Chat in a Virtual World*. Stanford, CA: Cent. Study Lang. Inf.
Christensen NB. 1999. *(Re)producing Inuit social boundaries on the World Wide Web*. 5th Circumpolar Univ. Conf. (CUA), Aberdeen, Scotland
Clark LS. 1998. Dating on the net: teens and the rise of "pure" relationships. See Jones 1998, pp. 159–83
Cole M, Engeström Y, Vasquez O, eds. 1997. *Mind, Culture, and Activity: Seminal Papers from the Laboratory of Comparative Human Cognition*. Cambridge, UK: Cambridge Univ. Press
Correll S. 1995. The ethnography of an electronic bar. *J. Contemp. Ethnogr.* 24:270–98
Crystal D. 2001. *Language and the Internet*. Cambridge, UK: Cambridge Univ. Press
Dery M. 1994. *Flame Wars: the Discourse of Cyberculture*. Durham, NC: Duke Univ. Press
Dery M. 1996. *Escape Velocity: Cyberculture at the End of the Century*. New York: Grove
Dickey S. 1997. Anthropology and its contributions to studies of mass media. *Int. Soc. Sci. J.* 49:413–32
Dietrich D. 1997. (Re)-fashioning the techno-erotic woman: gender and textuality in the cybercultural matrix. In *Virtual Culture*, ed. SG Jones, pp. 169–84. Thousand Oaks, CA: Sage
DiMaggio P, Hargittai E, Neuman WR, Robinson JP. 2001. Social implications of the internet. *Annu. Rev. Sociol.* 27:307–36

Downing JDH. 1989. Computers and political change: PeaceNet and public data access. *J. Commun.* 39:154–62

Downing JDH, Ford TV, Gil G, Stein L. 2000. *Radical Media: Rebellious Communication and Social Movements*. Thousand Oaks, CA: Sage

Ebo BL. 1998. *Cyberghetto or Cybertopia?: Race, Class, and Gender on the Internet*. Westport, CT: Praeger

Economist. 2001. Special report: geography and the net, putting it in its place. *The Economist,* pp. 18–20

English-Lueck J. 1998. Technology and social change: the effects on family and community. *COSSA Congressional Seminar.* 1 November 2001 http://www.sjsu.edu/depts/anthropology/svcp/SVCPcosa.html

Escobar A. 1994. Welcome to Cyberia: notes on the anthropology of cyberculture. *Curr. Anthropol.* 35:211–32

Ess C, Sudweeks F, eds. 2001. *Culture, Technology, Communication: Towards an Intercultural Global Village*. Albany: State Univ. NY Press

Fernback J. 1999. There is a there there. In *Doing Internet Research: Critical Issues and Methods for Examining the Net*, ed. S Jones, pp. 203–20. Thousand Oaks, CA: Sage

Foster GM. 1953. What is folk culture? *Am. Anthropol.* 55:159–73

Gal S. 1989. Language and political economy. *Annu. Rev. Anthropol.* 18:345–67

Garfinkel S. 2000. *Database Nation: the Death of Privacy in the 21st Century*. Beijing/Cambridge: O'Reilly

Gibson W. 1984. *Neuromancer.* New York: Ace

Giddens A. 1979. *Central Problems in Social Theory: Action, Structure, and Contradiction in Social Analysis*. Berkeley: Univ. Calif. Press

Ginsburg F. 1994a. Culture/media. *Anthropol. Today* 10:5–15

Ginsburg F. 1994b. Embedded aesthetics: creating a discursive space for indigenous media. *Cult. Anthropol.* 9:365–82

Goodwin C. 1994. Professional vision. *Am. Anthropol.* 96:606–33

Goodwin MH. 1990. *He-Said-She-Said: Talk as Social Organization Among Black Children.* Bloomington: Indiana Univ. Press

Gore AJ. 1991. Information superhighways: the next information revolution. *The Futurist* 25:21–23

Gray CH, Driscoll M. 1992. What's real about virtual reality?: anthropology of, and in, cyberspace. *Vis. Anthropol. Rev.* 8:39–49

Gupta A, Ferguson J, eds. 1997. *Anthropological Locations: Boundaries and Grounds of a Field Science*. Berkeley: Univ. Calif. Press

Hakken D. 1999. *Cyborgs@cyberspace?: an Ethnographer Looks to the Future*. New York: Routledge

Hakken D, Andrews B. 1993. *Computing Myths, Class Realities: an Ethnography of Technology and Working People in Sheffield, England.* Boulder, CO: Westview

Hamman R. nd. The application of ethnographic methodology in the study of cybersex. *Cybersociology* Vol. 1. http://www.cybersociology.com

Hamman RB. 1997. The application of ethnographic methodology in the study of cybersex. *Cybersociol. Mag.* 1. 10 October 1997 http://www.socio.demon.co.uk/magazine

Hamman RB. 2000. Computernetze als verb indendes Element von Gemeinschaftsnetzen: Studie über die Wirkungen der Nutzung von Computernetzen auf bestehende soziale Gemeinschaften. In *Virtuelle Gruppen: Charakterstika und Problemdimensionen*, ed. U Thiedeke, pp. 221–43. Opladen/Wiesbaden: Westdeutscher

Hannerz U. 1996. *Transnational Connections.* London: Routledge

Hannerz U. 1998. Transnational research. In *Handbook of Methods in Cultural Anthropology*, ed. HR Bernard, pp. 235–56. Walnut Creek, CA: AltaMira

Haraway D. 1993. A cyborg manifesto. In *The Cultural Studies Reader*, ed. S During, pp. 271–91. London: Routledge

Heath C, Luff P. 2000. *Technology in Action.* Cambridge: Cambridge Univ. Press

Heim M. 1993. *The Metaphysics of Virtual Reality.* Oxford: Oxford Univ. Press

Hiltz SR, Johnson K, Turoff M. 1986. Experiments in group decision making: communication process and outcome in face-to-face versus computerized conferences. *Hum. Commun. Res.* 13:225–52

Hollan JD, Hutchins E, Kirsh D. 2000. Distributed cognition: a new foundation for human-computer interaction research. *ACM Trans. Comput.-Hum. Interact.* 7:174–96

Hutchins E. 1995. *Cognition in the Wild.* Cambridge, MA: MIT Press

Hutchins E, Klausen T. 1996. Distributed cognition in an airline cockpit. In *Cognition and Communication at Work*, ed. Y Engeström, D Middleton, pp. 15–34. Cambridge, UK: Cambridge Univ. Press

Jacobson D. 1999. Doing research in cyberspace. *Field Methods* 11:127–45

Jones S. 1999. *Doing Internet Research: Critical Issues and Methods for Examining the Net.* Thousand Oaks, CA: Sage

Jones SG. 1998. *CyberSociety 2.0: Revisiting Computer-Mediated Communication and Community.* Thousand Oaks, CA: Sage

Keating EL. 2000. How culture and technology together shape new communicative practices: investigating interactions between deaf and hearing callers with computer-mediated videotelephone. *Texas Linguist. Forum* 43:99–116

Kelty CM. 2000. *Scale and convention: programmed languages in a regulated America.* PhD thesis. MIT, Cambridge

Kirshenblatt-Gimblett B. 1996. The electronic vernacular. In *Connected: Engagements with Media*, ed. GE Marcus, pp. 21–65. Chicago: Univ. Chicago Press

Kolko BE, Nakamura L, Rodman GB. 2000. *Race in Cyberspace.* New York: Routledge

Kottak CP. 1996. Integration, disintegration, and re-integration via advanced information technology. *Soc. Sci. Comput. Rev.* 14(1):10–15

Kroker A, Weinstein MA. 1994. *Data Trash: the Theory of the Virtual Class.* New York: St. Martin's Press

Latour B. 1992. Where are the missing masses? The sociology of a few mundane artifacts. In *Shaping Technology/Building Society: Studies in Sociotechnical Change*, ed. WE Bijker, J Law, pp. 225–58. Cambridge, MA: MIT

Latour B. 1996. *Aramis, or, The Love of Technology.* Cambridge, MA: Harvard Univ. Press

Lave JE, Wenger 1991. *Situated Learning: Legitimate Peripheral Participation.* Cambridge: Cambridge Univ. Press

Loader B. 1998. *Cyberspace Divide: Equality, Agency, and Policy in the Information Society.* London/New York: Routledge

Lyon D. 1988. *The Information Society: Issues and Illusions.* Oxford: Polity

Marcus GE. 1995. Ethnography in/of the world system: the emergence of multi-sited ethnography. *Am. Rev. Anthropol.* 24:95–117

Margolis M, Resnick D. 2000. *Politics as Usual: the Cyberspace "Revolution."* London: Sage

Markham AN. 1998. *Life Online: Researching Real Experience in Virtual Space.* Walnut Creek, CA: AltaMira

Marshall J. 2001. Cyber-space, or cyber-topos: the creation of online space. *Soc. Anal.* 45: 81–102

McEachern C. 1998. A mutual interest? Ethnography in anthropology and cultural studies. *Aust. J. Anthropol.* 9:251–61

Merrifield J, Bingman M, Hemphill D, Bennett deMarrais K, eds. 1997. *Life at the Margins: Literacy, Language, and Technology in Everyday Life.* New York: Teachers College Press

Miller D, Slater D. 2000. *The Internet: an Ethnographic Approach.* Oxford/New York: Berg

Morgan MM. 2001. Community. In *Key Terms in Language and Culture*, ed. A Duranti, pp. 31–33. Oxford/Malden, MA: Blackwell

Morse M. 1998. *Virtualities: Television, Media Art, and Cyberculture.* Bloomington: Indiana Univ. Press

Morton H. 1999. Islanders in space: Tongans online. In *Small Worlds, Global Lives: Islands and Migration*, ed. J Connell, R King, pp. 55–74. London: Cassell

Morton H. 2001. Introduction. *Soc. Anal.* 45:3–11

Morton H. 2002. *Tongans Overseas: Between Two Shores*. Honolulu: Univ. Hawaii Press

Negroponte N. 1995. *Being Digital*. New York: Knopf

Nichols B. 1994. *Blurred Boundaries: Questions of Meaning in Contemporary Culture*. Bloomington: Indiana University Press.

O'Brien J. 1999. Writing in the body: gender (re)production in online interaction. In *Communities in Cyberspace*, ed. MA Smith, P Kollock, pp. 76–106. London/New York: Routledge

Oldenburg R. 1989. *The Great Good Places*. New York: Paragon House

Paccagnella L. 1997. Getting the seats of your pants dirty: strategies for ethnographic research on virtual communities. *J. Comput. Med. Commun.* 3(1). http://www.ascusc.org/jcmc/vol3/issue1/paccagnella.html

Pfaffenberger B. 1988. The social meaning of the personal computer: or, why the personal computer revolution was no revolution. *Anthropol. Q.* 61:39–47

Pfaffenberger B. 1992. Social anthropology of technology. *Annu. Rev. Anthropol.* 21:491–516

Poster M. 1990. *The Mode of Information: Poststructuralism and Social Context*. Chicago: Univ. Chicago Press

Redfield R. 1947. The folk society. *Am. J. Sociol.* 52:293–308

Rheingold H. 1993. *The Virtual Community: Homesteading on the Electronic Frontier*. Reading, MA: Addison-Wesley

Rice RE. 1987. Electronic emotion: socioemotional content in a computer-mediated communication network. *Commun. Res.* 14:85–108

Robins K, Webster F. 1999. *Times of the Technoculture*. New York: Routledge

Ruby J. 2000. *Picturing Culture: Explorations of Film and Anthropology*. Chicago: Univ. Chicago Press

Ruhleder K. 2000. The virtual ethnographer. *Field Methods* 12:3–17

Schuler D. 1996. *New Community Networks: Wired for Change*. Reading, MA: Addison-Wesley

Sherry J. 2002. *Land, Wind and Hard Words: a Story of Navajo Activism*. Albuquerque: Univ. New Mexico Press

Spitulnik D. 1996. Social circulation of media discourse and the mediation of communities. *J. Linguist. Anthropol.* 6:161–87

Spitulnik D. 1998. Mediated modernities: encounters with the electronic in Zambia. *Vis. Anthropol. Rev.* 14:63–84

Spitulnik D. 2000. Documenting radio culture as lived experience: reception studies and the mobile machine in Zambia. In *African Broadcast Cultures: Radio and Public Life*, ed. R Fardon, G Furniss, pp. 144–63. Oxford: Currey

Spitulnik D. 2001. Media. In *Key Terms in Language and Culture*, ed. A Duranti, pp. 143–46. Oxford: Blackwell

Steiner P. 1993. Cartoon: Dogs on the Internet. *The New Yorker.* 69(20):61

Stephenson N. 1992. *Snow Crash*. New York: Bantam Books

Sterling B. 1986. *Mirrorshades: the Cyberpunk Anthology*. New York: Arbor House

Stone AR. 1995. *The War of Desire and Technology at the Close of the Mechanical Age*. Cambridge, MA: MIT

Thomas J. 1996. Introduction: a debate about the ethics of fair practices in collecting social science data in cyberspace. *Inf. Soc.* 12:107–17

Thomsen SR, Straubhaar JD, Bolyard DM. 1998. Ethnomethodology and the study of online communities: exploring the cyber streets. *IRISS '98 Conf. Pap. Int. Conf., Bristol, UK*, pp. 25–27

Turkle S. 1984. *The Second Self: Computers and the Human Spirit*. New York: Simon & Schuster

Turkle S. 1995. *Life on the Screen: Identity in the Age of the Internet*. New York: Simon & Schuster

Uimonen P. 2001. *Transnational. Dynamics@Development.Net: Internet, Modernization and Globalization*. Stockholm: Stockholm Stud. Soc. Anthropol.

Webster F. 1995. *Theories of the Information Society*. London/New York: Routledge

Wellman B, Gulia M. 1999. Virtual communities as communities: net surfers don't ride alone. In *Communities in Cyberspace*, ed. MA Smith, P Kollock, pp. 167–95. London/New York: Routledge

Wheeler D. 2001. New technologies, old cuture. In *Culture, Technology, Communication*, ed. C Ess, pp. 187–212. Albany: State Univ. NY Press

Wilson EJI. 2000. Closing the digital divide: an initial review. *Briefing the President*. Internet Policy Institute: http://www.internetpolicy.org/publications/index.html

Winston B. 1998. *Media Technology and Society: a History from the Telegraph to the Internet*. London: Routledge

Wolf ER. 1982. *Europe and the People Without History*. Berkeley: Univ. Calif. Press

Annu. Rev. Anthropol. 2002. 31:469–96
doi: 10.1146/annurev.anthro.31.040402.085453

First published online as a Review in Advance on June 26, 2002

TOWARD AN ANTHROPOLOGY OF DEMOCRACY

Julia Paley
University of Pennsylvania, Department of Anthropology, 323 University Museum, 33rd and Spruce Streets, Philadelphia, Pennsylvania 19104-6398; email: jpaley@ssc.upenn.edu

Key Words civil society, social movements, citizenship, governmentality, NGOs

■ **Abstract** Anthropologists, through their ethnographic method, relationships with people outside of formal and elite political institutions, and attention to alternative worldviews, bring to the study of democracy an examination of local meanings, circulating discourses, multiple contestations, and changing forms of power that is rare in the scholarly literature on democratic transitions, which has largely focused on political institutions and formal regime shifts. This review brings together the writings of ethnographers working in a wide variety of settings to generate lines of inquiry and analysis for developing an anthropology of democracy.

INTRODUCTION

Much ebullience greeted news of transitions to democracy worldwide in the 1970s and 1980s; yet in the wake of the celebrations, cynical phrases such as "low intensity democracy" (Gills et al. 1993) and "democracy lite" circulated widely, betraying a residual skepticism about the positive nature of political shifts. In academic literature, what had been hailed as "the third wave of democracy" (Huntington 1991) later came under critical scrutiny, as scholars aimed to understand different types and intensities of regime changes, their endurance ("consolidation"), and more recently still their "quality" ("deepening democracy").

By and large, these studies of democracy were conducted by political scientists whose concerns with political institutions, formal regime shifts, and comparative country studies shaped the questions and set the agendas for debate (see, e.g., O'Donnell & Schmitter 1986, Linz & Stepan 1996, Diamond et al. 1997, and the *Journal of Democracy*, published in part by the National Endowment for Democracy. But cf. Carothers 2002 as a critique of the transition paradigm, Putnam 1993 as an example of a widely read single country study, Yashar 1997 for an historical account, and Schaffer 1998 for an examination of democracy in cultural terms). Yet as anthropologists doing fieldwork in Eastern Europe, Africa, Latin America, and elsewhere have witnessed regime transitions in the places they study, democracy has emerged as a salient theme. Anthropologists' ethnographic method, their relationships with people outside of formal and elite political institutions, and

0084-6570/02/1021-0469$14.00

their attention to alternative worldviews have led them to look beyond official political transitions to the local meanings, circulating discourses, multiple contestations, and changing forms of power accompanying the installation of new political regimes.[1]

More often than not, anthropological observations on democracy are couched in other frameworks and embedded in other discussions. These have included social movements, human rights, law, citizenship, bureaucracy, violence, militaries, postcolonialism, the state, globalization, power, nongovernmental organizations, and civil society, to name just a few. Indeed at the 2001 American Anthropological Association meetings, an informal survey of presentations listed in the conference program and books on display revealed little work on the topic of democracy specifically (exceptions included Schirmer 1998, Paley 2001, Adams 1998; see also Gutmann 2002). The theme is nonetheless on the minds of many anthropologists, as I found when I wrote to over 70 scholars (mainly political anthropologists) to solicit their views. Over 50 replied, many with long and thoughtful commentaries detailing recommended reading, new areas of study, and ideas for analysis. Such a response indicates a dynamic field of study with the potential to deepen understanding, reconfigure frameworks, and rewrite the terms of debate.

The critical and ethnographic perspectives anthropologists are developing on regime transitions beg the question of whether similar processes could be studied in places whose governmental systems have not been subject to massive change. Such analytic approaches put democracy under an ethnographic lens not only in countries like the United States where political democracy is characterized by low voter turn-out, a powerful role of money in the political system, and widespread income, gender, and racial inequality; but also in Europe, where the European Union is said to entail a "democracy deficit" due to the myriad unaccountable committees operating secretively and without public record (Shore 2000, p. 220; Bellier 2000; on the EU, see also Darian-Smith 1999); and those hybrids such as Venezuela, Peru, and Colombia in which decades of prima facie democracy have been coupled with violence, corruption, and authoritarianism. In the words of Elizabeth Povinelli (personal communication 2001), "Democratization as an ongoing failed or semi-successful or imaginary project in the middle of the arch-typical democracies [is] seldom the object of analysis. When [it is] ... we are talking about the internal limits, contradictions, and tensions in democracy as they manifest in multicultural (or postcolonial) projects of material distribution." (See e.g., Povinelli 1998, Holmes 2000; see also political theorist Brown 1998) The challenge may be to turn critical perspectives on democracy emerging from fallen hopes in newly minted or recently returned democratic political systems toward places not

[1]Political theory (Brown 1995, Connolly 1999, Agamben 2000, Fraser 1997, Honig 2001) and political science, sociology, and other studies carried out with an anthropological or ethnographic sensibility (Jelin & Hershberg 1996, Barber & Schulz 1996, Keck & Sikkink 1998) have been stimulating resources for anthropological work. See also important cross-disciplinary collaborations (Escobar & Alvarez 1992, Alvarez et al. 1998).

undergoing overt institutional change. This interrogation of Western political ideals and institutions is especially apt given that the United States is regularly taken as an unexamined standard-bearer for the rest of the world (Gledhill 2000, pp. 7–8; political scientist Carothers 1999).

As the melange of uses in previous paragraphs suggests, both scholarly and colloquial accounts typically move all too fluidly among the terms "democracy," "democracies," "democratic," "democratizing," and "democratization," raising questions about democracy's status as an analytical category. The most straightforward assertion is that democracy is a political form, differentiable from other political forms such as monarchy and dictatorship (Borneman 1997, p. 3). Within that rubric there exist "different systems of democracy: advanced liberal democracy, parliamentary democracy, electoral democracy, socialist democracy" (Aihwa Ong, personal communication, 2001). Such an approach has the virtue of "disentangl[ing] democratic systems from the actual distribution of democratic values—equality in fundamental rights—that not even all people in advanced liberal democracies enjoy." In contrast, anthropologists who "deal only with imaginaries," who "look at how certain values associated with democracy—anti-colonialism, squatter claims, dreams of freedom, and the tensions between democratic values and cultural forms—have produced rather particular kinds of struggles or arrangements in different parts of the world" risk missing the "practical forms [such as electoral systems and other forms of government] that both deny or bring about the spread of democratic values" (defined differently in different contexts) (Aihwa Ong, personal communication). While the foregrounding of institutional concomitants to democratizing projects is fundamental, there is also a danger in setting the boundaries too clearly, for—as this essay shows—political forms are not neatly differentiable but rather complexly intertwined, and the discourses labeling certain regimes as democracies are strategically deployed by groups with strong interests in particular definitions and contested by others differently situated in relations of power. Noting the constitutive nature of those struggles, rather than establishing an a priori definition of democracy, is one of the central contributions of an anthropological approach.

This article proceeds as follows. I first give a brief historical view of anthropological studies done in the immediate postwar and postcolonial era, and I sketch out a second wave of interest accompanying the end of the Cold War. I then introduce a set of lenses anthropologists have used for viewing democracy: cultures and meanings, circulating discourses, qualities of citizenship, civil society and governmentality, and alternative democracies. Neither categories of study nor schools of thought, these headings are intended to capture entry points for anthropological analysis. Because competing modes of thought are at this stage largely emergent, this paper aims to offer questions and lines of inquiry for how one would go about constructing an anthropology of democracy. What emerges from the synthesis of the existing literature is a set of critical perspectives revealing contemporary democracies as enacting forms of power—perhaps less directly repressive than military dictatorships, but nonetheless falling short of democratic ideals. The final sections look at social movements' projects for alternative democracies and briefly overview anthropologists' own efforts to democratize ethnographic methodology.

HISTORICAL ANTECEDENTS

British social anthropology during the colonial period, known especially for its synchronic and structural-functional studies of African political systems, did little to interrogate the patterns and effects of colonial rule. After the countries' independence, however, synchrony and localism were no longer viable starting points given the undeniable occurrence of world-wide political change (Hart 1985, p. 250). In this context, U.S. anthropologists grouped into "The Committee for the Comparative Study of New Nations," which received funding from the Carnegie Corporation in 1959, set out to examine countries that had gained independence from colonial rule in the post–World War II period. According to political scientist David Apter (1963), who wrote the preface to the group's edited volume, what united all the authors was the goal of understanding "the problem of democracy in the new states, the forces that erode it, and the factors that might establish or strengthen it" (p. vii). Participants grappled especially with how to integrate local identities—"primordial sentiments," in the words of contributor and editor Clifford Geertz (1963)—into a unified civil order and modern political system associated with democracy. The New Nations Committee's interests were not merely academic, for participants sought to educate advisors to the newly independent states and to intervene in policy matters (Apter 1963, p. vii; Owusu 1970, p. 13). Full-length ethnographies written shortly thereafter evaluated the success (or lack thereof) of democracy in the social and institutional context of various countries and within local frameworks (Owusu 1970; see also Fox 1969). These early studies were born in the hopeful if chaotic years of the early 1960s, when independence from colonialism appeared to hold great promise, modernization seemed a feasible goal, and anthropologists sought to make their work relevant to political change. In this context, democracy was a universal political form signaling progress toward modernity. A second wave of anthropological interest in democracy would not surface until the 1990s, when the spate of transitions to democracy focused observers' attention worldwide.[2]

---

[2]In this article I focus on English-language publications written mainly by U.S.-based anthropologists. In contrast to them, Latin American and African anthropologists were grappling with questions of democracy in the 1970s and 1980s. Consequently, U.S.-based anthropologists may have had their interests piqued and analyses shaped not only by political transformations in their fieldsites but also by ongoing debates among those countries' intellectual communities. Their renewed attention to democracy in the 1990s may also have reflected heightened interest across the disciplines in questions of civil society and liberal democracy, and in turn stimulated the relatively recent turn by anthropologists to macro-political areas of inquiry including the state, globalization, and formal political institutions (Deborah Poole, personal communication).

CULTURES AND MEANINGS

Amid the Cold War's public discourse, democracy functioned ideologically as the antithesis to Soviet communism and was deployed in U.S. foreign policy to justify counterinsurgency efforts—as well as political transitions—in Latin America, Africa, Asia, and elsewhere. After the Cold War, the defeat of socialism as both actually-existing system and utopian ideal provoked a widely heralded triumphalism linking democracy with free market economics and a simultaneous disillusionment with actually-existing, if newly wrought, social, political, and economic conditions (Grant 1995, p. 31; Verdery 1996, p. 11). In both the 1980s and 1990s, democracy programs focusing most often on promoting elections and strengthening civil society and "good governance" were purveyed internationally by lending and donor agencies, with varying results.

For anthropologists, the latter part of the twentieth century brought not only changed political conditions, but also altered conventions in scholarly thought. Preceding and then intensified by the dismantling of the Berlin Wall and the breakup of the Soviet Union had come a crumbling of faith in metanarratives ranging from Marxist teleologies to development paradigms. In the spirit of then-reigning modernism, characterized by "the belief in linear progress, absolute truths, the rational planning of ideal social orders, and the standardization of knowledge and production" (PRECIS 6 1987, cited in Harvey 1989, p. 9), anthropologists writing about democracy in the postwar, postcolonial era had taken democracy to be a universal political form applicable to a wide variety of settings. In the 1980s and 1990s, this gave way to a postmodern-informed analysis of democracy's circulation, constructedness, discursive nature, and implication in power relations. The sense of democracy's contingent nature expressed in contemporary anthropological writings contrasted with still-modernist narratives by agencies such as the United States Agency for International Development (USAID) and the World Bank, which were promoting the expansion of democracy worldwide (see, e.g., USAID 2002).

It is in this context of international imports, regime transitions, and attendant dissonances between the discourse of democracy and the ways it played out in multiple locales, that anthropologists whose sights were set on other themes began to encounter democracy. Ethnographers working mainly in Africa applied to political transitions anthropology's classic task of identifying local meanings and institutions, thereby exploring how formal electoral processes and other components of Western-style democracy contrasted with, or had been interpreted and reappropriated by, culturally different native traditions. Their work demonstrates how official democratic procedures such as elections are reshaped in such idioms as sorcery in rural Mozambique (West 1998) and ritual practice among the Yoruba of Nigeria (Apter 1987). They also highlight linguistic counterparts to "democracy": words such as *Demokaraasi* (itself a concept derived from the French *démocratie*) for the Wolof in Senegal (political scientist Schaffer 1997) or *eddembe ery'obuntu* in Uganda (Karlström 1996). Such terms aggregate a range of colloquial meanings that, while at times overlapping, differ significantly from reigning conceptions of liberal democracy. Even apparently antidemocratic beliefs are revealed to be otherwise upon closer inspection; for example, the Comaroffs argue that support for a one-party state in Botswana is not a dismissal of democracy per se, but rather a rejection of procedural democracy in favor of a substantive democracy entailing both deliberation over policy matters and accountability by those who govern (Comaroff & Comaroff 1997). Unlike studies in the postwar period, these ethnographies use observation about cultural difference to problematize not primordial identities but rather the universalist assumptions of Western democratic practices themselves. While maintaining a modernist narrative of democracy's universal applicability, international agencies, donor institutions, and nongovernmental organizations seeking to implement democracy programs around the world have not always circumvented cultural conceptions and local political institutions; instead they have at times sought to mold apparently traditional political structures to electoral reform. This is true as well for national governments. Maxwell Owusu (1995), an anthropologist who participated in writing Ghana's constitution and took part in developing a decentralized District Assembly model in that country, sees potential in the "revival and proliferation of activist development-oriented civic organizations and mutual-aid societies based on village, town, ethnic, family membership, and similar affiliations" for creating a "grassroots participatory democracy." The system he describes "builds on indigenous political traditions of local self-government which assume the existence of consensual ethical and moral values shared within a community." These are based on chieftaincy, which, "despite its inherent social inequality, embodies shared values and virtues of accountability, service, probity; the tradition of voluntarism and self-help; and a spirit that extols the committed and total involvement of all the members of a community in the formulation and implementation of policies for the community's welfare." (p. 158)

Though local traditions may provide an important resource for democratic practice, other anthropologists have observed difficulties when "traditional authorities" are employed in the service of electoral democracy. West & Kloeck-Jenson (1999), for example, describe how "[e]veryone . . . from the United Nations to the World Bank to the United States Agency for International Development to NGOs such as Ox-Fam, CARE, and Save the Children—was talking about traditional authorities and their role in a democratized Mozambique." Specifically, USAID, which in 1995 and 1996 was holding workshops under its "'Democratic Development in Mozambique' project," aimed to incorporate "traditional authorities" into electoral structures. The authors explain in detail how complex the implications of this decision were. Historically, and in different ways in the precolonial, colonial, and postcolonial periods, tribal chiefs ("traditional authorities") had been used by dominating forces to brutalize, coerce, and exploit the populations they in theory represented. Traditional authority was therefore not entirely traditional at all—in the sense of enduring intact from a time prior to colonization—nor, by being local, was the institution necessarily democratic. Chiefs were, moreover, nested in a hierarchy of authority that the homogenized concept traditional authority obscures. Even more to the point, chiefs inherited their positions from ancestors; therefore, in the words of one chief, "to submit ... to elections is to *undermine* the power of the chieftaincy" (emphasis added; p. 71). These and other discrepancies show the ironies and unintended consequences of international agencies' blending of conceptions of cultural difference into universalizing democracy projects.

An explanation for the tensions is rooted in colonial history and the process of decolonization. Mahmood Mamdani (1996) argues that in Africa, democratization "would have entailed the deracialization of civil power and the detribalization of customary power .... A consistent democratization would have required dismantling and reorganizing the local state, the array of Native Authorities organized around the principle of fusion of power, fortified by an administratively driven customary justice and nourished through extra-economic coercion." He concludes that "the most important institutional legacy of colonial rule ... may lie in the inherited impediments to democratization" (pp. 24–25). In this interpretation, rather than being resources for democratization, the institutions of traditional authority may work to its detriment.

CIRCULATING DISCOURSES: THE USES AND ABUSES OF "DEMOCRACY"

Different definitions of democracy can be identified not only in the meaning systems of cultural subgroups, but also in state discourses and national self-understandings as well. Using a cognitive anthropological approach, Sabloff (2001) links Mongolians' concept of democracy with their 800-year-old political culture, manifested in their knowledge of basic democratic principles codified by Genghis Khan. Aihwa Ong (1999) indicates that in parts of Asia, democracy is presented less in terms of individual rights than as the state's ability to provide collective welfare benefits to citizens. In this sense, Singapore "prides itself on being a 'home-owning democracy'" in that citizens expect the state to ensure "universal home ownership, high-quality education, and unending economic expansion" (p. 208). Similarly China identified itself as a "socialist democratic society" based on state provision of access to housing, nutrition, schooling, and other benefits, at least until recent cutbacks. The point of these definitions is not to reify an "Asian" or "Chinese" cultural essence [though some may find it in their interests to do so (Ong 1997, p. 189)], but to suggest that democracy may have alternate meanings than elections and individual liberties—in this case, state provision for collective well being.

Yet what we know about the Chinese student movement's struggle for a very different kind of democracy (Calhoun 1994, pp. 237–60) impels us to look more closely at the strategic deployment of the term democracy, its power implications, competition over its meanings, its manifestations in institutions and social arrangements, and the way attendant discourses circulate within and among countries. In this vein Katherine Verdery (1996) considers democracy, along with "Europe ... civil society, and nation as key symbolic operators, elements in ideological fields, rather than as organizational realities." (p. 105). Matthew Gutmann (2002) suggests that "democracy's very multivalence is a key reason for the zeal with which so many people have employed the term to dramatically different ends in recent history" (p. 11). As these observations suggest, meanings of the term "democracy" are hotly contested among groups with interests in different outcomes, all of whom are linked to each other in unequal relations of power.

An example of a place where democracy took on a widely divergent set of meanings for actors differently situated in relations of power is Venezuela, which Fernando Coronil (1997) treats historically. Over time, meanings ranged from universal suffrage (ironically credited to the political party Acción Democrática, which in 1945 took power in a "violent coup against a constitutional regime that was widely acknowledged to be making steps toward democracy") (p. 132; see also Roseberry 2002, pp. 197–201) to the population's partaking in material benefits of large-scale public works projects (p. 167) while being excluded from political rights such as freedom of expression and participation in political parties under a military dictatorship (p. 176). Here military regimes, like single party states, call themselves democracies, invoking idiosyncratic meanings of the term to justify its use, and claiming the word democracy to legitimate their rule.

While military juntas may legitimate their power by labeling their dictatorship a "democracy," in other situations militaries exercise their power through procedural democracy itself, meaning that even after official regime transitions, the armed forces—and, correspondingly, violence and authoritarianism—continue to be embedded in the subsequent "democracy" (Warren 2000, Poole & Rénique 1992). The presence of the military is quite literally the case in postdictatorship Argentina, where former officers of the Dirty War have run for office and been elected to positions of political power (Taylor 1993). That phenomenon calls into question even the term "elected-civilian" regime that some analysts have used when the word "democratic" seems substantively inapplicable. Diane Nelson (1999) has warned against seeing democracy as nothing but a "mask for military rule" (p. 102) because "[s]uch an analysis of manifest (false) versus latent (true) content does little to explain either the power of the state or the many effects of contestatory practices." Seeking to "avoid the notion that the state and civil society are separate, enclosed entities (the former corrupt and repressive, the latter noble and liberatory)," she "instead . . . argue[s] that they are interpenetrated at every point." The centrality of the armed forces to the shape of democracy—and conversely the usefulness of democracy to the armed forces—is highlighted in the work of Jennifer Schirmer (1998), who shows that the repressive structures of the Guatemalan military are enacted and perpetuated through (not in spite of) civilian rule. She writes that "[a]fter decades of naked military rule, the Guatemalan military have crafted a unique Counterinsurgent Constitutional State in which *State violence has been reincarnated as democracy*" (emphasis added; p. 258). " . . . Rather than naked military rule based on emergency measures, juntas, and coups—instruments of power that have lost their legitimacy internationally—it is the appropriation of the imagery of the rule of law, of the mechanisms and procedures of electoral democracy, that is perilous to the human rights of Guatemalans" (p. 2). That is to say, military power that is enacted through electoral and constitutional systems gains legitimacy internationally through the rubric of democracy. Such an analysis reminds us to view even such seemingly positive terms as rule of law and democracy with caution. It also indicates that while "democracy" may at times seem to be a floating signifier that can be filled with any number of meanings, it is hardly "hyperreal" in the sense of being disconnected from institutional referents (Baudrillard 1988; see also McDonald 1993, pp. 100–101). Instead, political institutions, be they electoral systems or militaries or both, are central to the ways democracy's power is enacted.

Often the continuity between military and electoral rule takes place when political democracies are shaped through negotiations, reform, and pacts that largely uphold military structures. Begoña Aretxaga (2000) considers the case of Spain, where the parliamentary democracy arose out of negotiations following the death of Franco, with the result that his state's "army . . . police . . . [and] bureaucracy . . . remained largely unchallenged" after the transition (p. 47). Despite these continuities and complicities, the socialist party's election to power in 1982 was widely experienced as "a signifier of a *real* break with the dictatorship" (emphasis in original; p. 48). Reworking Michael Taussig's concept of state fetishism (Taussig 1992), Aretxaga calls this phenomenon "the power of democracy as fetish. It was a fetish produced by forgetting the traces that linked the Spanish democracy to the former regime (its nature as a reform of it), and its reinvention as the real Thing, democracy—an object of desire that held the promise of a new, European, modern, successful form of life. The fetishization of democracy endowed the Spanish state with a new aura and new body, a sacred one that came to replace the desacralized and profaned body of the Francoist state." She goes on, "Thus constituted as a fantasy of modern prosperity, democracy became under the socialist government the legitimizing discourse for a wide variety of authoritarian state practices" (p. 48). Her conclusion is arresting: "Perhaps state terrorism must be contemplated not as a deviation of democracy, a corruption of power or 'power gone awry,' but as an intrinsic part of contemporary practices of power" (p. 64). Such an analysis requires us to rethink the meaning and power functions of contemporary democracies, rather than assuming their benign or banal qualities.

Violence accompanying democracy may not only be the result of enduring legacies of prior military regimes. It may also be stimulated through democracy's procedures themselves. In his study of "ethnonationalist conflicts and collective violence in South Asia," Stanley Tambiah (1996) shows that in political democracy,

> the mobilization of the crowds and the wooing of their support—through election speeches, rallies, mass media propaganda, and the dispensation of favors through election machines—is the central process of persuasion and vote-getting. This reliance on crowds and mass mobilization opens the door to the invention and propagation of collective slogans and collective ideologies, to the appeal to collective entitlements for groups in terms of divisive 'substance codes' of blood and soil . . . (p. 261)

largely organized around ethnicity. Given the extent to which the mobilization of crowds is integral to electoral campaigns, "'democratic' political elections," themselves become, " a major contributor to collective violence" (p. 262) and ethnic violence in particular.

These examples suggest that what comes before transitions to democracy shapes what comes after them—not only because of pacts and negotiations between former military officials and incoming democrats, but also because emotions (particularly fear; see, e.g., Green 1999), ethnic cleavages, violence, bureaucracies, institutions, and other ongoing structures endure beyond political transition. Yet what appear to be remnants of former political regimes may actually be responses to new conditions. Burawoy & Verdery (1999) write that

> we challenge those analyses that account for the confusions and shortcomings of the transition process as 'socialist legacies' or 'culture.' Repeatedly, we find that what may appear as 'restorations' of patterns familiar from socialism are something quite different: direct *responses* to the new market initiatives, produced *by* them, rather than remnants of an older mentality. . . . [P]eople's responses to a situation may . . . appear as holdovers . . . because they employ a language and symbols adapted from previous orders. (pp. 1–2; see also Lass 1999, p. 274)

The degree to which different political forms are interwoven in practice suggests not only that "political forms . . . need to be related to each other in a field of contested possibilities" (Susan Gal, personal communication), but also that the very concept of transition from one system to another must be brought into question (Kideckel 2002, p. 115). Warren (2002) notes that " . . . transitions from socialist and capitalist authoritarianisms to varieties of market-driven democracy are neither linear nor unilateral processes" (p. 379), and Creed (1998) holds that the word "'[t]ransition' is . . . problematic because its common usage implies a temporary condition and an inevitable result. The social characteristics of transition may be quite enduring, and the outcome is certainly not predetermined. . . . " He goes on to note that although a "transition" may occur, " . . . what follow[s is] not invariably capitalist democracy" (p. xv). Some analysts have suggested that the word "transition" so mischaracterizes the phenomenon that "transformation" would be a more appropriate term (Verdery 1996, p. 15).

Writing in a different context and engaged in an overtly strategic project, David Scott (1999) has said that the present "global moment [is one] of considerable instability and uncertainty. It is a moment when hitherto established and authoritative conceptual paradigms and political projects . . . seem no longer adequate to the tasks of the present, and when, at the same time, new paradigms and projects have yet to assert themselves fully in the place of the old" (p. 10). The moment is, of course, dominated by "a resurgent liberalism that has stepped onto the stage to claim for itself a victory, to claim in fact that it constitutes our only possible future" (pp. 144–45). Refusing to accept that vision, Scott situates his strategic practice of political criticism in a "sort of Gramscian interregnum, a transitional moment that

I shall characterize as 'after postcoloniality'" (p. 10). His work raises the question of whether it would also be possible to envision the present as a moment "after liberal democracy" rather than its manifestation. Such a formulation might offer a way of breaking free of transition narratives positing a preordained outcome, envisioning political possibilities beyond actually-existing democracy, and—by taking the present as an instance of uncertainty—holding open the possibility for a range of alternatives. Ethnography would be a particularly apt research approach for such a project, in that it captures people's lived experience amid conditions of "political instability" and "dramatic political change" (Greenhouse 2002, p. 1; see also Moore 1993, p. 9), thereby revealing the complexity of conditions that might otherwise be assumed to fit predetermined teleologies (Verdery & Burawoy 1999, p. 2; Greenhouse et al. 2002).

QUALITIES OF CITIZENSHIP

The multiple meanings given to the term democracy, and the permeation of some posttransition societies by the armed forces, suggest that democracy is not a single condition that countries do or do not have, but rather a set of processes unevenly enacted over time. Holston & Caldeira (1998) note, for example, that while elements of political democracy such as elections, legislatures, and constitutions operate effectively in Brazil, the "civil component of citizenship" (exemplified by the justice system) is "ineffective" (p. 280) such that "the vast majority cannot rely on the institutions of state—particularly on the courts and the police—to respect or guarantee their individual rights, arbitrate their conflicts justly, or stem escalating violence legally" (p. 281). The authors term this uneven enactment of citizenship "disjunctive democracy," meaning that "the institutionalization, practice, and meaning of citizenship . . . are rarely uniform or homogeneous." To the contrary, "they are usually and normally unbalanced, irregular, heterogeneous, temporally and spatially arrhythmic, and even contradictory" (p. 280). Teresa Caldeira's (2000) ethnography of crime and fear in São Paulo further delineates how violence, police brutality, urban segregation, and privatized security arrangements combine to affect the quality and lived experience of democracy and citizenship in Brazil.

While liberal democracy is generally premised on equality of citizens under the law, ethnographic studies reveal the racialization and gendering of citizenship, as well as other inequalities. Anthropologists have focused, for example, on the ways in which "men and women are differently imagined as citizens" in democratizing East Central Europe (Gal & Kligman 2000a, p. 3; see also Gal & Kligman 2000b); the racialization of nationality and immigration legislation in Britain (Hall 2002); the exclusion as well as inclusion experienced by Salvadoran immigrants struggling for citizenship (Coutin 2000); the ways in which law both constitutes and naturalizes inequalities in the British Virgin Islands (Maurer 2000); the production of "sanitary citizens" and "unsanitary subjects," a distinction that helps determine "who is accorded substantive access to the civil and social rights of citizenship" amid a cholera epidemic in Venezuela (Briggs 2003, p. 28); and the formation of "citizenship regimes,"—the "political categorization of citizens by government agencies" in post-Soviet Russia, in which a panoply of laws create a multitude of "new social categories" (Humphrey 2002, pp. 75–76). Interestingly, the discourses of multiculturalism that might seem to remedy inequalities among citizens may in fact reinforce them. In her critical examination of liberalism in "constitutional liberal democracies," Elizabeth Povinelli (2002, p. 15) seeks to understand "[h]ow a state and public leans on a multicultural imaginary to defer the problems that capital, (post)colonialism, and human diasporas pose to national identity in the late twentieth century." Her study of court cases asserting aboriginal land claims in Australia shows that state acknowledgment of past discrimination ultimately legitimates and reinforces present discriminatory rule, leading Povinelli to suggest that "... state, public and capital multicultural discourses, apparatuses, and imaginaries defuse struggles for liberation waged against the modern liberal state and recuperate these struggles as moments in which the future of the nation and its core institutions and values are ensured rather than shaken ...." These usages are not unilateral, and Povinelli also seeks to investigate how multiculturalism "open[s] up a space for critical re-imaginings of social life as indigenous subjects creatively engage the slippages, dispersions, and ambivalences of discursive and moral formations that make up their lives" (p. 30). Basing his observations on interviews with staff of powerful organizations working in Guatemala, Charles Hale (2002) similarly finds that state-endorsed, neoliberal multiculturalism presents a mixture of "opportunity and peril" (p. 7). Acknowledging that cultural-rights movements have little choice but to take advantage of the openings that multiculturalist discourses and practices produce, he simultaneously cautions about the "cumulative effect" of these endeavors, warning that they "separat[e] acceptable demands for cultural rights from inappropriate ones, recognizing the former and foreclosing the latter, and thereby creating a means to 'manage' multiculturalism while removing its radical or threatening edge" (p. 25). His study of elite strategies well complements Kay Warren's (1998) ethnographic account of Guatemalan Maya's own proposal for a "multicultural (*pluricultural*) model for participatory democracy" (emphasis in original; p. 13) and the subsequent electoral defeat of a referendum aiming to recast Guatemala as a "'multicultural, ethnically plural, and multilingual state'" following the 1996 peace accords (Warren 2002, p. 10).

One of the markers of citizenship in a democracy is voting rights, and anthropologists have found wide variability in the significance and operation of elections. In some cases, procedural democracy is so falsified as to become not legitimation but farce, as Andrew Apter (1999) powerfully demonstrates in his study of Nigeria. He traces the "condition of verisimilitude and dissimulation" through which the "electoral charade of 'pro forma democracy'" operated in Nigeria—a situation in which the head of state choreographed elections as performance without really being elected through them. Miles (1988) provides a fascinating minute-by minute view of the infinitesimal manipulations, misunderstandings, and meanderings by individual Hausa in Yardaji during those same elections, revealing the myriad microencounters hidden behind the broad terms "voting" and "fraud." In her work on Bengal, India, Mukulika Banerjee (1999) finds that despite the fact that they have low opinions of elected officials, illiterate and poor citizens in India are among the most committed voters and use a language of "civic duty," citizenship, and rights to explain their decisions to vote. Anthropologists have also written about election monitoring (McDonald 1997), referendums (Warren 2002), political campaigns (Herzfeld 1985, pp. 92–122; Lomnitz et al. 1993), and the gendered aspects of elections (Gutmann 2002), often viewing elections and campaigns through the classic anthropological lenses of ritual, symbol, structure, and myth (McLeod 1991, 1999; Herzog 1987; Abélès 1988; see also Borneman 1992, pp. 316–19; Borneman 2002).

In many of these cases, the nation-state is the primary reference point for citizenship: the unit of sovereignty and suffrage, and the locus for racializing identities and distributing rights. Yet anthropologists have pointed out that in an age of globalization, citizenship is not purely a national phenomenon. They have noted that just at the moment that countries experience returns to formal democracy—thereby giving citizens the right to vote in national elections—major decisions about the economy and public welfare are being made not by national governments but by international financial institutions in places as distant from "Third World" locations as International Monetary Fund (IMF) offices in Washington, DC, or the closed-door meetings of the World Trade Organization (WTO) in their various locales. These decisions are made by specialists who take questions of resource distribution and economics to be not political issues open to public debate but rather technical and scientific questions to be determined by experts (Ferguson 1993, 1994). Such a vision directly contradicts normative theories of democracy that posit public debate, and its influence on elected legislatures, as centerpieces of democracy (Habermas 1996). Moreover, *who* performs state functions has changed, with international financial institutions contracting service provision to nongovernmental organizations and other agencies as easily as to national governments themselves (Ferguson & Gupta 2002), thereby raising questions not only about the "state effects" of such disparate processes (Trouillot 2001), but also about whom national citizens and social movements might hold accountable for material benefits and how. These phenomena raise the question of whether there can be a "cosmopolitan democracy" (Calhoun 2001). In this globalized context, citizenship must be understood as embedded in transnational processes. Aihwa Ong (1999) conceptualizes a "system of graduated sovereignty, whereby citizens in zones that are differently articulated to global production and financial circuits are subjected to different kinds of surveillance and in practice enjoy different sets of civil, political, and economic rights" (pp. 215–16). A spatial phenomenon, such differentiation among citizens, often manifests itself in ethnic and gender disparities. This system "has come about in the state eagerness to forge links with corporate interests," with the consequence that "democratic values are more available for some people than for others" (Aihwa Ong, personal communication).

Despite pervasive inequality, democracies are usually characterized by formal equality for all citizens under the law. In striking contrast is the case of the former

Yugoslavia where countries billing themselves as democratic enshrine in constitutions privileged membership for ethnic nationals, a phenomenon that Robert Hayden (1992) has called "constitutional nationalism." Not only do nonethnonationals residing in the territory have only partial citizenship rights, but ethnic nationals living abroad have, in some cases, full citizenship, thus granting these exiles and emigrants a say in further restricting citizenship rights of those living in the country (Verdery 1998, p. 296). Katherine Verdery points out that "[a]s external observers came to ratify that elections were free and fair, they failed to ask *who* 'the people' were who would be allowed into the social contract creating citizens and rights." Because in these countries "'people' connotes the sovereignty of an ethnic collectivity rather than the joint sovereignty of individual 'social contractors'[,] [t]he sovereign ... becomes the ethnic collectivity; democracy becomes ethnocracy. Constitutions and elections have traveled transnationally, then, but with unanticipated effects, producing transnational citizenships that nationalize" (p. 297). The case of Bosnia-Herzegovina presents another example of how "democratization is transnational" (Verdery 1998, p. 293), due to the central role of the "International Community" in its governance. Ironically, the (mainly European) representatives of international organizations whose assignment is to fortify the nation-state and instill democracy in Bosnia, themselves live outside the purview of Bosnian state institutions, engaging instead with "supra- or non-state institutions." This situation leads Kimberley Coles (2002) to note the paradox that "internationals may be sabotaging their own attempts at state creation through state displacement" (p. 13). The result is a variegated system in which people differently situated in national and international circuits have different citizenship experiences and relations to governing bodies.

CIVIL SOCIETY AND GOVERNMENTALITY

In the years leading up to the breakup of the Soviet Union and the fall of the Berlin Wall, and amid struggles against dictatorships, apartheid, and military regimes in Latin America, Africa, and Asia, the idea of "civil society" took on political importance in the self-concept of social movements contesting repressive regimes and seeking to bring about democracy (see, e.g., Kligman 1990). While in its initial contemporary uses civil society was a social movement category applied against totalitarian states, civil society has since become a key term used by international purveyors of democracy programs. Steven Sampson's (1996) ethnography of a Danish agency seeking to strengthen civil society in Albania indicates that civil society was virtually equated with democracy. Noting that "[t]he main focus of civil society development has been to increase the number of NGOs," he explains that "'[d]emocracy' was understood quantitatively. Few NGOs meant less democracy, more NGOs meant more democracy" (p. 128; see also Sampson 2002, Fisher 1997). Significantly, civil society and democracy promotion are closely linked to the advancement of market economies and the United States' global interests by donor agencies (Mandel 2002), leaving unexamined by these agencies the ways in which neoliberal market reform with its attendant income disparities and distancing of economic decision making might undermine rather than enforce a substantive version of democracy.

Recently anthropologists have asked "whether the discourse of 'strengthening civil society' ... is coherent, either from the point of view of actually existing historical situations or from the point of view of comparative, cross-cultural analysis ..." (John Gledhill, personal communication, referring to themes debated at the international conference "Citizenship and Political Culture in Latin America and Mexico's 'Transition to Democracy'," October 2001). Trying to explain why civil society discourse has been so ubiquitous and optimistic, others have argued that it is "civil society's" very incoherence that makes it so "good to think, to signify with, to act upon." That is, "[t]he less substance it has, the emptier its referents, the more this is so; which is why its very polyvalence, its ineluctable unfixability, is intrinsic to its power as panacea" (Comaroff & Comaroff 2000, p. 334; see also Coombe 1997, Comaroff & Comaroff 1999, Hann & Dunn 1996).

One of the attractions in international development circles of the idea of civil society—and related concepts such as "empowerment," "partnerships," "participation," and "community involvement"—is that this discourse and its attendant programs can involve poor citizens in providing (formerly public) services, thereby extending strapped budgets stretched yet thinner by structural adjustment programs, and involving people in their own self-management. Anthropological work on this subject has been informed by a multidisciplinary group of scholars who have elaborated on Foucault's (1991) concept of governmentality (see, e.g., Barry et al. 1996, Burchell et al. 1991, Mitchell 1991; see also Scott 1999, p. 17, 152–53). Nikolas Rose (1996), for example, emphasizes that in contrast to analyses that see a reduced role for government within free market economies, "Neoliberalism does not abandon the 'will to govern'." Rather, it "create[s] a distance between the decisions of formal political institutions and other social actors, and conceive[s] of these new actors in new ways as subjects of responsibility, autonomy and choice, and seek[s] to act upon them though shaping and utilizing their freedom" (p. 54). In her ethnography of postdictatorship Chile, Julia Paley (2001) shows, for example, that in aiming to prevent a cholera epidemic, the Chilean Ministry of Health conducted a publicity campaign instructing the population to take preventive hygienic measures such as washing one's hands and covering the trash. Here a state, which was unable or unwilling to make expenditures in public infrastructural improvements (such as improved irrigation systems that would have avoided the use of raw human sewage) to prevent the spread of the disease, created the conditions for citizens to engage in their own self-care (*auto-cuidado*). In a related example, an elected congressional representative called upon community groups to clean fields of trash, arguing that in democracy it was not the state, but rather organized groups of citizens, that should "participate" in keeping public spaces clean (pp. 166–67). Here governing officials used terms like "democracy" and "participation" as motivating discourses to involve citizens in service provision; they thereby sparked people's own complicity in contemporary forms of power. This ethnography of

Chile further describes how for a grassroots health group, whose method of work had been initiated under a repressive military regime in the mid 1980s, developing new strategies for resisting the state's efforts to incorporate citizens and organized groups into furthering the reach of neoliberalism became a central task during political democracy (see also Hyatt 1997, 2001; Cheater 1999; James 1999; and political scientist Schild 1998).

Invoking the writings of political theorist Barbara Cruikshank (1999), Lauren Leve (2001) makes explicit the ways in which not just national governments but also international organizations like the United Nations and USAID have used terms like participation and empowerment in the service of neoliberal economics. In the case of Nepal, they transformed women's literacy programs into ways of advancing market reforms by "prepar[ing] women to accept and initiate further socioeconomic transformation" (p. 115). In recognition that such efforts may transcend, bypass, or even subcontract to the state, James Ferguson and Akhil Gupta (2002) have coined the term "transnational governmentality" to refer to the "modes of government that are being set up on a global scale" (see also Gupta 1998, p. 321). They note that "[t]hese include not only new strategies of discipline and regulation, as exemplified by the WTO and the structural adjustment programs implemented by the IMF, but also transnational alliances forged by activists and grassroots organizations and the proliferation of voluntary organizations supported by complex networks of international and transnational funding and personnel" (p. 19). In this context, they are interestingly placed in relation to the processes of self-enumeration and self-surveying that Arjun Appadurai (2002), using a spacial metaphor that Ferguson and Gupta would problematize, has called "governmentality from below" or "countergovernmentality" (p. 24).

ALTERNATIVE DEMOCRACIES

For all the critiques of actually existing political systems by commentators and social movements themselves (for political commentaries expressed in performative and artistic genres, see e.g., Isbell 1998, Holland & Skinner 2001; but see Lemon 2000), democracy has been an aspiration for many who have lived within oppressive regimes. This is especially true for oppositional movements aiming to bring political democracies to their countries, be they Chinese students (sociologist Calhoun 1994), Nepali doctors (Adams 1998), or Thai demonstrators (Klima 2002). It has also been true in the immediate aftermath of regime transitions, when exhilaration and expectations run high. Nancy Scheper-Hughes tells the story of convening a conference on "Democracy and Difference" at the University of Cape Town in May 1994, just two days after Nelson Mandela had been elected president. Anthropologists flown in as speakers gave pessimistic analyses, pointing to difficulties with democracy in places around the world. In response, Albie Sachs, a former freedom fighter with the African National Congress who became a member of the South African Constitutional Court, asked "Can't we even celebrate for two days?!" South Africans wanted to dance following their victory, not begin an immediate cycle of skepticism and despair (Nancy Scheper-Hughes, personal communication). Even in the aftermath of imperfect transitions, opportunities created by the institutions of constitutional democracy, the principles of rule of law, and the discourse of human rights have opened unique spaces for prosecuting violent perpetrators such as those organized into death squads in Brazil (Scheper-Hughes 2001).

Yet while human rights, rule of law, and democracy itself have value as both aspiration and popular victory, the meanings attributed to democracy in various contexts and struggles do not necessarily match hegemonic definitions in actually-existing systems or even normative liberal democracy ideals. Instead, social movements have often created programs and practices that call themselves democracy movements while intentionally posing alternatives to standard definitions of the term. A case in point is the Popular American Revolutionary Alliance (APRA) operating in Peru in the 1920s and 1930s, which David Nugent describes as differing from "Liberal Representative Democracy" in seeking not only a set of basic freedoms from state intervention such as freedom of the press, speech, religion, and association (p. 20), but also citizens' engagement in economic decision making; direct decision-making by historically subordinated groups (namely indigenous peasants, laborers, and the middle class); full political participation for women; and a strong state "to guarantee the health, well-being, and democratic rights of its citizens" (Nugent 1999; see also Nugent 1997). What is most interesting about this prodemocracy movement is that no memory exists of it in the contemporary period, even by participants in social movements creating their own alternative visions of democracy, leaving the anthropologist to study it through interviews with octogenarians who were once its political organizers, and through written documentation from the time.

In recognizing the uniqueness of such alternative democratic programs and practices, anthropologists have noted that they are not pristine indigenous inventions. Rather, social movements strategically and selectively appropriate and transform transnationally circulating discourses, sometimes filling foreign words with their own meanings. The Zapatistas, whose declaration sets forth a "national proposal" for "democracy, liberty, and justice" (Nash 1997, p. 267) explain that "[o]ur path was always that the will of the many be in the hearts of the men and women who command .... Another word came from afar ... [and] gave the name of 'democracy' to our way that was from before words traveled" (p. 264). In their contemporary political context, their proposal embues the word democracy (as well as justice and liberty) with alternative meanings. Specifically democracy "requires 'not that all think the same, but that all thoughts or the majority of the thoughts seek and arrive at a good agreement'," an idea that June Nash interprets as a revision of "modernist ideals" for a "postmodern age" (p. 261; see also Mignolo 2000, p. 742; Stephen 2002). In thinking about the redefinition of existing terms, it is therefore important to ask: What aspects of other discourses are social movements drawing upon, what are the specific routes and networks through which discourses are accessed and dispersed, and what are the gains, losses, and transformations enacted in the process of translation? (Gal 2002). Such questions apply equally to related discourses such as human rights (Cowan et al. 2001, Wilson 1997). In this vein, anthropologists have asked: Through what process do people come to see themselves as being "rights bearing" subjects (Merry 2003), or, concomitantly, as democratic citizens?

If the presence of democracy discourse in diverse locations is notable, equally significant are its absences, and anthropologists are wise to pay close attention to the places where it blends into other discourses, or where it surfaces only when elicited. The use of the word "democracy" occurs neither alone, nor steadily, nor completely; it is, rather, ethnographically emergent. Therefore we must ask: Whose term is it? What does its usage in any particular case signify? Where does the term arise and where not? In this context, anthropologists are writing at the edges of the discourse, sighting its limits and boundaries, its instabilities and temporal fluctuations, the places where it emerges out of another discourse, or just as fluidly is subsumed into a different one. Social movements' invoking of democracy discourse may be a tactical move, a carefully selected appropriation of dominant logics, or a less reflective reproduction of dominant tropes; in a particular context it may also be a risky choice, one that plays into and legitimates a cold war discourse of democracy and its opponents, or a post–Cold War imaginary linking political freedom to liberated market forces.

At the same time, anthropologists sometimes invoke the term democracy where social movements themselves do not, using its aspirational content to highlight deeper significance of innovative social movement practice. Arjun Appadurai (2002) uses the term "deep democracy" to conjure up a kind of "'democracy without borders'" achieved through the process of "grassroots globalization." His work takes place in Mumbai (Bombay), where an alliance among a professional NGO, a strong grassroots organization, and an organization of poor women is doing innovative work on information collection, housing, and public toilets, in ways that are deeply local and simultaneously transnational. "Deep democracy," he says, "suggests roots, anchors, intimacy, proximity, and locality." At the same time, the "lateral reach of such movements—their efforts to build international networks or coalitions of some durability with their counterparts across national boundaries—is also a part of their 'depth'" (p. 38). So too is their ability to enable poor people to engage with powerful institutions whose stated mission—if not their effective practice—is the amelioration of poverty.

Some ethnographers have researched efforts to hold democracy to its highest ideals. Maintaining that "democratic legitimacy depends above all on a system of political and personal accountability that is institutionalized in the principles of the rule of law" (p. 3), for example, John Borneman (1997) studies how bringing former strongmen to justice can prevent cycles of retributive violence. (For a fascinating website tracing the significance of the ways dictatorships end, see Borneman & Fisher 1999.) At the same time that anthropologists have linked democracy to human rights and the rule of law, however, legal anthropologists have noted that law can be double-sided: While people use it to resist and contest power, they are also subjugated by it, a dynamic that operates in places as diverse as the United States (Yngvesson 1993), Kenya (Hirsch 1994), and the West Indies (Lazarus-Black 1994).

Other aspirational writings about democracy stem less from the practical activity of courts and social movements than from the normative theorizing of scholars. Here anthropologists have been in dialogue with political theorists, particularly those who—following Habermas (1989)—consider democracy to entail an active public sphere in which vibrant public discussions and a dynamic circulation of ideas can take place (see Calhoun 1992; for a "language-oriented perspective" on the creation of publics, see Gal & Woolard 2001). Pointing to the ways in which the emphasis on rational argument in theories of "deliberative democracy" excludes the communicative styles of women and other "socially marginalized" groups (p. 278), Rosemary Coombe (1998) offers "dialogic democracy" as an alternative normative framework. By involving "social systems of signification" open enough to provide the "cultural conditions for conversation" for a wide variety of people, dialogic democracy allows diverse groups to "express identity, community, and social aspiration in the service of imagining and constructing alternative social universes" (pp. 296–97). Coombe's formulation explicitly echoes political theorist Iris Marion Young's idea of "communicative democracy" (1996) and complements political theorist Nancy Fraser's (1994) notion of multiple subaltern counterpublics. Such ideas are explored ethnographically by Jacqueline Urla (2001) who considers the free radio of Basque radical nationalist youth to be a "partial public, a segment of a plural, rather than a singular counterpublic sphere . . . ." Urla argues that by "creat[ing] spaces for alternative modes of communication and cultural life," free radios "provide a soundtrack for minority languages, values, and cultural expression"; they thereby put into practice an "ideology of radical democratic communication" (p. 143).

Centered as they are in discourse theory, the public debates and discussions of which political theorists speak need not be detached from any specific locale; to the contrary, they need locations to happen. Radical Basque youth congregate in bars, bookstore/coffeehouses, and youth houses, even as the forms of communication they use are simultaneously transnational (Urla 2001, p. 160). Ritty Lukose (2001) shows how the space of a college in Kerala is contested, as the adminstration aims to produce an apolitical "civic public" that operates as a "space of consumption" to the exclusion of political public space. Emphasizing the need to preserve locations for the proliferation of democratic discussions, Setha Low (2000) argues that "public spaces, such as the Costa Rican plaza, are one of the last democratic forums for public dissent in a civil society. They are places where disagreements can be marked symbolically and politically or personally worked out." Given the importance of places like the plaza for the flourishing of public discourse, Low argues, there is a "need to make and remake public spaces, and to struggle relentlessly for the social and political availability of public space[. This] can be seen as a precondition for any kind of democratic politics . . . " (p. 240).

DEMOCRATIZING ETHNOGRAPHY

Anthropologists concerned with questions of democracy have, not surprisingly, been politically and personally invested in struggles for human rights, the rule of law, and a mitigation of harsh income disparities. As such, their work has at times involved not only observing, but also aiming to transform relations of power (see Gledhill 2000 for an analysis of engaged anthropology, Price 1998 for its history and costs, D'Andrade 1995, Scheper-Hughes 1995 for a debate, and Mahmood 1999 for an example of anthropological intervention in human rights). Anthropological activism has historical precedents in, among others, Franz Boas's anti-racist work and Margaret Mead's famed insistence that "... a small group of thoughtful committed citizens can change the world" (cited in Scheper-Hughes 2001). Currently, some anthropologists, including practitioners such as the medical anthropologists who founded Partners in Health, have aimed to make concrete impacts in living conditions and health, both by operating clinics in poor communities and by transforming the practices of major institutions such as the World Bank (Farmer 2001, Farmer et al. 1997, Kim et al. 2000). Others have initiated efforts to bring anthropologists' work to large audiences and illuminate issues central to public debates. Rob Borofsky describes Public Anthropology as an effort to

> make anthropology an intellectual engine for nurturing critical social transformations through providing the kind of thoughtful stories and analyses that make broad publics in democracies confront their own complicities in the status quo that oppresses others. Fostering democracy, fostering public anthropology in this context means enlarging public discussions regarding how we engage—and how we might engage better—with the critical issues and dilemmas of our time beyond our own zones of comfort. (Borofsky, personal communication; see also the University of California book series Public Anthropology 2002)

Peggy Sanday sees Public Interest Anthropology as encompassing two trends: "[m]erging problem solving with theory and analysis in the interest of change motivated by a commitment to social justice, racial harmony, equality, and human rights" and "[e]ngaging in public debate on human issues to make the results of anthropological analysis accessible to a broad audience" (Sanday 1998; see also Public Interest Anthropology 2002). These efforts put into practice the idea of "ethnography as an active form of democratic participation" (Greenhouse 1998, p. 3; see also Greenhouse 2002).

The practice of involving people affected by difficult situations in a problem-solving research process has historical precedents in anthropology. The primary example is Sol Tax, who, in the 1940s–1960s, developed action anthropology as "a participative ethnography in which the informants were coinvestigators and the investigators were students of the informants" (Bennett 1996, pp. S35–37). His line of work has largely faded, but it finds echoes in contemporary action and participatory action research (Greenwood & Levin 1998) including research on industrial democracy (Greenwood & González Santos 1992). Other efforts at participatory investigation have been carried out in conjunction with popular movements, some of whose own training in popular education inspired by Freire (2000) and Gramsci (1971) has already positioned them as popular intellectuals. Contemporary examples have included facilitating indigenous people's access to video production (Turner 1992, Ginsburg 1997) and teaching grassroots leaders to conduct ethnographic research of their own (Paley 2001, pp. 211–24). When anthropological engagement involves transforming power-knowledge relations of researcher, researched, and broader publics, anthropologists are engaging in the practice of democratizing ethnography.

ACKNOWLEDGMENTS

One of the most enjoyable aspects of writing this article has been gleaning ideas about democracy from a wide range of scholars. Their diversity of takes on the subject was truly remarkable, and while I have incorporated a great many suggestions, I regret that I could not cover the full range of ideas reflected in our correspondences. For their very perceptive comments on the précis and drafts to this article, and for discussions on democracy more generally, I thank Vincanne Adams, Sonia Alvarez, Arjun Appadurai, Andrew Apter, Mukulika Banerjee, Sandra Barnes, John Borneman, Rob Borofsky, Charles Briggs, Teresa Caldeira, Craig Calhoun, Lawrence Cohen, Kimberly Coles, Jean Comaroff, John Comaroff, Rosemary Coombe, Fernando Coronil, Susan Coutin, Eve Darian-Smith, Arturo Escobar, Paul Farmer, James Ferguson, William Fisher, Richard G. Fox, Susan Gal, John Gledhill, Carol Greenhouse, Davydd Greenwood, Matthew Gutmann, Charles R. Hale, Kathleen Hall, Chris Hann, Robert Hayden, Judith Adler Hellman, Michael Herzfeld, Sarah Hill, David Holmberg, James Holston, Susan Brin Hyatt, Billie Jean Isbell, John Kelly, Jim Yong Kim, Mindie Lazarus-Black, Lauren Leve, Claudio Lomnitz, Ritty Lukose, Kathryn March, George Marcus, Bill Maurer, James McDonald, Sally Engle Merry, Joyce Millen, Sally Falk Moore, June Nash, David Nugent, Aihwa Ong, Maxwell Owusu, Deborah Poole, Elizabeth Povinelli, Rayna Rapp, Paula Sabloff, Steven Sampson, Peggy Sanday, Frederic Schaffer, Nancy Scheper-Hughes, Daniel Segal, Orin Starn, Sidney Tarrow, Michael Taussig, Michel Rolph-Trouillot, Terence Turner, Greg Urban, Katherine Verdery, Kay Warren, Harry West, and Barbara Yngvesson. I would like to make special mention of the late historian Michael Jiménez, who in the early 1990s shared with me his emerging analysis of democracy in Latin America. Four students at the University of Pennsylvania made substantial contributions to this article, and it is with a great deal of appreciation that I thank Fernando Armstrong, Ana María Gómez López, Jonah Steinberg, and Todd Wolfson for engaging enthusiastically with the project and sharing their very perceptive insights. Ayako Kano offered moral and intellectual support, students in my graduate seminar "Urban Social Theory" stimulated my thinking on democracy during animated class discussions, and Gordon

Whitman was as always a crucial source of ideas on power, citizens' movements, and political processes. Finally, my appreciation goes to Bambi Schieffelin and the other editors of the *Annual Review of Anthropology* for approving my proposal to publish an article on democracy.

The *Annual Review of Anthropology* is online at http://anthro.annualreviews.org

LITERATURE CITED

Abélès M. 1988. Modern political ritual: ethnography of an inauguration and a pilgrimage by President Mitterrand. *Curr. Anthropol.* 29(3):391–404

Adams V. 1998. *Doctors for Democracy: Health Professionals in the Nepal Revolution.* New York: Cambridge Univ. Press

Agamben G. 2000. *Means Without End: Notes on Politics.* Minneapolis: Univ. Minn. Press

Alvarez SE, Dagnino E, Escobar A, eds. 1998. *Cultures of Politics, Politics of Cultures: Revisioning Latin American Social Movements.* Boulder, CO: Westview

Appadurai A. 2002. Deep democracy: urban governmentality and the horizon of politics. *Public Cult.* 14(1):21–47

Apter A. 1987. Things fell apart? Yoruba responses to the 1983 elections in Ondo State, Nigeria. *J. Modern Afr. Stud.* 25(3):489–503

Apter A. 1999. IBB = 419: Nigerian democracy and the politics of illusion. In *Civil Society and the Political Imagination: Critical Perspectives*, ed. JL Comaroff, J Comaroff, pp. 267–307. Chicago: Univ. Chicago Press

Apter D. 1963. Preface. In *Old Societies and New States: The Quest for Modernity in Asia and Africa*, ed. C Geertz, pp. v–viii. New York: Free Press

Aretxaga B. 2000. A fictional reality: paramilitary death squads and the construction of state terror in Spain. In *Death Squad: The Anthropology of State Terror*, ed. JA Sluka, pp. 46–69. Philadelphia: Univ. Penn. Press

Banerjee M. *Democracy: an Indian Variant.* Presented at the Visions and Voices Conference, Manchester University, Manchester, England

Barber BR, Schulz A. 1996. *Jihad vs. McWorld: How Globalism and Tribalism are Reshaping the World.* New York: Ballantine

Barry A, Osborne T, Rose N, eds. 1996. *Foucault and Political Reason: Liberalism, Neo-Liberalism and Rationalities of Government.* Chicago: Univ. Chicago Press

Baudrillard J. 1988. *Selected Writings*, ed. M Poster. Stanford: Stanford Univ. Press

Bellier I. 2000. The European Union, identity politics and the logic of interests' representation. In *An Anthropology of the European Union: Building, Imagining and Experiencing the New Europe*, ed. I Bellier, TM Wilson, pp. 53–73. New York: Berg

Bennett JW. 1996. Applied and action anthropology: ideological and conceptual aspects. *Curr. Anthropol.* 36(Suppl.):S23–53

Borneman J. 1992. *Belonging in the Two Berlins: Kin, State, Nation.* Cambridge, UK: Cambridge Univ. Press

Borneman J. 1997. *Settling Accounts: Violence, Justice, and Accountability in Postsocialist Europe.* Princeton, NJ: Princeton Univ. Press

Borneman J. 2002. Introduction: German sacrifice today. In *Sacrifice and National Belonging in 20th Century Germany*, ed. G Eghigian. College Station: Texas A&M Press. In press

Borneman J, Fisher L. 1999. *Death of the Father: an Anthropology of Ends in Political Authority.* http://cidc.library.cornell.edu/DOF/

Briggs CL, with Mantini-Briggs C. 2003. *Stories in Times of Cholera: The Transnational Circulation of Bacteria and Racial Stigmata in a Venezuelan Epidemic.* Berkeley: Univ. Calif. Press

Brown W. 1995. *States of Injury: Power and*

Freedom in Late Modernity. Princeton, NJ: Princeton Univ. Press
Brown W. 1998. Democracy's lack. *Public Cult.* 10(2):425–29
Burawoy M, Verdery K. 1999. *Uncertain Transition: Ethnographies of Change in the Postsocialist World*. New York: Rowman & Littlefield
Burchell G, Gordon C, Miller P, eds. 1991. *The Foucault Effect: Studies in Governmentality*. Chicago: Univ. Chicago Press
Caldeira TPR. 2000. *City of Walls: Crime, Segregation, and Citizenship in São Paulo*. Berkeley: Univ. Calif. Press
Calhoun C, ed. 1992. *Habermas and the Public Sphere*. Cambridge, MA: MIT Press
Calhoun C. 1994. *Neither Gods Nor Emperors: Students and the Struggle for Democracy in China*. Berkeley: Univ. Calif. Press
Calhoun C. 2001. Imagining solidarity: cosmopolitanism, constitutional patreiotism, and the public sphere. *Public Cult.* 14(1):147–71
Carothers T. 1999. *Aiding Democracy Abroad: The Learning Curve*. Washington, DC: Carnegie Endowment Int. Peace
Carothers T. 2002. The end of the transition paradigm. *J. Democ.* 13(1):5–21
Cheater A. 1999. Power in the postmodern era. In *The Anthropology of Power: Empowerment and Disempowerment in Changing Structures*, ed. A Cheater, pp. 1–12. New York: Routledge
Coles KA. 2002. Ambivalent builders: Europeanization, the production of difference, and internationals in Bosnia-Herzegovina. *PoLAR: Polit. Legal Anthropol. Rev.* 25(1):1–18
Comaroff JL, Comaroff J. 1997. Postcolonial politics and discourses of democracy in Southern Africa: an anthropological reflection on African political modernities. *J. Anthropol. Res.* 53(2):123–46
Comaroff JL, Comaroff J, eds. 1999. *Civil Society and the Political Imagination in Africa: Critical Perspectives*. Chicago: Univ. Chicago Press
Comaroff J, Comaroff JL, eds. 2000. Millennial capitalism: first thoughts on a second coming. *Public Cult.* 12(2):291–343
Connolly WE. 1999. *Why I am Not a Secularist*. Minneapolis: Univ. Minn. Press
Coombe R. 1997. Introduction: identifying and engendering the forms of emergent civil societies: new directions in political anthropology *PoLAR: Polit. Legal Anthropol. Rev.* 20(1):1–12
Coombe RJ. 1998. *The Cultural Life of Intellectual Properties: Authorship, Appropriation, and the Law*. Durham, NC: Duke Univ. Press
Coronil F. 1997. *The Magical State: Nature, Money, and Modernity in Venezuela*. Chicago: Univ. Chicago Press
Coutin SB. 2000. *Legalizing Moves: Salvadoran Immigrants' Struggle for U.S. Residency*. Ann Arbor: Univ. Mich. Press
Cowan JK, Dembour M-B, Wilson RA, eds. 2001. *Culture and Rights: Anthropological Perspectives*. New York: Cambridge Univ. Press
Creed GW. 1998. *Domesticating Revolution: From Socialist Reform to Ambivalent Transition in a Bulgarian Village*. University Park, PA: Penn. State Univ. Press
Cruikshank B. 1999. *The Will to Empower: Democratic Citizens and Other Subjects*. Ithaca, NY: Cornell Univ. Press
D'Andrade R. 1995. Moral models in anthropology. *Curr. Anthropol.* 36(3):399–408
Darian-Smith E. 1999. *Bridging Divides: the Channel Tunnel and English Legal Identity in the New Europe*. Berkeley: Univ. Calif. Press
Diamond L, Plattner MF, Chu Y, Tien H, eds. 1997. *Consolidating Third Wave Democracies*. Baltimore: Johns Hopkins Univ. Press
Escobar A, Alvarez SE. 1992. *The Making of Social Movements in Latin America: Identity, Strategy, and Democracy*. Boulder, CO: Westview
Farmer P. 2001. *Infections and Inequalities: the Modern Plagues*. Updated ed. Berkeley: Univ. Calif. Press
Farmer P, Connors M, Simmons J. 1997. *Women, Poverty, and AIDS: Sex, Drugs, and Structural Violence*. Monroe, ME: Common Courage Press

Ferguson J. 1993. De-moralizing economies: African socialism, scientific capitalism and the moral politics of "Structural Adjustment." In *Moralizing States and the Ethnography of the Present*, ed. SF Moore, pp. 78–92. Arlington, VA: Am. Anthropol. Assoc.

Ferguson J. 1994. *The Anti-Politics Machine: "Development," Depoliticization, and Bureaucratic Power in Lesotho*. Minneapolis: Univ. Minn. Press

Ferguson J, Gupta A. 2002. Spatializing states: toward an ethnography of neoliberal governmentality. *Am. Ethnol.* 29(4):In press

Fisher WF. 1997. Doing good? The politics and antipolitics of NGO practices. *Annu. Rev. Anthropol.* 26:439–64

Foucault M. 1991. Governmentality. In *The Foucault Effect: Studies in Governmentality*, ed. G Burchell, C Gordon, P Miller, pp. 1–51. Chicago: Univ. Chicago Press

Fox RG. 1969. *From Zamindar to Ballot Box: Community Change in a North Indian Market Town*. Ithaca, NY: Cornell Univ. Press

Fraser N. 1994. Rethinking the public sphere: a contribution to the critique of actually existing democracy. See Calhoun 1992, pp. 109–42

Fraser N. 1997. *Justice Interruptus: Critical Reflections on the "Postsocialist" Condition*. New York: Routledge

Freire P. 2000. *Pedagogy of the Oppressed*, tr. M Bergman-Ramos. New York: Continuum

Gal S. 2002. Movements of feminism: the circulation of discourses about women. In *Recognition Struggles*, ed. B Hobson. New York: Cambridge Univ. Press. In press

Gal S, Kligman G. 2000a. *The Politics of Gender After Socialism: a Comparative Historical Essay*. Princeton, NJ: Princeton Univ. Press

Gal S, Kligman G, eds. 2000b. *Reproducing Gender: Politics, Publics, and Everyday Life After Socialism*. Princeton, NJ: Princeton Univ. Press

Gal S, Woolard K, eds. 2001. *Languages and Publics: the Making of Authority*. Northampton, MA: St. Jerome

Gills B, Rocamora J, Wilson R, eds. 1993. *Low Intensity Democracy: Political Power in the New World Order*. Boulder, CO: Pluto

Geertz C. 1963. The integrative revolution: primordial sentiments and civil politics in the new states. In *Old Societies and New States: The Quest for Modernity in Asia and Africa*, ed. C Geertz, pp. 105–57. New York: Free Press

Ginsburg F. 1997. "From little things, big things grow": indigenous media and cultural activism. In *Between Resistance and Revolution: Cultural Politics and Social Protest*, ed. RG Fox, O Starn, pp. 118–44. New Brunswick: Rutgers Univ. Press

Gledhill J. 2000. *Power and Its Disguises: Anthropological Perspectives on Politics*. Sterling, VA: Pluto. 2nd ed.

Gramsci A. 1971. *Selections from the Prison Notebooks*. New York: International

Grant B. 1995. In *the Soviet House of Culture: a Century of Perestroikas*. Princeton, NJ: Princeton Univ. Press

Green L. 1999. *Fear as a Way of Life: Maya Widows in Rural Guatemala*. New York: Columbia Univ. Press

Greenhouse CJ. 2002. Introduction: altered states, altered lives. See Greenhouse et al. 2002, pp. 1–34

Greenhouse CJ, Mertz E, Warren KB. 2002. *Ethnography in Unstable Places: Everyday Lives in Contexts of Dramatic Political Change*. Durham, NC: Duke Univ. Press

Greenhouse CJ, Roshanak K. 1998. *Democracy and Ethnography: Constructing Identities in Multicultural Liberal States*. Albany: State Univ. N.Y. Press

Greenwood DJ, González Santos JL. 1992. *Industrial Democracy as Process: Participatory Action Research in the Fagor Cooperative Group of Mondragón*. Assen, The Neth.: Van Gorcum

Greenwood DJ, Levin M. 1998. *Introduction to Action Research: Social Research for Social Change*. Thousand Oaks, CA: Sage

Gupta A. 1998. *Postcolonial Developments: Agriculture in the Making of Modern India*. Durham, NC: Duke Univ. Press

Gutmann MC. 2002. *The Romance of Democracy: Compliant Defiance in Contemporary Mexico*. Berkeley: Univ. Calif. Press

Habermas J. 1989. *The Structural Transformation of the Public Sphere: an Inquiry into a Category of Bourgeois Society*, tr. T Burger, with F Lawrence. Cambridge, MA: MIT Press

Habermas J. 1996. *Between Facts and Norms: Contributions to a Discourse Theory of Law and Democracy*, tr. W Rehg. Cambridge, MA: MIT Press

Hale CR. 2002. Does multiculturalism menace? Governance, cultural rights and the politics of identity in Guatemala. *J. Latin Am. Stud.* In press

Hall KD. 2002. *Lives in Translation: Sikh Youth as British Citizens*. Philadelphia: Univ. Penn. Press

Hann CM, ed. 2002. *Postsocialism: Ideals, Ideologies and Practices in Eurasia*. New York: Routledge

Hann C, Dunn E, eds. 1996. *Civil Society: Challenging Western Models*. New York: Routledge

Hart K. 1985. The social anthropology of West Africa. *Annu. Rev. Anthropol.* 14:243–72

Harvey D. 1989. *The Condition of Postmodernity*. Cambridge, UK: Blackwell

Hayden RM. 1992. Constitutional nationalism in the formerly Yugoslav republics. *Slavic Rev.* 51(4):654–73

Herzog H. 1987. The election campaign as a liminal stage–negotiations over meanings. *Sociol. Rev.* 35:559–74

Hirsch SF. 1994. Kadhi's courts as complex sites of resistance: the state, Islam, and gender in postcolonial Kenya. In *Contested States: Law, Hegemony and Resistance*, ed. M Lazarus-Black, SF Hirsch, pp. 207–30. New York: Routledge

Holland D, Skinner D. 2001. From women's suffering to women's politics: reimagining women after Nepal's 1990 pro-democracy movement. In *History in Person: Enduring Struggles, Contentious Practice, Intimate Identities*, ed. D Holland, J Lave, pp. 93–133. Santa Fe, NM: Sch. Am. Res.

Holmes DR. 2000. *Integral Europe: Fast-Capitalism, Multiculturalism, Neofascism*. Princeton, NJ: Princeton Univ. Press

Holston J, Caldeira TPR. 1998. Democracy, law, and violence: disjunctions of Brazilian citizenship. In *Fault Lines of Democracy in Post-Transition Latin America*, ed. F Agüero, J Stark, pp. 263–96. Miami: North-South Cent.

Honig B. 2001. *Democracy and the Foreigner*. Princeton, NJ: Princeton Univ. Press

Humphrey C. 2002. *The Unmaking of Soviet Life: Everyday Economies After Socialism*. Ithaca: Cornell Univ. Press

Huntington SP. 1991. *The Third Wave: Democratization in the Late Twentieth Century*. Norman: Univ. Okla. Press

Hyatt SB. 1997. Poverty in a "post-welfare" landscape: tenant management policies, self-governance and the democratization of knowledge in Great Britain. In *Anthropology of Policy: Critical Perspectives on Governance and Power*, ed. C Shore, S Wright, pp. 217–38. New York: Routledge

Hyatt SB. 2001. From citizen to volunteer: neoliberal governance and the erasure of poverty. In *The New Poverty Studies: The Ethnography of Power, Politics and Impoverished People in the United States*, ed. J Good, J Maskovsky, pp. 201–35. New York: N.Y. Univ. Press

Isbell BJ. 1998. Violence in Peru: performances and dialogues. *Am. Anthropol.* 100(2):282–92

James W. 1999. Empowering ambiguities. In *The Anthropology of Power: Empowerment and Disempowerment in Changing Structures*, ed. A Cheater, pp. 13–27. New York: Routledge

Jelin E, Hershberg E, eds. 1996. *Constructing Democracy: Human Rights, Citizenship, and Society in Latin America*. Boulder, CO: Westview

Karlström M. 1996. Imagining democracy: political culture and democratisation in Buganda. *Africa* 66(4):485–505

Keck ME, Sikkink K. 1998. *Activists Beyond*

Borders: Advocacy Networks in International Politics. Ithaca, NY: Cornell Univ. Press

Kideckel DA. 2002. The unmaking of an East-Central European working class. See Hann 2002, pp. 114–32

Kim JY, Irwin A, Millen J, Gershman J, eds. 2000. *Dying for Growth: Global Inequality and the Health of the Poor*. Monroe, ME: Common Courage

Kligman G. 1990. Reclaiming the public: a reflection on creating civil society in Romania. *East Eur. Polit. Soc.* 4(3):393–438

Klima A. 2002. *The Funeral Casino: Meditation, Massacre, and Exchange with the Dead in Thailand*. Princeton, NJ: Princeton Univ. Press

Lass A. 1999. Portable worlds: on the limits of replication in the Czech and Slovak republics. See Burawoy & Verdery 1999, pp. 273–300

Lazarus-Black M. 1994. Slaves, masters, and magistrates: law and the politics of resistance in the British Caribbean, 1736–1834. In *Contested States: Law, Hegemony and Resistance*, ed. M Lazarus-Black, SF Hirsch, pp. 252–81. New York: Routledge

Lemon A. 2000. *Between Two Fires: Gypsy Performance and Romani Memory from Pushkin to Postsocialism*. Durham: Duke Univ. Press

Leve LG. 2001. Between Jesse Helms and Ram Bahadur: women, "participation," and "empowerment" in Nepal. *PoLAR: Polit. Legal Anthropol. Rev.* 24(1):108–28

Linz JJ, Stepan A. 1996. *Problems of Democratic Transition and Consolidation: Southern Europe, South America, and Post-Communist Europe*. Baltimore, MD: Johns Hopkins Univ. Press

Lomnitz LA, Lomnitz Adler C, Adler A. 1993. The function of the form: power play and ritual in the 1988 Mexican presidential campaign. In *Constructing Culture and Power in Latin America*, ed. DH Levine, pp. 357–401. Ann Arbor: Univ. Mich. Press

Low SM. 2000. *On the Plaza: the Politics of Public Space and Culture*. Austin: Univ. Texas Press

Lukose R. 2001. Between consumer and citizen: youth and the space of politics in Kerala, South India. Unpublished manuscript, Graduate School of Education, Univ. Penn., Philadelphia, PA

Mahmood CK. 1999. Writing the bones. *Human Rights Rev.* 1(1):19–33

Mamdani M. 1996. *Citizen and Subject: Contemporary Africa and the Legacy of Late Colonialism*. Princeton, NJ: Princeton Univ. Press

Mandel R. 2002. Seeding civil society. See Hann 2002, pp. 279–96

McDonald JH. 1997. A fading Aztec sun: the Mexican opposition and the politics of everyday fear in 1994. *Critique Anthropol.* 17(3):263–92

McDonald JH. 1993. Whose history? Whose voice? Myth and resistance in the rise in Mexico. *Cult. Anthropol.* 8(1):96–116

McLeod JR. 1991. Ritual and rhetoric in presidential politics. *Cent. Issues Anthropol.* 9:29–46

McLeod JR. 1999. The sociodrama of presidential politics: rhetoric, ritual, and power in the era of teledemocracy. *Am. Anthropol.* 101(2):359–73

Merry SE. 2003. Rights talk and the experience of law: implementing women's human rights to protection from violence. *Hum. Rights Q.* 25:In press

Mignolo WD. 2000. The many faces of cosmopolis: border thinking and critical cosmopolitanism. *Public Cult.* 12(3):721–48

Miles W. 1988. *Elections in Nigeria: a Grassroots Perspective*. Boulder, CO: Lynne Rienner

Mitchell T. 1991. The limits of the state: beyond statist approaches and their critics. *Am. Polit. Sci. Rev.* 85:77–96

Nash J. 1997. The fiesta of the word: the Zapatista uprising and radical democracy in Mexico. *Am. Anthropol.* 99(2):261–74

Nelson DM. 1999. *A Finger in the Wound: Body Politics in Quincentennial Guatemala*. Berkeley: Univ. Calif. Press

Nugent D. 1997. *Modernity at the Edge of Empire: State, Individual, and Nation in the*

Northern Peruvian Andes, 1885–1935. Stanford, CA: Stanford Univ. Press

Nugent D. 1999. *Democracy, modernity and the public sphere: Latin American perspectives on North American models*. Paper prepared for "The Anthropology of Politics and the Politics of Anthropology," Manchester '99: Visions and Voices. Univ. Manchester October 27–31

O'Donnell G, Schmitter PC. 1986. *Transitions from Authoritarian Rule: Tentative Conclusions About Uncertain Democracies*. Baltimore, MD: Johns Hopkins Univ. Press

Ong A. 1997. Chinese modernities: narratives of nation and of capitalism. In *The Cultural Politics of Modern Chinese Transnationalism*, ed. A Ong, D Nonini, pp. 171–202. New York: Routledge

Ong A. 1999. *Flexible Citizenship: The Cultural Logics of Transnationality*. Durham, NC: Duke Univ. Press

Owusu M. 1970. *Uses and Abuses of Political Power: a Case Study of Continuity and Change in the Politics of Ghana*. Chicago: Univ. Chicago Press

Owusu M. 1995. Culture, colonialism, and African democracy: problems and prospects. In *Africa in World History: Old, New, Then, and Now*, ed. MW Coy Jr, L Plotnicov. Ethnology Monographs no. 16. Pittsburgh, PA: Dep. Anthropol., Univ. Pittsburgh

Paley J. 2001. *Marketing Democracy: Power and Social Movements in Post-Dictatorship Chile*. Berkeley: Univ. Calif. Press

Poole D, Rénique G. 1992. *Peru: Time of Fear*. London: Lat. Am. Bureau

Povinelli EA. 1998. The state of shame: Australian multiculturalism and the crisis of indigenous citizenship. *Critical Inquiry* 24:575–610

Povinelli EA. 2002. *The Cunning of Recognition: Indigenous Alterities and the Making of Australian Multiculturalism*. Durham, NC: Duke Univ. Press

Price DH. 1998. Cold war anthropology: collaborators and victims of the national security state. *Identities* 4(3–4):389430

Public Anthropology. 2002. http://www.publicanthropology.org

Public Interest Anthropology. 2002. http://www.sas.upenn.edu/anthro/CPIA

Putnam RD, with Leonardi R, Nanetti RY. 1993. *Making Democracy Work: Civic Traditions in Modern Italy*. Princeton, NJ: Princeton Univ. Press

Rose N. 1996. Governing "advanced" liberal democracies. In *Foucault and Political Reason: Liberalism, Neo-Liberalism and Rationalities of Government*, ed. A Barry, T Osborne, N Rose, pp. 37–64. Chicago: Univ. Chicago Press

Roseberry W. 2002. Images of the peasant in the consciousness of the Venezuelan proletariat. In *The Anthropology of Politics: a Reader in Ethnography, Theory, and Critique*, ed. J Vincent. Malden, MA: Blackwell

Sabloff PLW, ed. 2001. *Modern Mongolia: Reclaiming Genghis Khan*. Philadelphia: Univ. Penn. Mus. Archaeol. Anthropol.

Sampson S. 1996. The social life of projects: importing civil society to Albania. See Hann & Dunn 1996, pp. 121–42

Sampson S. 2002. Beyond transition: rethinking elite configurations in the Balkans. See Hann 2002, pp. 297–316

Sanday P. 1998. *Opening statement: defining Public Interest Anthropology*. Presented at Annu. Meet. Am. Anthropol. Assoc., 97th, Philadelphia. See Public Interest Anthropology 2002

Schaffer FC. 1997. Political concepts and the study of democracy: the case of demokaraasi in Senegal. *PoLAR: Polit. Legal Anthropol. Rev.* 20(1):40–49

Schaffer FC. 1998. *Democracy in Translation: Understanding Politics in an Unfamiliar Culture*. Ithaca, NY: Cornell Univ. Press

Scheper-Hughes N. 1995. The primacy of the ethical: propositions for a militant anthropology. *Curr. Anthropol.* 36(3):409–40

Scheper-Hughes N. 2001. *Moralizing rhetorics: the uses of human rights discourses in the defense of children*. Presented at Annu. Meet. Am. Anthropol. Assoc., 100th, Washington, DC

Schild V. 1998. New subjects of rights? Women's movements and the construction of citizenship in the "new democracies." In *Cultures of Politics, Politics of Cultures: Re-visioning Latin American Social Movements*, ed. S Alvarez, E Dagnino, A Escobar, pp. 93–117. Boulder, CO: Westview

Schirmer J. 1998. *The Guatemalan Military Project: a Violence Called Democracy*. Philadelphia: Univ. Penn. Press

Scott D. 1999. *Refashioning Futures: Criticism After Postcoloniality*. Princeton, NJ: Princeton Univ. Press

Shore C. 2000. *Building Europe: The Cultural Politics of European Integration*. New York: Routledge

Stephen L. 2002. *Zapata Lives! Histories and Cultural Politics in Southern Mexico*. Berkeley: Univ. Calif. Press

Tambiah S. 1996. *Leveling Crowds: Ethnonationalist Conflicts and Collective Violence in South Asia*. Berkeley: Univ. Calif. Press

Taussig M. 1992. *The Nervous System*. New York: Routledge

Taylor J. 1993. The outlaw state and the Lone Rangers. In *Perilous States: Conversations on Culture, Politics, and Nation*, ed. GE Marcus, pp. 283–303. Chicago: Univ. Chicago Press

Trouillot M-R. 2001. The anthropology of the state in the age of globalization: close encounters of the deceptive kind. *Curr. Anthropol.* 42(1):125–38

Turner T. 1992. Defiant images: the Kayapo appropriation of video. *Anthropol. Today* 8(6):5–16

United States Agency for International Development. 2002. *Democracy and Governance*. http://www.usaid.gov/democracy

Urla J. 2001. Outlaw language: creating alternative public spheres in Basque free radio. See Gal & Woolard 2001, pp. 141–63

Verdery K. 1996. *What Was Socialism, and What Comes Next?* Princeton, NJ: Princeton Univ. Press

Verdery K. 1998. Transnationalism, nationalism, citizenship, and property: Eastern Europe since 1989. *Am. Ethnol.* 25(2):291–306

Warren KB. 1998. *Indigenous Movements and Their Critics: Pan-Maya Activism in Guatemala*. Princeton, NJ: Princeton Univ. Press

Warren KB. 2000. Conclusion: death squads and wider complicities: dilemmas for the anthropology of violence. In *Death Squad: The Anthropology of State Terror*, ed. JA Sluka, pp. 226–47. Philadelphia: Univ. Penn. Press

Warren KB. 2002. Voting against indigenous rights in Guatemala: lessons from the 1999 referendum. In *Indigenous Movements, Self-Representation, and the State*, ed. KB Warren, JE Jackson. Austin: Univ. Texas Press

Warren KB. 2002. Toward an anthropology of fragments, instabilities, and incomplete transitions. See Greenhouse et al. 2002, pp. 379–92

West H. 1998. Traditional authorities and the Mozambican transition to democratic governance. In *Africa's Second Wave of Freedom: Development, Democracy, and Rights*, ed. L Graybill, KW Thompson, pp. 65–80. Lanham, MD: Univ. Press Am.

West HG, Kloeck-Jenson S. 1999. Betwixt and between: "traditional authority" and democratic decentralization in post-war Mozambique. *Afr. Affairs* 98:455–84

Wilson RA, ed. 1997. *Human Rights, Culture and Context: Anthropological Perspectives*. Sterling, VA: Pluto

Yashar D. 1997. *Demanding Democracy: Reform and Reaction in Costa Rica and Guatemala, 1870s–1950s*. Stanford, CA: Stanford Univ. Press

Yngvesson B. 1993. *Virtuous Citizens, Disruptive Subjects: Order and Complaint in a New England Court*. New York: Routledge

Young IM. 1996. Communication and the other: beyond deliberative democracy. In *Democracy and Difference: Contesting the Boundaries of the Political*, ed. S Benhabib, pp. 120–35. Princeton, NJ: Princeton Univ. Press

Annu. Rev. Anthropol. 2002. 31:497–524
doi: 10.1146/annurev.anthro.31.040402.085420

First published online as a Review in Advance on June 28, 2002

African Presence in Former Soviet Spaces

Kesha Fikes[1] and Alaina Lemon[2]
[1]*The University of Chicago, Department of Anthropology, Haskell Hall, 1126 E. 59th Street, Chicago, Illinois 60637; email: fikes@uchicago.edu*
[2]*Department of Anthropology, University of Michigan, Ann Arbor, Michigan 48109; email: amlemon@umich.edu*

Key Words race, diaspora, displacement, Caucasus, USSR

■ **Abstract** This review traces accounts of African presence in the former USSR that are available in or have been cited primarily in English; many sources on this topic published in the USSR were strategically intended for Western consumption. This review tracks repetitions of tropes that link certain kinds of "blackness" to "Africa": It observes that treating blacks in the USSR as "displaced" confirmed Soviet humanitarianism, and produced and managed anti-Western/anticapitalist forms of Soviet nationalism and federalism. We scrutinize the ways accounts of African presence use evidence of "race remnants" that implicitly position black bodies as subjects of racial dissolution and/or cultural assimilation. This leads us to question the possibility of narrating African presence in contexts ruled by logics that wed spatial displacement/placement to racial impurity/purity. More broadly, the review addresses the utility of ideals of displaced racial communities within African diasporic criticism.

INTRODUCTION: REPRESENTING AFRICAN PRESENCE

To identify an African diaspora in the territories of the former USSR is a curious task. African presence outside of the contexts of slavery, or in spaces beyond transatlantic slave routes, has been a rare topic of diasporic inquiry. Research on African diasporic populations has centered on the transatlantic experience, with the exception of a limited number of works that attend to trans-Saharan and Ottoman slavery (Harris 1971; Fisher 1980; Toledano 1982, 1998; Blakely 1986; Fernyhough 1988; Jwaideh & Cox 1988; Ewald 1988; Clarence-Smith 1988; Ricks 1988; Lewis 1990; Hunswick 1992; Alpers 2000; Patterson & Kelley 2000). These authors stress that manifold historical and biographical trajectories urge radical transformations in the ways African presence can be geopolitically imagined. Migrations linking the Sahara to the Caucasus, such as those connected with Ottoman colonization and slave trafficking, suggest that African-identified populations reside in the territories formerly occupied by the Soviet Union. Accordingly, we raise questions about the criteria for discerning their presence, be it memory (Harris 1971, Alpers 2000), actual physical bodies, or other forms of material evidence (Savage 1992, Hunswick 1992). This review is concerned with the epistemological presuppositions upon which such inquiry around African presence is based. It sketches the historic processes that situate and name black bodies or materials that, within the former Soviet territories, are popularly referred to as *Negry* ("Negros") and *Africantsy* (the Russian term *chernij*, or "black," is applied to many non-European groups). It also addresses how race more broadly is used to articulate criteria for discerning diasporic presence.

Combining the terms "Sahara" and "Siberia" might seem farfetched: The cultural and geographic representations that delimit these spaces could hardly place them farther apart in the modern racial imagination. This conceptual distancing, one that chains notions of national and territorial legitimacy to spatial origins, biological inheritance, and racial purity, represents the ways that scholars, journalists, filmmakers, and authors have publicly treated African presence in the region. We might evoke a number of historical and biographical trajectories to close that distance: Ottoman slave trafficking affected not only the entire geography of Africa but also channeled slaves to and from Eastern Europe and the Balkans, as well as to and from parts of the Caucasus contested by the Russian Empire. Better known is the genealogy of nineteenth-century poet Aleksandr Pushkin. Pushkin's grandfather was Ibrahim Petrovich Hannibal, godson of Peter the Great and General-in-Chief of the Russian Imperial Army; some accounts argue that he was born in Cameroon (see Poe 1999) while others suggest Abyssinia (see Golden-Hanga 1966). Such trajectories, however, are most compelling if racial groupings and biological descent are treated as legitimate criteria for deciphering African presence; they fail to interrogate the social productions that make race recognizable, hence inadvertently reproducing race as real. Recognizing such occurrences within race-centered diasporic analysis, this review attends to parallel literatures that have treated race as a conceptual resource within diasporic inquiry.

Interpreting the details that constitute African diasporic presence poses a broader challenge to anthropologists. We intend this review to inspire exploration by analyzing writings about African presence in spaces not conventionally considered within reach of African diaspora. We aim thereby not only to illustrate how those writings use race as a concept but also to suggest ways to examine the work that race performs more widely within scholarship on diasporization. Diasporic populations, like any other, do not exist *sui generis*; rather, encounters among multiple subjects and institutions assign hierarchical "origins" and "placements" in space; this process constitutes conditions for diasporic subjectivity (Mercer 1994; Kondo 1997; Brown 1998, 2000; Fikes 2000). Thus, the theoretical challenge of this review is not to describe an African diaspora on former Soviet territories, per se; to merely plot dispersal over space and time would presuppose that physical movements or settlements truly evidence origins, belonging, or displacement. Rather, this review stresses the changing ways that people recognize bodies and populations as black and/or African. The authors attend to representations of dispersal or movement as tropes that legitimize images of temporal continuity and discontinuity, and thus belonging and exclusion. We build upon diaspora scholarship that has questioned impositions of predetermined collectivities that implicitly rely upon and thus generate racial or biological ontological distinctions (Apter 1991, 1999; Scott 1991, Butler 1993; Hall 1996, 1999; Kondo 1997; Brown 1998, 2000; Fikes 2000; Gilroy 2000). Frequent population movements linked the Russian and Ottoman Empires and marked Soviet and post-Soviet states. Our goal, however, is to draw attention to the contact practices that have constituted recognition of bodies as black and African (see Butler 1993, Hall 1996). Throughout this review, we often write "Africans," "Negros," and "blacks" not to refer, but to report and quote: The term "black" has different valences and references in Russian, as mentioned above and clarified below.

English-language historical and anthropological discussions of movements across the former Soviet territories are crosscut by accounts of contested borders and regime shifts. They address, for instance, 1990s return migrations to the Caucasus by Circassians, driven into Ottoman territories in the 1860s by Russian forces after the Caucasus wars (Shami 1995, 1998, 2000) (on exile of Circassians and others see Toledano 1982, 1998; Karpat 1985; Holquist 2001). Others focus on forced resettlements in the 1930s of certain "border" and "diaspora" nationalities to Siberia or Central Asia, populations (e.g., Finns, Germans, Kurds, Koreans, Crimean Tatars, Meshketian Turks, Kabardinians, Ingush, Chechens, and Kalmyks) believed to possess dangerous connections across Soviet borders. Prior to World War II such populations were singled out as "suspect" or "enemy" nationalities (see Conquest 1970; Gelb 1993, 1995; Naimark 2000; Martin 2001; Holquist 2001). Related work details the returns of resettled populations (Allworth 1998, Wilson 1998, Uehling 2000, Schoeberlein 2000). Another set of writings addresses ways that state policies and global market forces under Tsarist, Soviet, and later post-Soviet regimes compromised the political-economic practices of formerly mobile communities in Siberia and Central Asia (Slezkine 1994b, Fondahl 1995, Grant 1995, Balzer 1999, Humphrey & Sneath 1999, Anderson 2000, Liu 2000, Gray 2000, Schweitzer & Gray 2000, Rethmann 2000, Ssorin-Chaikov 2000). Finally, recent scholarship discusses post-Soviet movements of Russian and non-Russian refugees from Central Asia and the Caucasus into Central Russia (Naumkin 1994, Pilkington 1997).

Most of these works address transformations in modes of constituting cultural, linguistic, and national identities (Suny 1993, Laitin 1998, Platz 2000), some of which underwrite post-Soviet racialization or diasporization (Markovitz 1997; Lemon 2000b, 2002b; Goluboff 2001). Although none deal with specifically African nationalized or racialized identities (see Wolfe 2000), they are close to the agenda at hand. They point to the primary analytic obligation of this review—to identify criteria by which state policies, media, and even scholarship used discourses of race to categorize certain people as inherently displaced, unable to claim territorial legitimacy and public recognition. In this review we examine relationships between blackness and implicit assumptions of spatial or temporal displacement, in the Caucasus in particular. Examining such textual practices will help us understand the conceptual work that blackness performs, revealing that the only thing "inherent" about blackness is that it is realized through interaction with other subjects.

Shedding light on our approach are ways Soviets and post-Soviets have deployed tropes of "Africa," "decolonization," "slavery," "American Negros," or "blackness." Over the past several decades Soviets and post-Soviets employed such terms for various ends as shifting circumstances located Africans and other minorities in the USSR in diverse ways. Some, defending state ideologies, attributed the term "race" to alien political orders; they rejected the very applicability of it to Soviet life in order to affirm that Soviet nationalities policy did not discriminate according to racial difference (Schneider 1942, Golden-Hanga 1966; see also Blakely 1986). At the same time, however, some Soviet minorities used terms that indexed racial discrimination abroad precisely to portray Soviet conditions as similarly oppressive (see Fax 1974, Khanga 1992). To call themselves *bleky* or *Negry* rendered their experiences of discrimination or displacement more recognizable (Lemon 1995, 2000b). Soviets deployed racial tropes in ways that were markedly dialogical; they were aware of contradictions among ways various speakers and writers appropriated or rejected them. We observe how the simultaneous production and erasure of discourses on African presence in Soviet territories rely upon the disparate signifying capacities of blackness.

SEEKING AFRICAN ORIGINS

The spaces of the former USSR have been traversed by numerous mobile and settling populations, and many of its spaces and institutions were connected and severed by competing imperial regimes, including Mongol, Ottoman, Persian, Russian, Chinese, British, and Soviet governments. Today states recognize or deny resettlement claims to "home," perhaps especially in the long-contested Caucasus regions, in ways reminiscent of former imperial interests. But analysis of post-Soviet debates over migratory phenomena and resettlement regulations, or claims to territory and citizenship, is not the aim of this review (see Allworth 1998, Wilson 1998, Schoeberlein 2000, Uehling 2000). Instead, we build on recent scholarship about these debates, those calling into question popular and juridical assumptions about belonging and the production of legitimate discourses of spatial origins; we draw attention to the processes that territorialize and embody races and ethnicities (see also Williams 1989, 1991; Malkki 1995; Mamdani 2002).

How is it that formerly enslaved, African populations that settled within these spaces were never accorded territorial identities (see Harris 1971), while other formerly enslaved, likewise mobile—but "non-African"—populations were? Most accounts of how Africans appeared in Russia and the Caucasus stress their non-indigenous status and rely on reports of the slave trade—enmeshed as it was with military and diplomatic relations between Russia, Turkey, Western European nations, and the United States. Christian and Muslim slave records position African slaves in the Crimea, the Ukraine, northern Iran, and near Montenegro (see English 1959, Golden-Hanga 1966, Tynes 1973, Blakely 1986, Khanga 1992), both in groups and as individual workers, freed and enslaved (Schneider 1942). Whereas

Blakely insists that "among European states, Russia was highly conspicuous for her lack of involvement in the slave trade" (1986, p. 28) because of domestic serfdom, he documents the use of small numbers of young black servants in eighteenth-century Tsarist courts, imported from places as distant as Ethiopia and Holland as slaves "given personal freedom in exchange for a lifetime service obligation" (p. 15). Blakely (1986), English (1959), and Lamont (1946) mention the presence of once-enslaved Africans in Abkhazia, presumably purchased by Abkhazian royalty in Ottoman slave ports in Turkey some time around the eighteenth century. Imperial Russians called these people *arapy, efiopy*, and *negry* (blackamoors, Ethiopians, and Negros), linking their identities not only to African origins but also to Ottoman territories and circuits of influence (see Fisher 1980, Lewis 1990). According to Golden-Hanga (1966, p. 10), Russian statistical data in the nineteenth century categorized them as "Arabs" or "Jews."

However, not all accounts of African presence in the Caucasus trace it to the slave trade. According to English (1959), African communities in Abkhazia span a period beginning before the fifth century BC. He cites Herodotus (p. 49), who wrote of the inhabitants of Colchis (a Black Sea coastal region north of Georgia's border with Turkey) in 450 BC:

> [It] is undoubtedly a fact that the Colchians are of Egyptian descent. I noticed this myself before I heard anyone else mention it . . . My own idea on the subject was based first on the fact that they have black skins and woolly hair . . . and secondly, and more especially, on the fact that the Colchians, the Egyptians and the Ethiopians are the only races which from ancient times have practiced circumcision. (Herodotus Bk II/104; see also Du Bois 1970, p. 31).

Herodotus goes on to narrate an Egyptian story about Pharoah Sesostris leading an army northward through Syria and Turkey all the way to Colchis through the southern Balkans to Greece, returning home the same way, leaving colonists behind at the Colchian river Phasis (Poe 1999). Herodotus is not the only one to claim an early African presence: In the fourth century AD, church fathers St. Jerome and Sophronius described Colchis as the "second Ethiopia" for its black population (English 1959), and the nineteenth-century Abkhazian linguist and ethnographer Dmitri Gulia claimed parallels between Abkhazian and Abyssinian toponyms, names, and rituals to prove an ancient African origin (cited in Tynes 1973). Both visible signs (i.e., "black skin" and "woolly hair") and less visible signs (words, customs) serve as evidence.

Soviet journalists and scholars recycle both origin accounts in their own narratives of African presence. Golden-Hanga, for instance, mentions trade routes connecting the Caucasus with ancient Greece but attributes "the greatest flow of African slaves" to the sixteenth through eighteenth centuries (Golden-Hanga 1966, p. 10). Whichever origin they emphasize, they used neither to claim that African-identified people belonged in the Caucasus. Instead, they linked specifically "Negro" blackness to Africa, treating it as a sign of displacement. This review traces how.

READING RACE IN SOVIET AND FORMER SOVIET SPACES AND IN AFRICAN DIASPORA CRITICISM

Blakely's work falls outside canonical accounts of transatlantic diaspora by attending to Russian and Soviet spaces. He briefly recounts both Abkhazian-African origin narratives but more elaborately describes the voluntary, individual resettlements of African-Americans and Caribbeans to imperial Russia in the late nineteenth century and to the USSR in the twentieth (Blakely 1986). Lone sailors or performers from the United States chose to stay in Tsarist Russia, establishing families who would call Russia home, and later, African-American travelers and émigrés came to the USSR in search of racial equality. They and their descendents weave into their own autobiographies the stories of other Caribbean and African-American visitors or émigrés to the USSR (McKay 1937, Golden-Hanga 1966, Fax 1974, Robinson & Slevin 1988, Khanga 1992; see also Naison 1983, Quist-Adade 1996, Baldwin 2002). They and others detail how Soviet film studios, factories, and collective farms recruited (sometimes but not always through the Comintern—the Communist International, the association of national communist parties founded in 1919) African-American actors, workers, and engineers (Hughes 1934, 1956; Davis 1960; Smith 1964; Golden-Hanga 1966; Haywood 1978; Robinson & Slevin 1988; Khanga 1992). They also discuss the Soviet tours of performers (Robeson 1950, Hughes 1956) and describe the experiences of African and African-American students in Moscow universities (Davis 1960, Mulekezi 1961, Osei 1963, Blakely 1986, Robinson & Slevin 988, Khanga 1992). Furthermore, scattered press mention accounts of 1990s movements of black-African workers and asylum seekers from various African nations, in addition to black scholars, activists, artists, state officials, and professional elite athletes from across the globe.

Demographic information on black residents and black Soviets from the early Soviet period into the 1990s is difficult to assess; for one, no such category as "Negro" appears in the Soviet census or official records. They came to the USSR for varying reasons and under differing class and political circumstances. Khanga estimates 5000 to 10,000 "native black citizens and 40,000 African students in the former USSR" (1992, p. 22). However, the racial categories and politics implicit within such quantitative demographic reasoning ought to be questioned because such enumeration synthesizes disparate motives and conditions. That this spatial and temporal flattening occurs even within an autobiography claiming a hybrid genealogy ["I am a black Russian, born and raised in the Soviet Union—at least that's what we used to call it—and shaped by an extraordinary mixture of races and cultures" (Khanga 1992, p. 19)] illuminates a general crisis within discussions of African diasporas. As our own opening paragraph shows, to presume that persons we "know" to be black constitute the community or body under analysis constrains the project before it begins. Such logics, particularly ideals of racial authenticity, of diasporic community, or even collective resistance, commonly presuppose shared notions of cultural practice and political action (Williams 1995). More importantly, they obfuscate the practices creating that which is recognized as black. Approaches that do not temporally and spatially situate this recognition inadvertently render blackness inherent, rather than as a dialogically realized process.

More telling perhaps are the ways Khanga (1992), Mulekezi (1961), Davis (1960), Robinson & Slevin (1988), and Blakely (1986) detail black experiences of racial isolation and misery in the USSR. Drawing from accounts of African students, permanent resident African-American Soviets, and Soviet-born persons of "mixed-nationality" partnerships, the authors provide countless stories suggesting that opportunities for economic and spatial mobility were, despite policies that officially erased racial categories, aggressively racialized. Their narratives, reflecting mainly the Khrushchev and Brezhnev eras, describe difficulties in maintaining heterosexual partners or in receiving acceptance from white-identified families in Russia and the Ukraine (Robinson & Slevin 1988, pp. 299–310). They also, ironically, juxtapose the harsh classroom racism against African and African-American students in Moscow (Mulekezi 1961, Robinson & Slevin 1988) to African students' difficulties in forming racial-national organizations in universities, as opposed to political (communist youth) ones (Mulekezi 1961, p. 101). Other stories, told by professional, Soviet-born blacks who were barred from working in the West alongside their white Soviet colleagues (Robinson & Slevin 1988, p. 304), can be compared to narratives of African Americans visiting the USSR who were blocked from interacting with the isolated "African" communities in Abkhazia (see Khanga 1992) or who found it difficult to communicate with such communities, even with the assistance of translators (Blakely 1986, p. 78). These perceptions of "blocked" diasporic process, of difficulty in connecting with others who were popularly recognized as "Negro," suggest contradictory Soviet engagements with blackness, as we explore more deeply below.

At the level of our analysis, then, to identify African presence should entail that we rigorously assess the political processes that recognize blackness. We stress the tensions among accounts of disparately connected and separated black communities in the USSR, tensions arising from the mutually constituting celebration and erasure of black subject locations. In this review we primarily trace those celebrations and erasures in imperial and Soviet travel accounts and journalism in English; some were translated, but others were published specifically to impress Western audiences. We locate them in relation to Ottoman, Russian imperial, and Soviet policies and regime shifts.

We interpret these sources in ways to advocate inquiry into diasporic processes that neither presuppose racial-cultural collectivity nor generate some ontological biological reality that is often reproduced within the process of acknowledging or naming blackness. To accomplish this, we consider recent works in African diasporic criticism, such as Gilroy (2000). Gilroy's concept of "raciology" traces "the history of racial metaphysics ... as an underlying precondition for various versions of determinism: biological, nationalistic, cultural, and now genomic" (p. 52). He treats race not merely as a process that discerns how bodies are made socially meaningful, but as a site actively drawing upon murky distinctions among concepts such as biology, culture, and nationalism. Such sites, Gilroy suggests, must be wholly interrogated before we can judge how or why diasporas "problematize the cultural and historic mechanics of belonging" (p. 123). Departing from subjective emphases on diasporic subjectivity (Gilroy 1993a,b), Gilroy prioritizes the slipperiness of deterministic logics—those that seep into the roots of our research inquiries—that make recognition of race possible in the first place (Gilroy 2000). His dialogic management of race—where blackness works as both a subjective resource and an object of scrutiny—moves us closer to taking nothing about race for granted. Notwithstanding the commonalities of racial terror that inform black subject locations (Gilroy 1993b), Gilroy illuminates how actors can perform multiple and contradictory discourses of blackness within the same political field, or embrace and deny them in the same moment.

Brown's work (1998, 2000) on black diaspora narratives of spatial mobility and slavery also assumes a holistic approach to race as a dialogic site of discourse. A productive assessment of her two works reads them as parts of a whole. Brown (1998) observes the production of diasporic locality. She treats race as something that black subjects act upon through collaboratively repeating historic references that place them within transatlantic space and thus racialize subjectivity through imaginaries of mobility. Brown (1998) represents the possibilities of these imaginaries as "diasporic resources"—modes of reference that racially index and/or empower the dynamics of movement for black subjects. Whereas this work (Brown 1998) powerfully represents black subjectivity in practice, Brown (2000) uniquely positions blackness as a racial discourse whose referential potential cannot be realized without questioning the ongoing work of whiteness (see also Dominguez 1986), hence situating the dialogic reality of race. Here, Brown explores the ways black Liverpudlians in England "render slavery a potent signifier of whiteness" (Brown 2000, p. 341). That is, slavery as a signifier delivers the "white population beyond the reach of civilizing discourses on racial progress" (p. 341) so that slavery ceases to exclusively refer to blackness. Together, the articles suggest that diasporic subjectivity and racial positionality are mutually realized through contexts of contact, such that modes for race recognition, like slavery, can never pertain to blackness alone.

These representations of diaspora prioritize the discursive properties of race at every level of analysis. They attempt to unravel racial logics in ways that reconfigure diasporas less as groups and more as meaningful "contact sites" (Pratt 1992) that constitute power, place, and difference. In this sense, to evoke diaspora is never simply to describe subjective experiences of or within a community—it always also points to broader managements of cultural and political practice that transcend the community in question. Apter (1991, 1999) and Scott (1991, 1999) sound a similar call in connection to the conceptual status of "Africa" and "slavery" within African diasporic inquiry. Emphasizing "historic production" and "continuity," they treat these processes as contact spaces within which the mechanics of race are made knowable within research on black diasporization. In this sense, their projects attend to the ways in which representations of temporality are implicitly embodied, or perhaps "Africanized" through politicized origins and ideals of place.

Arguably then, recent African diasporic criticism demands acknowledging the heteroglossic properties of race as a sign that can bear multiple or conflicting referents and accents within accounts of diaspora (Bakhtin 1981). Considering the goals of this review, how then do we begin to interpret texts that so variously explain the supposed anomaly of black bodies in former Soviet territory, when accounts relate African presence to visible, physical, and even linguistic evidence? We might begin by tracing the citation path of one such report of evidence. The Black Sea coast of Abkhazia, in Caucasus Georgia bordering Turkey, is the site of several black communities reported in Russian imperial newspapers and periodicals in 1913. As Blakely notes, the presence of these "Negros" in Abkhazia was discovered repeatedly, first just before World War I, then after the Revolution (see Parry 1925), then during World War II (see Schneider 1942), and again in the Brezhnev period (see Golden-Hanga 1966, Tynes 1973), "each time with amazement but often in ignorance of prior such 'discoveries'" (Blakely 1986, p. 5). Yet each inquiry into the ostensibly mysterious origins of the Africans recycles texts and citations. One such text, a letter to the editor, was first published in 1913 in the Russian-language paper *Kavkaz*, printed in Tblisi, Georgia. It was sent by one E. Markov and was among a number of responses elicited by an article by Russian naturalist Vradii and another published by rival scholar Elius (cited in Blakely 1986). This letter, along with others, was collected and republished by Vradii in his 1914 volume, *Negroes of Batumi Province*:

> Passing for the first time through the Abkhazian community of Adzyubzha, I was struck by the purely tropical landscape around me: against the background of a bright green primeval jungle there stood huts and sheds built of wood and covered with reeds; curly-headed Negro children played on the ground and a Negro woman passed by carrying a load on her head. Black-skinned people wearing white clothes in the bright sun resembled a typical picture of some African village ... (Markov reprinted in Vradii 1914, pp. 16–17; quoted in Tynes 1973, p. 2 and Blakely 1986, p. 9).

The letter took up a debate generated by the first two articles over the numbers and origins of Negros in Abkhazia: Were they two dozen or two hundred? Were they ancient Colchians or the descendents of slaves? Markov argues for a relatively recent arrival with the Turks, for "they always had many African slaves whom they used to bring from their colonies in Africa." However, he anchors an otherwise surreal racial displacement, what he calls later a "chance phenomena," to African origins not through past events or relations, but through geographic images of present space. "Negro" physical features work together with exotic vegetation and substances at the Southern reaches of the Russian empire to create a world "resembling an African village." It is as if only transplanting an African environment to the Georgian Black Sea coast could justify the ongoing presence of black bodies.

In turn, African presence ranked the Caucasus as another Africa, confirming Russian imperial status. The 1913 debate had followed a century of colonial expansion and wars in the Caucasus. Until late in the nineteenth century much of the

Caucasus remained contested—a porous border zone in Russia's wars with Turkey. Throughout the nineteenth century most Russophone travel accounts of the Caucasus affected orientalizing wonder. Pushkin lyricized Circassians with Byronic envy as fabulous, romantically fierce mountain tribes, and Tolstoy later eulogized Chechens to criticize the cruelties of imperial expansion (Friedrich 2002). As literary critic Susan Layton (1994) notes, literary works' symbolic opposition of the North to the Caucasus helped confirm Russia's status as a civilized empire among European empires. The Caucasus played a role in the Russian imagination that was analogous to the role of Africa in the British imaginary, arguably in imitation of British and French imperial fantasy.

Markov's eyewitness account appears again in the Brezhnev era, in a 1973 article that likewise explains the supposed anomaly of a community that "continues to excite the minds of scientists who try to explain the African curly hair and dark skin color in some inhabitants of the Caucasus" (Tynes 1973, p. 2). Tynes begins by detailing for English readers the Colchian argument, citing Herodotus and Gulia, then he briefly touches on the slave-trade hypothesis and ends with an interview with a Soviet ethnographer (Vianor Pachulia) who poses a synthesis. The excited scientists he refers to, in the main, however, are not his contemporaries: Under the subheading "New Data on Africans in Abkhazia," he quotes the 1913 articles and Markov's letter. It seems that maintaining the anomaly of blackness required recycling familiar expressions of surprise. When accounting for Negros who voluntarily traveled to and settled in the USSR, Soviet and post-Soviet Russia media similarly framed blackness as anomalous and displaced, as addressed below.

To locate peoples via present, physical evidence of origin or race treats the moment of "contact" as continuous and as a biological reality, rather than as a nexus of processes and conditions in which subjects discern power and difference. Some historians grappling with similar evidence in other parts of the world suggest that the disappearance of African communities once engaged in trans-Saharan slavery is the result of high rates of mortality and assimilation (Savage 1992, p. 2; Hunswick 1992, pp. 25–26). However, assertions of death, genetic integration, or residual remnants all reveal something similar about practices situating blackness: Whether racial inheritance is observed as a survival or as failing to reproduce itself, race is treated as biologically real (Seshadri-Cooks 2000, p. 19). "Negro integration" depends upon the loss of physical evidence, the disappearance of "Negroid" features, whereas their survival verifies former black slaves' (but not white slaves') whereabouts. This review attempts to interrogate unified determinisms that float on unclear distinctions between biology and social relations; the objective is to clear a conceptual space to analyze the dialogic ways that people use race in meaningful social practice. The stakes for understanding such uses of evidence for race remnants are quite high. What's more, we need to challenge the ways that properties of blackness used to document African communities impose limits upon identification processes.

Across the globe various politics of blackness and "blackening" blur into each other as they transect disparate historical-political realities (see Hall 1994). No less so in the former territories of the USSR, where persons once officially recognized as minority nationalities are being blackened, or being labeled blacks. Both dominant and popular cultural representations of such minorities blacken them, as do communities undergoing such conscription themselves, in critical, reflexive expressions of black identity. These representations and expressions, though they index local political affiliations and rifts, are a part of international discourses about race and, in particular, global ideals of blackness. Decades of Soviet reportage on racism in the United States meant that Soviets were aware of competing pragmatic deployments racializing terms in the West. Thus, many post-Soviets use the phrase "white person" (*belij chelovek*) to mean not only "pale complexioned and/or biologically European person," but also "person enjoying civil rights" or "a normal life," as opposed to the more usual suffering of bureaucratic constraints in a crumbling Soviet infrastructure. Conversely, non-Russian minorities (Azeris, Georgians, Roma, Tartars, and others) in Russian-dominated metropoles forged imaginary connections with African Americans, combining the logic of rights with local understandings of blackness (in Russia any "swarthy," "southern," and "Asian" person might be labeled *chernij*, or black): "We are *negry*," one Romani man told Lemon (2000b, p. 75). "We are treated like second class here, like your blacks in America."

In the following sections this review calls attention to ways diasporic analysis could treat race by examining shifts in regimes that have constituted blackness through tropes of "displacement" and "continuity." Adding to related conversations in anthropology across colonial, postcolonial, socialist, and postsocialist contexts, it deconstructs implicit reasoning that links blood, purity, and miscegenation to spatial origins or to current territorial belonging and legitimacy (Hale 1994; Gilroy 1987; Williams 1989, 1991; Trouillot 1990; Gupta & Ferguson 1992; Alonso 1994; Malkki 1995; Amselle 1998; Fikes 2000; Lemon 2000b; Mamdani 2002) and/or to citizenship (Gilroy 1987, Stoler 1992, Wade 1993, Hale 1994, Harrison 1995, Ferreira da Silva 1998, Gordon 1998, Gould 1998, Grandin 2000, de la Cadena 2000, Fikes 2000, Lemon 2000a, Lomnitz 2001, Mamdani 2002, Brodkin 1998). Likewise, this review builds upon analyses of displacement and continuity that explore how such categories matter to communities whose public identities are constrained by representations that oppose settlement to travel and impermanence (Gilroy 1987; Scott 1991, 1999; Apter 1991; Brown 1998, 2000; Lemon 2000b; Fikes 2000).

Whereas our approach to textual sources works through and against certain representations of "Africa," "Africans," and "slavery," we by no means discount the effects of historically persistent conflations of "black" or "African" with "slave" (Scott 1991). Rather, we treat these terms as resources in a field in which various players act upon them: We wish to analyze that playing field. Hence, in the same sense in which Apter (1991) and Scott (1991, 1999) politicize "Africa" and "slavery" as tropes that naturalize "African" continuities, the following emphasizes the discursive work of crafting continuity and its absence. "Race" is a discursive regime whose real effects are negotiated into awareness by and among "producers" and "objects" alike. Recognizing Apter's (1991) call to attend to tensions between inventing and practicing discourses that rely upon these tropes, we focus upon state participation in the "inventive" process (Mudimbe 1988), in part because the available texts best document that process.

"Africa" and "slavery" establish a tension. They index limits of continuity, but they must also be publicly reinscribed to authorize their referential power to signify displacement or things officially silenced (see Trouillot 1990). We examine these processes by placing accounts of African presence amid disruptions to imperial regimes and the accompanying disruptions to modes of transmitting public memory. This approach both challenges readings of "continuity" and allows us to highlight the ways new regimes reappropriated "Africa" and "blackness" for new audiences (see Brown 2000); we situate the shifting ways Soviet and post-Soviet texts address both domestic and Western readers.

OTTOMAN AND RUSSIAN IMPERIALISM

This section draws from historians' accounts of imperial institutions, interrelations, and disruptions regulating Ottoman slave trade before and at the turn of the twentieth century. We lack oral accounts or texts to represent the voices of various agents and thus stress the political salience of African presence in available accounts. A more detailed study might, for instance, illuminate how in Russian and Turkish usage the categories black and African were variously politicized across the Ottoman and Russian empires.

To read across histories of Ottoman, Russian, and later Soviet Empires involves stressing that, although we refer to different imperial headings, they do not withstand the persistent contacts linking these regions to each other, as well as to western Europe and to Africa. Some African movements to Russian imperial territories were spurred by slave trading not only between the Ottomans and the Caucasus, but also across European-settled or colonized spaces (Clarence-Smith 1988). As mentioned above, Russian courts imported young black male servants from Holland (Blakely 1986). Some Africans en route via Europe to Turkey and to the Caucasus (particularly in the seventeenth through nineteenth centuries) were likely familiar with contemporaneous European understandings of race and of blackness in particular. Another node of intersection was the steady arrival to the Ottoman Empire of thousands of trans-imperial travelers and administrators. These visitors brought their own slaves and translators, many of whom were black Africans: These slaves' encounters with local slaves variably informed and helped situate representations of Ottoman (Tanzimat) enslavement and racializing practices (see Dorr 1999).

Britain urged the Ottomans to end slave trading in the early nineteenth century until the turn of the twentieth century, when Ottoman slavery officially ended. Ottoman slave populations included not only Africans, but also East European, Balkan, and Caucasus peoples, most particularly female Circassians. Beginning in the 1850s the British had been influential in slowing the African slave trade, but not the Circassian trade. The Russian Empire was all too happy to be rid of Circassians and other Caucasus peoples: After defeating the Ottomans in the Crimean War (1853–1856) it devoted full attention to sweeping resistant populations from the Caucasus. Also, the Circassian refugees brought their own Circassian slaves with them into exile. The Ottomans finally responded to British pressures to suppress the trade of Africans, most decisively in 1890 with the Brussels Act—but "white" slavery continued to be deemed by Ottomans and British alike as an internal issue (Toledano 1982). All this suggests that the racial marking of slaves was a profoundly trans-imperial and trans-spatial enterprise, a process that was constituted through dialogues that connected trans-Saharan and transatlantic practices. Regardless of the ideologies discerning enslavement, blackness was constituted as a sign indexing displaced peoples; the practices of traveling imperial bodies and the disparate imperial knowledges and institutions that these bodies represented confirmed this.

The Ottoman state instituted other measures that marked and separated black bodies. The 1890 Brussels Act not only added teeth to sanctions against the African slave trade, but also called for guesthouses in former trade centers along the Mediterranean and Red Sea coasts to protect emancipated persons "in transition" (Toledano 1982, p. 247). Near some of these guesthouses the state would give former slaves land to cultivate and to build settlements. At first, they were encouraged to marry other Africans to establish communities on that land, but by 1892 only married Africans were transported to such settlements (Toledano 1982, pp. 247–53). These guesthouses and settlements thus exhibit state involvement in creating and demarcating black-African-slave communities as such.

It is difficult to know to what extent Ottoman slave trading and manumission practices affected the creation of African communities in Abkhazia or of racial categories in the Caucasus or in Russia. More research is called for in this area. From the sixteenth century until 1810, the Abkhazian coast was dependent on the Ottomans, but the Ottoman reach did not include the Caucausus. Georgia, an autonomous Christian state since the fourth century AD, battled Seljuk forces, paid tribute to the Iranians and Mongols, and battled the Ottomans before declaring itself a Russian protectorate in 1783. Although those areas never came fully under Ottoman control (see Suny 1988), up into the seventeenth century the Ottomans were the dominant power across Transcaucasia. The area then suffered economic collapse, the slave trade becoming the only lucrative trade: The population of western Georgia was drastically reduced by warfare and the slave trade. The Russian Empire annexed Georgia in 1800 and controlled the rest of the Caucasus by the 1870s, after more than a century of struggles there with Turkish and Iranian forces and with local populations. The 1890 Brussels Act, coming into effect a generation later, marks a transition period from which a trans-imperial logic of race emerged—it effectively underwrote local constructions of place and belonging.

The cultural and political impact that Ottoman imperialism had on understandings of race and of spatial belonging—not only within the Ottoman Empire, but across Russian imperial and then Soviet Eurasian territories—has yet to be discerned in its complexity. Just as relations with Britain affected racialization in

Ottoman territories, so probably did Russian-Turkish relations render lasting effects. As we address below, global politics certainly affected Soviet and post-Soviet racializing discourses. Since World War I several overlapping political revolutions seem to account for a lack of information and thinking about these complex influences. The early Kemalist Turkish Republic, taking power in 1923, tried to disassociate itself from Ottoman history, rendering it conceptually distant and mythic to contemporary society (Gülap 1995). Across the borders the Soviet state similarly disassociated itself from Russian imperial history even as it reabsorbed the same Caucasus territories that the Russian Empire had annexed in the nineteenth century—territories once linked to the Ottoman slave trade. Finally, beginning in the mid-1920s, in line with this disassociation, the Soviets codified a rhetoric of cooperative equality to officially delimit certain forms of identity and erase others. These parallel events yielded historic narratives and territorial assignments that failed to recall the dynamics of contact that had woven Africa to the Caucasus (see Williams 1991). We do not review each in equal detail but mention them here in order to sketch a context for what follows and to suggest lines for further inquiry.

To review narratives that locate Africans within these contested territories (or to explore ways contemporary non-Africans appropriate narratives of race or slavery from other spaces and extend their tropes of "blackness" to local ones) requires that we assess the production of blackness as a trans-spatial enterprise—and relate it to particular political transitions. We have addressed international shifts that affected Ottoman slave trade. We turn now to shifts from Russian imperial to Soviet governance in 1918, roughly paralleling the shift from Ottoman to secular Kemalist rule in 1923. Both transitions drew upon and disregarded productions of racial difference.

TRANSITION TO SOVIET POLITICS

In 1921 the Bolsheviks assumed territorial control of all the Caucasus after defeating counter-revolutionary forces in a civil war (1918 to 1921). Beginning in the 1920s certain populations residing along the Black Sea (for instance, Crimean Tartars, Circassians, Abkhazians) were steadily classified as Soviet "national minorities" or "nations" and assigned autonomous districts, regions, or republics. The Russian term "nationality" carries senses closer to "ethnicity" than in English usage (though as we see below the term is multivalent): Key here are the ways policy makers and census takers used these categories and thereby cultivated national consciousness and a sense of inherent, "primordial identity" (Martin 2001; see also Suny 1993, Slezkine 1996, Hirsch 1997, Suny & Martin 2001).

After 1926 Soviet nationalities policy began in earnest to demarcate nationalities from each other (and "small peoples" from "national minorities" and from "nations") (Slezkine 1994a, Weiner 1999, Hirsch 2000). From this period until the mid 1930s, the commissar for nationality affairs interpreted Leninist nationalities policy this way: Imperial oppressions could only be redressed by recognizing national minorities, offering affirmative action–type education, job placements, and partial territorial autonomy. Lenin had urged that if the nation-state were to "wither away" under communism, the vanguard state should first strategically recognize oppressed nations in particular. Policies recognized nationalities based on several criteria, including common language, culture, historical, and territorial continuity. "Large nations" possessed all of these, while "minority nationalities" and small peoples might lack territorial continuity. Between 1923 and 1938 the state demarcated numerous national autonomous regions and republics, set up employment niches and quotas, and established presses and schools in almost 200 languages, which included those of many so-called small peoples and diaspora minorities that were not assigned regional territory. National minorities were to "raise their cultural level" and become politically literate in socialism through the mediation of their mother tongues: The rather Jesuitic slogan of the day was "nationalist in form, socialist in content."

The Soviets never recognized blacks in the Caucasus as a nationality in the same way that they recognized other peoples there (for instance, some Circassians had also been slaves, but they were recognized). Soviet propaganda in the early 1930s did refer to some peoples as "former slaves" (e.g., Roma) or as "former serfs" (Russians, Ukrainians) "freed" by the revolution, but this was a rhetorical move, not a basis for recognizing groups as historical entities. However, the Abkhazian Africans were not represented as originally "belonging" to that space: That alone ought not to have prevented a nationality classification because other populations lacking legitimated territorial continuity, such as Roma and Jews, were assigned nationalities based on perceptions of linguistic, historical, or cultural differences. According to sources cited above, however, black villagers in Abkhazia spoke Abkhazian and practiced local customs; with the ostensible lack of territorial continuity, this left "color" alone to index any sort of difference. However, Soviet policy could not explicitly use such racial markers to distinguish groups; in Soviet official discourse the color bar and antiblack racism were defined as evils of capitalist colonialism. As a result, no space (neither postemancipation nor postrevolutionary) opened up for these villages to constitute themselves as a group among other groups recognized as "oppressed minorities" in early Soviet Russia. As a corollary, early Soviet nationalities policy also erased opportunities to publish or otherwise publicly recollect any distinctive experiences of Africans in Abkhazia.

In 1936 Georgia was promoted to the status of a Soviet republic, with Abkhazia formalized as one of its minority regions. But by the late 1930s Stalin (born in Georgia and not himself a native Russian speaker) had reversed several aspects of Leninist nationalities policy. The Soviet Union shifted to a federative model in which Russian would serve as the "inter-nationality" lingua franca. In 1937 Russian became an obligatory subject, and presses and schools that had published and taught in minority languages of groups lacking recognized large territorial claims were shut down (Smith 1998; Lemon 2000b, 2002b; Martin 2001; see also Kreindler et al. 1985). "Small minorities" became subsumed under the more "advanced nationalities" (e.g., Mingrelians under Georgians) who, in turn, were accountable to Russophone institutions in Moscow. These moves would, according to party press, meld the nationalities into a "friendship of the peoples." The friendship of the peoples even more explicitly opposed racial discrimination abroad than had earlier policy, celebrating Soviet-style, "inter-national" hybridity as an alternative. Ethnographic data and statistics showing increases in inter-nationality marriage and bilingualism (see post–World War II, Russian-language publications of the Academy of Sciences Miklukho-Maklai Institute of Ethnography, *passim*) made a hybrid utopia seem real, while museum and folk displays and film and theater stereotypes instantiated the separate nations comprising the hybrid (Slezkine 1994b, Grant 1995, Petrone 1996, Lemon 2000b).

Safeguarded by the absence of explicit racializing criteria in official nationalities policies, the state could globally situate Soviet Republican, inter-nationality politics as more civil and humane than racial politics in the West. For example, children's books such as Samuil Marshak's 1933 *Mr. Twister* (translated into many languages over the decades; see Geldern & Stites 1995) depicted Soviets as equally hospitable to Africans and Europeans, housing them all in the same hotels—in the story, the white U.S. millionaire visiting Leningrad is enraged by this. In the 1936 film *Circus* (directed by Alexandrov), Moscow provides a haven from cruel bigotry to a white woman from the United States and her black baby, a "new home" where, at the end of the film, an audience of circus-goers representing dozens of Soviet nationalities pass the baby hand to hand, singing lullabies in their "national tongues." Note, however, that such narratives link African individuals in Russia to an origin somewhere else. They never link images of African communities to a more long-term presence.

However state media attempted to represent the USSR as eschewing racial categories (in order to signal opposition to racial discrimination both in the imperial past and in capitalist countries), state agents most likely did draw upon them when assigning access to education and employment and when implementing residence and resettlement policies (Abramson 2002, Hirsch 2002, Weitz 2002, Weiner 2002). Anecdotal evidence indicates that state agents in the Caucasus may have tried to erase African communities by deporting and dispersing them. Khanga (1992) notes that Svetlana Alijuevna, Stalin's daughter, wrote in her memoires that Khanga's mother, Golden-Hanga, had confided in her about a visit to the Abkhazian villages (1968; see also Blakely 1986, p. 78). The frightened villagers worried that Golden-Hanga's visit boded a relocation farther away; Blakely asserts that this suggests they had witnessed previous relocations. The years preceding World War II saw mass deportations of borderland and diaspora minorities, most notably from the Caucasus to Central Asia (see Conquest 1970; Gelb 1993, 1995; Naimark 2000; Martin 2001). Those orchestrating relocations may have used implicitly racializing criteria to remove several groups in the region, perhaps including Africans (see Weitz 2002; see also Holquist 2001, Martin 2001). The villagers thus either identified with resettled neighbors or remembered that soldiers had previously deported Africans.

Blakely (1986, p. 79) suggests that the Abkhazian blacks may have been relocated more than once to various parts of the Soviet Union, even in the 1970s. After World War II some resettled peoples returned. Such returns were no simple matter, neither was any relocation within the Soviet Union: All Soviet citizens carried passports that registered them at a particular address, and each citizen was allowed only one residence permit at a time. Registering for a permit was especially bureaucratically tortuous in desirable cites like Moscow; returning and registering in the Caucasus was likely fraught with bureaucratic obstacles as well—perhaps especially for people whom local bureaucrats may have de facto considered African, not belonging in the Caucasus. At any rate, according to Golden-Hanga's confidences, the Abkhazian blacks certainly experienced extreme poverty and lacked access to basic life necessities as well as to Soviet education and media.

THE SPECTACLE PRODUCTION OF BLOOD IN THE USSR

Paradoxically, the ways official delimitations of national identities rejected racial criteria constrained modes to publicly recognize and engage with African blackness. In this section we discuss ways African presence was, once again, produced as spectacle, in the context of the political transitions outlined above. We have addressed such spectacle-making in imperial times. Soviet representations, even as they linked racial discrimination to imperialism and capitalist "wage slavery," echoed imperial productions and reproduced the surprise and bewilderment the imperial papers had expressed upon discovering African communities in Abkhazia in 1913. In the 1940s, Soviet media accounts extracted African presence from the Ottoman and Russian imperial histories that 1920s Soviet policies had countered. They seemingly avoided imperial inequities without tracing its historical relations in detail. As discussed above, just before World War I, while the Caucasus was still under Russian imperial rule, press representations located the African villages as somehow displaced while also displacing the entire Caucasus as Russia's Africa. Later accounts of "Negro villages" drop the latter function but echo the former: Soviet logics of territorial placement and legitimacy appropriated imperial racial discourses in new, selective ways to embed spectacle in a new set of federative and international relations.

We can demonstrate these imaginaries in a wartime article published by Soviet journalist Isidor Schneider in the English-language Soviet public relations organ *Soviet Russia Today*. It was titled, "A Negro Citizen of Soviet Georgia: The Story of Bashir Shambe, Brought from Persia into Tsarist Russia as a Slave, Now one of Soviet Georgia's Distinguished Citizens":

> Following Bashir Shambe home one would note the respect and affection in the greetings received from his white neighbors .... Walking in with him would be introduced to Bashir Shambe's Russian wife and his slender, handsome, mulatto son. The boy wears the tie of a Young Pioneer, in whose organization only the youth who show determination, devotion, intelligence and other high

> qualities can hold membership. From his alert, eager and confident manner one realizes that the son of Bashir Shambe has never known that Negro blood be a bar to opportunity and to full participation in the life of the community (Schneider 1942, p. 148).

Shambe's distinguished citizenship is realized in a nonracist environment, brought about by transformations to Soviet forms of government. The phrase "the son ... has never known ... Negro blood [to] be a bar to opportunity" suggests that it is solely the political environment that alleviates otherwise certain suffering. Here, "Negro blood" is treated as real, and it is only the father's luck to have been brought to future Soviet territory (as an African can never be of it) that allows both to experience blackness without injury to spirit or body. As Seshadri-Crooks (2000, pp. 8–9) argues, race is treated as a neutral factor in human difference, as if racism (in the same conversation) merely misappropriated that factor.

Schneider distinguishes between race and racism earlier in her article when she quotes Shambe describing his life as a young slave in (Teheran) Iran, a country with a long history of conflicts with Tsarist and Soviet Russia:

> My new master was what could be politely described as whimsical. He decided to make me serve as a clown to entertain him and his guests. He instructed me in Persian dances. And he trained me to grin, opening my mouth as widely as possible and exposing my teeth. To laugh at my white teeth, showing against my dark skin, seemed to him remarkable entertainment. To grin before him and his guests, whether or not I had anything to grin about, became one of my chief tasks (Schneider 1942, p. 149).

Ventriloquizing Shambe, Schneider criticizes racist practice abroad. However, note that she shuns the category of race only insofar as notice of Shambe's body causes his suffering; she problematizes race only when the misguided visually index it. By contrast, in a section in which she marks race as invisibly "carried in the blood," inherent difference is commonsensical and legitimate.

Schneider continues Shambe's story as a Georgian prince visits Persia and decides to take him back to Georgia. He asserts that life in Tsarist-controlled Georgia was no different than life in Teheran, establishing imperial tyranny as the culprit in racist practices (149):

> The next day I was delivered to my new master ... To heighten what he considered the comic effect produced by his Negro servant my master bought me a white donkey to travel on ... I was given a corner in the dragoon stables to live in. There I slept and ate. The promised education was forgotten together with other promises. My mother and I never saw each other again. My work was menial and my Georgian master, like my Persian masters, used me as an object of sport. Then the Revolution came ... Finally the Mensheviks were defeated. Georgia became a Soviet Republic. If this meant real freedom and a new life for the Georgians you can imagine what a liberation it meant for me. To be accepted as an equal, to live as a human being and not as an object

of sport for bored rich people . . . You can understand with what eagerness I volunteered in the Red Army (Schneider 1942, pp. 149–50).

In juxtaposing this narrative of the past against that of present opportunities for Shambe's son—for whom "Negro blood" is irrelevant to education and organizational affiliation—the journalist affirms Soviet republicanism as the political solution to inhumanity, to racial and class segregation, and even to the destruction of the family. Recall that the article appeared in an English-language publication, aimed at a Western, English-speaking audience: Most important for its discursive positioning is not that Shambe's original enslavement occurred in Tehran rather than somewhere in the West, but that a Soviet journalist recoils from antiblack racism and champions the liberation of "Negros."

Of equal importance is that Shambe himself is not represented as a cultural participant in any broader community of Africans or blacks. Instead, the story emphasizes his comfort with white neighbors who honor and respect him. Such narratives resonate strongly with many Soviet assimilation tales, stories highlighting intermarriage and inter-national harmony and showcasing individual minorities as successful professionals within a broader, Russian speaking Soviet world: the hardworking Gypsy sports scholar or Chuvash surgeon. Yet Schneider never describes Shambe or his son as simply Soviets. Thus, however else they may have experienced their locality and however else their neighbors may have addressed them, this text's coherence rests upon identification of "Negro blood." Being "Negros" before anything else, though "Negro" was not a recognized nationality category, their figures imply an inherent relationship between race and nation (see Gilroy 1987; Williams 1989, 1991; Kondo 1997). Just in the moment when the journalist uniquely prizes their citizenship, she simultaneously indexes them as displaced.

Schneider's 1942 use of terms such as "blood" is not isolated: We can situate it within a broader frame of Soviet racializing discursive practice. We outline this frame by examining textual evidence from the past alongside the ways post-Soviet actors reproduce discursive practices that circulated in the Soviet past. In the 1990s many post-Soviet scholars argued that race was not a relevant category in the USSR because the relevant terms in official and academic use were not race but *natsional'nost* (nationality, ethnicity) or *narodnost* (folk identity, ethnicity) (cf. Hirsch 1997, Weitz 2002). As detailed above, these terms had particular uses in official policy. In many arenas, however (and as Schneider's article illustrates, including officially sanctioned media), Soviets did infer biological and inherited essences, drawing both upon external signs and nonvisible signs such as blood. Additionally, terms such as nationality were deployed to do the work of racial categories (see also Balibar 1989). Such practices have been amplified in post-Soviet times, as in this statement by an organization called Russian National Union (1995, p. 1): "[T]here are even people who . . . rush to mix with the Jewish nationality and expect all kinds of beneficial results. [A] man and wife who are both Russian and happen to want healthy, racially whole children are automatically labeled fascists." Connections and slippages among such categories change over time, and to project current configurations retrospectively would be unpersuasive. We can, however, assess how recent articulations strategically echo previous discursive practices for new audiences and new state interests and advocate more research on how changes in state policy and in international relations play into these strategies.

However firmly the Soviet state declared itself against racism, numerous racializing slurs circulated not only outside official discourse, but also among those who populated state institutions such as prisons and the army, at least from Stalin's time. Roback's multilingual dictionary of slurs, published just after World War II, gives numerous Russian colloquial pejoratives turning upon skin color and bodily features and linking biology to geography (Roback 1946); so also do dictionaries collecting Soviet prison slang of the 1960s (Rossi 1992[1987]). From such collections one can only hypothesize the actual social encounters through which terms such as *chernozhepy* ("black asses") or *negativy* ("photographic negatives") circulated beyond state disciplinary contexts in other social realms. Still, these collections belie attempts to explain post-Soviet racial thinking merely as imports from the West or to dismiss it as resurgence from the distant, imperial past.

Under Soviet rule, officially sanctioned cultural texts and unofficial popular discourse linked dark complexions to naturalized proclivities such as "cleverness in the market," "lusty dispositions," "hot blooded" temperaments, "traditional" patriarchal social organizing, and "clan-like" family networks. Anything isolated as a difference can be made to signal some ostensibly essential nature that connects generations. "Race" can be marked by accent or grammar (Irvine & Gal 2000), by forms of kinship, through spatial relations, or by other cultural practices. In 1990s Russia, post-Soviets often spoke of these traits as being carried unseen "in the blood" (Lemon 2000b, 2002a; also see Butler 1993, Hall 1996, Seshadri-Crooks 2000). Since at least the 1960s, Soviet films and television established a motif for detecting hidden identity "in the blood," playing on the trope of connections "under the skin" without naming those connections as "racial" (though some did use the language of "genes"). In Soviet times hybridity was presented as joyful—and not only by official media; counter-cultures, too, played with hybrid identities (see Rayport 1998). However, by the 1990s the problem of discerning racial and national identities intersected anxieties about authentic motives and values under a shifting regime, worries about cultural loss commonly aired in ethnographic and journalistic accounts of minority communities. Taxonomic dissolution had similarly vexed physical anthropologists in nineteenth-century Russia, who found "some Finns to be Balts, some Balts to be Slavs, and some Slavs to be Turks" (Slezkine 1996, p. 828). This slipperiness has been used to support arguments that Russian society is less racist than others. Yet reference to bodily forms and skin color were never the only racializing practices there or elsewhere: Observe the sliding discourses around hidden percentages of blood in the Unites States or the unmasking of geneologies in Nazi Germany. The accounts of displacement that we have traced here attest to still other slippery modes of making races.

THE DIASPORIC POLITICS OF RACIAL DISSOLUTION AND SPATIAL ORIGINS

Soviet political and social life was in part constituted through sliding engagements with blackness. The process of representing black individuals (from Pushkin's grandfather to Paul Robeson) as graciously welcomed, juxtaposed against official representations and policy that erased permanent black or African communities, representing them as not originally belonging, situates one of many playing fields within which Soviet federalism globally opposed capitalism and antiblack discrimination. This simultaneous celebration and erasure importantly confirmed Soviet civility while productively linking Russianness to whiteness. Both sorts of representation, each spectacular anomalies, worked as mutually constituting technologies; they internally managed distinctions among nationalities while globally representing Soviet identity. Effectively, this denial and erasure crafted both the invisibility of African communities existing in Soviet territory since imperial times (or earlier) and the celebrity of Soviet black émigrés, represented as short-term or individual residents in Russian space.

Khanga's perception of the ways Africans living in Abkhazia were kept apart from African Americans who chose to resettle in the USSR is telling. Khanga (1992) argues that when African Americans learned about and tried to connect with these communities, state officials made such meetings difficult. What could be read as an effort to silence (and as discussed above, disperse and dilute) the black Abkhazian can be observed against the accounts of Africans and African Americans who voluntarily relocated to the Soviet Union. These contradictions highlight processes constituting both discrete Soviet nationalities and the Soviet federalism that subsumed them. Curiously, then, the emergence of these tensions around blackness seems to have been ratified by the increasing presence in the USSR of Western blacks and African nationals who sought opportunities to experience their humanity without racial prejudice. Soviet-era voluntary émigrés played key roles in producing temporally situated images of blackness in Soviet space. Travelers and short-term residents sympathetic to the Soviet regime and to communist ideals, people such as W.E.B. Du Bois (1968), Paul Robeson (1950), Harry Haywood (1978), Langston Hughes (1934, 1956; see also Moore 1996), and William Patterson (1971) became living examples that Soviet press drew upon to depict the USSR as a place deemed desirable by U.S., Caribbean, and black-African intellectuals (see also Osei 1963, Fondem 1978, La Guma 1978).

Davis' (1960, p. 68) observation that Lily Golden-Hanga, daughter of such émigrés, did not recognize the name of Dr. Martin Luther King, while every Russian "loved" Paul Robeson, is significant. Blakely suggests that this sort of selective knowledge of prominent black intellectuals signaled implicit racism in Soviet nation-building (1986, p. 141): Soviet media depicted "Negros" abroad as victims only, acknowledging only the structural effects of racism. Other Soviets thus could conceive of them neither as people or communities successfully challenging U.S. racial politics nor as their own intellectual equals. Fax (1974, p. 167), however, reports that a decade later Uzbek children greeted him on the street by exclaiming "Angela Davis!" and "Mohammed Ali!" and raising a black power salute. Clearly, then, mundane Soviet engagements with international discourses about race were already, by the early 1970s, more complex than analysis of official media alone might show. What's more, Russian youths' post-Soviet appropriation of "skinhead" behavior, targeting Africans and other "blacks" in Moscow—in concert with other globally circulating skinhead ideologies—underscore what is at stake in understanding these engagements and articulations over time (see Banerjee 1998, Williams 1998). To confine post-Soviet interpretations of blackness to former Soviet territories, for instance, would neglect the new circumstances of contact, not to mention the various alignments with and against international racial discourses that shift during regime and global media transformations.

Assessment of the discursive production of African presence in the USSR poses important challenges to research on diasporas. We have focused on references and indexes of discontinuity and impermanence and of spatial displacement. Understanding the interplay of these representations—which rely upon origins and blood to mediate continuity—sheds light on the popular and bureaucratic regimes that safeguard racial practices that create the diaspora in question. We assume this approach in an effort to question that which race or racial community come to signify, both in political usage and at the level of analysis. The objective has been to think through how to avoid analyses of racialization that impose a predetermined sense of collectivity, one that implicitly relies upon and thus generates ontological biological distinctions. Within this process we question how, in acknowledging "black community," we come to create that which we refer to as black within diasporic analysis. These questions are raised not to suggest that black subject locations should not be treated as existentially or socially real. Rather, we aim to locate that which situates and confirms a black condition (be it forced labor regimes or citizenship practices) in an effort to recognize how we conceptually imply that a community or body is black (beyond obvious references to discrimination) within our analyses. As the particularities of African presences in these areas of the world are still to be fully explored, we hope this review will spur such exploration in ways that continue to clarify how race is treated and reproduced within diasporic criticism. Not interrogating how race is treated and deployed in any particular moment of articulation risks not only leaving African and other diasporic scholarship content with ambiguous readings of race, but also inadvertently reproducing race, even as it is questioned.

ACKNOWLEDGMENTS

Please note that this review's authors are listed alphabetically. The authors would like to especially thank the Editorial Committee of the *Annual Review of Anthropology* and Kevin Yelvington for their outstanding, copious critiques of this review. We are also grateful for the research assistance of Lonn Monroe and Dawn Fischer-Banks.

The *Annual Review of Anthropology* is online at http://anthro.annualreviews.org

LITERATURE CITED

Abramson D. 2002. Identity counts: nationality and the census in Uzbekistan. In *Categorizing Citizens: the Use of Race, Ethnicity, and Language in National Censuses*, ed. D Kertzer, D Arel. Cambridge, UK: Cambridge Univ. Press. In press

Allworth E, ed. 1998. *The Tatars of Crimea: Return to the Homeland*. Durham, NC/London: Duke Univ. Press

Alonso A. 1994. The politics of space, time and subsistence: state formation, nationalism and ethnicity. *Annu. Rev. Anthropol.* 23:379–405

Alpers EA. 2000. Recollecting Africa: diasporic memory in the Indian Ocean world. *Afr. Stud. Rev.* 43:83–99

Amselle JL. 1998. *Mestizo Logics: Anthropology of Identity in Africa and Elsewhere*. Stanford, CA: Stanford Univ. Press

Anderson DG. 2000. Fieldwork and the "doctoring" of national identities. In *Fieldwork Dilemmas: Anthropologists in Postsocialist States*, ed. H de Soto, N Dudwick, pp. 140–48. Madison: Wisc. Univ. Press

Apter A. 1991. Herskovits' heritage: rethinking syncretism in the African diaspora. *Diaspora* 1(3):235–60

Apter A. 1999. Africa, empire, and anthropology: a philological exploration of anthropology's heart of darkness. *Annu. Rev. Anthropol.* 28:577–98

Balibar E. 1989. Le Racisme encore un universalisme. *Mots* 18:7–19

Balzer M. 1999. *The Tenacity of Ethnicity: a Siberian Saga in Global Perspective*. Princeton, NJ: Princeton Univ. Press

Bakhtin M. 1981. *The Dialogic Imagination: Four Essays by M.M. Bakhtin*, transl. C Emerson, M Holquist. Austin: Univ. Texas Press

Baldwin KA. 2002. *Beyond the Color Line and the Iron Curtain: Reading Encounters Between Black and Red, 1922–1963*. Durham, NC: Duke Univ. Press

Banerjee N. 1998. Skinheads' attacks on visitors increase in Russia. May 20, *Dallas Morning News*

Berdahl D, Bunzl M, Lampland M. 2000. *Altering States: Ethnographies of Transition in Eastern Europe and the Soviet Union*. Ann Arbor: Univ. Mich. Press

Blakely A. 1986. *Russia and the Negro: Blacks in Russian History and Thought*. Washington, DC: Howard Univ. Press

Brodkin K. 1998. *How Jews Became White Folks and What that Says About Race in America*. New Brunswick, NJ: Rutgers Univ. Press

Brown JN. 1998. Black Liverpool, black America, and the gendering of diasporic space. *Cult. Anthropol.* 13(3):291–325

Brown JN. 2000. Enslaving history: narratives of local whiteness in a black Atlantic port. *Am. Ethnol.* 27(2):340–70

Butler J. 1993. *Bodies That Matter*. New York: Routledge

Clarence-Smith WG. 1988. The economics of the Indian Ocean and Red Sea slave trades in the 19th century: an overview. *Slavery Abolit.* 9(3):1–20

Conquest R. 1970. *The Nation Killers: the Soviet Deportation of Nationalities*. London: Macmillan

Davis W. 1960. How Negros live in Russia. *Ebony* 15:65–73

de la Cadena M. 2000. *Indigenous Mestizos: the Politics of Race and Culture in Cuzco, Peru*. Durham, NC: Duke Univ. Press

Domínguez VR. 1986. *White by Definition: Social Classification in Creole Louisiana*. New Brunswick, NJ: Rutgers Univ. Press

Dorr D. 1999. *A Colored Man Round the World*, ed. MJ Schueller. Ann Arbor: Univ. Mich. Press

Du Bois WEB. 1968. *The Autobiography of W.E.B. Du Bois: a Soliloquy on Viewing My Life From the Last Decade of its First Century*. New York: Int. Publ.

Du Bois WEB. 1970 [1915]. *The Negro*. Oxford: Oxford Univ. Press

English P. 1959. Cushites, Colchians, and Khazars. *J. Near East. Stud.* 18:49–53

Ewald JJ. 1988. The Nile Valley system and the Red Sea slave trade 1820–1880. *Slavery Abolit.* 9(3):71–92

Fax EC. 1974. *Through Black Eyes: Journeys of a Black Artist to East Africa and Russia*. New York: Dodd, Mead

Fernyhough T. 1988. Slavery and the slave trade in southern Ethiopia in the 19th century. *Slavery Abolit.* 9(3):103–30

Ferreira da Silva D. 1998. Facts of blackness: Brazil is not (quite) the US .... and racial politics in Brazil? *Soc. Identities* 4(2):204–34

Fikes K. 2000. *Santiaguense Cape Verdean women in Portugal: labor rights, citizenship and diasporic transformation*. PhD thesis. Univ. Calif., Los Angeles

Fisher A. 1980. Chattel slavery in the Ottoman empire. *Slavery Abolit.* 1(1):25–45

Friedrich P. 2002. Tolstoy and the Chechens. Presented at *2nd Chicago Conf. Caucasia*. Univ. Chicago, April 11

Fondahl G. 1995. Legacies of territorial restructuring for indigenous land claims in northern Russia. *Polar Geogr. Geol.* 19(1):1–21

Fondem JA. 1978. *Soviet Reality as Seen by an African*. Moscow: Novosti Press Agency

Gelb M. 1993. "Karelian Fever": the Finnish immigrant community during Stalin's purges. *Eur.-Asia Stud.* 45(4):1091–116

Gelb M. 1995. An early Soviet ethnic deportation: the far-eastern Koreans. *Russ. Rev.* 54(3):389–412

Geldern JV, Stites R, eds. 1995. *Mass Culture in Soviet Russia: Tales, Poems, Songs, Movies, Plays, and Folklore*. Bloomington: Ind. Univ. Press

Gilroy P. 1987. *There Ain't No Black in the Union Jack: the Cultural Politics of Race and Nation*. Chicago: Univ. Chicago Press

Gilroy P. 1993a. *Small Acts: Thoughts on the Politics of Black Cultures*. London: Serpent's Tail

Gilroy P. 1993b. *The Black Atlantic: Modernity and Double Consciousness*. Cambridge, MA: Harvard Univ. Press

Gilroy P. 2000. *Against Race: Imagining Political Culture Beyond the Color Line*. Cambridge, MA: Harvard Univ. Press

Golden-Hanga L. 1966. *Africans in Russia*. Moscow: Novosti Press Agency

Goluboff S. 2001. Introduction. In *Race Places: Changing Locations of Jewish Identities*. Special issue of *Identities: Glob. Stud. Cult. Power*. 8(2):163–71

Gordon ET. 1998. *Disparate Diasporas: Identity and Politics in an African-Nicaraguan Community*. Austin: Univ. Texas Press

Gould J. 1998. *To Die in This Way: Nicaraguan Indians and the Myth of Mestisaje 1880–1965*. Durham, NC: Duke Univ. Press

Grandin G. 2000. *The Blood of Guatemalans: a History of Race and Nation*. Durham: Duke Univ. Press

Grant B. 1995. *In the Soviet House of Culture*. Princeton, NJ: Princeton Univ. Press

Gray P. 2000. Chukotkan reindeer husbandry in the post-socialist Transition. *Polar Res.* 19(1):31–38

Gülap H. 1995. Turkey: questions of national identity. In *New Xenophobia in Europe*, pp. 358–67. London: Kluwer Law Int.

Gupta A, Ferguson J. 1992. Beyond culture: space, identity, and the politics of difference. *Cult. Anthropol.* 7(1):6–23

Hale C. 1994. *Resistance and Contradiction: Miskitu Indians and the Nicaraguan State, 1894–1987*. Stanford, CA: Stanford Univ. Press

Hall S. 1994. Cultural identity and diaspora. In *Colonial Discourse and Post-Colonial Theory: a Reader*, ed. P Williams, L Chrisman, pp. 392–401. London: Harvester Wheatsheaf

Hall S. 1996. The after-life of Frantz Fanon: Why Fanon? Why now? Why black skin, white masks? In *The Fact of Blackness: Frantz Fanon and Visual Representation*, ed. A Read, pp. 12–37. London: Inst. Contemp. Arts

Harris JE. 1971. *The African Presence in Asia: Consequences of the East African Slave*

Trade. Evanston, IL: Northwestern Univ. Press

Harrison FV. 1995. The persistent power of "race" in the cultural and political economy of racism. *Annu. Rev. Anthropol.* 24:47–74

Haywood H. 1978. *Black Bolshevik: Autobiography of an Afro-American Communist*. Chicago: Liberator

Herodotus. 1998. *Histories*, Book II. Oxford/New York: Oxford Univ. Press

Hirsch F. 1997. The Soviet Union as a work in progress: ethnographers and the category nationality in the 1926, 1937, 1939 census. *Slav. Rev.* 56:251–78

Hirsch F. 2000. Toward an empire of nations: border-making and the formation of Soviet national identities. *Russ. Rev.* 59:201–26

Hirsch F. 2002. Race without the practice of racial politics. *Slav. Rev.* 61(1):30–43

Holquist P. 2001. To count, to extract, to exterminate: population statistics and population politics in late Imperial and Soviet Russia. See Suny & Martin 2001, pp. 111–44

Humphrey C, Sneath D. 1999. *The End of Nomadism? Society, State and the Environment in Inner Asia*. Durham, NC: Duke Univ. Press

Hunswick J. 1992. Black Africans in the Mediterranean world: introduction to a neglected aspect of the African diaspora. See Savage 1992, pp. 5–38

Hughes L. 1934. *A Negro Looks at Soviet Central Asia*. Moscow: Coop. Publ. Soc. Foreign Work. USSR

Hughes L. 1956. *I Wonder as I Wander*. New York: Rinehart

Irvine JT, Gal S. 2000. Language ideology and linguistic differentiation. In *Regimes of Language: Ideologies, Politics, and Identities*, ed. P Kroskrity, pp. 35–84. Santa Fe, NM: Sch. Am. Res. Press, Oxford

Jwaideh A, Cox JW. 1988. The black slaves of Turkish Arabia during the 19th century. *Slavery Abolit.* 9(3):45–59

Karpat KH. 1985. *Ottoman Population, 1830–1914: Demographics and Social Characteristics*. Madison: Univ. Wisc. Press

Khanga Y. 1992. *Soul to Soul: a Black Russian American Family, 1865–1992*. Transl. S Jacoby. New York: Norton

Kondo D. 1997. *About Face*. New York: Routledge

Kreindler IT, ed. 1985. *Sociolinguistic Perspectives on Soviet National Languages: Their Past, Present, and Future*. Berlin: Mouton

La Guma A. 1978. *A Soviet Journey*. Impressions of the USSR Series. Moscow: Progress

Laitin D. 1998. *Identity in Formation: the Russian-Speaking Populations in the Near-Abroad*. Ithaca, NY: Cornell Univ. Press

Lamont C. 1946. *The Peoples of the Soviet Union*. New York: Harcourt, Brace

Layton S. 1994. *Russian Literature and Empire: Conquest of the Caucasus from Pushkin to Tolstoy*. Cambridge, MA: Cambridge Univ. Press

Lemon A. 1995. "What are they writing about us blacks": Roma and "race" in Russia. *Anthropol. East Eur. Rev.* 13(2):34–40

Lemon A. 2000a. Talking transit and spectating transition: the Moscow Metro. See Berdahl et al. 2000, pp. 14–39

Lemon A. 2000b. *Between Two Fires: Gypsy Performance and Romani Memory From Pushkin to Postsocialism*. Durham, NC: Duke Univ. Press

Lemon A. 2002a. Without a "concept"?: Race as discursive practice. *Slav. Rev.* 61(1):54–61

Lemon A. 2002b. "Form" and "function" in Soviet stage Romani: modeling metapragmatics through performance institutions. *Lang. Soc.* 31:29–64

Lewis B. 1990. *Race and Slavery in the Middle East: an Historical Enquiry*. Oxford: Oxford Univ. Press

Liu X. 2000. *In One's Own Shadow: an Ethnographic Account of the Condition of Post-Reform Rural China*. Berkeley: Univ. Calif. Press

Lomnitz C. 2001. *Deep Mexico, Silent Mexico*. Minneapolis: Univ. Minn. Press

Malkki L. 1995. *Purity and Exile: Violence, Memory, and National Cosmology among Hutu Refugees in Tanzania*. Chicago: Univ. Chicago Press

Mamdani M. 2002. *When Victims Become Killers: Colonialism, Nativism, and the Genocide in Rwanda*. Princeton, NJ: Princeton Univ. Press

Markovitz F. 1997. Diasporas with a difference: Jewish and Georgian teenagers ethnic identity in the Russian Federation. *Diaspora* 6(3):331–53

Martin T. 2001. *The Affirmative Action Empire: Nations and Nationalism in the Soviet Union, 1923–1939*. Ithaca, NY: Cornell Univ. Press

McKay C. 1937. *A Long Way from Home: an Autobiography*. New York: Farman

Mercer K. 1994. *Welcome to the Jungle: New Positions in Black Cultural Studies*. London: Routledge

Moore DC. 1996. Local color, global "color": Langston Hughes, the Black Atlantic, and Soviet Central Asia, 1932. *Res. Afr. Lit.* 27(4):49–70

Mudimbe VY. 1988. *The Invention of Africa*. Bloomington: Ind. Univ. Press

Mulekezi E. 1961. I was a "student" at Moscow State. *Read. Dig.* July:99–104

Naimark N. 2000. *The Fires of Hatred: Ethnic Cleansing in Twentieth Century Europe*. Cambridge, MA: Harvard Univ. Press

Naison M. 1983. *Communists in Harlem During the Depression*. Urbana: Univ. Ill. Press

Naumkin VV. 1994. *Central Asia and Transcaucasia: Ethnicity and Conflict*. Westport, Conn.: Greenwood

Osei J. 1963. *Moscow's Forbidden Fruit*. Moscow: Novosti

Parry A. 1925. Negroes in Russia. *Opportunity* Oct:306–7

Patterson TR, Kelley RDG. 2000. Unfinished migrations: reflections on the African diaspora and the making of the modern world. *Afr. Stud. Rev.* 43(1):11–45

Patterson W. 1971. *The Man who Cried Genocide*. New York: Int. Publ.

Petrone K. 1996. Parading the nation: physical culture celebrations and the construction of Soviet identities in the 1930s. Michigan discussions in *Anthropology* 12(spec. issue) *Post Soviet Eurasia*

Pilkington H. 1997. *Migration, Displacement, and Identity in Post-Soviet Russia*. New York: Routledge

Platz S. 2000. The shape of national time: daily life, history, and identity during Armenia's transition to independence, 1991–1994. See Berdahl et al. 2000, pp. 114–38

Poe R. 1999. *Black Spark White Fire: Did African Explorers Civilize Ancient Europe?* Roseville, CA: Prima

Pratt ML. 1992. *Imperial Eyes: Travel Writing and Transculturation*. London: Routledge Quist-Adade. Documentary film. *The Ones They Left Behind*

Rayport J. 1998. *Creating elsewhere, being other: the imagined spaces and selves of St. Petersburg young people, 1990–1995*. PhD. thesis. Univ. Chicago, Ill.

Rethmann P. 2000. Skins of desire: poetry and identity in Koriak women's gift exchange. *Am. Ethnol.* 27(1):52–71

Ricks TM. 1988. Slaves and slave traders in the Persian Gulf, 18th and 19th centuries: as assessment. *Slavery Abolit.* 9(3):60–70

Roback AA. 1946. *A Dictionary of International Slurs (Ethnoplaulisms)*. Waukesha, Wisc.: Maledicta

Robeson P. 1950. *The Negro People and the Soviet Union*. New York: New Century

Robinson R, Slevin J. 1988. *Black on Red: My 44 Years Inside the Soviet Union*. Washington, DC: Acropolis

Rossi J. 1992 [1987]. *Spravochnick po Gulagu (Gulag Handbook)*. Moscow: Prosvet

Russian National Union. 1995. O trebovanijakh k tem, kto nameren sozdat' sem'ju. *Shturmovik* 3:1

Savage E, ed. 1992. *The Human Commodity: Perspectives on the Trans-Saharan Slave Trade*. London/Portland, OR: Cass

Schoeberlein J. 2000. Shifting ground: how the Soviet regime used resettlement to transform Central Asian society and the consequences of this policy today. In *Migration in Central Asia: Its History and Current Problems*, ed. H Komatsu, C Obiya, J Schoeberlein, pp. 41–64. Osaka: Jpn. Cent. Area Stud.

Scott D. 1991. That event, this memory: notes

on the anthropology of African diasporas in the new world. *Diaspora* 1(3):261–84

Scott D. 1999. *Refashioning Futures: Criticism After Postcoloniality.* Princeton, NJ: Princeton Univ. Press

Schneider I. 1942. A Negro citizen of Soviet Georgia. *Sov. Russ. Today* 10(10):24–26

Schweitzer PP, Gray PA. 2000. The Chukchi and Siberian Yupiit of the Russian Far East. In *Endangered Peoples of the Arctic: Struggles to Survive and Thrive.* ed. MMR Freeman, pp. 17–37. Westport, CT: Greenwood

Seshadri-Crooks K. 2000. *Desiring Whiteness: a Lacanian Analysis of Race.* New York: Routledge

Shami S. 1995. Disjuncture in ethnicity: negotiating Circassian identity in Jordan, Turkey, and the Caucasus. *New Perspect. Turk.* 12:79–95

Shami S. 1998. Circassian encounters: the self as other and the production of the homeland in the North Caucasus. *Dev. Change* 29:617–46

Shami S. 2000. Prehistories of globalization: Circassian identity in motion. *Public Cult.* 12(1):177–204

Smith H. 1964. *Black Man in Red Russia: a Memoir.* Chicago: Johnson

Smith M. 1998. *Language and Power in the Creation of the USSR, 1917–1953.* New York: Moutton de Grayter

Slezkine Y. 1994a. The USSR as a communal apartment, or how a socialist state promoted ethnic particularism. *Slav. Rev.* 53(2):414–452

Slezkine Y. 1994b. *Arctic Mirrors: Russia and the Small Peoples of the North.* Ithaca, NY: Cornell Univ. Press

Slezkine Y. 1996. N. Ia. Marr and the national origins of Soviet ethnogenetics. *Slav. Rev.* 55(4):826–62

Ssorin-Chaikov N. 2000. Bear skins and macaroni: social life of things at the margins of a Siberian state collective. In *The Vanishing Rouble: Barter Networks and Non-Monetary Transactions in Post-Soviet Societies*, ed. P Seabright, pp. 245–61. Cambridge, UK: Cambridge Univ. Press

Stoler AL. 1992. Sexual affronts and racial frontiers: European identities and the cultural politics of exclusion in colonial Southeast Asia. *Comp. Stud. Soc. Hist.* 34(2):514–51

Suny R. 1988. *The Making of the Georgian Nation.* Bloomington: Ind. Univ. Press

Suny R. 1993. *The Revenge of the Past: Nationalism, Revolution, and the Collapse of the Soviet Union.* Stanford, CA: Stanford Univ. Press

Suny R, Martin T, eds. 2001. *A State of Nations: Empire and Nation-Making in the Age of Lenin and Stalin.* Oxford: Oxford Univ. Press

Toledano ER. 1982. *The Ottoman Slave Trade and Its Suppression: 1840–1890.* Princeton, NJ: Princeton Univ. Press

Toledano ER. 1998. *Slavery Abolition in the Ottoman Middle East.* Seattle: Univ. Wash. Press

Trouillot M. 1990. Good day Columbus: silences, power and public history (1492–1892). *Public Cult.* 3(1):1–24

Tynes S. 1973. When did Africans get to the Soviet Union? *Afro-American* 30:2

Uehling G. 2000. *Having a homeland: recalling the deportation, exile, and repatriation of Crimean Tatars.* PhD thesis. Univ. Mich. Ann Arbor

Vradii VP. 1914. *Negri Batumskoi Oblasti (Negroes of Batumi province).* Batumi, Georgia: Tavartkiladze

Wade P. 1993. *Blackness and Race Mixture: the Dynamics of Racial Identity in Colombia.* Baltimore, MD: Johns Hopkins Univ. Press

Weiner A. 1999. Nature, nuture, and memory in a socialist utopia: delineating the Soviet socio-ethnic body in the age of socialism. *Am. Hist. Rev.* 104(4):1114–55

Weiner A. 2002. Nothing but certainty. *Slav. Rev.* 61(1):44–53

Weitz E. 2002. Racial politics without the concept of race: reevaluating Soviet ethnic and national purges. *Slav. Rev.* 61(1):1–29

Williams BF. 1989. A class act: anthropology and the race to nation across ethnic terrain. *Annu. Rev. Anthropol.* 18:401–44

Williams BF. 1991. *Stains on My Name, War*

in My Veins: Guyana and the Politics of Cultural Struggle. Durham, NC: Duke Univ. Press

Williams BF. 1995. Review of "The Black Atlantic: Modernity and Double Consciousness," by Paul Gilroy. *Soc. Identities* 1(1):175–92

Williams D. 1998. From Russia with hate: Africans face racism. *Washington Post* Foreign Service. Monday, Jan 12:A12

Wilson Sir R. 1998. *Relation de la Campagne de Russie, 1812*. Paris: La Vouivre

Wolfe T. 2000. Cultures and communities in the anthropology of Eastern Europe and the former Soviet Union. *Annu. Rev. Anthropol.* 29:195–216

Annu. Rev. Anthropol. 2002. 31:525–52
doi: 10.1146/annurev.anthro.31.040402.085443

First published online as a Review in Advance on June 14, 2002

YOUTH AND CULTURAL PRACTICE

Mary Bucholtz
Department of Linguistics, 3607 South Hall, University of California, Santa Barbara, California 93106; email: bucholtz@linguistics.ucsb.edu

Key Words adolescence, agency, identity, modernity, youth cultures

■ **Abstract** The study of youth played a central role in anthropology in the first half of the twentieth century, giving rise to a still-thriving cross-cultural approach to adolescence as a life stage. Yet the emphasis on adolescence as a staging ground for integration into the adult community often obscures young people's own cultural agency or frames it solely in relation to adult concerns. By contrast, sociology has long considered youth cultures as central objects of study, whether as deviant subcultures or as class-based sites of resistance. More recently, a third approach—an anthropology of youth—has begun to take shape, sparked by the stimuli of modernity and globalization and the ambivalent engagement of youth in local contexts. This broad and interdisciplinary approach revisits questions first raised in earlier sociological and anthropological frameworks, while introducing new issues that arise under current economic, political, and cultural conditions. The anthropology of youth is characterized by its attention to the agency of young people, its concern to document not just highly visible youth cultures but the entirety of youth cultural practice, and its interest in how identities emerge in new cultural formations that creatively combine elements of global capitalism, transnationalism, and local culture.

INTRODUCTION

Despite a vast literature on youth cultures spanning many decades and disciplines, surprisingly little of this research was informed by anthropology until recently. To be sure, foundational ethnographies by Mead (1928) and Malinowski ([1929] 1987) established adolescence early on as a crucial topic of anthropological investigation, and as a result, issues closely associated with this life stage—initiation ceremonies, sexual practices, courtship and marital customs, intergenerational relations—have long been a focus of anthropological inquiry. But such research has usually approached adolescence from the perspective of adulthood, downplaying youth-centered interaction and cultural production in favor of an emphasis on the transition to adulthood. Thus anthropology concerned itself not primarily with youth as a cultural category, but with adolescence as a biological and psychological stage of human development. Now, however, shifts both in the discipline and in the world's cultures have expanded the range of anthropological inquiry, and as a result the field has seen much more investigation of youth cultural practices. From this small but growing body of work, it is clear that anthropology is particularly well situated to offer an account of how young people around the world produce and negotiate cultural forms.

The anthropology of youth has been overshadowed by the much larger and more visible project of the sociology of youth. It is here that youth cultures and practices are most widely studied, albeit only within late modern Western societies, particularly Britain and the United States. These countries are associated with two different but related sociological approaches to the study of youth: The American tradition examines the concept of deviance and its social consequences in young people's cultural practices, and the British tradition examines highly visible forms of working-class youth identities using Marxist theories of culture and poststructuralist semiotic analysis. The latter approach—which provided the foundation for the field of cultural studies—has had the most profound influence on how youth cultures have been studied. But if adolescence as the central concept for anthropological research on young people is at once too broad (because universalized) and too narrow (because psychologized), then youth culture is too burdened by its historical ties to particular theoretical positions. The anthropology of youth now emerging concerns itself not with the restrictive notion of culture that dominated early work in cultural studies but with the practices through which culture is produced. This formulation includes practices associated with age-based cultures, but also those that locate young people as other kinds of cultural agents.[1]

DEFINING YOUTH

It is a commonplace of much research on youth cultures and identities that the youth category lacks clear definition and in some situations may be based on one's social circumstances rather than chronological age or cultural position. In a given culture, preadolescent individuals may count as youth, while those in their 30s or 40s may also be included in this category. And youth as a cultural stage often marks the beginning of a long-term, even lifelong, engagement in particular cultural practices, whether its practitioners continue to be included in the youth category or not. Related categories like adolescent, teenager, or young adult provide a greater degree of specificity concerning age, but they also vary in their application across contexts. Moreover, potentially contrasting categories such as child, adult,

[1]Due to space limitations, this article does not attempt a comprehensive survey of the vast interdisciplinary literature on youth and adolescence. In general, I have focused more on recent work and on work done within anthropology, as well as research in other fields that is directly relevant to central anthropological issues pertaining to youth. Inevitably, however, even some studies that meet these criteria have been omitted for reasons of space; those that are included are not necessarily the best examples of current research on youth but serve as useful illustrations of specific points. Because ethnographic research on many aspects of youth cultural practice is often surprisingly scarce, I have at times turned to nonethnographic work in my discussion of particular topics.

or elder may shift to incorporate members of the youth category, and conversely. Thus in Soviet Russia, the category of teenager was collapsed into that of child in official discourse, and adolescents' dependent status was symbolically enforced in a variety of ways (Markowitz 2000). Historical changes such as population shifts that increase or decrease the number of adolescents, and economic circumstances that prevent young adults from assuming a new status as wage earners, may lead to redefinitions of the category as well (see also Neyzi 2001).

Such classifications, of course, are often strategic and contested. Labels like *child soldier*, *teenage mother*, and *youth violence* are socially meaningful, authorizing the interpretation of biological chronology in social terms that may shift according to sociopolitical circumstances; thus preadolescent children accused of committing violent crimes may be classified as adults in the U.S. legal system; by the same token, young people in their 20s have been labeled *children* in discussions of child labor (Gailey 1999). Likewise, the classification of young people as "youngsters" in England has shaped the way that youth sexuality is understood and addressed by sex educators and healthcare providers (West 1999). Hall & Montgomery (2000) argue that the division between children and youth in Britain is associated with several other divisions: sympathetic versus unsympathetic public perception, attention within anthropology versus sociology, and emphasis on young people overseas versus "at home." It is likely that the division between youth and adult is organized in similar fashion.

Youth or adolescence is not a highly salient life stage in all cultures, although this is changing in many societies. Condon (1990) documents the emergence of adolescence as a social category and the adolescent peer group as a social structure among Canadian Inuits as a result of rapid economic and cultural shifts. In many countries, a new category of adolescence as a relatively recent and ongoing media construct creates teenagers as a self-aware age grouping and targets them as potential consumers (Liechty 1995, White 1995). But a well-defined category for young people is not necessarily the result of modernity; the Marquesan youth category *taure'are'a*, for example, is carefully distinguished from both childhood and adulthood on the basis of established cultural principles and ideologies (Kirkpatrick 1987, Martini 1996). Moreover, even teenagers in late industrial societies may not experience adolescence as a distinctive life stage (especially one characterized by carefree indulgence, as is often popularly believed), due to economic and other constraints that move them quickly into adult responsibilities, and also in some cases because of a lack of sharp age and role differentiation between young parents and their children (Burton 1997). Aristocratic girls in modern Japan were forced to forgo adolescence because at an early age they were committed by their parents to arranged marriages intended to strengthen family alliances. Unlike the young adults Burton studied, such elite Japanese women did not experience this lack as a deprivation until postwar cultural changes led to the end of the aristocracy (Lebra 1995).

Given these difficulties in defining youth in any general way, Durham (2000) proposes applying the linguistic concept of a *shifter* (Jakobson [1957] 1971,

Silverstein 1976) to the category of youth. A shifter is a word that is tied directly to the context of speaking and hence takes much of its meaning from situated use, such as the deictics *I*, *here*, and *now*. Likewise, the referential function of *youth* cannot be determined in advance of its use in a particular cultural context, and its use indexes the nature of the context in which it is invoked. As a shifter, then, youth is a context-renewing and a context-creating sign whereby social relations are both (and often simultaneously) reproduced and contested.

THE ANTHROPOLOGY OF ADOLESCENCE

Where youth is a flexible and contestable social category, it has been argued on both biological and social grounds that adolescence is a cultural universal. As Schlegel (1995a) notes, sociologists have incorrectly maintained that the cultural category of adolescence is symptomatic of modernity, an assumption that overlooks the existence of similar categories in a wide variety of cultures, from nonindustrial to postindustrial. From this comparative perspective, the anthropological study of adolescence is a search for cross-cultural generalizations and variations in the biological, psychological, and social characteristics of this universal category.

Adolescence as a Life Stage

Western psychologists, who understand adolescence primarily as preparation for adulthood, theorize this period as a time of potential crisis brought on by the uncertainties of the physical and social transitions between life stages. A similarly physiological and psychological model of adolescence was a powerful influence on anthropological research on young people for most of the second half of the twentieth century (e.g., Fuchs 1976, Worthman 1987). Following Western psychological theories of youth, researchers propose general processes thought to be shared by individuals at this life stage regardless of culture, although these may be affected by specific cultural circumstances. Robinson (1997), for example, describes adolescence in general as a period of individuation and crisis, but one that—due to cultural shifts—presents special difficulties for Tiwi youth. And many scholars emphasize gender differences in the adolescent stage, in keeping with the perception that such patterns occur generally across cultures (Anderson & Anderson 1986, Condon & Stern 1993, Schlegel 1995b).

Given the influence of Western psychology, it is not uncommon to find explicit comparisons of adolescence in Western and other cultures. Such an overtly comparative stance is in keeping with the tradition established by Mead, who subtitled her enormously influential 1928 book *Coming of Age in Samoa* "A Psychological Study of Primitive Youth for Western Civilisation." However, cross-cultural research does not currently rely on comparisons with an undifferentiated concept of "the West." Schlegel & Barry's (1991) extensive statistical analysis of the sociocultural dimensions of adolescence in nearly 200 societies around the world represents the most comprehensive synthesis of what is known about the adolescent life stage across cultures. The most ambitious ethnographic undertaking within the cross-cultural framework is the Harvard Adolescence Project, which involves multidisciplinary investigations of the physiological and sociocultural dimensions of adolescence in seven different societies; four monographs reporting the results of the project have been published (Burbank 1988, Condon 1987, Davis & Davis 1989, Hollos & Leis 1989).

The emphasis on adolescence as a universal stage in the biological and psychological development of the individual usefully highlights selfhood as a process rather than a state, but it also inevitably frames young people primarily as not-yet-finished human beings. Indeed, for many years anthropologists studied adolescence almost exclusively as a liminal position between childhood and adulthood that is marked in many (but not most) cultures through some type of initiation ceremony (Schlegel & Barry 1979). Such ceremonies are means of socially managing, and indeed defining, this life stage in adult terms. While some coming-of-age rituals, like the Mexican American quinceañera (Watters 1988) and the U.S. high school prom (Best 2000), are shaped in part by youth themselves, most rites of passage that have been studied by anthropologists are in the hands of adult members of the community. The role of adults in the process of socialization is unquestionably a central element in the understanding of youth, yet the study of how adults guide adolescents into full cultural membership obscures the more informal ways in which young people socialize themselves and one another as they enter adolescence (e.g., Merten 1999).

Developmental Crises: Youth and Modernity

If many anthropologists of adolescence in previous decades concentrated on how adolescents around the world assumed new, culturally recognized roles through ritual activities that dramatized the liminality of youth (Turner 1969), the disappearance or alteration of these and other age-graded practices in the face of cultural pressures from without has raised a new question: What are the consequences of large-scale social and cultural transformations that disproportionately affect the lives of young people? This question continues to draw on the psychological foundation laid by earlier researchers, while emphasizing that cultural shifts are drastically revising the meaning of youth in many societies.

The impact of modernity and economic restructuring ("development") on youth in societies previously organized in other ways is often thought to give rise to psychological stress of a kind not unlike that associated with youth in industrialized societies, who are claimed to undergo "identity crises" as they resolve psychic conflicts with their adult roles (Erikson 1968). The difficulties believed to be endemic to this stage of life, however, may appear to be compounded among adolescents in societies undergoing rapid cultural change because such young people also face tensions between tradition and innovation. This issue has been discussed most extensively with respect to suicidal acts among youth, the etiology of which has been argued to be cultural rather than based in individual or family pathology.[2] While such phenomena are often at least partly ascribed to cultural traditions that may indirectly reinforce suicidal behavior, such as subordination of youth to elders and taboos against overt expressions of anger (Brown 1986, Minore et al. 1991), the emphasis of most studies is on the role of cultural contact and conflict in adolescent suicide. Thus the alarmingly high rates of suicide and suicide attempts by youth in some Pacific (Booth 1999; Hezel 1984, 1987; Macpherson & Macpherson 1987; Reser 1990; Robinson 1990; Rubinstein 1983) and Native American societies (Johnson & Tomren 1999, Novins et al. 1999), as well as in parts of Sri Lanka (Kearney & Miller 1985), have been attributed to cultural changes that disrupt traditional social roles and socialization processes. Despite this shared emphasis, specific patterns of suicide in each context are widely varied, and proposed explanations are likewise diverse: Among the suggested causes are the loss of traditional pathways of adolescent socialization, changes in family roles, and increased economic expectations coupled with decreased economic opportunities, or some combination of these (see Rubinstein 1992 for a critical overview of such explanations for the Pacific findings).

Other forms of psychological distress have been linked to the implementation of new educational structures among youth in changing societies. The stress of competition for educational access and the social mobility it promises has been cited as the source both of outbreaks of witchcraft-induced health problems among students in Botswana (Burke 2000) and of disordered and violent behavior caused by spirit possession among schoolgirls in Madagascar (Sharp 1990). However, such stress is also evident in more industrialized societies. In modern Japan, the diagnosis of "school refusal syndrome" medicalizes students' expressions of protest against perceptions of their inadequacy and morally frames this phenomenon within Confucian and capitalist ideologies of individual and family (Lock 1986).

These explanations for adolescent social crises have the merit of locating the cause of psychological or physical disturbance in specific social and economic processes. As O'Neil (1986) points out, social change in itself is an inadequate explanation for adolescent stress, which in turn is usually invoked to account for behavior perceived as problematic. But rapid social change need not be experienced as dramatic or unsettling by the young people living through it, as demonstrated by Markowitz's (2000) study of Russian teenagers during the period of the dissolution of the Soviet Union. Moreover, it is important to bear in mind that youth are as often the agents as the experiencers of cultural change. Burbank (1988), for example, shows how adolescent girls, taking advantage of the opening provided by other social shifts, are transforming the traditional marriage system in Aboriginal Australia by choosing premarital pregnancies. Thus although young people's

[2]In this regard, the study of adolescent suicide in industrialized societies lags far behind research on youth in other cultures, focusing instead on psychosocial dysfunction (Gaines 1990 is one important exception). Because of its lack of engagement with ethnography and culture, I do not treat this large body of scholarship here.

experiences of potentially socially threatening phenomena are thought to be the result of dramatic cultural changes that create unprecedented psychological pressure, there is another, creative dimension to these responses to new cultural circumstances. It is in this sense that youths' socially transgressive actions may be understood not simply as culture-specific manifestations of psychological distress but more importantly as critical cultural practices through which young people display agency. In accounts of such phenomena, a number of researchers in fact foreground the tension between young people's agency and the structural power of social institutions, thereby complicating the view of stress as an individual psychological state to which the young, with their age-based psychic fragility, are unusually susceptible.

The understanding of adolescents as the age group most vulnerable to the radical shifts of modernization also raises questions about relations between youth and elders. From one perspective, intergenerational conflict, like psychological stress, is exacerbated by the internal conflicts that young people experience in the process of cultural change. The tension between the tantalizing promises of modernity and the expectations of tradition-minded adults may be thought to create resentment among the young people caught in the middle. Yet this too-easy explanation has frequently been called into question in anthropological research. Admittedly, youthful challenges to adult authority are widely documented, but the phenomenon is neither so wholeheartedly rebellious nor so intimately connected to modernity as this imagined scenario suggests. Researchers in a variety of cultural settings have found that the divisions between youth and elder, modern and traditional, conflictual and consensual are blurry and ambiguous rather than clearly differentiated (Gable 2000, Rasmussen 2000, Rea 1998, Sharp 1995).

Moreover, as with psychological stress, it is unlikely that rapid social change in itself triggers disagreements between younger and older people. Although modernity has deservedly received a great deal of blame for intergenerational tensions (as well as for the rash of other problems plaguing many societies), Leis & Hollos (1995) argue that cultural factors, such as kinship structure, may also affect how smoothly change is negotiated between generations. In fact, in a number of societies undergoing rapid shift, intergenerational tensions are rare (Condon 1987, Davis & Davis 1989).

The anthropology of adolescence thus considers development and change at two levels: individual and cultural. These levels interact analytically in the social staging of adolescence in particular cultural contexts in which the universal developmental arc of adolescence is shaped by historically specific processes of social, political, and economic transformation, as well as by existing cultural practices. Although researchers are careful not to imply that cultural change has a teleology, they are less careful about this point in discussions of the changes that young people experience (and bring about) in the adolescent period. In fact, it is precisely the teleology of the developmental process from adolescent to adult that motivates this research tradition. The issues addressed in such studies are certainly part of the study of youth, but they paint an incomplete picture. The lived experience of young people is not limited to the uneasy occupation of a developmental way station en route to full-fledged cultural standing. It also involves its own distinctive identities and practices, which are neither rehearsals for the adult "real thing" nor even necessarily oriented to adults at all. These practices and identities, which might be classified as the concerns of youth rather than simply of adolescence, provide a firmer cultural ground on which to conduct research than the definitionally unstable terrain of adolescence alone.

FROM ADOLESCENCE TO YOUTH

In urging a scholarly shift from adolescence to youth, I am not simply calling for researchers to expand their scope from the teen years, puberty, or other chronological or biological measures of adolescence in order to incorporate the full range of ways that youth may be defined socioculturally. Indeed, many scholars are already taking this broader perspective in their work. Just as importantly, however, I want to interrogate the concept of adolescence itself, which contrasts and connects—etymologically as well as socially—with adulthood. *Adultum* is the past participle of the Latin verb *adolescere* "to grow (up)." The senses of growth, transition, and incompleteness are therefore historically embedded in *adolescent*, while *adult* indicates both completion and completeness (cf. Herdt & Leavitt 1998). This etymology is also reflected in the way in which the term adolescence has been put to use in the social sciences. This is not to say that the mere use of one term over the other determines analytic outcomes; as the discussion below demonstrates, work on young people's agency and creativity may go under the label of *adolescence*, and research within the developmental framework may advertise itself as a study of youth. My concern is therefore primarily conceptual, not terminological, but it is important to note that the selection of either term is itself a theoretical choice.

Youth foregrounds age not as trajectory, but as identity, where *identity* is intended to invoke neither the familiar psychological formulation of adolescence as a prolonged "search for identity," nor the rigid and essentialized concept that has been the target of a great deal of recent critique. Rather, identity is agentive, flexible, and ever-changing—but no more for youth than for people of any age. Where the study of adolescence generally concentrates on how bodies and minds are shaped for adult futures, the study of youth emphasizes instead the here-and-now of young people's experience, the social and cultural practices through which they shape their worlds (see also Wulff 1995a). And where adolescence is usually placed in relation to adulthood, an equally salient group for youth may be other youth—that is, the peer group—and relevant age contrasts may include childhood, old age, and other culturally specific stages, in addition to adulthood.

The difference between research on adolescence and research on youth may be illustrated by surveying studies of two widely problematized and highly sensationalized topics within scholarship on young people: violence and sexuality. These two issues are often approached from an adult-centered perspective as social problems; whether young people are understood as victims or perpetrators within this general approach, they are positioned as responding to, not shaping, cultural forces. Such an interpretation is challenged by research that takes seriously the fact that youth are cultural actors whose experiences are best understood from their own point of view.

Youth and Violence

The framing of adolescence as a psychological stage fraught with social problems is a prominent feature of a good deal of the anthropological work on youth violence. Hence, Sykes (1999) reports that youths in Papua New Guinea, unable to secure steady work, engage in acts of violence and excessive consumption; she argues that these acts produce alienation and strip the young men of identity. In a study of Chicano street gangs, Vigil (1988) takes a somewhat more positive view, suggesting that despite their violent activities, gangs provide a sense of self-identity and serve as a passage to adulthood. Yet it is clear from his discussion that this surrogate and illegitimate identity is held to be an inadequate replacement for legitimate cultural institutions such as the family or the school. Other researchers, by contrast, set the often sensationalistic topic of youth gangs and violence into broader perspective. Monsell-Davis (1986), cautioning against unremittingly negative representations of Papua New Guinean youth, points to the fact that many young people participate fully in village life, and some work on American gangs demonstrates that they are not simply symbolic substitutes for culturally approved social structures; more importantly, they function as one of the few avenues for entrepreneurship available to groups barred by race and class from other forms of capitalism (e.g., Jankowski 1991). Likewise, the understanding of identity in the problem-centered approach misses the crucial fact that the identity work of violence is neither anticultural, as Vigil would have it, nor acultural, as Sykes maintains, but is entirely cultural, if viewed on its own terms. Mendoza-Denton (1996) shows that for Latina gang girls, the capacity for violence, whether implied or enacted, is part of the production of a nonhegemonic femininity, while Leavitt (1998) argues that the violent practices of young men in Papua New Guinea should be seen not as rebellion against authority but as an appropriation of the authority reserved for political leaders through which a powerful masculine identity is constructed. Finally, Allison (2001) points out that some representations of violence in popular entertainment, often blamed for violent acts by youth, are conceptualized by fans as productive as well as destructive.

These differing perspectives on youth violence are especially clear in research on youth and war. West (2000) identifies two major strands in this scholarship. The first is a Western psychological approach that asserts that exposure to violence leads to youths' loss of innocence; proponents argue that such young people go on to perpetuate violence throughout their lives, whether as victims of violence or its (often coerced) perpetrators (e.g., Boothby 1986). The second approach centers on cultural agency and understands youth as able to adapt effectively to violent situations in culturally specific ways (Peters & Richards 1998, West 2000). Even when these two perspectives are combined, the romantic belief in a "lost generation" as the ultimate victims of war gives way to an analysis that recognizes both young people's agency in wartime and its very real constraints (Assal & Farrell 1992). Thus as producers and recipients of violence alike, youth maintain their agency as cultural and political actors (Bernat 1999, Diouf 1996).

Youth, Sexuality, and the Body

As with youth and violence, discussions of youth and sexuality within anthropology have been largely of two types: one, in the tradition of Mead, that focuses on culturally specific sexual practices and the extent to which adolescent and premarital sexual activity is culturally discouraged, tolerated, or encouraged (e.g., Barry & Schlegel 1984, 1986; Hollos & Leis 1986; Lepowsky 1998; Whiting 1986; Whiting et al. 1986); and a second, from a more medical perspective, that examines how young people themselves view sexual activity (Eyre et al. 1998, Lackey & Moberg 1998) and sexually transmitted diseases, especially AIDS (Leclerc-Madlala 1997, Obbo 1995, Paiva 1995, Sobo et al. 1997). Although the former tends to be more culturally grounded than the latter, the growing use of ethnographic and qualitative methods in medical anthropology and related fields has helped to emphasize the cultural agency of youth (see also Schensul et al. 2000 and Way et al. 1994 on drug use by young people). Both anthropological approaches have great advantages over many traditional sociological frameworks, which view certain youth practices as pathological or deviant, especially those that threaten hegemonic systems of authority and economy. By contrast, perspectives from anthropology offer cultural and structural arguments to account for the same practices. Thus Zigman (1999) views teenage sex workers in Philadelphia as adapting to complex social and economic forces and therefore rejects arguments that locate the cause in the family or the individual. The small but significant body of anthropological work on youth and same-sex desire (e.g., Herdt 1989, Leap 1999) likewise challenges the pathologizing frameworks that have dominated discussion of this topic in other fields.

However, much of the research on young people's sexuality places it in the context of adult activities and concerns. This is clearly the case in discussions of pregnancy and youth. The problematization of teenage pregnancy, so widespread in American public discourse (Luker 1996), is not common to all societies and has arrived only relatively recently in some parts of the United States: Reservation Navajos report that teenage pregnancy was once a cultural norm but that it is now desirable for young women to delay pregnancy (Dalla & Gamble 2001). Nor is adolescent sexual activity necessarily discouraged everywhere. Among the Kikuyu, adolescents were traditionally taught sexual practices that would not lead to pregnancy, but the effects of modernization and Christianization have eliminated the age-grade system on which the transmission of these practices depended (Whiting 1986, Worthman & Whiting 1987).

As Burbank & Chisholm (1998) point out, it is not adolescent pregnancy itself but the community's response to it that creates a social problem. Nader & González (2000) document the economically motivated rhetorical construction of teen pregnancy as an issue of "adolescent health" both locally and nationally by elements of the U.S. health care industry. This process of redefinition excludes from consideration young people's (and all nonexperts') views of teen pregnancy and prescribes a single appropriate community response. The operation of power illustrated here is therefore vital to the analysis of young people's sexual and other cultural practices. But the operation of individual agency is equally important. Youthful pregnancy in many contexts is not simply accidental, but a potentially tactical act of identity. McRobbie (2000) reports that teenage mothers in economically depressed South Birmingham view pregnancy both as a confirmation of womanhood and as a legitimation of sexual activity because it enforces an image of monogamy. Pregnancy can also be a way for Aboriginal adolescent girls in Australia to assert their autonomy and reject marital arrangements made by their parents (Burbank 1987, 1988). However, at the same time that these young women gain a certain degree of sexual freedom, safe in the knowledge that their child will be valued by the community, they may also be constrained in the range of options open to them, whether through ideologies of romance, the reality of male violence, or their own use of substances that may injure their fetuses (Burbank 1995).

It is worth comparing sexuality to a second arena of highly adolescent behavior: eating, dieting, and body size. Unlike pregnancy, this topic is not widely researched by anthropologists; Nichter's (2000) multi-method work stands as the most extensive ethnographic treatment of American girls' body image.[3] The virtue of Nichter's approach over the survey techniques that dominate in adjacent disciplines is that the latter have led to reports of a dieting epidemic among European American girls that in fact vastly overstate the extent of the problem. Nichter found that girls' cultural practice of "fat talk," in which the speaker's body is ritualistically problematized for a variety of interactional purposes, has no necessary relation to dieting or to negative body image, although white girls did tend to disparage their bodies more than girls of other ethnicities (see also Mendoza-Denton 1996, Parker et al. 1995). Such research demonstrates once again that practices often viewed as pathological are better viewed as sites of cultural agency.

The problem-based perspective on youth focuses on young people's actions as social violations rather than agentive interventions into ongoing sociocultural change. By contrast, the best work on the challenges facing youth emphasizes their own acts of cultural critique and cultural production in the face of often untenable situations. This view has also been instrumental in developing alternatives to theories of sociology that define youth practices solely in terms of their deviation from adult social norms. The most important of these, the extremely influential Birmingham School of cultural studies in England, opened up new directions for the investigation of youth cultures within sociology. However, this perspective has itself come in for a good deal of criticism (see Lave et al. 1992 for a history of the Birmingham tradition and a constructive critique of its achievements).

[3]There is a small anthropologically oriented literature on other facets of youth and body image such as race (Bloustien 1999) and disability (Butler 1998).

THE BIRMINGHAM SCHOOL: SUBCULTURE AND STYLE

The study of youth culture began in the United States in the first half of the twentieth century as an outgrowth of criminology and delinquency studies within sociology; the concern was not with youth directly so much as with deviant subcultures. The Chicago School of sociology took a strongly ethnographic approach to these issues, focusing on the ways in which subcultures, especially those created by young people, constitute alternative systems of shared symbolic meaning for their members (Cohen 1955) that take shape precisely by being labeled *deviant* by members of the dominant culture (Becker 1963).

This perspective had a significant impact on the work that is often identified as the foundation of youth culture studies—that produced by the Centre for Contemporary Cultural Studies at the University of Birmingham (Hall & Jefferson [1976] 1993). Influenced by Marxist cultural theory, the Birmingham School researchers shared with the Chicago School a focus on the working class but understood such youths' position as a result of material as well as symbolic positioning. Taking class as the foundation of youth culture, the newly emerging field of cultural studies focused primarily on youth cultural practices in late industrial urban British society (e.g., Mungham & Pearson 1976). However, some members of CCCS rejected the concept of youth culture altogether, replacing it with subculture, a term that they felt better emphasized the class positioning of such cultural formations (Clarke et al. [1976] 1993). *Youth culture*, however, is currently the preferred term of most researchers, not least because it allows for the inclusion of all youth in the study of culture, whereas the approach of Clarke and his colleagues very deliberately does not.

Unlike the Chicago School, the Birmingham School was not firmly committed to ethnographic methods. A favored technique was textual analysis of the media, through which researchers examined how "moral panics" are produced in media representations of youth (Cohen [1972] 1980). Another influential approach involved semiotic analysis of cultural forms (Hebdige 1979). Although theoretical concerns often overshadowed ethnographic details in such research, it combined a concern with cultural style and attention to economic consequences, thereby offering a clearer understanding of the cultural basis of class identity.

Nevertheless, one of the most widely read studies to emerge from CCCS was Willis's (1977) ethnography of a group of white working-class boys. Willis describes how these "lads" perpetuated their class position in the world of work by embracing an anti-school youth culture, in contrast to the "ear'oles," who accepted the authority of the school and the goals of schooling. This focus on the practices of groups understood as distinctive and separate from one another came to typify work in the Birmingham tradition. Thus Hebdige (1979) offers a semiotic interpretation of white British working-class styles, including the teddy boy, the mod, the skinhead, and the glam rocker, arguing that they are different responses to black culture and racial politics. Style itself is theorized by Hebdige, and earlier by Clarke ([1976] 1993), as *bricolage*, a borrowing from Lévi-Strauss (1966) that is perhaps the only significant influence of anthropology on the Birmingham School of cultural studies. On Clarke and Hebdige's reading, the *bricoleur* appropriates and combines existing elements in new ways to create a distinctive style. These acts of semiotic resignification subvert the meanings assigned to the appropriated objects within the dominant culture, often in ways that challenge class arrangements. Both the lads investigated by Willis and the working-class youths described by Hebdige are therefore understood as responding to the class-based subject positions assigned to them and as carving out distinctive semiotic spaces for themselves, although this dimension is much more fully elaborated in Hebdige's work.

The well-developed theory that characterizes the Birmingham tradition is both its strength and its weakness. Its engagement with a wide range of cultural theories fruitfully revised and extended American approaches to deviance and delinquency, but in privileging class in the analysis of youth culture, CCCS researchers and those who followed their example failed to take into account other crucial dimensions of young people's identities. For example, although Hebdige located white working-class youth cultures in relation to black culture, relatively little work on black cultural agency—as opposed to media representations of black youth (Hall et al. 1978)—was undertaken within cultural studies until much later (Gilroy 1991, 1993).

An early internal critique also pointed to the field's exclusive focus on male cultural actors (McRobbie & Garber [1976] 1993). Many scholars considered youth culture to be a male preserve almost by definition, and some even maintained that the primary purpose of such cultures is to work out issues of masculinity (e.g., Brake 1980). The problem is not that female cultural styles do not exist, but that they were not acknowledged as legitimate forms of culture. McRobbie & Garber note that the female-dominated teenybopper or preadolescent pop fan culture was often trivialized by male scholars as consumption-based and passive, in spite of its being highly agentive (see Rhein 2000 for a defense of teenybopper fan culture in Germany). Subsequent feminist research identified girls' trajectory into dating and marriage, but—like the work on their male counterparts—it did not address the full diversity of girls' cultural or gender styles (e.g., McRobbie [1977a] 2000).

Likewise, scholarly concern with "spectacular" or highly visible subcultural styles, as interpreted through the lens of semiotics, did not completely capture the range of orientations to gender, sexuality, class, race, and ethnicity that youth may display in their cultural practices. This concern with the symbolic representation of identity, manifested in the investigation of music, fashion, and other cultural forms as semiotic markers, also often enforced a view of youth cultures as clearly bounded and distinctive from one another, even as their semiotic resources, through *bricolage*, were drawn from diverse and overlapping sources and contexts.

Some of these limitations have been remedied in the more recent work of Stuart Hall, one of the founders of the Centre for Contemporary Cultural Studies. Hall's theorizing of "new ethnicities" redresses both the absence of racial and ethnic diversity in the early Birmingham studies and the rigidity of subcultural identity categories as initially conceptualized.

NEW ETHNICITIES

Although the notion of new ethnicities was first articulated in the context of film studies rather than the investigation of youth cultures, it was quickly extended to this latter domain. Hall's insight was that the strategic invocation of essentialized concepts of identity by black political activists in Britain was being supplanted by complex cultural blending both in representation and in practice. Following Hall ([1989] 1996, 1997), a number of British scholars embraced the concept of new ethnicities for the study of youth culture (e.g., Back 1996, Cohen 1999, Rampton 1999). Because such identities are not founded on static and essentialistic ethnic categories, but rather are emergent, hybrid, and local, the concept of new ethnicities can reveal nuanced social processes that the blunter tool of ethnicity could not expose. Such analytic work also has ample room for ethnographic methods, since new ethnicities are by definition locally constructed. Connections to anthropology are being reforged in other ways as well: Rampton (1999) revisits Turner's concept of liminality to develop the idea of new ethnicities as sites of cultural crossing, thresholds that young people move across as they carry on with their cultural business.

Although the utility of the concept of new ethnicities for promoting antiessentialist scholarship is evident, it should not be mistaken for a theoretical or political panacea. To begin with, it is not clear to what extent new ethnicities are really new or distinctive to late modernity and globalization, as Hall (1997) suggests. Cultural contact, appropriation, blending, and the resulting complex identities can be found in any number of societies, regardless of their relationship to modernity. The notion of new ethnicities thus seems to be not so much identifying an innovative cultural practice as urging a more delicate scholarly analysis. Nor is it clear how the framework would apply to cultures in which conceptions of ethnicity have very different meanings. Another issue that new ethnicities raise is the extent to which recent ethnic and racial configurations transcend historical patterns of racism rather than simply reinscribing them in less obvious ways. Here too, new ethnicities appear less than new: A number of researchers of race among British and American youth have noted that racist ideology and practice can exist side by side with cultural borrowing and even friendship (Back 1996, Bucholtz 1999a, Cutler 1999, Hewitt 1986, Schneider 1997; but cf. Wulff 1995b), and Hall himself is under no illusions that new ethnicities are synonymous with racial harmony. Finally, it is necessary to keep in mind that while the concept of new ethnicities may account admirably for current cultural practices in Britain—which has a small minority population and a relatively recent history of immigration—it takes on very different resonances in a country like the United States, with its long history of slavery and government-sanctioned racism and with its population quickly shifting, in the face of alarmist rightwing rhetoric, from predominantly white to "majority minority." In fact, both in racially homogeneous and in racially heterogeneous school settings young European Americans may counter the constitution of ethnicities, whether new or old, among youth of color by positioning themselves as "cultureless" (Perry 2001). Thus the great strength of the new-ethnicities approach—its emphasis on the local—should not be overridden by a desire to find racial convergence where more complex sociopolitical processes are at work.

Aside from some of the research on new ethnicities, much recent scholarship from a cultural studies perspective has lost even the Birmingham School's loose mooring of theory to ethnography. Some of the most influential work within cultural studies currently retains the Birmingham School's focus on music-based subcultures in capitalist societies, but it is now almost entirely historical and textual rather than ethnographic in orientation (e.g., Lipsitz 1994, Rose 1994, Ross & Rose 1994; but see Thornton 1995). Thus the participants in these cultures rarely come into view except in highly mediated ways. In many cases, too, cultural studies as currently practiced is virtually identical to popular cultural studies (Redhead 1997). As important as it is to investigate how youth cultures engage with both commercial and not-yet-commodified forms of popular culture, a full account of youth as cultural agents must look beyond these questions to understand the other ways in which youth styles emerge, the other dimensions of youth identities, and the other cultural practices in which youth engage. Most importantly, it must look not only to the United States, Britain, and other postindustrial societies for evidence of youth cultural practices, but also to young people's cultural innovations in other locations around the world.

YOUTH CULTURES OR CULTURAL PRACTICES OF YOUTH?

Although within cultural studies, youth cultures are understood as a response to the social class conflicts associated with industrialized societies, Lepowsky (1998) notes that nonindustrial societies may also have recognizable youth cultures. But even with this inclusion, the study of youth cultures, as productive as it has been and continues to be, is too limiting for research on youth from an anthropological perspective. Also necessary is an anthropologically based retheorizing of youth culture, in which static and inflexible cultural boundaries are replaced with the much more fluid and indeterminate collections of practices and ideologies that constitute culture in anthropology. In this way, social action that would not qualify as part of youth culture under the Birmingham School definition—for reasons of class, gender, or other factors—may be analyzed as a more dynamic form of youth culture: the cultural practices of youth. Such a recasting of youth research also serves as a corrective to some of the politically and ethically problematic elements of earlier approaches. Just as anthropologists have been drawn to the study of sexual practices among youth in non-Western societies, so too have spectacular and sensationalistic aspects of youth cultures preoccupied many sociologists of adolescence in industrial societies. Both groups have been accused of titillating readers at the expense of exploring other aspects of young people's lives. An emphasis on the ordinary, everyday activities in which youth engage, then, may act as an important counterbalance to previous work.

Research that contributes to these goals is already being done in a variety of fields. Both by critiquing the boundaries of traditional cultural studies research and by expanding them to include new groups, scholars in anthropology and related disciplines have begun to document the breadth of youth cultural production and practice.

Rethinking Resistance

The economic decline associated with deindustrialization in Britain in the 1970s and 1980s has often been cited as the reason for the emergence of oppositional and class-based youth styles. And as global economic restructuring continues, those whose entry into the working world has been deferred or rerouted have responded not only through the adoption of flamboyant styles but in other ways as well. McDermott (1985) found that a youth employment program established by the British government in this period served not to address the structural problems giving rise to high rates of unemployment or even to place young people in jobs, but to adapt workers to perform new kinds of work flexibly and without resistance. As Bridgman (2001) notes, even a job training program that emphasizes the dignity of teenage workers may clash with the reality of a work world that often strips young people of their agency. Despite efforts to produce a compliant workforce, resistance, or more properly, subversion, is widespread among youth in the workplace. Under conditions of underemployment and the lack of possibility of advancement, young American workers assert their autonomy through frequent job changing and rejection of the ideal of work as stimulating. Such solutions, however, are individual coping tactics rather than collective action (Willis 1998), in contrast to young people's challenges to workplace conditions elsewhere in the world (Mills 1999). Borman (1988, 1991) documents another tactic, "playing on the job," that allows adolescents to endure the tedium of routine work tasks. This practice recalls P. Willis's description of "having a laff" as a form of youthful resistance to school. There are thus many points of convergence between early cultural studies approaches to youth and employment and those taken more recently by anthropologists. But oppositionality takes many forms and may arise for many reasons in addition to or instead of class inequities.

Some scholars within the United States have suggested, for example, that a race-based oppositionality exists among students whose "involuntary minority" status (e.g., Ogbu 1988) makes academic achievement difficult. Fordham (1996) argues further that high achieving African American students must navigate carefully in order to avoid accusations of "acting white." But a number of scholars have challenged this claim, noting that many African American students are highly motivated to succeed in school (e.g., Hemmings 1996, Schultz 1996). If the oppositional identities of the "lads" and the "ear'oles" that Willis documented in England have counterparts in U.S. high schools, then, they necessarily differ on many key points due to differences in the local context. And the danger of framing oppositionality in terms of resistance is that identities are theorized as more dichotomous than is in fact the case. Certainly a wide variety of oppositional youth identities have been described by researchers (e.g., Bucholtz 1999b, Eckert 1989, Leblanc 1999, Lowney 1995, Kinney 1999), but despite the rigidity of these categories in local ideologies, they often prove to be flexible in practice. Hemmings (2000) documents a U.S. urban high school clique of unusual diversity, in which socially marginalized students of different backgrounds came together in ways that both allowed for individuality and precluded violent opposition with other groups.

Thus the explanatory power of resistance becomes less adequate as youth identities move further away from the class-based cultural styles that the concept was designed to account for. Where within the Birmingham School tradition musical subcultures were often explicitly linked to a broader political and economic context, many analyses of contemporary subcultures are striking for their frequent assertions that aesthetics rather than politics dominates cultural practice, especially in cultural styles associated with the middle class (Diethrich 1999/2000, Jerrentrup 2000, Roccor 2000). But as Thornton (1995) argues, such musical cultures are better understood as founded on a politics of distinction, in which musical taste is tied not only to pleasure or social identity but also to forms of power. This is a very different kind of oppositionality than is implied by the concept of resistance, for it is based not on a rejection of a powerless structural position but rather on a rejection of an undiscerning mainstream culture. Nor have youth cultures entirely abandoned overt political action, as shown by the Italian squatting movement, which has given rise to countercultural social centers that are often politically as well as musically based (Wright 2000). But the direct form that resistance takes here is once again quite different from the symbolic resistance that cultural studies scholars have described. Rather than reading resistance into these situations, analysts would do well to be attentive to local meanings of such practices.

Youth and Media

If youth cultures have generally been the heroes of the resistance movement in cultural studies, the media have historically been the villains of the piece. Viewed primarily as a threat to the vitality of youth cultures as forums for authenticity and resistance, the media are targeted for the ideologies that they promote both about and to young people. While some scholars focused on negative and panic-inducing media representations of youth—a tradition that continues today (Giroux 1996)—as part of the latter body of work, popular representations of femininity aimed at teenage consumers, such as romance novels (Christian-Smith 1990) and fashion magazines (Finders 1996, McRobbie 1977b [2000], Talbot 1995), have been analyzed for their ideological construction of a culture of femininity based largely on romance, beauty, and the domestic sphere. Similarly, in Japan, the rise of "cute culture" in the 1980s (Kinsella 1995), associated primarily with young women, ushered in an era of cuteness in advertisements, fashion, and even handwriting. Young women's widely documented trend away from highly gendered language use (e.g., Okamoto 1995) has also been associated with cute style

(Matsumoto 1996). In the context of modernizing societies, however, what is more immediately relevant than this ideological inculcation is the chasm between the representations of modern life presented by the media and the realities of limited economic opportunities for most youths (Miles 2000).

While youths' relationships to popular media are often associated with unattainable images and capitalist urgings toward consumption, media representations may also be a source of knowledge and agency. Fisherkeller (1997) found that young U.S. adolescents facing peer-group rejection often developed strategies and skills modeled on television in ways that negotiated rather than capitulated to hegemonic gender, racial, and social-class ideologies. In fact, commodification is not a barrier to the perception of authentic cultural practice: Despite the extensive commercialization of rave culture (Richard & Kruger 1998), many participants experience raves as sites of spiritual renewal (Hutson 2000). And media forms have been embraced by youth seeking like-minded others beyond the local community (Leonard 1998, Willard 1998). In any case, the relationship between resistance, authenticity, and cultural appropriation can be extremely complex. In the United States, body modification (piercing, tattooing, scarification, and so on) is understood by its practitioners both as a resistant desire that rejects capitalism—a "modern primitivism"—and as a therapeutic recovery of the authentic self (Rosenblatt 1997). Yet such practices also rely upon an unexamined construction of the exoticized cultural other, the never-to-be-modern primitive whose imagined existence authenticates these acts.

Styles of Appropriation

By contrast with the cultural appropriations that formed the basis of the Birmingham School's theory of style, or with those described above, many of the resources of present-day *bricoleurs* are in a certain sense self-appropriations—borrowings and adaptations of one's own cultural background to create new youth styles. The "Guido" cultural style of New York, for example, is predicated on Italian heritage but also involves a highly stylized performance of a particular commodified image of Italianness (Tricarico 1991). Dimitriadis (2001) describes how African American teenage boys in the Midwest used Southern rap music to construct a community around a nostalgic Southern tradition. Likewise, a great deal of cultural production among first- and second-generation immigrants to the United States involves a kind of neotraditionalism in which elements of the heritage culture are selectively appropriated and resignified. In the Indian American desi music scene in Chicago, diasporic and modern Indian musical genres such as film music and house bhangra are imagined as traditional (Diethrich 1999/2000; cf. Maira 1999). Such cultural forms lead to new ethnicities insofar as new panethnic identities emerge from this syncretic practice (see also Buff 1998).

New ethnicities, or at least new configurations of race and ethnicity, are also produced through acts of appropriation between self and other. Young people may negotiate in interaction among a variety of ethnicized and racialized subject positions, to which they may or may not have a culturally legitimized claim. In this process, language is often a privileged resource for staking identity claims (e.g., Bailey 2000, Bucholtz 1999a, Cutler 1999, Jacobs-Huey 1997, Lo 1999, Rampton 1995). This is not to say that ethnic reification does not occur or does not affect youth; the multivalent identities of youth in the Hungarian minority of Slovakia have recently become problematized, and young people are now forced to choose a single identity position as ethnic purity becomes a central ideology of the Slovak state (Langman 1997). In addition, cultural appropriations depend for their success on notions of cultural ownership even as they appear to repudiate them. Such questions become more vexed as cultural resources move globally as well as locally.

The global spread of popular culture is often viewed as symptomatic of cultural leveling, yet many scholars have pointed out that how cultural forms are taken up and assigned meanings far from their places of origin is a process that involves creativity and agency, not unthinking acceptance of cultural products. The same cultural resource can be put to use in radically different ways. Hence rap allows underemployed youth in Tanzania to participate politically in public discourse (Remes 1999), while in Zimbabwe, it enables privileged urban youth to display personal aspirations through cultural style (Neate 1994). Global black culture also provides the stylistic resources for young Surinamese Creoles in the Netherlands to create a panethnic black identity (Sansone 1995). Although hip hop is currently the cultural form most widely appropriated into new contexts around the world (see M. H. Morgan, forthcoming), other musical styles may also be resources for local identity making. In West Africa, reggae serves as a mediating link between Africa and the African diaspora, and reggae forms often become re-Africanized in local contexts through the addition of traditional linguistic and cultural elements (Savishinsky 1994). This racialized coding of cultural styles is highly mutable, however. In her study of a multiracial high school in South Africa, Dolby (1999) found that white students embraced techno music as part of a "global whiteness," but that when colored students began to participate in rave culture, racial divisions became less rigid as well. Thus cultural resources may be used locally in unpredictable ways.

CONCLUSION: GLOBALIZING YOUTH RESEARCH

Global youth research is not so much cross-cultural—a paradigm that is usually quantitative and comparative rather than qualitative and ethnographic—as it is transcultural or "multi-cultural" in the sense of Amit-Talai (1995). And some of the tools for the kind of work that is most urgently needed come from other disciplines, especially cultural studies. For example, the semiotics of fashion can be used to understand youth identities in the Congo, where the appropriation of European designer clothing is a political response to economic marginalization and to the prolonging of adolescence that is its consequence (Gondola 1999). Much like the teddy boys of England (Jefferson [1976] 1993), young Congolese *sapeurs* borrow the external trappings of an unattainable class status in order both to challenge inequitable state structures and to claim a new social identity. Likewise, O'Collins (1986) notes the parallels between the moral panics associated with the youthful "hooligans" of postindustrial Britain and those associated with the "rascals" who disrupt Papua New Guinean society.

This is not to say that cross-cultural research, including cross-cultural research within a single society, does not yield insights of use for the global study of youth cultures; indeed, such scholarship may bring to light issues that are addressed in complementary ways by other approaches. For example, although Brake's (1985) comparative study of youth cultures of the United States, Britain, and Canada often errs in its details, it provides useful generalizations that can be ethnographically tested, as well as offering a reminder that global cultural forms are taken up in diverse ways in local contexts.

The most productive view of youth cultures and youth identities, then, must admit both the ideological reality of categories and the flexibility of identities; recent work, especially in anthropology, draws from theories of practice, activity, and performance to demonstrate how youth negotiate cultural identities in a variety of contexts, both material and semiotic, both leisure-based and at home, school, work, and in the political sphere. Anthropological scholarship in youth culture is also distinguished by its geographic range and its concern with the local, which militates against the broad generalizations about youth that have emerged from other approaches. Some of the richest avenues for the anthropological exploration of youth culture include the development of global youth cultures, the blending of traditional cultural forms into new youth-based styles and practices, and the possibilities for cultural production offered by new technologies. Anthropologists working in these realms emphasize that youth-based cultural practices continue to be local phenomena, even when they take inspiration from mediated cultural forms. Further, anthropology problematizes the taken-for-granted nature of both "youth" and "culture" in much youth culture research by emphasizing the fundamental instability of these shifters across cultural settings.

An anthropology of adolescence, then, is not the same as an anthropology of youth. And while both are necessary to a full understanding of young people's perspectives and practices in cultures around the world, the latter task is more pressing, both because it is a newer project that raises less investigated questions and because youth cultural practices are becoming increasingly salient and central to the organization of all human societies.

ACKNOWLEDGMENTS

I would like to thank the Center for Humanities Research at Texas A&M University for providing financial support to assist in the researching of this article. For extremely helpful suggestions and comments, I am also grateful to Harry Berger, Giovanna Del Negro, Donna Goldstein, Kira Hall, Jen Roth Gordon, and an anonymous reviewer, none of whom are responsible for omissions or errors.

LITERATURE CITED

Allison A. 2001. Cyborg violence: bursting borders and bodies with queer machines. *Cult. Anthropol.* 16(2):237–65

Amit-Talai V. 1995. Conclusion: the "multi" cultural of youth. See Amit-Talai & Wulff 1995, pp. 223–33

Amit-Talai V, Wulff H. 1995. *Youth Cultures: a Cross-Cultural Perspective.* London: Routledge

Anderson WW, Anderson DD. 1986. Thai Muslim adolescents' self, sexuality, and autonomy. *Ethos* 14(4):368–94

Assal A, Farrell E. 1992. Attempts to make meaning of terror: family, play, and school in time of civil war. *Anthropol. Educ. Q.* 23(4):275–90

Back L. 1996. *New Ethnicities and Urban Culture: Racisms and Multiculture in Young Lives.* New York: St. Martin's

Bailey B. 2000. Language and negotiation of ethnic/racial identity among Dominican Americans. *Lang. Soc.* 29(4):555–82

Barry H, Schlegel A. 1984. Measurements of adolescent behavior in the Standard Sample of societies. *Ethnology* 23:315–29

Barry H, Schlegel A. 1986. Cultural customs that influence sexual freedom in adolescence. *Ethnology* 25(2):151–62

Becker H. 1963. *The Outsiders: Studies in the Sociology of Deviance.* Chicago: Free

Bernat JC. 1999. Children and the politics of violence in Haitian context. *Crit. Anthropol.* 19(2):121–38

Best AL. 2000. *Prom Night: Youth, Schools, and Popular Culture.* New York: Routledge

Bloustien G. 1999. The consequences of being a gift. *Aust. J. Anthropol.* 10(1):77–93

Booth H. 1999. Gender, power and social change: youth suicide among Fiji Indians and Western Samoans. *J. Polyn. Soc.* 108(1):39–68

Boothby N. 1986. Children and war. *Cult. Surviv. Q.* 10(4):7–8

Borman KM. 1988. Playing on the job in adolescent work settings. *Anthropol. Educ. Q.* 19(2):163–81

Borman KM. 1991. *The First "Real" Job: a Study of Young Workers.* Albany: SUNY Press

Brake M. 1980. *The Sociology of Youth Culture and Youth Subcultures: Sex and Drugs and Rock 'n' Roll?* London: Routledge & Kegan Paul

Brake M. 1985. *Comparative Youth Cultures.* London: Routledge

Bridgman R. 2001. I helped build that: a demonstration employment training program for homeless youth in Toronto, Canada. *Am. Anthropol.* 103(3):779–95

Brown MF. 1986. Power, gender, and the social meaning of Aguaruna suicide. *Man* 21(2):311–28

Bucholtz M. 1999a. You da man: narrating the racial other in the linguistic production of white masculinity. *J. Sociolinguist.* 3(4):443–60

Bucholtz M. 1999b. "Why be normal?": language and identity practices in a community of nerd girls. *Lang. Soc.* 28(2):203–23

Buff R. 1998. Gender and generation down the Red Road. In *Generations of Youth: Youth Cultures and History in Twentieth-Century America*, ed. J Austin, MN Willard, pp. 379–94. New York: NY Univ. Press

Burbank VK. 1987. Premarital sex norms: cultural interpretations in an Australian Aboriginal community. *Ethos* 15(2):226–34

Burbank VK. 1988. *Aboriginal Adolescence: Maidenhood in an Australian Community.* New Brunswick, NJ: Rutgers Univ. Press

Burbank VK. 1995. Gender hierarchy and adolescent sexuality: the control of female reproduction in an Australian Aboriginal community. *Ethos* 23(1):33–46

Burbank VK, Chisholm JS. 1998. Adolescent pregnancy and parenthood in an Australian Aboriginal community. See Herdt & Leavitt 1998, pp. 55–70

Burke C. 2000. They cut Segametsi into parts: ritual murder, youth, and the politics of knowledge in Botswana. *Anthropol. Q.* 73(4):204–14

Burton LM. 1997. Ethnography and the meaning of adolescence in high-risk neighborhoods. *Ethos* 25(2):208–17

Butler R. 1998. Rehabilitating the images of disabled youths. In *Cool Places: Geographies of Youth Cultures*, ed. T Skelton, G Valentine, pp. 83–100. London: Routledge

Christian-Smith L. 1990. *Becoming a Woman Through Romance*. New York: Routledge

Clarke J. [1976] 1993. Style. See Hall & Jefferson [1976] 1993, pp. 175–91

Clarke J, Hall S, Jefferson T, Roberts B. [1976] 1993. Subcultures, cultures and class. See Hall & Jefferson [1976] 1993, pp. 9–74

Cohen A. 1955. *Delinquent Boys*. Chicago: Free

Cohen P, ed. 1999. *New Ethnicities, Old Racisms?* London: Zed

Cohen S. [1972] 1980. *Folk Devils and Moral Panics: the Creation of the Mods and Rockers*. New York: St. Martin's. New ed.

Condon RG. 1987. *Inuit Youth: Growth and Change in the Canadian Arctic*. New Brunswick, NJ: Rutgers Univ. Press

Condon RG. 1990. The rise of adolescence: social change and life stage dilemmas in the central Canadian Arctic. *Human Organ.* 49(3):266–79

Condon RG, Stern P. 1993. Gender-role preference, gender identity, and gender socialization among contemporary Inuit youth. *Ethos* 21(4):384–416

Cutler CA. 1999. Yorkville crossing: white teens, hip hop, and African American English. *J. Sociolinguist.* 3(4):428–42

Dalla RL, Gamble WC. 2001. Teenage mothering on the Navajo Reservation: an examination of intergenerational perceptions and beliefs. *Am. Indian Cult. Res. J.* 25(1): 1–19

Davis SS, Davis DA. 1989. *Adolescence in a Moroccan Town: Making Social Sense*. New Brunswick, NJ: Rutgers Univ. Press

Diethrich G. 1999/2000. Desi music vibes: the performance of Indian youth culture in Chicago. *Asian Music* 31(1):35–61

Dimitriadis G. 2001. "In the clique": popular culture, constructions of place, and the everyday lives of urban youth. *Anthropol. Education Q.* 32(1):29–51

Diouf M. 1996. Urban youth and Senegalese politics: Dakar 1988-1994. *Pub. Cult.* 8:225–49

Dolby N. 1999. Youth and the global popular: the politics and practices of race in South Africa. *Eur. J. Cult. Stud.* 2(3):291–309

Durham D. 2000. Youth and the social imagination in Africa: introduction to parts 1 and 2. *Anthropol. Q.* 73(3):113–20

Eckert P. 1989. *Jocks and Burnouts*. New York: Teachers College Press

Erikson EH. 1968. *Identity, Youth, and Crisis*. New York: W.W. Norton

Eyre SL, Hoffman V, Millstein SG. 1998. The gamesmanship of sex: a model based on African American adolescent accounts. *Med. Anthropol. Q.* 12(4):467–89

Finders M. 1996. Queens and teen zines: early adolescent females reading their way toward adulthood. *Anthropol. Educ. Q.* 27(1):71–89

Fisherkeller J. 1997. Everyday learning about identities among young adolescents in television culture. *Anthropol. Educ. Q.* 28(4):467–92

Fordham S. 1996. *Blacked Out: Dilemmas of Race, Identity, and Success at Capital High*. Chicago: Univ. Chicago Press

Fuchs E. 1976. *Youth in a Changing World: Cross-Cultural Perspectives*. The Hague: Mouton

Gable E. 2000. The Culture Development Club: youth, neo-tradition, and the construction of society in Guinea-Bissau. *Anthropol. Q.* 73(4):195–203

Gailey CW. 1999. Rethinking child labor in an age of capitalist restructuring. *Crit. Anthropol.* 19(2):115–19

Gaines D. 1990. *Teenage Wasteland: Suburbia's Dead End Kids*. New York: Basic Books

Gilroy P. 1991. *"There Ain't No Black in the Union Jack": the Cultural Politics of Race and Nation*. Chicago: Univ. Chicago Press

Gilroy P. 1993. *The Black Atlantic: Modernity and Double Consciousness*. Cambridge, MA: Harvard Univ. Press

Giroux HA. 1996. *Fugitive Cultures: Race, Violence, and Youth*. New York: Routledge

Gondola CD. 1999. Dream and drama: the search for elegance among Congolese youth. *Afr. Stud. Rev.* 42(1):23–48

Hall S. [1989] 1996. New ethnicities. In *Stuart Hall: Critical Dialogues in Cultural Studies*, ed. D Morley, K-H Chen, pp. 441–49. London: Routledge

Hall S. 1997. New and old ethnicities, new and old identities. In *Culture and Globalization and the World-System: Contemporary Conditions for the Representation of Identity*, ed. AD King pp. 41–68. Minneapolis: Univ. Minn. Press. Rev. ed.

Hall S, Critcher C, Jefferson T, Roberts B. 1978. *Policing the Crisis: Mugging, the State and Law and Order*. London: Macmillan

Hall S, Jefferson T, eds. [1976] 1993. *Resistance Through Rituals: Youth Subcultures in Post-War Britain*. London: Routledge

Hall T, Montgomery H. 2000. Home and away: "childhood," "youth" and young people. *Anthropol. Today* 16(3):13–15

Hebdige D. 1979. *Subculture: the Meaning of Style*. London: Methuen

Hemmings A. 1996. Conflicting images?: being black and a model high school student. *Anthropol. Educ. Q.* 27(1):20–50

Hemmings A. 2000. Lona's links: postoppositional identity work of urban youths. *Anthropol. Educ. Q.* 31(2):152–72

Herdt G, ed. 1989. *Gay and Lesbian Youth*. New York: Haworth

Herdt G, Leavitt SC. 1998. Introduction: studying adolescence in contemporary Pacific Island communities. See Herdt & Leavitt 1998, pp. 3–26

Herdt G, Leavitt SC, eds. 1998. *Adolescence in Pacific Island Societies*. Pittsburgh: Univ. Pittsburgh Press

Hewitt R. 1986. *White Talk Black Talk: Inter-Racial Friendship and Communication Amongst Adolescents*. Cambridge, UK: Cambridge Univ. Press

Hezel FX. 1984. Cultural patterns in Trukese suicide. *Ethnology* 23(3):193–206

Hezel FX. 1987. Truk suicide epidemic and social change. *Human Organ.* 46(4):283–91

Hollos M, Leis PE. 1986. Descent and permissive adolescent sexuality in two Ijo communities. *Ethos* 14(4):395-408

Hollos M, Leis PE. 1989. *Becoming Nigerian in Ijo Society*. New Brunswick, NJ: Rutgers Univ. Press

Hutson SR. 2000. The rave: spiritual healing in modern Western subcultures. *Anthropol. Q.* 73(1):35–49

Jacobs-Huey L. 1997. Is there an authentic African American speech community?: Carla revisited. *Univ. Penn. Work. Pap. Linguist.* 4(1):331–70

Jakobson R. [1957] 1971. Shifters, verbal categories, and the Russian verb. In *Selected Writings of Roman Jakobson*. Vol. 2, pp. 130–47. The Hague: Mouton

Jankowski MS. 1991. *Islands in the Street: Gangs and American Urban Society*. Berkeley: Univ. Calif. Press

Jefferson T. [1976] 1993. Cultural responses of the Teds. See Hall & Jackson [1976] 1993, pp. 81–6

Jerrentrup A. 2000. Gothic and dark music: forms and background. *World Music* 42(1):25–50

Johnson T, Tomren H. 1999. Helplessness, hopelessness, and despair: identifying the precursors to Indian youth suicide. *Am. Indian Cult. Res. J.* 23(3):287–301

Kearney RN, Miller BD. 1985. The spiral of suicide and social change in Sri Lanka. *J. Asian Stud.* 45(1):81–101

Kinney DA. 1999. From "headbangers" to "hippies": delineating adolescents' active attempts to form an alternative peer culture. In *The Role of Peer Groups in Adolescent Social Identity: Exploring the Importance of Stability and Change*, ed. JA McLellan, MJV Pugh, pp. 21–35. San Francisco: Jossey-Bass

Kinsella S. 1995. Cuties in Japan. In *Women, Media and Consumption in Japan*, ed. L Skov, B Moeran, pp. 220–54. Honolulu: Univ. Hawai'i Press

Kirkpatrick J. 1987. Taure'are'a: a liminal category and passage to Marquesan adulthood. *Ethos* 15(4):382–405

Lackey JF, Moberg DP. 1998. Understanding the onset of intercourse among urban American adolescents: a cultural process framework using qualitative and quantitative data. *Hum. Organ.* 57(4):491–501

Langman J. 1997. Expressing identity in a changing society: Hungarian youth in Slovakia. In *Beyond Borders: Remaking Cultural Identities in the New East and Central Europe*, ed. L Kürti, J Langman, pp. 111–31. Boulder, CO: Westview

Lave J, Duguid P, Fernandez N, Axel E. 1992. Coming of age in Birmingham: cultural studies and conceptions of subjectivity. *Annu. Rev. Anthropol.* 21:257–82

Leap W. 1999. Language, socialization, and silence in gay adolescence. In *Reinventing Identities: the Gendered Self in Discourse*, ed. M Bucholtz, AC Liang, L Sutton, pp. 259–72. New York: Oxford Univ. Press

Leavitt SC. 1998. The bikhet mystique: masculine identity and patterns of rebellion among Bumbita adolescent males. See Herdt & Leavitt 1998, pp. 173–94

Leblanc L. 1999. *Pretty in Punk: Girls' Gender Resistance in a Boys' Subculture*. New Brunswick, NJ: Rutgers Univ. Press

Lebra TS. 1995. Skipped and postponed adolescence of aristocratic women in Japan: resurrecting the culture/nature issue. *Ethos* 23(1):79–102

Leclerc-Madlala S. 1997. Infect one, infect all: Zulu youth response to the AIDS epidemic in South Africa. *Med. Anthropol.* 17:363–80

Leis PE, Hollos M. 1995. Intergenerational discontinuities in Nigeria. *Ethos* 23(1):103–18

Leonard M. 1998. Paper planes: travelling the new grrrl geographies. In *Cool Places: Geographies of Youth Cultures*, ed. T Skelton, G Valentine, pp. 101–18. London: Routledge

Lepowsky M. 1998. Coming of age on Vanatinai: gender, sexuality, and power. See Herdt & Leavitt 1998, pp. 123–47

Lévi-Strauss C. 1966. *The Savage Mind*. Chicago: Univ. Chicago Press

Liechty M. 1995. Media, markets and modernization: youth identities and the experience of modernity in Kathmandu, Nepal. See Amit-Talai & Wulff 1995, pp. 166–201

Lipsitz G. 1994. *Dangerous Crossroads: Popular Music, Postmodernism, and the Poetics of Place*. London: Verso

Lo A. 1999. Codeswitching, speech community membership, and the construction of ethnic identity. *J. Sociolinguist.* 3(4):461–79

Lock M. 1986. Plea for acceptance: school refusal syndrome in Japan. *Soc. Sci. Med.* 23(2):99–112

Lowney KS. 1995. Teenage Satanism as oppositional youth subculture. *J. Contemp. Ethnog.* 23(4):453–84

Luker K. 1996. *Dubious Conceptions: the Politics of Teenage Pregnancy*. Cambridge, MA: Harvard Univ. Press

MacPherson C, MacPherson L. 1987. Towards an explanation of recent trends in suicide in Western Samoa. *Man* 22(2):305–30

Maira S. 1999. Identity dub: the paradoxes of an Indian American youth subculture (New York mix). *Cult. Anthropol.* 14(1):29–60

Malinowski B. [1929] 1987. *The Sexual Life of Savages in North-Western Melanesia*. Boston: Beacon

Markowitz F. 2000. *Coming of Age in Post-Soviet Russia*. Urbana: Univ. Ill. Press

Martini M. 1996. The July festival in the Marquesas Islands: "youth" and identity in a valley community. *Pac. Stud.* 19(2):83–103

Matsumoto Y. 1996. Does less feminine speech in Japanese mean less femininity? In *Gender and Belief Systems: Proc. 4th Berkeley Women and Language Conf.*, ed. N Warner, J Ahlers, S Wertheim, et al. pp. 455–67. Berkeley, CA: Berkeley Wom. Lang. Group

McDermott K. 1985. "All dressed up and nowhere to go": youth unemployment and state policy in Britain. *Urban Anthropol.* 14(1–3):91–108

McRobbie A. 2000. *Feminism and Youth Culture*. London: Routledge. 2nd ed.

McRobbie A. 2000. Teenage mothers: a new

social state? See McRobbie 2000, pp. 159–79

McRobbie A. [1977a] 2000. The culture of working-class girls. See McRobbie 2000, pp. 44–66

McRobbie A. [1977b] 2000. *Jackie* magazine: romantic individualism and the teenage girl. See McRobbie 2000, pp. 67–117

McRobbie A, Garber J. [1976] 1993. Girls and subcultures. See Hall & Jefferson [1976] 1993, pp. 209–20

Mead M. 1928. *Coming of Age in Samoa: a Psychological Study of Primitive Youth for Western Civilisation*. New York: Morrow

Mendoza-Denton N. 1996. "Muy macha": gender and ideology in gang-girls' discourse about makeup. *Ethnos* 61(1/2):47–63

Merten DE. 1999. Enculturation into secrecy among junior high school girls. *J. Contemp. Ethnog.* 28(2):107–37

Miles A. 2000. Poor adolescent girls and social transformations in Cuenca, Ecuador. *Ethos* 28(1):54–74

Mills MB. 1999. Enacting solidarity: unions and migrant youth in Thailand. *Crit. Anthropol.* 19(2):175–92

Minore B, Boone M, Katt M, Kinch P. 1991. Looking in, looking out: coping with adolescent suicide in the Cree and Ojibway communities of Northern Ontario. *Can. J. Native Stud.* 11(1):1–24

Monsell-Davis M. 1986. At home in the village: youth and the community in Nabuapaka. In *Youth and Society: Perspectives from Papua New Guinea*, ed. M O'Collins, pp. 65–78. Canberra: Aust. Natl. Univ., Dep. Pol. Soc. Change

Mungham G, Pearson G, eds. 1976. *Working Class Youth Culture*. London: Routledge & Kegan Paul

Nader L, González RJ 2000. The framing of teenage health care: organizations, culture, and control. *Cult. Med. Psychiatry* 24: 231–58

Neate P. 1994. Being a homeboy: youth culture around a bar in Harare, Zimbabwe. *Cambridge Anthropol.* 17(3):69–87

Neyzi L. 2001. Object or subject?: the paradox of "youth" in Turkey. *Int. J. Middle East Stud.* 33:411–32

Nichter M. 2000. *Fat Talk: What Girls and Their Parents Say about Dieting*. Cambridge, MA: Harvard Univ. Press

Novins DK, Beals J, Roberts RE, Manson SM. 1999. Factors associated with suicide ideation among American Indian adolescents: Does culture matter? *Suicide Life-Threatening Behav.* 29(4):332–46

O'Collins M. 1986. Urban youth and folk devils: reflections on International Youth Year. In *Youth and Society: Perspectives from Papua New Guinea*, ed. M O'Collins, pp. 155–67. Canberra: Aust. Natl. Univ., Dep. Pol. Soc. Change

O'Neil JD. 1986. Colonial stress in the Canadian Arctic: an ethnography of young adults changing. In *Anthropology and Epidemiology: Interdisciplinary Approaches to the Study of Health and Disease*, ed. CR Janes, R Stall, SM Gifford, pp. 249–74. Dordrecht: D. Reidel

Obbo C. 1995. Gender, age and class: discourses on HIV transmission and control in Uganda. In *Culture and Sexual Risk: Anthropological Perspectives on AIDS*, ed. H ten Brummelhuis, G Herdt, pp. 79–95. Amsterdam: Gordon & Breach

Ogbu JU. 1988. Class stratification, racial stratification, and schooling. In *Class, Race, and Gender in American Education*, ed. L Weis, pp. 163–81. New York: SUNY Press

Okamoto S. 1995. "Tasteless" Japanese: less "feminine" speech among young Japanese women. In *Gender Articulated: Language and the Socially Constructed Self*, ed. K Hall, M Bucholtz, pp. 297–325. New York: Routledge

Paiva V. 1995. Sexuality, AIDS and gender norms among Brazilian teenagers. In *Culture and Sexual Risk: Anthropological Perspectives on AIDS*, ed. H ten Brummelhuis, G Herdt, pp. 97–114. Amsterdam: Gordon & Breach

Parker S, Nichter M, Nichter M, Vuckovic

N, Sims C, et al. 1995. Body image and weight concerns among African American and White adolescent females: differences that make a difference. *Hum. Organ.* 54(2):103–14

Perry P. 2001. White means never having to say you're ethnic: White youth and the construction of "cultureless" identities. *J. Contemp. Ethnogr.* 30(1):56–91

Peters K, Richards P. 1998. "Why we fight": voices of youth combatants in Sierra Leone. *Africa* 68(2):183–210

Rampton B. 1995. *Crossing: Language and Ethnicity among Adolescents.* London: Longman

Rampton B. 1999. Sociolinguistics and cultural studies: new ethnicities, liminality and interaction. *Soc. Semiotics* 9(3):355–73

Rasmussen SJ. 2000. Between several worlds: images of youth and age in Tuareg popular performances. *Anthropol. Q.* 73(3):133–44

Rea WR. 1998. Rationalising culture: youth, elites and masquerade politics. *Africa* 68(1): 98–117

Redhead S. 1997. *Subculture to Clubcultures: an Introduction to Popular Cultural Studies.* Oxford: Blackwell

Remes P. 1999. Global popular musics and changing awareness of urban Tanzanian youth. *Yearbook for Traditional Music* 31:2–26

Reser J. 1990. The cultural context of Aboriginal suicide: myths, meanings, and critical analysis. *Oceania* 61(2):177–84

Rhein S. 2000. "Being a fan is more than that": fan-specific involvement with music. *World Music* 42(1):95–109

Richard B, Kruger HH. 1998. Ravers' paradise?: German youth cultures in the 1990s. In *Cool Places: Geographies of Youth Cultures*, ed. T Skelton, G Valentine, pp. 161–74. London: Routledge

Robinson G. 1990. Separation, retaliation and suicide: mourning and the conflicts of young Tiwi men. *Oceania* 60(3):161–78

Robinson G. 1997. Families, generations, and self: conflict, loyalty, and recognition in an Australian Aboriginal society. *Ethos* 25(3):303–32

Roccor B. 2000. Heavy metal: forces of unification and fragmentation within a musical subculture. *World Music* 42(1):83–94

Rose T. 1994. *Black Noise: Rap Music and Black Culture in Contemporary America.* Hanover, NH: Wesleyan Univ. Press

Rosenblatt D. 1997. The antisocial skin: structure, resistance, and "modern primitive" adornment in the United States. *Cult. Anthropol.* 12(3):287–334

Ross A, Rose T, eds. 1994. *Microphone Fiends: Youth Music and Youth Culture.* New York: Routledge

Rubinstein DH. 1983. Epidemic suicide among Micronesian adolescents. *Soc. Sci. Med.* 17: 657–65

Rubinstein DH. 1992. Suicide in Micronesia and Samoa: a critique of explanations. *Pac. Stud.* 15(1):51–75

Sansone L. 1995. The making of a black youth culture: lower-class young men of Surinamese origin in Amsterdam. See Amit-Talai & Wulff 1995, pp. 114–43

Savishinsky NJ. 1994. Rastafari in the promised land: the spread of a Jamaican socioreligious movement among the youth of West Africa. *Afr. Stud. Rev.* 37(3):19–50

Schensul JJ, Huebner C, Singer M, Snow M, Feliciano P, et al. 2000. The high, the money, and the fame: the emergent social context of "new marijuana" use among urban youth. *Med. Anthropol.* 18:389–414

Schlegel A. 1995a. Introduction. Special issue on Adolescence. *Ethos* 23(1):3–14

Schlegel A. 1995b. Cross-cultural approach to adolescence. *Ethos* 23(1):15–32

Schlegel A, Barry H. 1991. *Adolescence: an Anthropological Inquiry.* New York: Free

Schlegel A, Barry H. 1979. Adolescent initiation ceremonies: a cross-cultural code. *Ethnology* 18(2):199–210

Schneider JA. 1997. Dialectics of race and nationality: contradictions and Philadelphia working-class youth. *Anthropol. Educ. Q.* 28(4):493–523

Schultz K. 1996. Between school and work: the literacies of urban adolescent females. *Anthropol. Educ. Q.* 27(4):517–44

Sharp LA. 1990. Possessed and dispossessed youth: spirit possession of school children in northwest Madagascar. *Cult. Med. Psychiatry* 14:339–64

Sharp LA. 1995. Playboy princely spirits of Madagascar: possession as youthful commentary and social critique. *Anthropol. Q.* 68(2):75–88

Silverstein M. 1976. Shifters, linguistic categories, and cultural description. In *Meaning in Anthropology*, ed. KH Basso, HA Selby, pp. 11–55. Albuquerque: Univ. N.M. Press

Sobo EJ, Zimet GD, Zimmerman T, Cecil H. 1997. Doubting the experts: AIDS misconceptions among runaway adolescents. *Hum. Organ.* 56(3):311–20

Sykes K. 1999. After the "raskol" feast: youths' alienation in New Ireland, Papua New Guinea. *Crit. Anthropol.* 19(2):157–74

Talbot M. 1995. A synthetic sisterhood: false friends in a teenage magazine. In *Gender Articulated: Language and the Socially Constructed Self*, ed. K Hall, M Bucholtz, pp. 143–65. New York: Routledge

Thornton S. 1995. *Club Cultures: Music, Media and Subcultural Capital*. Hanover, NH: Wesleyan Univ. Press

Tricarico D. 1991. Guido: fashioning an Italian-American youth style. *J. Ethnic Stud.* 19(1):41–66

Turner V. 1969. *The Ritual Process: Structure and Anti-Structure*. New York: de Gruyter

Vigil JD. 1988. Group processes and street identity: adolescent Chicano gang members. *Ethos* 16(4):421–45

Watters B. 1988. Quinceañera: the Mexican-American initiation ritual of young women. In *The American Ritual Tapestry: Social Rules, Cultural Meanings*, ed. MJ Deegan, pp. 145–58. Westport, CT: Greenwood

Way N, Stauber HY, Nakkula MJ, London P. 1994. Depression and substance use in two divergent high school cultures: a quantitative and qualitative analysis. *J. Youth and Adolesc.* 23(3):331–57

West HG. 2000. Girls with guns: narrating the experience of war of FRELIMO's "female detachment." *Anthropol. Q.* 73(4):180–94

West J. 1999. (Not) talking about sex: youth, identity and sexuality. *Sociol. Rev.* 47(3): 525–47

White M. 1995. The marketing of adolescence in Japan: buying and dreaming. In *Women, Media and Consumption in Japan*, ed. L Skov, B Moeran, pp. 255–73. Honolulu: Univ. Hawai'i Press

Whiting J. 1986. Adolescent sexual training and behavior. *Cult. Surviv. Q.* 10(4):7–8

Whiting JWM, Burbank VK, Ratner MS. 1986. The duration of maidenhood. In *School-Age Pregnancy and Parenthood: Biosocial Dimensions*, ed. JB Lancaster, BA Hamburg, pp. 273–302. New York: Acad.

Willard MN. 1998. Seance, tricknowlogy, skateboarding, and the space of youth. In *Generations of Youth: Youth Cultures and History in Twentieth-Century America*, ed. J Austin, MN Willard, pp. 327–46. New York: N.Y. Univ. Press

Willis P. 1977. *Learning to Labor: How Working Class Kids Get Working Class Jobs*. New York: Columbia Univ. Press

Willis S. 1998. Teens at work: negotiating the jobless future. In *Generations of Youth: Youth Cultures and History in Twentieth-Century America*, ed. J Austin, MN Willard, pp. 347–57. New York: N.Y. Univ. Press

Worthman CM. 1987. Interactions of physical maturation and cultural practice in ontogeny: Kikuyu adolescents. *Cult. Anthropol.* 2(1):29–38

Worthman CM, Whiting JWM. 1987. Social change in adolescent sexual behavior, mate selection, and premarital pregnancy rates in a Kikuyu community. *Ethos* 15(2):145–65

Wright S. 2000. "A love born of hate": autonomist rap in Italy. *Theory, Cult. Soc.* 17(3):117–35

Wulff H. 1995a. Introducing youth culture in its

own right: the state of the art and new possibilities. See Amit-Talai & Wulff 1995, pp. 1–18

Wulff H. 1995b. Inter-racial friendship: consuming youth styles, ethnicity and teenage femininity in South London. See Amit-Talai & Wulff 1995, pp. 63–80

Zigman M. 1999. Under the law: teen prostitution in Kensington. *Crit. Anthropol.* 19(2):193–201

Subject Index

Cumulative Indexes

CONTRIBUTING AUTHORS, VOLUMES 23–31

CHAPTER TITLES, VOLUMES 23–31

Overviews

Archaeology

Biological Anthropology

Linguistics and Communicative Practices

Regional Studies

Sociocultural Anthropology

HISTORY, THEORY, AND METHODS

ECONOMICS, ECOLOGY, TECHNOLOGY, AND DEVELOPMENT

AFFECT, COGNITION, AND MEANING

MEDICAL ANTHROPOLOGY, NUTRITION, AND DEMOGRAPHY

Theme I: Aids

Theme I: Capitalism and the Reinvention of Anthropology

Theme I: Childhood

Theme I: Human Genetic Diversity

Theme I: Millennium

Theme II: Demographic Anthropology

Theme II: Diasporas

Theme II: Empire and Its Aftermath

Theme II: Nature of Anthropological Evidence

Theme II: The Anthropology of Everyday Life